Sustainability
for the 21st Century
Pathways, Programs, and Policies

K. David Pijawka

Kendall Hunt
publishing company

Cover Artwork
The Theme Work of Shanghai Expo – "City Rescue" on Immortal Love

On May 12th, 2008, an 8.0 magnitude earthquake struck in Sichuan Province, China. This horrific tragedy rocked the entire nation with sadness and sympathy. All of China responded with courage and aid as love and assistance flooded to the quake-stricken region. When the author rushed from Beijing to the quake-stricken area, he saw a hand calling for rescue from the debris. This scene was made such an impression that the author was inspired to create this *Immortal Love*.

On May 12th 2009, *Immortal Love* was unveiled in Hanwang, the epicenter of Wenchuan earthquake in the first anniversary of the quake.

The earth was shaking as the fragile nature of life was realized; this devastation reflects how we suffer from catastrophe and how we hope to be blessed by God. So *Immortal Love* was invited to appear in the theme exhibition in the Shanghai Expo of "City Rescue" on May 1st 2010. Billions of people show great concern for disaster relief and salvation of human beings hands by hands and hearts to hearts through this craft – *Immortal Love*.

798 Art Zone
Terroir Oriental
Peking University Art Capital Association

Cover image courtesy of K. David Pijawka with permission of James Healy, the photographer, and the artist, Dr. Lin Tianqiang

Kendall Hunt
publishing company

www.kendallhunt.com
Send all inquiries to:
4050 Westmark Drive
Dubuque, IA 52004-1840

Copyright © 2015 by K. David Pijawka

ISBN 978-1-4652-6671-2

Printed in the United States of America

DEDICATION

This textbook is dedicated to professors Robert Kates and Roger Kasperson, my mentors, co-authors and friends who developed sustainability ideas, concepts and practices that lead the way to today's conceptualizations and policies.

and to

My son Benjamin Michael and grandson Jack Ryder who will push for sustainable futures characterized in this book.

TABLE OF CONTENTS

Facing the Urban Age
with a Passionate Optimism

Foreword to *Sustainability for the 21st Century*

Tim Beatley, University of Virginia

There is an understandable tendency these days to be pessimistic about the future. To be sure, a planet of 10 Billion or more, with signs of serous climate change, severely constrained availability of water and food, and limited success to date at tackling global poverty, to name a few, are not trends that inspire confidence. As the planet continues its high-speed charge in the direction of cities, it remains to be seen whether this new global era of the urban will usher in new abilities to solve these many challenges, or will it simply exacerbate them, and make them intractable.

While the challenges facing the world today seem daunting, I frequently find myself feeling optimistic and excited about the possibilities, especially as a city planner (or perhaps because I am a city planner?) I am frequently heard saying that I can't remember a more exciting time to be in the urban planning and design disciplines, as I look back at a quarter-century career.

How cities and urban life will be designed and planned may be the single most important task ahead, and the book you are about to read, and the insights, knowledge, and case examples it offers, will help to steer the way. Sustainability, we all agree, will need to be the essential goal for everything we do from here on. It is no longer something optional, no longer simply lofty language, but an essential lens and metric against which we judge how well we are doing. You will need the depth of understanding and knowledge the editor and chapter authors so expertly provide here, but you will also need to be inspired, to be hopeful, and optimistic that your work in the future can make a discernible and significant difference.

But why be optimistic? There are many reasons, I think. There are new urban and environmental sensibilities afoot for one. The emergence of the local food movement, for instance, and the fact that many more people seem to want to know where their food comes from, how it was produced, and what impacts its production might have. And many want to be directly involved in the growing of some or all of that food. Cherishing and celebrating the unique flavors, origins, provenance of food has led to a global slow food movement that has now expanded to embrace slow wood, slow fish, even *slow cities*.[1] Slow is a pejorative word in many cultures and societies, of course, but it is the emphasis on quality of living, savoring experiences, and on deepening relationships between people and the communities and landscapes in which they live that is encouraging.

---

[1] http://cittaslowusa.org/

There are also promising new alliances that will aide in advancing community sustainability. The emergence of a new collaborative spirit between public health and urban planning, and new understanding of the importance of design for *healthy* cities and places—which actively foster walking and biking—is encouraging. Physicians, nurses, public health professionals of all sorts, are seeking out partnerships with city planners. And in planning we understand the powerful new frame that health and wellbeing can provide and the promising and potent new collaborations with medicine that can help to further elevate the importance of urban design and planning.

We also know much more now than we did about cities and what it will take to create livable, sustainable, healthy places. The last decade has seen an explosion of new research findings and scholarship, providing essential insights about the kinds of urban conditions and design strategies that will be needed to ensure that we make progress on advancing global health and happiness. There is much new research, for instance, on the important role that nature plays in our lives, and that we are likely to be happier, healthy, and lead more meaningful lives when we have daily connections to nature (even inside buildings). This has given rise to movements to return to nature (what we have been calling *biophilic urbanism or biophilic cities*).[2]

And there are new ways that average citizens are now participating and engaged in the life of places they care about, with the emergence of citizen science and crowd-sourcing, added by the technology of smart phones. With the world poised to go from 2 billion smart phones in 2015, to more than 5 billion by 2017,[3] the opportunities are tremendous to connect individuals not only to each other but to cultivate new understandings of communities and environments in which they live, and new pathways for activism and for cultivating connections with the nature around us (can the world change with 5 billion people using smart phone apps like *i-birds* and *i-trees*).

We have many new and inspiring design and planning ideas, on the way to re-imagining cities. A decade or two ago I would have had a hard time imaging buildings, or neighborhoods, that produce all or nearly all of their own energy from renewables, or high-rise apartment towers where sky-forests grow (such as *Bosco Verticale* in Milan). And while there are many project designs and plans that will forever remain at the level of renderings, there have been few times in history where there has been so much creativity and imagination aimed at cities and urban life. And never have we been closer to fully recognizing what livability requires—certainly access to shelter and food, and healthy living and working environments, but increasingly much more: walkable, vibrant community spaces, trees and greenery, community gardens, abundant nature all around.

Many cities around the world are rising to the fore, setting for themselves ambitious green targets and visions for the future. Several years ago the City of Copenhagen declared its intent to become the world's first Carbon Neutral Capital City. Vancouver, in 2012, declared its intentions to be the Greenest City in the World. For these two cities these are not empty rhetorical gestures or sound bites, or politics, but serous commitments, backed with detailed actions, plans, and targets.

---

[2] E.g. See Beatley, *Biophilic Cities*, Washington, DC: Island Press, 2011.

[3] "2 Billion Smartphone Users By 2015 : 83% of Internet Usage From Mobiles," Found at:http://www.dazeinfo .com/2014/01/23/smartphone-users-growth-mobile-internet-2014-2017/

Cities like Copenhagen and Vancouver reflect the important perspective that the production and consumption patterns of global cities, their ecological footprints, extend far beyond their borders, and that ethical duties exist to think and act at the global scale. How to harness the economic and political power of global cities on behalf of oceans, for instance (we are on the blue planet after all) is a challenge, yet possible. Working to educate and engage an urban citizenry about distant habitats and organisms (as well as closer ones that may be out of sight, beyond the land's edge) must be a key goal.

A recent article in the journal *Foreign Affairs* declared that "The age of nations is over. The new urban age has begun."[4] Cities will be expected to exert new forms of global leadership moving forward, and here is yet another cause for some optimism. In the absence of national leadership many cities have already taken the lead in addressing global problems, such as climate change, though obviously much more is needed. National and State governments will continue to be important, of course, but increasingly, it is the city-state that will carry sway and the sphere of influence that will perhaps have the most to do with shaping quality of life and global sustainability. The new era of cities suggest unusual opportunities. Increasingly, cities are negotiating their own city-to-city trade agreements, with a staff and organizational capacity to act unilaterally on the global economic stage. Large cities especially will need to be ready to spearhead global conservation treaties, negotiate and sign them, broker new global agreement regarding resource extraction, and generally exert new leadership on the global stage.

There has been a broadening of the city planning agenda that is also helpful and an increasing recognition that cities must at once consider many different challenges. Along with *sustainability*, there are now a newer suite of complementary words that make up the language of planners and urban designers and managers. A sign of the times that resilience has emerged as a potent word and aspiration in a world where Hurricane Sandy's will become more common, and where cities will become the first responders in periods of drought, heat waves, disease outbreaks. The news is good here, as foundations like the Rockefeller Foundation, with its 100 Resilient Cities Initiative, have significantly elevated the profile and importance of resilience, and tools available for advancing urban resilience. Initially 100 cities have funds to hire new Chief Resilience Officers (CRO).[5] And many cities, from New York to Rotterdam to Dhaka, are re-thinking the ways in which they occupy and inhabit the spaces on the edge of the dynamic coastal edge, suggesting new adaptive strategies but more profoundly, new modes of adaptive urban life.

Understanding the ability of coastal cities to move and shift and respond to sea level rise, and planning for and with this new dynamism, suggest new ways of seeing cities as ecosystems. And there are many other important ways of re-conceptualizing cities with implications for sustainability and livability. Importantly, we can take stock of and comprehensively understand cities in terms of the metabolisms, their complex flows of inputs and outputs. Sustainability and resilience will require that we understand these flows—for instance of energy, materials, food, water—and work to modify them, at once shortening supply lines where we can (e.g. growing more food

---

[4] Parag Khanna, "Beyond City Limits," Foreign Policy, 2010.

[5] http://www.100resilientcities.org/

locally and regionally, decentralized renewable energy), reducing the extent of these flows (e.g. designing homes and work spaces that use only tiny amounts of energy, for instance) and working toward a circular metabolism where possible (waste becomes an input to something else).

Partly this is a bold undertaking to re-imagine the very nature of cities and urban life. We need to plan cities, as architect William McDonough suggests, that act and function more like forests, like natural systems—producing the energy it needs, living off incoming solar energy, providing essential habitat for human and non-human species alike, recycling and reusing the material outputs (there is no such thing as waste in nature and so should not be in cities either). Understanding cities as places of abundance, bountiful and restorative as much as consumptive and destructive, is an essential mind shift and a more hopeful vision for the future.

Global sustainability will also require us to re-think the nature of economic relationships in an increasingly interconnected planet. No longer can large cities simply assume that massive flows of food, energy, building materials, are derived in benign and non-destructive ways, but there will be a need in the new urban era for city-states to be more engaged and proactive. Cities can and must be leaders in re-tooling these flows, to ensure global sustainability, but also global fairness. There remain relatively few examples, unfortunately. New York City's adoption of a policy of transitioning away from the purchasing of tropical hardwoods is an examples, but there will be many ways in which urban consumption, especially in the affluent cities of the global North will need to be accompanied by commitments to aid in the ecological restoration and enhanced health and quality of life of the cities in the Global South. The promise of a new model of global urbanism will is that it will harness the power of these metabolic flows and human demands on behalf of both planetary health and human welfare.

I believe, as well, that any compelling model of future urbanism must also take account of the need for daily contact with nature and the natural world. We increasingly recognize that as we advocate and work towards compact, dense and sustainable cities, that these be *nature-ful* places, places that provide us with a sufficient urban nature diet to be happy, healthy and to lead fully meaningful lives. Nature is not optional but essential, we have grown to understand, and by the way, can help to make cities more resilient in the face of climate change and the many other shocks we are facing.

Planners and urban designers, then, face serious challenges in creating just, sustainable, resilient and biophilic cities. But I am optimistic that this can be done, and that life on the urban Earth can be healthful, uplifting, and meaningful, as well as respectful of environmental limits.

We can harness the considerable new energy and thinking that exists around cities today (much of contained herein), new technologies, research, and new ways of re-imagining the very nature of what a city is. These are exhilarating times in sustainability education and the potential to make a positive difference has never been greater. You will need the skills, knowledge and inspiration too, and I can think of no better preparation than the articles and chapters contained herein. Sustainability, in all its flavors, and so clearly described and argued for in this book, is an essential pathway to our global future.

ABOUT THE AUTHOR

K. David Pijawká

David Pijawka is Professor and Associate Director of the School of Geographical Sciences and Urban Planning at Arizona State University (ASU) and a Senior Sustainability Scientist at the Julie S. Walton *Global Institute of Sustainability*. With other professors he teaches and leads the largest course on sustainability at the university and perhaps globally, *Sustainable Cities*. Professor Pijawka is also affiliated with the Schools of Tranborder Studies, Public Affairs, the Barrett Honors College, and the American Indian Research Institute, among others. He has published extensively on sustainability topics including research on energy related impacts, resiliency in disasters, planning for sustainable neighborhoods, and community well-being. He has also published on topics including transportation risk analysis, socio-economic impacts of nuclear waste storage, risk perceptions of hazards and climate change, neighborhood sustainable design, and environmental impacts on communities especially Environmental Justice studies. Dr. Pijawka has completed numerous planning studies on American Indian communities especially comprehensive plans, visioning and strategic planning. He was the director of a multi-year multi-university Center on the US-Mexico Border Region and developed a recognized indicators initiative on border urban quality of life.

Professor Pijawka has been recognized for his innovative teaching, and in addition to awards, has been invited to lecture all over the world on teaching sustainability. He has given key-note lectures at various universities and international conferences and has received grants from the National Science Foundation, US Department of Transportation, US Environmental Protection Agency, Nuclear Regulatory Commission, Department of Energy, among many others. Dr. Pijawka has been recognized with over 30 awards including an award from the NAACP for his work on Environmental Justice. He has authored over 30 books, monographs, and governmental reports on topics ranging from quality of life indicators to urban sustainability and disaster planning.

ACKNOWLEDGMENTS

This book would not have been possible without the feedback from students in Arizona State University's *Sustainable Cities* course over the past decade on the topics covered in the class and approaches used in meeting sustainability learning objectives—as well as the commitment of faculty involved in teaching and discussing this broad–based interdisciplinary and introductory course focused on cities. Initially given as class lectures, most of the textbook chapters were then written for this book after discussion with me about content coverage, perspective, structure, and cases. One challenging question was asked of each author: what are the concepts, cases, and ideas that you are conveying in your chapter that will elucidate the current problems in urban sustainability and how they may be solved over the next decades? Major thanks are given to those very special faculty members who are committed to sustainability education and who went the extra mile to write these chapters. These professors include: Anthony Brazel, Darren Ruddell, Rimjhim Aggarwal, Ariane Middel, John Meunier, Martin Pasqualetti, Charles Redman, Subhrajit Guhathakurta, Aaron Golub, Douglas Webster, Bjoern Hagen, Edward Cook, Judith Dworkin, and Ray Quay.

The book also benefitted from chapters written by doctoral and post-doctoral students who are making new and innovative advances in their research on the topics in this volume. These include subject matter on resiliency, indicator systems, history of sustainability, urban and environmental policy in China, and sustainability education. Thanks for their important contributions: Stephen Buchman (University of Michigan), Chad Frederick (University of Louisville), Nelya Rakhimova (University of Dresden, Germany), Feifei Zhang (Arizona State University), Devon McAslan (University of Michigan), and Craig Thomas (Arizona State University).

Thanks to Professor Timothy Beatley, from the University of Virginia, who wrote the book's Foreword, and in addition, provided material from his own book *Biophilic Cities* (Island Press) as an insert to one of the chapters. Dr. Beatley has had a continuous and close association with the sustainability program at Arizona State University, lecturing in the *Sustainable Cities* course and in the Julie Ann Wrigley Global Institute of Sustainability, as well as interacting with ASU's Barrett Honors College students on his Global *Biophilic Cities Initiative* where ASU is a partnership institution.

A large part of working with the authors on the book occurred during summer, 2014 while I was at the University of Kaiserslautern, Germany as a Visiting Scholar, and together with Bjoern Hagen, we carried out a study on the social and well–being sustainability of Freiburg, Germany that appears in the book. Much thanks to Kaiserslautern for hosting me and to the people in Freiburg who generously gave of their time to support our study. Thanks to Kevin McHugh, Nabil Kamel, Christopher Boone, Judith Dworkin, Bjoern Hagen, Katherine Crewe, Gloria Jeffery, and Kathrin Hab for their insightful reviews. This past summer I also visited a number of Chinese universities in Chengdu and Beijing and lectured on future trends of sustainable cities. Much thanks to the students and faculty in these universities and research centers for their high level of engagement and interaction, and especially to Douglas Webster,

Jianming Cai, and Feifei Zhang for producing a compelling chapter on the move toward sustainability in Chinese cities.

Walking along the sidewalks of Beijing's 798 Art District (once an old industrial warehousing quarter and now a vibrant area of galleries, restaurants, commercial establishments, and residences), I remember first seeing the sculpture that is now shown on the front cover of this book. The sculpted hand coming out from the sidewalk represents the devastation of the Sichuan region from an earthquake in 2008 with its loss of life and destruction, without its original vitality and strength; and the other hand coming down touching at the fingers, denotes support, hope, a new start, well-being, and reconstruction – the embodiment of sustainability. I am thankful to the artist, Lin Tianqiang, for granting us permission to use a photo of his artwork for the cover and to James Healy for taking numerous photos of the art piece for the book. Lin Tianqiang is the president of Peking University Art Capital Association and James Healy is with the China Daily newspaper.

Significant credit for this book and the course goes to Michael Crow, President of Arizona State University, who had the vision to invest in education programs, transdiciplinary research, and community engagement in sustainability. Over ten years, the *Sustainable Cities* course alone likely enrolled around 8,000 students, learning for the first time the compelling promise of sustainability science and its solutions for cities. Imagine, as it happened, the president of one of the largest universities in the U.S. coming in to the course to lecture to a class of 500 plus freshman on the importance of sustainability, and a panel of first-year students posing questions on the lecture. There are few places like this. I am also grateful to Angela Lampe, Kendall Hunt's national editor, for selecting this book for publication and for working with me, and with the authors, on every facet of its development. Lastly, all through 2014, Deborah Koshinsky, looked carefully at each chapter and edited them for language, grammar, references, flow, readability, placement of cases, and sometimes content. The book's impact through its readability and consistency will be largely due to her efforts.

David Pijawka
October, 2014

Introducing the Book: Pathways to a Sustainable Future

K. David Pijawka

Scope and Context

This textbook has developed for over a decade since the inception of a broad-based interdisciplinary course on *Sustainable Cities* conducted at Arizona State University. Its content, nature of the questions asked, range of topics, and sustainability concepts reflect a continual progression of ideas and initiatives as sustainability itself has changed. This book covers the essential topic areas, grappling with sustainable solutions at the urban scale. Each topic—like parts of a city—connects to other topics and issues and—like the field of sustainability—is complex, challenging, and interdisciplinary. Each chapter is presented holistically, exploring the urban connections while still covering the individual topic's essential dimensions and issues.

The guiding idea for this book is *interconnectivity*; that is, each individual aspect of the topic area has a temporal element, a connection between the past, present, and future; a connection by geographical and political scales; and connections among urban factors. For example, to understand and appreciate sustainable transportation fully, we need to show how making transportation more environmentally sustainable requires the understanding of land uses, goals for carbon reduction, economics of transportation, urban design, alternative transit systems, and environmental justice.

The objectives of this book are fourfold. The first objective is to deliver a broad-based textbook on urban sustainability to students, faculty who will become instructors in this field or are interested in current questions and the foundational core of urban sustainability, and the public, who look to see how sustainability can be applied to their communities, and to them, personally. An important audience also includes those individuals working in municipal, regional, and state governments—community planners, environmental resources personnel, policy-makers, and active members of nongovernmental organizations seeking information on the practice of sustainability science. Chapter authors, carefully selected as scholars in, and educators on, their respective sustainability specializations, are at the same time well informed about sustainability issues and trends that cut across cities.

All the authors contributing to this book are familiar with the interdisciplinary nature of sustainability, approaches used to address research on their topics, and underlying ethical issues. And, as much as possible within the constraints of a chapter, they connect their specific topic to other urban influences. The second objective of this book is to understand that "modern sustainability" has had its successes and disappointments. But now, 15 years into the new century, we are armed with relatively new tools and approaches, scientific urban predictor models, indicator systems, interdisciplinary methodologies, and policy and planning programs to tackle difficult challenges in restoring and transforming cities and their communities into resilient and livable places to live. This book promises to illustrate how cities are using these new methods and approaches. Especially relevant to this objective is Chapter 15 by Professor Guhathakurta who gives attention to urban simulation modeling for sustainability.

The reader and scholar of sustainability will also find several chapters that are not typically appearing urban topics (such as resiliency, sprawl repair, urban ecology, renewable energy, climate change, and neighborhood design). They are crosscutting new approaches for urban sustainability. For example, Chapter 6, by Stephen Buckman and Nelya Rakhimova, addresses the concepts and practices underlying community resiliency from the field's numerous perspectives. Chapter 14, by Devon McAslan, evaluates the role, history, and use of indicators to measure city progress along a number of dimensions important to sustainability. Further, Chapter 14 provides the reader with profiles of key indicator programs used by cities and discusses what makes indicators an effective tool in sustainability policy. During the last two decades, the work by landscape ecologists has taken root in planning for cities and is the basis for Edward Cook's chapter on urban ecological design (Chapter 7). That chapter stemming from the ecological sciences is indispensable for understanding urban sustainability. The author takes us from key principles in landscape ecology and networks and their importance in protecting and restoring urban land to the value of ecosystem services and their benefits for cities. Of significance, Professor Edward Cook and Timothy Beatley's insert on *Biophilic Cities* in that chapter examine the role that nature plays in cities—socially, psychologically and economically—as well as the importance of ecological restoration and preservation.

The third objective is to link the book to its educational value for sustainability learning. In Chapter 16, by Chad Frederick and I argue the case for developing and employing sustainable learning outcomes and competencies. As the principal instructor of the *Sustainable Cities* course for over 10 years, the editor as well as many of the authors contributed course material and developed the text chapters from the course experience. As such, most of the chapters have been tested for their educational value in the course.

The last objective of this book is to provide a model or framework of sustainable development that includes health and well-being factors, quality-of-life considerations, cultural restoration/cultural sustainability, and the full range of institutional capacity factors for decision making in the context of coupled human–ecological systems. For example, Judith Dworkin in Chapter 18 shows an application of an expanded sustainability framework in a case study of one American Indian tribe that uses a combination of innovative health services, adaptive resiliency, and cultural restoration.

Educational Value

Each chapter introduces the topic in terms of an issue for sustainability, provides a history of problems and their causes, and profiles the problems as manifest in cities with examples and solutions that have been attempted. Illustrations of practices and solutions tried by various cities are often shown in case studies with a particular focus on urban programs, strategies, or policies. As much as possible, the authors were asked to provide more than one case study solution for each sustainability problem.

The authors of this book are academic experts in sustainability science. As such, they are aware of the emergence of the new and briskly growing field of "education for sustainable development." There is an emergent literature on learning outcomes and competencies required for education in sustainability. Therefore, this book pushes the boundaries to direct and integrate some of its topics for such learning competencies as interdisciplinarity, systems thinking, anticipatory problem-solving approaches, and other venues, including ethical perspectives and assessments. Other competencies, such as sustainable methodologies involving adaptive governance and citizen engagement, collaborative experience, and strategic planning, are included. Chapter 16, by Chad Frederick and the editor, looks at these sustainable education competencies and how learning outcomes can be measured.

How sustainability education is delivered is critically important for the field to advance and the science to be accepted and applied. The growth of sustainability as a field of study has been recent, but it is now burgeoning with new conceptualizations, frameworks, methods, and applications. In the last decade, its vocabulary has expanded to include coverage of such topics as livability, resiliency, health and culture, adaptation, anticipatory governance, coupled human–ecological systems, and myriad forms of social-participatory processes in seeking acceptable solutions to achieve sustainable cities. This book engages the reader with knowledge and substance, and demonstrates how urban solutions are being accomplished. The pivotal role of transdisciplinary thinking and practice is threaded throughout the book.

Themes

The following section will briefly describe the major crosscutting themes and explorations in this textbook.

Can we measure progress in a city's sustainability? Developing measures for sustainability to determine progress over time has been central to sustainability analysis and policy development. To be able to express how well a city is performing in sustainability has become an important governmental and policy objective, especially when organizations track results of indicators and make city comparisons. Indicators enable city governments and the public to identify problems and then to place them onto a policy agenda. The objective of Chapter 2, by Bjoern Hagen and Ariane Middel, is to inform us of various programs and plans developed by three of the world's most sustainably advanced cities in areas of transportation, urban design, citizen engagement, protection and enhancement of natural systems, and housing. The chapter explores three of the principal indicators in use today for cities—the green city, resiliency, and livability—and through these, readers will be able to understand the criteria needed to fare well on the indicators and how to connect these to city plans. The development of the history of indicators, what makes for good and effective and long-lasting indicators, the type of indicators used in sustainability, and a profile of currently employed indicator systems also comprise the subject matter of Chapter 14, by Devon McAslan.

What constitutes a history of sustainability? The question—when did sustainability begin—is an important one to pose. For example, is the Malthusian question about the relationship of population growth, environmental resources, and scarcity important to discuss within modern sustainability science, or Ebenezer Howard's Garden Cities' utopian model for cities, because both emerged before the 20th century? Or, for that matter, is it important to know about the causes and impacts of America's first widespread natural disaster, the Dust Bowl, and the lessons learned from it? Or, should we now consider abandoning understanding the role of the naturalist philosophers for modern thinking on sustainability because they came before the Brundtland Commission's definition of sustainable development? Or, given the breadth and complexity of sustainability challenges, should there be a new, expanded role for the naturalists in sustainability education?

History comes into play in several ways in this book, but principally it does so in Chapter 3 by Craig Thomas. Here, the author does not start with the post-1980s United Nations initiatives, with its current debates over climate change, but identifies the central and essential intellectual discourses on sustainability and its meanings, and he links pre-1980 historical events to underlying concepts of sustainability thinking. The first use of the term *sustainable yield*, we learn, resulted from the product of scientific forest management concepts at the turn of the 20th century, and used later as an argument against *preservation of environmental resources.* The case of the Dust Bowl—its causes, impacts, and remedies—is seen in the context of current ideas of coupled human–ecological adaptive systems. Other histories and what they can tell us about sustainable systems are found in Chapter 4, by Charles Redman, which characterizes early cities and their evolution and what they can tell us about sustainability. Of particular interest are his insights on instances of societal "collapse" occuring at times when environmental resources were seriously diminished. The past matters!

What advances are being made in the social dimensions of sustainability? The most challenging part of the original Brundtland-based "three-pillar" framework centered around the articulation of the social dimensions of the framework. Over the last decade, substantial new approaches have been taken in advancing the social aspects of sustainability thinking and practices. Social well-being and resiliency indicator discussions are found in the chapters referenced earlier, especially those chapters specifically focused on resiliency and livability where (more often than not) the issues are embedded in ideas about community participation, social and neighborhood stability, social justice policies, leadership, and collaboration. For example, Chapter 2 "What Should Sustainable Cities Look Like", discussed earlier, has an insert on the social dimensions of building a neighborhood in Freiburg, Germany, one of the most sustainable cities in the world. Preliminary data from new research by Bjoern Hagen and the editor show the importance of acting on social sustainability goals right at the start—the role of citizen engagement in decision making, the importance of social networking and building community resiliency programs early—as in integrating social programs for the elderly and integrating different income levels into housing projects. Looking at desert cities in the world, John Meunier in Chapter 9 examines the role of urban design for maintaining water, shade, food, home, and social interaction and explores what can be learned building sustainable neighborhoods.

Within the social well-being sustainability coverage, environmental justice issues are threaded throughout the book as seen in discussions of differential impacts of access to transportation; diverse impacts among social groups and places related to climate action planning; disparities among social groups in relation to "food deserts"; and spatial differences in terms of heat island impacts across various social and income groups. While environmental justice concerns fluctuate across the urban landscape, the once hidden patterns of injustice, such as neighborhood access to urban parks, are becoming apparent. The beginning of the 21st century still continues to harbor urban legacy problems of the past, such as the lack of toxic cleanup in poor areas of cities, the staying power of Brownfield problems, and spatial variances in exposure to industrial toxics, especially among children. Sustainability challenges are now beginning to address serious health issues as part the social domain in the framework as well as the full range of quality-of-life issues. For example, Chapter 18 expands our understanding of the history of environmental justice and the criticality of sustainability for American Indian nations as we recognize the dire health crisis facing American Indian peoples, the unacceptable high levels of unemployment, and the purposeful destruction of Indian cultures as part of their history. Through a case study of one tribe, this chapter argues for a holistic model of sustainability that expands the three-pillar framework to include an additional and unique set of factors that include effective health services, restoration of lost and traditional culture, and adaptive decision-making organizations with emphasis placed on community resiliency and education.

Sustainability: A Trajectory from International Conferences to Local Actions

Nearly three decades have raced by since the 1987 Brundtland Commission's report on sustainable development that provided what has become the prevailing framework and definition of sustainable development, one which included maintaining our biocapacity (security of our ecosystems), meeting society's present needs (alleviation of poverty, food security, social justice), and securing intergenerational equity (resources for future generations) (WCED, 1987). These years can now be condensed into a short but vibrant history ranging from setting global environmental targets and measures to reduce global environmental threats to enhancing social resiliency through efforts by the United Nations, individual countries, and especially urban areas. Chapter 3 characterizes and contextualizes this history of successes and disappointments as part of a larger intellectual history of sustainability. Many of the principal initiatives and programs by the United Nations sustainability conferences that set targets did not meet those (even years later), and alternative programs and measures were then established. Many of the global conferences lacked targets, focusing instead on reaching agreements in establishing principles and recommendations for action upon which most countries could agree, such as Agenda 21. Attempts to reach a global consensus on these action programs and principles for sustainable development proved to be important in sustainability's staying power and a global influence and justification of initiatives at the local level.

It is at the city level where we see considerable progress and new trends toward urban initiatives in sustainability. For example, although there was a failure in reaching global carbon emissions targets, it was at the local level where we later (and currently) observe targets set for renewable energy generation, design standards to reduce carbon emissions, climate change adaptation plans (e.g., San Francisco, New York), local climate action planning, alternative transportation policies, renewable energy incentives, and green building programs, among others. It was the goal of the United Nations first Kyoto protocol to reduce carbon emissions by 5.2 percent below the emission levels of 1990 and to do so by 2012. Now in 2014, we know we have failed to meet this goal. We do know that the concentrations of carbon dioxide in the atmosphere rose 20 percent faster between 2000 and 2004 than in the 1990s. The first Kyoto protocol ended in 2012, and the second-phase commitment for eight additional years to reduce greenhouse gases (GHGs) to below 1990 levels was limited in scope because numerous countries were not committed or obligated. However, local level commitments to utilize renewable energy sources in 2012 alone did show promise by reducing GHGs by 6 percent. As I am writing this today, in September 2014, the CNN reported that in New York City hundreds of thousands of people protested for climate global change regulations at the start of a new United Nations global conference.

As this book demonstrates, the development of such programs and policies at the city scales have many obstacles. The start of the 21st century and the subsequent 15 years represent a noteworthy and foundational shift toward the acceptance and actualization of sustainability thinking, actions, and experimentation in cities. Such efforts will only expand and strengthen as new and robust sustainability frameworks are developed, policies are validated through practice, and sustainability planning becomes increasingly embedded in community culture. This book, then, identifies the urban problems in need of sustainable solutions, examines for each topical area the urban solutions attempted at conceptual and practical levels, demonstrates what can be done through comparative analysis, and identifies how we can improve and enhance city institutional capacities. This is the rationale for the book's title, *Sustainability for the 21st Century: Pathways, Programs, and Policies.*

Global Challenges at the Beginning of the 21st Century

The Brundtland Commission's report in 1987 informed us that we need to think carefully about how we consume our natural resources and the importance of alleviating poverty through sustainable development programs. The *Limits to Growth* update (2004) showed us that the planet's ecological footprint (EF) had exceeded its biocapacity. Each was a pivotal moment in sustainability. We are now at another pivotal period, at a crossroads in formulating ideas to take us through the coming decades of the 21st century. We are significantly more aware of the global threats and issues through international conferences and reports, global monitoring and indicator programs, scientific and social science research advances, and emerging sustainability education programs. Yet, global problems of climate change, ecological refugees, environmental injustice, declining biodiversity and marine life, lack of safe drinking water for many parts of the world, and food insecurity alarms are challenging and difficult to resolve. Global action on all aspects of sustainability, simultaneously, is a daunting prospect, yet work continues despite the lack of worldwide consensus and capacities.

Over the last decade, the three-pillar (i.e., environment, economy, and social equity) framework produced by Brundtland has expanded in practice to include ideas and programs about urban adaptation to disasters, resiliency, anticipatory governance, coupled human–ecological systems, benefits of ecosystem services in cities, and social well-being/livability, which include issues that fall into health and cultural domains. While advances in constructing new conceptualizations in urban sustainability in this new century are encouraging, there are continuing and unsettling threats questioning our ability to achieve a sustainable future at the urban, as well as the global level. Signed by more than 1600 scientists, a note introducing the book *Limits to Growth: the Thirty-Year Update* states:

> Human beings and the natural world are on a collision course. Human activities inflict harsh and often irreversible damage on the environment and on critical resources. If not checked, many of our current practices put at serious risk the future that we wish for human society and the plant and animal kingdoms, and may so alter the living world that it will be unable to sustain life in the manner that we know. Fundamental changes are urgent if we are to avoid the collision our present course will bring about.

These threats or challenges fall into several categories: (a) substantial and continuous global population growth well into the 21st century, particularly in the least-developed countries; (b) stabilization of urbanization rates at very high levels for developed countries, with major increases in urbanization for poorer countries; (c) increasing emissions of carbon dioxide and higher atmospheric concentrations of GHGs; (d) continuance of an ever-expanding global Ecological Footprint (e) food insecurity issues; and (f) continuance of disasters and catastrophes. The goal for sustainable development is to prevent, or at the very least, seriously diminish, the ongoing depletion and deterioration of natural capital that leads to "overshooting" the globe's biocapacity. What do we need to be aware of as we plunge into the 15th year of 21st century while searching for sustainable solutions for the world's cities? These challenges are deep and complex and will adversely impact cities through the 21st century. Society often does not have the experience or know-how or may not have the capacity to manage these growing, substantial, and intractable future threats. New ideas, skills, education, and institutional and policy tools will need to be advanced in sustainability science to meet these challenges.

Challenge: Population Growth Rates

The question of the connection between population, resources, and scarcity has been a protracted issue since Malthus; and, despite contemporary contentious debates, population growth continues to pose an underlying quiet threat into the future. In 2013, according to the United Nations *World Population Prospects*, the world's population stood at 7.5 billion people. Projections showed an increase to 8.1 billion by 2025, 9.6 billion in 2050, and up to 10.9 billion by 2100 (United Nations, 2013). These estimates were based on a median-variant projection assuming a decline in fertility, especially in countries with large families. Still, the expectation is for a 45.3 percent increase in the world's population by 2100. However, a more disquieting population scenario offered in the same report estimates much larger population increases based on higher fertility rates, showing 10.9 billion by 2050 and 16.6 billion people by 2100. A worst-case scenario can place the earth's population at just under 30 billion by 2100. Population estimates like these greatly exceed the earth's carrying capacity, estimated at 6 to 10 billion. The problem is further complicated by the fact that population growth largely will take place in the developing world and especially in the "least-developed" high-fertility countries, such as in Africa, Indonesia, and India. According to the United Nations, in contrast, little population change is expected in the industrialized and developed countries (United Nations, 2013).

These least-developed countries with generally large and young populations are concomitantly those areas with existing resource shortages and deteriorating environmental conditions, as well as areas prone to conflict. Based on population growth estimations, these areas will confront serious resources decline, challenges in adequately providing societal needs in employment, education, health services, and basic infrastructure. These populations will also be highly vulnerable in terms of coping with adverse health conditions. Already in 2014, several of these countries in West Africa are confronting a rapidly spreading Ebola health epidemic with the potential to be a global catastrophe if not contained. A principal objective of sustainability will involve determining how to reduce these massive vulnerabilities resulting from poverty and resource-deficient regions. We should start now. Lastly, the United Nations population report also tells us that at least 8 of the present "least-developed" countries in the world will be among the 20 most populated countries by 2100.

Aside from poverty-stricken areas, one of the most populated countries on earth, China, may have lessons for the rest of the countries over the next few decades. As Chapter 17 by Webster et al. on Chinese cities tells us, around 500,000 people die prematurely each year in China as a result of air and water pollution. Moreover, despite the investment in rail lines for mass urban transit, consumption of automobiles is expanding significantly, making it more difficult to reduce the carbon footprint, despite the fact that China is the world's leader in utilizing solar technologies and is eliminating coal power generation. To transform Chinese cities toward sustainability, major societal shifts will be necessary over the next decades. Chapter 17 documents that under the 12th National Plan, China is poised for transforming its cities toward sustainable structures through reducing coal burning power for their energy needs, enlarging major mass transit investment and construction, redistributing its industries to lessen the current high rate of rural-to-urban migration, and implementing policies to regulate loss of ecosystem services. This possible transformation may provide important lessons. Despite the threat of population growth relative to environmental resources, there is hope. The chapter tells us about initiatives taken in one of China's model sustainable cities.

Challenge: Urbanization Issues

Urbanization as the process by which cities grow, and how fast they grow is known as the urbanization rate. Not only will the next decades experience considerable population growth impacting the most vulnerable countries, rapid urbanization will result in growing and pronounced urban vulnerabilities. The largest cities in poorer countries will likely be the most vulnerable as they lack basic infrastructure, viable governance, as well as possessing markedly low levels of community resiliency. We observe that large cities in the least-developed countries show low ratings on the livability and resiliency indices as Chapter 2 documents. Like the Haiti disaster several years ago, and now the Ebola outbreak in West Africa, the levels of system resiliency (including institutional capacities to respond and tackle the immediate problem and build long-term solutions) are just not present.

This book informs us that sustainability solutions for highly vulnerable urban regions will require new long-term solutions to build resilient human–environmental systems, adaptable infrastructure systems, and the establishment of new, responsive and anticipatory governance. Developing these new urban governance systems for sustainable solutions over the next few decades will be a necessity in order to slow the adverse conditions of the most vulnerable regions. Several chapters consider the topic of resiliency in the context of sustainable development. Chapter 6 provides a full picture of the concepts and practices needed in advancing community resiliency. Augmenting this information is Chapter 18, which addresses the importance of applying resiliency ideas to the health services and cultural restoration of American Indian nations, regions often neglected in the past or exploited for their natural resources, but (in most cases) stripped of their assets, including their indigenous cultures. Sustainability is viewed as the basis for economic and cultural restoration and advancement.

The major global impacts that will confront cities and their sustainability also result from the rapid growth of cities and the structural changes beginning to be observed among the largest cities. In 2008, for the first time, the global population reached over 50 percent residing in urbanized areas of the world. This reflects a rapid climb from 1950, when cities represented only 30 percent of the world's population. Currently, it is at 54 percent according to the 2014 United Nations report, *World Urbanization Prospects* (United Nations, 2014). This reflects a major and noteworthy pull of cities that is transformational. The continual growth of the global population (especially the rapid rate of this growth into cities) sets off a present-day alarm for sustainability. This prospect establishes the clear need over the next decades to find viable solutions for urban regions that otherwise may not be able to build adequate infrastructure and resources in education, health services, employment, water security, and food systems. Further, such areas likely will not have sufficient resiliency to absorb and respond to (or even prepare for) environmental shocks, such as serious drought and water shortages for agricultural production. In these cities in poverty-stricken developing countries, sustainable development will need to be directed at reducing vulnerability to avoid what Jared Diamond calls "collapse" (Diamond, 2007). If the estimates of the United Nations are realized by 2100, 66 percent of the world will reside in cities, and many of these cities will be larger than any of our past experience with cities. Given today's knowledge, these cities will likely be highly fragmented, infrastructure deficient, with low levels of resilience to meet system shocks. Implementing resilient urban systems will not be optional.

In the developed industrialized countries, urbanization is already high, with Europe at around 73 percent and North America at 82 percent. It is the African nations and some Asian countries where rural areas are still between 40 and 50 percent (United Nations, 2014). High rates of urbanization result from natural population growth, rural-to-urban migration, and country-to-country migration. Even those countries with lower urbanization rates like those in Africa are changing very quickly. By 2100, the United Nations forecasts an urbanization rate at over 55 percent for that region. A frightening statistic by the United Nations–based report on population growth, is that 2.5 billion people will be added to urban populations between now and the next three and one-half decades. This issue of rapid urbanization rates would not be as daunting if urbanization was distributed equally, but the central, critical issue for sustainability is that population growth and urbanization rates are not projected to be equally distributed. In 1990, around the time of the Brundtland report, there were 10 megacities—defined as a city with over 10 million people. Twenty-five years later, there are 28 megacities. In about

15 years, we likely will have 41 megacities, with most of them growing well beyond the 10 million population mark. Added to the 41 megacities, there will likely be more than 60 other cities with populations between 5 and 10 million residents during this century.

From the perspective of sustainability, this may not be a crisis situation were these cities to be similar to Tokyo, a current megacity with around 38 million residents. Here, basic infrastructure is working well with mass transit and high-density residential districts coupled with consistent high levels of employment and characterized as a highly resilient city. However, most of the megacities are found in developing countries. Rapid growth is often unplanned and unmanaged, with poor infrastructure, underemployment, and mismatched development patterns. Many of the megacities are located along coastlines that may be impacted by climate-caused disasters over the next few decades. Adaptation policies to reduce the impacts of climate change will be a necessity for these areas. While these cities will require much attention in terms of adaptive capacities, because of the expected extreme impacts, there are also signs now of future food insecurity as rural areas are being depleted of natural resources and soil fertility. Innovative sustainability solutions will be required as the urban population in cities grows from 3.9 billion today to 6.3 billion in 2050, leaving us only a 35-year horizon for needed sustainability planning and intervention.

Challenge: Greenhouse Gases and Ecological Footprints (EF)

Two global issues confront and challenge our coping abilities for solutions in the 21st Century: carbon dioxide emissions and the expanding global EF. For these two challenges, the beginning of the 21st century is a continuation of the past as population numbers continue to increase, natural resources are diminishing beyond their sustainable yield, and regional conflicts disrupt communities and agricultural development. Some of the interesting points found in the sustainability literature related to GHG are that cities (through automobile fuel consumption, construction processes, and energy generation) prove to be the largest emitters of GHGs (around 75 percent of all GHG emissions), and they are also the areas most impacted by climate-based natural disasters.

What do the data tell us about these two challenges? The EF is a measure of environmental resource consumption and is used often to compare countries on a per capita basis of how much is taken from Earth's natural capital/resources and is usually conceptualized as a land area in hectares. We also examine the footprint in order to see trends and rate of diminishment of a country's resource base. For some countries, especially industrialized and developed countries with large populations, the size of the EF often extends beyond the boundaries of the country. The Global Footprint Network (GFN) for 2012 defined the EF as a measure of "human appropriation of ecosystem products and services in terms of bioproductive land and sea area needed to supply products" (Global Footprint Network, 2012). The report argues that in the early 21st century, we are experiencing natural resources constraints as demand in many countries has exceeded available resources.

The EF has two analytical dimensions: the demand for human consumption measured in land required for food crops, waste disposal, and absorption of carbon dioxide emissions; and, the availability of regenerative capacity to meet the demands. Some footprints are much more complex. The availability of regenerative land to meet each demand is termed *biological capacity*. In 2007, the EF consumption was estimated to be 2.7 global hectares per capita with a biocapacity measure of 1.8 global hectares per capita (GFN, 2012). The global deficit was then evident at 1.9 global hectares per capita—the level of consumption exceeded the earth's biocapacity. In the same year, the deficit for the United States was observed at 4.1 global hectares per capita. The GFN also shows the global ecological deficit in terms of number of earths: in 1961, the deficit stood at less than 1 earth at 0.8 earths, meaning we had residual biocapacity remaining. In the early 1970s, the deficit reached 1 earth; and from around 1990 to 2000, it stood at 1.2 earths. Five years back, the overshoot reached 1.5 earths according to the GFN. Clearly, over the last 50 years, the amount of ecological overshoot has increased. The growth of the EF over time suggests a serious and fundamental challenge regarding how to provide solutions for its reduction. The EF is a generalized indicator of resources consumption translated into amount of land required for that level of consumption. EFs can vary even for the same country depending on what factors are used to determine the footprint and can become complicated especially for determining EFs for cities.

There is a good degree of consistency, however, regarding the overshoot: by 2000, 1.2 earths appeared fairly consistently in the literature; and, there is general agreement in the literature at around 1.5 earths today. Interestingly, there are just a few projections of biocapacity deficits, one showing 3.0 earths by 2050, with absence of any planned interventions. Those developing the 2050 projections acknowledged that we can promote sustainability through interventions; for example, we may be able to reduce the deficit to 1.5 earths by 2050 if significant shifts to renewable energy are undertaken resulting in the reduction of carbon dioxide emissions (carbon emissions are part of the EF calculation). Here, then, is the tipping point that can influence whether we can become sustainable or not. If we continue at today's level of resource consumption and population growth, we may hit an overshoot of 3.0 earths by 2050 under one scenario. Or, we reduce GHGs through clean, renewable energy policies to return to the present-day levels by 2050. The scenario-based reduction to 1.5 earths by 2050 through renewables shows hope. Despite this one optimistic scenario, the deficit will still remain at 1.5 earths. This book shows that these pathways exist; the knowledge and policies are available; and plans can be implemented to transform our cities toward significantly improved levels of sustainability.

Challenge: Food Insecurity

At the urban level today, there are glaring concerns in the United States over food availability and quality, most often in central city areas. Chapter 8 addresses food insecurities and the conditions that bring them about and gives attention to these urban "food deserts." At the beginning of the 21st Century, it is surprising and disturbing that the United States, the richest country in the world, now has to confront and eliminate a new form of environmental injustice—"food deserts"—with their almost complete lack of fresh, healthy, and affordable food options that adversely and disproportionately impact inner city neighborhoods. Solutions for sustainable development in inner cities must include consideration of social justice, health, food security, social well-being, and legacy problems (such as toxics and pollution exposure), among other factors. To protect children's health in inner cities (including obesity, and other problems, such as violence and lack of access to quality education and medical services), innovative sustainability models need to be advanced that combine community resiliency in terms of well-being, support, leadership, and civic engagement, as well as sustainable neighborhood design and rebuilding. These efforts should include open space, public transit, engagement with nature, and places where families are secure from violence and food scarcity.

With respect to global food insecurity, since 1990, estimates show a decline of persons living with continuous hunger and undernourishment by 17 percent. This global decline is certainly a welcome improvement, and it signifies that something is working in our search for sustainability successes, whether from global economics, agricultural technologies, education, global drought reduction, or decline in desertification rates. However, for me at least, it still remains a global alarm that one-in-eight persons on earth currently suffers from malnutrition and hunger. Further, malnutrition is distributed unevenly with the largest concentrations located in developing countries, and certainly in countries with increasing desertification, mostly in Africa and areas where conflicts are apparent. A recent international report for these countries estimates an undernourishment rate of 14.3 percent (FAO, 2013). As I see it, there are three problems with food insecurity: (a) although food insecurity rates are declining, the total number of undernourished people remains massive (around 850 million persons); (b) most of the universally hungry are living in dire conditions in underdeveloped regions, so the solutions to underdevelopment are also the answers for hunger alleviation; and (c) the rate of progress to alleviate undernourishment is relatively slow and has not yet met any of the international targets. A recent report by the *New York Times* shows that there also may be serious problems with the data used by the United Nations in reporting reductions in the number of persons who are food insecure since 1990 due to numerous revisions in the baseline. Sadly, the image of faces of thousands and thousands of children in recently erected refugee camps waiting for a cup of rice to arrive tells the story of ongoing hunger and supports the rationale for teaching sustainability.

Challenge: Disasters and Extreme Events

Much of the growing interest in disasters currently stems from the emergence of *resiliency* as a principal area within sustainability science. Also, interest has increased because of the societal difficulties unaccounted for in long-term rebuilding and conjointly reducing human risk and vulnerability. Further, the systems thinking approach reflects developments in research in human–ecological coupled systems that address disasters as problems in complexity and uncertainty and products of failures in adaptation policies. Within sustainability, disasters are seen as products of the interaction between human settlements and environmental systems. As such, sustainability argues that over the next decades we should develop viable societal capacities to reduce human vulnerabilities to disasters and as much as possible to prevent or avoid disasters. Chapter 10, by Ray Quay, identifies the need for building "anticipatory governance" institutional processes for mitigating adverse future shocks in the areas of potential water shortages recognizing that these "wicked" problems are characterized by high levels of complexity and uncertainty.

For example, the emerging framework for sustainability solutions for natural disasters stemming from climate change is bifurcated into mitigation and adaptation policies. Mitigation applies to the source of the global warming problem, that is, reducing carbon dioxide emissions through alternative energy generation, especially renewables. The target set in the first Kyoto protocol involved the reduction of carbon dioxide emissions by 5.2 percent less than the prevailing 1990 levels. This reduction was never achieved. The alternative, as Martin Pasqualetti argues in Chapter 12, is to expand renewable energy generation (solar, geothermal, hydropower, and wind). The achievement of an 8 percent energy generation produced from renewables this year is clearly an important step, but not even close enough for the dramatic reduction presently needed for GHGs to decline to acceptable nonthreatening levels.

The second approach is adaptation, which entails admitting GHGs will continue to build and concentrate in the atmosphere causing the potential for adverse climate change impacts. Adaptation assumes that human actions can reduce climate-based impacts through: (a) significant investments in infrastructure to prevent extreme damages, in fact, to reduce the levels of extent and intensity of impacts; (b) land use planning policies to reduce vulnerabilities, including special land use zoning restrictions, open space regulations, flood insurance, and (in some places) wetlands protection; and (c) enhancement of community resiliency measures in terms of decision-making capacities. Chapter 5, on climate change, addresses both mitigation and adaptation response and policies. Adaptation responses to reduce risk among various different kinds of hazards are discussed in Chapters 5, 6, 10 and 13.

The first 15 years of the 21st century has left sustainability scholars in a quandary regarding the set of extreme events or disasters experienced around the world. What can these events tell us about societal responses to uncertainties? How can we improve our institutional capacities to prevent, respond to, restore, and rebuild damaged or destroyed communities? For example, we need to learn more about restoring the socioeconomic fabric of Detroit and turning it into a resilient community. As evidenced by the experiences after hurricanes Katrina and Sandy, we need to improve our knowledge about coastal cities and their protection. As important, we need to face the particularly problematic challenge of learning how we can perform better in collaborating with residents in rebuilding communities by creating a recovery process that takes into account well-being, participation, engagement, and social justice. The BP Gulf Coast Oil Spill, with its scale of possible decades-long ecosystem impacts, leads to sobering questions about energy policy, regulation of offshore oil drilling, response capacities, long-term hazard mitigation, and economic restoration. As unfortunate and even devastating as these extreme events are, there is much learning to be acquired from understanding their full human–environmental causes and subsequent effectiveness of remediation efforts.

I am especially troubled by two other disasters for entirely different reasons. Although persistently and complexly problematic, both events will inform us in meaningful ways about sustainability in our second decade of the new century. The disaster in **Haiti** conveyed to us how a colonial past, the loss of environmental resources, high levels of impoverishment, and poor health services, combined with low community support networks, can be the tipping point for amplified long-term ineffective recovery. The 2011 **Fukushima** nuclear disaster in Japan teaches us about the implications of living with risk and how we often make poor decisions by not being fully aware of the potential ramifications of human–technology–natural systems and human safety. While there is a current interest to invest again in nuclear technology as an approach to reduce and replace fossil fuel energy production in order to decrease atmospheric GHG, we need to remember the lessons learned from the Chernobyl, Three Mile

Island, and now Fukushima nuclear catastrophes. Sustainability will have to be positioned with sufficient methods, knowledge, and policies to handle these seemingly intractable trade-offs between human safety and GHG reduction.

Final Thought

In total, this book encompasses a focus on sustainability's past, present, and future, by using historical review and context; documenting current urban conditions and solutions; and the mapping out of issues, concerns, and possible new approaches cities can take for the future. Further, it urges a more capacious definition of sustainability and calls for an expanded role for sustainability education.

What Should Sustainable Cities Look Like? Programs, Policies, and Initiatives

Bjoern Hagen and Ariane Middel

Introduction

Today, more people live in city environments than in rural areas. Projections suggest that by 2050, approximately 75 percent of the world's population will live in cities. The ongoing rapid **urbanization** is transforming natural landscapes and ecosystems into artificial urban landscapes, creating complex social, economic, and environmental challenges, requiring sustainable development. The move of populations into cities is coupled with transformative changes including the growth of megacities, expansion of urban poverty, especially in developing countries, and growing concern over food security, among other issues. As shown in Table 1, there are already 29 cities with a population of over 10 million (Demographia, 2014). The Tokyo metro area has over 37 million inhabitants. It is expected in this century that numerous **megacities** will merge and transform into megaregions with potentially over 100 million inhabitants (UN Habitat, 2012). Some of the existing megaregions include the Hong Kong-Shenhzen-Guangzhou region in China with about 120 million people and the Rio de Janeiro-São Paulo region with more than 43 million people in Brazil.

The increasing number of cities and the number of people living in urban areas is also an opportunity to tackle environmental and social issues through thoughtful sustainable policies and development strategies.

There is a long history of sustainable urban planning and combining natural and man-made landscapes. In the last century, Ebenezer Howard's Garden City can be considered as a sustainable urban development concept (Parsons & Schuyler, 2002). In his book "Garden Cities of To-Morrow" (Howard, 1902), he outlines a settlement structure that creates self-contained communities including mixed residential, commercial, and recreational zones surrounded by greenbelts. However, only two garden cities were built: Letchworth and Welwyn; both located in England and loosely based on Howard. Although the Garden City concept can be viewed as mostly utopian, it incorporated many principles that underline today's sustainable urban development efforts (Caine, 2011). The Garden City concept aimed to combine the best of nature and urban environments in a planned and controlled way while providing high-quality urban fabric, economic development, community well-being, quality of life, and social equity. Transportation by rail between the urban villages was another idea that is showing promise today in the promulgation of transit oriented developments.

Early sustainable development concepts focused primarily on creating new cities and communities, but present day planners and urban decision-makers also face the

Urbanization - Urbanization describes the process of more and more people moving from rural to urban areas. As a result cities are growing in size and population.

Megacities - Megacities are cities or metropolitan areas with more than 10 million inhabitants

TABLE 1: Largest Urban Areas in the World

Rank	Urban Area	Country	Population
1	Tokyo-Yokohama	Japan	37,555,000
2	Jakarta	Indonesia	29,959,000
3	Delhi	India	24,134,000
4	Seoul	South Korea	22,992,000
5	Manila	Philippines	22,750,000
6	Shanghai	China	22,650,000
7	Karachi	Pakistan	21,585,000
8	New York	Unites States	20,661,000
9	Mexico City	Mexico	20,300,000
10	Sao Paulo	Brazil	20,273,000
11	Beijing	China	19,277,000
12	Guangzhou-Foshan	China	18,316,000
13	Mumbai	India	17,672,000
14	Osaka-Kobe-Kyoto	Japan	17,234,000
15	Moscow	Russia	15,885,000
16	Los Angeles	United States	15,250,000
17	Cairo	Egypt	15,206,000
18	Bangkok	Thailand	14,910,000
19	Calcutta	India	14,896,000
20	Dhaka	Bangladesh	14,816,000
21	Buenos Aires	Argentina	13,913,000
22	Tehran	Iran	13,429,000
23	Istanbul	Turkey	13,187,000
24	Shenzhen	China	12,860,000
25	Lagos	Nigeria	12,549,000
26	Rio de Janeiro	Brazil	11,723,000
27	Paris	France	10,975,000
28	Nagoya	Japan	10,238,000
29	London	United Kingdom	10,149,000

task of retrofitting existing cities with expanding populations (Vince, 2012) and the need for more resilient communities due to increasing climate change concerns. The rapid urbanization presents many dynamic sustainability challenges for the city's infrastructure, e.g., with regard to water and waste management, power usage, transportation, green building design, as well as greenhouse gas emissions and air quality issues. To achieve sustainability in urban communities, the existing literature points to five dimensions of sustainable development (Ahmedi & Toghyani, 2011): 1) economic sustainability, 2) social sustainability, 3) ecological sustainability, 4) sustainable spatial development, and 5) cultural continuity. Only if all five dimensions are considered, a city can evolve in a sustainable way. More recently, city governments have also started to recognize the necessity to plan for climate change by mitigating greenhouse gas emissions through a number of strategies and by increasing the resiliency of the urban fabric to adverse climate change related impacts (C40 Cities: Climate Leadership Group, 2014). A recent study (Zottis, 2014) shows that 75 percent of 350 surveyed cities perceive climate change as a pressing issue for consideration in their overall urban planning initiatives and sustainable development strategies.

In order to evaluate the efforts of cities to become more sustainable, recognize successful cases, and identify areas for improvement, cities are often rated and ranked according to their sustainability related performance. Different rating systems exist, measuring important aspects of sustainable development, such as the "The Green City Index" (The Economist Intelligence Unit, 2012a), the "Resilient Cities Ranking" (Grosvenor, 2014), or the "Livability Ranking" (The Economist Intelligence Unit, 2012b). All rating systems measure city performance based on specific indicators. Table 2 shows the top – ten city ranks for the three rating systems – green cities, residiency and livability.

For example, the Green City Index (GCI) assesses the environmental performance of over 120 cities worldwide based on up to 30 indicators depending on the region and data availability. The indicators are grouped into categories, such as CO_2 emissions, energy, effecient buildings, land use, transport, water and sanitation, waste management, air quality, and environmental governance. The categories are measured on comparative indicators (The Economist Intelligence Unit, 2012a). In terms of the European GCI, the top 3 cities are all from Scandinavia, whereas the bottom 3 cities are from Eastern Europe. In the United States and Canada, the top three green cities are San Francisco, Vancouver, and New York. On the other end of the spectrum, Cleveland, St. Louis, and Detroit comprise the bottom three.

The Resilient Cities Ranking examines the capabilities of cities to contend with negative impacts from events derived from climate change, rural to urban migration, and globalization, while simultaneously continuing to function as a hub for human, economic, and cultural development (Grosvenor, 2014). Assessing the resiliency of a given city is a two-step process. First, indicators are used to evaluate the vulnerability of the city and its infrastructure to occurring or projected environmental stresses or disasters. The indicators determine the vulnerability of the city to negative changes in climate, environment, availability in resources, infrastructure, and within the social fabric. A second set of indicators is used to determine the adaptive capacity of a city. In other words, how well prepared are the government and other vital institutions, the planning system, funding structures, and other key areas of a city to react to negative environmental, social, and economic events? In terms of urban resilience, the Canadian cities Toronto, Vancouver, and Calgary occupy the top three spots in a ranking of 50 cities worldwide.

The third rating system displayed in Table 2 ranks cities according to the quality of life they offer. Cities are scored based on over 30 indicators organized into five categories: a) stability, b) healthcare, c) culture and environment, d) education, and e) infrastructure. After the scores are collected, weighted, and combined, each participating city receives a score of 1–100. For a particular city, the higher the score, the better the living conditions. As illustrated by their ranking, the top three cities with the best 2012 living conditions were Melbourne, Vienna, and Vancouver. Similar to the resiliency ranking, Canada has the most cities in the top ten on the livability ranking. Out of the 140 cities surveyed, Port Moresby, Dhaka, and Damascus accumulated the fewest points.

TABLE 2: City Rankings

The Green City Index (GCI)				Resilient Cities Ranking		Livability Ranking		
European GCI		US and Canada GCI						
Rank	City	Rank	City	Rank	City	Rank	City	Score
1	Copenhagen	1	San Francisco	1	Toronto	1	Melbourne	97.5
2	Stockholm	2	Vancouver	2	Vancouver	2	Vienna	97.4
3	Oslo	3	New York City	3	Calgary	3	Vancouver	97.3
4	Vienna	4	Seattle	4	Chicago	4	Toronto	97.2
5	Amsterdam	5	Denver	5	Pittsburgh	5	Calgary	96.6
6	Zurich	6	Boston	6	Stockholm	5	Adelaide	96.6
7	Helsinki	7	Los Angeles	7	Boston	7	Sidney	96.1
8	Berlin	8	Washington DC	8	Zurich	8	Helsinki	96.0
9	Brussels	9	Toronto	9	Washington DC	9	Perth	95.9
10	Paris	10	Minneapolis	10	Atlanta	10	Auckland,	95.7
...		...		...		...		
21	Dublin	18	Orlando	41	Sao Paulo	131	Tehran	45.8
22	Athens	19	Montreal	42	Delhi	132	Douala	43.3
23	Tallinn	20	Charlotte	43	Guangzhou	133	Tripoli	41.7
24	Prague	21	Atlanta	44	Mexico City	134	Karachi	40.9
25	Istanbul	22	Miami	45	Rio de Janeiro	134	Algiers	40.9
26	Zagreb	23	Pittsburgh	46	Mumbai	136	Harare	40.7
27	Belgrade	24	Phoenix	47	Manila	137	Lagos	38.9
28	Bucharest	25	Cleveland	48	Cairo	137	Port Moresby	38.9
29	Sofia	26	St Louis	49	Jakarta	139	Dhaka	38.7
30	Kiev	27	Detroit	50	Dhaka	140	Damascus	38.4

Adapted from Green City Index, 2012; Resilient Cities Ranking, 2014 ; Livability Ranking, 2012

Although these indicator systems (among others) measure different dimensions of sustainability, the same cities seem to rank fairly well, demonstrating common characteristics, policies, and initiatives. North American cities like Toronto, Calgary, Vancouver, Washington DC, or Boston are often found among the highest ranked cities. In Europe, Stockholm, Vienna, Helsinki, Copenhagen, and Zurich always perform well when assessed for sustainably. The following sections of this chapter more closely examine three of the most sustainable cities in the world. Vancouver, Freiburg, and Stockholm are all well known for proactive policies and comprehensive planning, strategies emphasizing a commitment to becoming more sustainable, green, and resilient. They offer experiences from which other city governments can learn as well as best practices that can be transferred and implemented elsewhere. Although Stockholm and Vancouver often appear on different rating systems, Freiburg is usually too small in terms of its population to be part of most indicator rating systems that only focus on major metropolitan areas, yet it is internationally recognized for its sustainable principles in its plans and buildings (Beatley, 2010).

Vancouver, Canada

Background

Vancouver is a coastal seaport city in British Columbia, Western Canada. With a population of 600,000 people and a land area of 115 square kilometers (Statistics Canada, 2011), the City of Vancouver is the eighth most populous Canadian municipality and the most densely populated city in Canada. The Greater Vancouver area, with 2.3 million residents, is the third most populous metropolitan area in Canada. Archaeological finds suggest that the first settlements in Vancouver date back more than 3,000 years (City of Vancouver, 2014). Several Coast Salish First Nations, among them the Musqueam and Squamish indigenous peoples, had villages near the mouth of the Fraser River. Vancouver is named after British naval Captain George Vancouver, one of the first Europeans to explore the Pacific Northwest Coast in 1792.

Today, shipping and trade are key to Vancouver's economy. The Port of Vancouver is Canada's largest and busiest port and a major gateway for pan-Pacific trade. In 2013, the port traded goods worth $184 billion with more than 160 trading economies (Port Metro Vancouver, 2014). Other key economic sectors for the City of Vancouver include forestry, mining, film, and tourism. The Economist Intelligence Unit (EIU) has consistently ranked Vancouver as one of the top five most livable cities in the world. Although the city is one of the most densely populated urban areas in Canada, it features abundant green spaces and parks, waterfront activities, and nearby nature parks and mountains. Vancouver is also one of the most ethnically and linguistically mixed cities in Canada and home to worldwide cultural groups. Fifty-two percent of the population speaks a first language other than English (City of Vancouver, 2014). Vancouver's diversity and multiculturalism are seen as a major source of the city's vitality and prosperity, attracting visitors and investment. In the US and Canada Green City Index, Vancouver is ranked second overall, with top scores in the CO_2 and air quality categories (The Economist Intelligence Unit, 2012a). The concepts of sustainability and livability are centrally placed on the city's development and policy agenda and constitute the basis for several initiatives and campaigns to address environmental challenges. The following section touches on the "Greenest City 2020 Action Plan," an initiative to make Vancouver the greenest, most livable city in the world by 2020, as well as presenting key aspects of Vancouver's sustainability.

Greenest City Plan

Although Vancouver currently has the smallest per capita **carbon footprint** of all U.S. and Canadian cities as a result of policies promoting green energy and the dominance of **hydropower**, the city is not immune to future environmental challenges, such as continued population growth, uncertainties of climatic change, and rising fossil fuel prices. To address these challenges proactively and remain one of the most livable and sustainable places, Vancouver started an initiative in 2009 to become the greenest city in the world by 2020. The City Council developed a comprehensive plan, the "Greenest City 2020 Action Plan" (City of Vancouver, 2012), which builds on research findings from a team of local experts on best practices from sustainable cities around the world. Over 35,000 people helped develop the plan, providing input through social media, workshops, and events, setting an

Carbon Footprint - The amount of greenhouse gases (GHG) emitted in a given time frame to directly and indirectly support human activities. The carbon footprint is usually expressed in "equivalent tons of carbon dioxide" (tCO_2e) and calculated for the time period of a year.

Hydropower - Electricity that is generated using the energy of moving water.

example for best practices in government-citizen collaboration. The action plan establishes ten measurable and attainable targets, each with a long-term (year 2050) goal and medium-term (year 2020) goal, baseline numbers to describe the current status of each target, highest priority actions for the next three years, and detailed steps and actions required to achieve the goals. The ten targets focus on the overarching areas of carbon, waste, and ecosystems.

Climate Leadership

Renewable Energy - Energy sources which are natural, such as sunlight, wind, and geothermal heat. Due to peak oil and growing environmental concerns, more governments support the use of renewable energy sources

Vancouver's electricity mainly stems from **renewable energy** sources. The city benefits from its location close to mountains and draws most of its power from hydroelectric generating stations. **Hydropower** plants (usually situated at dams) use falling water to propel turbines to produce electricity. Renewable energy from water is highly efficient, with more than 95 percent of energy converted into electricity, with exceptionally low GHG emissions. Because of Vancouver's green energy portfolio, per capita GHG emissions are as low as 4.2 metric tons of CO_2, considerably less than the Green City Index average of 14.5 metric tons (EIU, 2012). Vancouver plans to further reduce its community-based GHG emissions 33% by 2020 from its 2007 levels (Table 3), despite expected economic growth and increasing population. A key strategy for realizing this goal is promoting local energy solutions and developing neighborhood energy systems, such as the Neighborhood Energy Utility (NEU). NEU provides a high-density residential area near the Olympic village with locally generated heat and hot water using thermal energy from sewage, a green technology that reduces GHG emissions for heating by more than 60 percent. Dense neighborhoods are particularly suited for this kind of renewable energy, as multiple buildings can be serviced simultaneously, making the system more cost effective.

Green Transportation

Due to Vancouver's geography and several municipal bylaws, Vancouver is one of the few Canadian metropolises without an extensive freeway network. Highway 1, the Trans-Canada Highway, is the only freeway within city limits, and it does not pass through the downtown area. A freeway through the center of the city was proposed in the late 1960's, but public protest by residents, activists, and community leaders prevented its implementation. Today, Vancouver has a long and dense public transit system (5.4 miles per square mile), a constantly growing network of bike routes, and the longest automated light rail system in the world (EIU, 2012). In 2012, the city adopted a transportation plan that sets targets for all transportation modes for the next 30 years, aiming for over 50% of all trips by foot, bike, or transit by 2020 and at least two-thirds by 2040. It is estimated that currently about 25 percent of the residents commute to work by public transit, bike, or foot.

Biking is the fastest growing transportation mode in Vancouver. The number of bike trips has steadily increased, with an overall trip number increase of 40 percent between 2008 and 2011 (City of Vancouver, 2011). Vancouver has an extensive bike network of over 300 painted lane-kilometers. Most of the bike routes are so-called bike boulevards, i.e., low-speed streets that have been optimized for biking and where traffic is calmed through circles and signals. In 2009, Vancouver added

TABLE 3: Greenest City 2020 Action Plan mid-term targets for reductions in carbon emissions and waste, and improvements to the City's ecosystems.

Goals	Targets	Indicator	Baseline	2020 Target
Green Economy	Double the number of green jobs over 2010 levels by 2020	Total number of local food and green jobs	16,700 jobs	33,400 jobs
	Double the number of companies that are actively engaged in greening their operations over 2011 levels, by 2020	Percent of businesses engaged in greening their operations	5% of businesses engaged	10% of businesses engaged
Climate Leadership	Reduce community-based greenhouse gas emissions by 33% from 2007 levels	Total tons of community CO_2e emissions from Vancouver	2,755,000 tCO_2e	1,846,000 tCO_2e
Green Buildings	Require all buildings constructed from 2020 onward to be carbon neutral in operations	Total tons of CO_2e from residential and commercial buildings	1,145,000 tCO_2e	920,000 tCO_2e
	Reduce energy use and GHG emissions in existing buildings by 20% over 2007 levels	Total tons of CO_2e from residential and commercial buildings	1,145,000 tCO_2e	920,000 tCO_2e
Green Transportation	Make the majority of trips (over 50%) by foot, bicycle, and public transit	Per cent of trips by foot, bicycle, and transit	40% of trips	50% sustainable mode share
	Reduce the average distance driven per resident by 20% from 2007 levels	Total vehicle km driven per person	N/A	20% below 2007 levels
Zero Waste	Reduce total solid waste going to the landfill or incinerator by 50% from 2008 levels	Annual solid waste disposed to landfill or incinerator from Vancouver	480,000 tons	240,000 tons
Access to Nature	Ensure that every person lives within a five-minute walk of a park, greenway, or other green space by 2020	Per cent of city's land base within a five-minute walk to a green space	92.6%	95%
	Plant 150,000 additional trees in the city between 2010 and 2020	Total number of additional trees planted		150,000
Lighter Footprint	Reduce Vancouver's ecological footprint by 33% over 2006 levels	Number of people empowered by a City-led or City-supported project to take personal action in support of a Greenest City goal and/ or to reduce levels of consumption.	600 people	to be determined
Clean Water	Meet or beat the most stringent of BC, Canadian, and appropriate international drinking water quality standards and guidelines	Total number of instances of not meeting drinking water quality standards	0 instances	0 instances
	Reduce per capita water consumption by 33% from 2006 levels	Total water consumption per capita	583 L per person per day	390 L per person per day
Clean Air	Meet or beat the most stringent air quality guidelines from Metro Vancouver, BC, Canada, and the WHO	Number of instances where air quality standards were not met	27 instances	0 instances
Local Food	Increase city-wide and neighborhood food assets by a minimum of 50% over 2010 levels	Number of neighborhood food assets in Vancouver	3,340 food assets	5158 food assets

Source: City of Vancouver, 2014.

Separated bike lane.

Olympic Line transit station.

separated bike lanes to key city streets in the cycling network. These dedicated bike lanes feature two-way travel for bikes on one side of the road. The bike lanes are separated from traffic using such physical barriers as medians, planters, bike racks, or car parking lanes. Thus making biking safer and more comfortable and attracting more participants. A research team at the University of British Columbia conducted a study on safe biking (Winters et al. 2012) and found safety issues to be the biggest concern amongst active and potential cyclists. Pedestrians also benefit from the separated bike lanes, because fewer cyclists ride on the sidewalks. The City of Vancouver plans to upgrade and expand the existing bike network to connect key destinations, such as schools, community centers, transit stations, and shopping areas. All city buses now have bike racks, and more bike corrals are being installed in and around Vancouver. In 2015, the City will implement a Public Bike Share (PBS) system, which will allow residents and visitors to rent bikes and helmets from automated docking stations distributed across the city center. The PBS system will add another green transportation option to Vancouver's transportation portfolio and help reduce personal vehicle trips.

Vancouver has the world's longest automated rapid metro system, the SkyTrain. Built for the 1986 World Exposition (Expo '86), it has been expanded to serve most of Greater Vancouver. As of 2014, the SkyTrain has a network of three lines, comprising 68.7 km of track and 47 stations. Fully automated trains run underground and on elevated guideways to keep the SkyTrain cars on schedule. A fourth line, the Evergreen line, will be completed in 2016 and add 11 km of tracks and seven stations. The SkyTrain has significantly shaped the urban areas close to the stations by sparking new development. From 1991 to 2001, the population living in walking distance to a Skytrain station has increased by 37 percent.

Vancouver plans to improve its transportation system further by re-establishing a streetcar network. During the 2010 Winter Olympics, a Downtown Streetcar called "Olympic Line" ran on the historic railway tracks in downtown as a showcase project and provided free public transportation. The City intends to continue operating this line, and three future line extensions are planned.

Access to Nature

The Vancouver region has historically been a temperate rainforest and the home of predominantly coniferous trees, such as the Western red cedar and Coast Douglas-fir. Although urbanization has changed the landscape of the city, Vancouver's mild climate and rainy weather have contributed to a green and lush environment. Today, around 12 percent of the city area is green space and 92 percent of Vancouver's residents live within five minute walking distance from a park, greenway, or other green space (EIU, 2012). Vancouver's Stanley Park, located in the heart of the city and designated a national historic site, is one of the largest urban parks in North America, covering approximately 400 hectares. In contrast to most large public parks, landscape architects did not design Stanley Park. Evolving over many years, parts of it are still densely forested with majestic trees that are hundreds of years old (City of Vancouver, 2014). Stanley Park is almost completely surrounded by the sea and famous for its Seawall path along Vancouver's waterfront that is a recreational hotspot for walking, jogging, cycling, and inline skating. The park attracts about eight million visitors every year and greatly contributes both to Vancouver's identity as a green city and its quality of life.

Green spaces and trees are important contributors to the livability of a place and the health of a city by creating a sense of community in providing space for recreational activities, but also for gathering and socializing (Beatley, 2010). Research has shown that urban green spaces improve the physical health and emotional well-being of urban dwellers, which is manifested in reduced blood pressure, cholesterol, and lower stress levels. In addition, green spaces provide various **urban ecosystem** services and socio-economic benefits: they absorb rainfall, reduce storm water runoff, filter out toxins, prevent flooding, reduce noise, create wildlife habitats, regulate air temperature through shading and evapotranspiration, and improve air quality by filtering out pollutants. Vancouver ranks first in the Green City Index air quality category with the lowest rate of particulate matter emissions compared to other index cities.

Urban Ecosystem - Ecological system within a city or urban area, i.e. the community of humans, animals, and plants in conjunction with the urban environment.

Despite the large number of parks and other green spaces in the city, Vancouver's tree canopy cover has declined 20 percent over the past two decades, mostly due to new developments, disease, and residents removing trees from their property. In response,

Stanley Park.

Street trees in Vancouver are part of the city's urban forest.

the City is developing an urban forest strategy to provide policy direction and a plan for actions to grow and maintain a healthy, resilient urban forest. An **urban forest** is not restricted to trees in parks and public spaces, it also includes street trees and trees in residential yards. While one of the goals outlined in the urban forest strategy is to protect and preserve existing trees, it also calls for an expansion of the current tree canopy cover. This goal is highlighted further in the Greenest City 2020 Action Plan, which calls for 150,000 additional trees in Vancouver between 2010 and 2020. Since 67 percent of the existing urban forest are on private property and 54,000 of the additional trees will have to be planted in people's yards, educating Vancouver residents about the benefits of trees and engaging the broader public to support new trees in the city is key to achieving the urban forestry goals. Therefore, the City of Vancouver and the non-profit organization Tree City, in conjunction with the Environmental Youth Alliance, launched "Treekeepers" in late 2012 (TreeKeepers, 2012). Treekeepers is a $215,000 city funded three-year initiative aimed at encouraging residents and businesses in Vancouver to plant more trees on their property. Various tree species suited to Vancouver's climate are available for purchase at subsidized rates between $10 and $20. The tree program provides a unique opportunity for private citizens to support the City of Vancouver's goal to become the greenest city in the world by 2020 and to continue to be named one of the most livable cities on Earth.

Freiburg, Germany

Background

The city of Freiburg is located in the southwest corner of Germany, at the edge of the Black Forest, and very close to the borders of Switzerland and France. Founded in the year 1122, the city was strategically located at a junction of trade routes between the Mediterranean Sea and the North Sea. Freiburg was heavily bombed during World War II and carefully reconstructed based on the city's medieval plan that includes a unique system of small waterways throughout its historic center.

Today, the purpose of the small canals/waterways is no longer to channel fresh water into the city, rather they add to the pleasant and comforting atmosphere of the city's pedestrian environment. The city's population of approximately 220,000 people

© katatonia82/Shutterstock, Inc.

City Center of Freiburg.

is a hub for regional eco-tourism and center for academia and research. The Albert Ludwig University in Freiburg is one of the oldest universities in Germany and has been the largest employer since the end of World War II.

Green Movement

Because of the large academic community, Freiburg became a center of the country's **"green" movement**, which started in the

Pedestrian zone with historic waterway canal.

1970s. The movement led in 1979 to the founding of the Green Party, with a political agenda containing numerous environmental goals such as the nuclear energy phase-out and stricter environmental protection laws (Bündnis 90/Die Grünen, 2014). An important event that led to the Freiburg of today stemmed from the successful 1975 citizen protest against the plans to build a nearby nuclear power plant. Many protest leaders and other people involved in Freiburg's green movement remained in the area and became involved in local and regional politics, often involved in the city administration and found employment in educational or research activities, or founded environmentally-based companies. As a result, the mayor and more than 25 percent of the council are currently members of Germany's Green Party (City of Freiburg, 2014). Over the last few decades, Freiburg focused heavily on becoming a recognized green and sustainable city. The City has won various national and international environmental awards for their policies and developments. Freiburg is especially well known as a green city or **eco-city** for its efforts in transportation, alternative energy systems, and sustainable place-making (Newman et al, 2009). The city administration emphasizes other sectors as well to increase sustainability such as land conservation and the promotion of a green economy (Green City Freiburg, 2014).

Transportation

Transportation plays a pivotal role in Freiburg's urban development policy. Since 1969, the city has established its **Global Transport Concept (GTC)**, which is a traffic management plan that is updated every decade. The main goals are to reduce total automobile traffic volume in the city and support the advancement of public transit, cyclists, and pedestrians. Furthermore, the GTC focuses on creating a rational balance between all modes of transportation. In 1969, the first GTC policy implemented created a bicycle path network. This network was quickly followed by a considerable expansion of the light rail network and the conservation of the city center into a pedestrian zone in 1972. More than 300 miles of bike paths and bike-friendly streets exist throughout the city, as well as 8,000 public bike parking spaces.

The light rail network is now the most used transit system of the city, Almost 75 percent of all public transit users rely on the light rail for their daily travel. Furthermore, 70 percent of the population lives within 550 yards of a tram stop. This short distance promotes walking to a transit station and the creation of Transit Oriented

Green Movement - Green movements are often grassroots movement advocating social reforms and the protection of the natural environment and resources

Eco-City - Eco-cities, or sustainable cities, consider environmental impacts in their design and policy decisions. In addition, eco-cities strongly support the use or renewable energy sources, public transit, and compact and walkable neighborhood design.

Global Transport Concept (GTC) - The Global Transport Concept is a traffic management plan that is updated every 10 years. The main goals are to reduce traffic in the city and support public transit, cyclists, and pedestrians. Furthermore, the plan focuses on creating a rational balance between all modes of transportation.

Development around stations or higher density development. During peak hours, the tram runs every 7.5 minutes. All stations have park-and-ride as well as bike-and-ride facilities. What makes Freiburg's public transit system truly sustainable, however, is that it is powered by renewable energy sources. Approximately 80 percent of the energy used to power the system is generated by hydropower, and the remaining is provided by solar and wind energy.

Besides aiming to make public transit convenient, fast, reliable, and comfortable, the city administration strives for affordability as well. A monthly transit pass costs about 50 Euros, providing unlimited access to more than 1,800 miles of routes from numerous transportation companies throughout the entire region. This is much cheaper than the monthly costs of owning and operating a private car. Because of Freiburg's transportatiopn policies, the vehicle-miles traveled by car fell significantly, and as a result, greenhouse gas emissions declined as well. Between 1982 and 1999, the contribution of bicycling to the city's total volume of traffic increased from 15 to 28 percent. The number of people using public transit also increased in this period, from 11 to 18 percent. Among university students nearly 90 percent use public transit or bike. Simultaneously, only 30 percent of the entire traffic volume is generated by private automobiles.

Green Energy

In addition to the GTC, Freiburg is characterized by a progressive energy policy. The city's energy policy is based on three pillars: energy saving, efficient technologies, and renewable energy sources. Since 1992, the city has enforced strict building design standards for new houses. These standards have reduced heating oil consumption from about 12–15 liters to 6.5 liters per square meter. To improve energy efficiency in existing buildings, Freiburg instituted a comprehensive support program for home insulation and energy retrofits. Due to the expenditures for this program, which cost around 1.2 million Euros in subsidies and 14 million Euros of investments, energy consumption declined by around 38 percent per building.

In terms of efficient energy technology, Freiburg relies heavily on **combined heat and power plants (CHP)** by developing and maintaining more than 100 such plants. These power plants reuse the waste heat from electricity production to generate more electricity and useful heat for buildings. The majority of the CHP's are small scale and located directly in the neighborhoods they serve. In addjtion, 14 large, combined heat and power plants are located at the city's outskirts. CHP plants are powered by natural gas, **biogas**, landfill gas, **geothermal** energy, wood chips, and heating oil. The steady increase in the number of CHP power plants has allowed Freiburg to decrease its reliance on nuclear power from 60 to 30 percent (The EcoTipping Points Project, 2011). Germany's policy is to reduce dependence on nuclear power for creating electricity. Today, slightly more than half of the city's electricity is produced by CHP plants or other renewable energy sources. Freiburg's renewable energy sources consist of solar, wind, hydropower, and biomass. The remaining energy is imported, about a third of which comes from external power plants. For the near future, Freiburg's goal is it to further increase the amount of renewable energy and to reduce reliance on nuclear power and fossil fuel.

Although all four renewable sources are utilized, the city is most famous for its support of **solar energy**. Throughout the city, the use of solar energy is highly visible,

Combined Heat and Power Plants (CHP) - These power plans reuse the waste heat from electricity production to generate more electricity and useful heat for buildings. CHP plants can be powered by natural gas, biogas, landfill gas, geothermal, wooden chips, and heating oil.

Biogas - A renewable energy source created by the biological breakdown of organic matter without oxygen. Common organic waste used for biogas production are dead plants, animal materials, animal feces, and kitchen waste.

Geothermal - Geothermal power stations generate electricity by extracting heat from the lower layers of the earth. This heat is used to power turbines, which in turn are linked to generators that produce electricity.

Solar Energy - This technology allows generating energy by converting sunlight into electricity using solar panels. Solar panels use solar cells made up of photovoltaic material.

with more than 400 photovoltaic installations occurring on both public and private buildings. The 1.6 million square feet of photovoltaic cells produce more than 10 million **kWh/year** of energy. However, solar still only provides a small fraction of the city's electricity needs. The total electricity demand is well over 1,000 million kWh/year. Nevertheless, solar energy also became an important element of Freiburg's sustainable economy. The

Solar Settlement in Freiburg.

kWh/year - kWh stands for kilowatt hour and is used as a unit of energy

highly visible solar installations attract eco-tourism, and the support of solar energy has attracted numerous scientific and educational organizations to the city (Newman et al., 2009). For example, 1,500 companies from the green economy sector employ nearly 10,000 people. The green economy sector includes research facilities, environmental education programs for university students, as well as for solar technicians and installers, and manufacturing. Various companies produce solar cells and machinery to create the cells. In addition, these companies have attracted numerous suppliers and service providers in a green-supply-chain system. In the solar industry alone, more than 80 businesses employ 1,000 people or more.

Sustainable Living and Place-making

Vauban is one of the most sustainable neighborhoods in Freiburg, relying heavily on solar energy. This neighborhood is 38 hectares in area (Vauban, 2014) and located in an area of a former French military base close to the city center. The final development plan was approved in 1997; Vauban is now an attractive and family-friendly community of about 5,000 people. Due to carefully designed zoning regulations and policies, low-energy buildings are obligatory in this district and **zero-energy** or **energy-plus buildings** with solar technology are prominent. The 60 energy-plus homes in this neighborhood create more energy than they consume. Their residents earn, on average 6,000 Euros per year by selling the surplus energy back to the grid.

Zero-Energy Buildings - Zero-energy buildings use different technologies such as solar and wind to harvest energy on site. These type of buildings are very energy efficient and do not have to rely on the city's energy grid. Furthermore, zero-energy buildings and energy-plus buildings do not produce any carbon emissions.

Based on the Vauban district master plan, the neighborhood is characterized by a dense pattern of primarily attached housing and multifamily housing. Green spaces between the housing clusters ensure good climatic conditions and provide play areas for children. The green corridors channel fresh air into the neighborhood while vegetation filters the air and reduces the air temperature during the summer. A set of U-shaped access roads limits access of cars to the neighborhood. Instead, the life of the community takes place in the interior pedestrian spaces where cars are not allowed. The extensive set of walkways and paths connects the different housing areas and makes the entire neighborhood both bicycle and pedestrian friendly. Furthermore, Vauban has its own CHP plant using wood chips from local forestry, which provides all residents and local businesses with power.

Energy-Plus Buildings - Due to good insulation, special design guidelines, and the use of renewable energy sources, energy-plus buildings create more energy than they consume. Residents can make extra money by selling the extra energy back to the grid.

In addition to the efforts of implementing solar energy, promoting walkability, and creating a sense of community, the neighborhood has received much attention internationally for its efforts to promote car-free living. Before the construction of Vauban, the

Zero-Energy and Energy Plus buildings in Vauban.

state zoning law required builders to provide parking space for every housing unit. The law was changed due to organized lobbying by the so-called Forum Vauban, a group of people advocating for a car-free neighborhood. Today, Freiburg can waive any parking requirements if the developer can prove that the future residents will not own a car and that extra land is available to create parking spaces if residents subsequently choose to own a car. In the case of Vauban, costs of housing and parking are separated, and if residents choose to own a car, they must cover the costs of a garage parking space at the fringe of the neighborhood. The onetime charge is about $14,400 per car. This cost is a strong incentive for residents to find alternatives for getting around, such as using the tram system or a bicycle. New residents are offered a special mobility package as an alternative to owning a car. The package includes membership in a car-sharing company, a one-year local transit pass, as well as a 50 percent reduction on train tickets. Official numbers report about 250 motor vehicles per 1,000 Vauban residents, much lower when compared to the national average in Germany of 500 automobiles per 1,000 residents.

Stockholm, Sweden

Background

The capital of Sweden, Stockholm, has a population of close to 900,000 and is located at the country's south-central east coast (City of Stockholm, 2014). Often referred to as the "Venice of the North," Stockholm consists of 14 islands that are connected by 57 bridges. The history of the city dates back to the thirteenth century when it became the formal capital of Sweden in 1634. Following the Great Northern War early in the eighteenth century, Stockholm became an economic hub and cultural center experiencing strong population growth. Since then Stockholm has fully evolved into a modern and cosmopolitan city. Presently, just over 2 million people live in the greater Stockholm metropolitan area which accounts for almost one quarter of the country's total population (Statistikomstockholm, 2013). The core of the city is rather densely populated, although the total area of the municipality is spread out over 73 square miles, only one third is urbanized. The remaining two-thirds are equally water and green space (Berggren, 2013) Furthermore, 31 percent of the population only occupies 8 percent of the total land area, suggesting a high population density.

© Aleksei Andreev/Shutterstock, Inc.

The City of Stockholm.

In the past few decades, Stockholm has also been associated with sustainable urban development and planning. Due to the city's commitment to preserve nature, reduce greenhouse gas emissions, as well as to implement sustainable development policies and urban designs, Stockholm received the 2010 European Green Capital Award (www.europeangreencapital.eu). One of the key challenges the city faces pertains to balancing the demands of an increasing population and the infrastructural needs of a modern city while aspiring to meet the requirements of sustainable development and the policy goal of becoming 100 percent fossil fuel-free by 2050.

Transportation

One of the key challenges Stockholm is facing today rises from rapid population growth. Forecasts suggest that by the year 2030, Stockholm's number of inhabitants will increase by 25 percent compared to today (City of Stockholm, 2012). As a result, roads and public transit systems need to be updated and extended without compromising the overarching goal of becoming more sustainable and 100 percent fossil fuel-free by 2050. A specific area of concern is the transportation sector's ongoing reliance on fossil fuels and the resulting relatively high degree of air pollution resulting from carbon emissions (LSE, 2013). Nonetheless, in recent years a number of performance targets were set and policies implemented to make the transport system more environmentally friendly and to reduce emissions. The main purpose of these policies is to encourage the residents of Stockholm to rely less on the private automobile, by switching to alternative modes of transportation such as bicycle, public transit, or walking for their daily trips.

Overall, the initiatives used by the city of Stockholm are not much different to the policies discussed in the previous cases of Freiburg and Vancouver. Similar to other cities, Stockholm uses regulations and **zoning ordinances** that lead to compact and **mixed use development** that support public transit, encourages walking and cycling through extensive path networks, and invests heavily in a green transit fleet. Some

Zoning Ordinances - Consist of regulations and laws dictating how property in specific areas can be used. They determine whether particular zones within a municipality can be used for residential, commercial, or recreational purposes.

Mixed Use Development - Are developments that are not limited to a single use. Instead mixed use developments often combine residential and commercial use in the same building.

transportation policies and strategies do stand out and have contributed substantially to today's Stockholm's environmentally friendly image and sustainable development pattern. Notably, the bicycle is a major component of Stockholm's efforts to make the transportation sector more sustainable, while accommodating an increasing population. Today, more than 150,000 people commute daily to work by bike, while taking advantage of the over 750 kilometers of bike paths within the city limits (Fourteenislands.com, 2014). To increase safety and to encourage even more people to use the bike for daily travel, many bike lanes are situated between sidewalks and roadside parking, providing a buffer between moving cars and cyclists. In addition to the already existing extensive network of bike paths, the city's current mobility plan emphasizes bicycles not only for recreation but also as an important form of transportation. As a result, automobiles are no longer considered a priority in the city's transportation concept and overall development (Berggren, 2013).

Another aspect of the city's transportation policy that has reduced reliance on the private automobile is the high intermodal connectivity of the different modes of public transit. In Stockholm, one can quite easily switch between public-transit services such as regional trains, trams, or buses using the same fare card. The different transit stations are in close proximity, and the schedules are timed accordingly to accommodate each other. Since the public transit lines run every five to ten minutes, people can commute to work or travel within the city with minimal walking involved and without needing a car. The single transportation policy Stockholm is probably best known for is its congestion charge, which was first tested in 2006 (LSE, 2013). After London, Stockholm was only the second European city to introduce such a system. Since its full implementation in August 2007, traffic volumes have decreased significantly together with carbon emissions and other harmful air pollutants. Cars that enter the downtown area of Stockholm have to pass unmanned electronic control points (as shown in Picture 16), which recognize the license plate and the owner is charged a fee depending on the time of the day. The maximum amount that can be charged is about $8.20 a day. Due to the congestion charge and the other transportation policies, downtown traffic has decreased on average by 20 percent annually since 2007 (OECD, 2013). This has led to 10 to 15 percent reduction in CO_2 emissions by motor vehicles. This reduction is quite remarkable, considering that the city's population is growing by around 40,000 people a year. Simultaneously, public transit use has increased continuously by about 7 percent and now accounts for roughly 70 percent of all motorized trips within the city (Stockholm, 2012).

Land Use & Urban Form

Land use and urban form are other key areas of Stockholm's efforts to reduce energy consumption and become fossil fuel free in the foreseeable future. In order to reduce the use of fossil fuel, one of the main goals is to limit the number and length of trips people need to take on a daily basis for work, shopping, or recreation, as well as to improve the cost effectiveness of public transit systems through a high density and mixed use settlement structure. By developing land use policies that create an urban form characterized by shorter commuting distances, increased use of public transit and a high degree of walkability, the city hopes to further reduce energy consumption and greenhouse gas emissions. Therefore, in 2010 the city developed a new city plan called "The Walkable City" (City of Stockholm, 2011). The plan outlines 4 core strategies to achieve a more integrated and interconnected settlement structure. The overarching objective is to create space for about 200,000 new residents by the year 2030—without compromising the attractiveness or the city's commitment to a sustainable development pattern. The first strategy focuses on the strengthening of the downtown area by densifying the urban environment while simultaneously protecting the high quality of ex-

Hammarby Sjöstad District.

isting green infrastructure such as parks. A special focus is placed on the border region between the center of Stockholm and its surrounding districts. As a result, the second strategy focuses on the concept of node development to establish strong links between the public transit network and the adjacent neighborhoods. These corridors not only guide the extension of the public transit system into the suburban regions of the city but also the city's efforts to densify neighborhoods along public transit lines (OECD, 2013). One of the most important public transit expansions, to improve the connection between different parts of the city, is the cross-town rail tunnel of which its completion is the main focus of the third strategy. The tunnel especially creates a strong link between southern and northern Stockholm and further improves the integration of suburban neighborhoods in these areas to the core of the city.

A very good example of such an environment is the brownfield redevelopment Hammarby Sjöstad. Started in 2000, this eco-neighborhood is located south of Stockholm's south island and, when fully completed, will have 11,000 residential units for about 25,000 inhabitants. The underlying masterplan addressing the infrastructure of the development focuses on new public transit routes, centralized heating and cooling as well as an underground waste collection system (Ignatieva & Berg, 2014). Furthermore, the city set highly ambitious targets for the neighborhood, such as a very low car ownership rate of only 0.5 cars per household and integrating twice as much nature compared to other similar housing projects in Stockholm. What makes this neighborhood unique is its "closed loop" system for treating water, waste, and energy (Future Communities, 2014). Now often referred to as the *"Hammarby Model"* (City Climate Leadership Awards, 2013) this infrastructure system allows water, waste, and energy to support each other, thus reducing the energy and natural resources needed to operate the neighborhood. In addition, technologies such as fuel cells, solar cells, and solar panels are also integrated into the neighborhood, allowing its residents to produce half of all the energy they need themselves once the area is fully developed. Moreover, the city imposed, from the very beginning, stringent environmental restrictions on buildings, technical installations, and traffic, hence limiting their impact significantly on the surrounding natural environment compared to other Stockholm neighborhoods. Overall, the build environment is characterized by high density and modern architecture utilizing mostly sustainable materials. Although Hammarby Sjöstad will not be completed until 2025, it is already considered a success story attracting over 10,000 visitors a year (Ignatieva & Berg, 2014).

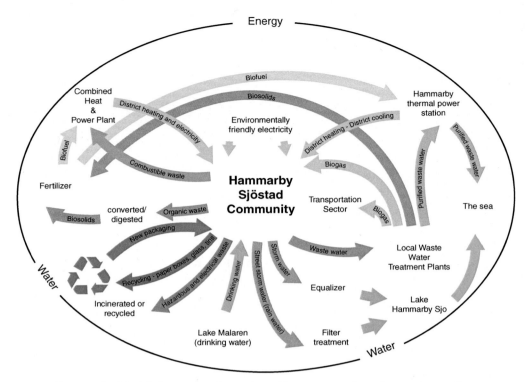

Hammarby Model demonstrating a closed-loop system for urban regeneration.

Brownfield redevelopment in general, plays is an important role in Stockholm. Going back to the mid-1980s, densification and revitalization of old industrial complexes have been an integral part of Stockholm's sustainable development strategy. In recent years more than half of urban development taking place inside the city involve infill developments (City of Stockholm, 2012a). Between the years 2000 and 2007, approximately 25,000 new housing units were built of which more than one third were built on large scale brownfield redevelopments.

Integrating and Preserving Nature within the city

The integration and preservation of nature plays an important role in the city's determination to become more sustainable and resilient. In order to preserve important green areas and protect surface and ground water as well as integrate new parks, open spaces, and green corridors, Stockholm developed the "City Plan 99" in 1999 and a regional development plan in 2001, which was the first of its kind for the metropolitan area. Furthermore, these plans specifically identify sites for brownfield redevelopment to accommodate the increase in population while limiting the destruction of existing green spaces due to urban expansion.

Today, different forms of natural infrastructure are clearly visible throughout the city. For example, connective green corridors spread out like wedges from the city center to the suburbs, providing recreational space as well as ecological services to maintain the local natural biodiversity. In addition, 12 large parks function as green anchors throughout the city. Each park is at least 200 acres and together account for approximately one third of the city's open space. Among these parks is the so called "Ekoparken," which became the first urban national park in 1995. This park is considered of high cultural value to the residents of Stockholm and is home to rare insects and birds (Nelson, 2014). Smaller neighborhood parks and community gardens make up another third of the overall park network. Moreover, the vast majority of Stockholm's shoreline is accessible as well. Today, the city of Stockholm offers 160 km of shoreline, 13 percent of the city's land area is covered by water and 42 percent by parks and forest (OECD, 2013). To further increase the number of green spaces, the city also supports and provides assistance to households and property owners in creating greener and more sustainable courtyards.

Ekoparken.

Characteristics & Principles of Sustainable Cities

If we examine cities such as Vancouver, Freiburg, Stockholm, and other cities alike, various characteristics and principles emerge that make these cites more sustainable, the observations are as follows:

1. Low Ecological – Environmental Impact

   Through the use of solar structures on private and municipal buildings as well by utilizing passive energy designs and homes that are carbon neutral, the cities can significantly reduce carbon dioxide emissions. Moreover, the associated reduction of fossil fuel use for energy production is a very effective strategy to reduce greenhouse gas emissions and thus mitigate climate change.

2. Cluster Housing and Densification

   New housing developments are zoned and designed as high compact and high density neighborhoods, while simultaneously preserving and integrating nature and walkways into the areas. Overall, many of these new settlements combine solar-based housing, cluster development, open space, and connections to public transit.

3. Green Employment

   Concomitant with implementing ecological friendly and sustainable designs, city polices also focus on boosting the green economy. For example, as Freiburg became known as a solar energy community, it utilized that recognition to generate green jobs in energy research at the university, employment through eco-tourism, and manufacturing of solar technologies.

4. Pedestrian & Bicycle- Friendly Environment

   These cities implement policies to support and encourage walking and bicycling. They provide extensive bicycle pathways, monetary incentives for not owning a car, punitive action for requiring a garage, well organized and widely available public-transit options, and a settlement structure that encourages walking short distances. These kinds of sustainable urban design and planning efforts also result in numerous social benefits, including: the creation of viable areas for social space and interaction, community building, and an enhanced quality of life and satisfaction from a sense of wellbeing and community efficacy.

5. Emphasis on Resilience

Another dimension that sets sustainable cities apart from other places is often their diverse set of small energy systems located in neighborhoods. The "Hammarby Model" or Freiburg's energy mix consisting of wind energy systems, solar collectors, hydropower, biogas, and geothermal add to the community's resilience. They provide security because the small technologies are not dependent on fossil fuel and its attendant political and economic constraints and fluctuations.

6. Place-Making

Sustainable cities also recognize the importance of building or restoring special places of history, culture, and community. These elements are an important part of the social domain in sustainable development. In the case of Freiburg, the historic medieval city that was destroyed in World War II was rebuilt with a similar spatial organization, using open public spaces and compact development without suburban sprawl. Later, the small canals that once brought water into the cities were reestablished as a means of visually reintroducing history to the community and enhancing aesthetics. Open space in the form of a farmer's market surrounding Freiburg's central church and largest structure provides a dominant place-making, pedestrian, and cultural experience

7. Political and Policy Support for Sustainable Development

The policies of "sustainable urbanism" are highly entrenched in cities that are focusing on becoming more sustainable. City government support for solar research and manufacturing, high-density living, habitat protection within the city, or increasing public-transit all work toward the greater goal of an overall sustainable development pattern. This particularly applies to urban planning for sustainable development that is central to governmental activity such as solar housing requirements, housing design, pedestrian environments, and bike trails.

8. Interconnectivity of Economic, Ecological, and Social Dimension

Following the sustainable development framework developed by the Brundtland Commission, sustainable cities encourage and advance sound ecological and environmental goals (such as the reduction of greenhouse gas emissions or a significant increase in public-transit ridership) and support an agenda of green employment in universities, research centers, and the private sector. Social and community based objectives through urban planning are also advanced and supported.

Social Dimension of Sustainable Neighborhood Development: CASE STUDY Freiburg – Rieselfeld

When it comes to sustainable development projects and environmental friendly neighborhood design, the social dimension often receives less attention compared to the environmental and economic side of sustainability (Vallance et al., 2011; Murphy, 2012; Woodcraft, 2012). Too often decision-makers tend to focus only on technical aspects such as energy reduction, sustainable building materials, or compact settlement structures, without acknowledging the importance of building social capital or social networks. Although different definitions exist, the main purpose of social sustainability is to create strong, vibrant, and healthy communities, which enhance the quality of life and the overall resiliency of the neighborhood and its population by establishing a built-environment of high quality that provides appropriate and accessible local services, contributing to the overall physical, social, and cultural well-being (Department of Communities and Local, 2012; Bacon et al., 2012).

A good example of a development where the social dimension of sustainable neighborhood design was considered through all stages of the planning process is the Rieselfeld neighborhood in the city of Freiburg. Very similar to the previously described Vauban district, Rieselfeld is characterized by simple building designs, mixed use, strong support for public transit, as well as many green spaces, playgrounds, and other public areas. Divided into four construction stages, the building of the neighborhood began in the year 1994 and was fully developed in 2010. The first residents moved to the district in 1996 and today about 12,000 people live in Rieselfeld's 4,500 housing units.

As mentioned above, the social aspects played an important role during the development of Rieselfeld. One of the major goals of development concept for Rieselfeld was to establish social and cultural life simultaneously with the construction of the physical build environment. As a result, the whole neighborhood development process was not only guided by design, transportation, and ecological

Light Rail and Community Center in Freiburg – Rieselfeld.

principles, but also by a social concept acknowledging the need for a community based participatory foundation. In particular, the social concept addressed the following community – based infrastructure (Siegl & Kaiser, 2002):

Childcare, Schools, Youth Programs

One of the cornerstones of Rieselfeld's social concept was to provide facilities for childcare, education, and youth programs as quickly as possible and before the completion of all the residential units. From the start is was very important to provide kindergarten space for every child as well as specifically tailored childcare for children between 1–3 and 6–10 years old. Therefore, the first elementary school was ready only 2 months after the first people moved into the neighborhood and the first Kindergarten was completed in 1998. Just 8 month after the completion of the elementary school, the high-school was also completed in September of 1997. Today, the elementary school has the highest enrollment statewide. Because all these institutions were present from the beginning and children did not have to leave the neighborhood to attend kindergarten or school young families not only felt comfortable moving to Rieselfeld, but also built strong social networks among each other. Since 2002 a community center was also established with a children library and youth workers on site, offering different recreational activities in the afternoon ant creating another opportunity for social interaction.

Healthcare for Elderly People

Another important aspect of social sustainability is the provision of healthcare inside the neighborhood, especially for the elderly. Riselfeld does not only have medical practices, but also offers a private nursing home next to regular housing units. Although, only a minority of the people living in Rieselfeld belong to the elderly age group of 65 and higher, the early construction and central location of the nursing home allows its resident to be still an active part of the community. Moreover, people who grew up in the district do not have to leave their social network and support system behind, once they are in need of care.

Church, Community Center, Public Space

Both major congregations in Germany, Catholic and Protestant, were present in Rieselfeld from the beginning and play a central role in the district's social and cultural life. The joint store, offering faire-trade products, was one of the first public spaces available to the residents to establish contacts with others. Moreover, both congregations celebrate interfaith services on a regular basis which is greatly supported by the residents and offers another opportunity to strengthen social ties. Whereas, at the beginning of Rieselfeld church services took place at the local gymnasium, both congregations built an integrated religious center in the most central location of Rieselfeld offering not only religious services, but also common community services and public meeting spaces.

The Community Center "Glashaus" was finished in 2003 and is the main social meeting point of Rieselfeld and located next to the church in the center of the neighborhood and in very close proximity to the elementary and high school. In addition, to the already mentioned youth library, which is a very popular meeting point after school, the "Glashaus" also has office space for the local citizen's organization K.I.O.S.K, which stands in German for Contact, Information, Organization, Self-Help, and Culture. Part of K.I.O.S.K and also located inside the community center is a café that is run by volunteers from the neighborhood.

The well planned public spaces such as parks and playgrounds also contribute to today's strong social network in Rieselfeld. Green infrastructure and path networks were established early on in the development process, providing a high quality public realm before the settlement structure was completed and all units were occupied. Especially the concept of creating semi-public spaces inside the courtyards of the different building blocks, strengthened the social networks between neighbors and improved the overall quality of life. Besides the green infrastructure, streets were also designed to encourage social interaction and provide a safe environment for children. With the exception of the main road with its light rail line all roads a very narrow and the maximum speed limit in the entire neighborhood is less than 19 miles per hour. In many areas the allowed speed limit is only walking speed.

Quatiersarbeit and Public Participation

Public participation plays a major role in Rieselfeld and started even before the first residents moved into the neighborhood. The first public participation projects started in April 1996 with the goals to engage future residents in the early stages of the design and implementation of social and cultural infrastructure as well as to help create the district's culture of everyday life. Furthermore, the city founded project, provided an opportunity for the public to provide feedback on the proposed project during the planning stage and thus influence the final design of Rieselfeld. Involving citizens from the beginning of the process created a strong sense of identity and responsibility among today's residents. People who live in Riselfeld generally care about their environment and value the social infrastructure and networks they helped to put in place so many years ago.

References

Bacon, N., Cochrane, Douglas, Woodcraft, S., 2012. *Creating strong communities: how to measure the social sustainability of new housing developments*, London: The Berkeley Group

Department for Communities and Local, 2012. National Planning Policy Framework. Available at: http://www.communities.gov.uk/planningandbuilding/planningsystem/planningpolicy/planningpolicyframework/ (accessed 8.18.2014)

Murphy, K. (2012). The social pillar of sustainable development: a literature review and framework for policy analysis. *Sustainability: Science, Practice & Policy, 8*(1)

Siegl, K., Kaiser, P. 2002. *Rieselfeld: Wo Freiburg wächst*. Stadt Freiburg: Baudezernat Bauverwaltungsamt/Geschäfstelle Rieslefeld.

Vallances, S., Perkins, H.C., Dixon, J.E. 2011. What is social sustainability? A clarification of concepts. Geoforum, 42: pp. 342–248.

Woodcraft, S. 2012. Social Sustainability and New Communities: Moving from concept to practice in the UK. *Social and Behavioral Sciences, 68*: 29–42.

An Intellectual History of Sustainability

Craig Thomas

Introduction

According to sustainability scholar David Orr (2002), the term sustainability has become "the keystone of global dialogue about the human future" (p. 145). And, it is well known by its framework of the three pillars of "environment, economy, and society." The term "**sustainable development**" was introduced to development discourses of the early 1970s, such as during the United Nations Conference on the Human Environment (Balboa, 1973), *Limits to Growth* (Meadows, Randers, Meadows & Behrens, 1972) published the same year and the *Brundtland Report* (WCED, 1987). The sustainability discussion has contributed to what might be thought of as a new "paradigm" or "worldview" that looks toward the future with respect to actions in the present. By 1992's *Rio Convention* (Summit, 1992), "sustainable development" had become the catch-all phrase, as it is found in 12 of its 27 principles. Over the past two decades, the concept has enjoyed a surge in public and academic visibility, encompassing wide ranging applicability, such as the valuing of ecosystem services, food security, urban design, building materials and construction, and energy systems.

> **Sustainable development -** economic growth and development that does not deplete natural resources nor damage ecosystems. The *Brundtland Report's* (1987) definition is commonly used as a definition of sustainability: "Sustainable development is development that meets the needs of the present, without compromising the ability of future generations to meet their own needs" (WCED, 1987).

When discussing the origins of *sustainability*, most people refer to the "three pillars of sustainability" and the *Brundtland Report* (WCED, 1987)—also known as "Our Common Future"—as the source. While the *Brundtland Report* was transformational, the *Oxford English Dictionary* (*OED*) dates the first usage of 'sustainable,' as "capable of being maintained at a certain level," to 1965. But American foundations for the concept reach back to at least during its first use in American forestry practices at the turn of the twentieth century, and in Europe much earlier.

Defined simply, sustainability is *the capacity to endure*; it has been a main concern of society as far back as we are aware. Sustainability discussions have guided societies whenever signs of dwindling resources and collapse make themselves apparent. Archeologists and geographers like Jared Diamond have exposed how soil loss, changing climates, population growth, and the homogenization of natural systems have been an abiding concern for naturalists (American and otherwise) for centuries, as stated in *Collapse: How Societies Choose to Succeed or Fail* (2006): "problems of toxic wastes, forests, soil, water (and sometimes air), climate changes, biodiversity losses, and introduced pests" are all among "the dozen types of problems that have undermined pre-industrial societies in the past" (p. 35). *Sustainability* can also be defined as the polar opposite of collapse.

In this chapter, an intellectual history of sustainability thinking is covered from the eighteenth century seeds of the Industrial Revolution to the present. Who are the key historical thinkers—including ecologists, economists, philosophers, historians and scientists—and their ideas, values, and concepts that preceded the current term sustainability in becoming as Orr (2002) called it, the "keystone" to our futures?

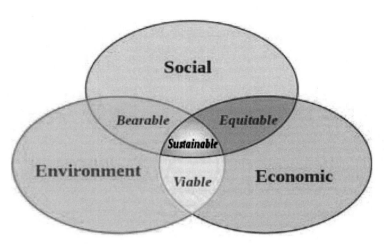

The three pillars were introduced with the 1987 *Brundtland Report* but since have been expanded, interpreted, and reinterpreted in attempts to define *sustainability*.

This chapter will begin by examining the nature of socio-ecological problems and the "**Dust Bowl**" of the 1930s. It will then look at historical influences in Europe and America on sustainability thinking, including major thinkers of the "environmental movement" in the US. Next, it examines the sustainability tradition as framed by the United Nations (UN) and other international conferences designed to address sustainability problems and define sustainability. Finally, it offers an alternative tradition posed by naturalists and ecologists to enhance our understanding of the UN tradition and shape a contemporary understanding of sustainability.

Socio-Ecological System (SES) Problems

"Peak oil," soil depletion, loss of biodiversity, growing urban squalor, and twenty-first century global traumas/crises such as the Fukushima disaster are just some of the highly complex problems vexing our institutional abilities to anticipate and respond effectively to such problems—especially over the long-term. Many immense, global challenges call for a change in the worldview commensurate with the magnitude of complex and integrated *socio-ecological systems* (SES, or "coupled system").

This kind of problem explicitly advocates that what is often divided into 'natural' and human systems be considered a single, complex SES (Redman, Grove & Kuby, 2002, p. 161). The resolution of SES problems (such as climate change, environmental degradation, and increasing human population growth and consumption) must be approached from an integration of knowledge systems. In order to be effective, this approach needs to cross normal disciplinary boundaries and employ a worldview that transcends or transforms traditional ideas of how knowledge and institutional systems should function.

Complex SES problems like climate change, biodiversity loss, and population growth that lower the natural carrying capacity on global, regional and local scales are sometimes characterized as *wicked* problems—which are of sufficient complexity

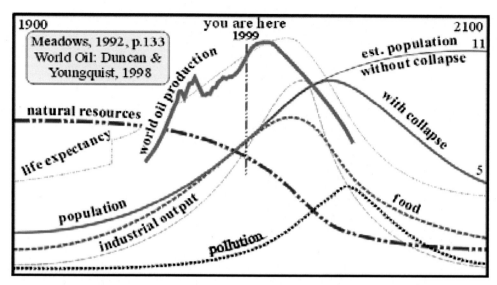

In *Beyond the Limits* (1992) Meadows, Meadows & Randers illustrates intertwined and overlapping problems that require an understanding of SES—coupled human-natural systems—to solve.

that they require the integration of knowledge from many disciplines coupled with experiential and empirical knowledge from various fields (Kates & Parris, 2003). As if wicked problems were not sufficiently daunting, SES problems have been characterized as *super-wicked*, given that the time available to solve many such problems is running out at the global level. Further, they worsen with each passing day of inaction, and they have no viable testing ground, meaning that they cannot be solved by trial and error, since we have but one planet with which to experiment (Rittel & Webber, 1974).

A discussion of terms like *coupled, socio-ecological systems (SES)*, and related terms like *resiliency* and *adaptive management* (covered later in this book) has origins at least as far back as the 1960s and 1970s, particularly in the work of ecologist and systems-thinker C. S. Holling, and in findings by international and interdisciplinary groups such as the authors of **Limits to Growth** (Meadows, et al., 1972). Holling's work also linked natural and social sciences in new fields like *urban ecology.* In recent decades, writers on sustainability such as Robert Kates and William Clark (1999) have expanded this work. In addition, important research bodies, like the Proceedings of the National Academy of Sciences (PNAS), have recognized SES as inextricably intertwined with this new *transdisciplinary* science that examines important *wicked problems,* such as the decline of land health in the form of ecosystem diminution, agricultural erosion and depletion, and annual biodiversity losses at a rate estimated at 100 to 10,000 times past extinction rates (Wilson, 2002). Along with climate change, these are among sustainability's most urgent problems.

Solving these complex problems requires integrating theory and practice, as well as understanding that the linkage of minute, individual actions in the present to collective consequences may manifest many generations in the future. What the great majority of scientists and citizens alike failed to appreciate at the time of the Industrial Revolution (1760–1840) was that while it "freed people from that land," it was an

The Limits to Growth (1972) - a book that suggested we would soon reach the Earth's carrying capacity, and launching the term *sustainable development* into the modern sustainability discourse.

evolutionary action. Not only did it free people from working on the land, it affected a paradigm-shift; the relationship that had existed between human beings and the land for thousands of years changed. Presently, many sustainability scholars speak of that time in history in terms of *decoupling* agricultural and natural systems. They call for a *recoupling* of social and environmental systems based on traditional farming and production practices that keep society more aligned with its natural and local environmental limits.

All these concepts will be covered in detail in this book, but the next section will first examine the nature of SES through the historic lens of the "Dust Bowl" as it took place in the 1930s in the United States and is reflective of a significant SES collapse.

America's First Major SES Problem: the "Dust Bowl"

The United States' first modern, national, socio-ecological tragedy occurred nearly 80 years ago. As massive clouds of dirt, silt, and important minerals laid down over thousands of years of geological history rose up to 8,000 feet high filled the sky for hundreds of miles, destroying entire communities across 11 states within the span of a few years. As environmental historian Donald Worster (1979) puts it, the "Dust Bowl" as it came to be known signified "the final destruction of the old Jeffersonian ideal of agrarian harmony with nature" (p. 45). Ten million tons of soil eventually dropped on Chicago alone (Worster, 1979). For most of US history, American farmers held a progressive doctrine of reaping ever higher and higher yields—but now "Nature" was striking back, eradicating viable agricultural environments and creating over 100,000 *ecological refugees.*

"Houses were shut tight, and cloth wedged around doors and windows, but the dust came in so thinly that it could not be seen in the air, and it settled like pollen on the chairs and tables, on the dishes," writes the great American novelist John Steinbeck illustrating this event in *Grapes of Wrath* (1939). The novel opens by portraying farmers staring numbly at a wasteland of dying crops. As the farming families looked fearfully to their leaders, believing if they and the community could remain "whole," there was still hope in their own work ethic, and later the federal government would come to the rescue. But, day after day, as thousands of tons of topsoil flew into the air, and as huge gusts of wind carried the miasma all the way from the Great Plains to the Atlantic, hundreds of thousands of people were completely displaced from their livelihoods and homes.

Gutherie produced the "Tom Joad Ballads" based on his views of the terrible human conditions in America after seeing the movie based on Steinbeck's book.

What caused this SES problem? It was not just natural causes like strip winds and tornados that are endemic to the Western prairies and Great Plains of America; nor was it only traditional natural climatic cycles, and the 50 to 100 year drought and flood cycles. What was it then that led to a positive feedback loop that depleted Western agricultural soils for over a decade, creating what might be America's first mega-disaster?

For decades prior to this event, farming and ranching in this area stripped the land of its natural vegetation and the sod that kept the land alive. When droughts came, the wind easily lifted the dead soil, carrying it across the country as far as New York City, where on many days the "black blizzards" prevented one from seeing more than a meter in front of one's face.

Historians generally agree that early Americans embraced a view that misunderstood the ecology of the Great Plains by assuming the agricultural principles of the East and its temperate climates could be applied to the Southwest by the mere addition of water. In 1909, Congress passed the Enlarged Homestead Act that granted settlers 320 acres of "dryland farming" and brought thousands of "sodbusters," settlers to the main area from 1910–1930, who would irrevocably alter the biotic community of the West. Vast irrigation networks eventually diverted the flows of the West's major rivers; but only a few independent farmers were successful on these dryland farms that were over a thousand acres smaller than later recommendations (Worster, 1979).

Day after day, year after year, for up to a decade in many places of the Great Plains, the "Dust Bowl" brought tragedy to many Americans.

Ranchers given 4,000 acre parcels in the original Homestead Act (1862) transformed the land through enormous cattle drives that destroyed many endemic species of plants and animals and eroded the soil, especially disturbing river beds whose flow was already greatly diminished due to expanding settlements. While scientists and researchers made great advancements at the time in ecosystems, in practice, farmers did not heed warnings to rotate crops and let significant-sized patches lie fallow annually. Instead, the scientific advances in the ecological sciences did not manifest in regional agricultural policies. Hence, ranching practices also resulted in soil degradation and loss of nutrient-rich topsoil.

While the Central Plains had been a vast sea of grasses that held the earth together, it was highly alkaline unlike the areas east of the Appalachian Mountains. Further, settlers viewed the land as subservient to their purposes. These inappropriate practices ultimately deprived the land of much needed minerals like nitrogen and phosphorus, and simultaneously it robbed the land of the many benefits of its natural cycles. Mono-cropping, especially of certain strains of wheat, was designed for maximum yields and used ubiquitously. For instance, while it was well-known that legumes and alfalfa could be rotated with wheat to build a more sustainable humus soil, "progressive farming" following the stock market crash drove machinery intensive farming practices to increase national production from 112 to 375 million bushels in the three years from 1929–1932 alone (Worster, 1979). So, with the utilization of mono-agriculture, new strains of wheat, lack of crop rotation, etc. developed in those years produced an agricultural culture that would, in time, wholly lose its resiliency. Nutrients set down over millions of years were quickly depleted by these intensive, widespread farming practices, causing vast quantities of dirt to be loose enough for seasonal winds to easily lift off the ground.

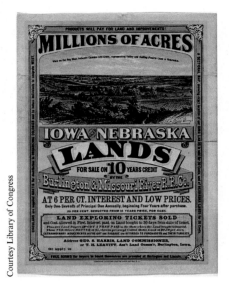

The government encouraged mass migrations west. Settlers often did not have the land and water resources to sustain a farm through the generational and seasonal climate changes.

At the turn of the twentieth century, scientific advancements in agricultural machinery, the development of early pesticides and herbicides, and new petro-intensive practices like mass chemical fertilization also contributed to the collapse of the agricultural region. The fragility of biotic communities collided with conservation laws geared toward agricultural and ranching efficiency and the steady increase in the production of yields. Warnings against these methods were not heeded, and by the 1930s, citizens watched as six million acres of taxpayer-funded land filled the air from west to east across the country.

It would serve us well to remember, as population ecologist Lester Brown (2011) put it, "the archeological record indicates that civilizational collapse does not come out of the blue . . . economic and social collapse was almost always preceded by a period of environmental decline" (p. 9). While the "Dust Bowl" was an important lesson that helped the US to change its agricultural practices, this same integrated SES problem is now occurring in places like Africa and China And, as our country faces prolonged drought, such an event could strike again. Global drought, flooding, massive human migrations, premature deaths due to poor air-quality, and agricultural yields far below than expected due to changing climates are central to today's sustainability discussions. These kinds of problems have plagued humankind; important historical analysis can benefit us in understanding the key tenets of sustainability as we will discuss next (Diamond, 2006).

"Maximum Sustainable Yield"

The modern concept of sustainability began with forest management in America, which reflects long-held philosophies and practices in Europe. The dwindling timber supplies following the Thirty Years War (1614–1648) in France and Germany and the seeds of industrialism were inextricably integrated with their treatment of nature. This short background section will describe the contributions of Carl von Carlowitz, Thomas Robert Malthus, and American forester and conservationist Gifford Pinchot who all influenced the intellectual understanding of "**sustainable yield**" as it spread from Europe to America through forestry management and the maintenance of natural capital.

Sustainable Yield - the harvesting a given natural resource without diminishing its natural capital or lowering ecosystem productivity.

The origins of sustainability in America begin with the appearance of the concept *sustainable yield*, advanced by the first Chief Forrester of the U.S. Forest Service (1905–1910), Gifford Pinchot. He applied European concepts of good use, conservation, and sustainable yield to develop the first national park system in the United States as one that was designed to increase the wealth of the country. To understand Pinchot's concept, we must first examine two European economists who influenced him.

Von Carlowitz and Sustainable Forestry Management

Seventeenth-century Germany greatly accelerated the destruction of forests by nearly stripping them clean for the sake of building its navy and for the copper and iron ore smelting during the seeds of European industrialism, which began arguably during this era. They helped initiate industrialism by being among the first to venture into global markets fueling exploration and colonization.

Hans Carl von Carlowitz began his work in mining (1645–1714) when the degraded state of the forests in Germany started to present problems in economics, governance, and social equity. As the environmental realities of a small country with limited resources constricted the growth and development of the population, he led Germany in turning forestry management into a science.

After touring Jean-Baptiste Colbert's (1619–1683) managed forests in France in 1713, von Carlowitz published *Sylvicultura oeconomica, oder haußwirthliche Nachricht und Naturmäßige Anweisung zur wilden Baum-Zucht* (loosely translated as *Forestry Economics' Nature Decree: Moderate Instructions for Wild Tree Breeding*) in 1732. Under Louis XIV (1638–1715), Colbert began managing forests, primarily for Louis's shipbuilding. This manuscript was a comprehensive treatise that tied the endurance of the mining industry directly to the development of German forestry. Von Carlowitz employed economics as the dominant metaphor and wrote primarily to keep the copper and iron mines running and the German colonial apparatus running (Grober, 2012).

In this book, von Carlowitz coined the term of *nachhaltigkeit* or "lastingness." He used *nachhaltigkeit* to describe forests that remain eternally productive and autonomously regenerative, while still producing enough harvest to profit economically. Thus, von Carlowitz firmly established economics as integral to sustainability. During the early enlightenment, new "forest managers" employed von Carlowitz's term in increasingly strict regulatory measures that geared forests toward the productivity of the nation.

Malthus and Population Ecology

Thomas Malthus (1766–1834) may be most remembered for economics being named "the dismal science," but he is probably the most referenced historical figure among writers on sustainability. As one of our first population ecologists, Malthus would set the stage for the modern economy as well as a very early understanding of how ecological limits would affect the economy. Environmental historian Donald Worster (1994) claims Malthus introduced ecology to classical economics, but Malthus' viewpoint was strictly instrumental, placing an economic value on ecosystems only in terms of supporting the maximum possible number of human beings, for maximum happiness, part of the utilitarian philosophy of Jeremy Bentham (1748–1842) and John Stewart Mill (1806–73) that dominated the thinking of this era of English history.

In his essay, "A Principle of Population," Malthus explores the production of food, population growth, and their effects on the future improvement of society. He states that food production grows *linearly* while population grows *exponentially*. This incongruity suggests that we will one day surpass the carrying capacity of the Earth, or the amount of life that can be sustained by available resources.

While Malthus is often referred to as an early sustainability thinker, environmental policy historian Lamont Hempel (2012) argues, "[t]he condition of overshoot

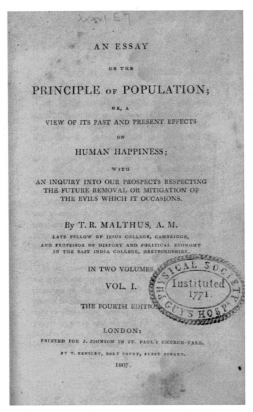

Thomas Malthus' 1798 book shockingly depicted a human race that would outgrow its environment.

Source: King's College, London. (2014). Online Collections http://www.kingscollections.org/exhibitions/specialcollections/charles-dickens-2/victorian-tight-fi stedness/scrooge-and-malthus.

described by Malthus was based on immutable mathematical logic, but offered very little of what we would call today insights on human behavior from social scientists or notions of resilience and sustainability" (p. 70). Presently, it can be seen that current population growth with unfulfilled food production with unsustainable practices not being mitigated, "food security" is becoming one of the critical wicked problems of our time, vindicating Malthus's earlier arguments, with the production of such outcomes as disease, famine and war.

Since the beginnings of the Industrial Revolution, Malthus' importance has waxed and waned in social sciences discussions. Climate change and other SES problems, however, have reopened sustainability conversations that are often characterized as "Malthusian" and "neo-Malthusian" because they involve the acceptance of the idea that the human race is outstripping its resources. Malthusian thought also feeds directly into the very controversial tradition of population ecologists like Henry Fairfield Osborn who wrote *Our Plundered Planet* in 1948, Paul and Anne Ehrlich

in the 1960s who authored *The Population Bomb*, and the highly influential document *Limits to Growth* in 1972, all of which suggest human economic development endangers the life-support systems of the Earth.

Gifford Pinchot and *Sustainable Yield*

The first prevalent use of the Greek root *sustene* in America can be traced to Gifford Pinchot (1865–1946), the first Chief of the U.S. Forest Service. Pinchot was a friend of naturalist President Theodore Roosevelt (1858–1919) who was instrumental in creating America's first national park system. During his tenure, Pinchot's department began using the term *sustainable yield* as a guiding objective in the long-term commercial management of American forests—meaning, in forestry, the largest harvests that can be made without degrading long-term productivity. In sustainability, it has meant preserving natural capital. But in practice, obtaining the *maximum **sustainable yield*** or the maximum level at which a natural resource can be routinely exploited without long-term depletion (*OED*, 2014) from an ecosystem without also damaging an ecosystem has been hard to achieve. Few ecosystems, especially during Pinchot's era, had been studied over the long-term.

Pinchot, whose family made a small fortune in harvesting the Pennsylvania forests for profit, studied directly under Sir Dietrich Brandis, (1824–1909), a minor but textbook utilitarian forester. Pinchot's philosophy was geared toward Colbert's *bon usage* (Pinchot's "wise use" is a direct translation), and his 1905 manual "The Use of the National Forest Reserves" is a document dedicated to the supply and demand of forests. These ideas would guide not only the United States Forest Service, but also the first school of Yale School of Forestry in 1910 (which Pinchot's family founded). Pinchot was trained in the European and heavily relied upon the von Carlowizian tradition of sustainable yield. His introduction of *sustainable yield* to the American dialogue had a longstanding impact and led to the wide acceptance of the concept maximum sustainable yield.

To summarize, the modern American concept of sustainability really began with forest management and the dwindling timber supplies following the Thirty Years' War in France and Germany. This short background section described the defining roles of von Carlowitz and Malthus, and the American forester and conservationist Gifford Pinchot who, in turn, greatly influenced the intellectual understanding of sustainability as it developed in the first half of the twentieth century and into the 1960s. Pinchot, a devout utilitarian, represented the *conservationist* worldview of the times—one that valued the environment but framed it primarily in terms of its value for economic development. Pinchot, and his brand of *conservation*, has since been caricaturized in much of the literature as a villain (Minteer, 2006). He is often contrasted with the naturalist John Muir, who alternatively, advocated that a *preservationist* approach to sustainability be defined in **non-anthropocentric** terms, valuing the environment for its own sake, as we will see in more detail next.

Controversies within Environmentalism and Sustainability

Most people refer to the *Brundtland Report's* (1987) definition of "future generations" and "**three pillars**" as the ultimate definition of *sustainability*. This focus has evolved partly out of a polarized political world of communist vs. democratic beliefs (Cronon, 2011), human-first vs. environment-first interpretations, and trade-offs between oppositions. Several ideological polarizations have been observed throughout the course of environmental discourse. Although these are avoidable, and it may be best argued that we need a variety of lenses with which to view sustainability problems. And, while there is no "silver bullet" solution to such problems, it is wise to be familiar with several key debates. This section will examine *conservation* vs. *preservation* in the early twentieth century, issues of *developed* vs. *developing* in the post-WWII economic development discourse, and *anthropocentric* vs. *non-anthropocentric* views as they have taken shape over the last few decades.

Conservation versus Preservation

The controversy between Gifford Pinchot and John Muir first separated American environmentalists into conservationist/preservationist and anthropocentric/non-anthropomorphic camps, one side stressing instrumental values (or values that represent human interests only), and the other side emphasizing intrinsic values (or values that represent ecosystem needs). While this controversy has often been misinterpreted

Non-anthropocentric values - values that consider the environment for its own health and well-being, rather than for instrumental (*anthropocentric*) human uses (*biocentric, ecocentric, preservationist values* have a similar gist).

Three pillars - the three guiding areas of sustainability problems and solutions: *environment, economy,* and *social equity* (aka the *three e's*) as outlined in the *Brundtland Report* (1987) and the Rio "Earth Summit" Convention (1992).

Courtesy Library of Congress

John Muir was a friend of President Roosevelt's but when it came to the management of our national forests, Roosevelt eventually sided with Pinchot.

through oversimplification, similar issues of ideological polarization among interpreters of sustainability and environmentalism persist today.

A devout utilitarian, Pinchot as we have seen earlier in the chapter, represented the *conservationist* worldview of his times—one that valued the environment but primarily in terms of its value for economic development. Subsequently, Pinchot has been caricaturized in the literature as a villain. A more grounded characterization would be as an interdisciplinary scholar who identified the dwindling resources of the nation as a threat to national security and a pragmatic ecologist and forester who sought to preserve American forests in the best way, which he saw as appealing to the private and collective economic interests.

Pinchot's early sustainability worldview is one that was inextricably tied to the "progressive movement" of his era—utilitarianism and mass production. His terminology resonated into the next age of rapid growth in America with the "Multiple-Use Sustained Yield Act of 1960," which explicitly characterized forests as recreational, renewable resource, and watershed management in orientation (Hempel, 2012, p. 96). Char Miller (2009), a contemporary Pinchot scholar, describes Pinchot as someone who saw the dwindling resources of the nation as a threat to *national security* and a pragmatic manager who sought to preserve American forests in the best way he could. But, Pinchot is probably most remembered as an early interdisciplinary conservationist outside of the naturalist vein. He is also viewed as one who helped unite the fields of ecology and economy and instigated environmental regulation in an era when none existed. John Muir, however, advanced a *preservationist*-based approach to conservation, lobbying his friend Roosevelt to accept his views. "When one tugs at a single thing in nature, he finds it attached to the rest of the world," said John Muir, taking an holistic view of the natural world. A naturalist, Muir advocated a biocentric, or non-anthropocentric view toward the rights of nature (Minteer, 2006). One of the first people to write about the Central Valley of California, Muir dedicated a large portion of his life to documenting its wildlife abundance. "He waded ankle-deep through the blooms, lay at night on them for a bed, shared their fragrance with the larks, antelopes, hares, and bees" (Worster, 1985, p. 9). Major dam-building projects like Hetch Hetchy in California eradicated this biodiversity and seemingly along with it, Muir's preservationist vision for the national parks.

A controversy between Muir and Pinchot resulted from the flooding (and ruination of) the Hetch Hetchy Valley. This first separated American environmentalists into conservationist/preservationist camps, with the former side stressing instrumental values of natural resources and the latter side emphasizing the intrinsic values of

Nature (Minteer, 2006). But the flooding of the Hetch Hetchy Valley in California to create a hydroelectric power plant for San Francisco was one of America's first clear trade-offs between environment and economics.

Issues between Environmentalists

In ecology, *sustainability* refers to "a state that can be maintained over an indefinite period of time" (Du Pisani, 2006, p. 91); but, it has a variety of meanings when referring to human activity, particularly in the context of legal arguments, land management, and other contemporary applications that include environmental considerations (*OED*, 2014). The majority of these definitions view nature and natural resources primarily for their economic value to human society--this is especially true within the context of economic development. As stated in the introduction to this chapter, the concept of sustainability began to gain strength during the development discourse of the 1960s and 1970s. This section will briefly look at another public and intellectual debate between environmentalists.

As early as 1947, ecologist Barry Commoner (1917–2012) showed signs of deep concern for the planet's well-being. Commoner began to bring important scientific debates of high risk into the open, as well as to press the American Association for the Advancement of Science to begin to play a more ethical role. Later in 1952, he formed the Committee on the Social Aspects of Science. Commoner and Rachel Carson inspired a wave of activism that persisted through the 1960s and early 1970s. Commoner was a harsh critic of technological optimism and conveyed this message in his seminal works, *Science and Survival* (1966) and *The Closing Circle* (1971). "In the eager search for the benefits of modern science and technology we have become enticed into a nearly fatal illusion: that through our machines we have at last escaped from dependence on the natural environment" (Commoner, 1971, p. 8).

Commoner argued that the "environmental crisis" (as it became to be known in the 1970s) resulted primarily from the technological advances designed to achieve a more sustainable future like the Green Revolution, rather than in lieu of them–an old idea, but one that seemed to be increasingly obfuscated when infused with capitalistic notions of progress (p. 17). Commoner also thought that most Americans had mistaken the "good life" as one primarily of affluence. He equated it to kitchen appliances, sporty automobiles, and national security in the form of the atomic bomb for Americans after WWII. Commoner based his three-pronged platform to create a new scientific structure based upon 1) the necessity of dissent; 2) transparency of technical information; and 3) public discussions and decision-making (Egan, 2007).

Commoner resisted what he termed as Paul Ehrlich's "barbaric" assault on population growth; something he called the "lifeboat ethic" through distributing birth control, coercively if necessary. The debates between Ehrlich and Commoner in the late 1960s and early 1970s serve to illustrate this ongoing ideological debate and division within human development discourse. Commoner critiqued Ehrlich's views on population control in *The Population Bomb* (1968) as "coercive" in his seminal publication. Ehrlich, a neo-Malthusian locating the problem primarily in population growth and aggregate consumption, was perceived as both pessimist and alarmist.

Ehrlich's view was reinforced through Hardin's article, "The Tragedy of the Commons" (1968), with Malthusian Ehrlich publically attacking Commoner's views that social action constituted the best arena for solving population, consumption, and pollution problems, saying in a review of *The Closing Circle* (1971), "uncritical acceptance of Commoner's assertions will lead to public complacency regarding both the population and affluence" (Bulletin 1972, p. 55). Commoner fired back in the *Bulletin of the Atomic Scientists* a month later:

"Ehrlich took the position that ecological catastrophe is inevitable if the peoples of developing countries...are left to regulate population growth by their own actions . . . [which] include improvement of living conditions, urgent efforts to reduce infant mortality, social security measures, and the resultant effects on desired family size" (p. 55).

Ongoing Anthropocentric vs. Non-anthropocentric Worldviews

While the concept of sustainability has sought to integrate opposing views, it does not seem to have completely resolved ideological polarizations such as preservationist vs. conservationist and environmentalist vs. economist that manifest into instrumental and intrinsic value divisions among environmentalists; in fact, the construct of sustainability has often exacerbated ideological differences. Divergent social issues are the most hotly debated of the three sustainability pillars because they are the most vaguely defined and because frameworks often ignore issues such as environmental justice and poverty, despite sustainability's inherent concerns over these matters.

The environmental movement of the late 1960s and early 1970s would also be marked by polar opposite stances on the state of the world and how to address its major problems. While substantial gains in pollution legislation occurred in the 1970s, people also began to view the world as a place that would one day become "uninhabitable." Within a few years of the first Earth Day in 1970, many social and environmental advocates became polarized over the approaches needed to interpret and solve environmental issues (Sale, 1993). These approaches transformed into issues that favored an environmental justice worldview and stressed social concerns vs. a much deeper ecologist point of view that favored the intrinsic values of Nature as valuable, and its utmost consideration was perceived the only way to preserve the planet.

Norwegian Arne Naess, who introduced the term "deep ecology" in *The Shallow and the Deep* (1973), revived thinkers from the distant past such as Baruch Spinoza (1632–77), who saw all "particularity" within Nature as equally representative of God, linking the human and natural world (Hay, 2000, p. 26). Naess described the differences between deep and "shallow ecology" in detail: with regard to pollution, a shallow approach would seek a technology to help purify emissions that cause acid rain, while a deep approach would attack the causal economic and technological mechanisms responsible for the diminishing of biospheric integrity. This theory would facilitate the application of ethics to ecosystems. Ecocentrism was a concept that applied to "the ecosphere as a whole" (Naess & Sessions 1984: 5).

As the concept of environmental justice captured momentum during the Reagan Era of the 1980s, the forefront of the public debate became skeptical of what was thought to be the biocentric or ecocentric views that were perceived as only a luxury of educated elite in developed countries. Environmental justice placed precedence on the distribution of the environmental costs and benefits unequally between the Global North and Global South, as well as within the Global North itself. Like Commoner's social platform, environmental justice advocates saw the capitalistic economy as the source of many of the problems, and social programs designed to increase transparency and encourage pluralism in decision-making as the cure.

The Environmental Movement

During the 1960s and 1970s, many American ecologists were also writers and activists like Barry Commoner. Among the most well-known and influential is Rachel Carson, whose book *Silent Spring* (1962) brought the problems caused by pollution around the globe into people's homes, helping to inspire an "environmental movement" among various interest groups in America. This short section will focus on the contributions of intellectual thinkers like Commoner and Carson who inspired the environmental movement in America.

Rachel Carson (1907–1964), whose 1962 book *Silent Spring* brought forward concerns about the pervasiveness of pesticides in our daily life into public discourse, ushered in a new perspective on production and consumption. Carson's greater body of work, including her letters and books on the natural history of the sea, presents a new ecological vision for holism by focusing on multi-generational environmental problems and risks. This approach was novel, marking a break from some of the earlier conservationist writers and a transition to "environmentalism." In *Silent Spring* (1962), Carson addressed pivotal issues like industrial pollution, persistent pesticides, and the bioaccumulation of toxins as they traveled up the food chain to human beings. Carson contributed to the understanding of coupled human-natural systems through her interdisciplinary work at Wood's Hole Naval Research Laboratory prior to and during World War II, when disciplines from all areas of epistemology came together to respond to the threat of global domination, but also during groundbreaking work like mapping the ocean floor and the discovery of plate tectonics.

Before 1962, Carson had written many books about the interconnectedness of nature. Her poetry was so compelling she won the 1951 National Book Award with *The Sea Around Us*. But soon after that, Carson felt the need to switch gears, after realizing that in her local natural haunts along the East Coast, much of the biodiversity was disappearing. Specifically, she noted that in springtime, fewer birds could be heard singing, which she found was due to the widespread use of DDT (*dichlorodiphenyltrichloroethane*). Ubiquitous DDT spraying was responsible for the thinning bird eggs so badly they could not hatch. By using her connections as a government scientist, she acquired what were then confidential reports of the deadly effects of DDT, allowing her to become an expert on the effects of herbicides and pesticides that could be found in everything everyone ate and drank, even the air breathed.

Carson's passion for writing about ecology and human ecology linked ethical and scientific values, notably in a manner important to sustainability discourse. As Carson herself writes, "The history of life on earth has been a history between living things and their surroundings" (1962, p. 297). Carson's primary contribution to sustainability includes developing an understanding of *human ecology* as the link between science and ethics, and advancing a vision for a new and vital role for science and the scientist alike in creating transparency between government and knowledge systems.

Although he would not come from such an aesthetic appreciation of nature as Carson, Commoner likewise concluded in *Science and Survival* (1963) "[t]he age of innocent faith in science and technology may be over" (p. 14). During the era of environmentalism (sometimes referred to as the "age of ecology" in Carson and Commoner's time), Commoner expanded Carson's thoughts on science and technology, and he would inject them into the political arena for over three decades (and long after Carson's death from cancer in 1964).

Commoner, like Carson, identified another problem—science was declining in prestige as well as being the cause of new social concerns. Commoner saw the gap between science and social science widening and took it upon himself to fill that gap. As a result, "by 1960, Commoner's popular identity took on the issues of toxic substances and knew that someone in the realm of science had to make value-laden decisions" (Egan, 2007, p. 42). As early as 1966, Commoner warned we were "mortgaging future generations" with our industrial practices (Egan, 2007, p. 83). Like Carson, he conducted research during WWII, especially working on projects to use DDT to kill the mosquitoes at Normandy prior to invasion, which influenced his beliefs. During the war and for some time afterward, social issues of science were put on hold and R& D gained primacy and escalated rapidly.

Because of writers like Carson and Commoner, the environment became a pivotal political theme during the late 1960s and early 1970s, but their writings also shifted the dialog toward quality of life issues like the human health effects of pollution. Regardless of individual rationale, motivation, or philosophy, a social-environmental movement coalesced across a broad spectrum of society and mobilized to remedy environmental degradation and its effects. In the United States, a platform of very positive environmental laws were enacted, the likes of which have not been seen since. A number of the most well-known pieces of legislation during this time included the Clean Air Amendments of 1970, the establishment of the Environmental Protection Agency 1970, Federal Water Pollution Control Amendments of 1972, the Endangered Species Act of 1973, the Safe Drinking Water Act of 1974, and the Resource Conservation and Recovery Act of 1976. National environmental policy was promulgated though the 1969 National Environment Policy Act that had a global influence and provided a process for decisions regarding environmental impacts.

During this period with *Limits to Growth* (1972), the term "sustainable development" became the foreground of environmental and development discourses, serving as a meeting place for human and ecological values. This document initiated sustainability discourse in its modern form, forecasting humankind's new global problems with the first computers and equations derived by Jay Forrester from MIT, *Limits to Growth* (Meadows et al., 1972), constituting the beginning of the concept of sustainability's first global toehold.

United Nations Literature and International Conferences

The United Nations (UN) Conference on the Human Environment (UNCHE) held in Stockholm (Balboa, 1973) and underlying intellectual documents such as *Limits to Growth* (1972) published the same year, introduced the term *sustainable* to the development discourse focusing on the economic value of resources. The *Brundtland Report* (which reinforced the outcomes of UNCHE) further propagated and entrenched the human- and economic-centered focus of sustainable development. Preliminary and follow-up discussions such as the 1972 *Earth Summit* of Rio also embraced this definition, firmly establishing its framework for global discussions. **Sustainable development** had become the catchall phrase for environment and development (i.e., *sustainability*) discourses.

This section examines three important UN documents side by side with three other revolutionary documents that all used sustainability terminology: *Limits to Growth* (1972), *The World Conservation Strategy* (1980), and *Our Common Journey: a Transition for Sustainability* (1999)

The *Stockholm Declaration* and *Limits to Growth*

The 1972 United Nations Conference on the Human Environment (UNCHE) held in Stockholm, or *Stockholm Declaration*, considered "the need for a common outlook and for common principles to inspire and guide the peoples of the world in the preservation and enhancement of the human environment" (Balboa, 1973). The *Stockholm Declaration* lays out 26 principles and is considered by authors of the **Brundtland Report** to be the first of the lineage that led to Brundtland and the three-pillar framework of sustainability thinking.

The *Stockholm Declara*tion was praised by subsequent bodies (WCED, 1987; Summit, 1992), despite its predominant interest in the growth of economic markets for the developed and developing worlds alike. Their discussion influenced later UN documents like the *Brundtland Report* and the *Earth Summit*.

In the first part of the 26 principles of the Stockholm Declaration, one can see ideals of protecting the ocean, wildlife, and preserving non-renewable resources; but, in looking further, we begin to see many of sustainability's inherent contradictions. For instance, Principle 8 states, "[e]conomic and social development is essential for ensuring a favorable living and working environment for man and for creating conditions on earth that are necessary for the improvement of the quality of life" (Balboa, 1973). This places the two broad fields of inquiry *development* and *environment* at odds as well as placing *development* in the position of operationalizing the benefits of the environment. Principle 11 goes even further by placing development first,

"[t]he environmental policies of all States should enhance and not adversely affect the present or future development potential of developing countries, nor should they hamper the attainment of better living conditions for all, and appropriate steps should be taken by States and international organizations with a view to reaching agreement on meeting the possible national and international economic consequences resulting from the application of environmental measures."

As we travel further down the list of principles, the terms we see most are those framing sustainable development in terms of human-centric benefits. For example, Principle 14 states that conflicts (i.e., what we call tradeoffs today) "between the needs of development and the need to protect and improve the environment" will be solved by "rational planning" (Balboa, 1973). Principle 18 focuses on science and technology and "their contribution to economic and social development." It further states that they "must be applied to the identification, avoidance and control of environmental risks and the solution of environmental problems and for the common good of mankind." Finally, Principle 21 boldly claims that "[states] have . . . the sovereign right to exploit their own resources pursuant to their own environmental policies, and the responsibility to ensure that activities within their jurisdiction or control do not cause damage to the environment of other States or of areas beyond the limits of national jurisdiction" (Balboa, 1973). This last statement is considered impossible from most contemporary sustainability theorists' understanding of global interconnectedness and presents an illogical from a naturalist perspective.

In the same year, the ***Limits to Growth*** (Meadows, et al., 1972) framed sustainability quite differently, *Limits to Growth* (1972) predicted that population would overshoot the earth's **carrying capacity**, impairing the ability of the planet to support human and other biological life. The authors stated that global transformations were needed in five categories: *population, industrialization, pollution, food production,* and *resource depletion.* These were clearly anthropocentric in scope; yet, the document linked humanistic and scientific horizons of interpretation. In this way, it paved a course for a new rapport between the previously bifurcated studies of social and hard sciences and named this new marriage *sustainable development.* Supporters of the concepts advanced by the authors of *Limits to Growth* (1972) realized that both developed and developing countries needed to change their patterns of economic and population growth.

The findings in *Limits to Growth* (1972) were highly controversial at its issuance, as they remain today. While limits to economic growth implied developed countries must show constraint in production and consumption; for developing countries, it meant reinforcing the gross inequities between their countries and developing countries. As a result, it immediately received backlash from the business world, conservative think tanks, and from the left as well for its neo Malthusian thinking. *Limits to Growth* (1972) would demonstrate that the term *sustainable development* began to take hold in the global discourse.

Carrying Capacity - the maximum sustainable population an area will support before undergoing environmental deterioration.

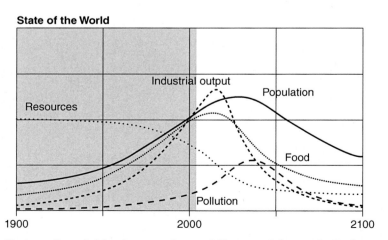

State of the World

Limits to Growth **(Meadows, et al., 1972) illustrated that ecological limits dictated human limits of economic growth and expansion.**

Source: Limits to Growth (1972) p. 40. Publisher: Chelsea Green Publishing Company (August 1993)

The *Brundtland Report* and the *World Conservation Strategy*

Commonly known as the *Brundtland Report* (WCED, 1987), "Our Common Future: Report of the World Commission on Environment and Development" was the first publication to use the term *sustainability* in its current usage (i.e., noun form). Its definitional "development that meets the needs of the present without compromising the ability of future generations to meet their own needs" (WCED, 1987, 1:1) may the most often quoted definition for sustainability. Certainly future generations are crucial to sustainability, anything otherwise would defy its definition. Its **"three-pillar"** framework has been an important foundation for sustainability discussions and can be found in many sustainability education textbooks and sustainability coursework at the university level.

Brundtland's central ethical and material issue concerned the rights of developing and developed countries to expand economically, while also maintaining ecosystems for future human and economic use. The document directs developing countries to develop and grow sustainably, yet it sets no clear boundaries for similar sustainable development of developed countries. While opening up important normative discussions, Brundtland only *began to include* the subject of environmental resources in discussions about development previously absent from such discussions. Until its publication, strictly economic bodies like the International Monetary Fund and the World Bank were the hegemons of all global development issues. Brundtland's intended scope was merely to add environmental resources as yet another dimension. It did not recognize the ecological phenomena that contribute to making a SES-problem, like positive feedback loops, cascading socio-ecological effects, *ecological limits*, and *thresholds*. Nor did its authors intend to address or remedy the complex web of ethical issues surrounding development (Minteer, 2011; Orr, 2002).

What is commendable regarding "Our Common Future" is its premise that ecological sustainability required addressing social inequities through democratic pluralism (Minteer, 2011). This is the basis for contemporary sustainability theory, which posits that a sustainable society rests on three interlinked foundations—social equity, efficient economic allocation, and respect for ecological limits. These have come to dominate human development discourse, shaping sustainability initiatives around the globe for 25 years.

The Brundtland's Report's (1987) strength lay in its addressing of social inequities through democratic pluralism as a necessity for ecological sustainability (Boone & Modarres, 2006). Nowhere before had universal social justice as an immediate goal been indissolubly linked to issues of conservation. Also, often overlooked is the report's dedication to *intra*-generational equity. It inextricably linked the planet's well being to peoples of all generations and races, and it solidified the link between the eradication of poverty and sustainability theory. The successful mediator was the concept of sustainability.

For example, not only did the report secure sustainability's place at the center of human development discourse, but it also provided women with an equitable share of the discussion. It recognized "the changing role of women" and "the right to self-determination" (WCED, 1987: 2.51, 4.6). Child rearing responsibilities in developing

The *Brundtland Report* (1987) - the source of the modern paradigm of sustainability. It is significant for demanding ethical issues such as gender and economic equity be part of sustainability's definition.

countries—and often in developed countries—rest primarily on women. The report also made important claims about women's shifting roles, including the observation that women were producing 60 percent to 90 percent of the food in Africa (WCED, 1987: 5.86).

It may have been in part the acceptance and endorsement of the term *sustainable development* by a group of ecologists in the *World Conservation Strategy* (1980) that created Brundtland's success. This group's mission targeted "living resource conservation for sustainable development" (p. 18), opening the door for the term's universal use in dialogues about the environment.

The *World Conservation Strategy* (1980), was penned by the International Union for the Conservation of Nature (IUCN), one of the most prestigious non-governmental agencies for the protection of the environment today (aka the World Conservation Union). Established in 1956, the IUCN was the preeminent body of global ecological preservation and conservation. It tackled the most difficult environmental issues like diminishing biodiversity, climate change, natural resource depletion, and endangered species. This non-UN conference was applauded for being able to link inextricably the interest of human rights in developing countries to conservation efforts—this time from the point of view of biologists and ecologists.

The commission that produced the *Brundtland Report* (1987) was the World Council on Environment and Development—the very name of which suggests its aim to establish a compromise between conservation and growth (Du Pisani, 2006). Once Brundtland had captured the attention of development and planning theorists and practitioners, "trading-off" among the three pillars became an intrinsic reality in sustainability planning.

The *World Conservation Strategy* (1980), contrary to Brundtland, should be commended for defining humans in ecological terms as a significant "evolutionary force" (IUCN, 1980: 3.1). In fact, the specific wording in the document makes clear the use of sustainability as a socio-ecological interface. "The separation of conservation from development together with narrow sectorial approaches to living resource management are at the root of living resource problems. Many of the priority requirements demand a cross-sectorial interdisciplinary approach" (IUCN, 1980, 8.6). This admission by biologists, chemists, and ecologists—scientists dedicated to the study of natural systems—helped underscore sustainability's basic transdisciplinary premises, but with the understanding that environmentalists and developers should work together. This compromise may be flawed because the marriage of conservation and economic growth seems to increase efficiency, but not reduce the overall consumption of environmental resources.

The *Earth Summit* and *Our Common Journey*

The UN's Rio Convention of 1992, also known as the *Earth Summit*, was a large, enthusiastic, and optimistic gathering of businesses and non-governmental organizations (NGOs) around environmental and social issues of combatting poverty, deforestation, and the transfer of technology. National leaders from 180 countries attended the conference along with about 30,000 overall attendants. Coincidentally, this was 20 years following The Stockholm Declaration as well as occurring at the same time as *Limits to Growth* (1972) and during the publication year of Meadows' follow-up book,

Beyond the Limits (1992), which reported that although the world had not collapsed as predicted, the carrying capacity of the Earth had been exceeded.

The *Earth Summit* (1992) concentrated on the environmental problems of new sources of pollution, the depletion of tropical rainforests, and the ozone layer. New approaches for contending with complex SES problems like climate change and biodiversity loss, including important new concepts like Agenda 21. Agenda 21 is a non-binding but important pledge that encompasses four areas: social and economic dimensions, conservation of resources in development, the strengthening of minority groups, and probably most important, the means of implementation often lacking in other treaties.

However, because the *Earth Summit* was not a formal treaty, the ideas in it lost momentum over time. At the Rio + 10 Conference in Johannesburg, some of these ideals were considered but became watered-down as the discussions were "almost paralyzed by a variety of ideological and economic disputes, by the efforts of those pursuing their narrow national, corporate, or individual interests" (Meadows et al, 2004). But many businesses adopting a "eco-efficiency" policy simply worked using more with less—especially with energy. Energy efficiency became the emphasis for sustainability in addition to replacements of some non-renewable energy. With Agenda 21, a shift occurred from global ideals and principles to city initiatives, policies, and plans. Municipal Climate Action Plans illustrate this.

A few organizations, however, have embraced sustainability concepts. These outside organizations have helped promote Rio's key principles, an improvement over Brundtland, but nonetheless, modeled on an inherent contradiction. For example, Local Governments for Sustainability, originally founded as the International Council for Local Environmental Initiatives (ICLEI)) supports local governments in implementing sustainability plans. It has been instrumental in fostering urban and voluntary emissions cuts in over a thousand cities in America and many more around the world.

Sustainability became a formalized science when the National Academy of Science (NAS) published: *Our Common Journey: a Transition for Sustainability* (Kates & Clark, 1999) echoed the language in "Our Common Future" stressing sustainable transitions with a "normative vision." In examining what has happened since Brundtland and providing a map to the year 2050, this body and many other experts predict there will be approximately 9 billion people on the planet. One document outside of the UN that precipitated the *World Conservation Strategy* (1980) was *Caring for the Earth: A Strategy for Sustainable Living* (1991). Another important consequence of the *Brundtland Report* (1987) concerned the creation of bodies like the Intergovernmental Panel on Climate Change.

Our Common Journey (1999), written by scientists, links the ideals of Brundtland to the real world. Especially important is the second chapter that outlines the historical trends of population, economy, resource use, and pollution as humankind becomes an ecological force and begins to shape the planet in terms of changes to the life support system. It also outlines the largest threats to humans and the environment. Finally, this report is one of the first to establish reporting methods through the use of "indicators" of human and land health, and further establishing sustainability as a science

To summarize, UN literature and international conferences of the 1970s to the present tell conflicting stories. UN documents trace the term sustainability from its first use in the early 1970s to its centrality in environmental discourse in the late 1980s. Together these distinct yet complementary documents tell the story of sustainability's rise from a virtual unknown to the leading term in development discourse. Each written by an international group of scientists and academics, they hoped to lead a logical and ethical discourse to solve global problems. These three documents helped bring sustainability into governmental, business, academic and environmental discussions. But, they did not tease out a gamut of values that have made sustainability irreplaceable in contemporary environmental and policy discourse.

The Naturalists: An Alternative Tradition

As we saw earlier, John Muir, a life-long naturalist, represented a different worldview than the common instrumental view of nature. The use of the term **naturalist** has changed over time, but during the height of its use in the eighteenth and nineteenth centuries, it denoted, first, a natural philosopher or student of natural history, and second, a field biologist engaged in direct observation and experimentation. Naturalists at this time were synonymous with "*scientist*: in practice those whom we would call physicists or biologists" (Williams, 1976, p. 216). The term naturalist also had a very important third aspect. The best naturalists systematically took their findings of direct observation and deductions, and applied them to the larger body of knowledge as a whole. This *holism* provided a more creative, frontier aspect that provides a broader focus, which is often overlooked within today's intensely focused disciplinary tracts (Wilson, 1998). Was Muir part of a dying breed? Or, can naturalist principles help guide and enhance sustainability thinking today?

> **Naturalists** - the first scientists; field biologists and studentsof natural history.

When we consider some of the most iconic and influential of naturalists—Aristotle, Linnaeus, Darwin, E.O. Wilson—we think of generalists claimed by a multitude of disciplines, although most people know the naturalists by the influence their literature had on the environmental movement. This section will examine three American naturalists who had an affinity for coupled human-nature systems and SES.

Henry David Thoreau (1817–1862) was a naturalist during the rise of industrialism in America whose seminal 1854 work *Walden: or Life in the Woods* has inspired those looking for an antidote or alternative to the alienating effects of industrial development. Despite this, little attention has been devoted to his critique of society, and especially economics, in America. Thoreau's contributions to sustainability come *not* from his allegedly impracticable ideas about ethics or spirituality alone, but from his ability to integrate a widely varied spectrum of thought and values toward a wide range of practical applications and SES problem solving. His broader worldview is still an ongoing challenge to sustainability thinking.

First, Thoreau created a roadmap for not only efficiency but also consuming less just a little over a mile outside his hometown of Concord, Massachusetts. *Walden* (1854) is the first book to describe in detail how to (what we would today call) live "off the grid." In describing his daily transactions of building his own home, obtaining fuel and clothing, and living a contemplative life he fully explains how to have a low impact on the environment. Second, Thoreau's activism as described in "Civil Disobedience" (1949) a written protest against American capitalism and expansionism which has provided a template of how to stage a non-violent protest for leaders such as Mohandas Gandhi (1869–1948) and Martin Luther King Jr. (1929–1968) as well as the aforementioned leaders of the environmental movement. Finally, his merging of philosophy and science through his own special breed of transcendentalism—can guide us in linking the disparate fields of ecology economics and society with which sustainability thinking is most concerned.

A hundred years later, naturalist, ecologist, conservationist, land manager, amateur philosopher Aldo Leopold (1887–1948) conducted his own Thoreauvian experiment with his family at a place in Wisconsin called "the shack." But unlike Thoreau, Leopold had devoted his entire life to conservation issues all over America, applying concepts devised by generalists like Thoreau who could link science and philosophy. Leopold (1949) was also able to consolidate intrinsic and instrumental values through his worldview of "the land ethic." Leopold explained ecosystem conservation in his manifesto, *A Sand County Almanac* (1949), "If the land mechanism as a whole is good, then every part is good, whether we understand it or not. . . . To keep every cog and wheel is the first precaution of intelligent tinkering."

Leopold is among the most widely recognized of pre-sustainability thinkers. Through practical applications in real-life scenarios in the United States Forest Service, as well as complemented by the university setting, Leopold's comprehensive land ethic advanced both the fields of environmental ethics and ecology. His extensive work with the US Forest Service across the states of the mid- and southwest, as well as his university teaching experiences, led him to propose expanded roles for both individuals and governments by instilling them with a sense of environmentally based moral obligation. His "land ethic" presents a vision for inclusiveness, cooperation, and simplicity that people of all walks of life could support. Because Leopold was a hunter, outdoorsman, land owner as well as a scientist, he often appealed to non-anthropocentric and anthropocentric views simultaneously and for that reason provides a template suitable for pluralistic discussions of sustainability.

Edward O. Wilson (1929-) is the only living and self-proclaimed naturalist mentioned in this section. Analysis of Wilson's work over the past five decades provides a contemporary, scientific, and comprehensive view of natural and social systems together. It covers an impressive breadth of topics, from evolutionary theory and genetics, to his 300-year history of the sciences and humanities that examines the role of disciplines like economics, ecology, genealogy and many more as they arrive upon the academic scene. Interestingly, Wilson's own writing largely avoids the rhetoric of sustainability. In particular, his sophisticated understanding of sociobiology, biophilia, and conservation ecology contributes to an ethic of enlightened self-interest—an evolutionarily based argument for the human affiliation with nature, and a worldview driven by planetary survival that can help frame sustainability in such a way as to counteract the "natural economy crumbling beneath our busy feet" (Wilson, 2002, p. xxiv).

Edward O. Wilson is an enormously prolific writer, having authored hundreds of articles and over 50 monographs. Nevertheless, his lifetime's work in the study of animal and human social behavior culminates in *Consilience* (1998) and *The Future of Life* (2002), and provides a broad platform for arguing for a changed economy, preserved biodiversity, and greatly improved social systems in order to survive. His work highlights the need for stability in bio- and socio-diversity, convergence of human and natural values, and the essential nature of multi-scalar coordination and public-private partnerships.

Thoreau wrote Walden (1854) just a little over a mile outside his hometown of Concord, Massachusetts in the little shack depicted on the cover, providing a roadmap for an "alternative" lifestyle.

The Future of Sustainability

Today, the United States is riddled with *socio-economic* problems such as widening income disparity, poor education status, high levels of poverty, and poor national health care. As significant as these problems are, there are parallel SES problems that increasingly threaten the climactic integrity of our global life-support systems. Much of America's environmental footprint is well externalized beyond our borders, depleting arable resources and causing biodiversity loss around the world. As the US population nears 400 million, and the world at 9 billion, the growth of middle-class consumers will further reduce our carrying capacity. This creates great uncertainty and complexity that can only be resolved by transdisciplinary, SES, and sustainability thinking.

Meadows, Randers and Meadows (2004) in their follow up to *Limits to Growth* (1972), confirmed their predictions. Their chart depicting our growth begs the question, which of the following scenarios are more likely: a slow easing down of resources or a sudden event that will shock socio-economic and ecological resources? These scenarios are: (a) where environmental resources are very plentiful, and population growth will not erode the carrying capacity, energy is abundant and/or efficiency will exponentially multiply the available energy; (b) where we have not reached carrying capacity, and signals from physical limits to the economy are instant or accurate; (c), where we have passed the carrying capacity, and signals and responses are delayed;

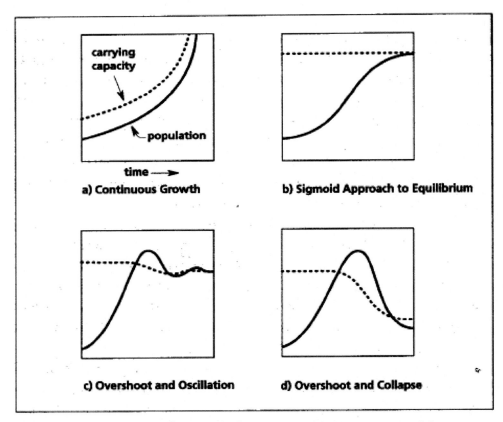

Scenarios of growth. In *Limits to Growth: The 30 Year Update*. Scenarios c. and d. are most likely.

or (d) where we have passed carrying capacity and signals are delayed and limits are irreversible (Meadows, Randers & Meadows, 2004, p. 158). This is the harsh reality—sustainability must be about cutting back net impact as an individual, as a community, as a nation, and as a global community. Most sustainability initiatives do not have such a transformational vision in mind, and, thus, will not address the scale and magnitude of the problem at hand.

Urban development has become the main forum for a sustainability discourse, especially since William Rees and Mathis Wackernagel (1996) coined the term *ecological footprint*. In same year as the release of *Beyond the Limits* (1992), the authors reported that though some of their calculations were off, the human race had indeed surpassed the Earth's carrying capacity. Earlier that same year, the Canadian ecologist William Rees (1992) came out with a seminal argument using what he called the *environmental footprint*. He argued that we are indeed in "overshoot mode" and estimated our deficit environmental spending at about 1.5 planets. In Rees and Wackernagel's (1996) "Urban Ecological Footprints: Why Cities Cannot be Sustainable—And Why They are a Key to Sustainability," they describe how the ecological footprint of cities extends far beyond a city and its traditional hinterlands. In doing so, they address the foundational ecologist Eugene Odum's (1971) lament that "Great cities are planned and grow without any regard for the fact that they are parasites on the countryside which must somehow supply food, water, air and degrade huge quantities of wastes" (p. 371).

While conferences brought people from all around the world together, the majority of the resulting agreements are not binding. As a result, little has been done to insure the protection of land health worldwide and preserve carrying capacity (IUCN, 2004) with many institutions and business failing to significantly change their behavior. What changes have been implemented have decreased our per-capita carbon and environmental footprints; however, they have failed to decrease our *net* footprints. Making matters worse, the environmental footprints of most developed countries extend far beyond their borders.

As developing countries' populations continue to emulate developed countries' economies, population growth and consumption among the global middle class is likely to decimate the ecologies of many biodiversity hotspots, and increase the rate of historical over-consumption patterns (Brown, 2011; Wilson 2002). Some scenarios estimate the United Nations estimate that the world's population will level out at 11.5 billion people, far beyond the carrying capacity that most population ecologists estimate. This will be exacerbated even further by climate change (Rees & Wackernagel, 1992; Wilson, 2002).

The *Brundtland Report* (1987) can be thought of as the sustainability shot heard round the world, as it promoted a new "paradigm" for thinking about the environment in terms of human development (Cronon, 2011). Insofar as their interpretations of sustainability are founded on this, this type of thinking is inadequate to solve wicked problems and provide a very narrow basis on which to build a useful framework of sustainability. Centered on efficiency issues, Brundtland-type thinking, however, contributed to further production and consumption and continued exploitation of the environment (Radkau, 2009).

Legislators and leaders from around the world struggle now to give treaties and conferences some teeth to overcome these impediments. However, international agreement is proving difficult. This was evident in the Copenhagen and 2014 Warsaw conferences that witnessed ever-growing frustrations, especially by representatives from developing countries who often walked out of the proceedings in protest or to form their own sub-groups and decision-making bodies.

Yet despite all the difficulties of bringing together diverse ideas, institutions and knowledge systems, people who would have never before sat down together have reached agreement within the framework of *sustainability* and *sustainable development*. Keeping all these problems in mind we must reinvent programs and policies based on efficiency only to those that preserve natural resources, biodiversity, and our life-support systems for many generations to come. The future success of the sustainability paradigm, or its failure as a constructive discourse, depends on its dedication to pluralistically-driven debates that address the serious and global crises that face us today.

Earliest Urbanism

Charles Redman

What can History Tell us about Sustainability?

History holds many lessons for better understanding the operation of modern cities and possible directions for developing urban sustainability. Although more people reside in modern cities than in the past and the technologies we use are dramatically different, human interactions and the ways in which we organize ourselves are very much the same. If utilized carefully, history can provide seemingly countless examples of how people around the world cooperated to live in ever larger settlements, how they solved problems, and, in many cases, how they sowed the seeds for their own collapse. Sustainability is about solving problems as societies confront change, successful human interaction over long periods, and preventing imbalances between the extraction of resources from our natural environment and its ability to regenerate those resources. There are numerous advantages of using history over relying only on contemporary studies. Among them is our ability to monitor slowly emerging long term processes and cycles which allows us to know how decisions and actions played out over time, and whether they led to further growth or to decline and abandonment. Another is the large number of case studies many of which include important processes such as experiencing global climate change or the introduction of fundamentally new technologies. One particularly insightful message from the past is that the collapse of many cities and states occurred when they appeared to be at their peak of power and sophistication, and not after long periods of decline. This message may have direct relevance to our own situation and lead to a better understanding of how and why such collapses could have happened repeatedly to the "great" societies of the past; it may help us redirect our trajectory toward sustainability instead of collapse.

One of the most significant and informative milestones in the history of human societies was the growth of the first cities in the Near East. This process, often called **The Urban Revolution**, involved much more than just an increase in the size of settlements: it included fundamental changes in the way people interacted, in their relationship to the environment, and in the very way they structured their communities. Processes and institutions that began at this time, some 5,000 years ago, have continued to evolve, forming the basic structure of urban society today. Although ancient cities emerged in various regions of the world, this chapter focuses on the process as it occurred in the Near East, and in particular, Mesopotamia, for three important reasons. First, cities appear in Mesopotamia as early as, or earlier than, anywhere else; second, cities and their societies have direct links with developments in neighboring regions and can be traced as ancestral to developments in many parts of the modern world; and third, we can identify early examples of **human-environmental dynamics** that are still operating today.

The Urban Revolution - processes that originated during the growth of the first cities in the Near East; encompasses the behaviors that simultaneously occurred as people began to reside in urban communities, such as the cultivation of crops, herding of animals, the mass production of goods, and the development of a writing system.

Human-environmental dynamics - the study of complex interactions between natural systems and human activity that examines the causes and consequences of human impacts on the environment and human adaptations to environmental change.

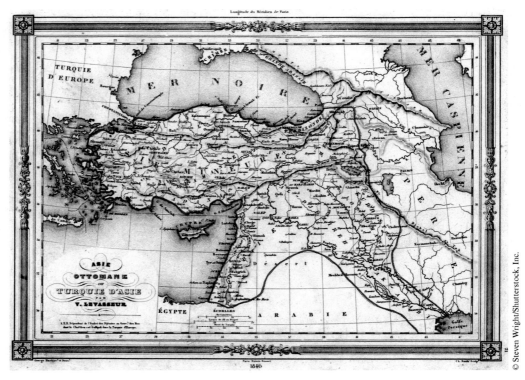

Historic map of Iraq dated 1872 showing "Mesopotamien," which is German for Mesopotamia.

Writing, a system of laws, the wheel, the plow, metallurgy, mathematics and engineering principles—all commonplace in our modern world—were first developed in the cities of Mesopotamia (present-day Iraq and southwestern Iran). Despite the vast scope of these technical innovations, the most significant developments were those of **social organization**. A quantum leap occurred in the number of inhabitants living in the largest settlements, and with this growth, transformation occurred in the way people dealt with each other and with their environment. The physical environment of Mesopotamia and the surrounding regions provided promising ecological conditions for the early introduction of agriculture and the subsequent growth of the first urban society. An awareness of these conditions, and how they supported the human-nature relationships that were to emerge, is essential to a thorough understanding of **coupled human-nature interactions** today.

Social organization - how people interact with each other, including the kinship systems they use and how they assign communal tasks, decide who has access to goods and knowledge, and make communal decisions.

Coupled human-nature interactions - the connections or links between humans and their environment; expressed as a feedback loop, many of humans' actions affect the environment and in turn, changes in the environment affect the human population.

The Environmental Stage

Mesopotamia is a large, arid alluvial plain created by two major rivers—the Tigris and the Euphrates—and is surrounded on two sides by better-watered mountainous zones. The region's climatic pattern is one of summer drought and winter rainfall, although the lowland plain receives minimal rainfall and the people there derived most of their water from the rivers. In the south, where the Tigris and Euphrates rivers join and eventually empty into the Persian Gulf, the land is almost flat and there are many marshy areas. Moving upstream, to the northwest, the slope is small, but it increases perceptibly, giving rise to more clearly defined watercourses surrounded by arid plains.

Effective natural levee formation in the southern reaches of the Mesopotamian plain strongly influenced their selection for settlement locations.

Furthest from the rivers were lowland areas that were marshes during the flood season and supported natural grasses the rest of the year, making them useful for grazing animals. Nearer the rivers, farmlands developed if they were within reach of irrigation water from the river.

Those fields closer to the river were preferable in that they often were better drained, more productive, and had more secure access to irrigation. Along the riverbanks were the natural levees, which were higher and better drained than the surrounding plain. These were the best locations for intensive cultivation and settlement. The levees had several natural advantages: they were fertile, quickly drained after floods, and were least vulnerable to winter frosts. Equally important, as the population density of farmers increased, the levees gave access to river water during years in which the river level was low and not all fields could be adequately irrigated.

Moving further upstream, to the northerly areas of the Mesopotamian plain, the gradient increases, the landscape becomes rolling, and the rivers cut deeper into the landscape, making irrigation more difficult. Continuing further north, the major rivers and their tributaries cut across a series of increasingly high ridges and ultimately reach the Taurus Mountains, to the north, and the Zagros Mountains, to the northeast.

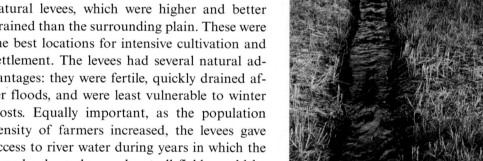

Flat alluvial plain.

Irrigation canal.

© Envyligh/Shutterstock, Inc.

© Vlue/Shutterstock, Inc.

Proximity to these uplands and the large tributary rivers provided natural advantages to settlement in the north, such as access to stone and timber for building, while the vast stretches of relatively easily irrigated land in the south facilitated population growth there.

Pre-urban, Neolithic settlement (8000–5000 BC) of Mesopotamia concentrated in the uplands, with only a few settlements around the margins of the lowlands where the upper reaches of the rivers and their major tributaries intersected in what are now southeastern Turkey and the Irano-Iraqi borderlands. The earliest that researchers have found evidence of any substantial settlement in southern Mesopotamia is approximately 5500 BC. Between 6000 and 4000 BC, however, the area of settlement

Upstream Euphrates River in SE Turkey.

expanded from the uplands to include more and more of the Mesopotamian plain. This was not a rapid migration in terms of a single lifetime; it took many generations to learn how to manage crops and animals in the heat and aridity of the lowlands. At first, expansion was limited to areas of possible, although unreliable, rainfall. Subsequently, with the aid of primitive irrigation systems, settlers moved into areas of the plain that previously could not be cultivated by rainfall alone.

Processes of Change

History offers many lessons relevant to sustainability about how humans and their societies have recognized and responded to challenges and opportunities of their human-natural environment. Three of the basic approaches to problem solving in antiquity were: (a) mobility of people to available resources; (b) **ecosystem management** to secure enhanced local growth of produce; and (c) increasing social complexity encoded in formal institutions that guided an ever-expanding range of activities. These solutions were fundamental to the rise of early civilizations, are instrumental in the design of sustainable cities in the future, and continue to evolve.

The mobility of people to available resources has dominated the human approach to securing adequate subsistence for the vast majority of human existence. Until approximately 10,000 years ago (and more recently in many regions), virtually all people had to move among several locations each year to take advantage of the seasonality of ripening resources.

This movement pattern was disrupted by the introduction of agriculture, which allowed the establishment of year-round settlements in most regions of the world. Agriculture is an example of the second approach to problem solving noted above, ecosystem management for *enhanced productivity.*

This has proven to be an astonishing successful solution to feeding an ever-increasing global population, thereby allowing virtually all people to live in permanent settlements. In fact, the advancement of agriculture and the infrastructural improvements made to enhance productivity were strong incentives for the spread and growth of sedentary communities. Scholars believe that a highly effective socio-natural pattern emerged from millennia of experimentation—called the village farming community—and became the dominant settlement form across the globe. Made up of between 1 and 500 people, village farming communities were the most enduring and widespread type of community because they had flexibility in their sources of subsistence, and they achieved balance between the extraction of natural resources and the

Ecosystem management - the use, protection, and conservation of our environmental resources in a way that seeks to ensure their long-term sustainability. This concept considers humans and the environment as a single system rather than as individual parts.

Families on annual migration near border of northern Iran.

resulting regeneration of the local ecosystem. Although beginning as early as 10,000 years ago in the Near East, the concept spread to most continents, and similar descendent communities housed over half the world's population as recently as the middle of the twentieth century!

Something similar to this village farming community emerged in most regions of the world and endured as the dominant commu-

Traditional plow near village farming community in SE Turkey.

nity form for millennia because it proved to be a highly **resilient socioeconomic unit**. The resiliency allowed it to adapt and survive in the face of many challenges both natural and human induced. The modest number of people in a village meant that traditional face to face social organization was effective, the economy was flexible, being based on a wide range of resources, and for the most part villages did not over-exploit the productive potential of their region to regenerate fertile soil. However, over time some of these communities expanded on their approach to ecosystem management to the point where larger aggregations of people were necessary to supply the required labor. These larger populations also underwent a transformation in the social order, which was largely achieved through innovations in social complexity. This is at the heart of what scholars call The Urban Revolution, and it appears to have occurred first in Mesopotamia.

Resilient socioeconomic unit - characterizes the interconnectedness between the human inhabitants and the economy of a place in a way that promotes the ability to bounce back and recover after a disturbance or crisis.

The First Cities

The formation of the first cities and their linking together as one civilization on the Mesopotamian plain was relatively rapid, considering the scope of the social and technological changes involved. Only approximately 2,000 years after the earliest known occupation of this region, in about 5500 BC, cities emerged, along with attendant

Early farming communities in the Middle East.

traits of urbanism, such as writing, the construction of monumental buildings, and craft specialization. The rise of these early cities was not simply the growth of large collections of people—rather, it involved communities that were far more diverse and interdependent than their predecessors. Relative independence and self-sufficiency characterized village farming communities, but they also limited the growth of these communities. Specialization in the production of various goods and complex exchange networks helped urban societies grow. Cities were also interdependent with their surrounding towns and villages, and they developed ways to obtain goods and services from them. The development of effective irrigation agriculture, the manufacture and widespread exchange of goods, and the advance of science and mathematics were fundamental to the growth of cities. Additionally, changes in the social realm, such as class-structured society, formalized systems of laws, a monopoly on the use of coercive force, and a hierarchical, territorially based government made cities possible and continued to characterize their successful operation.

A landscape-productivity-human relationship evolved in villages and towns, enabling the growth of large, diverse populations that aggregated into cities. As positive as these "advances" were in terms of productivity and competitiveness, they also have led to maladaptive relationships and created an increase in long-term risks. One set of new relationships was established as the concept of private property emerged to replace both a generally weak sense of ownership and the concept of community ownership. It is hard to say what came first, but these new relationships evolved when farmers could both produce more food than their families required and find ways to store this surplus for later use or trade. This led some farmers to produce a surplus to guard against future bad harvests; however, one could only eat so much, and a variety of factors limited the amount of food that could be effectively stored. Hence, the stimulus to produce a surplus remained limited in most farming villages. What may have changed this relationship, and was key to the growth of urban society, was the ability to transform locally produced surplus food and goods (through purchased, specialized labor, and exotic goods) into enduring prestige items associated with elevated status. This only existed in areas where a new social order occurred that acknowledged classes with differential wealth (access to productive resources), power, and status. An ideology (through religion, myth, constructed history, and law) legitimized the existence of elite classes and their precious goods that helped identify them. Another dynamic that coevolved with private property, surplus production, elite goods, and hierarchical class society was the reliance on inheritance for membership in these classes. Merit, strength, agility, and intelligence certainly were important, but which family, clan, or class a person was born into set limits on his future potential in the age of early cities, and to some extent, continues to operate today in certain cities.

Cities Going Global

Organizing society into hierarchically stratified classes became widespread along with urbanism, coming to characterize most regions of the world up to the present day. This social framework, along with a widely accepted ideology legitimizing it, was an effective means of organizing large groups of people and large-scale productive activities. People have always sought to make sense of the world around them and to determine how to relate to other people. Myths, histories, and ethics often were organized into formal religions that helped people understand their place in the world, and simultaneously, justified the unequal allocation of rights and prescribed appropriate ways to behave.

In time, territorially based authority also emerged, largely through successful military action and monopolies on the use of coercive force. This secular authority also needed a source of legitimization, which emerged as constructed histories, legal codes, and institutions of management and enforcement. Although they often cited different rationales, governing authorities based on religious or secular justification served many similar purposes in creating a framework for the effective functioning of large populations and controlling vast tracts of land. Not surprisingly, the two interacted closely, and they have often been unified into a single entity or a closely cooperating team. Hence, in the newly emergent urban society of Mesopotamia, and later elsewhere across the globe, people produced more goods, and larger numbers of people could live in a single community and be marshaled as a labor force. This was possible because sacred orders were established and widely accepted that legitimized the social order and prescribed appropriate behavior, and because security was provided through a monopoly on the use of force and formal systems of laws. Respect for this new social

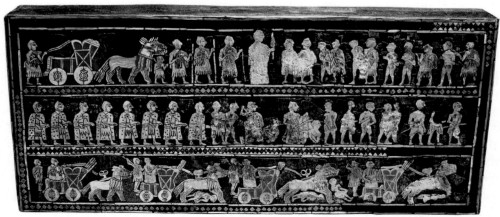

© Kamira/Shutterstock, Inc.

Legitimizing the social order.

Dating back to 3500 BC, Mesopotamian war art intended to serve as a way to glorify powerful rulers and their connection to divinity.

and governing order was often reaffirmed through the construction of massive monuments, the performance of complex rituals, and expression through large-scale representational art. The concentration of people, stored supplies, and elite goods led to early cities being targets for raiding and organized military activity, prompting further investment in defensive walls and armies to defend cities. This cyclical relationship of the concentration of wealth leading to military aggression leading to the investment in armies is a cycle that dominates all of human history and can be seen operating today.

Are Cities Maladaptive?

Unfortunately, other responses that originated to aid the facilitation of solutions to help solve problems have also established detrimental cycles that threaten the very existence of the societies that developed them. That is resilience can be a favorable characteristic if it perserves positive characteristics, but it also can act to preserve undesirable dynamics. For example, large numbers of people aggregating into cities allowed for specialization of labor and other efficiencies, but it also meant that most people would not be able to grow their own food. Hence, people in the rural countryside were responsible for growing enough food for both themselves and city dwellers in an amount to offset the cost of transport and distribution. This arrangement put a tremendous burden on farming communities to produce much more than they would if the farmers alone made the decisions. As differing segments of the population grew more divergent in their societal roles, so did their objectives and understanding of the situation. For instance, farmers in the earlier village farming era more intimately understood the landscape and productive systems and were inclined toward conservation practices wherein they balanced extractive activities with the **regenerative capabilities** of the land. The urban elite, on the other hand, were more focused on the net produce they could extract from the countryside and insisted on maximum production, with little knowledge of or concern for the potential deleterious effects on the rural landscape. In an ideal hierarchical society, even though decision-making authority is concentrated at the top, knowledge would travel up the hierarchy, and informed decisions would thus be made. However, it is somewhat surprising that this was seldom the case and that the dominant pattern was **maximizing short-term returns with little concern for long-term consequences**. Archaeological evidence attests to repeated instances of intense environmental degradation in the region around cities, and the impact of urban demand on the rural countryside is still evident today.

In addition to making ill-advised decisions leading to excess extraction of resources, individuals and societies are regularly forced to make decisions in response to changing

Regenerative capabilities - the processes of renewal, restoration, and growth that make ecosystems resilient to natural events in order to prevent irreversible damage.

Maximizing short-term returns with little concern for long-term consequences - this concept encompasses the idea that many decisions made by those individuals with authority and power often focus solely on increasing short-term benefits, such as the accumulation of money, without considering long-term consequences of those decisions, such as degradation of the environment.

conditions. These conditions might be a change in climate, such as less rainfall, a change in local environment, such as soil erosion, or a change in the cultural or technological context, such as new neighbors or the introduction of new subsistence strategies. Changes like these are normal, and they were frequent in the past and are common today. Jared Diamond, in his book *Collapse: How Societies Choose to Fail or Succeed*,[1] points to errors in decision making as a primary cause of social collapse. Such errors occurred in a variety of contexts, such as not recognizing the significance of an important change in conditions; recognizing the change, but misdiagnosing the appropriate response; or waiting too long before responding. Unfortunately, many of today's leaders have apparently not learned from the past and are unable or unwilling to respond to the varied significant changes currently taking place around us. This is strikingly similar to the behavior of the collapsed civilizations about which Diamond warns us. Fortunately, Diamond also points out that leaders and citizenry have also acted in perceptive, positive ways to maintain and even enhance their human-environmental relations. He recounts how in the early 17th Century Japan was at a crossroads where war and population growth could have led to serious environmental degradation and potential collapse, yet the new dynasty of Tokugawa shoguns (emperors) made the top-down decision to protect and restore large areas of forests both as a potential natural resource and also to protect against major soil erosion, providing the foundation for subsequent centuries of high population density coupled with environmental stability.

Other "urban efficiencies" create their own challenges. Many of the world's devastating contagious diseases were virtually nonexistent until the growth of dense urban populations. The spread of the plague, small pox, measles, cholera, and many other diseases can be traced to a combination of close association between humans and domestic animals, and living in large, dense populations. Cities were the centers of people, economic activity, and the arts, but until public health innovations of the twentieth century, they were also the centers of disease, many of them fatal. Large urban populations also created new challenges that were unknown when the largest communities were only several hundred people or less. For example, knowing who everyone is in the community and how to act toward them is no longer feasible when the community's population exceeds 500 people. Similarly, less tranquility and security breakdown are evident as the population grows larger, requiring the introduction of formal, impersonal solutions to human interactions and security. Certain other challenges become more complex as the population enlarges, such as the transport of people and goods, sanitation, and an adequate supply of potable water and food. Often, these issues are addressed by formal institutions that unfortunately raise the monetary cost of being an urbanite and also increase residents' dependency on the central authority.

Speculations for the future based on the past

Several lessons are apparent from this review of earliest urbanism. First, humans are amazingly successful at self-organization to promote their survival in the face of virtually any environmental challenge, but many of these solutions have unanticipated costs, with continuing impacts on future societies. People manage their socio-ecosystems according to how they perceive the opportunities and risks and how they value the alternatives. However, this valuation process may appear very different to people in different social positions, and the true "costs" of some alternatives are not recognized at the time, and may even threaten the society's very survival. There is also the problem that challenges may take unrecognized forms because they occur in a new context and people have not retained the knowledge of the past occurrences. Moreover, people may choose to ignore or minimize the expected impact of the challenge because they believe that they may be unwilling to bear costs to responding appropriately. However, once there is recognition, people do respond to problems and opportunities, and they do so by transforming biota (the flora and fauna of the region), landscapes, technologies, and their built environment so that the immediate, net yield for humans is increased even though native biota and earth systems may be degraded. Unfortunately, we do not yet know how serious these threats are and if they will eventually undermine the sustainability of cities. Nevertheless, we must devote ourselves to forming a better understanding of the impacts of our decisions and the pathway toward a more sustainable existence.

Several lessons that inform sustainability stand out from the past. The first is that environmental, social, and technological change is to be expected and, therefore, individuals and societies must prepare themselves to respond to those changes in sustainable ways. The second is that there will be tradeoffs in taking virtually any action to respond to these challenges. That is, some parts of the system will benefit, but other parts of the system will likely be diminished. Hence, we must continually strive to gain a thorough understanding of the interconnectivity of all social-ecological systems and recognize that cascading and unintended consequences will often result to even our best-intentioned actions. Third, the world and its challenges are perceived and valued differently by people in different positions within society. What may appear to help one segment of society may hurt another. All too often, because decision makers are in positions of power, they act in ways that further their own power and wealth, often at the expense of other segments of society. This inequality in power, wealth, and access to resources that characterizes our contemporary world has very old origins. In designing a more sustainable world, we would be well advised to carefully study how the formation and growth of early cities resulted in societal inequality, and strive to discern and implement solutions to reverse this disparity.

Supplemental Readings

Diamond, J. (2005, January 1). "The ends of the world as we know them [Op-ed]." *New York Times*. Retrieved from http://www.nytimes.com/2005/01/01/opinion/01diamond.html?_r=1

Butzer, K. W. (2012). "Collapse, environment, and society." Proceedings of the National Academy of Sciences of the United States of America, 109(10), 3632.

Choi, C. (2012, May 28). "Huge ancient civilization's collapse explained." LiveScience. Retrieved from http://www.livescience.com/20614-collapse-mythical-river-civilization.html

Global Climate Change: A Key Issue for the 21st Century

Bjoern Hagen

Introduction

Global **climate change** is one of the most important scientific and societal issues facing the twenty-first century. Climate change is often perceived as a global issue and its impacts can already be observed in both the national and local scales (Pittock, 2009; NRC, 2010). This global trend does not exclude the United States. Extreme weather events are increasing in frequency and scale impacting various regions and sectors across the country. Areas are facing climate conditions that have never been experienced before. Among other impacts, ongoing drought and increasing temperatures in the southwest United States have led to an earlier start of, and longer lasting, wildfire season. Prolonged droughts have also increased the competition for limited water resources among people and ecosystems. In other regions such as the Northeast, Midwest, or the Great Plains, weather and climate data show that over the past century heavy rainfalls (which frequently exceed the capacity of infrastructure systems such as storm drains and sewer systems) have increased. This has resulted in a demonstrable uptake in flooding events, land erosion, and landslides (IPCC, 2013).

The majority of the scientific community is in agreement that human behavior and current urban patterns, especially automobile usage, are key factors in the rapid increase of the average global temperature in recent decades (Calthorpe, 2011). Cities cover less than one percent of the earth's surface yet carry disproportionate responsibility for **greenhouse gas emissions** and constitute the leading cause of global climate change. Most of the world's energy consumption either occurs in cities or is a direct result of the way cities function. Cities are not only a major contributor to climate change, but they can also play a major part in solving current and future challenges stemming from climate change. Urban sustainability establishes a key role in the discussion about the causes, impacts, and solutions of climate change.

In recent years there has been growing acknowledgement among scientists and policymakers that the challenges of climate change can be met, or at least abated, through the design, development, and redesign of urban space and structure. Making cities more sustainable will not only reduce the causes of climate change **(mitigation)** but also improve our **resiliency** toward the effects of climate change that can no longer be avoided **(adaptation)**. Therefore, this chapter presents not only the issues and science behind climate change, but it also examines the importance of urban sustainability through mitigation and adaptation policies and applications, as well as building **institutional capacity** to make more effective decisions under **high levels of uncertainty.**

Climate change - Statistically significant changes over long time scales of the global average temperature are referred to as climate change.

Greenhouse gas emissions - Greenhouse gases are gases in the atmosphere that absorb and re-emit solar radiation back to the earth's surface. The four most common greenhouse gases (GHG) released by humans are carbon dioxide (CO2), methane (CH4), halocarbons, and nitrous oxide (N2O).

Mitigation - Mitigation in the context of climate change refers to measurements that reduce the causes of climate change. The majority of mitigation strategies aim to reduce greenhouse gas emissions.

Resiliency - In the context used in this book, resiliency refers to the ability to cope with potential negative impacts of climate change.

Adaptation - Adaptation in the context of climate change refers to adjustments and measurements undertaken by natural or human systems in response to current and possible future impacts of climate change.

Institutional capacity - The term institutional capacity describes the ability of an institution, such as the federal government, to perform functions, solve problems and set and achieve objectives that will reduce the threats and impacts of climate change.

High levels of uncertainty - Climate change is cauterized by high uncertainties regarding the types and severity of future impacts. The high levels of uncertainty are a result of the very complex climate science itself, the possible future behaviors and decisions by humans, and from internal processes in the climate system.

Climate Change

Climate is the most significant component of the world as we know it. Landscape, plants, and animals are greatly influenced by long-term climate conditions, and urban areas are often affected by short-term climate fluctuations. Prior to the introduction of irrigation and the start of industrialization in human cultures, climate determined food supplies, trade, trade routes, and where people could live. In general, the term 'climate' is the typical range of weather and its variability experienced at a particular place (Archer & Rahmstorf, 2010) People speak of 'climate variability' in describing the irregularities of weather at a particular location from one year (or decade) to another. Changes over longer time scales are referred to as 'climate change.' Although modern technology allows people to live in places where previously it was impossible to live, local climate should still be a pivotal factor when determining an appropriate design for buildings and urban areas. Aside from some natural variations, scientists concur that the rapid changes experienced in climate during the last several decades are mostly caused by human activity or are anthropogenic, i.e., resulting from the influence of human beings on nature (IPCC, 2013). It is well known that climate can change over time. Yet, the precipitous acceleration of the rate of change and the observability of the **global warming** trend recorded in the last few decades is alarming. As shown in Figure 1, worldwide surface temperatures have increased since 1901. Each of the last three decades has been warmer than any other decade since 1850. Between 1880 and 2012, the average combined land and ocean surface temperature has increased by 0.85 degrees Celsius (33.53 °F). Simultaneously, climate data indicates that since 1950 the number of unusual and extremely cold days and nights are decreasing, whereas the number of abnormally warm days and nights are becoming more frequent.

Global Warming - The term global warming is often used to describe the rapid increase of the global temperature in recent decades caused by natural factors, natural process, or human activities.

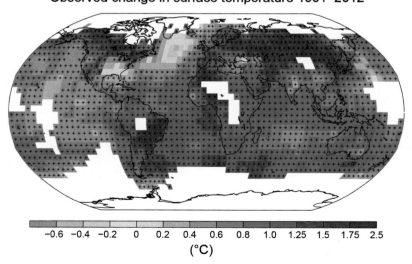

Observed change in surface temperature 1901–2012

−0.6 −0.4 −0.2 0 0.2 0.4 0.6 0.8 1.0 1.25 1.5 1.75 2.5
(°C)

FIGURE 1: Observed annual and decadal global mean surface temperature anomalies from 1850 to 2012 and map of the observed surface temperature change from 1901 to 2012.

Source: IPCC, 2013: Summary of Policymakers. In: *Climate Change 2013: The Physical Science Basis. Working Group I Contribution to the Fifth Assessment Reprot of the Intergovernmental Panel on Climate Change*, Figure SPM.1. [Stocker,T.F., D.Qin, G.-K. Plattner, M.Tignor, S.K.Allen, J.Boschung, A.Nauels, Y.Xia, V.Bex and P.M. Midgley (eds.)] Cambridge University Press, Cambridge, UK and New York, USA.

Figure 2 shows the temperature trends by continent, global averages between 1910 and 2010, and it compares these observations with simulated climate change emphasizing the impact of human behavior on the significant increase of temperatures over the last 50 years. The black lines show the actual measured temperatures. The blue band shows simulated temperatures from various **climate models** assuming that only natural causes are impacting climate conditions. The pink band shows the spread of model outputs resulting from human actions, such as greenhouse gas emissions as causes for climate change. Consistently, the observed temperatures overlap with the simulated temperatures assuming anthropogenic climate change, suggesting that global temperature trends, especially since 1950, cannot be explained through natural causes alone. Research shows a larger than 95 percent level of confidence (IPCC 2013)

Climate models - Climate models sophisticated computer programs and a quantitative way of representing the interactions of the atmosphere, oceans, land surface, ice, and human behavior. There is a wide range of climate models available, ranging from relatively basic models that focus on the basic aspects of the Earth's heat balance to very complex and detailed simulations, that aim to show possible future impacts of global climate change under a variety of different assumptions.

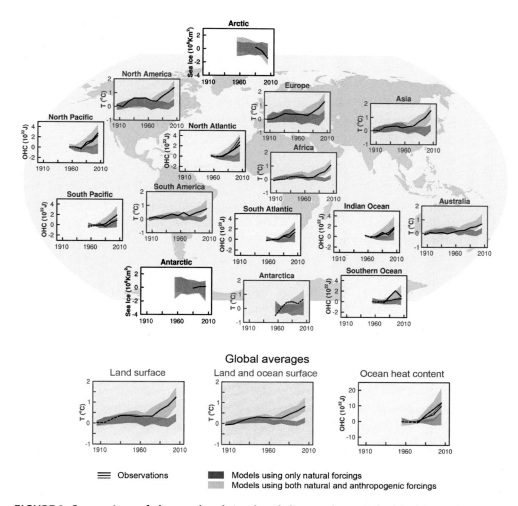

FIGURE 2: Comparison of observed and simulated climate change. The black lines show the actual measured temperatures. The blue band shows the expected temperatures if climate would only be influenced by natural causes. The pink band show possible trends of temperatures if human actions are acknowledged as causes for climate change (Intergovernmental Panel on Climate Change, 2013).

Source: IPCC, 2013: Summary of Policymakers. In: *Climate Change 2013: The Physical Science Basis. Working Group I Contribution to the Fifth Assessment Reprot of the Intergovernmental Panel on Climate Change*, Figure SPM.6. [Stocker,T.F., D.Qin, G.-K. Plattner, M.Tignor, S.K.Allen, J.Boschung, A.Nauels, Y.Xia, V.Bex and P.M. Midgley (eds.)] Cambridge University Press, Cambridge, UK and New York, USA.

that the majority of the observed increases in global average surface temperatures since 1951 resulted from human induced greenhouse gas emissions. Overall, from 1950 to 2000, the warming trend was around 0.13 degrees Celsius per decade, almost twice as much as in the e previous century (IPCC, 2007). This trend continued to the beginning of the twenty-first century and is expected to accelerate even further in the future. Worldwide, the years between 2000 and 2009 are the warmest decade ever measured (NASA, 2010). More recently, the National Oceanic and Atmospheric Administration (NOAA) concluded that the year 2013 was the fourth-warmest year on record (NOAA, 2013). Spanning back to 1880, the records show that the current top 10 warmest years have all occurred since 1998.

Science Behind Global Climate Change

National Academy of Sciences - The National Academy of Sciences (NAS) is a private nonprofit institution whose members as advisers to the nation on science, engineering, and medicine.

Since 1979, when the **National Academy of Sciences** first raised concern about global warming, the body of knowledge and the amount of scientific data documenting this phenomenon has grown. The year 1988 marked the start of the Intergovernmental Panel on Climate Change (IPCC), founded by the World Meteorological Organization (WMO) and the United Nations Environment Programme (UNEP). Today, the IPCC is considered the leading institution for the assessment of climate change. Its mission is to monitor the worldwide scientific research regarding climate change.

With the help of thousands of scientists, the IPCC regularly assesses the available scientific information relevant for improving the understanding of climate change and its possible environmental and socioeconomic impacts. The participating scientists are divided into three "Working Groups": 1) the scientific assessment of today's research regarding global climate change (IPCC 2013); 2) the potential impacts of climate change to socioeconomic and natural systems and how they can be reduced (IPCC, 2014a); and 3) evaluating options for avoiding the causes of global climate change (IPCC, 2014b). The results are summarized and published in specific chapters of the "Assessment Reports of the Intergovernmental Panel on Climate Change."

IPCC Assessment Reports

Since 1988, the IPCC has released five Climate Change Assessment Reports. The first report (1990) did not find sufficient scientific proof to demonstrate a relationship between human behavior and global climate change. Nevertheless, the report projected that by the year 2000, the connection between human actions in the emission of greenhouse gases and global climate change would be made. The second report, released in 1995, concluded that evidence of human induced climate change has already been found, and that finding surfaced five years earlier than projected by the first report. The third report in 2001 supported this claim and provided further evidence that the increase in temperature over the past 50 years can be linked to GHG emissions. In 2007, the fourth report finally stated that (with a likelihood of 90–99%) global climate change is driven by human-caused emissions of heat-trapping gases and projected serious environmental damages could be expected in the future. The reports of the three different working groups for the fifth assessment report were released between

September 2013 and April 2014. Given the usual tenor of scientific reports, these documents use strong language emphasizing the urgency to take action against global climate change. The latest assessment report concludes with a 95% certainty that human behavior (human induced greenhouse gas emissions) stands as the main reason for global warming since 1950.

Causes of Global Climate Change

The basic principle of the earth's climate is that the energy entering the atmosphere from the sun is reflective and has to go out again. The sun's energy is mostly submitted by sunlight either in the form of visible or ultraviolet light. A considerable proportion of incoming radiation is reflected back to space by snow, ice, and clouds. The sunlight that is reflected back away from the earth is referred to as the earth's **albedo** and does not "deposit" energy. If this steady exchange between incoming and outgoing energy becomes historically unbalanced, meaning that less energy is being reflected back to space than in the past, then the temperature from the earth's surface and atmosphere changes. The lower the albedo, the greater the heat absorption is on earth. Various factors that can change the earth's temperature are called **climate forcing agents**; and, the strength of these factors is called **radiative forcing**.

The human-caused emissions of greenhouse gases have played a significant role in the changes of the earth's temperature in recent decades. This phenomenon, called the **greenhouse effect**. Greenhouse gases such as CO_2 and methane (CH_4) function as **heat trapping gases**, preventing the earth's albedo from reflecting the sun's energy back into space. Instead, those gases trap the energy inside the earth's atmosphere and send parts of it back to the surface. As a result, over time, the atmosphere and the earth surfaces warm up more and cool down less.

Greenhouse Gas Emissions

The four most common greenhouse gases (GHG) released by humans are carbon dioxide (CO_2), methane (CH_4), halocarbons, and nitrous oxide (N2O). Overall, GHG emissions have increased 70 percent between 1970 and 2004, with carbon dioxide being the largest contributor to greenhouse gas composition (IPCC, 2007). Systematic measurements of the concentration of carbon dioxide in the earth's atmosphere began in the 1950s. Since then, the concentration of CO_2 has been rising at an accelerating rate. For example, the concentration of CO_2 rose 20% faster between the years 2000 to 2004 compared to the 1990s. The majority of the emitted CO_2 has been captured and stored by the ocean, resulting in increased levels of seawater acidification. In addition to its high percentage in the earth's atmosphere, CO_2 also has a notably longer lifetime than many other gasses emitted by humans. Its persistency factor is quite high.

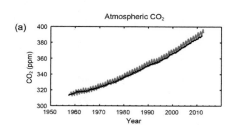

FIGURE 3: Atmospheric concentrations of carbon dioxide from Mauna Loa and South Pole since 1958.

Source: Intergovernmental Panel on climate change, 2013

Albedo - The term albedo is a measurement used to determine the reflectivity of the earth's surface. The earth's albedo states how much solar energy is reflected from earth back to space.

Climate forcing agents - Many cities and states have developed in recent years "Climate Change Action Plans" to mitigate and adapt to climate change. "Climate Change Action Plans" help states and cities to identify and evaluate feasible and effective policies to reduce their greenhouse gas emissions through a combination of public and private sector policies and programs. In addition these plans provide a framework to change current development patterns and establish a sustainable way of living in the future, which reduces the vulnerability to climate change and increases the adaptive capacity of communities.

Radiative forcing - The terms radiative forcing is used to describe the strength of climate forcing agents in changing the earth's temperature.

Greenhouse Effect - The greenhouse effect in the context of climate change and global warming describes the phenomenon of increasing global temperatures. So called greenhouse gases prevent the earth's albedo to reflect the sun's energy back into space. Instead, those gases trap the energy inside the earth's atmosphere and sends parts of it back to the surface. As a result, over time, the atmosphere and the earth surfaces warm up more and cool down less.

Heat trapping gases - Heat trapping gases prevent the earth's albedo to reflect the sun's energy back into space. Instead, those gases trap the energy inside the earth's atmosphere and sends parts of it back to the surface.

Greater CO_2 concentration in the atmosphere is, to a large extent, due to an increase in human caused CO_2 emissions from fossil fuel combustion, deforestation, and cement manufacture. Burning of fossil fuels, mostly by private automobiles, is the largest single source of CO_2 emissions (IPCC, 2013). The transport sector alone accounts for about 23 percent of the overall CO_2 emissions from **fossil fuel combustion** (International Transport Forum, 2010). Another source of significant CO_2 emissions can be found in the building sector. In the United States, buildings account for approximately 40% of the total CO_2 emissions (USGBC, 2012). This large amount of emissions by the building sector results from their high electricity consumption and that much of that electrical energy is created by the burning of fossil fuels, such as coal or natural gas. Deforestation causes high CO_2 emissions from burning or decomposing of trees and soil carbon.

Methane is the second most frequent greenhouse gas found. Compared to a molecule of CO_2 the radiative forcing from a molecule of methane is about 30 times stronger. However, with a current lifetime of about eight years, the lifespan for methane molecules is much shorter than CO_2. Another difference with CO_2 pertains to the concentration of methane in the atmosphere has not increased since 1993 (Archer & Rahmstorf, 2010). Natural and artificial wetlands, as well as oil wells, comprise the largest sources of methane emissions. Although methane concentrations are currently stable, methane sources are expected to increase due to thawing permafrost, another example of climate change impacts. Halocarbons and nitrous oxide have a significantly smaller impact on climate change than carbon dioxide and methane. The concentrations of halocarbons in the atmosphere, however, are declining as a result of international efforts to protect the ozone layer (NOAA, 2005).

Current Climate Change impacts

An average temperature increase of 0.85 degrees Celsius (33.53 °F) since the beginning of the 20th century might sound insignificant. However, the impacts of climate change are already visible in the United States and globally. Increases in air and water temperature have reduced the number of frost days. A higher frequency and magnitude of heavy rainfall, a rise in sea level, reduced snow cover, and changes in glaciers, permafrost, and sea ice are also observed. Such changes can affect human health, water supply, agriculture, coastal areas, and the natural environment. One recent conclusion is that in many areas of the world, global climate change impacts are occurring faster than once expected (Pittock, 2009).

Sea Level Rise and Ice Sheets

The increase in ocean temperatures and the melting of ice sheets are both direct results of global climate change and are the main contributors to ocean expansion and the **rise of the sea level**, observed since the beginning of the twentieth century. The process of ocean water enlarging as it becomes warner is called "**thermal expansion.**" Considering that the oceans are on average 3,800 meters deep, even an average expansion of one hundredths of one percent would result in the ocean rising by 38 centimeters – hence posing a significant risk to coastal cities and their inhabitants.

The impact of ice sheet melting is a far bigger issue. If all ice sheets melted entirely, the sea level could rise by as much as 70 meters, which would change the world's coastal landscapes forever. Currently, data shows that the sea level has risen 19 centimeters since the beginning of the twentieth century (IPCC 2013). More important, recent studies summarized in the latest IPCC reports strongly suggest that the rate of sea level rise has accelerated since 1901. Between 1901 and 2010, the global average sea level rise was 1.7 millimeters (mm) per year, the annual average for the time period between 1971 and 2010 was 2.0 mm, and since 1993 the annual average increase in sea level ranges from 2.8 to 3.6 mm. The two ice sheets with potentially the greatest impact on sea level rise are Greenland and Antarctica. The melting of the ice sheet of Greenland alone could raise the sea level by seven meters. Measurements in Greenland show that the ice closest to the sea is already melting on the surface, creating meltwater ponds, increasing the volume of water streaming toward the open sea. Both ice sheets are decreasing, and if temperatures continue to rise, it could only be a matter of decades before the ice sheets of Greenland are melted completely, and the Antarctic ice sheets become unstable. Sea level rise is not the only outcome of melting ice (Archer & Rahmstorf, 2010). Another consequence is the loss of surfaces that reflect sunlight back into space, decreasing the earth's surface albedo and adding more heat to the earth's surface [See earlier discussion of this chapter.]

Compared to ice sheets, mountain glaciers and ice caps contain significantly less water, but this water melts much more quickly under increasing temperatures. Glaciers have been retreating since the eighteenth century, but only since the 1970s has the rate of the melting increased. This trend is shown in Figure 4. The four photographs were taken at four differnt times of the Muir glacier in Alaska – or, what remains. The two pictures on the left were from August 1941 and September 2004. The pictures on the right were taken in Spetember 1976 and September 2003. It can be seen that over a timespan of 65 years, the glacier retreated more than seven miles, and the resulting runoff created a mountain lake. The glacier's sustancial shrinking illustrates the dramatic impact an increase in temperature can have. Mountain glaciers and snow packs store winter precipitation and release it slowly over the summer, providing a fresh water source when it is needed for agricultural irrigation. With glaciers retreating and snow packs declining, fresh water from mountain streams could cause decreases in dowstream storage of water supplies [See the Chapter in this book by Ray Quay – Chapter 10]. The melting of permafrost soils is another problem that has the effect of increasing the concentration of greenhouse gases in the atmosphere. Arctic permafrost underlies almost one fifth of the planet's land surface and usually contains methane hydrate. As long as it is frozen, methane hydrate does not present any danger for the environment, but once the ice thaws,, the methane converts to a very potent heat trapping gas.

Precipitation and Drought

In addition to increasing global temperature, climate change impacts precipitation patterns. Unlike temperature, which has increased almost everywhere on the planet, precipitation is increasing in some parts of the world and decreasing in others. The warmer the air becomes, the more water it can store and then release it during colder days. This can lead to storm floods and heavy damage in areas where the

Field, William Osgood. 1941, Muir Glacier. Glacier Photograph Collection. Boulder, Colorado USA: National Snow and Ice Data Center/ World Data Center for Glaciology. Digital media.

Molnia, Bruce F. 1976, Muir Glacier. Glacier Photograph Collection. Boulder, Colorado USA: National Snow and Ice Data Center/World Data Center for Glaciology. Digital media.

Molnia, Bruce F. 2004, Muir Glacier. Glacier Photograph Collection. Boulder, Colorado USA: National Snow and Ice Data Center/World Data Center for Glaciology. Digital media.

Molnia, Bruce F. 2003, Muir Glacier. Glacier Photograph Collection. Boulder, Colorado USA: National Snow and Ice Data Center/World Data Center for Glaciology. Digital media.

Figure 4: Retreat of the Muir Glacier in Alaska from 1941 to 2004. Clockwise from the top left: August 1941, September 2004, September 1976, September 2003.

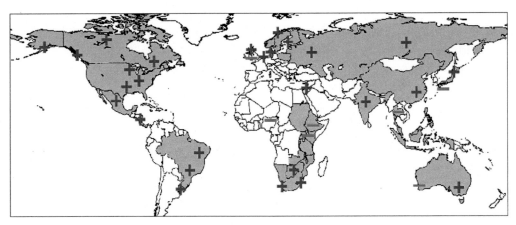

FIGURE 5: Changes in heavy rainfall around the world both increases and declines (*Intergovernmental Panel on Climate Change*, 2007).

Source: Climate Change 2007: The Physical Science Basis. Working Group I Contribution to the Fourth Assessment Report of the Intergovernmental Panel on Climate Change, FAQ 3.2, Figure 1. Cambridge University Press.

infrastructure is not able to handle the release of exceptionally large amounts of water in short amounts of time, as with last year's storm damage in the Northeast United States. The map in Figure 5 shows the areas where heavy rainfalls increased or decreased.

For example, heavy rainfall increased on the east coast of the United States, but decreased in Africa, where food shortages and hunger are already a major concern. In 2012, Hurricane Sandy caused extraordinary rainfall on the east coast causing floods, heavy property and land damage, and even human casualties. In total, hurricane Sandy caused 117 deaths in the US and 69 in Canada (CNN, 2013). According to the United States Department of Commerce (2013), the total economic loss caused by the hurricane in New Jersey for travel and tourism spending alone, has been estimated at $950 million. In addition the New Jersey State Government concluded that it would cost approximately $29.5 billion to repair all damage caused by Hurricane Sandy.

Besides the increases in frequency and magnitude of heavy rainfall, seasonal changes in precipitation are occurring. These changes are especially important to land ecosystems and the agricultural sector. Farmers are concerned about seasonal changes of rainfall impacting their growing and harvesting seasons. Heavy rainfall is already delaying spring planting in some areas of the United States, jeopardizing the live-lihoods of farmers. The resulting flooding of the fields during the growing season causes low oxygen levels in the soil, which destroys crops and increases the likelihood of root diseases. In addition, research suggests that increasing temperatures will most likely reduce livestock production during the summer season.

Without causing any changes in the annual average rainfall, in some regions pre-cipitation has decreased in the summer but increased in the winter, resulting in increas-ing risks of flooding during the winter and drought in the summer with potentially devastating results for the agricultural sector. Seasonal changes may also impact areas that rely heavily on tourism and winter sports. In some areas, precipitation that used to fall as snow during the winter is now falling as rain. Consequently, the reduction in the snowpack not only shortens the winter sports season but also reduces the water runoff during the summer when water is most needed for agriculture. We find this occurrence in the Southwestern United States, where there is concern about the persistence of a long-lasting drought condition.

Droughts are another major result of changes in precipitation. There are different ways to define and measure the severity of droughts. The most common measure-ment used is the **Palmer Drought Severity Index** (PDSI), which considers not only

Palmer Drought Severity Index - The Palmer Drought Severity Index (PDSI) is the most common measurement used to define and measure the severity of droughts. The index considers not only the monthly amount of precipitation but also the regional average temperatures. The severity of the drought is shown in terms of minus numbers and excess rain is reflected by plus numbers.

FIGURE 6: Flooded neighborhood in Little Falls, N.J. after Hurricane Irene.

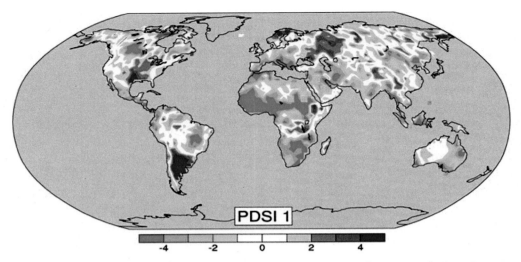

FIGURE 7: Drought severity from 1990 to 2002 according to the Palmer Drought Severity Index. In this index the severity of the drought is shown in terms of minus numbers and excess rain is reflected by plus numbers (*Intergovernmental Panel on Climate Change*, 2007).

Source: Climate Change 2007: The Physical Science Basis. Working Group I Contribution to the Fourth Assessment Report of the Intergovernmental Panel on Climate Change, FAQ 3.2, Figure 3.39 (bottom). Cambridge University Press.

the monthly amount of precipitation but also the regional average temperatures. As shown in Figure 7, according to the PDSI, droughts became more severe between 1990 and 2002 and are increasing. In this index, the severity of the drought is shown in terms of minus numbers and the plus numbers reflect the excess rain. Although heavy rainfall has increased, the risk of droughts has only decreased in very few regions of the world. Instead, the amount of dry areas has more than doubled in size since the 1970s (IPCC, 2007).

Human Health, Food Insecurity, and Ecological Refugees

In addition to environmental impacts, global climate change can also cause or intensify health and social issues. The impact of climate change on human health is a relatively new research field, and at this point not much data is available. Nevertheless, existing research shows a strong correlation between heat waves and increased mortality rates. In 2003, the European heat wave was responsible for at least 35,000 deaths, many of them in highly industrialized countries that were considered less vulnerable to weather extremes compared to developing countries in Africa or South America. Furthermore, data indicate that ticks spreading Lyme disease, the Anopheles mosquito carrying Malaria, and other viruses are spreading northward. An increase of pollen allergies is another impact of climate change, since the increase in temperature causes the pollen season to start earlier in the year. For those interested in this topic, please see the following Internet sites:

- World Health Organization: http://www.who.int/globalchange/en/
- Environmental Protection Agency: http://epa.gov/climatechange/effects/health.html
- United States Global Change Research Program: http://www.globalchange.gov/

Another problem area reinforced by global climate change that is becoming more and more visible is food insecurity. The United Nations Food and Agriculture Organization (FAO) warned in 2008 that climate change would negatively impact all aspects or dimensions of food security. Those dimensions consist of food availability, food accessibility, food utilization, and food system stability (FAO, 2008). Although food systems in all countries will be further impacted by climate change in the future, the world's poorest and most food insecure countries will be affected the greatest.

The Global Food Security Index is another measurement developed to assess food security (Global Food Security Index, 2014). The main categories from which the index is compiled includes a) affordability, b) availability, and c) quality & safety. According to the latest ranking the majority of the 109 countries included in this measurement have improved their food security from 2013 to 2014. However, the rankings also show that several developing nation still struggle with providing sufficient infrastructure, political unsettlement, and food cost inflation – all of which pose significant barriers to reaching a satisfying level of food security. In the latest ranking from 2014 the top ten nations are all located in North America, Asia, and Europe with the Unites States being on top followed by Austria, Netherlands, Norway, Singapore, Switzerland, Ireland, Canada, Germany, and France. On the other hand, the ten countries with the lowest scores are all located in Africa such as Burkina Faso, Mozambique, Niger, Haiti, Tanzania, Burundi, Togo, Madagascar, Chad, and in last place the Democratic Republic of Congo.

According to the IPCC, the environmental impacts of climate change discussed above will also lead to social problems causing ecological refugees and even leading to concerns of national security.

Future Impacts of Global Climate Change

Climate Models and Scenarios

Future climate change is already built into the system by past greenhouse gas emissions, which will take decades to disappear from our atmosphere. Thus, ongoing impacts will still occur even if we act immediately to reduce GHG emissions. The first **Kyoto Protocol** had as a goal to reduce GHG emission by 5.2% below the emission levels of 1990 by 2012. This goal failed as, in fact, the amount of worldwide GHG emissions is still increasing. Research calls for the strong likelihood that extreme weather events and sea level rise will continue to increase and droughts will become longer and more severe. Additional impacts in the future might be major alterations in oceans, ice, or storms, as well as massive dislocations of species, pest outbreaks, and major shifts in wealth, technology, and societal priorities (Stern, 2006). There is a wide array of climate models available, ranging from relatively basic models that focus on the aspects of the earth's heat balance to very complex and detailed simulations, which aim to show possible future impacts of global climate change under diverse assumptions.

The models compute different outcomes or **scenarios** based on different assumptions regarding possible future amounts of greenhouse gas emissions, policy selections, behavioral actions, and other aspects that might impact future climate trends.

Kyoto Protocol - Initially adopted in December 1997, the Kyoto Protocol is an international treaty with the goal to reduce greenhouse gas emissions to prevent further increases in the global temperature. Today, more than 190 countries have signed the treaty.

Scenarios - Scenarios are possible future circumstances computed by climate models. The scenarios are based on different assumptions regarding possible future amounts of green-house gas emissions, policy selections, behavioral actions, and other aspects that might impact future climate trends.

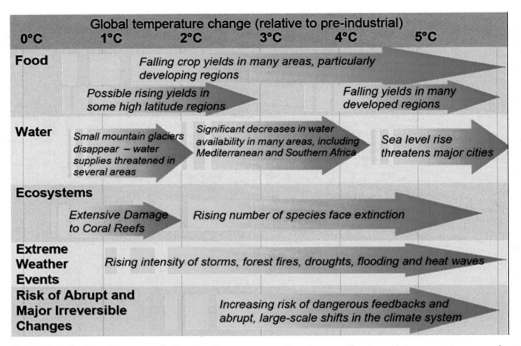

FIGURE 8: Project impacts of climate change according to specific rises in temperature-used in OBP 155-selection 46 (Stern, 2006).

Source: From The Economics of Climate Change: The Stern Review-Executive Summary by Nicholas Stern, Cabinet Office-HM Treasury. Copyright © 2006 by Cambridge University Press. Reprinted by permission.

It is important to understand that these models do not predict the future, rather they simply offer possible future scenarios. The future of climate change, to a large degree, depends on human behavior, which is impossible to predict. The scenarios, however, do provide important data to decision-makers, which allow them to make better-informed, long-term decisions to impact the future positively. Based on different scenarios, Figure 8 shows impacts of climate change by sector as temperatures increase. Although some areas show short-term benefits, in the long run (as temperatures keep increasing), the scenarios indicate significant negative consequences in all sectors.

Future Global Temperatures

According to the 5th IPCC Assessment Report (2013), between 1986 and 2005 the global mean surface temperature will likely increase by 0.3°C to 0.7°C between the years 2016 and 2035 compared to temperatures measured between 1986 and 2005. As shown in Figure 9, projections reaching further into the future suggest average temperature increases ranging from 0.3°C to 1.7°C—all the way to 2.6°C to 4.8°C by the year 2100 depending on the emission scenario. Moreover, the IPCC concludes with a very high degree of certainty that there will be more hot weather extremes in the future and fewer cold temperature anomalies.

Future Precipitation Patterns

In addition to rising temperatures, changes in precipitation rates will also impact society and the natural environment. A secure water supply is fundamental for our food supply and for the livelihood of plants and animals. Yet, a possible future change in

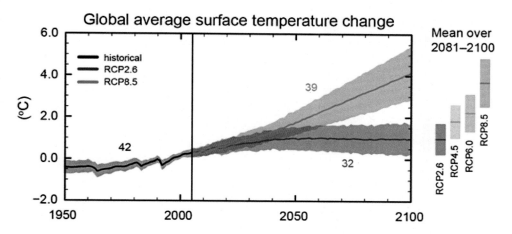

FIGURE 9: Projected change in global annual mean surface temperature relative to 1986–2005 (*Intergovernmental Panel on Climate Change*, 2013).

Source: IPCC, 2013: Summary of Policymakers. In: Climate Change 2013: The Physical Science Basis. Working Group I Contribution to the Fifth Assessment Reprot of the Intergovernmental Panel on Climate Change, Figure SPM.7(a). [Stocker,T.F., D.Qin, G.-K. Plattner, M.Tignor, S.K.Allen, J.Boschung, A.Nauels, Y.Xia, V.Bex and P.M. Midgley (eds.)] Cambridge University Press, Cambridge, UK and New York, USA.

precipitation is much harder to predict than other features of climate change. By and large, current climate models operate on a large spatial scale, making it very difficult to capture and focus upon important regional differences in rainfall. Therefore, the uncertainties regarding possible future trends of rainfall extremes or droughts can be quite large.

Despite the uncertainty in terms of the severity of the precipitation changes, all models anticipate future droughts, heavier rainfall, and floods (IPCC, 2013). The different scenarios that indicate the difference in precipitation between wet and dry regions will increase, meaning that wet areas will become wetter and dry areas will become even drier. Furthermore, as mean surface temperatures increase, extreme precipitation events will most likely have also intensified by the end of the twenty-first century. Climate models show that heavy rainfall will become strong and more frequent, especially over most of the mid-latitude landmasses and over wet tropical regions. Monsoon seasons are also likely to start earlier in the future and last longer in many regions. Risks of droughts on the other hand are forecasted to amplify in Australia, the eastern parts of New Zealand, as well as in the Mediterranean, central Europe, and Central America. In terms of snowfall, decreases in the length of the snow season can be expected in most of Europe and North America.

Future Impact on Water Security

One of the most significant impacts of climate change on human society in the future is on water security (IPCC, 2007). The wide range of possible impacts is summarized in Figure 10. Regions in the Mediterranean, southern Africa, Western Australia, and in the southwest United States will likely face serious future droughts. According to the 2007 IPCC report, by the year 2050, one to two billion people could suffer from the effects of droughts and decreasing water quality. Moreover, water stress in regard to quality and availability will increase, affecting up to two-thirds of the global land area. In turn, this will affect food security and water quality and can adversely impact human health.

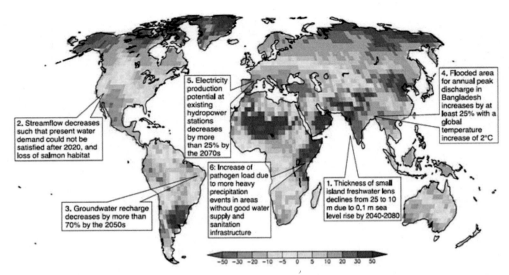

FIGURE 10: Possible threat to water security worldwide in the future. Blues show increased runoff, red decreased runoff in percent. (Intergovernmental Panel on Climate Change, 2007).

Source: Climate Change 2007: Impacts, Adaptation and Vulnerability. Working Group II Contribution to the Fourth Assessment Report of the Intergovernmental Panel on Climate Change, Figure 3.8. Cambridge University Press.

Uncertainty in Climate Change Projections

All future climate change impact scenarios are characterized by uncertainties. The uncertainty arises from very complex climate science, possible future behaviors, decisions by humans, and from internal processes in the climate system. Future human behavior is very unpredictable and is influenced by attitudes toward quality of life and wealth. Future emission trends will depend heavily on the development and availability of new technologies, the implementation of different environmental policies, and by their level of acceptance and support by the public. Currently, the U.S. federal policy through executive order is advancing regulations to reduce CO_2 emissions in coal plants. Internal processes in the physical climate system might involve impactful changes in vegetation, variations in the earth's orbit around the sun, or volcanic eruptions. Given these large uncertainties, it is quite challenging to anticipate and employ the appropriate adaptation strategies to ameliorate future climate change impacts. Traditional approaches such as making decisions based on "worst case" scenarios do not translate readily to the highly complex and uncertain issue of climate change. Instead, a more flexible framework is required that allows decision makers to develop strategies based on highly variant potential scenarios with feedback loops. This approach is referred to as **advanced scenario planning** and is a key component of the **anticipatory governance framework** (Quay, 2010) [See chapter 10 by Ray Quay].

The concept of "anticipatory governance" can be described as "a system of institutions, rules, and norms that provide a way to use foresight for the purpose of reducing risk and to increase capacity to respond to events at early rather than later stages of their development" (Fuerth, 2009, p. 29). It presents a new model for decision making, interpolates high uncertainties, and consists of the anticipatory future steps and feedback creation needed for flexible adaptation strategies, monitoring, and action. Anticipation and future analysis is based on advanced scenario planning and

Advanced Scenario Planning - Advanced scenario planning presents a flexible framework that allows decision makers, to develop long-term strategies based on many different possible scenarios. Advanced scenario planning includes methods such as aggregated averages, risk assessments, sensitivity analysis of factors or decisions driving the scenarios, identification of unacceptable or worst case outcomes, and assessment of common and different impacts among the scenarios.

Anticipatory governance framework - Anticipatory governance relies on the development and analysis of a range of possible scenarios, rather than a forecast or selection of a single scenario. It presents a new model for decision making while dealing with high uncertainties and consists of the anticipatory future steps and feedback creation of flexible adaptation strategies, monitoring and action.

includes methods such as aggregated averages, risk assessments, sensitivity analysis of factors or decisions driving the scenarios, identification of unacceptable or worst case outcomes, and assessment of common and different impacts among the scenarios. Due to the uncertainties surrounding climate change and the changing impacts over time, the final step 'monitoring and action' demands that policy makers and decision makers revise adaptation strategies on a regular basis.

Climate Change Governance and Strategies

A great amount of political intervention, public behavioral change, and support for climate strategies and policies will be necessary in the next decade to confront the causes of climate change and to reduce the negative potential consequences. Action to reduce the production of carbon dioxide is called mitigation. Comprehensive changes in numerous aspects of society and the built environment are required to recognize and cope with the effects of global climate change impacts that are already unavoidable. These are referred to as adaptation. Adaptation and mitigation strategies are considered the two main policy responses to global climate change. However, they are not independent; in fact mitigation and adaptation are driven by the same set of problems, and the more mitigation that takes place, the less adaptation will be needed, and vice versa. Improving the climate resiliency of urbanized areas and their inhabitants through successful implementation of mitigation and adaption strategies will be one of the major societal challenges resulting from global climate change in the twenty-first century.

Climate Treaties and Frameworks

On the international scale one of the most important and well-known policy frameworks was signed by more than 150 countries following the 1992 Earth Summit in Rio de Janeiro. The initial goal of the "United Nations Framework Conventions on Climate Change" (UNFCCC) involved the reduction of GHG emissions to a level that would prevent any negative impacts on the climate system (UNFCCC, 2014). Focusing on climate change, mitigation, and adaptation, while also acknowledging issues of social equity and sustainable development, the framework entered into force in 1994, this in turn led to the Kyoto Protocol in 1997. As mentioned in the previous section "Climate Models and Scenarios," developed countries that did sign the Kyoto Protocol committed to reduce GHG emissions by an average of 5.2 percent below 1990 levels during the period of 2008–2012 (United Nations, 1998). The reduction target for the United States was set at seven percent. However, the US only signed but never ratified the protocol and withdrew in 2001 and the goal of a 5.2 percent reduction did not happen. The United States did not ratify the treaty mainly due to economic concerns, arguing that the protocol would harm the economy and result in the loss of jobs (NBC. 2005).

In addition to the Kyoto Protocol, the UNFCCC also established yearly climate summits among its members called the "Conferences of the Parties" (COP), which have led to numerous international agreements on contending with the issue of climate change. Major milestones were reached in 2007 during the COP 13 in Bali, Indonesia that led to the "Bali Road Map" and the "Bali Action Plan"—which outlined a negating process with the goal to achieve a legally binding climate treaty (UNFCCC, 2008). Two years later in 2009 at COP 15 in Copenhagen, 114 countries signed the "Copenhagen Accord" re-emphasizing the need to cut GHG emissions and establish financial support mechanisms for mitigation efforts in developing countries (UNFCCC, 2009). In 2010, COP 16 in Cancun, Mexico led to the "Cancun Agreement", which included recognizing the efforts by developing countries to reduce GHG emissions, the "Cancun Adaptation Framework", which improved the planning and implementation processes of adaptation projects, and actions to further reduce emissions caused by deforestation and forest degradation (UNFCCC, 2011). In addition, countries continued negotiations about extending the Kyoto Protocol past the year 2012, which marks the end of the first commitment period (2008–2012), as well as making their new emission reduction pledges official. The 2011 climate change conference (COP 17) in Durban, South Africa focused mostly on the continuation of the work started with the "Bali Roadmap" and the "Cancun Agreement". Nevertheless, a decision was made to adopt a new, universal, legally binding agreement on climate changes no later than 2015 during the COP 21 in Paris, France.

The year 2012 marked the end of the initial phase of the Kyoto Protocol, and therefore was a major talking point at COP 18 in Doha, Qatar (Doha, 2012). Governments advanced initiatives to establish a second commitment period for another eight years, which started January 1, 2013. However, compared to the first commitment period, the second phase is appreciably more limited in scope. The renewed agreement only covers about 15 percent of the global carbon dioxide emissions—due to the lack of participation of USA, Canada, Japan, and Russia, and the fact that developing countries like China (the world's largest emitter), India, and Brazil are not subject to any emissions reductions under the Kyoto Protocol. The last meeting took place in Warsaw, Poland in late 2013. During this conference, consensus was reached among the members in terms of finances to support developing countries in their efforts to reduce GHG emissions and adapt to impacts already occurring (Warsaw, 2013). Countries confirmed their commitment to reach a climate agreement by 2015, but the summit was highly criticized for the lack of urgency by negotiators.

On the national scale, many cities have come to terms with the fact that something needs to be done about climate change and are starting to take responsibility instead of relying on the international community or comprehensive global treaties. Cities are often considered a significant part of the climate change problem and are now actively engaged in finding solutions [See Chapter 12 by Martin Pasqualetti]. Since cities frequently occupy locations along coastal regions or rivers, they are seen as sites for climate vulnerability. Today, rapid **urbanization** further increases the vulnerability of cities to climate change since urban centers are already overstressed, and new city dwellers, particularly the poor, are often relegated to live in high risk areas. In developing countries, many poor individuals are forced to construct their own homes in informal settlements on floodplains, in swamp areas, or on unstable hillsides, all of which lack necessary infrastructure and basic services (Rosenzweig et al. 2011). As cities also consume major amounts of energy, they are the main producers of GHGs, hence serving as a considerable source of the risks of climate change in the first place. The spatial concentration of industry and transportation, as well as domestic and

Urbanization - Urbanization describes the process of more and more people moving from rural to urban areas. As a result cities are growing in size and population.

commercial buildings assign cities a key role in how (and how much) energy is produced and GHGs are emitted.

Cities are both the victim and perpetuator of climate change; nonetheless, they are a primary part of the solution. Municipalities have a significant say in aspects of urban planning, building codes, the provision of transportation, and the supply of energy, water, and waste services that determine vulnerabilities and the production of GHG emissions. As a result, city governments are in an advantageous position to address climate change mitigation and adaption. Cities are centers for innovation with the potential to develop new technologies and urban policies and strategies to address climate change. It is at this level where effective solutions with climate change will be discovered.

To improve local climate change strategies and learn from experiences in different places, cities have begun to organize themselves in transnational municipal networks. One such network is the "C40 Cities Climate Leadership Group", a network of the world's largest cities willing to address climate change (http://www.c40.org). Among the network's tasks are raising finances, sharing knowledge, and providing additional partners and expertise to its member cities to engage in specific climate change related projects. For example, the C40 networks share knowledge and support one another in areas such as bus rapid transit systems, climate risk assessments, sustainable urban development, and sustainable solid waste systems. Another well-known transitional city network with similar goals and approaches is the "Local Governments for Sustainability" (ICLEI), established in 1990 (http://www.iclei.org/). ICLEI has member cities in over 85 countries ranging from mega-cities to small and medium-sized towns. Within the United States, the lack of political action on the federal level has led to the formation of the US Mayor's Agreement (http://www.usmayors.org/). By signing the agreement, city mayors commit to take three decisive actions against climate change. First, meet the GHG reduction targets outlined by the Kyoto Protocol for their own community. Second, lobby at the state and federal levels to implement more mitigation policies and reduce GHG emissions below the benchmark set by the Kyoto Protocol for the entire USA. Third, work toward the implementation of a national emission trading system. So far, over 1,000 mayors have signed the Climate Protection Agreement (The United States Conference of Mayors, 2014).

Mitigation

Mitigation addresses the core cause of human-induced climate change, namely the large amount of energy consumption and the resulting greenhouse gas emissions. The concept of mitigation is clearly understood by scientists and decision makers. As a result, various international treaties exist such as the Kyoto Protocol (1997) and the Copenhagen Accord (2009), signed by many countries, setting greenhouse gas reduction goals and strengthening the international cooperation in the fight against climate change. The fact that greenhouse gas emissions are easy to assess and can be monitored quantitatively has led to the development and implementation of numerous mitigation strategies.

Overall, cities and urban areas consume about 75 percent of the world's energy and are responsible for up to 75 percent of GHG emissions. The burning of fossil fuels, mostly by private automobiles, is the largest single source of CO_2 emissions with about 57 percent. However, cities are not only part of the climate problem, but their development can also serve as part of the solution. The following sections address three major sectors of energy consumption, especially in urban environments and discuss how much mitigation strategies can reduce their GHG emissions.

Transportation Sector

The transportation sector is among the fastest growing areas of energy use. The heavy reliance on combustion engines fueled by oil has led to a significant increase in greenhouse gas emission over the past decades. Although gas prices are increasing, many consumers still seem to prefer large vehicles with powerful engines that rely on fossil fuel. Thus, the free market with its seemingly unpredictable price swings for oil has little impact on the people's travel behavior and the mode of transportation they choose. In contrast, mandatory regulation regarding fuel economy has been much more effective in reducing greenhouse gas emissions while also encouraging research toward higher fuel efficiency (IPCC, 2007). As a result, new technologies have emerged that already make automobiles up to 40 percent more efficient compared to the cars relying entirely on fossil fuels. Technologies such as hybrid vehicles, turbo diesels, and biofuels will decrease greenhouse gas emissions even further with new technologies becoming available for the mass market in the near future.

Strategies that provide a technological alternative for the use of fossil fuels in the transportation sector, however, are not the only measurements available for the mitigation of climate change. Current research also suggests that greenhouse gas emissions from the transportation sector can be reduced by establishing specific settlement structures and densities, which reduce the necessity to drive and decrease the overall amount of vehicle miles traveled. The underlying strategies include the mixing of land uses, the implementation of compact development patterns, the creation of walkable environments, and the allocation of transportation alternatives such as public buses or light rail systems. The possible reductions in vehicle miles traveled by implementing these strategies are still heavily debated among scientists. The existing literature suggests that in the best case, a reduction of 25 percent in vehicle miles traveled (NRC, 2009) can be achieved utilizing all the strategies mentioned above—though it may take over 30 years to achieve.

Building Sector

Changing the energy use of buildings can also reduce greenhouse gas emissions significantly. The building sector provides low cost opportunities to reduce CO_2 emissions. Many energy-saving efficiency measures regarding the heating, cooling, or lighting of buildings are being implemented. Energy efficiency can be improved and heating costs reduced by improving the insulation of buildings, sealing leaks, and using energy-efficient windows. Depending on the climate, these measures alone have the potential to decrease heating costs by up to 90 percent (Archer & Rahmstorf, 2010).

Reducing emissions from air conditioning and decreasing cooling costs is also relatively simple. This can be achieved through architectural design and siting choices, such as orienting the long axis of a house east-west, so that wall areas receiving hot morning and afternoon sun are minimized. Another possibility to save energy is by using reflective materials and light colored surfaces, which reflect most of the heat away from the house. Providing shade through specific landscaping is also an effective way to cool buildings and reduce cooling costs by up to 40 percent. In recent years concepts as the ten smart growth principles (Smart Growth Network, 2014), new urbanism (CNU, 2014), or assessments tools like LEED (USGBC, 2014) were developed and introduced into planning policies to establish a sustainable development pattern for neighborhoods and communities.

Especially the LEED certification program is very comprehensive. Since 1993, the U.S. Green Building Council (USGBC) is developing rating systems to define and measure existing sustainable buildings and new developments under the LEED program. Currently the USGBC has five LEED rating systems for a) Building Design and Construction, b) Interior Design and Construction, c) Building Operations and Maintenance, d) Neighborhood Development, and e) Homes.

In order to receive LEED certification, projects that fall within the five different rating systems need to earn a certain number of credits for meeting different sustainable design categories and performance benchmarks. For example, development projects such as a master planned communities are awarded points based on the materials used, water efficiency, energy use, site location, level of access to public transit, and others. In total the LEED program offers four types of certification (certified, silver, gold, and platinum) depending on the points scored on the rating system.

Industry Sector

The industrial sector is third major source of energy use and significant contributor to global climate change. It is responsible for roughly 8.4 G ton of CO_2 being emitted into the atmosphere. Compared to the transportation and housing sector, however, the annual increase in emissions from the industrial sector is relatively low with only 0.6 percent. Within the industrial sector, the metal and chemical production industries are the most energy intensive and account for 85 percent of the sector's total greenhouse gas emissions. The highest potential for reducing emissions offer the steel, cement, and petroleum industries through investments focusing on the use of cleaner industrial processes or stricter environmental laws. The latest IPCC report argues that emission cuts of up to 40 percent are possible if the responsible company would be charged $20 for each ton of CO_2 or any other greenhouse gas emitted into the atmosphere (IPCC, 2014a).

Adaptation

Adaptation strategies focus on avoiding or reducing harmful impacts caused by global climate change. They are essentially adjustments with the aim to increase resilience or decrease vulnerability to current or expected impacts of climate change. Even if current mitigation measurements prove to be successful in reducing greenhouse gas emissions, global climate change is already occurring and further climate change is already built into the system by previous emissions. This development makes the design and implementation of adaptation strategies a clear necessity to reduce the impacts that can no longer be prevented and to prepare for possible future threats.

Compared to mitigation strategies that focus on the global and national scale and require international cooperation, adaptation is more a regional and local challenge. Another difference is that the effectiveness of adaptation strategies is influenced by high uncertainties because their effectiveness depends on the accuracy of regional climate and impact projections. Moreover, many governments agreed on GHG emission targets and time frames to reach that goal. On the contrary, there are no targets and schedules for adaptation: they are a local concern determined by local, serial, and geographical effects.

Adaptation Strategies and their Impact

Reducing greenhouse emissions will take time, and benefits of reduction will not be fully experienced for decades. Adaptation measurements on the other hand provide a much shorter lead-time. Due to the strong links with development initiatives and the implementation mostly on the local or regional scale, adaptation efforts and their results are much faster and visible when compared to mitigation measures. Furthermore, the efficiency of adaptation strategies is less dependent on the actions of others and does not need international agreements.

Since adaptation is primarily a local and regional problem, the appropriate strategy has to be evaluated on site. Without the successful implementation of adaptation strategies, it will be impossible to minimize the economic costs of climate change impacts, protect human health and welfare, and limit harm to infrastructure, ecosystems, and biodiversity. Adaptation measurements are required either to protect settlements threatened by sea level rise, floods, and droughts, or to enable the population to relocate. In the case of water shortage, development of new supplies or the implementation of conservation measures will become necessary. Adaptation measures also play an important role in the agricultural sector. Farmers and ranchers might need to react to the impacts of climate change by changing crops, raising different livestock, or by relocating. Furthermore, vulnerable settlements need protection from increasing heat-related events. Already occurring shifts in disease and insect pattern also emphasize the need for adaptation measures for the public health sector.

Real world examples of implemented adaptation measurements include coastal defense planning and flood gates, as shown in Figure 11, and early warning systems to prepare for sea level rise and storm floods. Different regions are starting to prepare for water shortages by creating water storage systems, implementing conservation measures, and by building seawater desalination plants. In addition, land management plans and zoning laws are being updated to prevent soil erosion. Regions, depending on winter tourism, are shifting ski slopes to higher altitudes and cities are preparing emergency plans to deal with future heat waves or other extreme weather events.

© Gertje/Shutterstock, Inc.

FIGURE 11: Storm surge barrier in Zeeland, Netherlands built after the storm disaster in 1953.

Local Climate Change Action Plans

A majority of the world's energy consumption either occurs in cities, or as a direct result of the way cities function (e.g., through transport of goods to points of consumption in cities). Nevertheless, the concentration of resources in cities can be a useful weapon in fighting climate change. Cities are often centers of new thinking and policy innovation; they are in an excellent position to lead the way for other municipalities to follow. In recent years, many cities and states have developed "Climate Change Action Plans" to mitigate and adapt to climate change. "Climate Change Action Plans" help states and cities to identify and evaluate feasible and effective policies to reduce their greenhouse gas emissions through a combination of public and private sector policies and programs.

The first generation of Climate Action Plans focused mainly on improving municipal operations in terms of energy use and GHG emissions with the most prominent strategies as follows:

- Creating building codes and standards that include practical affordable changes that make buildings cleaner and more energy efficient.
- Conducting energy audits and implementing retrofit programs to improve energy efficiency in municipal and private buildings
- Installing more energy efficient traffic and street lighting
- Implementing localized, cleaner electricity generation systems
- Developing bus rapid transit and non-motorized transport systems
- Using clean fuels and hybrid technologies for city buses, rubbish trucks, and other vehicles
- Implementing schemes to reduce traffic, such as congestion charges
- Creating waste-to-energy systems at landfills
- Improving water distribution systems and leak management

Today, these plans are also addressing adaptation strategies and jurisdiction wide policies such as land-use planning (Millar-Ball, 2010). By the end of the last decade, at least 141 local jurisdictions had developed Climate Action Plans in the United States. Climate Action Plans and their recommendations present a great opportunity. They provide a framework to change current development patterns and establish a sustainable way of living in the future, which reduce the vulnerability to climate change and increase the adaptive capacity of communities.

A very good example of a Climate Action Plan that considers mitigation and adaptation strategies can be seen in the 2008 plan developed and published by the city of Chicago. After consulting with dozens of experts, an internationally recognized research advisory committee, and numerous business, labor, civic, and environmental leaders from Chicago, the city revealed plans to achieve a 25 percent reduction of the 1990 level greenhouse gas emissions by 2020, an 80 percent reduction of the 1990 level greenhouse gas emissions by 2050, and to prepare the city for the effect of global climate change (City of Chicago, 2008). Chicago's Climate Change Action Plan outlines five main strategies, which provide 26 actions for mitigating greenhouse gas emissions and nine actions to prepare for climate change. The plan identifies key opportunities to meet the emission goals by improving the energy efficiency of residential, commercial, and industrial buildings or upgrading power plants and improving their efficiency. The plan also emphasizes the need to reduce greenhouse gas emissions by decreasing the amount people who drive and improving vehicle fuel efficiency. The different strategies include supporting principles of transit-oriented development and policies encouraging car sharing and carpooling, improving fleet efficiency, and achieving higher fuel efficiency standards. In terms of adaptation the five strategies focus on the management of possible heat waves, the protection of air quality, the preservation of plants and trees, the engagement of the public and local businesses, green urban design, and innovative cooling. In addition to the environmental benefits of these actions, the Climate Action Plans also point to other benefits such as the potential for thousands of new jobs once the policies are implemented.

Portland, Oregon is another city that is well known for its efforts to become more sustainable and prepare for climate change. In 1993, Portland became the first local government in the United States to adopt a plan to address climate change. The Local Action Plan on Global Warming was developed under the guidance of a steering committee and involved extensive input from residents, businesses, non-governmental organizations, and public sector representatives. Because the plan addresses issues such as public transportation and energy supply, for which other entities hold ultimate decision-making authority, the process and final plan are highly collaborative and involve a broad network of partnerships. The plan identified strategies to reduce greenhouse gas emissions in six areas: land-use planning, transportation, energy efficiency, renewable energy, solid waste and recycling, and urban forestry. Activities targeted both city government operations and community-wide initiatives, all building on a tradition of stewardship of natural resources and the high value Portland residents place on local quality of life. The fundamental goal of the Local Action Plan on Global Warming (City of Portland 2001) aimed to reduce greenhouse gas emissions in Multnomah County, Oregon, to 10 percent below 1990 levels by 2010 while minimizing costs and maximizing co-benefits.

In 2007, Portland City Council and the Multnomah County Board of Commissioners adopted resolutions directing staff to design a strategy to reduce local carbon emissions 80 percent by the year 2050 (City of Portland 2001). The resulting 2009 Climate Action Plan leads future efforts by the City and County and provides a framework for the region's transition to a more sustainable and climate-stable future. The visions of the Climate Action Plan are the following:

- Each resident lives in a walkable and bikeable neighborhood that includes retail businesses, school, parks, and jobs

- Green-collar jobs are a key component of the thriving regional economy, with products and services related to clean energy, green building, sustainable food and waste reuse and recovery providing living-wage jobs throughout the community

- Homes, offices and other buildings are durable and highly efficient, healthy, comfortable, and powered primarily by solar, wind, and other renewable resources

- Urban forest, green roofs, and swales help cover the community, reducing the urban heat island effect, sequestering carbon, providing wildlife habitat, and cleaning the air and water

- Food and agriculture are central to the economic and cultural vitality of the com-munity, with productive backyard and community gardens and thriving farmers markets. A large share of food comes from farms in the region, and residents eat healthily, consuming more locally grown grains, vegetables and fruits

Resilience: An Innovative Approach to Social, Environmental, and Economic Urban Uncertainty

Stephen Buckman and Nelya Rakhimova

Resilience as a New Approach

The rapid explosion in urban population in the second half of the 20th and first half of the 21st century have brought on uncertainties and complex challenges for urban regions not experienced any time in history. In relation to these challenges urban and regional researchers together with city officials have been exploring the concepts of resiliency and sustainability as an approach to confront and cope with these challenges. Resilience, much like sustainability, has become a new and compelling topic within academia focusing on interdisciplinary systems thinking and new approaches to deal with future uncertainty. Both terms have and are driving the fields engaged in urban sustainability thought in directions that make them more inclusive. While both terms are driving the field and are often spoken of in the same breath they are different in scope. The concepts of resilience can offer useful starting points for understanding some of the mechanisms that hinder or enable cities to cope with structural change, disruptive events, situations of crisis, and sometimes to recognize slow changes and to find ways to manage these.

In this chapter we will review and discuss the historical components of resiliency which grew out of ecological and engineering resilience and the importance of adaptation to resiliency thinking in terms of urban systems. We will also describe the various levels of resiliency which include economic, social and environmental capital as well as adaptive governance as ways to deal with shocks and slow burns to a system. Lastly we will discuss how certain cities rank when it comes to resiliency.

Historical Background, Sustainability and Key Concepts

Resilience has been studied across a range of disciplines ranging from environmental research to materials science and engineering, psychology, sociology, and economics. Resilience has been defined as "the ability to recover quickly from illness, change, or misfortune. Buoyancy. The property of a material that enables it to assume its original shape or position after being bent, stretched, or compressed. Elasticity" (Smith et al., 1998). The concept of resilience has been applied to describe the ability for ecosystems, individuals, urban communities, and larger societies to recover after disturbances or long-term debilitating processes.

The concept of resilience emerged from ecology in the 1960s and early 1970s in scientific journals and research in ecological studies. A primary work emerging from this era was the ecologist C.S. Holling's 1973 paper entitled *Resilience and Stability of Ecological Systems* which defined resilience as "a measure of the persistence of systems and of their ability to absorb change and disturbance and still maintain the same relationships between populations or state variables ", illustrating the existence of multiple stability domains and how they relate to ecological processes, random events or disturbances.

Expanding on Holling's (1973) definition, it is important to understand there are neither natural or pristine systems without people nor social systems without nature. Social and ecological systems are invariably looked at as interdependent and constantly co-evolving. As a result, a key concept in the resilience framework is the concept of **social-ecological systems**. A social-ecological system is defined as a system that includes societal (human) and ecological (biophysical) subsystems in mutual interaction (Gallopín, 1991). The social-ecological systems can be specified for any scale from the local community and its surrounding environment to the global system constituted by the whole of humankind and the ecosphere, provide the biophysical foundation and ecosystems services for social and economic development.

While resiliency may be a relatively new term within the urban planning arena, as noted it is born out of engineering and ecology (Holling, 1973; 1996). From an engineering perspective resilience centers on how quickly a system can return to equilibrium after a disturbance as in infrastructure or city's electrical system. On the other hand the ecological perspective, looks at how a system adapts and persists, with the main difference being that the ecological definition acknowledges the existence of multiple **equilibria** and the ability to change into alternative stability domains. It is within this concept and definition of adaptation that we can use the "idea" of resiliency as an intervention technique to strengthen a system, community or neighborhood. Each of these notions rely heavily on the idea of a hazard or disturbance offsetting the balance of a system creating the need to reconcile that balance. Thus these notions often are aligned with the area of hazard mitigation and response time of entities such as the Federal Emergency Management Agency (FEMA) in the wake of a hurricane or other disasters, but even more so with the idea of adaptation.

Social-ecological system - a system that includes societal (human) and ecological (biophysical) subsystems in mutual interaction: ecosystems, from local areas to the biosphere as a whole, provide the biophysical foundation and ecosystems services for social and economic development.

Equilibrium - the condition of a system in which competing influences are balanced, resulting in no net change. Ecological equilibrium is a point or period in time in which the state of an ecological system is at climax, wherein it stops to grow or decline.

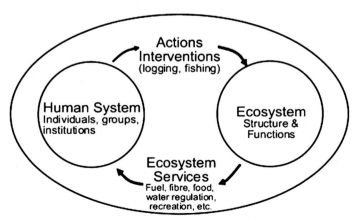

Social-Ecological System

FIGURE 1: The Social-Ecological System.

Emerging out of both engineering and ecology, evolutionary resilience (also known as socio-ecological resilience) has come forth to question the idea of equilibrium, advocating that systems can change over time with or without a radical shock as in a slow onset draught. Implying not only that disasters will shock the system but also the idea of slow evolving change or a "slow burn" to the system such as climate change. This idea of resiliency does not see the world as an orderly system but rather as a chaotic and complex changing system, which challenges the utility of relying on past forecasting to determine and plan for uncertainties (Davoudi,S. in Davoudi et al, 2012).

Therefore, there is another empirical concept of complex systems called the **adaptive cycle**, which is a model that helps expose the mechanisms that can support or prevent resilience in systems (Resilience Alliance, 2014). This model shows that change is a part of urban systems and that internal and external shocks can change the local structure and function of neighborhoods, districts, or entire urban agglomerations.

Adaptive cycle - a model that can be used to describe a variety of phenomena such as ecological succession, where ecosystem goes through exploitation, conservation, release and reorganization.

Generally, the pattern of change in adaptive cycles is addressed in a sequence of four phases from a rapid growth phase through to a conservation phase in which resources are increasingly unavailable, locked up in existing structures, followed by a release phase that then moves into a phase of reorganization, and after these four phases another growth phase starts. In reality multiple possible transitions among the four phases are possible and the pattern may not reflect a cycle. The growth and conservation phases together constitute a relatively long developmental period with fairly predictable, constrained dynamics; the release and reorganization phases constitute a rapid, chaotic period therefore, resilience research focus on these phases to understand the nature of vulnerabilities and shock and their prevention, or possible opportunities for reorganization if release phase already has occurred (Figure 2).

To illustrate adaptive cycle we can refer to an example of the history of Detroit, Michigan. In the growth phase Detroit had a dynamic and diverse growth in the late 19th and early 20th centuries, when the city was a rapidly expanding center for a wide variety of manufacturing, including the automobile. In the conservation phase, when the system becomes more inflexible and less diverse, as resources become more

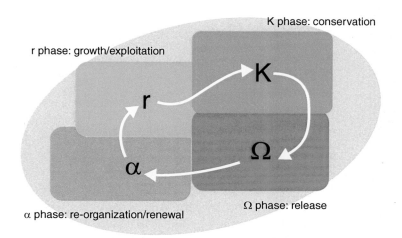

K phase: conservation

r phase: growth/exploitation

Ω phase: release

α phase: re-organization/renewal

FIGURE 2: The Adaptive Cycle.

concentrated and tightly interconnected, Detroit's consolidation of the auto industry in the early and middle decades of the 20th century occurred. The breakdown of the auto-dominated economy during the second half of the 20th century represents the third phase of adaptive cycle phase. The relevant pressures consisted of the business cycle, class tensions, racial unrest, and mobile capital; the results of the collapse were unemployment, vacancy, poverty, pollution, and violence. The final phase of the adaptive cycle is reorganization or regeneration, in which the city of Detroit may now be entering a stage of its development that parallels this phase of the adaptive cycle. The evidence for this new stage is not found in the public sector so far, but rather the innovative wings of the private and associative (nonprofit, philanthropic, and civic) sectors (Enelow, 2013).

In regards to the mentioned key concepts of resiliency theory, urban practitioners then must see places as not being static but as socio-spatial systems that are unpredictable. This means that urban planners must not be fixed in their thinking but rather must produce plans that are fluid and adaptable to change. This shows that resilience should not take the engineering or ecological approach to bouncing back but must rather think in terms of bouncing forward (Shaw in Davoudi et al, 2012). Reaction and actions must come before the shock rather than after the shock to reverse adverse impacts.

Thus a *resilient city* is one that has developed the systems and capacities to be able to absorb shocks and stresses, maintaining essentially the same functioning, structure, systems, and identity, while implementing strategies to mitigate future chocks and disturbances. Resilience in cities translates into a new paradigm for urbanization and influences the way we understand and manage urban hazards and stresses, as well as urban planning in general. It provides practical rules that can guide stakeholders' decisions to incorporate the proper management into urban investments.

Resilience and Sustainability

Both sustainability and resiliency are focused on how the changing environment is affecting the way we live and how we can confront adverse changes, yet each takes a different route to get there. The very idea about sustainability is imbedded in the word itself. The root of sustainability is "sustain" which means to maintain or to revert back. As shown throughout this book the role of sustainability is to prevent and reverse change via measures that look to cope with these changes through mechanisms that attempt to halt issues such as global climate changes. Measures taken range from greening cities to slowing the "heat island effect", construction of compact housing to increase pedestrian traffic and reduce car emissions, the use of solar energy, and the application of LEED principles in building construction to name a few examples. All of these processes look to slow or revert the negative global environmental forces that are taking shape.

Resiliency, in contrast, takes a different tact to global climate change than sustainability. Rather than looking to slow or revert the process of global climate change community resiliency looks to adapt to the process within in a urban context. The community resiliency field while acknowledging the need to slow the climate change process and administering many of the same techniques that are used by the sustainability field, takes a much more proactive view towards the changing landscape. The field of community resiliency looks not to revert to what was but to change and adapt to potential impacts by stewardship of community infrastructure and governance to build adaptive mechanisms. The idea of adaptation is key to the notion of resiliency in that change is viewed as inevitable and that for a community to be resilient and for that matter sustainable it must be prepared to adapt to change and move forward.

Examples of resilient adapting cities abound. In a recent list the Rockefeller Foundation listed the 100 most resilient cities and how each city adapted to key vulnerabilities to make it more resilient. Some these cities and their efforts include:

- Durban which is one of the poorest urban areas in South Africa which Has been dealing with issues of extreme issues of poverty. In combating extreme poverty Durban in attempt to build a more resilient economy has been looking to adapt institutions, systems and processes to facilitate integrated and innovative and flexible planning techniques.

- El Paso Texas has worked across the Mexican border with Ciudad Juarez to combat issues of drought and water shortages but planning for a future with less water and adapting to that future by lessening their water usage. These two cities show that climate change does not have a border that both sides of the border must work together to lessen the impact of waterless future.

- Tokyo Japan not only is a city that is an international economic powerhouse but is also extremely prone to earthquakes inspired by the1995 Kobe Earthquake the city constructed the Honjo Bousai-kan (Life Safety Learning Center) which serves as a fire station and as a public training facility for residents of the city to prepare and survive numerous disasters such as typhoons, tsunamis and earthquakes that could hit the city. By training residents the city has taken a proactive stance towards natural disasters, thus adapting to the very fact idea of not "what if" a disaster happens but to "when" it happens. (The Rockfeller Foundation).

Therefore with the importance of adaptation, resiliency is often considered as a cornerstone of sustainability. The sustainability of any system, including cities, requires resilience. Enhancing resilience of a city will make it not only more sustainable but has the potential to provide a higher quality of life in economic, social and environmental terms for its residents as the community will be inherently strengthened and connected together (Beatley, 2009). For that reason, Sustainable Development Solutions Network (SDSN), which was launched by UN Secretary-General Ban Ki-moon in August 2012 and mobilizes scientific and technical expertise from academia, civil society, and the private sector, proposed to include resiliency of cities in new 10 Sustainable Development Goals for the years 2016–2030 (post-2015 development agenda) following up Millennium Development Goals:

SDG 7: Empower inclusive, productive and resilient cities. The goal is to make all cities socially inclusive, economically productive, environmentally sustainable, and secure and resilient to climate change and other risks. Success in Sustainable Development Goal 7 (SDG 7) will require new forms of participatory, accountable and effective city governance to support rapid and equitable urban transformation. (Sachs, 2014)

Urban and Community Resilience

As previously touched upon, resilience research is focusing on two stages of the adaptive cycle, and this part of the chapter will look at the "release phase" or shocks and disturbances cities and communities are facing. Urbanization and rapid population growth leads to the concentration of population in cities as cities grow rapidly in the beginning of the 21st century both in population and areal extent. Urban areas provide a number of socio-economic advantages as jobs and income generation, but are also simultaneously becoming increasingly more hazardous, especially for low-income residents of cities, particularly large cities in developing countries which are confronting growing air and water contamination, food insecurities and expanding slum areas. Both metropolitan areas and medium- or small-sized cities represent different concerns for various shocks. For example, modern cities are highly vulnerable to natural and human-made disasters. According to the 2007 UN Report entitled *Mitigating the Impact of Disasters,* since 1975, there has been a fourfold increase in the number of recorded natural disasters. Human-made disasters have seen a tenfold increase from 1975 to 2006, with the greatest rates of increase being in Asia and Africa. Therefore, cities are facing different problems today than in the past and future urban planning needs to understand the factors which are shaping the socio-spatial aspects of cities and the institutional structures which attempt to manage them in order to prevent or recover from shocks and disturbances that occur with alarmingly greater frequency.

In the resilience framework, the types of shocks are defined by origin, lasting time, frequency, predictability, and scale of impact (See Table 1). For instance, natural disasters recently have gotten the most attention from scientists over the last four decades. The reason for the uptick in concern is that natural disasters, which are especially destructive in urban areas where there is a concentration of people and resources, have

TABLE 1: System Shocks

		Example
Origin	Natural:	earthquakes, weather events
	Economic:	market shocks, employment, recessions, poverty
	Biological:	diseases
	Social:	demographic, riots, revolutions
	Technological:	industrial accidents
	Political:	change government, wars
Lasting time	Minutes:	earthquakes, landslides
	Days:	hurricanes, riots
	Weeks:	stock market crashes, weather events
	Month:	housing prices, revolutions
	Decades:	famine, droughts, demographic change
Frequency	Chronic:	weather events
	Frequently:	hurricanes
	Rarely:	industrial accidents
Scale of Impact	Neighborhood:	riots, diseases
	City:	heat island effect
	Region:	weather events
	Global scale:	climate change, peak oil

caused more than 3.3 million deaths and 2.3 trillion dollars in economic damages, worldwide statistics reveal an increasing number of disasters over that the last four decades.

While natural disasters are press worthy for its sheer immediate shock value, a lasting period of shock, slow disturbances, or so-called "slow-burns" are the most challenging for urban and community planning and development. These lasting disturbances, as long-term demographic change, economic decline or degradation of the environment sometimes can be avoided during the planning process because they can be considered as "normal process" that has been happening already during several generations. For US cities, aging and poverty are a good example of such disturbance. For instance as the "Baby Boomer" generation (born between 1945–1964) enters retirement there will be an increasing strain on inadequate savings, social welfare services and especially on an already stressed Social Security system. Considering Social Security support will be not enough to cover basic needs and with the majority of baby-boomers living in cities, urban communities have the potential to face major problems in next decades with a significant percentage of older adults living in poverty.

Disturbances and shocks can occur at different spatial scales. Consequently, resilience research operates at different levels of spatial development as the local effects of global environmental change and economic, political and cultural globalization are adding greater uncertainty to development and planning. As cities and communities are facing the same disturbances, sometimes the impacts are completely different. This depends not only on ability to respond to shock but also on weak points or vulnerabilities of the system. Urban areas are not disaster and risk prone by nature; rather the socio-economic structural processes that accelerate rapid urbanization; population movement and population concentrations substantially increase **vulnerability**. For example, cities that are historically located on coastlines have an economic advantage as trading centers such as New York or Seattle, yet at the same time are vulnerable to current climate change that can cause significant sea level rise such as New Orleans. Some cities, on the other hand, can have vulnerabilities in human created infrastructure, such as a monopoly in transportation which can cause a serious problem in critical situation in cities limiting resource supplies.

Operating on multiple spatial scales policy-makers have a lot of uncertainties to deal with both at

© Zack Frank/Shutterstock, Inc.

Flooding from Katrina in New Orleans.

Vulnerability - an inability of system to withstand the effects of a hostile environment; exposure to hazard factors.

Uncertainty - a system's state of having limited knowledge where it is impossible to exactly describe the existing state, a future outcome or events.

the regional and local level. **Uncertainty** is an essential element of any disaster; it is always necessary to deal with disaster impacts that cannot be quantified or are completely unknown. To cope with uncertainty cities need a robust approach to decision making. Therefore, decision-makers should take into account potential weak spots and system failures, preparing for a wide range of futures rather than focusing on optimal design solutions. At the same time, there is increasing difficulty to rely on extrapolation of different events in the past when the physical and human conditions that contextualized a past event is being re-shaped by local and global forces. When uncertainty and disempowerment are felt by decision-makes, there is a danger that investment in disaster preparedness and mitigation will be left outside of urban development strategy (Pelling, 2003). To combat this situation scenario planning or anticipatory governance, which in essence empowers decision-makers with a list of worst and best case options can be instilled as a tool to foresee and plan for change (Quay, 2010).

Most importantly however cities can be socially vulnerability when people, organizations, and societies are not able to withstand adverse impacts from multiple stressors to which they are exposed. Usually social vulnerability in cities is partially the product of social inequalities, that lead to different susceptibility of various groups to harm and that also govern their ability to respond (Cutter et al., 2003). As a result, social vulnerability is not only demonstrated by exposure to hazards alone, but also expressed in the sensitivity and resilience of the system to prepare, cope and recover from such hazards (Turner et al., 2003).

How a City or Community Can Be Resilient

The key component of resiliency research is learning how a city or community can enhance its resilience to uncertainty. Key approaches to resilience can be categorized into four major views, resilience as **stability**, **recovery**, **transformation**, and **adaptation**, with the common thread being the ability to withstand and respond positively to stress or change (Adger, 2000, Resilience Alliance 2007, Maguire and Cartwright 2008). The resiliency approach to stability relates to a system's efforts to endure a disaster and its consequence; the recovery view of resilience relates to a system's ability to 'bounce back' from a change or stressor to return to its original state. While the transformation view of resilience is concerned with concepts of renewal, regeneration and reorganization (Folke 2006) such as when a disturbance has the potential to create opportunities for innovation and for development. It is especially applicable in cities and communities where a system is already degrading and efforts to get it back into a desirable stable phase are no longer possible without innovative policies, financial support, and system change.

Of the four major views, adaptation has received the widest attention in the academic and practitioner communities. It must be understood that adaptation can be both reactive and proactive. Reactive or autonomous adaptation represents a response to a stress that has already occurred. However, reactive adaptation does not always end well as it can be too late to take some actions. As humans we have the unique ability to anticipate future stresses and the capacity of taking proactive adaptation measures to lessen the negative impacts from these future events. That is why, cities and communities can *"bounce forward"* to prevent or mitigate some shocks and disturbance. Such approaches depend on one's ability to understand what the future might resemble, but are also influenced by one's ability to have learned from past experiences, particularly what

Stability - ability of a system to withstand a disaster and its consequences, simply saying it is when a city or community be able resist some particular shock and demonstrates its resilience.

Recovery - ability of a system to 'bounce back' from a change or stressor to return to its original state.

Transformation - renewal, regeneration and reorganization of a system after stress event; disturbance has the potential to create opportunity for doing new things, for innovation and for development when to get back into a desirable regime are no longer possible.

Adaptation - a physical or behavioral characteristic that has developed to allow a system to better survive in its environment under particular stress. Adaptation causes the system to better survive and redevelop.

worked (and did not) in similar circumstances. Moreover, the adaptation must take place is multi-faceted. There is not just one aspect of a community that must be resilient rather a community must take a holistic approach. Resiliency within a community must embrace economics, the environment, socio-cultural dynamics and civic institutions.

Adaptation is also closely connected with the concept of **adaptive capacity**. The reason for that is that adaptive capacity constitutes the ability or capability of a system to modify or change its characteristics or behavior to cope better with actual or anticipated stresses. Adaptation includes actions taken to reduce vulnerabilities and to increase resilience, and adaptive capacity is the ability to take those actions. In this sense, both adaptation and adaptive capacity may be seen as relating to the ability of social and political institutions to think and act towards anticipatory events and reduce vulnerability. Often, vulnerabilities are difficult to identify in complex systems.

Adaptive capacity - the capacity or ability of a system to adapt if the environment where the system exists is changing.

Cities and communities with high adaptive capacity are able to re-configure themselves without significant declines in crucial functions in relation to primary productivity, social relations and economic prosperity. A consequence of a loss of resilience, and as a result of adaptive capacity, is loss of opportunity, constrained options during periods of reorganization and renewal.

Therefore, as highlighted urban and community resiliency is concerned not about controlling change but adapting to change. Thus, it is best to think of it as an ever evolving process rather than a set in stone outcome. In essence, for a community, resiliency "is the existence, development, and engagement of community resources by community members to thrive in an environment characterized by uncertainty, unpredictability and surprise" (Magis, 2010: 401). The way a community or city deals and adapts to unpredictability in terms of economic, social and environmental stresses will determine its success making it vital to social sustainability. Thus it is best conceptualized by how a community develops social, economic and environmental capital that are usually considered as basic adaptive capacities. And more importantly how they are shared throughout cities and communities.

Adaptive Capacities of Cities and Communities

In establishing a strong resilient community various entities or pillars must be adhered to. Like a building, each pillar must be strong enough to keep the building standing. If one pillar is not holding its weight the entirety of the structure will collapse. Thus, the analogy of a strong resilient community is that of a strong well-constructed building or in more technical terms a community's adaptive capacities. There are primarily four pillars that are the basis of community resiliency: **economic capital**, **social capital**, **environmental capital**, and **adaptive governance**. While each of these areas can be seen as separate, like a building they work holistically reinforcing one another, if one area is not sufficient the brunt of the weight must be taken up by another pillar. Ideally a community will be equally strong in all four areas allowing it to be 100 percent resilient yet in reality this is rarely the case.

Adaptive governance - a concept that focuses on the evolution of formal and informal institutions for the management and use of shared assets, such as common pool natural resources, environmental assets, existing infrastructure, social capital and so on.

Economic Capital

It is easily understood that the economy would have an important role to play within community resiliency. The stronger a community's economy the more that community can rebound from disaster as they would have the economic resources to rebuild,

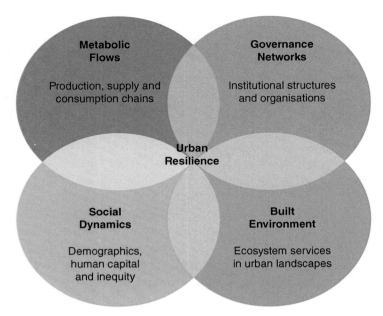

FIGURE 3: Urban Resilience Pillars.

retrofit, and restore the important functions of the community that keeps it moving. On a individual level money of course equals access to resources, power and prestige and the same holds true for a community. Yet other factors, beyond just wealth are important to consider in terms of economic capital.

The role in economic terms for community resiliency entails making sure a community's wealth increases its citizen's standard of living for the present and the future. This is done though a few key ways. First, the level of economic resources is important meaning that levels of corporate taxation, property tax, business turnover as well as other standard economic variables. A second important aspect is the degree of equality in the distribution of resources. A resilient economic structure will not have huge disparities between the poorest economic members in a society and the wealthiest economic members of the society, hence the polar the level of wealth in a community the less economic resilient that community becomes. Lastly the scale of diversity of economic resources is important. The more diverse area's economic resources the easier a community can weather an economic storm. One only needs to look at already mentioned City of Detroit and the collapse of the blue collar car industry to see how the lack of economic diversification can create significant vulnerabilities in an urban area (Sherrieb et al, 2010).

Courtesy Stephen Buckman

**Abandoned Michigan Train Station:
Symbol of the power and decay of Detroit.**

Social Capital

Another important area to judge a community's resiliency is by examining its social capital. This is especially important in times of distress such as in federal post disaster recovery, where the brunt of the actual on the ground recovery effort, enabled by federal subsidies, is often taken up not by the government but by the local community. The context of social capital involves the level of citizen participation, place attachment and a sense of community. It is premised on the fact that communities have many other resources that are not economically driven but rather are based on social, spiritual, cultural and political foundations (Magis, 2010). As Putnam (2001) and others have shown the stronger social capital is the more balanced a community is in terms of mutual aid and non-governmental support and invariably the weaker a community's social capital is, the more that community is susceptible to collapse.

There are three types of social capital that are important in terms of community resiliency. The first of these is bonding, which entails the close ties and cohesion of groups within a community. The second is bridging, which entails the loose ties that groups in a community have with each other. The third important aspect vertical linkage between groups usually lower economically with those with more power, is important for poorer communities to tap into resources (Magis, 2010). Thus social capital is about social support, social participation and community bonds (Sherrieb et al, 2010).

Engaging in these approaches, especially from the evolutionary perspective, the idea of social resilience becomes the foundation for which community resiliency can be built. Social resilience in essence is the ability for groups to cope with and adapt to disturbances as a result of social, political and environmental change (Wilson, 2012). A strong community then will development adaptive capacity that harnesses social, economic, ecological, and community resources in an ever evolving process to deal with change. In a sense by instilling social resilience planners that are looking to establish resilient communities are taking a proactive position rather than a reactive position.

A prime example of both economic and social resiliency in action is the "Local First" movement. Local First is an economic and social campaign that communities under take to keep economic and social resources local. This entails employing local labor, eating from local farms, buying from local companies and in turn circulating money locally. This type of local buying and producing creates a greater pride in one's local area and connection with the local community and insulates communities form economic shocks that take place outside of the community. An example of this is Local First of Western Michigan which encourages local consumption in the Western Michigan region. As stated on their webpage their mission is "to foster the development of an economy, grounded in local ownership, which functions in harmony with our ecosystem, meets the basic needs of our people, encourages joyful community life, and builds wealth" (Local First) The economic impact as stated by localfirst.com can be seen in Figure 4 which shows the impact to the local community in economic terms of buying locally.

Environmental Capital

Urban landscapes are subject to a rapid rate of change, continuing disturbances, and complex interactions between various processes. This together with landscape

Opera de Arame: Wire framed opera house in a former quarry as part of the Curitiba park system.

fragmentation affects the capacity of urban landscapes to continue to generate ecosystem services that sustain urban quality of life.

Original ecosystems can play an important role to prevent various shocks and disturbances, especially natural disasters. For example the disappearance of wetlands and the barrier islands south of the City of New Orleans has been identified as a major factor in the devastation from Hurricane Katrina because it failed to offer a natural barrier to coastal flooding. It is often that during the planning process some features of natural landscapes are ignored that can lead to vulnerable condition of communities. For instance, in many cases of flooding, the original shape of river valley of its historical path has been ignored during urban development. However, there is an opposite example in the famous city of Curitiba in Brazil with its Seasonal Parks. Curitiba's Seasonal Parks were designed respecting natural flow of rivers that transformed flood plains into useful and beautiful parks using natural adaptive capacity of ecosystems. Allowing for dual purpose of protecting the city from flooding and establishing beautiful parks that have become recreational areas for citizens and tourists with facilities such as restaurants, amusement parks, and other services that offset the economic costs of park construction.

The built environment and infrastructure is also an important adaptive capacity. For instance, the physical location of roads, railways, airport, etc has a significant influence on the flow of commerce and people in and out of cites, which is important during a period of crisis. New urban development should focus on changing the built environment in line with changing needs and requirements of urban populations providing them opportunities for prevent and avoid any harm during various kinds of disturbances. New innovative means of urban complexity are needed to exclude major vulnerabilities.

Adaptive Governance and Collaborative Planning

There is a need for new flexible, integrated, holistic forms of governance that can deal with the complexity of urban areas, and their associated services. New challenges of urban development require networks and institutions that are able to capture and share knowledge in a transparent way, adapt to social, ecological, economical, political changes and built capacity for long term observation, monitoring and perspective. The roles of local, regional and international governance and institutional structures need to increasingly take into account collaborative participatory approaches through development of adaptive co-management and community self-management, including the development of academic initiatives (Resilience Alliance, 2007b).

Adaptive co-management is an emerging approach for governance of urban areas where all mentioned characteristics could be combined. If adaptive management is a systematic management paradigm that assumes natural resource management policies and actions are not static, but are adjusted based on the combination of new scientific

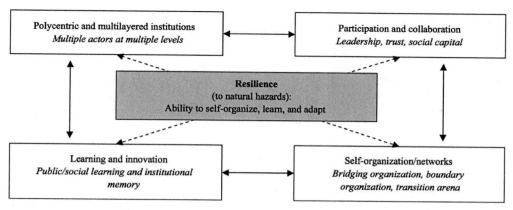

FIGURE 4: Adaptive Governance Linkages.

and socio-economic information, adaptive co-management combines the learning dimension of adaptive management and the linkage dimension of collaborative management in which rights and responsibilities are jointly shared. Multiple stakeholders participate in learning and developing a shared understanding about establishing goals, objectives, and management decisions.

Adaptive co-management promotes place-specific governance approaches in which strategies are sensitive to social and ecological feedback and oriented towards urban resilience and sustainability (Olsson et al, 2004). Thus adaptive co-management allows for open flows of information for a well-functioning recovery process during and after a disaster situation. When individuals see that that there is a well working government that communicates freely and openly with the community, individuals and NGOs have a better sense that the governance and community structure will properly deal with adversity (Norris et al, 2007).

Yet even before an actual disaster event, communication and empowerment become important. One of the most effective ways to achieve these levels of communication is through open participation within the governance process. An example of this is the collaborative planning process when constructing a master or disaster plan. In contrast to a traditional top-down approach to planning, collaborative planning allows citizens to have open dialogue with the planning commission and city council.

In essence collaborative planning allows for multiple viewpoints to come to the table. As Margerum (2011: 6) states, "collaboration is an approach to solving complex problems in which a diverse group of autonomous stakeholders deliberate to build consensus and development networks for translating consensus into results." What is especially valued in planning of this nature—at least by scholars promoting collaborative planning—is candid and explicit discussions that break down power hierarchies (Brand et al, 2007). Toward that end, collaborative planning involves four key variables to achieve success: stakeholders who spend time understanding the problems; a deliberative process between stakeholders that allows everyone to debate the issues; consensus among stakeholders and the public; and networks that can translate consensus into results (Margerum, 2011). This form of planning helps to empower disenfranchised members of the community and allows for further transparency which opens veins of communication which is a key aspect of community resilience.

Resilience Indicators and Rankings

To measure urban resilience is not an easy task. One of the biggest scientific topics is how to measure urban resilience and find the gaps where governance solutions are needed. One way to assess urban resilience is by its qualities to cope with future challenges. The Building Resilient Regions network in 2011 has developed a tool called the Resilience Capacity Index (RCI) which is a single statistic summarizing a region's score on 12 equally weighted indicators—four indicators in each of three dimensions encompassing Regional Economic (income, quality economic diversification, regional affordability and business environment), Socio-Demographic (educational attainment, lack of disability and poverty, high level of health insurance), and Community Connectivity attributes (civic infrastructure, metropolitan stability, homeownerships, voter participation). RCI reveals strengths and weaknesses of 361 United States metropolitan areas allows regional leaders to compare their region's capacity profile to that of other metropolitan areas.

The collaborative urban planning process.

If we take into account the RCI, areas in the North and Midwest of the U.S. tend to have higher scores of index in contrast to the lower propensity of resilience capacity in the south and southwest states. High RCI can be found in slow-growing regions where metropolitan stability, regional affordability, homeownerships, and income equality is usually higher. And opposite are metropolitan areas with rapid growth of population in southern and western states.

Rochester, MN, Bismarck, ND and Minneapolis-St. Paul, MN-WI were ranked highest in term of overall resilience. However, having the capacity to be resilient is no guarantee that in the face of a stress the region will effectively respond to and recover from the disturbance. Having higher capacity does imply, however, that the region has factors and conditions thought to position a region well for effective post-stress resilience performance. Lacking capacity to be resilient is no sentence that a region will falter in the face of a stress. Having lower capacity does imply, however, that the region lacks factors and conditions thought to position a region well for effective post-stress resilience performance.

Grovesnor Group, an international development and management company, in 2014 released a report on international ranking of cities in terms of resilience. In this ranking resilience comes from the interplay of vulnerability and adaptive capacity. Vulnerability and adaptive capacity for each of 50 cities was defined through five main themes: for vulnerability - climate, environment, resources, infrastructure and community characteristics; for adaptive capacity – governance, institution, technical and learning features, planning system and funding structures.

According to the report, the three most resilient cities in the world are in Canada. Canadian cities have a strong combination of low vulnerability and high adaptive capacity. There is a high level of resource availability, and Canadian cities are well governed and well planned.

Most U.S. cities do not score particularly well in our vulnerability rankings. Social inequality in US cities leads to social tension, utilities lack investment, and urban sprawl leads to the over consumption of land resources. However, adaptive capacity of US cities is quite high, where resources, public accountability of elected officials and the technology of the US are dominating factors.

Most European cities fall into middle of the ranking. For example, London is 18th in the ranking: it suffers increasingly from social tensions due to lack of affordable housing, but it has relatively strong institutional capacity and the ability to track progress of government policies. The weakest European cities are Moscow, Milan and Madrid; the strongest are Zurich, Amsterdam and Frankfurt.

The weakest 20 cities are in developing countries. Recent economic growth so far did not lead to the quality and long term resilience of these cities. Vulnerability in these cities derives from inequality, poor infrastructure provision and environmental degradation, and, to a lesser extent, climate vulnerability. Invariably,, these cities are weak in all of the dimensions of adaptive capacity.

Lessons Learned

This chapter has been geared to introduce the concept of resiliency it pertains to urban systems. Key lessons that should have been learned in this chapter include:

1. That community resilience deals with both abrupt shocks to the urban system such as a natural disaster akin to Hurricane Katrina but just as important and often times harder to plan for are slow-burns such as the impact of climate change which includes the increase in temperature, droughts and economic impacts such as the slow loss of a manufacturing base.

2. Urban environments are socio-spatial systems that are unpredictable and thus must be looked at in terms of bouncing forward not back bouncing back. Thus adaptation and the adaptive cycle which constitutes a series of changes that rebalances the system only to start anew, are key to understanding resiliency. Implying that resilience is a constantly moving situation that is relies on change as its life source.

3. Resiliency is composed of various pillars that together strengthen the larger whole. These key pillars or approaches to resilience can be categorized into four major views, resilience as **stability**, **recovery**, **transformation**, and **adaptation**, with the common thread being the ability to withstand and respond positively to stress or change.

As stated throughout this chapter resiliency thinking is beginning and will continue to play a greater role in the way we plan for and adapt to issues of changing economic, social and environmental impacts in our cities. The static view of planning our cities that was dependent on predicted models no longer holds true, now the name of the game is unpredictability and resiliency thinking allows for urban regions to combat and adapt to times of unpredictability.

Supplemental Readings

Kapucu, N, C. Hawkins and F. Rivera (eds) 2013. *Disaster Resiliency: Interdisciplinary Perspectives.* London: Routledge

Pearson, L., P. Newton and P. Roberts, 2013. *Resilient Sustainable Cities: A Future.* London: Routledge

Wilson, G., 2012. *Community Resilience and Environment Transitions.* London: Routledge

Urban Ecology, Green Networks and Ecological Design

Edward Cook

Introduction

This chapter examines how the scientific field of **urban ecology** and the emerging planning concept of **green networks** and **ecological design** can contribute to making cities more sustainable. The scientific basis and relevance of urban ecology for sustainable cities is reviewed and an overview of green networks and ecological design is provided with discussion of particular challenges and opportunities of working with this concept in urban settings. The importance of **hierarchy in ecology** and planning for green networks is illustrated through exploration of multi-scalar plans that range from continental to individual local sites. A set of examples are provided that illustrate how urban ecological design helps realize the goal of creating more sustainable cities. Finally, a discussion is provided that clarifies how linking science, policy, planning, and design can ultimately lead to making green networks and ecologically designed sites in cities a reality providing a foundation for urban sustainability.

Urban ecology - The study of the interactions of organisms and their environment in an urban context

Green networks - The system of interconnected patches and corridors that provide and sustain ecological functions and values within human-dominated landscapes

Hierarchy in ecology - The order of interactions and relationships within an environment

Urban and Landscape Ecology

The scientific field of ecology focuses on the study of interactions between organisms and their environment. Historically, ecologists have largely tended to study organisms within more natural ecosystems and have undertaken less research in **human-dominated ecosystems**, such as cities. With global shifts toward increasing urbanization and the understanding that impacts on the environment are seldom contained locally, in recent decades urban and landscape ecology have emerged as important topics of increasing interest to ecologists, urban and regional planners and designers, landscape architects, social scientists and others.

Human-dominated ecosystems - Ecosystems that are managed and transformed by Humans

The integration of ecology in planning and design of cities took hold in the late 1960's as a result of the environmental movement and contributions of a number of influential academics and practitioners. In 1969, Ian McHarg, a professor of landscape architecture and urban and regional planning at the University of Pennsylvania, published his seminal book "Design with Nature," issuing a plea for integrating ecological thinking into planning and design decisions for cities and regional landscapes. He also articulated a method for gathering, analyzing and synthesizing ecological information to inform planning and design decisions. Several others who studied and worked with McHarg continue to contribute to the development of ecological planning and design. Frederick Steiner, currently Dean of the School of Architecture at the University of Texas at Austin, is making ongoing contributions to the development of ideas and applications of ecological planning and design. He is among the most prolific writers on this topic with numerous books and articles of his own (see The Living Landscape: An Ecological Approach to Landscape Planning 2002; Human Ecology: Following Nature's Lead, 2002; Design for a Vulnerable Planet, 2011) but also leads a growing effort to document exemplary work that demonstrates ecological planning and design as it is realized. Michael Hough, another disciple of McHarg and founder and former head of the landscape architecture program at the University of Toronto, developed an urban focus to his ecological planning and design work through his practice and his contributions as an educator and author. He took the lessons of McHarg's approach to ecological planning to the city and helped transform sterile urban environments into living urban ecosystems. His book, City Form and Natural Process (1984), laid a foundation for many others who then saw the potential of the city to become a living and much more sustainable environment. John Tillman Lyle, a professor of landscape architecture at California State Polytechnic University in Pomona (CSPU Pomona), made important contributions through the establishment of the Center for Regenerative Studies at CSPU Pomona to explore and test theories and principles of regenerative design as articulated in his books "Design for Human Ecosystems" (1985) and "Regenerative Design for Sustainable Development" (1995).

In addition to the efforts of planners and designers, ecologists have crossed into the realm of urban planning and design to provide greater levels of scientific understanding as a basis for making decisions about the future of cities. Richard T.T. Forman's books Landscape Ecology (1984), Land Mosaics (1995), Urban Regions: Ecology and Planning (2008) and Urban Ecology: Science of Cities (2008) are now used regularly by planners and designers as they incorporate more knowledge about how ecosystems work and how human interactions with natural systems change the dynamics and in turn the relationships that exist. Forman, an ecologist, is a professor in the Harvard University Graduate School of Design and works with landscape architects, urban designers and architects informing the planning and design process with sound ecological science. Following this model, teams of scientists, planners and designers are being formed to work on urban ecological problems in an attempt to increase the potential for urban sustainability. New movements are emerging that are embracing nature in the city, recognizing that humans and nature must inevitably co-exist in the same space discarding old notions that humans and nature are better separated or managed independently. Timothy Beatley's growing organization promoting biophilic cities (see insert by Beatley) and other efforts that are increasing "urban wildness" by fostering urban woodlands, re-naturalizing or re-wilding rivers or re-creating urban meadows are embracing the idea of true forms of nature occupying the same space as humans.

Ecological functions - The interactions that occur between organisms and their environment

Cities impact **ecological functions** in many ways. Alberti (2005, p. 169) notes that urbanization "fragments, isolates and degrades natural habitat; simplifies homogeneous species composition; disrupts hydrological systems; and modifies energy flow

BOX 1: Imagining Biophilic Cities—(Tim Beatley)

That we need daily contact with nature to be healthy, productive individuals, and indeed have co-evolved with nature, is a critical insight of Harvard myrmecologist and conservationist E.O. Wilson. Wilson popularised the term *biophilia* two decades ago to describe the extent to which humans need connection with nature and other forms of life. More specifically, Wilson describes it this way: "Biophilia . . . is the innately emotional affiliation of human beings to other living organisms. Innate means hereditary and hence part of ultimate human nature."[1]

To Wilson, biophilia is really a "complex of learning rules" developed over thousands of years of evolution and human-environment interaction: "For more than 99 percent of human history people have lived in hunter-gatherer bands totally and intimately involved with other organisms. During this period of deep history, and still further back they depended on an exact learned knowledge of crucial aspects of natural history . . . In short, the brain evolved in a biocentric world, not a machine-regulated world. It would be therefore quite extraordinary to find that all learning rules related to that world have been erased in a few thousand years, even in the tiny minority of peoples who have existed for more than one or two generations in wholly urban environments."[2]

Stephen Kellert of Yale University reminds us that this natural inclination to affiliate with nature and the biological world constitutes "'weak' genetic tendency whose full and functional development depends on sufficient experience, learning, and cultural support".[3] Biophilic sensibilities can atrophy and society plays an important role in recognising and nurturing them.

The Nature of Cities

While we are already designing biophilic *buildings* and the immediate spaces around them, we must increasingly imagine biophilic *cities,* and should support a new kind of biophilic *urbanism.* As the planet barrels rapidly down the path of urbanisation the need for green and *nature-ful* cities is an ever more urgent need.

There is already much nature in cities, of course, more than we realise. It is both big and small, visible and hidden. It is intricate, yet sweeping. It is amazing in its biological functioning, ever-present yet highly dynamic, and vastly underappreciated for its ubiquity in cities. In understanding the nature of cities it is necessary to think beyond our usual approach to visualising or imaging space and place, and to understand that nature is everywhere in cities if we look: it is above us, flying or floating by, it is below our feet in cracks in the pavement, or in the diverse micro-organic life of soil and leaf litter. Nature reaches our senses, well beyond sight, in the sounds, smells, textures, and feelings of wind and sun. Understanding the natural history of a city helps us to see cities as ever-changing. Ever-evolving palettes of life.

In the higher reaches of our cities, the rooftops and façades also harbour nature, sometimes by design, and sometimes by accident and naturel volunteerism. New forms of nature are being created in cities all over the nation in the form

Continued

of ecological rooftops and rooftop gardens, hosting grasses and sedum, and increasingly found (over time and with the right design elements) to harbour great diversity in terms of invertebrates, bird and plant life. We know, for instance, that butterfly species will visit rooftops on high-rise structures, and food, for humans and nature alike, can be grown here as well.

This nature in cities is the raw ingredient for a new global urban society organised around wonder. Few have made a more compelling and eloquent plea for the importance of wonder in the natural world than Rachel Carson more than half a century ago. In a 1956 essay entitled "Help Your Child to Wonder", she describes the value and pleasures of exposing her young nephew to the nature found along the Maine coast: "If I had influence with the good fairy who is supposed to preside over the christening of all children I should ask that her gift to each child in the world be a sense of wonder so indestructible that it would last throughout life, as an unfailing antidote against the boredom and disenchantments of later years, the sterile preoccupation with things that are artificial, the alienation from the sources of our strength."[4]

Carson counsels looking at the sky, taking walks, uncovering and experiencing nature, even if (as parents) we are not able ourselves to identify a species or a constellation. It is about cultivating an awareness of the sights, sounds, natural rhythms around us, paying attention and learning to see the mystery and beauty in everything around us.

We need wonder and awe in our lives, and nature has the potential to amaze us, stimulate us, people us forward to want to learn more about our world. The qualities of wonder and fascination, the ability to nurture deep personal connection and involvement, visceral engagement in something larger than and outside ourselves, offers the potential for meaning in life few other things can provide.

My landscape architecture colleague Beth Meyer argues that with matters of environment and sustainability we need also to emphasise the beauty and pleasure and enjoyment we derive. We often forget about the aesthetics, or try to reduce them to monetary values. At the end of the day, watching that circling hawk or turkey vulture, walking or bicycling through an urban woods, harvesting and eating produce from one's garden, listening to the sounds of kadydids and tree frogs on a humid August evening, are deeply pleasurable: they are the building blocks of a life enjoyed. We climb trees as kids because this is a fun and enjoyable thing to do, and as adults unfortunately we often forget these pleasures (and of course rarely climb trees!).

In our recent documentary film *Nature of Cities* we spent a stimulating several days in Austin, Texas, filming the 1.5 million Mexican free-tailed bats that have inhabited the underside of the city's Congress Avenue bridge during the summer months. People line-up hours before nightfall to get a good look at the wondrous columns of bats emerging from the bridge. Merlin Tuttle, founder of Bat Conservation International (BCI), dutifully recites the many environmental (and economic) benefits provided the city by these bats. And they are considerable, including the millions of mosquitoes they eat each day. But ultimately the sight of thousands of bats flying off in distinct columns that can be seen for several miles, is an immense and beautiful thing. It is the raw emotion and beauty of the natural word, a primordial spectacle unfolding against a backdrop of high-rise buildings and a human-dominated (at least we think) urban environment.

In many American cities the biodiversity is aquatic and sometimes offshore, as in Seattle, which has abundant and wondrous life in the not-far depths of the Bay and Sound. Much of the biodiversity of King Country, in which the City of Seattle lies, is found in the "deep subtidal habitat" of Puget Sound in some places almost 900 feet below the surface, and including "over 500 benthic and 50 pelagic invertebrates."[5] And while some are known and recognisable to residents, such as the king crab, many are not. That the Seattle metro region is also home to such unique marine critters as the giant Pacific octopus and giant Acorn Barnacle suggests a wildness and mystery very close at hand.

And new forms of nature can be fostered in the many leftover spaces of the city. A visit to the Green Roofs Research Center, in Malmo, Sweden, shows the extent of possibilities–here they have planted and monitor hundreds of green roof test plots, testing different plant and soil combinations. Some of these plots are for so-called brown rooftops-places in the urban environments (there are many) were plants can be used to restore end even take up pollutants in highly contaminated and degraded settings (Phytoremediation). And the Malmo centre's immense research rooftop also shows the potential of different, sometimes surprising delivery methods–their standard green roof, as Trevor Graham who runs many of the centre's green city efforts explains, is made from recycled polyurethane car seats, and in several places there are small mounted frames, with sedum growing vertically, showing the potential for a kind of natural artwork suitable for hanging in one's living room!

These new forms of nature are catching on, and are now encouraged and in some places mandated by codes, and we will see more of this happening in every city around the world. And new creative developments in cities–such as *Via Verde* (the green way), a 200-unit complex of affordable housing planned for a 1.5-acre site in the South Bronx of New York–will find many ways to insert and grow nature. In this case, the nature takes the form of a connected multi-functional garden "that begins at street-level as a courtyard and plaza, and spirals upward through a series of programmed, south-facing roof gardens that end in a sky terrace".[6] Increasingly biophilic cities will understand rooftops, courtyards, and façades as places to cultivate nature.

What is a Biophilic City?

Exactly what is a biophilic city, and what are its key features and qualities? Perhaps the simplest answer is that it is a city that puts nature first in its design, planning and management it recognises the essential need for daily human contact with nature as well as the many environmental and economic values provided by nature and natural systems.

A biophilic city is at its heart a *biodiverse* city, a city full of nature: a place where in the normal course of work and play and life residents feel, see, and experience rich nature–plants, trees, animals. The nature is both large and small–from tree-top

Continued

lichens, invertebrates, even microorganisms, to larger natural features and ecosystems that define a city and give it its character and feel. Biophilic cities cherish what already exists in and near cities (and there is much as we have already seen) but also work hard to restore and repair what has been lost or degraded, and to integrate new forms of nature into the design of every new structure or built project. We need contact with nature, and that nature can also take the form of shapes and images, integrated into building designs, as we will see.

A biophilic city ought to be judged by the existence of nature and natural features, but also in some way its biophilic sensibilities or *spirit:* how important is nature and how central to the lives and *modus operandi* of the city, its leaders and its populace? A bit harder to quantify, this *biophilic spirit* or sensibility, suggests a value dimension the sense that residents and public officials alike recognise the importance and centrality of nature to a rich and sustainable urban life. This quality could easily fit as both an activity and an approach to governance.

Every city will have its natural spectacles–some large, others more nuanced–but a biophilic city is one that pays attention, a city that sees and conveys this sense of beauty and wonder and caring. It may be the running of the Steelhead trout in the Niagara River, or the appearance of Orcas in Price William Sound, or the migratory return of robins along the east coast of the US. A biophilic city celebrates this wonder and sees in these events the opportunity to connect, to strengthen bonds to mark the cycles of life and seasonality. This celebrating often involves the direct experience of that biodiversity and nature, such as watching migratory birds, or visiting a park or green area, or it might be a more referential form of biophilic expression.

As the accompanying Table 1 suggests, how actively citizens enjoy the nature around them and actively participate in this nature is also an important measure of a biophilic city. Participation is an interesting word to use here because it implies a level active engagement beyond just passively observing something: it suggests a keen and active interest in the subject Citizens or a biophilic city, and their leaders, are not removed from nature around them, but are highly aware of it and present in its midst. A biophilic city is a city in which a large percentage of its population is actively enjoying nature. This enjoyment and engagement can take many different forms. of course from walking and hiking in natural areas, to bird-watching and plant and tree identification, to organised nature events and activities, from fungi forays to nature festivals.

Biophilic cities help to make it easier to enjoy nature and reflect an understanding that exposure to and enjoyment of nature are key aspects of a pleasurable and meaningful life. There are many potential outlets and venues for our need to connect with nature, and most are also intensely social. Facilitating contact with nature has the great potential to help create new friendships and build social networks, in turn helping to make urbanites healthier and happier. In San Diego, the activities of a number of "friends" of the canyons help to conserve and protect the canyon as a neighbourhood and community resource, but also provide opportunities for neighbours to interact and socialise in a way and to an extent that would otherwise not occur. In the Rose Canyon, for instance, residents from different sides of the

TABLE 1: Some Important Dimensions of Biophilic Cities (and Some Possible Indicators)

Biophilic Conditions and Infrastructure
- Percentage of population within a few hundred feet of metres of a park or green space
- Percentage of city land area covered by trees or other vegetation
- Number of green design features (e.g. green rooftops, green walls, rain gardens)
- Extent of natural images, shapes, forms employed in architecture, and seen in the city
- Extent of flora and fauna (e.g. species) found within the city

Biophilic Behaviours, Patterns, Practices, Lifestyles
- Average portion of the day spent outside
- Visitation rates for city parks
- Percent of trips made by walking
- Extent of membership and participation in local nature clubs and organisations

Biophilic Attitudes and knowledge
- Percent of residents who express care and concern for nature
- Percent of residents who can identify common species of flora and fauna

Biophilic Institutions and Governance
- Priority given to nature conservation by local government; percent of municipal budget dedicated to biophilic programmes
- Existence of design and planning regulations that promote biophilic conditions (e.g. mandatory green rooftop requirement, bird-friendly building design guidelines)
- Presence and importance of institutions, from aquaria to natural history museums, that promote education and awareness of nature
- Number/extent of educational programmes in local schools aimed at teaching about nature
- Number of nature organisations and clubs of various sorts in the city, from advocacy to social groups

Source: Beatley, 2010

canyon have places and opportunities to converse and come together, something that would have been difficult without the pull of nearby nature.

Cities must also begin to see the value and importance of facilitating such connections with nature, and perhaps offering help and support in the Australian Bushcare model. Here local groups of citizens and community volunteers organise around a specific urben ecosystem–a patch of green space, a stream, a park–and with the help of a municipal staff person ("bushcare officer" usually), spend weekends and spare hours cleaning up, repairing, and tending over these spaces. The result is not only ecological repaid, but also making friends and the rebuilding of community, as well as becoming more embedded in place and environment.

Creatively involving citizens in the conducting of science is another way to intimately engage people with the nature around them. In San Diego, citizens have been trained to become "parabotanists" (like paralegals), helping to collect plant specimens in this highly biodiverse country. There are now 200 citizens serving as parabotanists, working to collect plant data for the San Diego Country Plant Atlas Project (begun in 2002). The project records plants on a three-square-mile grid. Parabotanists are now steered to collecting on grid squares where less plant date exists. Once they sign up for a square they are mailed maps and permits from the Museum. A biodiversity "hotspot" and most floristically biodiverse county in the US, recording and protecting this biodiversity takes on special importance. The

Continued

Plant Atlas will eventually result in an "internet-accessible, plant atlas based upon vouchered specimens". There are more than 1,500 native species of plants in San Diego County and so there is much to document and record, and citizens here play an important role. Volunteers go through training by San Diego Natural History Museum, and once trained, collect and press the plants and record date about the plant's location. A museum botanist verifies the plant's identification.

A biophilic city then is a city with an extensive and robust *social capital,* to extend Robert Putnam's concept.[7] Evidence is compelling that we need extensive friendships and social contact to be healthy and happy, as well as our contact with nature, so finding creative ways to combine these needs becomes an important goal in the biophilic city. I have been calling this *natural* social capital, acknowledging that there are many ways that learning about and experiencing nature can also help to nurture friendships and help to overcome the increasing levels of social isolation felt at least by Americans. How many social organisations or clubs, or community events or activities, explicitly focus around the unique nature of cities? The extent of creative social possibilities is almost limitless: weekend fungi forays, wildlife tracking clubs, *bioblitzes* and nature festivals, wildflower and birding clubs, among many others.

Judging what happens is often a function of the range of the organisations, some public, some private, that exist in a city and that can help in supporting the educating and engagement of citizens. One measure of a biophilic city is the extent of the organisational support, the quality and reach of the biophilic organisations that exist in a city that can actively work towards nature. Bird watching and nature hikes through the city might be one option, but there should be many: swimming, canoeing, and kayaking in urban waters, visiting parks near and far, experiencing nature on a sidewalk or rooftop or building façade as one walks to work or to the subway, among many others.

Many cities around the world are located on or near water bodies and a measure of their biophilic tendencies is how easy it is for residents to enjoy these aquatic environments. In some cities such as Boston, non-profit organisations have worked to make it economic and easy to learn how to sail. In that city a junior sailing programme run by the non-profit Community Boating Inc offers kids the chance to learn how to sail for only $1, for the entire June-August season. Many American cities, moreover, have worked hard to reestablish direct physical contact and connection with rivers, creeks, harbours, through waterfront parks and trails and opportunities to get out on a kayak or canoe.

Biophilic cities are cities that work to expand the opportunities to spend time outside and in close proximity to nature. Partly this means rethinking the ways parks and green spaces are used. New York City has been a leader in creating opportunities for urbanites to camp on weekends in city parks. The programme occurs in the summer months and is quite popular. In 2009, family camping took place in every borough of the city. These camping evenings are especially from the perspective of kids quite enjoyable and exciting. The City's Parks and Recreation Department provides the tents and sleeping bags, and there are typically barbeques, night hikes, skywatching and even S'mores!

Biophilic cities are to be identified not just by the presence or absence of nature, of green spaces, and green infrastructure, but other forms of investment that also facilitates a biophilic life. A biophilic city invests in a robust network of public (and private) institutions that will educate about, restore and protect, and nudge residents toward enjoying nature. These include traditional environmental education and natural science institutions such as local botanical gardens, zoological parks, and natural history museums, among others. Environmental education centres have been very effective in some cities, and in some cases based in urban neighborhoods.

And biophilic cities are also concerned about and work to protect nature beyond their borders. Each city has opportunities to express care about the environment and other life in the world. Large cities exert a tremendous pressure on global biodiversity through their material flows and consumption patterns, and one measure of a biophilic city is the extent to which it seeks to moderate or reduce those impacts.

New York City, for instance, has recently acknowledged that it purchases a large amount of tropical hardwoods, an estimated $1 million worth each year. The city uses this wood–South American species such as *Ipe* and *Garapa*–for such things as benches, boardwalks, and ferry landings. The ten-mile long Brooklyn Bridge Promenade is constructed of *Greenheart,* another South American hardwood. In recognition of the destructive impact of such purchases Mayor Bloomberg announced a plan in 2008 to significantly reduce the city's purchasing of such wood–a 20 percent reduction immediately and larger reductions later as the city researches and pilots alternative wood sources and alternative materials that could be used.[8] Describing tropical deforestation as an "ecological calamity", and noting that it may be responsible for as much as 20 percent green-house gas emissions. Mayor Bloomberg has made an eloquent plea for cities to become better stewards of the global environment. "New Yorkers don't live in the rain forest. But we do live in a world that we share. And we're committed to doing everything we can to protect it for all of our children."[9] City purchasing policies and decisions is an important opportunity for biophilic values to gain expression.

Biophilic Cities In Our Future?

What constitutes a biophilic city is still very much a matter of discussion and debate. Less a definitive list or set of principles, the categories described above are meant to identify at least some of the potential building blocks of a biophilic city. It is unlikely that a singular coherent vision of a biophilic city will emerge. Rather, perhaps there are many different *kinds* of biophilic cities, and many different expressions of urban biophilia. And they might be expressed by different combinations and emphases of the qualities and conditions described here. At the simplest level, through, a biophilic city is a city that seeks to foster a closeness to nature–it protects and nurtures what it has (understands that abundant wild nature is usually a lot), actively restores and repairs the nature that exists, while at the same time finding new and creative ways to insert and inject nature into the streets, buildings, and urban living environments. And a biophilic city is an outdoor city, a city that makes walking and strolling and daily exposure to the outside elements and weather possible and a priority.

Continued

But as the above discussion also indicates a biophilic city is not just about its physical conditions or natural setting, and it is not just about green design and ecological interventions–it is just as much about a city's underlying biophilic spirit and sensibilities, about its funding priorities, and about the importance placed on support for programmes that entice urbanites to learn more about the nature around them. A biophilic city might be measured and assessed more by how curious its citizens are about the nature around them, and the extent to which they are engaged in daily activities to enjoy and care for nature, than more the physical qualities or conditions, or for instance the number or acres of parks and green spaces per capita that exists in a city.

There are a variety of important research questions about designing and planning biophilic cities in the future. We still have, for instance, relatively little knowledge of the *cumulative* recuperative and healing powers of urban nature. How do the many smaller green features in a city or urban neighbourhood contribute to our closeness with nature and what are the interactive effects? Is access to a large forest more effective than a neighbourhood full of smaller green features, such as street trees and green rooftops? And what is the actual daily minimum level of nature needed by urbanites, and in what form, to live a healthy life?

There are also a host of research questions that relate to how effective our biophilic strategies in fact are–what are the most effective planning and policies for getting people outside? What will it take to nudge urban populations to adopt a more outdoor nature-oriented lifestyle? As well, our very understanding of the science and ecology of cities remains quite limited and there is much work to be done here as well. New research is needed to better understand the biology and lifecycles of fauna found in cities and how it changes or is modified in an urban setting (e.g. think of coyotes!), as well as the management implications therein. There are many, almost countless, research questions and opportunities that arise from the agenda of biophilic cities.

A major task in the future, certainly for those in city planning and urban design, will be in offering an alternative future vision of cities and urban neighbourhoods. As Stephen Kellert of Yale University has said: "We need to do more than just avoid all the bad things that we have done in terms of our adverse effects on natural systems. We also have to create the context for thriving, for development, for meaningful exchange with the world around us, and the people around us, And for that we need to restore that sense of relationship with the natural world which has always been the cradle of our creativity."[10] That vision will be of dense, sustainable, walkable cities, and places that are also full of nature, and are profoundly restorative, magical, and wondrous.

References

1. Wilson, E.O. 1993. "Biophilia and the Conservation Ethic," in Kellert and Wilson, *The Biophilia Hypothesis*, Washington, DC: Island Press.

2. Wilson, op cit, p. 32.

3. Stephen Kellert, *Building for Life: Designing and Understanding the Human-Nature Connection*, Washington, DC: Island Press, 2006, p. 4.

4. Rachel Carson. "Help Your Child to Wonder," *Woman's Home Companion,* July, 1956, p. 46.

5. King County, Washington, King County Biodiversity Report, 2008, p. 57.

6. New Housing, New York Legacy Project, "Phipps-Rose-Dattner-Grimshaw Selected to Develop City-Owned Site in South Bronx," press release, January 17, 2007.

7. Robert Putnam, *Bowling Alone: The Collapse and Revival of American Community,* Simon and Shuster, 2001.

8. See "Mayor Announce Plan to Reduce the Use of Tropical Hardwoods." February 11, 2008. found at www.NYC.gov, accessed on February 17, 2009.

9. ibid.

10. Stephen Kellert interview, in *The Nature of Cities*, documentary film, 2009.

and nutrient cycling." **Urban ecosystems** and natural ecosystems have similar interactions. Urban ecosystems, however, are a blend of natural and human-created elements and as such, the interactions are significantly affected by human intervention as well as natural processes.

Integrating ecology into cities should be an important sustainability goal because: 1) it may help ameliorate human impacts on ecosystems, 2) it enhances **ecosystem services**, 3) it adds **biodiversity value** to cities, 4) it ensures equitable access to nature and resources, and 5) it maintains a healthy functioning planet for future generations. Urban and landscape ecology are interdisciplinary sciences dealing substantially with the interaction of natural and human processes (Forman and Godron, 1984; Forman, 1995). Landscape ecology addresses how spatial variation in the landscape affects ecological processes. Theories and applications provide a rigorous scientific methodology that can be integrated into urban planning, design processes, and urban sustainability policies, providing the bases for urban planning and design decisions that affect the sustainability of cities.

The goal of green networks and ecological design is to preserve or restore the ecological integrity of critical natural systems while allowing for compatible human activities while to continue productive use of the landscape for human benefit. **Ecological integrity** is a concept that refers to the health of an ecosystem or a landscape. It can be considered to be the level at which the system is functionally viable. Forman (1995) notes that to achieve ecological integrity, near-natural levels of production, biodiversity, soil, and water characteristics must be present. He also notes "ecological integrity could be measured as the single most important or sensitive attribute of an ecological system" (p. 499). As a measure for sustainable development the challenge becomes the quantification of the idea of "near-natural." It is quite simple to assess many areas and determine that they are not near-natural because of the evidence of excessive deterioration. But, because there are too many natural attributes that are often difficult to quantify, determining that areas are near-natural may be a major challenge.

Urban ecosystems - Dynamic ecosystems that have similar interactions and behaviors as natural ecosystems, but consist of a hybrid of natural and human-made elements whose interactions are affected not only by the natural environment, but also by culture, personal behavior, politics, economics and social organization

Ecosystem services - The combined outcomes of an ecosystem that are beneficial to humans and nature including processes such as the production of oxygen, decomposition of waste and the production of clean water

Biodiversity value - An intrinsic value of achieving biodiversity that is work protecting regardless of its value to humans

Ecological integrity - The healthy compositions, structure and functioning of an ecosystem consisting of near-natural levels of production, biodiversity, soil and water

Noss (2004) characterizes ecological integrity as an "umbrella concept," embracing all that is good and right in ecosystems. It encompasses other conservation values, including **biodiversity**, **ecological resilience**, and "naturalness." Noss also notes that although urban areas will never have the biodiversity, naturalness, and ecological resilience of pristine wilderness areas, there are reasonable standards that can be met. He outlines an index that considers composition, structure, and function of the urban ecosystem. These effectively align with the three basic tenets of landscape ecology: structure, function, and change. Utilizing these and other concepts from landscape ecology, planning and design strategies are developed within a nested hierarchy that relates to various levels of ecological functioning and correlated levels of human activity and management.

Landscape structure refers to the spatial and structural characteristics of the landscape. Vegetation, soils, hydrology (rivers, streams, lakes, etc.), and topographic conditions, including slope and landform, are all integral to understanding landscape structure. Landscape function refers to the interactions that occur between organisms and the environment. Landscape change occurs constantly. As living dynamic systems, landscapes are in a constant state of flux. These three concepts (landscape structure, function, and change) are interrelated and fundamental to understanding and working with urban ecosystems.

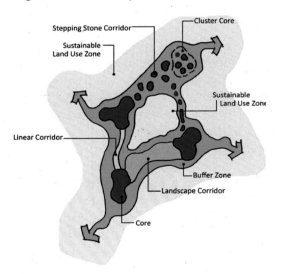

FIGURE 1: Conceptual Diagram of a Green Network.

Landscape structure includes patches, corridors, edges, and the matrix (see Figure 1). These are useful terms for describing and understanding the physical nature of landscape patterns. As was noted previously, landscape structure and function are interrelated and by understanding how landscape structure affects ecological functions, we can plan for spatial arrangements to facilitate ecological functions and restore or strengthen sustainable urban ecosystems. Patches are the irregularly shaped elements in the landscape mosaic whether it is developed or not, that differ from their surroundings. Corridors are linear elements that traverse the landscape mosaic and facilitate flows and connectivity between landscape elements. Connectivity, in ecological terms, refers to the interactions that occur between species and landscape structure across landscape elements.

Edges are those areas that bound patches and or corridors and are zones of critical interaction with adjacent ecosystems. There are a variety of types of patches and corridors and a range of different ways that edges accommodate interaction between ecosystems. By understanding landscape structure and the relative inherent ecological value of different types of patches and corridors, a process can be developed by which we can structure spatial arrangements on the landscape that facilitate high levels of ecological functioning and create opportunities for efficient, but ecological friendly land-use activities. Resilient urban ecosystems require effective balances of socio-ecological systems.

Ecological functioning occurs at many scales and is linked between scales. Many of the global environmental challenges we face today are a result of aggregation of many actions that have occurred on small scales but taken together have a global impact. It is also true that organisms function at numerous scales ranging from micro-biotic activity to interactions of meta-populations at broad scales. This hierarchy of systems doesn't always correlate between levels of ecological functioning and levels of government or other organizational structures that may be intended to manage land-use and environmental objectives. However, it is important to find ways to allow organizations at various scales to collaborate in order to facilitate the range of levels of ecological functioning that must occur to sustain ecosystems and continue to provide ecosystem services to the population. However, this often does not work. One goal in sustainability is to develop new institutional objectives for governance specifically for socio-ecological systems.

There are several deleterious effects of human habitation of the landscape that the concepts of green networks and ecological design are specifically intended to help mitigate, including problems resulting from fragmentation, isolation, and edge effects. Fragmentation of landscapes is a pervasive and significant problem. Prior to human occupation, natural systems were connected and sustained by the flows that occurred within and between various ecosystems. Examples of these flows are the movement of water through rivers, streams, and drainage corridors, the movement of air in and around various landscape elements, the migration of various organisms, and the associated movement of nutrients, energy, and genetic material.

For example, a river system does not just move water from one location to another through gravity flow. Along the way, drops of water moving to lower elevations carry particles of soil and other organic material. This sediment that the river accumulates is deposited along the way in various locations changing landscape structure, but also providing nutrient-rich soil for the germination of new plants that then become food and habitat for other organisms in different locations. Fish and other aquatic species move up and down rivers to lakes and the sea, become food themselves for other animals, and spawn to create new populations while adding nutrients to the ecosystem.

Many other types of flows are just as critical, but may not be so obvious. The movement of cold air from higher elevations to low-lying areas creates microclimatic variation in the landscape. Since cold air is denser than warm air, it naturally flows to lower elevations. The movement of this cold air creates cooler zones in which more cold hardy plant communities that differ from the surrounding areas can become established. This variation creates the opportunity for increased diversity and, as a result, a broader range of species and potential ecological value. Human interventions such as building roads across valleys, drainage corridors, or other low-lying areas can introduce blockages of cold air drainage changing the microclimate. This may lead to extinction of some species in these areas that require certain climatic conditions, ultimately increasing the level of fragmentation of ecosystems. Fragmentation leads to the isolation of various landscape elements and populations that inhabit them. Over time, isolated areas that are no longer connected to a larger supporting structure will decline in richness and diversity. Often the decline is not immediately observable because the landscape structure changes slowly and the organisms that inhabit these areas are not always easy to observe and document. Because these areas are no longer connected to a larger system, the opportunity for introduction of new genetic material to renew populations becomes less likely. The subsequent decline in populations and the reduced level of ecological functioning causes decline in ecological viability and resiliency of the ecosystem. Biodiversity is declining through the loss of species, as well as a loss of the ecosystems they inhabit. Essential habitats are lost, in part due to urbanization, pest invasions, disease and overharvesting. The loss of biodiversity has a direct effect on a system's capacity to be resilient, which is the ability to respond and bounce back from disturbances and retain vital functions and structure.

Edge effects occur where natural or near natural landscape elements are adjacent to other types of ecosystems. Interactions between ecosystems occur naturally, but when human activities are introduced adjacent to natural areas, new stresses can be placed on ecosystems that are not always able to adapt to the changing conditions. As a result, even though some areas may still remain designated as natural areas or as important green areas, they may become less viable from an ecological perspective because of the incompatibility of adjacent land uses. It is important, therefore, to maintain and facilitate connections in the landscape or accommodate the flows that are vital to maintaining healthy functioning ecosystems.

From an ecological perspective, it is also important to understand the landscape morphology or history of the evolution of ecosystems with which we interact. Since landscapes are dynamic and constantly evolving, it is helpful to understand how landscapes or particular ecosystems have come to be the way that they are now. Although we cannot predict how landscapes will change or evolve, we may be able to identify tendencies that give us knowledge that we can use to make decisions about how we might best interact with them. Ecological systems often have what we call a **deep structure**; that is they have remnant or latent characteristics and long-term tendencies that often reemerge. Within developed areas, such as cities, it is useful to understand what these are so that plans can accommodate and take advantage of the rhythms and changes that occur naturally in these ecological systems.

One important dimension of urban sustainability is to allow nature to continue to thrive and essentially manage itself without the infusion of energy and resources to keep urban ecological systems functioning. The problems associated with maintaining viable ecosystems in urban areas are significant. Specific challenges often surface, such as the development, conservation, landscape restoration, edge effects, and site-scale ecological design (Van der Ryn and Cowan, 1996). These can be addressed through the planning and design processes in urban sustainability. Urban landscapes are a finely structured mosaic of property owners and land uses where competing interests for undeveloped land are intense. Over time, cities have largely been formed as a result of many political, economic, cultural, and physical determinants. Resulting urban forms are an amalgamation of the most resilient human creations and ecological processes. However, nature's deep structure is ever present in our cities and continues to provide evidence that when ecological processes are ignored in city design, a natural response is to recapture parts of the city either through catastrophic natural events or through incremental change. Often, valuable resources are used to hold back the forces of nature or to rebuild urban infrastructure after reoccurring natural disruptions such as floods, soil movement, or weathering. The main goal of urban ecology is to understand these forces and work together with natural processes to achieve a sustainable future for cities.

Deep structure - rhythms, changes, long-term tendencies and latent characteristics that occur naturally in an ecological system

Ecosystem Services and Socio-economic Benefits

The principal reason green networks and ecological design are gaining acceptance as strategies to increase urban sustainability is that there are a variety of ecosystem services (Daily 1997) and cultural benefits that can result from these planning and design strategies. Ecosystem services are the result of the function of ecosystems that provide many benefits that we often take for granted. They are derived from nature and are used extensively to maintain our society. We depend on ecosystem services to provide breathable air, clean and plentiful water, food, pharmaceuticals, clothing, fuel, climate, waste disposal, and pollination of plants, carbon sequestration, and much more. In addition, green networks and ecological design provide a number of socio-economic and cultural benefits that might include increased property value, recreational opportunities, sense of community, and identity. A recent report by Odefey et al. (2012) quantifies economic benefits of green infrastructure for cities. These are things that we have historically relied upon for basic human existence. However, as ecosystems become more stressed both locally and globally, a decline in ecosystem services and associated cultural benefits is experienced. Following is a brief description of a variety of ecosystem services and cultural benefits that are often realized through the establishment of green networks and employing ecological design.

Increased biodiversity—The diversity of life on this planet is immense and it is difficult to fully comprehend never mind document the variety of species that exist. Both habitat and conduits for species migration are among the most important ecological functions that can be accommodated. Within an urban context, some areas may not be entirely suitable as primary habitat for all but a few species, but as islands for refuge or places to forage they may be quite suitable if connected to node or primary source areas. Plants and animals, both are dispersed through corridors and patches of natural systems. These zones serve as conduits for nutrient, energy and gene flow.

Hydrologic Processes—The functions of hydrologic processes are among the most critical to preserve and restore. These areas are well suited to serve as the foundation of a network since they are often left as undeveloped because of flood danger. They are also among the most environmentally rich and sensitive. When in a viable state, drainage corridors serve as filters for surface runoff, helping to purify water before it returns to water supply sources. They also serve as sinks for groundwater recharge. Flood containment and protection against soil erosion are also important (Cook 2007). Groundwater is another important resource that many cities rely upon for municipal water supplies. However, in many locations groundwater is being extracted more rapidly that it is being naturally replenished. Ecosystems located in areas where ground water recharge is most viable can be incorporated into green networks and surface water can be filtered and allowed to percolate to replenish groundwater resources.

Climate Amelioration—Specifically in urbanized areas, climate modification can be achieved by increasing vegetative cover in appropriate locations. In many metropolitan areas, and particularly in hot arid climates, an "urban heat island effect" has significantly increased average temperatures, reducing human comfort and causing increased energy consumption (Bowler et al. 2010). Street trees and other green spaces help to mitigate increased temperatures through shading and evapotranspiration. McPherson (1992) calculated that there are significant energy savings that can be achieved with urban tree plantings. Negative effects of wind can also be mitigated through increased plantings.

Recreation—The most commonly recognized human activity that may occur in more natural areas is that of recreation. Suitable activities would likely be passive, such as hiking, cycling, horseback riding, nature observation, picnicking and light camping in specific locations. As concern increases over lack of fitness, increased obesity and rising associated health costs, opportunities for urban recreation become increasingly important.

Carbon Sequestration—As noted in Chapter 5, the emission of carbon into the atmosphere is creating significant environmental problems. In addition to poor air quality in urban centers, the aggregation of carbon in the global atmosphere is known to be causing changes in climate that may have serious implications for future generations. Many scientists and engineers are exploring ways to artificially sequester carbon to help offset these anticipated climate changes. Natural ecosystems, particularly wet ecosystems, can sequester carbon from the atmosphere. Maintaining viable functioning ecosystems can help to preserve natural carbon sequestration processes throughout the planet.

Reduced Management and Maintenance Costs and Aesthetics—Elements of green networks that are predominantly comprised of more natural ecosystems can be self-sustaining and thus provide areas in which a range of other activities can occur without having to be maintained and managed using public resources. Although it is difficult to place specific monetary values on beautiful scenery, it is generally understood that aesthetic qualities are important. Research has shown that properties adjacent to nature areas have increased in economic value. In many cases, the image of an entire district is formed because of the existence, or lack of, natural landscape characteristics. The spiritual or emotional value of beautiful natural areas should also be recognized.

Education and Human Psychology—Education and human psychological ties with nature can be reinforced by having accessible nature areas within cities. As society becomes more urbanized, the danger of losing touch with nature becomes real. Functioning natural areas within an urban setting can provide opportunities for city-dwellers to learn more, first-hand, about natural processes and green spaces can provide sanctuary from the strains of urban life. In the long term this may promote a stronger environmental ethic in society (see Box 1 by Timothy Beatley).

A number of other functions could be identified, but these are some of the most relevant in urban areas. All of these ecosystem services or functions would likely not occur simultaneously throughout a green network. However, there may be several compatible functions with varying levels of priority in certain segments.

Green Networks

The concept of green networks embraces urban ecology as an essential determinant of city form that provides a guiding philosophy for sustainable new urban development and opportunities to retrofit existing urban structure to the ecological patterns nature has shaped over time. A green network can be described as a system of interconnected or related patches and corridors that provide and sustain ecological values within a human-dominated landscape mosaic. The concept of green networks is a human interpretation of relationships that have occurred in nature since the beginning of time. Related terms or concepts include ecological networks (Cook and Van Lier, 1994, Jongman and Pungetti, 2004), green infrastructure (Benedict and McMahon, 2006), greenways (Hellmund and Smith, 2006), green or ecological structure (Werquin et al., 2005), habitat networks and dispersal networks (Asbirk and Jensen, 1984). The concept grew out of the Dutch planning. It is an emerging planning idea that when applied effectively can create an "ecological infrastructure" for cities and contribute to long term urban sustainability.

It is also a response to deleterious effects of fragmentation and ecological degradation. If a green network is designed as a coherent system of natural or semi natural landscape elements configured and managed with the objective of maintaining or restoring ecological functions as a means of conserving biodiversity it will provide opportunities for sustainable use of natural resources and ecosystem services for the public. The principal benefit is that this concept allows nature to thrive and essentially manage itself without the infusion of energy and resources to keep urban ecological systems functioning. Figure 1 is a conceptual diagram of the various components of a green network.

The elements indicated as core areas represent relatively large natural or semi natural open space or landscape elements that would provide secure habitats for a variety of species and the range of ecological functions. These areas are often critical as prime habitat for a variety of organisms that are not tolerant of significant levels of human activity or deterioration in ecological value. One of these core areas is labeled as a clustered core. This element illustrates how it may be possible to organize a collection of smaller natural or semi natural open space elements into a larger core. This approach may be necessary when working in developed landscapes such as cities where ecosystems are already fragmented and the only way to achieve ecological functioning at a higher level is to attempt to **adapt** through retrofitting.

Each of the core areas are linked by corridors. There are three different types of corridors highlighted in this diagram - landscape corridors, linear corridors and stepping stone corridors. Landscape corridors link the core areas with wide continuous landscape elements that would allow use of the zones in similar ways as core areas but would also facilitate flows and migration between cores. Linear corridors are narrower and function primarily as connections from one core area to the next and do not provide sufficient area to be used as prime habitat zones. Stepping stone corridors allow for connectivity between core areas into different way that may require migration across less hospitable zones in the landscape with stepping stones operating as points of refuge and temporary habitat as organisms move along the corridor.

Surrounding all of these areas is a buffer zone. The buffer zone plays a critical role in filtering contaminants, invasive species, unnatural predators and other negative impacts that may be introduced by human activity such as noise and toxic materials. It provides protection for core areas and corridors, minimizing edge

Adapt - The ability to evolve or maintain based on changing circumstances, including environmental conditions

effects, while allowing the effective area of the core or corridor to function at its maximum potential.

The arrows show that connectivity to other green network elements should exist illustrating that the system carries on throughout a larger region as an interconnected system of core areas (patches), corridors, buffer zones and other landscape elements. Surrounding the green network elements, the diagram shows sustainable use areas. These are zones that are dominated by human activity that could be agricultural areas, heavily urbanized zones, suburban development or dispersed types of human settlement. In each situation where the green networks concept is applied, it will have varying sizes and numbers of core areas, corridors and buffer zones depending upon the inherent characteristics of the landscape and the opportunities available for implementation and acquisition of various landscape elements. In some locations it may be possible to design green networks based largely on the remaining natural ecosystems and habitats, however, in urban settings ecological restoration will be necessary or designing "synthetic" corridors that mimic natural systems may be appropriate to establish linages where no natural connections are possible. The concept of green networks is also applicable at multiple scales. It can be applied at a continental scale, a national scale, city scale or even on a local level. In fact, it is important that this concept be linked between these various scales to ensure the long-term resiliency of the green network.

The Nested Hierarchy of Green Networks

To be most effective, green networks should be linked at multiple scales. Although the scales or levels may vary depending on the situation, in most cases we can identify four principal scales at which this nested hierarchy can be established. At the broadest scale or "mega"- scale, the focus would be on linking green network elements of significant size that may have relevance at the continental level. The next level or "macro"- scale, national or regional level significance is important. Cities would typically occur at the next level or "meso"- scale. And, at the finest level or "micro"- scale individual projects or sites become relevant. Linking all of these scales together creates possibilities for connectivity and flows between these levels that are essential for their long-term sustainability.

There are several initiatives that are focusing on implementation of green networks from continental scale down to individual sites or projects. In North America, a proposal entitled "Yellowstone to Yukon Conservation Initiative" (Schultz 2005) aims to establish a conservation corridor that extends from Yellowstone National Park following the Rocky Mountains up through Canada to the Northern Territory of the Yukon. This conservation initiative is intended to protect critical habitat for bears and other large mammals that need vast undisturbed areas to maintain their long-term viability. More than 100 organizations partnered in this conservation initiative that links major national parks and wilderness areas and other critical habitat as a part of a **continental scale conservation strategy**.

In Europe, after 20 years of planning, the first complete version of the Pan European Ecological Network has begun to be implemented (Jongman et al., 2011). This was undertaken in three distinct pieces: one plan for Western Europe; another for Central Europe; and the third for South Eastern Europe, including Turkey. This extensive

Continental scale conservation strategy - An approach to ensure the ecological integrity and connectivity of vital habitats across entire landscapes or regions and establish strategic partnerships involving mixed land uses to promote ecological restoration in the reconnection of large ecosystems

effort required the generation of national plans that were then integrated into a continental scale initiative. Important European bird migration routes and habitats as well as varying levels of conservation for a variety of other species and critical ecological sites were protected and conserved through this planning effort.

In Central America, the Mesoamerica Biological Corridor (MBC) project (Miller et al. 2001) ranges from the Yucatán Peninsula of Mexico through all of Central America to the southern reaches of Panama. This plan was started at the initiative of a number of international nonprofit conservation organizations. They worked with national governments in a cooperative effort to identify important habitat and ecological zones throughout the region. The plan was initiated as a conservation strategy entitled "Paseo Pantera" (Path of the Panther) which was intended to protect biodiversity by providing protected corridors and patches that extend from Mexico to Panama (Carr et al. 1994). Over the following five years, this plan was broadened to incorporate many other areas of ecological importance. Each of the participating countries developed a plan and coordinated their efforts with adjacent national governments. The national governments also developed strategies and incentives for formulation and implementation of local level plans.

An example of how a multiple scale strategy has been implemented is the case of Hacienda Baru in Costa Rica (Ewing 2005). Costa Rica participated in cooperative international planning effort of the MBC. Costa Rica also has a strong national-level plan identifying national parks and other conservation areas that have significant ecological importance. Over 25% of the total land area of the country is National Park or some other protected status. Part of Costa Rica's economic development strategy is also to embrace the idea of ecologically-based tourism in order to preserve their critical natural resources and the ecological integrity of the landscape. As a part of the national strategy, initiatives were launched in the form of tax incentives, preservation easements, education, decentralized administration, partnerships with international organizations and land purchased to secure the most important ecological zones and encourage more sustainable land use activities (Ewing, 2005).

Hacienda Baru went through the process of converting an 820 acre parcel of land from an active cattle ranch to an eco-lodge, helping to re-establish critical wildlife habitat and support sustainable tourism. The landscape transformations that occurred on the land occupied by the Hacienda Baru Ranch was vast. In 1971, it was a working cattle ranch owned by an US meat packing company. The land was completely deforested and open for cattle grazing. Several years later this company decided to concentrate only on the production and meat packing operations in the US and sold the land to ranch employees. The new owners created a series of pastures separated by a fence lines. Something that is common in this region is to create fences using cuttings from live trees as stakes in the ground and then take root and leaf-out become living trees while still serving as fence posts. This protects the fence posts from rot and insect infestations and provides a lasting and living fence system. As the fence lines became established, monkeys, kinkajous, opossums, iguanas, and olingos from the upland forested areas started to use them as migration corridors to travel down to lowlands near the water's edge (Ewing 2005). The new landowners created a site-scale green network that facilitated the migration of certain of the species in the area.

Subsequently, the landowners embraced the opportunity to convert this series of pastures into an eco-lodge complete with nature trails, rustic lodging, environmental education opportunities and guided tours. Over time, the pasture naturally regenerated and the former barren landscape of Hacienda Baru is now completely reforested and is home to a wide range of plants and animals that coexist with visitors and eco-lodge owners and employees.

Ecological Design

The more encompassing concept of urban sustainability and the planning strategy of green networks can only be realized through implementation on a site-by-site basis. This is where ecological design becomes an essential element of creating a more sustainable future for cities. Nature has provided and does provide us with exceptional examples of functional, efficient ecological systems. We can use these to inform the process of design and restoration of urban ecosystems. The more we know about how nature functions, the better we will be at designing systems that will provide the benefits we seek. We also have to embrace technology along with natural sciences to develop effective strategies for designing urban ecosystems, resulting in a range of ecosystem types from natural to artificial. This section provides a series of examples of ecological design that are intended to illustrate how knowledge of patterns and processes of nature can inform design and be applied in urban situations to contribute to the long-term sustainability of cities.

Re-wilding Urban Rivers and Streams

Rivers, streams and other riparian zones are among the most biologically diverse and rich areas in most landscapes. They are also critical lifelines since they are essential for providing connectivity that facilitates flows and many other ecological functions. Where these rivers and streams are in a natural or near natural condition, it is important to preserve or conserve these critical corridors. In many places, however, humans have settled near rivers and streams, primarily for water supply and disposal of waste. In most cities, rivers and streams and their drainage basins are usually significantly modified from the original condition, and so the corridors are sometimes channelized or straightened in an attempt to manage flooding and maximize adjacent land for urban development. While this sometimes remedies short-term problems in the zone immediately surrounding the watercourse, many unintended complications often arise. Channelization and straightening rivers increases the speed of water flow, which in turn increases the force causing erosion of stream banks and furthers instability downstream. As the water moves more rapidly it also carries more sediment, reducing water quality. Additional problems occur downstream when the river is no longer channelized. The sediment load that is carried by the rapidly moving water drops once the river returns to its normal meander cycle and over time the channel fills with the sediment reducing the capacity to carry water, resulting in flooding beyond historical flood zones. Many rivers and streams that have been previously modified are now being restored and **re-naturalized**, reintroducing the meander and reestablishing stream bank vegetation.

  An example of the river that was formerly channelized and has been re-naturalized is the Enz River in Pforzheim, Germany. Pforzheim is a city of about 120,000 people that sits at the edge of the Black Forest in Germany. The Enz River runs through the center of the city and was channelized and straightened in the early 1900s. The land area adjacent

Re-naturalized - A habitat or ecosystem that was brought back into conformity with nature, including reintroduction of ecological functions

FIGURE 2: Channelized Enz River in Pforzheim, Germany.

FIGURE 3: Re-naturalized Enz River in Pforzheim, Germany.

to the river within the city has been developed through the decades as urban housing, industrial complexes, shops and other forms of intense urban development. The river restoration project was part of a larger scheme to create a new urban park following the course of the river for about 15 kilometers through the city. The design was undertaken in the late 1980s and construction was completed by 1992. Figure 2 shows the river in its channelized and straightened condition and Figure 3 in its re-naturalized condition.

The re-naturalization process reintroduced the normal meander cycle based on historical analysis of the river form, prior to channelizing and straightening. Trees and shrubs were replanted in locations where they would typically be found in a natural river channel structure. The landscape architects who designed the project followed ecological design principles, using lessons from nature to inform their design strategies (bio-mimicry). Some 20 years later, the river corridor is now well re-established in its natural regime, vegetation has matured providing habitat for many species and the river corridor now looks much like it did in its original natural condition. Most importantly, it has reestablished many of the ecological functions that were lost when the river was channelized and straightened and it has now once again become an important ecological corridor linking the Black Forest to other important ecological zones.

Preserving Urban Nature

Source and core areas are large areas of natural or near natural landscape, although they do not need to be natural or near natural if they show high levels of ecological functioning. There are many examples of landscapes that have been restored after some significant disturbance or deterioration that provide many of the same benefits as natural or near natural source or core areas. They are important elements in a green network to provide stability because they are generally somewhat

FIGURE 4: Open Space Preserves in Phoenix, Arizona, USA

resistant to external influences. These areas normally function as prime habitat for a variety of species and may contribute to shaping climate, hydrological, and other biological functions within the larger context of the urban area. The term source area simply refers to the fact that these large areas are places where there are significant populations from which genetic material may spread to other zones and the green network. Because these areas are usually covered by vegetation, they supply oxygen and absorb carbon helping to improve air quality. The presence of vegetation also can help to mitigate urban heat island effects by keeping the surface cooler and through the process of evapotranspiration returning moisture to the air. Depending on the specific characteristics of the core or source area they may perform important hydrological functions such as

Sonoran Preserve Land Ownership and Location

	In Acres
State land within city limits	14,800
State land outside city limits	2,000
Total State Land	16,800
Private land within city limits	2,800
Provate land outside city limits	1,900
Total Private Land	4,700
Total Sonoran Preserve Land	21,500

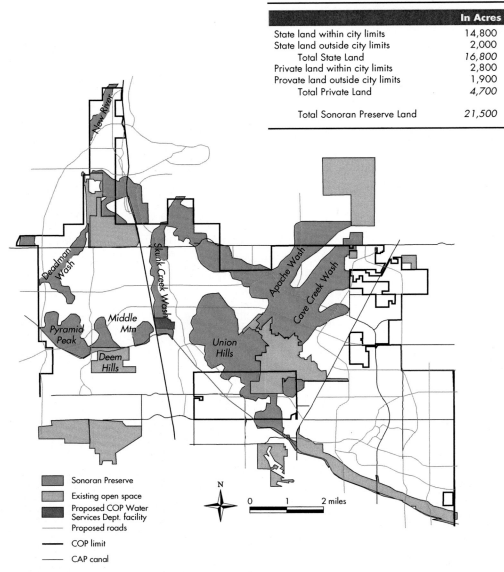

FIGURE 5: Master Plan Map from the Sonoran Preserve, Phoenix, Arizona, USA

Source: From *Sonoran Preserve Master Plan* by James P. Burke. Copyright © 1998 by James P. Burke. Reprinted by Permision.

water retention, groundwater recharge and filtration of surface water. From a biological perspective, these areas usually occupy sufficient terrain to provide habitat and range for migration for many species that may not be tolerant of frequent interaction with, or influence from, humans.

The Phoenix Mountain Preserves in Phoenix, Arizona, USA, are an example of a series of open space elements in an urban area that function as multiple core or source areas. Figure 4 shows open space preserves that are all part of the city of Phoenix Park system, but are all natural or near natural condition. The first of these preserves, South Mountain Park, was established in 1924 and occupies 16,500 acres. It is the largest city park in the United States. An additional 10,500 acres were added to the preserve system in 1972 with the establishment of the North Mountain Range. The most recent addition to the preserve system came with the establishment of the Sonoran Preserve Master Plan (Figure 5) which identifies approximately 21,500 acres in North Phoenix to be added to the system.

Grey to Green Infrastructure: Transportation and Utility Corridors

Most roads, rail lines, utility corridors and other infrastructure elements form barriers, interrupt flows and accelerate fragmentation and isolation. Strategies such as ecological bridges and eco-ducts are being employed to overcome these barriers. It is most effective, however, to research natural systems and understand how alternative road alignments or making infrastructure corridors more compatible with ecological functions can be accomplished. In addition to mitigating barrier affects, designing or retrofitting infrastructure systems as ecological corridors creates opportunities for establishing linkages within urban areas in places where there are no natural connections. Most roads, rail lines and utility corridors travel through rights of ways that are much wider than the actual infrastructure element. The residual space, either beside the road or rail line, underneath overhead utility lines or above underground utility lines, can become an ecological corridor by simulating natural corridors through ecological design. These areas can also become useful as recreational corridors for hiking, running, cycling, and horseback riding.

Figures 6 and 7 show how an ecological bridge and an eco-duct can help to mitigate the barrier affects of major transportation elements. An ecological bridge would

FIGURE 6: An Ecological Bridge along the A-50 Highway in the Netherlands

FIGURE 7: An Eco-Duct Passing Under a Major Road in Eindhoven, Netherlands

Image courtesy author

FIGURE 8: Green Streets in Portland, Oregon, USA with Curb Extensions to Capture runoff Water from the Street

Image courtesy author

FIGURE 9: Green Streets in Portland, Oregon, USA with Curb Inlets Directing Runoff Water to Landscape Strips in Sidewalk

typically be situated at the location of known migration corridor for animals that inhabit the landscape of that region. On initial inspection, the cost might seem prohibitive to accommodate the movement of animals. However, in addition to ecological benefits, these bridges provide greater safety for motorists because they minimize the potential for accidents involving wildlife. An eco-duct is a simple inexpensive way to facilitate movement of small animals underneath roadways rather than limiting migration possibilities to crossing roadways risking the animal's lives.

Portland, Oregon has established a progressive "Green Streets" program to manage urban storm water by localizing collection. Figure 8 includes curb extensions in a typical residential neighborhood. This is a very simple adaptation to a typical street curb and gutter, where the curbs are extended into the street narrowing the roadway at the corners, leaving gaps along the existing curb line to allow water to flow from the street into a landscaped area at the end of each block. The water that runs off the streets usually carries contaminants from automobile exhaust, oil and other elements and while the landscaped zone helps to filter out contaminants, the water also provides sustenance for the plants. Figure 9 is another example from Portland Green Street program. In this case, water that runs off the street collects along the gutter and drains through inlets into the landscape zones rather than being carried below ground in the pipes in the storm sewer system.

In many cities, parking lots occupy extensive areas and are sterile, hot environments. Figure 10 shows a parking lot in Essen, Germany that incorporates a bio-swale that collects water from the adjacent paved areas, allowing it to percolate into the soil. The actual parking spaces are made up of a permeable paving system that incorporates unit pavers with gaps between the stones to allow the water to percolate through rather than running off. The increased green space also helps to cool these areas can improve the aesthetic quality of parking lots.

Courtesy author

FIGURE 10: Green Parking Lot in Essen, Germany with Bio-swales Between Parking Bays to Capture and Infiltrate Runoff Water from Paved Surfaces

Forgotten Space: Vacant Land, Underutilized Sites, and Brownfields

Vacant and underutilized land and derelict or **post-industrial brownfield sites** represent an opportunistic resource in most cities. Pagano and Bowman (2000) have determined through their research of 70 cities in the US that on average 15% of the land area was vacant. Often these vacant parcels remain fallow for decades. Since they are privately owned, it is sometimes difficult to establish programs for temporary use. However, many cities are now exploring ways to use these parcels until they are transformed to a more permanent land-use activity. Vacant parcels can play important roles in green networks as stepping stones within the more developed urban structure, providing linkage between other more stable ecological zones. Strategies such as **interim re-vegetation**, temporary urban agriculture or in some cases **natural regeneration** can return some ecological value to these sites.

Brownfields are sites that have been previously occupied, often in some industrial capacity, that are now abandoned and may have significant site contamination issues. Typically, brownfields require intensive research and site investigation to determine appropriate strategies for site restoration to remove contaminants before or integral with developing suitable strategies for re-use. Ecological approaches to site remediation, including phytoremediation (Suresh and Ravishankar, 2004), bioremediation (Diaz 2008), and in-situ oxidation (Huling and Pivetz, 2006) can provide many ecological benefits beyond just cleaning up hazardous waste or other contaminants.

There are also many new parks being created on sites of former industrial facilities or other land-use activities that cause degradation and contamination. These projects turn formerly undesirable or unusable space into useful public sites that contribute to improving ecological functions in urban areas. The Westergasfabriek Culture Park in Amsterdam, Netherlands is an example of how an urban park can transform a derelict site into a vital ecologically functioning system. The site is located in the central part of Amsterdam and occupies approximately 36 acres. The site was originally developed as a coke gas production facility in 1898. It operated in that capacity for about three quarters of a century but in 1967 ceased operations. The site was left with serious soil contamination. The cleanup and restoration process began in 2000 and it was determined that the site would be converted into a new urban park. The design for the park established a number of ecological elements that help to manage some of the contamination problems and infuse the site with a wetland that provides habitat, helps filter and clean water and incorporates a naturalistic aesthetic element in the heart of the city. The photographs in Figures 11–13 show a variety of elements in the park integrated with the old industrial structure.

Post-industrial brownfield sites - Underused or vacant land previously used for industrial or commercial purposes often containing hazardous substances and contamination that are made available for redevelopment

Interim re-vegetation - Plant species used to stabilize the soil and nutrients of an idle site in an effort to provide barren land with productive use

Natural regeneration - A dynamic process by which life recolonizes when vegetation, land and/or ecology has been partially or completely destroyed

Image courtesy author

FIGURE 11: Constructed Wetlands in Westergasfabriek Park in Amsterdam, Netherlands

Image courtesy author

FIGURE 12: Wood Deck Pedestrian Pathway through Constructed Wetlands in Westergasfabriek Park in Amsterdam, Netherlands

Image courtesy author

FIGURE 13: Foundations of Old Gas Storage Tank now used in Designed Wetlands in Westergasfabriek Park in Amsterdam, Netherlands

Conclusions

While it is clear that a need exists for maintaining the viability of critical ecological systems in urban areas, it is uncertain whether this goal can be achieved over the long term given the current strategies many cities employ in urban planning. Ecological and urban theories have evolved in different directions and are only now starting to meet at a point in time when many urban areas have deteriorated ecosystem values that require substantial efforts to restore. Numerous perspectives exist on how to conserve existing viable systems and restore those with degraded quality. Understanding urban ecology, employing the planning concept of green networks and incorporating ecological design provides promise that urban areas can indeed become more sustainable. Linking science, policy, planning and design is the most effective way to integrated ecology into cities and help provide a foundation for a more sustainable future.

Landscape metrics can be used to assess the viability of these strategies. Landscape metrics are tools used to analyze landscape structure, inherent characteristics of landscape elements and the interrelationships between landscape elements and external factors affecting the functioning of landscapes (Boutequila et al., 2006; Cook, 2002; McGarigal and Marks, 1995; Dramstad et al. 1996). Interrelationships between individual landscape elements and the urban landscape mosaic can be assessed through several indicators. The use of metrics provides the opportunity to have more objective conversations about ecological outcomes or urban planning decisions. The most important issue is generating public awareness and support for sound concepts such as green networks and ecological design. If the public is knowledgeable about the potential contribution toward actually realizing a sustainable future for cities, then the urban development community, government agencies and politicians will likely follow.

Supplemental Readings

Cook, E.A. and J.J. Lara (2013). Remaking Metropolis: Global Challenges of the Urban Landscape. Routledge: New York

Forman, R.T.T. (2008). Urban Ecology: Science of Cities. Cambridge Press: Cambridge.

Sustainable Agricultural Systems for Cities

Rimjhim M. Aggarwal and Carissa Taylor

Introduction: The Challenge of Feeding Cities

As the world becomes increasingly urbanized, with cities moving to former agricultural land and farmers moving to cities, the question of who will feed the cities and how has become critical. The world today is very different from nineteenth-century Europe when productivity in agriculture was rising. This meant that as people moved to cities, they could be fed by the shrinking number of farmers in rural areas, but the rate of production in farmlands had to continue to increase. In the twentieth century, farming in cities was discouraged or ignored as urban planners drew a clear distinction between rural areas as primarily agricultural and urban areas as primarily industrial and residential. The same model was carried to other regions of the world by the colonial rulers, and it was believed that farming had no place in the building of modern cities. Despite this objective, several cities in Europe continued to have significant urban land devoted to urban farming.

Now, we live in a world where the majority of people live in cities, far from the primary sources of food production. The whole process, from growing the food to bringing it to consumers, has become highly energy intensive, and there are large ecological impacts associated with each step of the lifecycle process, from the local to the global scale. Rising rates of food deprivation and obesity within neighborhoods of even relatively rich cities have raised concerns about the **accessibility of healthy food** within cities. As our **food systems** become highly integrated globally, questions about food safety are regularly raised, and we seem to be less and less in control of what gets into our plate. In the United States and Western Europe, in particular, this feeling of disconnect and loss of control over something as intimate as the food we eat has motivated people to look for alternative ways of securing their food. In some cities in Africa and Asia, where the rate of migration into urban areas is very high, widespread poverty and unemployment has driven residents to find ways of growing their own food in cities to survive.

Given the centrality of food in our lives and the dominant role played by the **global food system** in shaping resource use on this planet, it is clear that we cannot achieve sustainability without fundamentally restructuring our food system. By 2050, the world population is expected to increase to 9.1 billion, with around 70% of people living in cities. Feeding all those people will require increasing food production by 70%, according to the UN's Food and Agriculture Organization[1]. The conventional model of keeping cities and agriculture distinct and separate cannot

Accessibility of healthy food - limited availability to purchase healthy food normally seen in low-income neighborhoods.

Food systems - the infrastructure and process needed in feeding a population (growing, harvesting, processing, packaging, consumption, etc.).

Global food system - decisions made by countries and companies regarding who produces food, what food is produced and when, and where and how the food is produced creates social, economical, and political impacts on everyone.

continue for long. In fact, if we look closely, we realize that agriculture has always been practiced in and around cities in different forms (see Howard's Garden City). The problem has been that agriculture in cities is generally treated as a marginal or fringe activity and not systematically integrated within city planning and decision making until now.

In the context of urban sustainability, we need to ask a different set of questions regarding the relation between cities and agriculture: In your vision of a sustainable city, how would the food system be designed to meet the diverse food needs of city residents? Does it make sense to bring sources of food production closer to the consumers? If so, to what extent is agriculture an appropriate use of city space and other scarce resources, such as water? Thinking beyond food provision, what other services (or disservices) does agriculture provide within cities? How can we better incorporate the beneficial services that agriculture provides within urban development? Addressing these questions requires us to fundamentally rethink what sustainable agriculture means in an urban context and how we can transition toward it. This is an exciting new area of research and action, where we have more questions than ready-made answers.

The rest of this chapter is organized as follows. We begin by discussing how sustainable agriculture has generally been defined. Then we describe three different agricultural systems that currently provide for the food needs of cities. Each system has its own unique characteristics, and we critically examine the sustainability implications of each of these systems. Then we broaden the discussion to think about agriculture as not only providing food but also other kinds of services and disservices. Lastly, given this broader understanding, we discuss how we might integrate agriculture into urban planning and development to better design cities of the future.

What Is Sustainable Agriculture?

Many definitions of the term sustainable agriculture exist today. One particularly useful and overarching definition represents the legal definition of Sustainable Agriculture in the United States today:

> *An integrated system of plant and animal production practices having a site-specific application that will, over the long term:*
> * *Satisfy human food and fiber needs*
> * *Enhance environmental quality and the natural resource base upon which the agricultural economy depends*
> * *Make the most efficient use of nonrenewable resources and on-farm resources and integrate, where appropriate, natural biological cycles and controls*
> * *Sustain the economic viability of farm operations*
> * *Enhance the quality of life for farmers and society as a whole.*

Embedded within this definition we can clearly see the core elements of sustainability: meeting social, environmental, and economic needs over the long term. Achieving agricultural sustainability, however, is much easier said than done and may involve making difficult tradeoffs. For example, providing low-income populations with affordable fruits and vegetables may come in direct conflict with maintaining economic viability of farms. In the next section, we discuss the sustainability of the different agricultural systems that provide food for cities.

Agricultural Systems for Feeding Cities

Much of our food takes a very complex path from farm to plate. Examining the **food supply chain** from a **lifecycle approach**, we understand that the process begins with production on a farm. From there, food is processed, packaged, and distributed either directly to consumers, or to retailers. Consumers purchase the food and then prepare and consume it, disposing of the wastes. This process sounds simple enough, but at each step along the way, there are different stakeholders, decision-makers, and regulations involved.

The food system is defined as the chain of activities connecting food production, processing, distribution, consumption and waste management, as well as the associated actors and the regulatory and institutional environment. Next, we discuss the sustainability implications of three different kinds of food systems that provide food for the cities: the **industrial food system**, the **organic** food system, and the local food system. These three systems compare in terms of the sustainability criteria we outlined above.

Food supply chain - a network of business related to food moving from production to consumption.

Lifecycle approach - making decisions on food purchasing and intake based on convictions, philosophies, the "want of something better," and the intangible attributes it adds to one's life.

Industrial food system - the way we eat and how the food is created in mass quantities to supply that demand.

Organic - foods produced not using synthetic pesticides or chemical fertilizers, additives or solvents.

The Industrial Food System

Today, most of us participate in what we call the industrial food system. This is the system we all know and love (or hate). But, let's take a moment and un-package it. How much do we really know about all the things we put in our grocery cart?

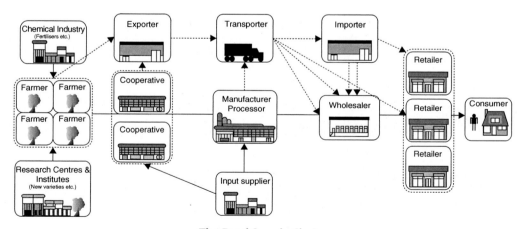

The Food Supply Chain.
From Supply Chain Management: An International Journal by Georgios I. Doukidis, A. Matopoulos, M. Vlachopoulou, et al. Volume 12, Issue 3, Pages 177–186 (May 08, 2007). Copyright © 2007 Emerald Group Publishing Limited.

© Studio 1a Photography/Shutterstock, Inc

Over the past century, the food system has undergone a dramatic shift. Development of high-yielding hybrid crops, widespread irrigation, application of synthetic fertilizers and pesticides, and the increasing use of machinery to replace human and animal labor all contributed to an increase in agricultural yields. Farms focused on efficiency, with each specializing in producing a limited set of crops to streamline their efforts and maximize yield. These practices spread throughout the globe in what is now known as the "**Green Revolution.**"

Development of high yielding, synthetically fertilized, widely irrigated crops has created the Green Revolution. Four-fifths of the world's food production now comes from **industrial agriculture.**[2] This industrial system was initially heralded as widely successful. The new "industrial" techniques doubled the yields of many staple grains and increased the amount of food available for the developing world's growing population, from below 2,000 calories per person in the early 1960s to more than 2,500 calories per person by the mid-1980s.[3] Would feeding the world be possible without industrial agriculture? From a perspective of sustainability, what are the broader impacts of the industrial food system—environmentally, socially, and economically? What are the advantages of this system? What are the disadvantages?

Green Revolution - occurring between 1940 and the late 1970s, development and technology innovations that increased agriculture production.

Industrial agriculture - innovation in technology, farming methods, production, consumption markets, and global trade that effects the production of crops, animals and fish.

Economic Impacts—Rise of Large Farms and Agribusiness

Green Revolution technologies were expensive and required substantial capital investment up-front. Despite widespread government subsidies for agricultural inputs such as fertilizers, pesticides, and water, the additional costs were too much for many small farmers. In the 1950s and 1960s, the number of farms in the United States was reduced by half. Meanwhile, large farms thrived and consolidated, and the average U.S. farm size nearly doubled.[4, 5] These trends have continued. Since 1982, there has been a 40% decrease in the number of small and mid-sized farms.[6] As large farms increased in size and market share, they outgrew the regional and local markets and began integrating horizontally (i.e., with other farms) or vertically (i.e., with processors, distributors, retailers) so they could operate at national or international scales. Over time, this integration has led to the rise in **agribusiness**—large multinational corporations that now control much of the food system worldwide.

Agribusiness - all of the business and the range of activities involved in food production including farming, seed supply, farm machinery, transportation, processing, distribution, and retail sales.

Globalization of the food system - acceleration of urbanization creating a strain on agriculture and how food is produced.

Environmental Impacts and the Ecological Footprint

With the expansion and **globalization of the food system**, its ecological footprint has also increased significantly. The conventional food system requires extensive use of nonrenewable fossil fuel resources for use in agricultural chemical production, on-farm machinery, processing, packaging, and transportation. In the United States, agriculture is estimated to account for approximately 17% of the country's fossil fuel consumption. Recent studies suggest that in the United States, food travels approximately 1,500 miles from "farm to plate," and the average American meal contains ingredients from at least five different countries.[7,8] Ultimately, the large **food mile** system is highly inefficient—producing 1 unit of food energy for every 7.3 units of fossil fuel energy input.[9] Global estimates of total agricultural greenhouse gas emissions (GHG) range from 20–22% of all anthropogenic GHG emissions.[10] Agriculture also accounts for over two-thirds of water extracted from lakes, rivers, and aquifers worldwide.[11]

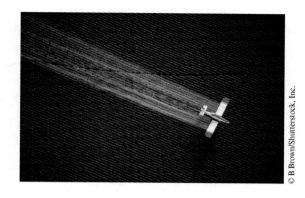

© B Brown/Shutterstock, Inc.

Food mile - distance food travels from production to consumer.

The increased application of synthetic fertilizers and pesticides has also had significant impacts on ecosystem health and integrity. Synthetic fertilizers and pesticides create eutrophication, affecting environments within many miles of the agriculture

From 1960 to 2000, the use of synthetic nitrogen fertilizers increased 800% in the United States. However, it is estimated that approximately 30–80% of the nitrogen applied to crops is never taken up by the plants themselves. Much of this ends up in streams and lakes, where it can lead to **eutrophication**. Eutrophication is a process in which algae bloom due to the sudden influx of nutrients. When the algae die, the bacteria that decompose them consume oxygen in the region, triggering a chain reaction of dieoffs that can ripple across the aquatic ecosystem. Fertilizer runoff from farms along the Mississippi River flows into the Gulf of Mexico, generating a "Dead Zone" of approximately 5,000 square miles.[12, 13] Excessive and improper use of agricultural chemicals has led to loss in **biodiversity** and severe impacts on human and animal health.

Eutrophication - the reaction of an ecosystem to an addition of natural and/or artificial nutrients or substances.

Biodiversity - the variety of life forms within an environment, region, or ecosystem first used referencing wildlife but now widely adopted.

Food Security, Nutrition and Health

Despite a 25% increase in the amount of food available per person worldwide, and a doubling in food production in the United States, many go without adequate food. In 2008, nearly 15% of the U.S. households were **food insecure** – meaning that they did not have access to enough food for an active, healthy lifestyle at all times throughout the year.[14] The urban poor and minorities feel the worst of the effects. While the Green Revolution was able to increase the total amount of food available worldwide, it could not address people's inability to afford or otherwise access that food.[15, 16, 17]

Food insecure - access to adequate food varies throughout the year.

Growing concerns about obesity and other diet related diseases, have led to research on how food intake may be influenced by the access that consumers have to different food outlets (such as supermarkets, convenience stores and fast food outlets) in their neighborhood. Recent research has indicated that in some low income and minority neighborhoods, referred to as food deserts, residents have limited access to affordable nutritious food because they live far from a supermarket or large grocery store and do not have easy access to transportation. Box 1 provides further details on the varied definitions of food deserts, their prevalence within the US, their impacts, and the various policy and non-policy options being explored to address the problems they pose.

Food deserts - low-income neighborhoods in rural and urban areas that are more than one mile from a grocery store. This equates to 23 million Americans, including 6.5 million children.

The term '**food desert**" was reported to be first used in the early 1990s, in Scotland, by a resident of a public housing sector scheme (Cumins and Macintyre, 2002). Since then a number of different definitions have been proposed. The US Department of Agriculture (USDA), has defined a food desert as "a census tract with a substantial share of residents who live in low-income areas that have low levels of access to a grocery store or healthy, affordable food retail outlet" (USDA, 2014). The USDA defines low access as "based on the determination that at least 500 persons and/or at least 33% of the census tract's population live more than one mile from a supermarket or large grocery store" (USDA, 2014).

A study conducted by USDA in 2008-9 estimated that 23.5 million people (or 8.2 percent of the total U.S. population) lived in low-income areas that are more than 1 mile from a supermarket or large grocery store (USDA, 2014). For residents in these areas, convenience stores and other small grocery or corner stores may be more common than supermarkets. These smaller stores generally stock energy dense unhealthy foods and little or no produce, and they often charge more for the healthier foods that are available (Walker et al., 2010). Poverty, lack of access to transportation, poor development of public transportation, high crime rates and low awareness about nutrition further compound this problem of accessibility to healthy food options.

There are several different theories on how food deserts have come into existence. The most popular explanation pertains to the changes in demographics in large US cities between 1970 and 1988, when economic segregation became very prominent, with several affluent households moving from inner city to suburban neighborhoods. This movement led to a decline in median income in the inner city (Walker et al., 2010). This was also the time at which supermarket chains were growing. These supermarket chains found the suburban areas more attractive because of larger availability of space and greater demand. With the spread of supermarkets, several smaller stores in the inner city were driven out of business, thus leaving a void and creating a food desert. Other theories view food deserts as yet another manifestation of the process of deprivation of inner city neighborhoods which can be traced back to structural problems of poverty and racial segregation, declining demand for low skilled workers, high crime rates, and zoning laws.

What can be done to mitigate or eliminate food deserts? At the policy level, The Food, Conservation, and Energy Act of 2008, also known as the 2008 Food Bill, implemented by the USDA prioritized the need to address domestic food accessibility and nutrition issues. The subsequent 2014 Farm Bill authorized funding for the Healthy Food Financing Initiative (HFFI) to provide start-up grants and affordable loan financing for food retailers, farmers' markets and cooperatives that sell and deliver healthy goods to "food deserts" (CDC, 2014). However, while the bill seeks to improve the retail environment for nutritious food, it also cuts, by around $8 billion, the food stamp program that 15 percent of Americans rely on to purchase food, thus limiting its effectiveness (FRAC, 2104).

Several states have also enacted legislation to attract full-service grocery stores and supermarkets to underserved communities and to improve the quality of the foods that are sold at small corner stores (FRAC, 2014). In addition to the direct health benefits of such initiatives, communities may also realize indirect economic benefits as well, including job creation and community-wide revitalization. An often-cited example of these direct and indirect benefits is the The Pennsylvania Fresh Food Financing Initiative, which helped develop supermarkets and other fresh food outlets in 78 underserved urban and rural areas, through a successful statewide public-private initiative (Treuhaft and Karpyn, 2010).

CASE STUDY: Phoenix Metropolitan area

USDA has developed a Web-based, Food Locator Tool (http://www.ers.usda. gov/data/fooddesert) , which enables users to view a map of the US that identifies census tracts, that qualify as food deserts. Users can scan the map and zoom into an area and download other statistics on population characteristics of a selected tract. Using this tool you can map the food deserts in your local area. For example, the map below constructed using this tool, shows food deserts in Maricopa county, which encompasses the Phoenix and other neighboring towns that comprise more than half of Arizona's population. Based on the Locator's statistics, approximately 57 percent of the population in Maricopa County has low access to a supermarket or large grocery store.

The availability and access to food, or food security, is an issue that Arizona is addressing through assistance programs such as Supplemental Nutrition Assistance Program (SNAP), Nutrition Assistance (formerly the Food Stamp Program), Coordinated Hunger Program and the Emergency Food Assistance

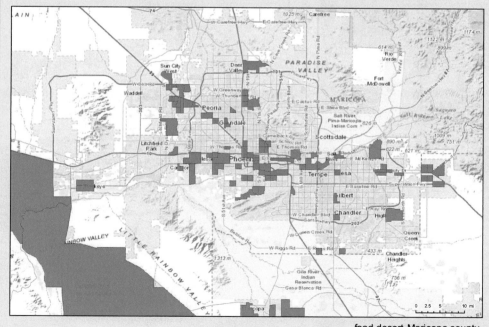

food desert-Maricopa county

LILA at 1 and 10

Date: 7/13/2014   Source: USDA Economic Research Service, ESRI. For more information:
http://www.ers.usda.gov/data-products/food-access-research-atlas/documentation.aspx

Continued

BOX 1: FOOD DESERTS *Continued*

Program. Other initiatives being promoted by community activists as part of the development of a holistic community food system include:

- encouraging farmstands and community supported agriculture programs;
- increasing the stock of fruits, vegetables, and other healthy foods at neighborhood corner stores or small groceries;
- growing food locally through backyard and community gardens;
- improving transportation to grocery stores and farmers' markets; and
- promoting education about nutritional value of different food options.

References

Centers for Disease Control (CDC) (2014). State Initiatives Supporting Healthier Food Retail: An Overview of the National Landscape. Retrieved July 7, 2014 from http://www.cdc.gov/obesity/downloads/healthier_food_retail.pdf.

Cummins S, Macintyre S. (2002). "Food deserts - evidence and assumption in health policy making." British Medical Journal 325(7361): 436–8.

Food Research and Action Council (FRAC, 2014). Farm Bill 2014. Retrieved July 7, 2014 from http://frac.org/leg-act-center/farm-bill-2012/.

Treuhaft S. and A. Karpyn (2010). The Grocery Gap: Who Has Access to Healthy Food and Why It Matters. PolicyLink and The Food Trust.

United State Department of Agriculture (USDA) (2014). Food Deserts. Retrieved July 7, 2014 from https://apps.ams.usda.gov/fooddeserts/foodDeserts.aspx.

Walker, Renee E., Christopher R. Keane, Jessica G.Burke (2010). "Disparities and access to healthy food in the United States: A review of food deserts literature." Health and Place 16: 876–884.

BOX 2: EBENEZER HOWARD'S GARDEN CITY

A need for closer integration between agriculture and cities is not a new concept. In the late 19th century, concerned with the downsides of capitalism and the increasing urban-rural divide, English stenographer Ebenezer Howard sought to develop an approach to urban planning that would help re-connect people to their agricultural land and surrounding ecosystems. In his 1898 publication Garden Cities of Tomorrow Howard explained that the current rural-urban divide was untenable. Towns provided employment but squalid living conditions, while the country was healthy and beautiful but lacked modernization and job opportunities. Thus, he argued "town and country must be married" and this must be done in a carefully planned way. He called his utopian idea the "garden city."

Each household would receive a plot of land enough for a small garden, and would be located in close proximity to a community park or open space which also would contain some sort of public amenity such as a theater, museum, hospital, or library. A central city park would also contain the city's major shopping and business center. All this would be bounded by an agricultural greenbelt, which could provide the city with much of its food, and rail would connect garden cities to one another. Under his urban planning model, each garden city would be small – bounded to 6000 acres and no more than 32,000 people. Consider for a moment how small this is. New York City is 193,000 acres and has over 8 million residents. Even Phoenix, Arizona's "little" suburb of Tempe is far larger – with over 25,000 acres and more than 158,000 residents. His vision was taken up and adapted for use in England, and later the U.S. as a model for town and city planning.

The first city built under the garden city model was Letchworth, England – established in 1904. Other examples of towns and suburbs designed using "garden city" principles include Hampstead Garden, England; Fairfield, AL; Kincaid, IL; Goodyear Heights, OH; Greenbelt, MD; Yorkship Village, NJ; Forest Hills Gardens and Sunnyside Gardens in Queens, NY; and Beloit and Kohler, WI (Gillette, 2010). Ultimately, the garden city movement was not widely adopted, though many of the communities that were created were considered successful. Some blamed the lack of political support for new modes of urban planning, the rampant culture of individualism. Others suggested that Howard's designs were too rigid to account for the evolving and diverse nature of modern cities (Gillette, 2010; Batty, 2008).

References

Batty, M. (2008). The Size, Scale, and Shape of Cities Science 319, 769–771 (2008).

Gillette, H. (2010). Civitas by Design: Building better communities, from the garden city to the new urbanism. Philadelphia, PA: University of Pennsylvania Press.

Long-Term Resilience

Long-term resilience - an environments ability to "bounce back" from external stress or events.

Reliance on distant food sources can undermine local resilience—increasing regional vulnerability to shocks from fluctuating markets, mass-scale food contamination, rising fuel costs, breakdowns in the global transportation system, while decreasing communities' capacity to respond to such stresses.[18] Global food prices rose by 80% between 2006 and 2008, significantly affecting the household budgets of urban dwellers.[19] Due in part to the large separation between consumers and producers, people are often unaware of the impacts of their purchasing decisions, making change difficult. However, there have been some attempts at agricultural reform. Next, we look at the organic food system, which seeks to address some of the negative effects associated with the industrial food system.

Organic Food

The organic food movement began as a much more holistic and transformative endeavor than is sanctioned by the official organic certification processes we see today. Sir Albert Howard (1873–1947) is generally regarded as the founder of the modern organic movement. Howard's philosophy of agriculture was much broader than the organic-inorganic debate he has become known for today. He advocated proactive measures to prevent soil erosion, raising mixed crops (polyculture), integrating

How Sustainable Is Organic Food?

Organic agriculture is grown without the pesticides or petroleum/sewage-based fertilizer being used.

livestock farming with crop farming, recycling plant and animal waste back to the soil in the form of compost, and rainwater harvesting. Despite his call for a more holistic view of agriculture, and his followers' later advocacy toward understanding the farm as an "organic whole," the debate over chemical applications was what was galvanized the organic movement.[20] We cannot discount the importance of Barry Commoner's and Rachel Carson's books, which suggested the long-term hazards of pesticide applications for humans.

So, what exactly does "being organic" mean? According to the U.S. Department of Agriculture's National Organic Program (NOP) regulations, organic crops are grown and processed without most conventional pesticides, petroleum-based fertilizers, or sewage-sludge-based fertilizers. Animals raised organically must be fed only organic feed, receive no antibiotics or growth hormones, and have access to the outdoors. In terms of processing and handling, the regulations further prohibit the use of ionizing radiation and genetic engineering.[21]

For several decades, organic agriculture has served as the poster child of the broader sustainable food movement. In fact, many consumers equate "**organic**" with sustainability as far as food is concerned. In recent years, organic food has increased dramatically in popularity. In 1992, the United States was home to fewer than 1 million organic acres, but by 2008, it contained over 4.8 million acres of certified organic farmland.[22] Consumers have been found to purchase organic products primarily for the following reasons: health, taste, environmental benefits, food safety concerns, animal welfare concerns, support for small and local farms, wholesomeness, agricultural heritage, and trendiness. So how well do our desires match up with reality? How sustainable is *organic*? Let's take a look at some of its key impacts to the environment, the society, and the economy.

Reduction in Synthetic Chemicals—Pros, Cons, and Gray Areas

The core purpose of the organic certification process is to minimize the amount of harmful synthetic chemicals that are used in the production and processing of our food. Here is where organics truly meet sustainability goals. The rejection of synthetic fertilizers forces farmers to re-think the way they interact with soil. Soil health may be improved using organic fertilizers and **nitrogen-fixing cover crops**, as well as innovative techniques such as low-tillage, crop rotation, and **inter-cropped polyculture**. Many organic farmers employ a combination of these procedures to maintain soil health, but proper management of nutrients still remains a challenge. For instance, recent research suggests that organic inputs tend to have adequate nitrogen but too little phosphorus and potassium, leading to a slow depletion of these key nutrients over time on organic farms.[23]

Nitrogen-fixing cover crops - crops planted, also known as catch crops, to retain soil nitrogen that is then released back into the soil and absorbed by other nitrogen needing crops.

Inter-cropped polyculture - growing several different crops in one area creating individual growing patterns and higher return.

Lower chemical pesticide use translates to fewer non-target plant and animal species being killed off by potent chemicals. Studies show that biodiversity, and in particular, species abundance and richness tends to be significantly higher on organic farms.[24] Fewer pesticide applications on farms also means less pesticide exposure for farmers and consumers. In the United States, an estimated 300,000 **acute pesticide poisonings** occur each year, and worldwide, this figure may be as high as 26 million.[25] Past studies have found that chemicals present in pesticides are known or suspect carcinogens, endocrine disruptors, and neurotoxins. Intuitively, these seem like good things to keep away from something so intimate to us as our food. Complicating the matter, however, is the fact that many organic products are grown in close proximity to nonorganic ones. This can result in pesticide-drift and contamination of otherwise organic products. It is also important to keep in mind that although under NOP organic regulations, most synthetic substances are banned, there is a long list of allowed synthetic substances.

Acute pesticide poisonings - extensive use and exposure of pesticides and agro-chemicals in local agriculture and food production primarily in low- to middle-class communities due to the commercialization and globalization of agriculture.

Organics—Energy Reduction?

Studies suggest that organically grown crops tend to use less energy than their conventionally grown counterparts. How much less is a matter of debate. Organic farms don't use fossil fuel intensive pesticides and fertilizers, but depending on the crop and the level of mechanization on the farm, fewer pesticides can mean more mechanical weeding—hence, some of the savings are lost. A **lifecycle assessment** of the U.S. food system as a whole indicates that only about 8% of the energy use of the entire system is embodied in the production of chemical fertilizers and pesticides. Some suggest that because organics avoid these chemicals, energy inputs per acre can be 30%–50% lower for organic crops.[26, 27, 28]

Lifecycle assessment - environmental impacts associated with a particular crop or agriculture.

Organics—More Nutritious?

Many perceive organic foods to be more nutritious. Is this really the case? Currently, the research is inconclusive. Studies tend to indicate that vitamin C concentrations are significantly higher in organic produce. However, a recent review of 39 studies comparing organic and conventional produce found that results can vary widely depending on the types of nutrients and the specific crop. For example, vitamin C concentrations were higher in organic tomatoes than conventional ones, but for carrots and potatoes, the reverse was true. Studies reveal no consistent, significant differences between conventional and organic products in terms of many other nutrients, such as vitamin B, vitamin A or beta-carotene.[29, 30]

Organics—Lower Yield?

One critique levied against organic agriculture is that organic agriculture results in lower yields. A 22-year study performed at the Rodale Institute indicated that fields grown organically can see up to 20% *lower yields* than fields grown conventionally, and other studies have found organic yields to be up to 50% lower.[31, 32, 33] In part, the lower yields are compensated by saving in expenses on chemical fertilizers and pesticides, but potentially higher costs for seeds, labor, and machinery. Thus, price premiums are a key factor in ensuring that farms profit from their organic venture. Some research suggests that a premium of 10% above conventional products may be necessary to ensure comparable farm profits. This has not been a problem in the past because some consumers appear to be willing to pay up to 180% more for their organic products.[34, 35, 36]

More problematic is the following lingering question: with lower yields, could organic agriculture ever feed the world? Critics argue that with 20% lower yields, up to 25% more land would need to be cultivated to supply the same amount of food. Environmental arguments for curbing the expansion of agricultural land aside (deforestation, biodiversity loss), some argue that as populations rise, there will simply not be enough land nor enough organic fertilizer available to feed the world organically.[37, 38] Additional research needs to be done to determine how much yields could be improved by changing on-farm management practices. Could a shift to organic agriculture increase agricultural land use and heighten food insecurity worldwide? It's possible, but it is also important to realize that food insecurity isn't just about availability of food—it's about the lack of stable access to healthy, usable food. This brings us to the next critique of organic agriculture, its inaccessibility due to cost.

Organic Food's High Price Tag: Are Industrial Organics a Solution?

People who try to fill their shopping cart with organic products soon realize that these products are much more expensive than their conventional counterparts. The higher cost and relative unavailability of organics significantly diminishes the movement's potential to meet the dietary needs of mid-to-low income populations. But, whereas organics used to be found only at farm stands and small grocers, many organic products have begun to infiltrate our mainstream supermarkets, at increasingly affordable prices. Much of this is due to the entry of large-scale farms into the organic market. These farms are able to achieve **economies of scale** and levels of efficiency that many small farms are incapable of, and as a result, can pass on the savings to their customers.

However, these large organic farms don't come without a cost. For many of us, the term "organic agriculture" conjures up images of small, pristine, family farms, where farmhands work the good soil with nothing between them and the earth but their own bare hands, or perhaps a shovel. However, for much of the food labeled USDA Organic, this is far from the truth. Organic farms that are 500 or more acres control over 60% of the organic farmland in the United States. Furthermore, the size of organic farms is trending upward. In 1997, organic farms averaged 268 acres; by 2005, this figure was 477.[39]

Many would argue that the creation of the label "organic" has done little to transform the industrial food system. This could be seen as both a blessing and a curse. Proponents of large-scale organic farming argue that by working within the industrial system, it is easier to convince farmers to adopt the practice. Critics argue that large-scale agribusiness has simply created a new forum in which business-as-usual agricultural practices may occur, with may be a little less pollution and a lot more profit—a world of **industrial organics**. In 2008, approximately half of all organic purchases were made in mainstream supermarkets and big-box stores.[40] These stores require large volumes of consistent product, and the small-scale organic farms quickly get outcompeted.

To summarize, organic regulations restrict chemical use, and this means reductions in fossil fuel use and **embodied energy**. Overall, lower chemical use seems to translate to greater energy efficiency of organic crop production, better soil health,

Economies of scale - factors that affect the cost per unit to drop based on increased output.

Industrial organics - organically fed non-antibiotic animals or crops that are raised or grown indoors.

Embodied energy - energy used to produce/create a product during its entire lifecycle.

improved biodiversity, less risk of human exposure to pesticides. However, there are tradeoffs. Yields appear to be lower in organic fields than conventional ones, which could mean we need more land to produce the same amount of food, which is a sustainability problem since bioproductive land is decreasing at the global scale. For a variety of reasons, organic products are typically far more expensive than conventional ones, limiting their capacity to serve low-income populations. Finally, organic agriculture, for better or for worse, does little to challenge the mainstream, globalized system of industrial agriculture where small-scale farms lose out.

We need to ask ourselves: is this all we want from a sustainable agricultural system? What about other environmental issues such as water use, greenhouse gas emissions, soil erosion, nutrient runoff, deforestation, and biodiversity loss? What about farm livelihoods, the loss of small-scale farms across the United States, and the domination of the industry by large corporate agribusiness? What about the inequities in our food system, rising obesity, rising costs of nutritious food, and the many hungry and food insecure in our midst? On all these issues, the organic movement as we see it today is silent. These are the principle questions of sustainable agriculture and cities for which we need answers.

Local Food

There is a growing argument that both the industrial and organic models of agriculture fail to address the bulk of the world's food system problems. Both models operate primarily within a structure of an intensely globalized agricultural system in which producers and consumers are distanced, and local regions remain highly vulnerable to global shocks. **Local food systems**, on the other hand, seek to minimize the distance from farm-to-plate and often use direct marketing approaches, where farmers sell directly to consumers. When talking about cities, local agriculture is often called **urban and peri-urban agriculture (UPA),** which takes place inside the city itself or in the periphery. UPA includes horticulture, aquaculture, arboriculture, and poultry and animal husbandry. It can be found in the form of greenbelts around cities, community gardens, farming at the city's edge and in vacant inner city lots, fish farms, farm animals at public housing sites, municipal compost facilities, schoolyard greenhouses, restaurant-supported salad gardens, backyard orchards, rooftop gardens and beehives, window box gardens, and much more (see Box 2).

In the United States, agriculture in metropolitan regions accounts for about 33% of total crop sales, and 61% of the production of fruits and vegetables by acreage.[41] The **local food** trend is growing. Today, the United States is home to more than 5,200 farmers' markets, and at least 2,500 Community Supported Agriculture programs. Direct sales of farm products have increased from $812 million in 2002 to $1.2 billion in 2007.

Local food systems - how food is being produced and delivered to consumers within a community to increase food security.

Urban and peri-urban agriculture (UPA) - growing, harvesting, producing, and consuming food in an urban area of a city, town, or metropolis.

Local food - food being produced and delivered to consumers within a geographical area.

© Malivan_Iuliia/Shutterstock, Inc.

Rooftop Garden

What Is Local Food?

Defining this term is more complex than one might guess at first glance. Unlike organic or fair trade, there is no formal, overarching certification system that defines what makes a product *local*. The definition of local, therefore, varies from region to region and person to person. Geographical or political boundaries such as "state" or "county" are often used by academics, because datasets are readily available at this level. These types of definitions may also tend to be employed by retailers for marketing purposes.[42] However, many consumers tend to conceive the term "local" in narrower terms expressed in "food miles" from their home—for example, a 50- or 100-mile radius.[43, 44] Consumers also often inherently associate particular values with the term *local*. Often implicated in people's definition of local are attributes associated with *who* produced the food, *how* they produced it, or perhaps *where* the food was *purchased*. According to these definitions, large corporations and agribusinesses, or farms without environmentally sound practices, may be excluded from consideration as truly local. The definition of local may be even further constrained to include only products that are bought directly from producers, or those purchased from particular outlets branded as local.[45]

Why Go Local?

Consumers buy local food for many reasons. Some of the most commonly cited reasons include: improved quality, freshness and taste, environmental concerns, nutritional benefits, a desire to support local farms and economies, direct purchasing from farmers, obtaining organic products, and gaining a sense of knowing where their food came from.[46, 47, 48, 49] So, again, we must ask, how well do these expectations match up with reality? How sustainable is local food? Without clearly defined standards, the answer is often "*it depends*." It depends on the specific practices of the particular farm or local food outlet in question, and on whom you are asking. So, let's take a look.

Is Local Food Sustainable?

Urban demand for local produce can provide profitable avenues for metropolitan area farms to maintain a sustainable livelihood. But, direct-marketing isn't for everyone. Only 6.2% of farms in the United States participate in direct-marketing.[50] So, why don't more farmers participate in local food systems? Research suggests a variety of reasons, most of which have to do with our mass conversion to industrialized, specialized agriculture. For many large farms, selling products exclusively at a local level is no longer feasible. They produce in quantities beyond what the local markets could consume, and their use of machinery, fertilizers, and pesticides allows them to produce with great efficiency. Working on a small-scale farm can be extremely hard work, and there is a great deal of physical labor involved. In addition, marketing directly to consumers is time-consuming, and many farmers describe feelings of "burnout" associated with producing and marketing their products locally.

Competition with the 24-7, one-stop-shopping, highly subsidized, supermarket experience is difficult. Americans are used to getting what they want, when they want it, and many don't want to be restricted to the seasonal produce that local farms have to offer. Because of this, local farmers have to spend extra time and effort educating the public and seeking out niche markets for their products. Why is it that small-scale farms do not sell their products at regional supermarkets? Supermarket chains—as well as large-scale foodservice, restaurants, and catering companies—typically only buy from large farms that can supply consistent and substantial quantities of product to all their stores.[51, 52] Typically, they purchase products from regional food distribution farms because of market security and diversity of products.

Many people buy local to support their local economy. Does buying local improve the local economy? Unlike supermarket purchases, where much of the profits "leak" to distant corporate headquarters, money spent on local food is more likely to go to a local

Local foods effect the local economy greater and more quickly than supermarket purchases. Local food outlets such as farmers' markets may create new job and volunteer opportunities, both directly and indirectly. One study calculated that for every person employed at an Oklahoma farmers' market, an additional 2.44 jobs were created throughout the state.[60]

farmer or retailer, who in turn, is more likely to spend it in the local region. It is estimated that for each dollar spent on local food, more than double this amount is then able to re-circulate in the local economy.[53]

Noncommercial forms of urban agriculture, such as household and community gardens, can play a particularly significant role in contributing to health and nutrition, especially in food-insecure communities. In developing countries, where poor, urban residents are estimated to spend 60–80% of their meager incomes on food, a few homegrown crops can go a long way to meeting nutritional needs while freeing up financial resources for other investments.[54, 55] Household gardens can also be vehicles of empowerment for women living in regions of the world that still discourage them from seeking a job or participating in economic activities. So, it would seem that for some farmers, and in terms of the local economy, a local food system can contribute a lot. But, what about the rest of the world? What happens when we choose to buy locally rather than import our products from somewhere else?

Defensive Localism—A Cautionary Tale

Buying something produced locally sounds like a simple idea. But, as you start unpacking what it really means in terms of sustainability, things can get complicated. What if a better, more sustainable, product could have been sourced non-locally? *Buying local for local's sake is at best lazy sustainability, and at worst, irresponsible.* Thus, scholars argue, we need to be careful not to fall into the "local trap"—assuming that local is better without looking more closely at the issues. Assuming that local is better can lead to a sort of **defensive localism**, in which nonlocal products are shunned without a second glance. Along with this can come an array of cascading effects, some potentially positive, others negative. As we have seen, there are *local* economic benefits to buying local. But, this may be at the expense of a job in another community elsewhere. Furthermore, the local scale may be just as susceptible to power imbalances, injustices, and irresponsible practices. In this sense, the *local* label can run the risk of appearing to embody a set of sustainability principles and values that inherently

Defensive localism - aversion to agriculture products not produced within the community.

The use of transportation that delivers food from farm to plate creates Food Miles, which average between 1,500 and 2,000 miles for what ends up on our plates.

have, in fact, very little to do with the local scale.[56, 57, 58] Let's take a deeper look at some of the other factors that need to be considered when thinking about sustainability.

Local Food—Better for the Environment?

Is eating local better for the environment? One widely used argument for local food is that it travels less distance from "farm to plate." Many argue that fewer *food miles* entails less fossil fuel use and lower greenhouse gas (GHG) emissions. While this seems to make sense intuitively, reality is much less straightforward. What *is* well established is that in the conventional system, food travels a long way to get to our dinner plate. Most studies peg this number at an average of 1,500–2,000 miles for U.S. consumers.[59]

Things get complicated, however, when you start to factor in the *type* of transportation used to deliver food from farm to plate. Personal vehicles and small trucks used by farmers and consumers to transport food on a local scale have lower capacity, and therefore, they transport fewer pounds of food per gallon of gas consumed, despite the fact that these vehicles have relatively good fuel efficiency. It comes down to economies of scale. When carrying substantial amounts of food, large refrigerated trucks can actually be more fuel efficient *on* a per-pound basis.

Moreover, when considering the energy impact of local food, transportation isn't the whole story. In fact, the energy used in food miles to transport a food from farm to plate only accounts for a tiny 14% of the overall energy consumption of the food system.[60, 61] If we truly care about reducing the fossil fuel use and greenhouse gas emissions of our food purchases, we have to think about the big picture and perform a life cycle assessment.

Different regions and different farms may produce food with far less fuel used and far fewer GHGs emitted per unit of product than others—giving them a comparative advantage over local regions. This may be due to a variety of factors, such as soil type, climate, farm-management practices, and the nature of processing and packaging. The question becomes, how much energy is embodied in the product as a whole by the time it hits your refrigerator? For example, one study revealed that tomatoes purchased locally in the United Kingdom in the wintertime came from heated greenhouses and used more energy than would have been used to ship them to the United Kingdom from Spain.[62] Therefore, it is important to consider seasonality, crop yield, regional geography, and on-farm management practices before universally labeling local food as having lower energy use and a smaller carbon footprint. It must be stressed here that it is important to calculate energy use per unit of farm product produced. Some farms may be more productive than others, and therefore, though their energy consumption overall may be greater, they yield more crop per unit energy input.

It's also important to remember that energy use is just one of many indicators that we could use to assess the impact of a local food product on the environment as compared to another, non-local option. But, there are many other aspects to consider. We must compare local and nonlocal options in terms of their use of other nonrenewable and scarce resources such as water and phosphorus-based fertilizers. We must compare them in terms of their impact on air, water, and soil quality, as well as overall biodiversity and ecosystem health. We must do all of this in terms of assessing not only the farm, but also the entire processing, packaging, and distribution **phases of the food system** as well.

Phases of the food system - production, processing, distribution, consumption and post consumption.

Local Food—Better for People?

Today, one of the key reasons that people in the United States turn to local food systems is that, through them, they have a better sense of where their food comes from. Local food systems reconnect producers and consumers and heighten "agricultural literacy" in urban dwellers. They begin to understand what goes into their food, how it's grown, the seasonality of production, and the local environmental characteristics of their region. Because of this increased knowledge, consumers feel that they can make more informed choices when they buy or grow. Furthermore, direct contact with customers and the increased visibility of farms and their practices have been shown to be related to increases in on-farm biodiversity, and environmental and ethical farm management.[63, 64, 65]

Local Inequities—Who Gets a Seat at the Local Table?

Who buys local food? Participation in local food outlets is very limited. A growing body of research suggests that local food systems primarily serve the urban elite and that low-income or minority customers are less well served.[66, 67] If local food is ever to be the answer to our food sustainability problems, its inequities must be addressed. The reasons behind low-income and minority consumers' lack of participation in local food markets are complex and not well understood. Much research is yet to be done in this field. One lens that can increase understanding of the issue is that of **food security**. The Food and Agriculture Association of the United Nations states that for food security to be achieved, food must be available, accessible, usable, and stable.[68, 69] The United States has more than enough quality food available, but what about the other factors? We'll address each in turn.

How accessible is local food to consumers? **Food accessibility** encompasses a number of factors—typically aspects of affordability, physical accessibility, and cultural acceptability. Many consumers cite the high cost of local foods as a major barrier to purchasing it.

Food security - access and availability of food to an individual to live a healthy lifestyle.

Food accessibility - access and availability of food to an individual.

© marlee/Shutterstock, Inc.

Farmers markets that are accessible for consumers are very important for continued sustainability.

Providing food subsidies to low-income and other vulnerable groups, through food stamps and food vouchers , and making these redeemable at local food outlets such as farmers' markets is one way of addressing the affordability issue. But, affordability is not enough to ensure food security.

Local food outlets such as farms, farm stands, farmers' markets, or Community Supported Agriculture drop-off locations are not always physically accessible for consumers, or that access may be unstable, varying from season to season. A given market must also provide culturally acceptable food. In terms of food, the culture with which we identify can unwittingly play a significant role in what we come to regard as acceptable food and how we utilize it.[70, 71, 72]

Thus, to conclude, it would appear that local food, just like organic options, is not a miracle cure. On a regional scale, local food can bring many benefits. It stimulates the local economy, provides a profitable avenue for many small farmers, and can contribute to increasing resilience and food security. But, we have also seen that local food tends to be unaffordable and inaccessible for many city residents. We have also discussed that although local food may reduce fossil fuel use, this is not *always* the case. Similarly, depending on the region, sourcing non-locally could mean savings in water inputs, fertilizer applications, pesticide use, or even improvements regarding issues of social justice, fair wages, or humane treatment of animals. In this light, it's not *local* in and of itself that is so important as what's actually happening in the process from seedling to dinner plate. However, one could argue that it is much easier to know what's happening on the farm and in the distribution process when the farm is local—and of course this is one of the major reasons people buy from local farms.

Beyond Food: Ecosystem Services (and Disservices) of Urban Agriculture

Ecosystem services - benefits and resources a human receives from its surroundings or ecosystem.

Farms can offer urban regions much more than just food. Scholars increasingly recognize the many **ecosystem services** that agricultural lands can provide. Essentially, ecosystem services are the benefits people obtain from a given ecosystem, and agriculture can be thought of as a managed ecosystem. In the case of agriculture, these include food provisioning, waste and nutrient cycling, water runoff management and groundwater recharge, maintenance of soil fertility, provision of educational, recreational and economic opportunities, increased wildlife habitat and biodiversity, reduction in the urban heat island effect, and other microclimate and aesthetic improvements.[73, 74, 75] We'll explore some of these concepts below, as well as some of the potential *disservices* of urban and peri-urban agriculture.

City Metabolism—Rethinking "Waste"

Currently, our cities operate in a **linear** manner. We bring in vast quantities of food and other resources, and emit vast quantities of waste—much of which is processed through our wastewater treatment plants, eventually ending up polluting our waterways or being trapped in our landfills. There is very little active recycling of any kind, and as a result, we see a slow, but persistent removal of nutrients—especially phosphorous—from our agricultural lands.[76] Phosphorus is a nutrient that is absolutely essential to plant growth. It is also a nonrenewable resource, harvested primarily in the form of rock phosphate. Farmers apply it to their fields as fertilizer to maintain soil fertility. Some of this is lost to runoff before the crops can take it in. The part that plants do uptake is shipped off to cities, embedded in our food. Nearly 100% of the phosphorus humans eat is excreted—mostly in urine. Eventually it ends up in our waterways or sewage sludge in landfills. Only 10% of this is estimated to recirculate back to agricultural lands—a serious problem when you recall that global phosphate rock resources will likely be depleted within the next few hundred years.[77, 80]

Because of this, many increasingly argue that it is crucial that we begin to think of the **metabolism** (inputs and outputs) of our cities as **circular** rather than linear.[79] Here, the development of closely integrated urban-agriculture systems could help. Sewage water, if properly treated, could be used to fertilize agricultural lands. In fact, many regions in China have had long-standing traditions of successfully recycling waste back onto cropland near urban areas using **aquaculture ponds**. Of course, recycling human waste into a form that can be applied to edible crops does not come without its own challenges. Improperly treated wastewater can increase exposure to diseases such as cholera, typhoid, giardia, dysentery, and more. Furthermore, urban soils may be contaminated with heavy metals from automobile exhaust and industry.[80] However, there are many examples of such ecological sanitation systems worldwide, and this is promising for a move toward more closed-loop, regenerative urban-agriculture systems.[81, 82]

Metabolism - inputs and outputs of ourselves and our ecosystem.

Aquaculture ponds - ponds installed and modified to produce grow and harvest fish, other animals, and irrigation of plants.

Wildlife Habitat & Biodiversity

Urban areas have become notorious for their destruction of ecosystems. As cities have grown, they have literally paved over much of the world's prime agricultural land and biodiverse habitat.[83, 84]

In the United States, much of this land now lies vacant. Urban agriculture provides an opportunity to provide cities not only with food, but also with much needed green space. Many studies show that due to their high plant diversity, backyard and rooftop gardens can provide key urban habitats for native pollinators, birds, and other wildlife.[85] However, urban agriculture doesn't *always* provide vibrant wildlife habitat. Chemical monocultures, heavy tillage, or farms producing vast amounts of nutrient runoff, for example, don't improve soil and ecosystem health or wildlife habitat; they degrade it. So again, we see that local, urban agriculture isn't *necessarily* a good thing, but that when practiced properly, it could be.

Growth of cities can destroy ecosystems.

Microclimate Improvements

There are a number of ways in which urban agriculture can lead to microclimate improvements. Plants help minimize the movement of dust and resulting air pollution. As plants respire, the water they've taken in evaporates, cooling the surrounding region. In desert climates, this urban heat island mitigation can play a critical role in making the city livable and reducing the amount of air conditioning required. Of course, the tradeoff here is water. For evaporative cooling to work, water is needed, and this can be problematic for areas in which water is scarce.[86]

Integrating Agriculture in Cities: Innovative Urban Design, Policy, and Community Efforts

In the above section, we discussed the various ecosystem services and disservices that agriculture potentially provides in cities. Given this discussion, a central urban design and policy question is whether and to what extent agriculture is an appropriate use of city space and scarce resources such as water. In most places, it has been observed that as a city grows and land prices rise, land held in agricultural production is out-competed by other uses. This is because the market values only the agricultural products (food and fiber); other forms of ecosystem services that we discussed above—such as microclimate regulation, green spaces, biodiversity, and cultural services—are provided free. As a society, we may value these other services for a healthy and resilient city. But, if these services do not earn a market return, then we either need some sort of policy support or we need to think about alternative models of urban design and architecture, together with community efforts, so that we can make urban agriculture viable.

A wide range of policy instruments have been designed to manage urban growth and protect or promote agricultural production.

This vacant lot in an inner-city neighborhood has been transformed into a community garden.

Agricultural zoning has been used widely by cities across the world to protect land use in agriculture. Land use plans often indicate the areas within the city in which urban agriculture is allowed. Sometimes these plans may also include guidelines from planners on the types of urban agriculture that are permissible. In Botswana, for example, the City of Gaborone has set up poultry zones on land considered of low potential for development for other land uses.[87]

In addition, in the United States, legally recognized geographic areas called *agricultural districts*, or *agricultural preserves*, are designed to keep land in agricultural use. The agricultural preserves differ from exclusive agricultural zoning areas because enrollment in them is voluntary.[88] Farmers who join an agricultural district may receive a variety of benefits, such as differential tax assessment, which implies that they are taxed at a lower agricultural value rather than the higher values associated with developed uses.[89] Another popular approach, widely used not only by government agencies but also a large number of private land trusts, for protecting agricultural land is the *purchase of development rights* (PDR). Under PDR, the landowner retains title to the land but voluntarily sells the development rights that prohibit future subdivision and development.[90] Conservation easements are also being increasingly used to delineate environmentally vulnerable lands that then can be used for agriculture. Several municipalities are also exploring the option of promoting *multifunctional land use,* wherein, through encouraging community participation in the management of open spaces, food can be grown in combination with other urban functions such as recreation and city greening.

Another innovative policy option gaining ground in recent years is the use of vacant public and private land for urban agriculture. With the growing "sprawl" into the suburbs, the last couple of decades have seen a common pattern of inner-city neglect in most cities across North America. For example, it is estimated that Chicago now has 70,000 vacant parcels of land. The economic recession of the past few years has led to depopulation and rise in abandoned properties in several cities across the United States. Urban agriculture can play a regenerative role by transforming these vacant lands, which are often neglected, to vegetable gardens that meet the food needs of the city.

The challenge here is negotiating a deal between the owners and potential users of these properties. Without a title or three- to five-year leases, the users risk losing their investment when the land is taken away for other purposes. The temporary nature of use may also make it difficult to secure other resources, such as water.

All these policy options and challenges are leading to a great deal of creative thinking around the question of how food production can be incorporated into the built environment. Architects are finding ways to fit food production into buildings, for instance, through rooftop gardens (which also provide cooling). Unused spaces such as riverbanks, median strips, schoolyards, and hospital lawns are being incorporated into a broader vision of creating green infrastructure within cities. New citywide coalitions are emerging to advance the goal of food security, both at the household and community level. Health and nutrition advocates are joining with community gardeners, university extension services, emergency food distributors, and city planners to design these new food systems. It is through these collaborations that the potential of urban agriculture in providing different types of ecosystem services can be realized.

Conclusions

In this chapter, we have reviewed several of the key food systems utilized in urban areas and discussed their sustainability implications. We have seen that much of the food that passes through U.S. cities today comes not from the local region, but from farmlands and pastures hundreds or even thousands of miles away. In terms of sustainability, there may be some sound economic, social, and environmental reasons for sourcing food from far away—perhaps rain-fed agriculture is possible there, the land is more fertile, or the farm is large enough to achieve greater on-farm efficiency. But, there are costs as well. Buying into the globalized, industrial system may mean that more fossil fuels and chemicals were used to produce the food that arrives on our plates. Furthermore, relying solely on distant sources of food may make urban dwellers more vulnerable to shocks in the global system. Climate change, economic crises, food contamination, and increasing fuel costs could all result in price hikes, dramatically reducing the affordability and availability of food within a city.

One increasingly popular response to the many problems with the mainstream, industrial food system is to source more food *locally*—either within or very close to cities themselves. Urban and near-urban agriculture can take on many forms, including commercial farms and markets, or community and household gardens. Urban agriculture brings consumers back into close contact with the source of their food and can allow them to make more informed decisions about what they are buying into. It can enhance urban resilience by maintaining a city's capacity to feed itself, and furthermore, by providing a number of ecosystem services such as waste recycling, wildlife habitat, economic opportunities, and microclimate improvements.

Supplemental Readings

Arnould, E. J. & Thompson, C. J. (2005). Consumer culture theory (CCT): Twenty years of research. *Journal of Consumer Research*, 31.

Barrett, C. B. (2010). Measuring food insecurity. *Science, 327*, 825–828.

Born, B. & Purcell, M. (2006). Avoiding the local trap: scale and food systems in planning research. *Journal of Planning Education and Research, 26*, 195–207.

Making Desert Cities Sustainable: The Role of Urban Design

John Meunier

Introduction

Modern desert cities, such as Phoenix, Albuquerque, Tucson, Las Vegas, and even Riyadh and Dubai, are being made in ways that reflect the capacity of **postindustrial technology** to overwhelm the limitations that constrained the forms of older, preindustrial, desert cities. This chapter questions whether both the technology and the living patterns that typify such modern desert cities are sustainable. It also looks at some older desert cities to see what they may have to teach us about how to live well in desert cities without an excessive dependence on nonrenewable resources, and without placing so much stress on the environment. At the same time, as some scholars have suggested, we must recognize that the forms in which cities are made respond as much, or more, to **cultural imperatives**, as to issues of climate and technology. We need to be cautious, therefore, as we derive these lessons and attempt to apply them. Nonetheless, many of these older cities, such as Yazd in Iran, Shibam in Yemen, Jaisalmer in India, and Marrakesh in Morocco, have evolved in response to their desert contexts over extended periods. Some have even survived significant cultural shifts, such as in Sana'a in Yemen, with the arrival of Islam after many centuries of growth. It is argued that they may provide valuable models, regarding **compact urban form**, alternative house forms, climate control and its optimization, water usage and its celebration, low energy construction materials and methods, even the nature of windows, in the making of modern desert cities.

Desert cities in the United States, such as Phoenix or El Paso, even Los Angeles and San Diego, face a unique responsibility as they provide models for what it means to live a "modern" life in a desert environment. Following these models can multiply by many times the stresses placed on other ecological and political systems as they are emulated, partially or wholly, throughout the world—first by the wealthy in their suburban villas, and then, over time, by others in the population—abandoning the old, dense city centers as they seek the benefits of a life that begins to match their images of twenty-first century **urbanism**.

City of Shibam in Yemen.

© John Meunier

Postindustrial technology - a period in the development of an economy or nation in which the relative importance of manufacturing lessens and that of services, information, and research grows; examples of postindustrial technologies include biotech, artificial general intelligence, intelligence amplification, and molecular technology.

Cultural imperatives - a belief or belief system that is unconsciously imposed on a group or individual by the greater society; the social norms that are found in all societies that presumably express the basic social needs of all people.

Compact urban form - the physical layout, land use pattern, and design of a city; includes things such as land use mix and distribution, transit availability, infrastructure phasing, and resource management. It comprises a land use pattern that encourages efficient use of land, walkable neighborhoods, mixed land uses (residential, retail, workplace), proximity to transit, and the reduced need for infrastructure.

Urbanism - the characteristic way of life of city dwellers; the study of the physical needs of urban societies; used by archaeologists to describe the process that drives people to live in cities.

This chapter aims to address a growing concern by many regarding the long-term prospects of cities, such as the rapidly growing cities of the American Southwest, with both an **urban form** and an array of building types that have largely ignored their desert settings. It also is a response by the author based on extensive travel to desert cities around the world, particularly, but not solely, to older cities whose cores were built in a preindustrial era, in search of lessons indicating more appropriate ways to live in the desert. This work is not informed by nostalgia or cultural conservatism, although these forces certainly stay the hands of those who would destroy, indeed in some places have already destroyed, the patrimony of ancient cultures in the name of "modernization," and in response to the ineluctable forces of the marketplace. It is informed by a deep commitment to what Vitruvius, an ancient Roman writer, called "propriety;" by a belief that the best way to live is not by dominating the context but by optimizing its benefits and gently ameliorating its challenges; and that the power of modern technology should be used only as a last resort when all other means cannot meet the demands of twenty-first century life.

Urban form - the physical layout and design of a city. Growth management issues such as urban sprawl, growth patterns, and phasing of developments heavily influence urban form.

Background

The advent of twentieth-century technology has radically changed the nature of desert city living in many parts of the world. Widespread use of automobiles, increased access to large-scale urban water and sewage systems, almost universal access to electrical power and, in some cases, full climate control through air-conditioning have eroded the need for a careful relationship with both the social and physical environment. Satellite receivers, powered by that electricity, have infiltrated almost every household with images of ways of life that challenge **indigenous cultural norms** of both behavior and artifacts. This barrage of images, reinforced by the communications from international commerce, has promoted the uses of the new technologies as a means to "modern" life patterns.

Indigenous cultural norms - agreed upon expectations, rules, or behaviors that are characteristic of a specific group living in a particular region.

There are still many desert settlements in the world where access to all of these modern technologies is very limited. Auto mobility is at best a motorcycle, and minibuses or shared taxis enable much travel. Although electricity may be available via a tangle of overhead wires, water may be available only for a few hours a day or a few days a week, or must be brought in containers from communal taps or wells. The building of sewer systems often has been less than satisfactory in some desert cities, because leaking pipes have both polluted the ground and dissolved the foundations of older buildings. Further, effluent is often left untreated as it leaves the system. But these transitions to "modern" living, even when incomplete, have still been eroding ways of making desert cities that evolved over centuries and were adapted to the physical demands and opportunities of their physical and cultural contexts.

Is this process reversible? Some political and religious leaders have attempted to resist this tide of "modernization." Countries such as North Yemen had rulers who refused to let their community participate in twentieth-century developments throughout the first two-thirds of that century. The resistance to this western model of modernization may be reflected in some of the political turmoil in the world today among those who value the traditional ways of life and fear their destruction under the wheels of the juggernaut of western modernization. However, even in countries that profess a cultural hostility to the west, many of the forces of modernization seem to be irresistible. What is needed is an alternative model that retains much of what is valuable from the past but that also accommodates with a new sensibility the demands of the present.

Modern Desert Cities

Greater Phoenix is a prototypical modern desert metropolis in the American Southwest. This city anticipates achieving its full realization as a major urban center in the twenty-first century and is accumulating the necessary elements of a metropolis. It is becoming a "major league" city more than simply in terms of sports. At the beginning of this century the population of the metropolitan area of Phoenix already had exceeded 3.5 million, with a land area of more than 1,200 square miles. By 2050, the population is projected to be between 9 and 28 million, depending on which previous growth trend is extrapolated. Phoenix has had most of its growth as an automobile city. As in other automobile-dependent cities, its **population density** has been low, averaging about 2,750 people per square mile.

Housing Expanding into the Desert in Scottsdale, Arizona.

© John Meunier

What could be the model for a different urban density in a desert city? Older American cities such as Boston, New York, and San Francisco have much higher densities and more urbane lifestyles, and are among the most desirable places to live. But they are not desert cities.

What makes a city have a higher density? Typically, such factors include high-rise dwellings, closer proximity to goods and services, less driving, and more walking, biking, and the availability of public transport. The concept of urban density is important in understanding how cities function. Generally, it refers to the number of people living in an urban area, and it can affect that area's economics, health, innovation, psychology, geography, and sustainability. Many advocates of increasing urban density argue that higher-density cities are more sustainable than lower-density, dispersed cities that rely heavily on auto transport. In general, a compact and denser city is a more efficient city, in part, because many services such as schools, shops, and public transportation are within walking distance. Additionally, residents of compact cities with increased inner suburban density are less dependent on cars, resulting in a decrease in fossil fuel, thus improving air quality and decreasing greenhouse gas emissions. The use of undeveloped land and the costs of providing infrastructure, real estate development, and public services are all considerably less for managed and denser growth than for conventional sprawl development. School, road, and utility costs per residential unit vary

Shade: Arcades onto the Main Plaza in Cuzco, Peru.

depending on development density. Compared to denser urban development, sprawl costs are about 60 percent more. In fact, in recent years, planning strategies, especially in the United States, have focused on increasing urban densities; these strategies include New Urbanism, Transit Oriented Development (TOD), and smart growth. These strategies rely on evidence that suggest that the lower a city's density, the more energy it consumes.

This chapter looks at lessons for making successful desert cities. It explores examples in Iran, Tunisia, Morocco, Rajasthan, Egypt, Yemen, Australia, Chile, and Peru. This is not a comprehensive array. Rather, it is a survey of a diverse set of long-enduring desert cities. Each has its own lessons, not only at the urban scale, but also at the scale of the building types. Within this survey, some shared characteristics are identified.

Among them are: shade, **pedestrian scale** and mass transit, courtyards, efficiency in water and energy use, natural ventilation and evaporative cooling, and enduring building materials; but most of all they share the characteristic of **compactness**. A brief description of these characteristics follows.

Shade

Shade is an essential component of desert living, particularly for the pedestrian. When one consults early photographs of the centers of cities like Phoenix, and of older Hispanic cities, porches and arcades (portales) are in front of almost every building, and awnings often shade the windows. In older cities in Australia, such as Adelaide, such portales are still to be found, somewhat like the cast-iron arcades of the French Quarter of New Orleans. In newer parts of cities such as Brisbane, high steel arcades have been constructed upon which shading plants climb. Major city streets are often lined with shade trees. Sometimes, as in Isfahan and Yazd in Iran, they are growing directly out of the irrigation ditches that flow alongside the sidewalks. In other North African desert cities, water is too scarce for all but the occasional street drinking fountain, often built as a philanthropic gift to the community by some well-to-do citizen. Here, the buildings themselves are the source of shade as they form the edges of the often narrow pedestrian alleyways. In cities such as Shibam in the Hadramawt of South Yemen, the tower houses that line the street are so high that they create a great deal of shade, and the narrow city streets are noticeably cooler than the surrounding countryside.

Shade is particularly difficult to achieve at the scale of the typical automobile dominated street. The roadway almost inevitably will be exposed to long-term solar radiation and will itself become a **radiant heat** source. This can be reduced by substantial shade trees along the sidewalks and in the medians, but such trees are rarely water

Pedestrian scale - an urban development pattern where walking is safe and efficient.

Compactness - high-density or monocentric development; some concentration of employment and housing, as well as some mixture of land uses.

Radiant heat - heat transmitted by radiation as contrasted with that transmitted by conduction or convection.

conservative and would not meet the requirements for indigenous xeriscape plants often adopted by desert cities like Phoenix. This suggests that the higher-density, pedestrian dominated parts of the desert city should be served, not by streets predominantly conceived of as vehicular roadways with pedestrian sidewalks, but as relatively narrow, shaded pedestrian ways, with limited access for service and emergency vehicles as well as purely local traffic. This is the arrangement for many of the streets of older desert cities. Physical conditions limit vehicular traffic to small service and public safety vehicles, or two wheeled vehicles such as bicycles or mopeds. The widths of streets in the "medinas" of Morocco or Tunisia were often thought of in terms of the required number of laden donkeys or camels walking side-by-side. In a modern desert city, the dimensions could follow the minimums required for specially designed or selected essential vehicles, while recognizing the priority of the pedestrian, as do the malls on many of our university campuses.

Shade structures Brisbane, Australia.

Narrow shady street in Sana'a, Yemen.

Pedestrian Scale

Pedestrian scale creates a very different built form than the scale of the automobile. Pedestrians need an intimacy of encounter with the environment, whether natural or human-made. They also need short-range destinations. This leads not only to a smaller scale environment but also to the possibility of a more varied geometry. Since 1785 when the Jeffersonian Land Ordinance established a neoclassical subdivision of land west of the Appalachians, the plans of most American cities have been dominated by the rectilinear mile square grid. The interest in the picturesque that emerged in the mid-nineteenth century introduced the curvilinear street pattern, originally in our cemeteries and parks and eventually in our suburbs. The desert city, however, in providing for pedestrians, will often have an even more complex geometry in its pattern of major and minor streets. A few examples appear in the history of desert cities planned for princes, such as Jaipur in Rajasthan, that are almost completely on a rectilinear grid, but the majority do not respond to a single dominant geometric concept. This is not to suggest that they are illogical, but that the logic is not that of simple geometry. Rather, as scholars have suggested, it is often the logic of religiously derived and legally enforced social relationships, and the creation of a hierarchy in street networks linking small communities to the larger city.

The dense network of intimate shady streets typically will lead to a major communal space. In the Hispanic colonial cities of South and North America, built under the influence of the Laws of the Indies, this will be a formal plaza, focused on a major fountain, flanked by arcades, and framed by the buildings of government and religion. In Isfahan in Iran, there is an enormous central square, or "maidan," whereas in cities such as Marrakesh in Morocco the major open space lacks such geometric clarity, but comes to life in the cooler evenings with food stalls and crowds clustering around storytellers, snake charmers, tribal bands, acrobats, and even dentists. In most Islamic countries, formal geometry is reserved for the paradise gardens of palaces or mosques, not for urban spaces. Nonetheless, the central plaza is the focus of the community. The major Friday Mosque also will be nearby, and at dusk, the air will be filled with the electronically amplified and distorted wail of the call to prayer from the loudspeakers mounted on its minaret. The vitality and identity of the city are relished by both its citizens and its visitors in such places. In the modern city similar public places are still necessary, and could relate to the transit systems that bring people from the further reaches of the city, thereby reducing the necessity for the major roads and parking garages that erode the intensity and thermal comfort of urban life in the desert.

In the ancient desert cities it is often from such places that the market, bazaar, or souk heads off as a shaded linear pedestrian passageway, burrowing its way through the fabric of the city. Typically, this linear market will be flanked by occasionally fountained service courts, workshops, and storerooms from which laden trolley carts head off to refill the emptying shelves of the small stores that line the pedestrian way, and also by the fondouks or inns that accommodate the visiting merchants. Bazaars or souks are often vaulted or domed, and illuminated and ventilated from round windows that let narrow shafts of sunlight in and the heated air out. Such spaces, neither interior nor exterior, which are shaded but open to the fresh air, are crucial to the success of desert city buildings. Whether such a form of retail would work in the modern world may be questioned but it certainly has its parallels in cities such as Scottsdale in Arizona that has a naturally day lit, and

© John Meunier

Main Plaza Santiago, Chile.

in certain seasons, naturally ventilated, shopping mall a half mile long. The major difference is that the means of access via the automobile has isolated the modern mall from the rest of the city behind a moat of parking. With increased access provided by mass transit, and a higher density of residences within walking distance, such physical isolation of shopping from the surrounding community can be significantly reduced.

Courtyards

Courtyards have been the focus of buildings in compact cities for millennia, but particularly in desert cities. The central courtyard allows the building to be constructed out to the very edges of its site, gaining most of the necessary light and air from within, rather than depending on a wasteful buffer around it of often relatively useless space. That courtyard becomes the focus of the building from which the major rooms are reached directly, and into which those rooms may open at cooler times of the day and depending on the season. In very hot desert cities, as in Fez or Marrakesh in Morocco, the courtyard will have provision to be shaded when necessary with sheets of fabric stretched on ropes, or by open-weave mats laid across a metal grille that protects the courtyard from the heat from above. Typically, within the courtyard there will be a fountain or pool and leafy plants that provide both physical and emotional cooling.

Buildings of this courtyard type were designed in the late 1950s for the campus of Arizona State University. The Farmer Education Building and the Social Science Building there have central fountains and planted courtyards around which the open to the air circulation of the building, both stairs and galleries, is located. These stairs and galleries share the shade of the light mesh canopy over the courtyard. Only on entering the rooms off that circulation does one experience full mechanical climate control. The courtyard also becomes the major social focus for the inhabitants of the building. In some courtyards in Iran, for example in the desert city of Yazd, the pool in the courtyard may have a wooden platform straddling it on which a family and friends may gather in the evening to eat and converse. The courtyard will have on its southern edge, facing north, an open porch or iwan for use in the summer,

Courtyard of Social Science Building at Arizona State University in Tempe, Arizona.

Wind tower and courtyard of the Lari house Yazd, Iran.

and on its northern edge, facing south, a winter space, that in the nineteenth century may have been furnished with moveable windows glazed with colored glass. The air movement through these courtyards and iwans is stimulated by windtowers, or baudgir, which climb above the rooftops and channel air from all directions down into the houses, iwans, and courtyards. In many older desert cities there is also space below ground to which people may retire in the heat of the day for rest, quiet, and contemplation.

Such below-ground space in Iran often surrounded a small pool through which the water from the qanats flowed. The qanats are underground channels hand tunneled from the base of the distant mountains to bring water to the city. The residents of major institutions and the important houses of the city were served directly by these qanats. Others had to go to a communal cistern into which water would flow from the qanats. This space is covered by a dome and ventilated by an array of windtowers. Qanats are also found in North Africa, although there they are called khettaras.

Water

Water is obviously crucial to the survival of desert cities. Many were built on rivers that brought the water from far beyond the sparsely precipitated desert environment. Cairo is the most extreme example of this, but many other desert cities—such as Lima in Peru, where the local rainfall is almost zero—are served by rivers fed from distant mountain watersheds. In the Chilean Atacama Desert, one of the driest in the world, there are richly vegetated fissures in the arid desert surface through which streams flow from the distant volcanic mountain ranges. Small oasis towns, such as Toconao, capture that water and guide it in narrow channels through their orchards, much as with the acequias in New Mexico and the great date palm groves of North Africa.

Another source of water has been groundwater in aquifers built up over millennia and replenished by seasonal rains (see Chapter 10). Surface water is the water that flows or is impounded on the surface of the Earth, such as that found in rivers and lakes. Some of this surface water percolates into the ground and into groundwater aquifers. Water in the aquifers moves underground eventually reemerging at springs that flow back to the oceans via streams and rivers. Unfortunately, the time it takes for recharged water to move into and through an aquifer can vary from decades to centuries. Compounding the problem is that the rate of pumping groundwater is much greater than the rate of recharge.

Sadly, in many ancient desert cities, such as Sana'a in North Yemen, the wells that almost every house had in its basement no longer reach the aquifer. This source of water has retreated

Water in the Atacama Desert leading to the oasis town of Toconao in Chile.

beyond the reach of those wells because of profligate mechanical pumping caused by increased per capita use, multiplied by rapid population growth. Water is now piped into Sana'a, as is the case in most of the smaller towns and villages of Yemen where it is usually connected to communal taps in the street rather than directly to the houses.

In both ancient and contemporary desert cities, the modern technology of pumps and pipes, as well as canals that bring water from great distances, has changed patterns of water use as well as cultural attitudes toward water. The sense of water as a scarce and precious commodity, to be celebrated architecturally through noble fountains and the building of great cisterns and magnificent stepwells into which

© John Meunier

A monsoon tank in Rajasthan, India.

the monsoon rains are carefully channeled, can be seen in Yemen and Rajasthan. This sensibility has been displaced more recently by a purely utilitarian attitude that appears to have encouraged wastefulness. In beautiful old cities such as Jaisalmer in India, this newly excessive use of water overloads the inadequate drainage systems and erodes the foundations of older buildings that were not built to withstand the rising dampness.

In our modern desert cities there appears to be a growing consciousness of the need to be thoughtful about water. Many cities have adopted xeriscape as the standard for landscaping. Development also is constrained by the need to demonstrate the long-term availability of water, and an attempt is being made to avoid the exhaustion of the aquifers. In Phoenix, for example, the local press educates the public through articles about the loss of natural rivers because of the unconstrained increase in the number of wells within the watershed.

In fact, given the scarcity of water in deserts and the amount of time it takes depleting aquifers to recharge, some desert cities, such as Las Vegas, Nevada, have adopted water conservation measures. According to the Las Vegas Water District's website, southern Nevada has reduced its demand of gallons per capita per day by 29 percent in 2011.[1] Ultimately, their goal is a further reduction of 11 percent by 2035. Sadly, however, not all desert cities (such as Phoenix, Arizona) have yet adopted such sensible conservation measures (see Chapter 10).

What techniques and attitudes can then be learned from the history and recent experiences of these desert cities?

Water cisterns in White Cliffs, Australia.

The town cistern in Hababa, Yemen.

Water harvesting - the activity of direct collection of rainwater, which can be stored for direct use or can be recharged into the groundwater.

Water Harvesting

Water harvesting is a term that needs to be understood and embraced. Desert cities throughout history have practiced it. The modern desert city may harvest water at the scale of the watershed and the region but, at the scale of the individual building and the small community, many still have lessons to be learned. For example, throughout Australia many older homes have under their eaves a great round steel cistern into which the rainwater drains. It is used to relieve dependence on the main water supply in old mining towns such as White Cliffs or Coober Pedy, where many live in underground houses converted from the opal mines and harvest water from the ground above.

An older example is in the courtyard in the middle of the great mosque in Kairouan, Tunisia. Below the center of the courtyard sits a cistern into which the rainwater that falls on that courtyard is drained, and it is then available as a well for the ablutions required before prayer. At the center of the beautiful small town of Hababa, in Yemen, is the town cistern into which the winter rains are drained and stored; it is surrounded by a wall of houses and a small mosque. In India, water harvesting is now a requirement for all new developments. All other desert cities could benefit from such a fine

Tower houses around a vegetable garden in Sana'a, Yemen.

grain attitude towards water conservation. The continuing use of water already used for ablutions is evident in Sana'a, the capital city of Yemen, as it irrigates gardens where fresh vegetables are grown. The Waqf, the local religious foundation, manages these gardens as well as the adjacent mosque.

The celebration of water as a scarce and valuable commodity should be expressed in civic and private architecture, in urban form, and in management policies. As an example of what not to do, in a recent drought in Phoenix, the fountains were left dry to symbolize a commitment not to waste water, but this practice was actually misguided. The savings were negligible because the water used in the fountains is recirculated and the only slight loss would be through evaporation. Historically, fountains have been used to provide respite from the arid heat of the desert and to honor the cleansing and life-giving power of water. To keep the fountains flowing is to demonstrate the ability to continue life and civility in the desert. To turn them off is to admit defeat. The lesson here is in the appropriate use of civic architecture to celebrate the value of water as it is harvested and enjoyed.

Earth

Earth is the material most used in the construction of many of the older desert cities. Adobe and rammed earth, or pise, often are dug from the immediately adjacent land. From the North African settlements of Morocco, Algeria, and Tunisia to most of the Middle East the communities are made of it. The towered city of Shibam in Yemen, for example, is built of mud brick from the great wash of the Hadramawt. Local stone also is used, as in Rajasthan, India, where the indigenous sandstone is extraordinarily versatile and can be used for columns, beams, floor slabs, as well as intricately carved screens and brackets. In Jerusalem, the city benefits from the continuing commitment to the use of its beautiful locally quarried Jerusalem stone on all of its buildings, giving a consistency and coherence lacking in many modern cities.

© John Meunier

Rammed earth construction in Morocco.

Building Materials for the Desert

In contemporary desert cities, many architects of the Southwest have been exploring the use of rammed earth, adobe, and other more enduring materials and techniques that extend their palette to make a thoroughly modern architecture that fits their context as well as the contemporary needs of their clients. Eddie Jones in Phoenix and Rick Joy in Tucson are two of a rapidly growing school of regional architects whose work is being recognized far beyond the bounds of the region, and who have incorporated rammed earth as a valuable contribution to their architectural resources. Inorganic materials that will not deteriorate under the fierce attack of sunlight and dry air, such as earth and metals, have replaced wood as the primary raw material for the structure, or as cladding on the exteriors of buildings. Even the great wooden beams at Taliesin West, located in Scottsdale, Arizona and Frank Lloyd Wright's former winter home and school, have now been replaced by steel. In the arid air of the desert, steel often can be left unpainted in the knowledge that the rusting process will be extraordinarily slow. Will Bruder has been an architectural leader in exploring the use of metals, and his work at the Phoenix Central Library is sheathed in locally mined copper that has been corrugated by the same machines that mold the steel sheets that form the walls of agricultural silos.

Air

Air in the desert has been one of its greatest assets. Many very talented people, such as New Mexico's great architect John Gaw Meem, as well as Frank Lloyd Wright, came to the desert to benefit from the clear dry air as a part of a treatment for their lung-based illnesses. For many months of the year, fresh desert air can be allowed to circulate freely through the buildings. The great mosques in the older desert cities of the Middle East are open to the air, without glazed windows. Indeed, one mosque type is little more than great arched porches, or iwans, on the four sides of an open fountained courtyard. In the older desert cities, many fresh air environments use architecture to create exterior microclimates rather than closed interior environments. These courtyards, kiosks, porches, shaded souks or bazaars, gardens, or naturally ventilated major rooms, often domed and even fountained, lend much of the quality and richness to the fabric of older desert cities, particularly those of ancient Persia, Egypt, and the Arab world.

Some modern desert based architects have understood the continuing value of these architectural elements as they build in Arizona, New Mexico, and other arid regions. Taliesin West, the winter home of Frank Lloyd Wright and his school, also had

© John Meunier

**Shutters below clerestory windows
in Sana'a, Yemen.**

no glazed windows in its early years—just shutters that could be closed to keep out the wind or the cold night air. Similarly, older desert homes in Yemen also had shutters only in their lower windows, with the higher windows "glazed" with thin sheets of alabaster to diffuse light into the rooms. High-level ventilation through lantern vents, or simply holes in the roof similar to that of the Pantheon in Rome, have ensured the evacuation of hot air from both major halls and linear vaulted souks or bazaars throughout the history of architecture in arid lands.

In an Islamic city, because of Koranic laws against overlooking into the private courtyards of neighboring houses, there is a consistent height for all the houses. This permits a continuous stream of breezes above the rooftops. The wind towers of Iran, such as in the great desert city of Yazd, reach into that stream to play an important part in stimulating air movement within the courtyard houses, both through scooping air down on the positive pressure side of the tower and through drawing air out on the negative pressure side.

Compact Urban Form

What form should higher-density urban living take in a twenty-first century desert city? High and low-rise condominiums currently being built, particularly close to existing centers with an array of services available within walking distance, follow models established in San Diego and Dallas. For some people in the urban area, notably young professionals and older people without children, this may be an appropriate although relatively expensive housing type. Higher density traditional houses also are being built. The open space around many of these houses, though, has shrunk to a margin measured in feet rather than yards. This limits the use of the open-air space that is one of the rewards of desert living where, for much of the year, it is possible and enjoyable to be in appropriately positioned and shaded outdoor spaces connected to the house.

The older desert cities, built before the days of the automobile and air-conditioning, have much to teach us about ways to live comfortably and well at higher urban densities. The late Norbert Schoenauer wrote in "6,000 Years of Housing":

> In a world where no nation is wealthy enough to afford waste, the land-use efficiency of the oriental urban residential pattern is worthy of emulation in terms of both land use and energy conservation. This is not to say that the oriental urban environment should be duplicated, but merely that some of its urban design principles should be adopted, such as, for example, the hierarchical order in street networks that bring about a safer residential environment.

> Moreover, planning small precincts for residential neighborhoods without through traffic would afford a more intimate identity with the residential community. In addition, a compact urban development pattern with no waste space would result in reasonable walking distances to many community facilities and would create the population density required for efficient mass transportation systems. Finally, the courtyard concept could be applied successfully in the design of both single-family dwellings as well as multiple housing in which each dwelling would have some semblance of privacy and indeed also a "well of heaven."[2]

The following comparison illustrates the urban land use efficiency that Schoenauer analyzed. The typical North American suburb has 23 percent of its area devoted to public rights of way, 6 percent to driveways and garages, 17 percent to built-up areas, and 54 percent to private yard space, much of it just a buffer between the houses and the road. He compared this pattern to several other oriental urban patterns: Tunis, Medina, 9 percent public rights of way, 74 percent built-up areas, 17 percent private courtyard space; Ahmedabad, Kadwa Pol, 18 percent public rights of way, 69 percent built-up areas, 13 percent private courtyard space; Baghdad, Iraq, 16 percent public rights of way, 72 percent built-up areas, 12 percent private courtyard space. In the oriental examples, instead of only one-sixth of the land being used for dwelling, between two-thirds and three-quarters of the land is in residential use, and that does not count the private open space, nearly all in the form of central courtyards that are an intrinsic part of the home. This makes it possible to achieve much higher densities without building high or losing contact with the ground. It also allows the use of building and paving areas to collect the runoff from rains and support the plants that can flourish in its courtyards and along its pedestrian ways.

This comparison does not mention the great value of the roof surface of the desert house. Typically flat, it is accessible and usable. Residents use it at night, under the clear desert sky, as a cool place for sleeping. In the early morning, with the appropriate shade from the early morning sun, it can be a delightful place for breakfast. In the winter, the gentler sun can be enjoyed directly. In an Islamic city, due to the strict rules about overlooking, the neighboring houses will not block the distant views. This becomes a welcome contrast to the introversion of the rest of the house. Even without the rule of the Koran, such height limitations could be easily assured within the planning controls of the western world.

Past and Future

Desert cities have been around since the beginnings of civilization thousands of years ago. Largely due to the extraordinary technological changes of the last century and a half, modern life has alienated us from much of the evolved wisdom of those millennia of urban desert living, even for those who grew up within such ancient patterns. For many contemporary desert dwellers, the term "sustainability" has attached to it a question mark. It would seem appropriate as we confront an uncertain future, where the optimism of modernity is being tempered by our growing concerns about the price it is exacting on our natural and social environments, for us to reconsider our heritage, not as something to be discarded, but as a source of valuable concepts. The past is not to be copied, but to be used as a reservoir of societal wisdom.

Supplemental Readings

Ouroussoff, N. (2010, September 25). In Arabian Desert, a sustainable city rises. *New York Times*, p. A1. Retrieved from http://www.nytimes.com/2010/09/26/arts/design/26masdar.html?ref=nicolaiouroussoff

Biello, D. (2011, August 19). Can a sustainable city rise in the Middle Eastern Desert? [Special issue.] *Scientific American*, retrieved from http://www.scientificamerican.com/article.cfm?id=masdar-sustainable-city-in-desert

Alshuwaikhat, H. M., & Nkwenti, D. I. (2002). Developing sustainable cities in arid regions. *Cities, 19*(2), 85–94.

Managing Water and Its Use: The Central Issue for Sustaining Human Settlements

Ray Quay

Introduction

Water sustainability, though in itself it represents a critical challenge, cannot be separated from the general concepts of social, environmental, and economic sustainability. Water is critical to each of these three aspects of sustainability. Water is required to sustain human life, but it also plays an important role in lifestyle and culture. The landscapes that we find desirable, our preferences for recreation, and our habits and technologies of hygiene and health depend on adequate water. The ecosystems of our lands heavily depend on freshwater. Riparian areas, wetlands, lakes, and rivers provide critical habitat and ecosystems services, which depend on adequate water to sustain them. Our economies also heavily depend on adequate water supplies. Agriculture and most industrial processes require water. Goods are shipped via rivers. Most tourism-based economies depend on water and snow for recreation. Thus, water is a foundation in multiple aspects of sustainability, which likely will mean that as we manage sustainability of our communities, tradeoffs in water use may be required. We may need to change some aspects of water use for lifestyle, to ensure adequate water for the environment or economy. Or we may need to accept some loss of environmental quality or ecosystem services because less water is available for the environment.

Water is essential for the survival of life as we know it, and its abundance or lack thereof has been a major factor in the growth or decline of almost every human civilization. Today, adequate **water supplies** to meet current and future worldwide needs of humans and the environment could be one of the greatest challenges of the twenty-first century. This challenge is in response to an emerging global water crisis of three interrelated dimensions: the lack of sanitary water and wastewater conditions in developing countries; degradation of freshwater supplies and associated habitats by human action such as pollution; and a looming shortfall between freshwater supply and demand in urban and rural areas. These problems are further complicated by the fact that they are not uniform for all parts of the globe. Since the adoption of the United Nations Millennium Development Goals in 2000, the percent of people worldwide that do not have access to sanitary water decreased from 24% to 11%, and those who do not have access to sanitation facilities decreased from 51% to 33%. These are significant achievements, but in sub-Saharan Africa, 60% do not have access to sanitary water and 70% do not have access to sanitation.[1] In 2010, it was estimated that 80% of the world's population lived in an area impacted by degradation of a river system. This impact also has global spatial patterns. Some countries are able to deploy technology to reduce these threats, while others, such as Africa and South Asia, are more limited in their ability to do so.[2] This creates a significant regional problem given that, in 2005, it was estimated that 54% of China's seven main rivers were unsafe for human consumption.[3] Lastly, many developed and undeveloped countries already have highly **stressed** water supplies. It is estimated that globally 1.4 billion people live within **watersheds** where demand exceeds available water supplies[4] and that half of the world's 16 largest cities are experiencing freshwater shortages.[5] This gap in **water supply** and demand will likely increase with continued growth and possible **climate change** impacts. Discussion of these three issues of water crisis would require more space than afforded by this book, thus, this chapter focuses on this last issue. How we manage demand and supplies of water to maintain a sustainable water supply, especially in our cities, under conditions of change and **uncertainty** will be the most critical issue to our future.

Water sustainability can be defined in the terms of the 1987 Brundtland Commission report as the ability of institutions to manage water in a manner that meets the needs of present social and environmental systems without impairing the ability of future generations to do the same. There is no silver bullet to accomplishing this goal. As this chapter will present, water sustainability is a complicated issue fraught with high uncertainty about the future state of social and environmental systems. Four conditions of water resource sustainability should be considered:

1. Availability of freshwater supplies under conditions of uncertainty, including long-term drought, climate change, and regional growth.
2. Ability to provide infrastructure needed to store, withdraw, treat, recycle, and deliver water for power, agricultural, and domestic use.
3. Ability to manage power, domestic, industrial, and agricultural demand for water.
4. Ability of private and public water management institutions to anticipate and adapt to changes within social and environmental systems.

Though water sustainability is a global issue, this chapter focuses primarily on sustainability of water in the United States. It will examine each of these four conditions of urban water sustainability.

Water as a Renewable Resource

Water is essential for life and development, and fortunately, it is plentiful. On earth, 97% of the surface is covered by water and only 3% by land. However, most of the life that exists on land needs freshwater, which represents only a small portion of the earth's total water supply. Less than 2.5% of the earth's water is freshwater, and over half of this freshwater is for now locked in ice caps, glaciers, and permanent snow mass. Less than 1% of the earth's total water is freshwater available for use by life on the earth's landmasses.[6] Even this 1% is not evenly distributed across the earth's landmasses; some areas such as the northern and tropical forests have more, and desert areas of the southwest United States and northern Africa have less.

Stress - the result of a change that threatens the functionality of a system.

Watersheds - the geographic extent from which rainfall will eventually flow into a river or lake.

Water supply - the total amount of water available to be used to meet water demands.

Climate change - long-term deviations from historical records of precipitation, temperature, and storm intensity.

Uncertainty - lack of knowledge about when or what will be a future state.

Water sustainability - based on the Brundtland Commission definition of sustainable development, the ability of institutions to manage water in a manner that meets the needs of present social and environmental systems without impairing the ability of future generations to do the same.

Water, including freshwater, exists within a natural cyclic system that moves water from the oceans to the land and back. Solar radiation evaporates water from the oceans and **surface water** on land. This evaporated water condenses into clouds and eventually precipitates as rain and snow on land and over the oceans. On land, some of the rain and melted snow becomes surface water flowing into streams and rivers and eventually back to the oceans. Some surface water is stored in lakes. Some percolates into the ground and into **groundwater aquifers**. Water in the aquifers moves underground, eventually reemerging at springs that flow back to the oceans via streams and rivers. This **water cycle** makes freshwater a **renewable resource** that is constantly replenished as water moves from the oceans to the land.

Not all paths of the water cycle occur in the same time frame or in the same place. The time it takes for **recharged** water to move into and through an aquifer can vary from decades to centuries. Shallow water aquifers are more closely linked to surface waters and can often be found in association with a river. Water will percolate into these aquifers quickly; however, the volume of supply is often limited, and high-volume pumping quickly can deplete these **aquifers**. They are also susceptible to contamination from surface sources such as septic tanks. Deepwater aquifers contain water that may be centuries old. Typically, they are within geologic formations that can span hundreds of square miles and contain large volumes of water. Although their location is independent of surface water features, they are often recharged where rivers and streams cross over them. Given their volume and depth, recharge can take decades to centuries. Surface water can also take a slower path as glaciers and permanent snowpacks can store water for decades to centuries. One growing problem is the pumping of groundwater supplies at a rate faster than they are being recharged.

Surface water - the water that flows or is impounded on the surface of the earth, such as that found in rivers and lakes.

Groundwater - water found underground in aquifers.

Water cycle - the cyclic process that continuously moves water back and forth between the land, oceans, and the atmosphere.

Renewable resource - a resource that continually renews itself through natural processes.

Recharge - the flow of water into an aquifer, typically from the land surface.

Aquifer - an underground feature of porous stone or river gravel/sand that is saturated with water.

Demand for Water

The availability of freshwater has been a key factor in the rise and fall of ancient civilizations.[7] Humans use water for numerous purposes. Obviously, we need water to drink. We use it to bathe ourselves, wash and cook our food, and dispose of human waste. We use it to irrigate our crops and raise animals. We use it to produce raw materials and goods, to produce electricity, and occasionally, to fight fires. We also use it for less critical activities such as for watering lawns and gardens, swimming pools, and fountains. It is estimated that for 2005 in the United States, 210 billion gallons of water per day were withdrawn from various sources of water for these activities. Not all of this was freshwater; 15% came from saltwater sources. Thermoelectric power production was the largest use of this water in 2005, using 41% of the total freshwater withdrawn and almost all of the saltwater. With 37% of the total, irrigation was the next largest use of freshwater. Public systems represented 13% of the freshwater withdrawn.[8] One of the goals of sustainability is to assure long-term safe drinking water supplies for every person in the world. Unfortunately, this goal has not been reached.

Most people in the United States get their water from a public system. These public systems vary from a single well serving a dozen customers to large systems serving millions of people using multiple sources of water. These systems deliver water that must meet national **water quality standards**. Typically, the water is collected from a groundwater or surface water source, treated within a water treatment plant, and delivered via pipes to individual customers. How much water each of these public systems uses and for what purpose can vary widely between systems and regions. Several key factors can account for these differences. Climate has an impact on water use. Dryer and hotter climates will require more water to meet demands for outdoor water use, such as landscape irrigation, pools, and cooling towers. Southern parts of the United States, such as Southern California, Arizona, and Florida, can have two or three growing seasons. Thus, agriculture water use can be much higher on an annual basis. Cities with older water systems, such as Boston, have high rates of unaccounted for water, essentially water that leaks from main water lines, in some cases, as high as 30% to 40%. Newer cities such as Phoenix, Arizona, may have less than 6% unaccounted for water. A common standard measure of the efficiency of water use for a public system is total **gallons used per capita per day (GPCD)**. GPCD varies between and within regions, ranging from as low as 50 to as high as 400. When compared to other countries, the United States has some of the highest GPCDs in the world.

Within these public systems, residential or domestic uses represent the largest volume of water use, on average, 60% to 70% of total public water supplies in the United States. Domestic water use can be separated into two types of uses, indoor water use and outdoor water use. Unfortunately, measuring indoor and outdoor water use is not easy, and estimates of what percent is used for each are generally based on methods that amount to being educated guesses. Estimates of the percent of outdoor water use vary from 15% to 60%, with the range a function of how much water is used outdoors, not how much is used indoors, and primarily due to local climatic conditions. Outdoor water is used for a variety of purposes with irrigation of grass, gardens, and trees being the largest, and cooling towers and pools in warmer climates representing a second major use. Most of suburban America is landscaped with turf, utilizing significant water volume. Cities in northern latitudes with high amounts of annual rainfall, such as Seattle, Washington, have natural rainfall that is adequate to support most landscapes and thus less water is needed for irrigation. Cities in dryer regions, such as Phoenix, have high rates of evapotranspiration and less rainfall requiring more water to maintain turf and pools. Outdoor water use is also a factor of the seasons, with more being used in the summer months than winter months.

Examples of this are outdoor and indoor water use for Atlanta, Las Vegas, and Seattle. Though total GPCD varies from 165 for Las Vegas to just over 60 for Seattle, indoor water use only varies from 54 to 71 GPCD. Average per capita indoor water use does not vary much between regions in the United States or from one season to the next, but can vary based on the age of the home and the number, income, and age of residents in the home. Typically, over half of indoor water use occurs in the bathroom with most of that coming from the toilet. Another 25% is used in the laundry room by the clothes washer. But these ratios are changing. In the United States, federal standards for water efficiency have greatly increased the efficiency of new toilets, shower heads, and faucets, and most manufacturers now produce more efficient clothes washers and dishwashers. As a result, newer homes will typically have more efficient appliances and thus lower average water use. Much of the decline in per capita water use over the last 20 years can be attributed to these efficiency improvements.

Most water-resource planning focuses on the human uses of water, but water is also critical to the function of natural environments. **Riparian areas** adjacent to streams and rivers depend on shallow groundwater replenished by the river or stream and often are critical habitat for wildlife. Some habitats require year round streamflows, while others have adapted to intermittent streamflows. Habitats in upland areas are dependent on seasonal rainfall and snowmelt. Many species of fish require specific levels of streamflow to breed. Changes that reduce streamflow can result in changes to these habitats. Such changes arise from several causes. Damming rivers and streams, over pumping or altering natural recharge of aquifers that are a source of water for streams, and reduced precipitation due to climate change all can result in reduced streamflows. Such changes are one factor in the steady loss of riparian habitat in the United States.[9]

Riparian areas - natural areas of flora and fauna that are dependent on shallow groundwater that is recharged by an adjacent river or stream.

Water Supply

In ancient times, humans relied on three primary sources of freshwater: rainfall; surface waters that could be found in rivers, lakes, and springs; and groundwater available from shallow wells. From the earliest periods of human civilization, humans built infrastructure such as canals, wells, and impoundments to store and convey freshwater from where it was found to where it was needed for agriculture and consumption. As civilization advanced, our methods of obtaining, storing, and delivering freshwater allowed us to withdraw, store, and deliver more water over longer distances. Today, this technology varies globally from methods not much more advanced than those used by ancient civilizations to highly advanced systems of reverse osmosis to remove salt from seawater. Sources of freshwater vary from one region to another. In some regions, groundwater from shallow aquifers is widely available, while other regions must use modern pumps to access aquifers that exist thousands of feet below the surface. Some regions have access to surface water from lakes and rivers, while in other regions, water supplies are scarce and the lack of surface or groundwater limits human activities. Many major urban areas, such as Boston, New York, San Francisco, Los Angeles, and Phoenix, move water from watersheds hundreds of miles away to meet the **water demand** of their region. The below image shows the 337-mile long **Central Arizona Project** canal that diverts water from the Colorado River to Phoenix and further south to Tucson mostly for municipal water needs plus water for Indian tribes, who have regained their historic rights to water through federal legal challenges.

Freshwater supplies can be organized into three major sources: groundwater, surface water, and **reclaimed water**. In the United States, on average, the primary source of freshwater is from surface waters (77%) with the rest coming from groundwater (23%).

Water demand - the consumption of water to support human and environmental activities.

Central Arizona Project - a quasi-governmental agency that manages the delivery of a portion of Arizona's allocation of the Colorado River to central Arizona primarily using a canal that stretches from the Colorado River to Tucson, Arizona.

Reclaimed water - sewage treated to a level of water quality suitable for reuse or recycling.

Courtesy author

BOX 1: Drought: A Natural Disaster Worth Paying Attention To

Usually, natural disaster news in the United States is about earthquakes, tornadoes, hurricanes, floods, landslides, forest fires, or extreme winter storms. Rarely today in the US does one hear drought described as a natural disaster, nor does it get the same news coverage as other disasters, even though droughts occur frequently with potentially devastating impacts. Is this warranted or are we overlooking drought as a potential natural disaster?

There are likely four reasons for this current view of drought: 1) a drought unfolds slowly over many months and years and, thus, does not create the same sense of emergency as other natural disasters; 2) in US cities, even during the most severe droughts, it is rare that water will not flow when the water faucet is turned on or a toilet is flushed; 3) urban dwellers will see the biggest impact of drought indirectly and eventually in higher prices at the grocery store; and 4) deaths are attributed to heat waves not drought, even though the weather conditions that cause summer heat spells are the same as those that that cause drought. Generally the term "drought" implies an extended period of time, usually a year or more, of abnormally low rainfall resulting in a water shortage that makes it difficult to meet the normal water demand for agriculture, urban, or natural environmental systems. However, what constitutes a drought, its scale, severity, length, and impacts, varies widely with geography and climate. All watersheds are dynamic systems that undergo cycles of wet and dry conditions; however, the magnitude and duration of these cycles are unique for each watershed. Thus, droughts are not universal events and can vary from place to place. As of 2014, Arizona has been experiencing drought conditions for almost 15 years, yet it is just approaching a point where some of its surface water supplies may be restricted. In contrast, two years of drought in Texas in 2011 led to the entire state being declared a national disaster area. Thus, talking about drought in Texas is different than talking about drought in Arizona.

Even the impacts of drought will vary based on a region's ability to respond to drought. In regions where water management and agricultural practices are less sophisticated, even short-term droughts can eliminate the ability to meet a region's water demands. In western Africa, drought conditions regularly create disastrous conditions that result in hundreds of deaths from thirst and famine (Gettleman, 2011; Lacey, 2006). US history includes cases where droughts have created disasters on a regular basis. The Dust Bowl drought in the 1930s devastated the farms of the Great Plains, forcing thousands of people to leave the area; in the late 1950s another severe seven year drought killed livestock and crops in Texas, resulting in a similar exodus of people from their ranches and farms (Burnett, 2012); and in 1988 a Midwest drought destroyed half the nation's corn crop, forcing thousands of farmers out of business (Schneider, 1993) (see Chapter 3 on the Dust Bowl).

There is a growing perception in the US that drought is occurring more frequently and more severely (Travis, Gangwer, & Klein, 2011). In the past decade, drought conditions have begun to affect more than just rural agriculture regions. In late 2007, after 18 months of drought conditions, many cities in the South reached a point where they had only enough water to last a few months. As a result, the state of Georgia and a number of cities enacted mandatory restrictions on urban outdoor water use, with some requiring a 50% reduction in water use (Goodman, 2007). In 2013, during one of California's worst droughts of the last 100 years, the governor of California called for cities to encourage their residents to reduce their water use by 20%. But, even in these cases, signs of complacency still exist. In 2012, following another two years of extreme drought in Georgia (Davis, 2012), there was little public discussion in Atlanta about actions needed to manage water (Jones, 2012). In California, voluntary water use restrictions did not work as well as expected. State surveys have shown that urban water use in May actually increased by 1% over May use in previous years, mostly driven by consumption in Southern California. In response the state has adopted mandatory water restrictions with fines (Boxall, 2012).

Defining whether drought is getting worse is difficult to do because even the study of drought impacts has taken a back seat to disasters like floods and tornadoes, which cause sudden fatalities, and we have limited information to assess if trends are changing (Travis et al., 2011). Our anecdotal record seems to imply that droughts are occurring more frequently, but this could be due to growth in cities putting more strain on limited water resources, which are then more easily strained by drought. Regardless, it is likely in the future that drought will get worse as the US experiences higher temperatures and changes in precipitation due to climate change. Given this, and our recent experience, perhaps it is time to give drought more attention as a potential natural disaster, which will manifest itself in different ways for each region.

References

Boxall, B. (2012). California approves big fines for wasting water during drought. LA Now. http://www.latimes.com/local/lanow/la-me-ln-water-wasting-fine-20140715-story.html

Burnett, J. (2012). How One Drought Changed Texas Agriculture Forever. NPR News US Around the Nation. http://www.npr.org/2012/07/07/155995881/how-one-drought-changed-texas-agriculture-forever

Davis, M. (2012). 'Exceptional' drought wreaks havoc in south-west Georgia. ajc,com. http://www.ajc.com/news/news/local/exceptional-drought-wreaks-havoc-in-southwest-geor/nRMSt/

Gettleman, J. (2011). Misery Follows as Somalis Try to Flee Hunger. The New York Times. http://www.nytimes.com/2011/07/16/world/africa/16somalia.html

Goodman, B. (2007). Drought-Stricken South Facing Tough Choices. The New York Times. http://www.nytimes.com/2007/10/16/us/16drought.html

Jones, W. C. (2012). Georgia's newest drought stirs less political interest. The Augusta Chronicle. http://chronicle.augusta.com/latest-news/2012-08-22/georgias-newest-drought-stirs-less-political-interest

Lacey, M. (2006). In Deep Drought, at 104°, Dozens of Africans Are Dying. The New York Times.

Continued

Schneider, K. (1993). Recalling '88 Drought's Disaster, Farmers Say Deluge Is Not as Bad. The New York Times. http://www.nytimes.com/1993/07/08/us/recalling-88-drought-s-disaster-farmers-say-deluge-is-not-as-bad.html?pagewanted=print

Travis, W. R., Gangwer, K., & Klein, R. (2011). Assessing Measures of Drought Impact and Vulnerability in the Intermountain West: Western Water Assessment.

The availability of surface water for each region is a function of the climate, topography, and the dynamics of the water cycle within the region. For most regions, surface water comes from seasonal precipitation that gathers on upland areas flowing into streams and rivers to lower areas. Large watersheds with high volumes of rainfall, such as the Mississippi River, can sustain flow across the whole year with some ebb and flow resulting from the season. Smaller watersheds and those with low rainfall may only flow during the wet season. Some areas have natural storage within snowpacks at higher elevations. Snow accumulates in the winter, slowly thawing in the spring delivering water to streams and rivers. Some parts of the United States, such as the southwest, have built dams to catch and store water during the wet season so it can be released during the dry season.

This variability in streamflow is not just seasonal; precipitation is influenced by climate cycles that can vary in length from decades to centuries. For the last 5,000 years, the southwest has experienced oscillations in its regional climate between wet and dry periods. These oscillations are highly uncertain but can be characterized by periods of wet and dry from 10 to 100 years in length. For the Colorado River, we have a written record that is only for the last 100 years, but we have been able to estimate past streamflows using tree ring records to estimate precipitation in past years. In this record, periods of drought as long as 35 years can be seen, but there is little evidence of a normal pattern of wet and dry periods. Even within these periods, high variability can occur. The southwest recently experienced a 15-year dry period from 1996 to 2011, but within this period, 2005 and 2006, respectively, were the driest and wettest years in the last 100 years. In other regions, this oscillation between wet and dry can be very slow, sometimes centuries long, thus there may be low variability in streamflow records. For some regions, a 500-year record of streamflow does not exist, thus the severity of dry years, like that which affected Texas and Georgia in 2011, seem like abnormal events, when actually they may be part of a climate profile that is longer than we have written records. Typically, surface water requires some level of treatment to be usable for potable purposes. How much treatment is required varies with the nature of the watershed and water source. Streams fed by mountain runoff that provides water supplies to Colorado Springs, Colorado and Portland, Oregon, require minimal treatment because the water has low suspended solids and organic material. Memphis, Tennessee, which uses the Mississippi River as a water source, must provide extensive treatment to remove suspended solids and organic material like bacteria that come from stormwater runoff and other sources.

From ancient times, groundwater has been a source of water for human settlements. But the technology limited the depth from which wells could draw water to the surface in any usable quantity. This limitation changed in the middle of the twentieth century when advances in drilling and turbine pump technology allowed large volumes of water to be pumped from aquifers thousands of feet below the surface. Today, groundwater is a major supply of water worldwide. Groundwater typically requires little, if any, treatment. Although the natural variability of groundwater supplies is not as high as that for surface waters, its variability is typically a function of the depth of the aquifer providing the supply. Shallow aquifers, where the time of surface water to recharge the aquifer can be measured in years, will be responsive to climate patterns of less than a decade. Thus, such groundwater can be susceptible to drought conditions. Deeper aquifers, where the recharge time can be measured in decades, will only be responsive to climate patterns that last for several decades or longer.

Groundwater is not an inexhaustible water supply. Withdrawal from aquifers at rates higher than they are recharged is a growing global problem. Aquifers in India and China are experiencing declining levels because of groundwater pumping. The Ogallala Aquifer, one of the largest in the United States, stretches under 174,000 square miles of the eight high plain states and has been the primary source of water for this region for the last 100 years. Unfortunately, it is being pumped so fast that estimates suggest it may be pumped dry in the next 25 to 30 years. The below image shows an estimate of global groundwater depletion in the year 2000. The aforementioned "Water use per residential customer" image shows the location by state of total water, surface water, and groundwater withdrawal in the United States.

Reclaimed water is water extracted from sanitary sewage. Today, only a small percentage of total freshwater comes from reclaimed water. In the United States, **wastewater treatment** plants generate effluent that is at or above the federal standards of the raw water source for drinking water supplies; however, federal and state regulations restrict use of this water to non-consumptive uses such as irrigation and cooling

Wastewater treatment - the process of removing material from sewage that is harmful to humans or the environment.

Total withdrawals

Key

Water withdrawals, in million gallons per day

- 0 to 200
- 200 to 500
- 500 to 1,000
- 1,000 to 2,000
- 2,000 to 7,000

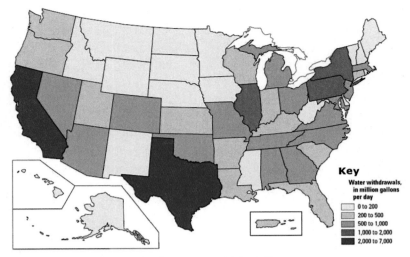

Surface-water withdrawals

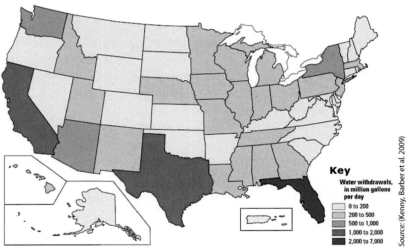

Groundwater withdrawals

Source: (Kenny, Barber et al. 2009)

towers. Reclaimed water used in this manner is considered reuse because it is used once and then returned to the environment by percolation to groundwater or evaporation to the atmosphere. In the United States, some limited recycling of this water as a source for toilets has begun to emerge because of the Leadership in Energy and Environmental Design (LEED) building standards. Such reclaimed water is flushed down the toilet, eventually to be recycled back to the toilet. Other countries, such as Singapore, have now taken this idea to a new level where reclaimed water is used as a source for drinking water.

The Challenge of Water Resources Sustainability

Sustainable yield - the balance between the rate in which a resource is renewed and the rate at which it is harvested.

The concept of water resources sustainability has been around a long time and has its roots in the concept of **sustainable yield** for renewable resources. Sustainable yield is the balance between the rate at which a resource is renewed and the rate at which it is harvested and consumed. At first glance, this seems to be a simple concept to implement, that is, to identify the rate of renewal and manage demand so it does not exceed this renewal rate. If the social and environmental systems that generate demand for water and the natural cycle of water renewal were simple and stable, such an approach to water sustainability could be easily achieved. Unfortunately, this is not the case. Social and environmental systems are highly **complex adaptive systems** that are constantly changing in response to a number of internal and external forces. Our ability to understand how these forces impact the complex relationships within these systems and our ability to predict the future of these forces and their impacts is very limited.

This reliance on stationarity in natural-water supplies has been at the heart of sustainable yield for the last 100 years. "Stationarity—the idea that natural systems fluctuate within an unchanging envelope of variability—is a foundational concept that permeates training and practice in water-resource engineering."[10] Such a viewpoint suggests that a future yield can be predicted, and based on this prediction, a plan to allocate it can be developed. An example of the folly of this viewpoint is the 1926 **Colorado River Compact**. In 1926, the seven basin states of the Colorado River **watershed** (Upper Basin: Colorado, New Mexico, Utah, and Wyoming; Lower Basin: Arizona, California, and Nevada) agreed through the Compact to allocate to each state a share of the Colorado River. This allocation was based on an assumption that the last 20 years of instrument gauging (1906 to 1926) of the river's flow was representative of the normal pattern of wet-dry cycles for the river. This assumption of stationarity yielded an average flow for the Colorado of 17.5 million acre feet per year. Today we have been able to reconstruct the flows of the Colorado River back almost 500 years. This record shows the Colorado River has experienced very high unpredictable levels of fluctuation between extreme highs and lows and that this 20 year record was among the wettest periods over the last 500 years. The result was an over allocation of the river's resources, which are now estimated to be closer to an average of 15.5 million acre feet per year.

The impact of this misjudgment has been minor to date. The upper-basin states are not using their full allotment, and thus, river flows have been adequate to store sufficient water in the reservoirs to meet the lower-basin state allocations. The long-term effect will be that periods of flow less than 17.5 million acre feet per year will occur more often than above, and thus, over time, shortage conditions for the lower-basin states will happen sooner and more often than originally estimated. Since Arizona's and Nevada's rights are lower than California, these states will experience such shortages first.

Climate change introduces a new layer of uncertainty for water supplies. Current estimates of temperature resulting from climate change generally agree it will increase globally with only the magnitude of the change in question. However, exactly what impact this will have on water supplies and demand is less certain. The relationships between snowpack volumes, snowpack melting, and streamflows are quite complex. Rising temperatures may cause more rain and less snow, reducing the volume of water stored in snow packs and causing snowpacks to melt sooner. For areas that rely on snowpack for storage of water, such as Boston, California, Denver, Phoenix, Portland, and Seattle, this could create problems for existing systems of water storage and flood control. Temperature increases will also result in higher evapotranspiration rates, which may increase water demand for landscape irrigation, fountains, and pools.

Complex adaptive systems - systems that have complex internal dynamics and functionality that are costly changing in response to internal and external stresses.

Colorado River Compact - an agreement signed in 1926 that allocated to Wyoming, Colorado, Utah, Nevada, New Mexico, Arizona, California, and Mexico, different portions of the Colorado River's normal and stored river flow.

More air conditioning may be required, increasing demand for power and water for cooling towers.

Current estimates of the impact of climate change on, location and magnitude of precipitation are not as certain as temperature. Generally, in the United States, most of the 26 **global climate models** (GCM) included in the Intergovernmental Panel on Climate Change Fourth Assessment Report indicated higher levels of precipitation in the northern parts of the country and decreases in precipitation in the southwest. Yet, some models indicate the opposite—less precipitation in the north and more in the southwest. Our ability to use GCMs to understand possible changes in extreme events and seasonality of precipitation is still limited. It is possible that a region may experience a decline in overall average precipitation but experience an increase in the severity of individual precipitation events. Temperature increases will affect how much snow falls in higher elevations and when it will melt.

Social systems are also subject to high uncertainty regarding their future. For the last two decades, regional growth has been considered a certainty, but the recent downturn in the economy and the collapse of the housing market has caused regional planners to pause and reconsider the future of growth in their regions. But even during the past periods of growth, there was a lot of uncertainty associated with what type and where growth would occur. These uncertainties make it difficult to estimate the future demand for water.

Financial resources are needed to fund water supply projects, but financial markets undergo cycles of bear and bull. Predicting the timing and magnitude of these cycles remains limited. Thus, the question of whether financial resources will be available when needed is uncertain.

The factors that affect demand are complex, and our understanding of them is limited. For example, how people will behave in response to increases in the price of water is not well established. We generally know that increases in price will result in declines in demand, but how much reduction and how fast it might happen are unclear because few regions have experienced rapid and significant changes in the cost of water. How technology will affect water use is also unclear. Is there a limit on how little water can be used to flush a toilet or wash a load of clothes? How increased temperatures will affect outdoor water use is unclear. Though we have experienced variations in temperature from one year to the next and can document the impact such changes have had on outdoor water use, these variations have been minor and our experience is over a small range of change. Is the affect linear, or will it decrease or increase over a larger range of change that may occur because of climate change?

Our experience with drought response to reduce demand is also limited. Normal water conservation activities focus on reducing people's water use without negatively impacting their quality of life. Such actions include improving the efficiency of water using appliances such as installing low-flow toilets and water-efficient clothes washers, changing habits to use water more wisely, and low-water use landscape design and maintenance. These actions can be implemented with little, if any, impact on a family's lifestyle. Drought response is when people are asked to take actions to reduce water use that will likely impact their quality of life or the economics of their business, hopefully for only a short period. Such actions include removing landscaping (grass, trees, and gardens) or allowing it to die, not filling a pool, taking fewer showers, not planting

Global climate models - models that simulate the complex functions of global climate systems over many years.

water-intensive crops, raising or lowering the thermostat, using water at off-peak periods, or reducing production of water-intensive products. Some utilities have had experience with managing a drought response from their customers for short periods of a year or two. What will the response and impact of drought response be over a decade? Will people or businesses leave the region for places with more water?

So, how do we achieve sustainability of water resources when there is so much uncertainty about the future? The answer does not lie in efforts to reduce uncertainty by better understanding social and environmental systems. That has not been our past experience where the more we understand about these systems, the more uncertainty we realize exists within them. The answer is within the complex adaptive systems themselves. **Resiliency**, the capacity of a system to absorb change or reorganize and retain essential functions, has emerged in the literature as a key concept for long-term sustainability of social-ecological systems. This is what happens within natural systems when they are stressed by external forces. The system changes to adapt to the external force and maintain essential functionality. Adaptability, the capacity of the actors in a social system to manage the system to successfully adapt to change, is one of the major components of resiliency. History shows many examples of where social systems were subject to some social or environmental forces such as drought and war. In some cases, the social systems were unable to adapt and a civilization collapsed. Others were able to anticipate change and effectuate a response, successfully adapting. These are two key factors of successful **adaptation**, anticipation and response. Unfortunately, even with the advancements in the science of systems modeling our ability to forecast the future is still significantly limited and our social-political systems seem lethargic in all but the most critical of situations. Thus, to achieve water-resource sustainability in an uncertain environment, we must create tools and methods that allow us to anticipate the future and develop flexible strategies that can be quickly implemented as the future slowly unfolds.

Resiliency - the capacity of a system to absorb change or reorganize and retain essential functions.

Adaptation - reorganization of a system in response to internal or external change, in a manner that still retains the essential functions of the system.

Anticipatory Governance

A new model of planning and implementation called **anticipatory governance** is being used by water utilities to anticipate a range of futures, prepare a range of flexible strategies to respond to these futures, and then implement these strategies over time as anticipated. Anticipatory governance has three basic steps: 1) Futures analysis: Develop an ensemble of possible futures that represents the full range of futures that we can currently foresee for a particular issue. This can be based on expert opinion or can be developed using a model that forecasts future conditions across a range of values for one or more factors. Then, distill strategic concepts or trends across the entire ensemble that explores the sensitivity or risk of various factors and impacts. 2) Anticipate adaptation: Using the futures analysis, develop possible actions to adapt (react to change or effect change) to individual or groups of possible futures. Such actions may be important to preserve future options or respond to specific changes that may occur. 3) Monitor and adapt: On a regular basis, monitor the present to identify change that may indicate the realization or exclusion of one or more of the anticipated futures. Then, act to adapt as anticipated. The City of Phoenix is one of the communities that has embraced this anticipatory governance model.[11]

Anticipatory governance - the process of using foresight to anticipate a wide range of possible futures, plan adaptation strategies for these futures, monitor changes over time, and act to adapt to change as anticipated.

Phoenix Water-Sustainability Planning Model

The City of Phoenix is located in central Arizona at the southern edge of the arid southwest United States with an average precipitation of eight inches per year. In 2008, Phoenix had an estimated population of 1.57 million people located in the center of a region of 3.5 million people. In 2008, Phoenix delivered just under an average of 300 million gallons per day to its customers, 184 gallons of water per capita per day. It has a robust water supply portfolio that consists of surface water, groundwater, and reclaimed water. Though Phoenix has substantial groundwater supplies (650 billion gallons, or 2 million acre feet of credits), it has chosen to rely primarily on its two surface-water supplies: the Colorado River delivered via the Central Arizona Project canal and the Salt and Verde rivers delivered via the Salt River Project reservoirs and canals. Phoenix is one of a few cities in the United States that reuses almost 100% of its effluent, 30% for agriculture and turf irrigation, 30% for power production, and 40% for environmental uses. Phoenix estimates it has enough **water supplies** to meet its needs today and growth for the next 100 years under normal conditions. But **water supplies** in the southwest are anything but normal.

Given these conditions, management of surface **water supplies** in Arizona over the last 100 years has been based on storage of **water supplies** during wetter years and delivery during dryer years. Reservoirs on the Colorado River provide this system of storage for California, Nevada, and Arizona, and reservoirs on the Salt and Verde rivers provide storage for central Arizona. During Phoenix's growth boom in the 1960s and 1970s, agricultural and urban uses were increasing their reliance on groundwater, which threatened to drain central Arizona's aquifers. Surface water delivered via the Central Arizona Project canal in the 1970s provided an opportunity to reverse this trend. In 1980, the state adopted the Groundwater Management Act (GMA), creating Maricopa **Active Management Areas** in the central part of the state where groundwater withdrawal was required to achieve sustainable yield by 2025. It is anticipated that the primary method for accomplishing this goal would be to switch groundwater use to surface-water use. This Act also requires all subdivisions to demonstrate that they have adequate **water supplies** (surface and groundwater) to meet the subdivision's water needs for 100 years. However, the GMA assumed that surface **water supplies** were stationary and did not account for climate variability or long-term droughts.

In 2002, as the City of Phoenix began the update of its Water Resource Plan, it wanted to move away from the stationarity model of predicting and planning embedded in Arizona's standard requirements, and move to a model of anticipatory governance. This effort included elements of **foresight** and flexible adaptive strategies.

Foresight

Phoenix began by identifying three key factors that had the most potential significance for water-resource planning and had high degrees of future uncertainty: 1) delivery of surface-water supplies (Salt River Project and Colorado River), 2) growth and development patterns, and 3) water conservation levels. Phoenix defined ranges of possible future conditions for each of these factors. Relying on tree-ring stream reconstructions to provide a wider range in variability in wet and dry periods for the Colorado and Salt/Verde river systems, Phoenix estimated allocations from these systems under normal, moderate, and severe drought conditions. Using a trends approach, Phoenix

Active Management Area - a regulatory term used in Arizona to identify regions of the state that must comply with the 1980 Groundwater Management Act goal of sustainable yield for the regions' ground-water resources.

Foresight - the process of anticipating a possible future.

developed several spatial scenarios of growth, such as accelerated growth rate, changes in the type of economy, higher density in peripheral areas, higher densities in the core area, and a transit-influenced growth pattern. These scenarios were used to estimate demand based on residential and employment growth. Three levels of customer water use were anticipated based on past trends and possible future trends. These factors were combined to generate 144 scenarios of water supply and demand.

In developing its 2010 plan, Phoenix incorporated climate change as part of its foresight. Phoenix participated in a partnership of local, regional, and federal agencies with state universities (City of Phoenix, Salt River Project, Central Arizona Project, Bureau of Reclamation, University of Arizona, and Arizona State University) to regionally downscale scenarios of precipitation and temperature estimates from several global climate change models, estimate the impacts of these scenarios on the stream-flow of the Salt/Verde river system, analyze impacts on reservoir management, and estimate impacts on local municipal water allocations. These new scenarios are being used to create new scenarios of surface-water supplies under average and extended drought conditions.

Flexible Adaptive Strategies

As part of its 2005 Water Resource Plan, Phoenix identified two types of flexible strategies: robust short-term strategies and a worst-case infrastructure timeline for drought response. Robust strategies are those that can be implemented immediately and work well across a wide range of scenarios. For example, an analysis of all the scenarios showed that if no more growth or only little growth were to occur, adequate water supplies were available to meet existing demand even under the most severe surface-water shortage scenarios with moderate drought response to decrease water demand. However, if growth were to occur even at moderate rates, this growth would require infrastructure to deploy existing water supplies and, under conditions of water shortage, acquisition of supplemental supplies would be required. In response, the City placed the burden of financing new infrastructure and supplies for new growth under normal and shortage conditions on growth itself by increasing its water-acquisition impact fee, a fee required to be paid with the building permit of each new home or building. This strategy works well under normal and shortage conditions, and under conditions of slow or fast growth.

Water supplies are essential to a community, and the failure to meet demand can result in the community's economic failure. Various strategies can be used to aggressively reduce demand or enhance supply in critical water shortage conditions. Yet, if these strategies fail to meet a community's essential water needs, sustainability will be lost. One approach to minimize such failure is to anticipate a worst-case scenario and develop flexible strategies to implement incrementally as a worst-case situation unfolds. The basis for Phoenix's worst-case scenario was to assume that current trends were proceeding to the most severe water-shortage scenario that could be reasonably anticipated, a 35-year dry period. A timeline was developed that estimated the magnitude of water shortages and when they would occur over a 25-year time frame. (Phoenix was in its 10th consecutive dry year in 2005.) Using a worst-case projection of demand based on aggressive growth, a timeline of trigger points was developed that identified when new water resources or drought-demand reductions would have to be deployed to meet basic community water needs. Phoenix, like most utilities in the United States,

Decision tree - for a specific problem, a diagram of questions (nodes) and answers (branches) that guide the decision maker to a recommended solution to the problem. Deficit: When demand exceeds supply.

has been experiencing substantial stress on its financial resources that will limit its ability to adapt to long-term drought and climate change in the near term. Using its infrastructure timeline as a just-in-time **decision tree** will be essential to minimize the investment needed to adapt over time. Each potential strategy can be assessed by water volume, certainty of availability, cost, and time to deploy. This assessment can be used to create a decision tree that indicates the latest point in time action would be required to preserve future options, plan future options, or fund and deploy future options. Using the decision tree, short-term plans of appropriate near-term actions can be created. Indicators of climate, drought, and certainty of supplies can be monitored, and the decision tree and short-term plans reassessed and updated as conditions change.

Summary

The social and environmental systems that support water resources and water management are complex adaptive systems that are constantly changing in response to internal and external forces. Our limited ability to predict the future of these forces and their impact on these systems creates a high level of uncertainty about the future of water resources. This need not limit our ability to achieve a state of sustainable water resources. Using foresight to anticipate a range of possible futures and to plan flexible response strategies will increase the resiliency of our institutions, allowing us to successfully adapt as changes in environmental and social systems occur. Our view of sustainable water resources will need to extend beyond the concepts of sustainable yield. We will need flexible strategies that allow us to reduce our demand, enhance supplies, and finance and build the infrastructure needed to treat and deliver freshwater under a variety of possible future conditions.

Supplemental Readings

John Cronin and Robert F. Kennedy, Jr. (1997), *The Riverkeepers: Two Activists Fight to Reclaim Our Environment as a Basic Human Right,* Touchstone, New York, 304 pages.

Milly, P. C. D., J. Betancourt, et al. (2008). "Stationarity Is Dead: Whither Water Management?" Science 319(5863): 573.

Holway, J. and K. Jacobs (2007). Managing for Sustainability in Arizona: Linking CLimate, Water Management and Growth. Water Resources Sustainability. L. W. Mays, McGraw-Hill: 73–98.

Gammage, G. (2011). Watering the Sun Corridor: Managing Choices in Arizona's Megapolitan Area, Morrison Institute for Public Policy, Arizona State University. (available online)

Sustainable Transportation

Aaron Golub

Introduction

Some of the world's most pressing problems result from how its urban systems operate. These systems consume huge amounts of energy and materials and create intense local "hotspots" for emissions, solid waste, water pollution, congestion, safety, and other challenges to livability. Of course, well-managed urban systems can be fairly efficient and effective at providing sustainable livelihoods for large numbers. Urban transportation systems, in this vein, can be both an asset and a liability to the development of sustainable cities. In the United States, a large share of energy consumption, carbon emissions, and preventable death and injury result from urban transportation systems. For example, because of enormous growth in urban travel, about half of Americans currently live in counties that fail the now four-decades-old National Ambient Air Quality standards, even after spending billions of dollars on technology to reduce emissions from automobiles.

In this chapter, we explore the sustainability challenges and solutions of urban transportation systems in three steps. First, we define the sustainability problem as a special class of urgent and harmful multi-scale and multi-sector problems. We can then clarify sustainability problems that United States urban transportation systems create.

Next, to move from defining a problem to solving it, we must understand the problem's drivers or causes.. Looking at cars' exhaust pipes is just not enough to understand urban air pollution; we need to investigate all of the connections between the different factors to uncover the forces behind the pollution and the impacts. If we could snap our fingers and eliminate the pollution, we would have solved the problem a long time ago. We need to recognize that some segments of society benefit from the air pollution, and that pollution is an outcome of a complex system of institutions with their own web of rewards and feedbacks.

Next, we can move toward solutions; understanding the causes allows us to uncover solutions. We can also develop intervention strategies, areas of policy and practice to focus efforts for change. We can uncover "low-hanging fruit," the easy changes in practice that yield large benefits, as well as the deeper underlying forces and values that may take decades to change.

This chapter will follow these steps, first introducing and defining the special class of problems that are sustainability problems, and then exploring the various problems that stem from urban transportation systems in the United States. Then, it will explore the various drivers of those problems, which form barriers to moving forward toward solutions. Finally, examples and cases from places within both the United States and internationally show some promise toward solving these urgent and messy problems.

Sustainability Problems and Solutions

Human-ecological systems - humans are dependent on natural systems, such as the water cycle or other nutrient cycles. On the other hand, humans alter these cycles by their effects on the natural environment. This combination of dependence and effects are characteristic of human-ecological systems.

Complexity - a characteristic of a system based on webs of interrelated and interdependent institutions and subcomponents. Complexity means that changes in certain inputs yield unforeseeable and unintended consequences.

Multiple sectors - urban systems are built on various sectors, such as housing, transportation, and the various systems that supply them with the resources they need, such as fuels, electricity, and other materials.

Not all problems we face are sustainability problems. Sustainability problems are a special class of problems that pose a particularly urgent threat to **human-ecological systems**. Their urgency is compounded by their **complexity** and their involvement of **multiple sectors** and actors across multiple scales. This complexity means that they are best tackled by using interdisciplinary approaches as diverse as the many systems that affect the problem or by applying new methods to these problems.

An example of a sustainability problem is urban air pollution. It poses significant harm to the health of many urban residents, and it causes billions of dollars in damage to infrastructure and crops, lost worker productivity, and additional burdens on the healthcare system. It is caused by a complex array of factors: emissions from electric power generation, exhaust from trucks and automobiles, and emissions from construction and industrial sites, among others. Obviously, to tackle such a problem would require understanding of such diverse issues as household energy use, freight logistics, the demand for automobile and air travel, and the technological and regulatory factors governing automobile, freight, industrial, and construction site emissions. It gets even more complex when governments must set air pollution standards, implement strategies to meet these standards, and monitor them. Something as simple as clean air, as we can see, is not a simple matter, but requires a team approach involving efforts from across many different disciplines, such as urban planning, engineering, business, and public policy. Cultural and psychological factors may underlie certain household practices that result in pollution, and these need exploration as well.

We can now move to the focus of this chapter—sustainable urban transportation. We will explore the underlying sustainability problems current transportation practice poses, uncover the sources of problems in urban transportation systems, and then explore sustainability solutions.

Urban Transportation and its Sustainability Problems

Following from such a definition of a sustainability problem, we can see that urban transportation is not a sustainability problem in and of itself, but it is a significant direct and indirect cause of several sustainability problems. This chain of causation means that focusing on urban transportation is an effective approach to solving those problems it causes. Here, we introduce some of these urgent problems that urban transportation systems cause, grouped into different realms; some, such as petroleum dependence, cause a set of other "indirect" problems.

Most urban travel in the United States is by automobile; thus, the urgent problems urban transportation systems create here derive from the particular issue of using automobiles for mass transportation. The problems from urban transportation in other countries may relate to different issues particular to systems there. In 2000, 88 percent of United States workers drove or were driven to work, and fewer than 5 percent took public transit.[1] For all trips, not just those to work, only about 6 percent are by human power (biking or walking). Compare this statistic with other industrialized countries like England, where 16 percent walk and bike, or Germany, where more than 34 percent bike or walk.[2] Thus, when we investigate the significant problems arising from our transportation system, they largely result from using the private automobile for mass transportation. Here, we review briefly some of these problems, grouped along social, economic, and environmental realms.

Car Crash.

Social Problems
Social disruption from traffic fatalities and injuries

Around 3,000 people—roughly the same number that perished during the September 11 attacks—die *every month* on the nation's roadways from traffic crashes. Americans have been dying on our roadways at that rate for the past 700 months. On top of these fatalities are about 200,000 injuries from traffic crashes monthly, resulting in thousands of permanent disabilities and days, weeks, or months of physical therapy and recovery and countless days lost from work or school.

Social inequality, exclusion, and isolation

Planning a transportation system around the need to own and operate a personal vehicle means that, for those who are unable to do so, the system will be poorly configured. In most metropolitan areas, around 25 percent of the population is too old to drive, too young to drive, or not able to afford an automobile. The dispersion and suburbanization of jobs and housing and the resulting automobile dependence means that those who cannot afford or cannot operate an automobile have greater difficulty finding work, and they can become isolated and excluded from the mainstream of society. In many central cities where low-income populations lack access to automobiles and decent transportation, a lack of access to healthy food and grocery options results in what is known as a "food desert." The reliance on cheaper but less healthy food options has been shown to create health problems, especially in inner-city neighborhoods. The "Food Desert" is discussed in Chapter 8.

Sedentary lifestyles and detrimental health impacts

Studies have shown that transportation has a significant impact on how active people are, and in turn, on their health. The lack of "walkability" in many metropolitan areas leads to low rates of cycling and walking, and this inactivity is linked to higher body mass indexes and poorer health. Obesity and diabetes are at alarming rates in many segments of the population, including children.

Ethical dilemmas of petroleum dependence

The strict reliance on petroleum for the operation of the economy is called "petroleum dependence." Today, U.S. demand for petroleum overwhelms the country's own domestic supply: more than half its petroleum needs are imported from other countries (See Box 1). Ethical problems arise because dependence on oil imports forces the United States to make political decisions that may often betray its own ethics. More fundamentally, however, dependence on oil means we are forced to use it, even if we do not want to. U.S. citizens in several cases were basically powerless to react by choosing

BOX 1: OIL AND UNITED STATES—A short history

Oil was initially used in the United States to produce kerosene for illumination. It was discovered in large quantities first in Pennsylvania in the 1850s, though it would not be until the 1890s when demand for it rose because internal combustion engines were becoming more commonplace in industry and transportation. Oil was discovered in California and Texas around 1900, during which time a single company dominated the system for distributing and refining it—Rockefeller's Standard Oil Company. After 1900, the demand for oil products exploded—and so did Standard's wealth, along with threats from new competitors and government displeasure with Rockefeller's ruthless anti-competitive behavior. In 1911, Standard was broken up into more than a dozen independent companies, many of which still exist today, such as Chevron, Exxon, Mobil, Amoco, ARCO, and Conoco, among others. The international system of oil production and distribution also began during the last years of the 1800s, with tight competition between Standard Oil and Royal Dutch Petroleum Company (now Shell) in Indonesia. Soon after, Mexico, Venezuela, Iraq, and Iran became locations of significant oil extraction.

While in 1900 only about 25 percent of the few thousand existing automobiles ran on gasoline—most were steam or electric—in a short time, gasoline would emerge as the dominant fueling technology. Significantly as well, military prowess became linked to petroleum as World War I (1914 to 1918) showed for the first time how important planes and tanks would become to the future of warfare. After 1920, the demand for gasoline in the United States would explode and the number of automobiles reached 27 million in 1939 (Philip 1994, 36). Thus, the die was set—our economy would become increasingly dependent on petroleum, and those firms who could supply it would become increasingly powerful. On the eve of World War II, the United States contained over 80 percent of the world's automobiles and consumed 65 percent of the world's oil produced (Philip 1994, 36–37).

Between the late 1930s and 1950, large oil deposits were discovered in the Gulf countries of Saudi Arabia, Iran, Iraq, and Kuwait, completely rearranging the world oil map. Initial dominance of the British in the Middle East followed from their colonial administration of it after the fall of the Turkish Empire during World War I. During and after World War II, diplomacy was increasingly used to support oil production by U.S.-based companies in the Middle East and to edge out British competition. By the 1950s, five U.S. oil companies, together with two European firms, controlled nearly all of the Middle Eastern oil resources. These "Seven Sisters" include British Petroleum, Royal Dutch–Shell, Gulf Oil, Chevron, Exxon, Mobil, and Texaco.

This close relationship between the U.S. government, private oil companies, and the governments in the Middle East would become problematic. Rapidly rising demand for oil in the United States following the full shift to Fordist consumption after World War II would put pressure on the U.S. government to preserve these special relationships in the name of oil supply stability. (The U.S. demand for oil would outstrip its own internal production in the 1960s.) The power struggle over oil, while complicated by the tension caused by the presence of the Soviet Union in the Middle East, forced the United States to support many anti-democratic regimes over the years. The relationship between the United States and Saudi Arabia is particularly close—it provides the United States with access to some of the largest known oil reserves on the planet in exchange for guaranteed revenues and protection of the Saudi government against external or internal aggressors. In another example, the United States supported a coup against Iran's Mossadeq government after it nationalized (converted from private to public ownership) the Anglo-Iranian Oil Company in 1951 (ironically, the Anglo-Iranian Oil Company was itself a national company of the British government). This coup installed the pro-U.S. Shah as ruler. A similar coup was supported in Iraq when it too threatened to nationalize its oil system, leading eventually to the rise of Saddam Hussein. His desires to restrict oil production to raise prices were, in part, responsible for the 1991 U.S. invasion. While Hussein had always cooperated with the United States, his new activism did not follow U.S. plans. U.S. strategy in the region also forced the United States to overlook Iraq's attack on the Kurds in 1973 and forced it to arm groups such as the Mujahedeen in Afghanistan.

The United States and Europe became so dependent on Middle East oil that changes in oil production policies among Middle East oil producers had profound effects on their economies. In late 1973, responding to U.S. and European support for Israel during its war with Egypt and Syria, several countries in the region restricted or completely halted oil production. This quickly quadrupled the world price and caused shortages throughout the United States. World prices would soon stabilize, but spike again during the 1979 Iranian revolution over the U.S.-backed Shah. To this day, oil prices continue to rise and fall with changes in production and policy in the few oil producing countries. The United States has reduced some of its dependence on Middle East oil by improving its energy efficiency and moving to alternative sources for oil, such as Mexico, Venezuela, and Nigeria. Still, it remains in a highly vulnerable position in the world system: in 2008, it imported 57 percent of its petroleum needs, about one-third of that from the Persian Gulf.

For more information on the history of oil and the development of U.S. policy, see *The Political Economy of International Oil* by George Philip (1994) and *The Prize* by Daniel Yergin (2008).

alternatives, which were simply not available at any reasonable scale. Examples include the 2010 BP oil spill in the Gulf of Mexico, when the Exxon-Valdez oil tanker ran aground in 1989 off the coast of Alaska, and when the government of Nigeria executed indigenous activists in 1995 who were questioning its oil export practices. What is worse is that even these significant spills are dwarfed by the total amount of routine spills that result from the normal operation of the oil distribution system. Petroleum dependence poses a significant ethical dilemma for those urban residents hoping to choose freely how their lives affect the larger world.

© Nate A/Shutterstock, Inc.

Bird killed in Gulf of Mexico oil.

Economic Problems
Costs of traffic fatalities and injuries, traffic congestion, and petroleum dependence

Traffic fatalities and injuries impose large financial costs on our society. Some of these costs are borne by car insurance holders, and others fall on society at large. These "externalized" costs are estimated to be between $46 and $161 billion per year.[3] In good traffic conditions, driving is normally the fastest way to travel in U.S. cities, however, during rush-hour, the average traveler can suffer from long delays. At a value of $10 per hour, these delays are estimated to cost between $63 and $246 billion per year.[4] Petroleum dependence imposes several kinds of financial costs on the U.S. economy. Significant costs, estimated to total between $7 and $30 billion per year,[5] result from lack of flexibility in the economy to respond to changes in price. Additional costs result from the non-competitive structure of the oil industry, resulting in prices that are higher than what a competitive market would charge. The sum of these costs since 1970 is estimated to be over $8 trillion. Finally, the United States military incurs costs for its presence in locations of strategic importance to the oil industry, amounting to estimates of between $6 and $60 billion.[6]

Local air pollution

The Clean Air Act, enacted in 1970 and enforced by the U.S. Environmental Protection Agency, has had a major impact on regulating and reducing pollution emissions from automobiles for more than 40 years. Most pollution is reduced to just a small percent of what it was before regulation. But, large increases in driving and worsening congestion in metropolitan areas means that although each vehicle is cleaner, local air pollution remains a national problem. More than 120 million Americans live in counties that fail at least one of the National Ambient Air Quality Standards that define what levels of pollution in the air are safe to breathe.[7]

Infrastructure barrier effects

Infrastructure for automobiles, such as freeways and arterial roads, are large, intrusive, and can separate neighborhoods from each other and cause barriers to mobility. Studies show that these "barrier effects" exacerbate automobile dependence because they can deter residents from walking or cycling for even short trips.

Greenhouse gas emissions

Greenhouse gasses in the atmosphere manage the planet's greenhouse process, whereby temperatures are regulated. Most greenhouse gases are created from the burning of fuels to create energy either in electric power plants, factories, or in vehicles which burn fuels for energy. Overwhelming evidence suggests that the significant greenhouse gas emissions created by human activity, rivaling the amount of gases produced by natural ecological systems, are influencing the planet's normal climate. Reducing greenhouse gas emissions is essential to avoid the worst effects of climate change. Unfortunately, because human-induced climate change has already begun, we are already too late in avoiding some significant climate change effects.

Transportation systems burn fossil fuels, which create greenhouse gas emissions such as carbon dioxide and methane, either in the vehicle's own engine or in power plants that make electricity for electric vehicles' batteries. Transportation is responsible for about one-third of our country's greenhouse gas emissions. About 70 percent of that is for cars, light trucks,

A lot of used cars in the junkyard.

and SUVs.[8] The net effects of high automobile use are evident when we compare cities' energy use, which is related to their greenhouse gas emissions. U.S. cities consume an average of 2.4 MJ of transportation energy for every dollar of regional product, ranging from a high of 3.1MJ/$ in Phoenix to lows of 1.7 MJ/$ and 1.8 MJ/$ in Washington, D.C., and New York, respectively. In contrast, European cities consume around 0.8 MJ of transportation energy per dollar of product, contributing to their much lower greenhouse gas emissions rates.[9]

Production and disposal of vehicles

Cars and lights trucks use a large amount of non-renewable steel, glass, rubber, and other materials. Data from 1990 showed that automobile production consumed 13 percent of the total national consumption of steel, 16 percent of its aluminum, 69 percent of its lead, 36 percent of its iron, 36 percent of its platinum, and 58 percent of its rubber. Around 10 million automobiles are disposed of every year.[10]

Environmental impacts of petroleum extraction, transport, and refining

Negative environmental effects occur throughout the supply chain—from spills and flares at the local sites of oil extraction, to spills and toxic pollution emissions at ports and refineries, to local service stations where fuels can cause groundwater contamination. Oil spills, large and small, are part of our transportation system, which

is so reliant on international extraction, transportation, and refining of oil. Roughly 10 million gallons are spilled into U.S. waters every year.[11] This does not include the large spills such as the 2010 BP oil spill of around 170 million gallons, or the 1989 Exxon Valdez spill of 11 million gallons. Worldwide, more than 3 billion gallons have been spilled into waters since 1970.

Gulf shores Alabama.

Agents of Automobile Dependence

Urban transportation systems in the United States are driven by a complex set of historical and institutional factors giving current practices great momentum and resistance to change. Its complexity results from the combination of numerous histories, cultural norms, expectations, and practices. Urban transportation is shaped and reshaped, produced, and consumed across several groups of actors. Entering into a discussion about fundamentally changing urban transportation systems in the United States means one must consider the needs of these various actors, how they interact with each other, and how they respond to demands for change. We must understand that a web of actors *benefits* from the current system. In this section, we briefly consider these different actors and how they interact. This discussion will then lead us into our final section, where we discuss strategies for change.

The Individual and the Household

The individual and household sit at the most micro level of activity, making daily decisions about how to travel and less regular decisions about home location or vehicle ownership. These decisions are made mostly on rationally minimizing travel times and maximizing convenience. As work and home became more decentralized in most cities, the automobile was a clear choice for travel: the automobile system delivers significantly higher performance than public transit systems. This is due entirely to the government's much greater attention and resources placed on guaranteeing the performance of driving. It is not a result of any technical or "natural" advantage that cars have over public transit.

What is more, however, is that individuals and households engage with larger cultural forces. For instance, car ownership in general and specific vehicles in particular are often powerful tools of an individual's identity formation in our society. Automobile ownership is seen as a symbol of status, patriotism, and of belonging to and supporting mainstream (referred to as Fordism) society (see Box 2). These cultural contexts can become significant shapers of decisions regarding automobiles.

BOX 2. FORDISM: The Marriage of Mass Production and Mass Consumption

Throughout human history, a dynamic interaction has existed between social organization and its technologies and techniques. New ideas about the organization of work and production lead to technological innovations, which in turn reveal even new ways of organizing work and production. A complex series of changes to the U.S. economy during the late 1800s led to a shift from small-scale to industrial production and to a corporate form of private investment management. Large companies' capacities for investment and further innovations in mass production during the early 1900s led to incredible improvements in industrial productivity. The limited capacity for the society to absorb all of the outputs of mass production, along with other factors, led to the crash of the U.S. economy and the Great Depression of the 1930s.

The response to the Depression was a new way of thinking about the interaction between the economy and society and between production and consumption.

Through the theories of British economist Keynes and the political negotiations between industry, organized labor, and the government through the New Deal, a plan to stabilize the economy was developed. This plan, sometimes called Keynesianism, would emphasize government intervention in the economy to stimulate consumption to solve the crisis of the Great Depression. The government would borrow and tax to play a more significant role in building infrastructure, regulating business and finance, subsidizing and insuring credit, and stabilizing the overall size of the economy. Together with wartime spending and an employment boom during World War II, the plan succeeded, causing relatively stable and sustained growth for the 30 years following the end of the war.

This new form of society is known as Fordism—named after one of the originators of the assembly line, Henry Ford. Government intervention in infrastructure and credit meant that highly productive and well-paid workers could afford to purchase much more of the goods they produced, such as automobiles and houses, and even become investors themselves. The suburb and the single-family home, the freeway and the automobile, along with the oil and other resources needed to power them all, became the centerpieces of the Fordist society. Indeed, many of these processes remain alive today, though conditions have changed. Fordism was linked to the incredible manufacturing capacity of the U.S. economy, along with the existence of inexpensive oil, conditions which have changed drastically over the past 40 years.

Today, the Fordist links between worker productivity, production, and consumption are weakening. An increasingly global production system supplies ever cheaper goods for the U.S. economy, while the role of domestic workers has changed from production to service for this new "Post-Fordist" arrangement. The implications for urban development, automobile ownership, and suburban growth are only weakly understood.

For more information on the history and inner workings of Fordism, see *The Public and Its Possibilities* by John Fairfield (2010), *A Consumers' Republic* by Lizabeth Cohen (2003), and *The Condition of Postmodernity* by David Harvey (1991).

Planners and Developers

Urban planning emerged as an important force in the process of urban development in the United States. Early last century, planners felt that suburban areas offered a better quality of life compared to the crowded and dirty industrial cities of the time. To this day, much professionalized urban planning practice merely reproduces the suburban, automobile-oriented models. Since this is often what the public and governments request, this is what planners deliver.

Developers reproduce the suburban model, not out of a particular preference, but mostly because

Modern suburban neighborhood.

© Wade H. Massie/Shutterstock, Inc.

Greenfield - urban growth that happens on previously undeveloped "green" land, such as agricultural or forested areas. This is in contrast with urban growth, which happens by reusing previously developed land within the city's areas.

that is what seems to be the least risky endeavor. Banks are more likely to lend construction loans to build traditional suburban developments, and developers will find it easier to develop fresh **"greenfield"** sites on the edge of cities, compared to dealing with potential neighborhood conflict and higher or unpredictable construction costs in urban infill sites.

The State and Federal Government

State governments have a special role in urban transportation systems because they are tasked with overseeing the design and construction of the interstate highway system. Most states also collect their own gasoline taxes, mostly used for investment in roads and freeways. The federal government has an important role for supporting automobile use and urban development around automobile dependence, as well as regulating it and supporting alternatives to the automobile. Federal funds have long been used to support automobile use. Federal funds were first used to build roads in significant amounts during the 1920s and the 1930s New Deal stimulus package. The 1956 Interstate Highway Act solidified support into a set of financing systems, based on the national gasoline tax and federal planning support, to build the national network of interstate highways we have today. Furthermore, U.S. foreign policy is heavily tied to the stability of oil supply in order to keep gasoline prices low and predictable (see Box 2). Urban historians point to two federal policies that spurred suburban development after World War II—the Interstate Highway Act and federal support for home mortgages.

Federal policies have also been important in managing automobile use. These include regulations to control safety, pollution from automobiles, and fuel economy standards that all automobile companies must follow. Federal funds also support public transportation systems, though in small amounts compared to the monies spent for roads.

Industrial Structures: Oil and Automobiles

The oil and automobile sectors are some of most heavily concentrated in the entire United States economy—relatively few companies account for nearly all of their industry's production. (Fordist society is built around large companies that can direct the mass production and consumption process more efficiently – see the Box 2 on Fordism.) This concentration means that they can together easily coordinate their concerns, influence public policy, and shape consumer demands through organized action. Thus, we must see urban transportation systems' use and dependence on petroleum and automobiles as being tied directly into the needs of the oil and automobile-related industrial pillars.

Automobile manufacturers became the focus of the emerging Fordist economy, riding the wave of public investments in freeways and suburbia, and overcoming competition from transportation alternatives, such as streetcars, in most cities. The 1956 Interstate Highway Act, passed by a federal commission with ample automobile-related representatives, solidified the course toward automobile dependence, guaranteeing financing and planning support for freeways. Though homebuilding in the suburbs predated the Highway Act, the pace of suburbanization exploded after its passage.

Surrounding larger pillar industrial sectors sit countless small companies—automobile parts suppliers, independently owned car dealers, service stations, repair shops, along with other related sectors such as automobile insurance companies, drive-through restaurants, and suburban homebuilders. In the 1970s, one study found that all together, the automobile-related industries contributed one-seventh of the total U.S. economy.

Sustainability Solutions: Toward Sustainable Transportation in the United States

Thus far, the chapter has explored the particular sustainability problems urban transportation systems produce and then discussed some of the most powerful drivers of the current transportation system. Now, we can envision sustainability solutions to particular problems by appreciating the drivers of those problems. Understanding the drivers will help us formulate specific strategies. Because we have emphasized the social nature of these problems, we will emphasize a social approach to their solution by looking at examples of social change and social movements that work toward advancing sustainable transportation. This approach generally involves challenging and reducing automobile dependence, which, in turn, would reduce driving, which would reduce fatalities, emissions, costs, among other things. Challenging the broader role of driving in society would yield compounding benefits across different problem areas.

As we saw earlier, the social production and maintenance of automobile dependence occurs at various scales and institutions. In this section, we explore several solutions that build on the social context of transportation systems across those various scales and institutions. The first is an urban planning approach that reorients the city away from traditional automobile planning. We look at the cases of Curitiba, Brazil, and Portland, Oregon, as inspiring examples where social change and social movements led to the rejection of the automobile-dependence model. Then, we look at the international movement in **car-sharing**, and how technology has been used to facilitate automobile sharing. Rather than redesigning the automobile, these systems redesign how people use the automobile, replacing ownership with short-term usage. Finally, we consider the social movement around bicycling in the United States, looking at the specific example of San Francisco. Here, we can see glimpses of challenges to Fordist society by challenging dominant paradigms about urban efficiency and the use of road space.

Proactive Urban Planning Paradigms

Research shows that urban planning, and reflecting variations in the mix of land use and transportation systems in a region, can have profound effects on automobile dependence and the accompanying problems that automobile use produces. Travelers in urban areas are always faced with the choice of different modes of travel—between walking, bicycling, public transportation, and driving. The relative convenience and costs of the different options affect how travelers decide to travel. Some modes become more or less convenient depending on the arrangement of land uses and the prices of using those modes, such as gasoline, parking, and bus fares. Strategies to reduce automobile use then rely on a range of land use and price changes.

Car-sharing - a system that allows members to use cars on a short-term rental basis. The car-sharing system owns and maintains the cars, and allows members to access and use them at any time of the day, for as little as 30 minutes, removing the hassle of going to a rental car facility. The cars are placed in public parking facilities or on streets to facilitate easy access. As of 2012, there are an estimated 500,000 car-sharing members in North America.

The transportation systems in many cities in the United States were designed to facilitate **mobility**. This paradigm of mobility planning refers to the dedication of urban resources and space to moving people and goods between different destinations including residences, workplaces, and shopping areas. Mobility is expensive, however, requiring substantial resources, including fees (e.g. tolls or parking), fixed costs (e.g. costs of automobile ownership or infrastructures), but also time costs, and other costs such as health or environmental damages, as were described earlier. Mobility is only made to seem convenient and inexpensive by a coordination of investments by the institutions described above – from the government to each household.[12] Without significant public investments in traffic engineering, road construction, parking systems, and emergency systems, mobility by automobile would be very inconvenient and few people chose it for their travel.

Related to mobility is the idea of **accessibility**, which considers more explicitly the objective of travel. Ultimately, the value of mobility results from the value derived from the completed trip. Accessibility is the attainment of that value from the trip. Ultimately, accessibility is the aim of any mobility system. Thus, in urban areas where origins, say residences, and destinations, say workplaces, are far apart, accessibility results from being mobile. But, accessibility doesn't have to be provided by mobility.[13] Locating destinations close to origins or placing them close to a coordinated public transit network can improve access. This can be referred to as accessibility planning. For instance, the density of jobs or houses in an area dictates how proximate origins and destinations are in space. When jobs, houses, and other uses are close together, it makes walking or bicycling relatively more convenient and a more likely option for a greater number of travelers. If land uses are spread out, then the average distances between places is much farther, making travelers rely on faster modes such as driving or public transportation. Making land uses closer together is a key strategy to reduce the reliance on automobiles. It can also help to improve the walkability of a place.

More specifically, there is a strategy of integrating the location of public transportation and land uses such as job and housing centers; the strategy is called **transit oriented development (TOD)**. TODs combine the idea of density, with the convenience of being located at a public transportation facility such as a light rail or **Bus Rapid Transit (BRT)** station. Evidence shows that compact development approaches such as TODs reduce the need for driving by around 20 to 35 percent, depending on the specific design.[14] In fact, residents in one TOD area in Atlanta drive only one-third as much as the average Atlanta resident.[15] Combining land use strategies such as TOD with measures such as increasing the supply of public transportation, reducing the rate of highway construction, and increasing fuel prices (whether by raising taxes or through the natural increase in petroleum prices) have been estimated to reduce total driving by about 38 percent.[16]

It is clear that the arrangement of land use and transportation in a region dictate how people travel. Knowing this fact, however, does not get us any closer to solutions—implementing alternative land use and transportation systems is not easy, considering the array of institutions listed earlier in this chapter. We proceed with three cases showing how citizens and elected officials worked to change their land use and transportation planning in an effort to reduce automobile dependence.

Transit oriented development (TOD) - the practice of mixing land uses, such as retail and housing, and increasing the density of urban development near public transit stations. This enables more residents and workers to use public transit for their travel.

Bus Rapid Transit (BRT) - using buses to offer rail-like public transit services. BRT systems are based on using normal buses in exclusive, dedicated lanes that allow them to avoid traffic. BRT also relies on passengers prepaying their fares at kiosks or stations like rail systems to speed up passenger boarding.

Curitiba, Brazil

Curitiba is generally considered an example of best practices in terms of urban transport planning in the world. The city's history shows the importance of the relationship between investment in public transport improvements and urban development. An important element of its success was a master plan adopted in 1966 to direct the city's growth and development.[17] It was decided at this early stage that the city's growth would be directed along certain corridors and that these corridors would be focused around public transit, not automobiles. This was, in effect, a rejection of the U.S.-originated model of automobile-based urban development being exported around the world, especially in Brazil, during the post-war period. In fact, at around the same time Curitiba was growing, Brazilian planners had just completed Brasilia, the capital city, based on a decentralized, automobile-oriented model. It has since needed retrofitting with heavy and light rail systems to improve its functioning.

The relationship between land use planning and public transport was solidified when higher densities were enforced along the bus corridors through a strict zoning code. This makes public transit very attractive to most residents of the city, since most live close to the various bus routes and most destinations are also close to the bus system. In addition, these plans were made before there were residents—the proactive planning channeled development with explicit goals rather than having to respond to ad hoc development after problems arose.

Jaime Lerner, mayor of Curitiba during this period, favored a bus-based system over the often-proposed rail systems because of its relative lower cost and ability for flexible and fast deployment. In 1974, a hierarchical bus system was developed with the introduction of express and local buses and the single ticket. A "trinary road system" was developed wherein an exclusive bus way (lanes only for buses) and slower travel lanes make up the main axis of the system. Buses in the bus way, sometimes called Bus Rapid Transit, act like light rail—they use mini-stations with platforms that help speed boarding. The exclusive bus lane speeds the buses up ahead of crowded local streets. The rail-like boarding system makes boarding much faster since passengers have already paid to get into the bus stop, thus eliminating the need to pay the driver.

Lerner's proposals were not always accepted by the car-owning public in Curitiba. He engaged in several political battles with proponents of the automobile model, and was forced at times to use drastic measures to protect the public spaces he was trying to remove from the automobile network. In one instance, car drivers threatened to drive through a pedestrian plaza he had created by closing several downtown streets; in response, Lerner brought hundreds of schoolchildren to play in the plaza.[18] Curitiba's comprehensive and proactive planning, in contrast to more typical piecemeal and reactive planning in U.S. cities, makes it an inspiring example. Curitiba's thinking has gone on to influence urban planning and sustainability thinking around the world. Bogota, Colombia, recently implemented a city-wide BRT system to inexpensively add significant capacity to its public transit systems.

A recent national study showed that these new planning approaches linking land use and public transportation will be essential for the United States to reach carbon dioxide targets (60–80 percent below 1990 levels) required for climate stabilization.[19] Though nothing as sweeping as Curitiba's approach can be found in the United States, there is an increasing awareness of the interaction between transportation, land use, energy, and emissions. Dozens of new transit-oriented developments are appearing in public transit station areas across the country. New-Urbanist principles are being increasingly used in what would have been more conventional suburban master planned communities. Moreover, Curitiba's BRT innovations are now being built in dozens of cities across the country with funding and planning support from the Federal Transit Administration.

Portland, Oregon

During the 1950s and 1960s, when many U.S. cities were being retrofitted for automobile use, communities in Portland, Oregon rejected a significant part of freeway plans developed for it by the State of Oregon's Department of Transportation. The Mt. Hood freeway was slated to connect downtown Portland to the southeast, running through established neighborhoods as it made its way to connect to an outer interstate running north-south. The Mt. Hood, as a designated interstate, was to be funded by the federal gas tax—only 8 percent of the funds would need to come from local sources. Regardless, neighborhoods in the area organized themselves to challenge the freeway using new regulations in the National Environmental Protection Act of 1969 and the Clean Air Act of 1970. These acts required environmental impact analyses for infrastructure projects—tests never required before for freeways. Using these procedures and growing support from local political bodies, the community and city government got the freeway cancelled in 1974. New rules in the 1973 renewal of the 1956 Interstate Highway Act allowed the use of federal highway funds for mass transit, and the $180 million planned for the Mt. Hood freeway was redirected to build light rail in Portland.

Dozens of other communities across the United States successfully fought freeway plans in their communities. The most famous cases include San Francisco's cancelling of the planned Embarcadero Freeway connection to the Golden Gate Bridge, and Boston-area residents' stoppage of the "inner beltway" around Boston. For more on the history of freeway revolts, see "Stop the Road: Freeway Revolts in American Cities," written by Raymond Mohl in 2004.[20]

Phoenix, Arizona

While Phoenix, Arizona may not initially conjure up images of urban living, the city has been making great strides towards accessibility planning over the past decade. In fact, streetcars played an important role in the development of the city and by the late 1800s streetcars provided a significant part of the city's transportation needs.[21] From the 1950s, however, the Phoenix metro area experienced rapid exurban and suburban growth based around the mobility planning paradigm. In 1999, however, several cities in Maricopa County created a proposal for the Central Phoenix / East Valley Light Rail project and the 20-mile, 28-station line opened in December of 2008 and passes through central and east Phoenix and connects with neighboring cities of Tempe and Mesa to the east. Current weekday ridership averages around 43,600 per day, up substantially from 34,800 per day in 2009, its first year of operation.[22]

Supporters argued that it would stimulate and re-center growth and revitalize downtown Phoenix and the surrounding neighborhoods. To try and jumpstart development, the cities of Tempe and Phoenix developed special land use regulations such as station area plans and (TOD) zoning. The City of Phoenix planning department then partnered with Arizona State University and the Saint Luke's Health Initiative on a federally-funded project called "Reinvent Phoenix" to assist neighborhoods located

Courtesy Aaron Golub

Native American Connections manages the Devine Legacy complex, an example of Transit Oriented Development in Phoenix, Arizona.

along the light rail to create long-term visions of station area development.[23] The project synthesized land use, economic, transportation, housing and health assessments into a participatory planning processes to create long-range plans in contextually sensitive ways while revitalizing and preserving the existing stable neighborhoods. For example, housing market analyses revealed a lack of affordable housing in some neighborhoods along the Light Rail, while **Health Impact Assessments** carried out with community members showed that some neighborhoods are "food deserts," lacking easy access to healthy food (see Chapter 8). Adaptation to climate change was also a focus of the project, and plans were created to reduce temperatures through tree, shade and park investments. Community members active during the planning process were asked to create a steering committee for their neighborhoods to steward the plans forward into the future.

An example of the kind of TOD proposed in the Reinvent Phoenix plans can already be found in Phoenix. A local non-profit housing developer called Native American Connections builds and manages apartment complexes for low-income families in Phoenix, one of which is located right along the light rail.[24] The proximity to rail allows families to be accessible to many destinations without the burden of owning an automobile and many essential services such as schools and medical care are close by.

Health Impact Assessments - Detailed assessments, often led by community members, of the various health impacts of a project or planning process used to highlight important concerns or risks.

Rethinking Automobile Ownership

At first glance, trading the convenience of one's personal, private car for the occasional use of a shared car, owned and maintained by others and located somewhere out in the public realm seems supremely countercultural in the United States. It appears that there are places all over the nation, however, where this idea makes sense and has increased in popularity. Car-sharing is a system that allows members to use cars on a short-term rental basis—for as short as 30 minutes in some systems. The cars are placed in public areas in cities, rather than in car rental agencies. Then, members can use them by swiping a smartcard any time of the day. Though no car-sharing programs existed before 1994, in mid-2009, there were roughly 280,000 car-share members sharing about 5,800 vehicles in the United States,[25] with these numbers growing roughly 20 percent per year.

Courtesy Aaron Golub

Car-share in Berkeley, California.

Courtesy Aaron Golub

Car-Share in San Francisco, California.

Car-sharing dates back to the 1940s in Northern Europe, and most notably, with the electric car-sharing system in central Amsterdam during the 1970s and 1980s.[26] San Francisco saw an early experiment in car-sharing in its Short-Term Auto Rental program, though it only lasted from 1983 to 1985. Eventually, with improvements in communications technologies, modern car-sharing took off with systems introduced in Europe and Canada in the early 1990s. Portland, Oregon, was the site of the first car-sharing system in the United States, with its CarSharing-PDX opening in 1998.

Car-sharing takes place when a member makes a reservation online or by phone through a voice-operated menu some time before he or she needs it (though the reservation can be made instantly, so long as the car is available). The system shows, based on the person's location, where vehicles are available for the reservation period requested. The user can specify the kind of vehicle they want or do searches anywhere in the system—even in other cities, for members of a multi-city network like Zipcar. The car is available to the user once the reservation is made; a cardkey activates the car. Reservations can be extended on-the-go as long as the car is still available.

Numerous studies have been made of the transportation impacts of car-sharing. Car-sharing can have effects on several aspects of transportation systems, such as

Courtesy Aaron Golub

The windshield-located card reader on a car-share vehicle in Berkeley, California.

household car ownership and parking demand, car use, and demand for "alternative" transportation such as public transportation, cycling, and walking.[27] Research across North America shows extremely significant effects: after joining car-sharing groups, households went from owning an average of 0.47 vehicles (already somewhat lower than typical North American households) to 0.24 vehicles. Put another way: in the group of about 6,000 surveyed households that joined car-sharing, almost 1,400 vehicles were "shed"—equal to almost half of the vehicles the group owned. Even more vehicles were reduced because car-sharing households avoided planned purchases of vehicles.

The Rise of Bicycle Activism in the United States

Bicycling makes up a very small share of daily travel in the United States, with only about 1 percent of all trips. But, with increased gasoline prices and traffic congestion, growing concern about climate change, and interests in physical activity, bicycling has experienced a boom in many U.S. cities.[28] Chicago, New York, Portland, Seattle, and many smaller university cities have experienced significant increases in utilitarian bicycling. In San Francisco, it is estimated that 5 percent of adults use bicycles as their main mode of transportation (up from 2 percent in 2001), and 16 percent ride a bike at least twice a week.

Bicycling is poised to be a substitute for many short-range automobile trips and has enormous potential to contribute to reductions in **vehicle miles traveled** (a measure of the total distance in vehicle travel). Nationally, roughly 72 percent of all trips less than three miles in length are by car, a spatial range that an average cyclist can cover easily. Bicycles do not require expensive, long-term capital investment or operating costs like that of transit and so can be deployed quickly. And, in many respects, bicycling is among the most equitable forms of transportation because it is affordable and accessible to almost everyone. **Bicycle space**, or an interconnected, coordinated, multifaceted set of safe bicycle lanes, paths, parking racks, and accompanying laws and regulations to protect and promote cycling, has been extremely difficult to implement in the United States. Lack of political will to develop bicycle space has been a major barrier. There is no strong national bicycle policy with dedicated funding programs as there are for automobiles. Advocacy for bicycling has been a largely local, fragmented, and isolated effort. Therefore, the few cities, such as San Francisco, that have established a political will to promote bicycling—and that have seen significant increases in bicycling—are worth considering.

Vehicle miles traveled - a measure of total travel by all vehicles. If 100 vehicles travel each 100 miles, the total vehicle miles traveled is 10,000.

Bicycle space - coined by Jason Henderson, the well-connected set of bicycle-related infrastructure, such as bike lanes and paths, as well as bicycle storage facilities like bike racks and larger storage facilities at public transit stations.

San Francisco, California

In San Francisco, an 11,000-member bicycle organization has lobbied hard for the production of bicycle space, and the city has experienced a rapid upsurge in bicycling. Between 2005 and 2009, bicycling increased 53 percent, accounting for 6 percent of all trips in 2009 and amounting to 128,000 daily trips. In some inner neighborhoods of San Francisco, the mode share of bicycling is above 10 percent for all trips. This is despite the fact that much of the city terrain is quite hilly. How did this happen, when so few people bicycled there in 1990?

Through the early and mid-1990s, despite a growing and vocal San Francisco Bicycle Coalition (SFBC), the City of San Francisco's unspoken priority was to ensure that bike lanes did not impact car space. It was a lonely and sometimes daunting existence for San Francisco cyclists in those days. The frustration over the lack of political will to create bicycle space led bicyclists to create their own spaces. These were the spaces of **Critical Mass** bicycle rides which, beginning in 1992, occurred on the last Friday of every month in downtown San Francisco. Similar Critical Mass rides

Critical Mass - a number or amount large enough to produce a particular result; in this case, the number of bicyclists that can recapture urban space from the automobile, enabling the mass to progress through streets unimpeded, forcing motorists to have to wait for its passage. As such, critical mass is an act of civil disobedience meant to illustrate what a city might be like without automobiles and if street space were used for bicycle travel.

Bicycle demonstration in Budapest.

eventually spread to New York City, Chicago, and globally to cities like Rome and Vancouver. The name Critical Mass is as implied: a critical mass of cyclists that once reached, can recapture urban space from the automobile, enabling the mass to progress through streets unimpeded, and forcing motorists to have to wait for its passage. Critical Mass helped reframe the questions about urban sustainability, pushed open the debate about the use of street space, and showed the possibilities of a humane city.

Eventually, struggles between Critical Mass and the City's mayor led to a particularly violent clash in the fall of 1997. In response, the mayor directed his traffic department to hold hearings around the city in 1997 and 1998. Hundreds of cyclists attended these meetings, and the SFBC took a more aggressive position in its lobbying efforts. Although the SFBC made pains to differentiate itself from Critical Mass, the outfall from Critical Mass strengthened the SFBC, which had 1,700 members by 1998 and was gaining allies with some members of the city's board of supervisors.

Some key streets were made more welcoming to cyclists. When bicycle lanes were added to Valencia Street in 1999, bicycling increased by 144 percent. The success of the Valencia Street project further emboldened activists and proved that, with adequate infrastructure, more people would choose to bicycle. By 2004, 16 percent of all trips on the street were by bicycle. By the mid-2000s, and with almost 5,000 members, the SFBC had almost every local elected official concerned about the "bicycle vote" and very few elected officials spoke against bicycling, although ambiguity about how to implement bicycle space was widespread among many politicians. In 2005, with a clear pro-bicycle majority on the city's board, the SFBC pushed through a bicycle plan that is now adding 34 new bike lanes to the existing 45 miles.

Conclusions

Taking a social view of the problems leads us to a social view of the solutions. The social arrangement of industry, government, along with individual choices for convenience and identity formation create a complex web built around automobile dependence. Challenging this process will require profound and difficult social changes. Although there are few good examples of these changes, those examples assembled in this chapter give us a flavor of what social change can look like.

The public-transit oriented example from Curitiba showed a clear departure from standard models at the time. This model was developed and supported by a team of active citizens, planners, architects, and elected officials. Finding similar examples of such sweeping efforts will be difficult, but the efforts of Portland communities are inspiring nonetheless. Their rejection of transportation planning paradigms integral to the Fordist model was in effect a rejection of that model. The need for high-performance driving to serve an ever-expanding suburban fringe was traded for less traffic congestion, lower automobile use, and improved public transit capacity. Trade-offs also may have occurred, such as lower economic performance and growth from the diversion of investments to other regions.

Similarly, the explosion of car-sharing illustrates that, indeed, many communities are willing to sacrifice convenience for other goals. Of course, for many, car-sharing is a rational approach to high parking or automobile ownership costs. But, those costs are integral to the Fordist model—they are the costs of identity because the automobile becomes part of how a person is valued. Rejecting car ownership on purely rational grounds is still irrational according to the model. We must wait and see how large of a dent car-sharing can make into the dominant model—right now, it appears that in places where the finances make sense, there is a willingness to reject Fordist roles.

Finally, in a similar vein, we find bicycle activists challenging the dominant urban management of roadways for automobiles, asserting an alternative vision for urban streets filled with bicycles rather than cars. That is, filled with things not extracted, produced, nor distributed by the international oil conglomerates or international automobile conglomerates. Producing bicycles is a minor part of the national economy, yet it can provide a significant amount of our mobility if that possibility were made real. Urban streets were used for thousands of years by humans, horses, bicycles, and streetcars before automobiles came along. There is nothing natural about any one of their roles in the streets—it is purely a social decision. Thus, moving forward with the understanding that our problems and our current state is socially produced, we can see more clearly how our solutions will require social changes involving a constellation of actors across multiple scales and approaches.

Several important lessons are found in the efforts of cities and citizens attempting to reduce their automobile dependence. The larger lesson is that urban practices, such as automobile dependence, water or energy use, and pollution, are results of webs of institutions, from citizens and neighborhoods to city and state governments, to federal policies. Effective action for achieving sustainability begins with understanding these institutions and how they respond to and resist change. We saw how important the Fordist framework of mass consumption was to the overall production and maintenance of automobile dependence.

Effective cases of reducing automobile dependency can be found across all of these scales and institutions. We examined how at the regional scale, proactive citizens, neighborhoods, and city governments led movements against the expected city planning paradigm. They emphasized goals of walkability and public transportation over the typical reliance on roads and automobiles.

Other citizens have implemented visions for reduced reliance on automobiles by proposing reasonable alternatives. Groups around the world have implemented car-sharing services that reduce the need to own an automobile. The impacts on urban travel have been shown to be profound. Likewise, groups around the world have used the civil disobedience of Critical Mass to illustrate what cities more reliant on bicycles would look like. These acts of theater have successfully translated into real policy changes at the city and regional scales.

This chapter emphasized the role of citizens and activists together at a variety of scales to show that it is not enough to have a "right answer"—that with such technology or such a density we can reduce automobile use by such an amount. The importance is in how citizens and governments implement these solutions. Thus, we can see that sustainability is achieved when we join with others with similar visions and create the social change needed to challenge the dominant urban planning and practice of automobile dependence.

Supplemental Readings

Urban Land Institute. (2010) *Growing Cooler—the Evidence on Urban Development and Climate Change*. Retrieved from http://www.smartgrowthamerica.org/documents/growingcoolerCH1.pdf

Wray, Harry J. (2008) *Pedal Power: The Quiet Rise of the Bicycle in American Public Life*. Boulder: Paradigm Publishers.

Schiller, L. (2010) *An Introduction to Sustainable Transportation: Policy, Planning and Implementatio*n. Routledge.

Cities as the Mirror of Energy

Martin J. Pasqualetti

Cities are terrestrial 'black holes'. They gorge on energy. Their appetites are without limit and the network that supplies them can spread hundreds and even thousands of miles in all directions. Looking at our cities, we see a reflection of the energy they consume. Skyscrapers needing to be heated and cooled, concrete rivers loaded with cars burning refined oil, street lights and neon signs turning night into day. Big cities mean big energy, and their existence depends on a ceaseless supply of it, in every form imaginable, including gasoline, electricity, natural gas, ethanol, wood, and dung. Cities are the largest consumers of energy on the planet.

And they are multiplying. Presently in China, for example, new cities are appearing by the hundreds even before there are people to occupy them, all in anticipation that by 2020 one in every eight people in the world will live in a Chinese city. Worldwide, almost 5 billion people—about 60 percent of the global population—will live in cities by 2030. Such growth will require massive amounts of energy and expanded infrastructure. The problem is that, with no exceptions, big cities are unsustainable in their current configuration and operation. This fact is recognized by many organizations and funding agencies, although progress to modify these trends is difficult to implement.[1]

Smaller cities usually have more of a chance at sustainability than larger ones because their energy needs are smaller, their economies less complex, their supply lines are typically less extensive and complicated, their commuting distances are shorter, they can be closer to food supplies, and they are unlikely to stew in the heat of their own heat island. While small cities may not be able to provide all the services of a large city, they have several advantages when it comes to energy requirements.

Cities normally start out small, and they rarely grew to great size before industrial times. Cities in Central Mexico might have exceeded 100,000 individuals, although they were possible only because of slave labor and a mild climate. After about 1750, cities would grow to ten times that size and larger, usually because they had ready access to energy reserves that could fuel the factories of the Industrial Revolution. Glasgow and Manchester in the UK, Cleveland and Pittsburgh in the US, Essen and Frankfurt in Germany, and many similar cities expanded because of their proximity to energy supplies, the industrialization of the local economy, and the decreased need for everyone to grow their own food. At the same time, such industrialization produced the wealth necessary to underpin the growth of service-cities which were relatively more distant from energy reserves, such as London, New York, and Berlin.

When we look around the world, we see hundreds of cities that are overcrowded, polluted, and congested to such a degree that it seems hopeless to believe their problems can ever be resolved. São Paolo, Beijing, Kolkata, Cairo, Mexico City, and many other urban areas, all needing food, shelter, and transportation for many millions of people, are grinding to a halt under the weight of the humanity concentrated in each city. The question is: can big cities ever be sustainable?

The problem faced by those who would hope for sustainable cities is that sustainability has never been a major consideration in their design or operation. Rather, cities have usually grown 'organically', not by some pre-considered plan. That means that they have expanded incrementally, a freeway here, a building there, pushing up hillsides and across farmlands. Is there anything to be done to improve the sustainability of cities? While the answer is 'yes', one must caution against any optimism that major changes can be accomplished quickly. The reason is simple: the form and function of cities is complex, there are vested interests to argue against upsetting the status quo that serves them well, and there are few policies that can help remedy conditions in the short term. Like a massive aircraft carrier under full power, it is not easy to turn this ship around.

Cities as Energy Creations

We cannot ignore the most obvious purpose of cities; as nodes of convenience, trade and mutual protection, cities rely on steady and reliable supplies of energy. Early on, the more successful cities controlled water for drinking and farming and later, for water power as well. In places where food surpluses were common, such as Mesopotamia and the Indus River Valley, people were able to settle down, becoming more stable and less nomadic. After thousands of years of little change in form, function or size, cities began a rapid growth in size and complexity after fossil fuels become a more common fuel, replacing wood and other non-commercial fuels. Once this happened, spatial dependency was reduced with heavy-goods transport and the eventual introduction of electricity. Cities could literally crop up anywhere.

London—today receiving its energy by wires and pipes—first relied on the coal carried up the Thames in ocean-going caravels plying the waters of the **North Sea** from Newcastle. Other cities on the British Isles such as Cardiff and Edinburgh would also prosper because of coal, both through its combustion, but—unlike London—also from its mining and export. Over time, the development of energy resources would nurture to maternity many other cities including Baku, Azerbaijan; Dhahran, Saudi Arabia; Valdez, Alaska; Harcourt, Nigeria; Charleston, West Virginia; Kogalym, Russia; and the city-state of Singapore.

As urban economies, particularly those of the US and Europe, have changed from an industrialized to a service orientation, people have gained greater freedom to choose where they wish to live. This trend, in turn, has stimulated the expansion of a more elaborate, expensive, and complex energy infrastructure to service the increasingly more scattered and less dense pattern of settlement. No longer were energy supplies going to be converging mainly on a few big urban demand nodes, such as those of the industrialized centers of the northeastern US. Rather, energy would be needed *wherever* anyone preferred to live, particularly as they selected warmer and less crowded southern and western states. As a result, transmission lines and pipelines were installed over vast distances to service places like Tucson, Los Angeles, San Diego, Miami, and Denver, none of which is close to the great energy reserves necessary to support them.

North Sea - A marginal sea of the Atlantic Ocean located between Great Britain, Scandinavia, Germany, the Netherlands, Belgium, and France. It connects to the ocean through the English Channel in the south and the Norwegian Sea in the north. It is more than 970 kilometers (600 mi) long and 580 kilometers (360 mi) wide, with an area of around 750,000 square kilometres (290,000 sq mi).

It has been a natural evolution. Early US cities tended to be near energy resources such as water and wood; the growth of large industrial cities was only possible when **fossil fuels** became more abundant and cheaply available. Pittsburgh, Pennsylvania, for example, was near coal supplies and easy river transport. Later, once artificial canals and railroads were available to bring steady coal supplies from Appalachia, even more distant cities such as Philadelphia and Baltimore began a substantial upward trend toward major urban status.

Today, proximity to energy resources plays is not necessary for the growth of large cities. Major urban centers such as Atlanta and Phoenix, for example, hold millions of people, even though these places are hundreds of miles from significant supplies of oil, natural gas, coal, uranium, or hydro-power. Unlike many of the early major cities of the northeastern US, virtually all the energy in these two cities is imported from far away. People living in such places—especially those who migrated there—realize that they can enjoy a better quality of life without having to tolerate the environmental and social costs that often accompanied the cities they left. However, on the down side, they are living in places that are entirely dependent on steady re-supply. For this reason, the are vulnerable to supply interruptions, either natural or intentional in origin. None of these conditions are part of a model of sustainable urban living.

Fossil fuels - Carbon-based fuels in the forms of coal, oil, and natural gas. They all derive from animals and mostly plants. In other words, they are stored solar energy. They are created over millions of years under conditions of heat and pressure.

Energy and Transportation in Large Cities

Owning a car brings status and independence. Along with privacy and greater flexibility, however, it is notably very inefficient. Consider the difference in energy (and air pollution) necessary to transport a 180 pound man inside a 4000 pound car compared to the same man riding a 25 pound bicycle an equal distance. The Chinese have learned this lesson the hard way in the 20 years since cars have displaced bicycles as a popular mode of transportation. The explosive expansion in car ownership in Beijing has resulted in some of the worst air pollution on the planet (Figure 1).

Smog, however, is not been the only problem in Beijing. Congestion has increased as well (Figure 2) Beijing's 19 million residents and 5.3 million cars have turned streets and highways into parking lots. A massive traffic jam that formed on August 14, 2010 extended for 100 km (60 mi) and lasted more than 10 days. Many drivers were able to move only 1 km (0.6 mi) per day; some were stuck in the traffic jam for five days.[2] Some people are already are calling for a return to the good old days when cars were not so coveted and prevalent.[3]

Smog - Originally, air pollution caused by the burning of coal. Modern smog, as found for example in Los Angeles, is a type of air pollution derived from vehicular emission from internal combustion engines and industrial fumes that react in the atmosphere with sunlight to form secondary pollutants that also combine with the primary emissions to form photochemical smog.

FIGURE 1: Notorious Beijing air pollution blankets Tiananmen Square.

FIGURE 2: Traffic congestion in Beijing is representative of conditions in many of the world's large cities.

FIGURE 3: A return to use of bicycle has become increasingly popular in Beijing.

In the early 2000s, people preferred to use bicycles to move around the city.[4] It was a time with 40 percent of Chinese, the "kingdom of bicycles" cycled to work and school.[5] The 'car revolution' stimulated a rapid rise in the demand for transportation fuels. Fifteen years ago, there were few private cars in the country, and the principal commute choice was the bicycle. Today, China alone accounts for about 40 percent of the world's demand for oil, burning twice as much now as it did a decade ago. In response, the Chinesse government is ceaselessly scouring the world to find more oil to feed the skyrocketing new demand.

The transition from bicycles to cars was intentional. As a mechanism to stimulate the economy and provide incentives to individual Chinese, the government encouraged the consumption of automobiles, even subsidizing their purchase in 2009. Over 1.6 million cars were acquired in just two years. In Beijing the streets are now clogged with so much traffic and pollution that government officials have begun considering policies to return to the use of bicycles, but this is ironically happening at the same time as Beijing suburbs are becoming too distant for the convenient use of bicycles (Figure 3).

One of the principal reasons that bicycles have been an effective mode of personal transportation has been the high density of population within the city. Such density also works to the advantage of mass transit schemes. The density around the Forbidden City is about 25,000 persons per km². This allows for an effective system of mass transit. The Beijing Subway, begun in 1969, was expected to have 30 lines, 450 stations, and 1,050 km in length by 2012. It is first in the world in annual ridership with 3.21 billion rides delivered in 2013.[6]

The California cities of San Francisco and Los Angeles offer a further example of the effects of population density, a difference that affects mass transit options. San Francisco at about 121 km² with a population (in 2013) of 837,000 is confined by San Francisco Bay and the Pacific Ocean. Los Angeles, at 1215 km² is ten times larger, with four times as many people at about 3.8 million (in 2012), but with few natural barriers to expansion (Figures 4a and 4b).

San Francisco is the second most-densely settled city in the US (after New York) at 6,898 people per km² As a result of this density, living in San Francisco without owning an automobile is not only feasible but increasingly popular.[7] By contrast, in

FIGURE 4 A-B: The population density of Los Angeles (Left) is 8,225 people per sq. mi (with downtown at 4770 per sq. mi), while the population density of San Francisco (Right) is more than twice that at 17,867 per sq. mi. The greater density of population within the confined space of San Francisco facilitates robust mass transit systems, which save fuel and shortens commuting distances.

Los Angeles—as in Houston, Dallas, Phoenix, and other horizontal cities—owning a car is almost mandatory because the low population density makes mass transit so costly on a person-mile basis.

City form is not only influenced by natural settings, it also has historical roots. For example, population densities tend to be higher in European cities than in cities in western North America because the older cities took shape before electricity and automobiles afforded increased spatial flexibility. Once electricity and cars became ubiquitous, the inclination toward high density living relaxed and people moved to the suburbs to enjoy greater individual space and privacy. As population densities declined, commuting distances increased, freeways became requisite, and congestion soon followed. None of these trends portend a future of sustainability within such cities.

In Asia, we find that despite the scorn heaped on Beijing for its heavy traffic and air pollution, it is by no means the sole example of a congested city, nor is it the most polluted. This distinction belongs to Delhi, which ironically was originally designed to reduce travel distances. Nevertheless, it has become crushingly reliant upon automobiles.[8] In Beijing and Delhi, not to mention places like Los Angeles and San Francisco, traffic can come to a standstill, and there is no easy solution in sight because we are dealing with two problems at once. Even if everyone in these cities converted to zero-emission vehicles overnight, congestion would still continue, as would the need for more roads and parking spaces, and all the other costs that accompany an automobile economy. Cars may bring status and the luxuries of independence and convenience, but these privileges come at a high cost when it comes to sustainability.

The Energy-Sustainable City

Recognizing the rising energy use in cities, several organizations are addressing what can be done to bring it down. In the United States, for example, the American Council for an Energy-Efficient Economy (ACEEE) has developed a City Energy Efficiency Scorecard.[9] Boston tops their list as the most efficient city, followed by San Francisco, Portland, and New York. Jacksonville and Detroit rank at the bottom, meaning that they are particularly wasteful in their use of energy. The ACEEE developed their Scorecard by evaluating **energy efficiency** in each of the following

Energy efficiency. Using an energy resource for the maximum benefit least waste - A typical internal-combustion car, for example, has a low energy efficiency and substantial waste. When energy efficiency is increased, waste is reduced. As a result, mileage of the vehicle rises.

categories: Local Government Operations; Community-Wide Initiatives; Buildings Policies; Energy and Water Utility Policies & Public Benefits Program; Transportation Policies. You can develop a scorecard for your own city by accessing the ACEEE web site: http://aceee.org/local-policy/scoring-tool. When you do, you will gain an understanding of how they came up with the rank order.

A second organization, the European Institute for Energy Research (EIFER), specifically addresses the role of energy in all future decisions concerning urban development, spatial use and settlements. In order to understand urban change, to build up innovative strategies, and to implement them, EIFER targets their research in the following fields:[10]

- Analyzing the urban development, dynamic, and impact on energy demand using approaches to assess and understand the urban transitions

- Analyzing local energy and climate change policies

- Understanding urban governance and its interaction with energy planning, efficiency, and climate change policies

- Assessing innovative urban mobility by evaluating urban policy, technological trends, spatial simulation and its interaction with the built environment

- Integrating concepts for sustainable energy use, taking into account acceptability studies, analyses of lifestyle, models for the diffusion of new technologies, analyses of the legal framework and of stakeholders, studies on governance, and the interactions between the different influence factors

Both the ACEEE Scorecard and the EIFER programmatic assessments are based on the presence of various policies dealing with operations, energy use, and transportation to enhance sustainable solutions. We can supplement this approach by recommending the development of sustainable cities adopt one or more strategies in each category.

Category One – Measures toward more sustainable cities already taking place

- Increase the efficiency of the energy used
- Increase the proportion of sustainable energy resources to power cities

Category Two – Measures toward sustainable cities making slow progress

- Introduce more efficient designs in cities
- Reduce the dependency on automobiles
- Rethink the concept of urban spaces

Let's look at each of these in turn.

Category One – Measures toward more sustainable cities already taking place

Increase Efficiency. Amory Lovins has been the most visible champion of energy efficiency, calling it the "soft energy path".[11] In contrast to relying on technical solutions for energy demand, he argues there are better alternatives. Soft energy is tantamount to energy efficiency; that is, getting the job done while using less energy. His approach was called **Demand-Side-Management** (DSM) and was the opposite of **Supply-Side-Management** (SSM). That is, instead of generating more electricity to meet rising demand, he showed that we can achieve the same personal and communal benefits by cutting our use of electricity and other energy through greater efficiently.

Demand-Side Management (DSM) - An approach toward energy efficiency often used by electric utility companies that meets customer needs by lowering the demand for the energy, rather than increasing the supply. This can be accomplished by using more energy efficient appliances, and better insulated materials.

Supply-Side Management. The opposite of DSM, it tends to satisfy demand by increasing the supply of energy. For example, building a new power plant, instead of building more efficient buildings.

As it is often said, it is always cheaper to *save* a kilowatt of power than to *produce* a kilowatt of power.

Here's an example. Say we provide $1 billion to build a 1,000 megawatt power plant to serve one million people. That would be a supply-side approach. However, if we spent the $1 billion (or much less) to make every house and building in the city more efficient, we would have the same result but with none of the costs. That would be a demand-side approach. Along the way, we would also avoid everything associated with having the power plant, including fuel development and refining, air and water pollution and product transportation for the entire life of the power plant, usually 30-40 years!

Despite the seemingly foolproof logic of a DSM approach, it has taken several decades for the concept to sink in. Nevertheless, we do find rising evidence of its acceptance if we look hard enough. Anyone traveling to Switzerland, Norway, and Germany, for example, has noticed that doors and windows seal tightly, lights switch off when rooms are empty, air conditioners shut down when windows are opened, and incandescent lights are nowhere to be found. The US and other countries are trying to catch up to this example.

Large energy consumers were the first to get on board the efficiency wagon. Chief financial officers quickly understood in a time of rising energy costs, how much money they could save with simple changes such as lighting, the installation of motion sensors, and the use of window screens and other coverings. And payback was often quick and impressive. For example, 20 years ago at Arizona State University (ASU), the first significant experiment with DSM was to retrofit the lighting fixtures and install motion sensors in every room of six campus buildings. Soon, the university was saving over $200,000 per year, with a return on investment of only a few years. Increasing energy efficiency measures at ASU continue to be implemented to this day for the entire university with savings approaching $1 million per year. The goal now is to entice entire cities to follow this example.

Whereas Arizona and other states are just catching on to the benefits of DSM, such improvements in energy efficiency have been aggressively pursued elsewhere, particularly in California, starting in the 1970s. Today, California has one of the lowest rates of per-capita energy consumption in the U.S., a rate that is on par with that of the mild tropical islands of Hawaii.[12] All this success in California results from one of the most robust and varied catalogs of energy efficiency measures and policies anywhere.[13] As such examples have gained traction, further progress towards urban sustainability has accompanied the acceptance of the internationally recognized green building certification system program known as **LEED** (Leadership in Energy and Environmental Design).[14] Today there are over 44,000 LEED-certified building in the US alone.[15]

Increase the Use of Renewable Energy. The impacts of urban energy use extend beyond city boundaries, and run back up the supply paths of railroads, highways, pipelines, shipping routes, and transmission lines. The more we can rely on renewable energy resources, the greater the decline of environmental and human costs of supplying urban energy demands will be. Movement in this direction began in the mid-1980s, and accelerated abruptly from the late 20th century until today, when we are witnessing an unexpectedly quick growth of wind power and solar power worldwide (Figure 5).

By 2011, the percent of power produced by renewables exceeded that generated by nuclear energy, which accounts for about 19% of the total electrical generation in the US. Wind alone generated over 140 billion kWh in 2012.

Leadership in Energy and Environmental Design (LEED) - A set of rating systems for the design, construction, operation, and maintenance of green buildings, homes and neighborhoods. LEED-certified buildings generally operate with greater energy efficiency and, therefore, less environmental impact.

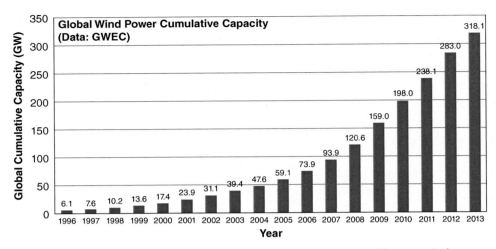

FIGURE 5: The rising capacity of wind generation (and other renewable energy), the smaller the impact of growing energy demand in cities.

By 2013, it was producing about four percent of total electricity generated, compared to less than one percent from solar photovoltaics (PV). PV, however, has been quickly catching up, due to a yearly growth rate of about 156 percent in 2012 and 85 percent in 2013.

Rising demand for electricity in our large cities continues to drive the quick emergence of renewable energy for this generation, as does the widespread adoption of state targets for renewable energy use called **Portfolio Standards**. California, is leading the way with a standard set for 33 percent by 2020. That is, 33 percent of the electricity used in California in 2020 must be from renewables. Today, more than 20 percent of California's electricity demand is met by renewables, with about half that from hydropower. As population continues growing, renewable energy is expected to keep pace and perhaps exceed increased demand, including the adoption of roof-top solar installations. According to the California Public Utilities Commission (CPUC), its California Solar Initiative (CSI) is well on the way to meeting its goal of installing 1,940 megawatts of solar capacity by the end of 2016. Operating these installations produces no air emissions and leaves behind no waste, and they supplant generation from energy sources that do. It is one way to reduce some of the more pernicious environmental impacts of cities and render them more sustainable.

This progress is part of a pattern that can be witnessed especially well in those European countries that have used **Feed-In Tariffs** (FITs) as incentives. In Denmark, wind power production sometimes exceeds the level of power consumption, helping make their cities more sustainable.[16] While China cannot claim anything close to this level of penetration, it has had the fastest growth in the development of solar, wind, and hydropower in recent years. Moreover, the Chinese have also been installing solar water heating throughout the country, something that is common in other places such as Israel and Palestine—further action that reduces the demand of energy development from fossil and nuclear fuels and demonstrates how city life can become more sustainable.

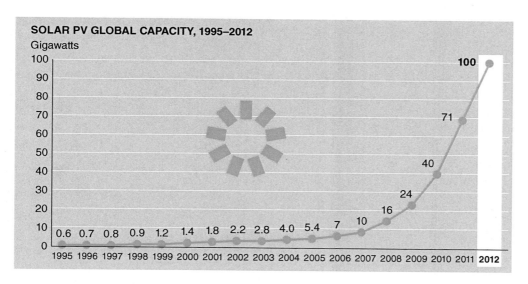

SOLAR PV GLOBAL CAPACITY, 1995–2012

Gigawatts

100 — **100**
90
80
70 — 71
60
50
40 — 40
30
24
20 — 16
10 — 0.6 0.7 0.8 0.9 1.2 1.4 1.8 2.2 2.8 4.0 5.4 7 10
0

1995 1996 1997 1998 1999 2000 2001 2002 2003 2004 2005 2006 2007 2008 2009 2010 2011 **2012**

FIGURE 6: As with wind power, solar PV has risen abruptly in recent years, a result of favorable policies, cheaper manufacturing costs, and higher conventional power prices.

Category Two – Measures toward sustainable cities making slow progress

Improve the design and operation of cities. Naturally, redesigning cities for greater sustainability is no easy task. The basic elements of such revisionist design include greater walkability, designated bike lanes, recycling, mass transit, urban farming, and—most important of all—the willingness to address this need in the first place. Some of the cities that have demonstrated such a willingness include Melbourne, Australia; Ottawa, Canada; Masdar City, UAE; and Älvstaden, Sweden. While revamping urban spaces to make them more energy sustainable is a large task, it is being done here and there with some notable success, such as in Freiburg, Germany, as Bjoren Hagan and Arian Middel fully describe in Chapter 2.

Reduce the dependency on automobiles. Efforts to reduce the use of automobiles have produced little net benefit in most cities, especially in cities with low population densities or no history of mass transit. There, however, are some exceptions. The Bay Area Rapid Transit (BART) light-rail system in the San Francisco Bay Area is very popular with 20 million rides in 2013, albeit these numbers are small compared to cities like New York and Beijing. Moreover, San Francisco has had over a century of familiarity with mass transit in the form of its Municipal Railway system, so people there were more accustomed to leaving their cars at home. Some cities have opted for bus rapid-transit instead of fixed rails and it has had some success, for example in

FIGURE 7: Bus Rapid Transit is a flexible alternative to fixed-rail systems.

Brazil, Indonesia, Australia, and Europe (Figure 7). (see Chapter 11 on Sustainabile Transportation.) The reality, however, is that people who can afford them tend to prefer cars, even though the cars themselves rarely carry more than just the driver. In consequence, every person who drives a car contributes much more than their share of global warming gases than they would if they were to walk, car pool, use mass transit, or ride a bicycle. It is estimated that each gallon of gasoline used in a passenger vehicle results in about 18 pounds of greenhouse gas. For a car traveling 12,000 miles per year, this means that it emits over 8,000 pounds of carbon dioxide, or more than twice its own weight. It is yet another example of why it is difficult to make cities sustainable.[17]

Rethink the concept of urban spaces. Undoubtedly, the most radical experiment in restructuring the form and function of urban spaces has been Arcosanti, an '**archology**' developed by Paolo Soleri in Arizona to describe his designs for ecologically sound human habitats[18].

Among the many elements of such archaeologies is the use of passive solar design, miniaturization, elimination of the automobile, sustainable agriculture, and emphasis on building upward rather than outward. As is common for someone with such ideas, Soleri has attracted ridicule as well as praise, but he is probably on to something.

Final Thoughts

Absent existential threats like permanent traffic jams, deadly pollution, and rampant street violence, cities will be slow to overcome the inertia of their own unsustainable ways, both in the manner we construct them or in the way we operate them. We cannot expect conditions to improve in the future as long as we continue the pattern of rural-to-urban migration, love of suburbs, the dominance of the private automobile, or the use of nonrenewable energy to fuel transport systems, heat and cool buildings, and power factories.

All urban considerations we have just discussed—including cars, highways, congestion, building design, personal comfort, landscaping, pollution, and growth trends—are spokes on a wheel fixed together at the hub of energy. Cities cannot move forward toward a sustainable future without considering the central importance energy places in how they operate and what shape they take. This chapter demonstrates that cites are currently unsustainable because they are not designed or operated with energy efficiency as a primary consideration, and because they rely on unsustainable forms of energy to operate. We need to reduce consumption of fossil fuels, bolster the development of renewables, and increase our attention to energy efficiency in every decision we make about our urban spaces. If we do this, we will accelerate our pace toward the sustainable cities of the future.

The Urban Heat Island Effect and Sustainability Science: Causes, Impacts, and Solutions

Darren Ruddell, Anthony Brazel, Winston Chow, Ariane Middel

Introduction

As Chapter 4 described, the urban experiment began approximately 10,000 years ago when people first started organizing into small enclave settlements of permanent residence. While people initially used local and organic materials to meet residential and community needs, advances in science, technology, and transportation systems now support urban centers that utilize distant resources to produce engineered surfaces and synthetic materials. This process of **urbanization**, which is manifest in the growth of cities in terms of both population and spatial extent, has increased over the course of human history. For instance, according to the 2014 U.S. Census, the global population has rapidly increased from one billion people in 1804 to 7.1 billion in 2014. During the same period, the percent of the global population living in urban centers grew from 3 to over 52 (U.S. Census, 2014).

As previously stated, the number of cities is also rapidly growing. For example, in 1950, there were 86 cities in the world with a population of more than 1 million. In 2010, 400 cities fit this criteria, and by 2015, it is projected that at least 550 cities will have more than 1 million residents (Davis, 2006). **Megacities** (urban agglomerations with populations greater than 10 million) have also become commonplace throughout the world. Megacities in developed countries include Tokyo, New York, Los Angeles, London, and Paris; however, the highest rates of urbanization and most megacities are located in the developing world, particularly in South America (i.e., Sao Paulo, Buenos Aires, Rio de Janeiro), Asia (i.e., Jakarta, Delhi, Mumbai, Shanghai, Dhaka), and Africa (Cairo, Lagos).

One common thread found in all cities, regardless of population size and urban extent, is that urbanization inadvertently alters the local climate system. Although impacts vary at different **spatial scales**—such as at the scale of an individual building, neighborhood, city, or urban region, clear differences occur in climate between urban and rural areas, as witnessed in patterns of temperature, precipitation (rainfall and snowfall), humidity, particulate matter, and wind speed (Landsberg, 1981). This chapter examines the best-known urban-induced alteration of climate: the Urban Heat Island (UHI) effect. By the end of this chapter, you will understand:

- The **morphology** (i.e., form and structure) of UHIs, as well as different UHI types

- Factors causing or modifying **UHI intensity**

Urbanization - the process whereby native landscapes are converted to urban land uses, such as commercial and residential development. Urbanization is also defined as rural migration to urban centers.

Megacities - urban agglomerations with a population exceeding 10 million residents.

Spatial scale - the extent or coverage of a given area, such as a county, state, or nation.

Morphology - the study of the form, structure, process, and transformation of the urban heat island.

Urban heat island (UHI) intensity - a global phenomenon generally seen as being caused by a reduction in latent heat flux and an increase in sensible heat in urban areas as vegetated and evaporating soil surfaces are replaced by relatively high impervious, low albedo paving and building materials.

Mitigation - strategies to reduce greenhouse gas emissions and increase carbon sequestration in order to slow the rate of climate change.

Adaptation - adjustment strategies to increase a system's ability to adjust and reduce vulnerability to the effects of climate change.

Land Use and Land Cover (LULC) - land use refers to the syndromes of human activities (e.g., agriculture, urbanization) on lands. Land cover refers to the physical and biological cover of the surface of land. The vegetation, water, natural surface, and cultural features on the land surface.

Anthropogenic waste heat - heat generated by humans and human activity, such as emissions from factories and transportation systems, among other sources.

- The impacts of the UHI on residents
- Linkages between the UHI effect and urban sustainability
- Various **mitigation** and **adaptation** strategies to reduce the UHI effect

The UHI Effect

Formal scientific study of the UHI first began with the English meteorologist Luke Howard (Howard, 1833) who noted that temperatures within the City of London were different from the surrounding climate of the countryside:

> "The temperature of the city is not to be considered as that of the climate; it partakes too much of an artificial warmth, induced by its structure, by a crowded population, and the consumption of great quantities of fuel in fires."

He hypothesized that **land use and land cover (LULC)** change (the conversion of the Earth's natural surfaces, such as grasses, shrubs, trees, bare soil, into urban surfaces (e.g., asphalt, concrete, buildings, glass) for human socio-economic activities, and the generation of **anthropogenic waste heat** (such as emissions from factories and/or transportation systems, among other sources) were key factors in causing the UHI. It turns out Howard was not far off!

The UHI effect quantifies the temperature gradient between urban and nearby rural areas, which often depicts a given urban area as an "island of heat" amid the native landscape (as illustrated in Figure 1). This pattern is similar to the

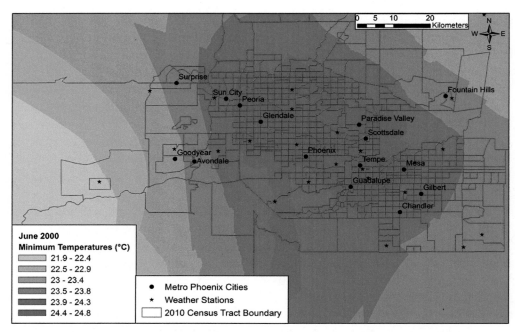

FIGURE 1: The spatial form of the Phoenix, Arizona Metropolitan UHI in June 2000, as measured by minimum temperatures (T$_{min}$) taken from several weather stations. T$_{min}$ is considered a good indicator of UHI, as the urban influence on temperatures is significantly stronger during nocturnal periods as opposed to daytime conditions.
Source: Author – WTLC.

geomorphic land/sea interface of an island, with a notable "cliff" separating the urban and rural temperature fields. There are four distinct **UHI subtypes**: 1) subsurface, 2) surface, 3) urban canopy layer (the atmospheric air layer between the ground surface and average building roof height), and 4) urban boundary layer (the lowest portion of a planetary atmospheric boundary layer that is directly influenced by an underlying urban area) (Oke, 1995). Observation of each UHI subtype has distinct methodological platforms. For example, urban canopy layer studies use data either obtained from point measurements taken at weather stations or taken during mobile traverses (Brazel et al., 2000). Surface and subsurface UHI studies often utilize data from handheld, infrared thermometers, or from instruments mounted on remotely sensed platforms such as airplanes, helicopters, or satellites. Lastly, the urban boundary layer UHI can be investigated through radiosonde data collected by weather balloons that travel up to the top of the lower atmosphere.

Typically, scientists measure the UHI effect either by the increase of minimum temperatures (T_{min}) of a weather station as its surrounding environment "urbanizes" over time, or by the difference in temperatures between urban and rural areas (ΔT_{u-r}) (Landsberg, 1981). Maximum magnitudes of ΔT_{u-r} are generally found at the urban core (e.g., downtown). A "plateau" of elevated temperatures can also be found in other areas that have distinct urban land-use categories (e.g., commercial, residential, and industrial). A third approach to measure the UHI effect was recently introduced that utilizes the concept of Local Climate Zones (LCZs); a scheme to systematically classify UHI study sites based on the urban structure, cover, materials, and anthropogenic activity (Stewart and Oke, 2012). The scheme relies on 17 standardized classes to assess differences between urban and rural landscapes within the given study area.

Parks, lakes, and open areas within cities generally observe lower temperatures than the surrounding urban area and can disrupt urban temperature peaks; these are sometimes called a **park cool island (PCI)** (Figure 2). Dense urban areas can also be

Urban heat island (UHI) subtypes -

1. subsurface: below the surface of the Earth

2. surface: the skin of the surface of the Earth

3. urban canopy layer: the atmospheric air layer between the ground surface and average building roof height

4. urban boundary layer: the lowest portion of a planetary atmospheric boundary layer that is directly influenced by an underlying urban area

Park cool island (PCI) - zones in the urban landscape reporting relatively cooler temperature conditions, which are often associated with parks, lakes, or open areas

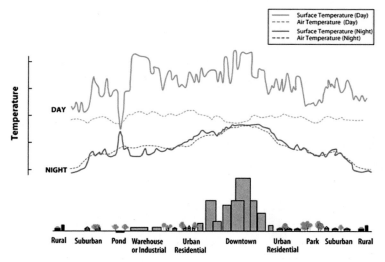

FIGURE 2: Surface and atmospheric temperatures over different land use areas for a city.

Source: EPA -http://www.epa.gov/heatisland/about/index.htm

cooler during the day than sprawled urban areas due to reduced incoming solar radiation and more shading (Middel et al., 2014). If daytime temperatures in the urban area are lower than in the surrounding areas, this is called an oasis effect. The oasis effect is mainly driven by moisture availability and shading, as observed in the Phoenix metropolitan area. Knowledge about the cooling influence of PCIs within cities is important in discussing ways to sustainably mitigate the UHI, as we shall see later in this chapter.

The UHI is also a dynamic phenomenon that arises from different urban and rural temperature cooling rates. Under clear and calm weather conditions for a hypothetical city, ΔT_{u-r} usually varies in a consistent manner during a 24-hour period (Figure 3). Canopy layer temperatures generally start cooling in the late afternoon and evening, with urban areas cooling at slower rates than rural areas. This difference results in the growth of ΔT_{u-r} reaching a maximum about three to five hours after sunset (Oke, 1982). It is important to understand the physical factors that cause the UHI (and

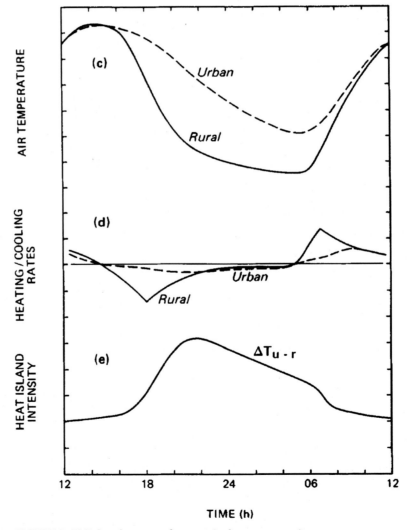

FIGURE 3: UHI development for a typical temperate city as seen through air temperature changes (a), heating/cooling rates (b), and heat island intensity (c) (Oke, 1987).

modify its maximum intensity) when modeling its occurrence and development within different cities and at different scales. Atmospheric models can range from relatively simple statistic-based regression models based on observed data to highly complex, physics- based numerical models that require enormous computational power (Masson, 2006). Results from both observation and modeled studies have great potential in urban planning and policy toward alleviating the negative impacts of the UHI.

What Factors Cause the UHI?

The key to understanding how a UHI is caused is to examine alterations to the urban surface-energy balance, which is expressed in equations 1 and 2.

$$Q^* = K_\downarrow - K_\uparrow + L_\downarrow - L_\uparrow = K^* + L^* \qquad \text{(eq.1)}$$

$$Q^* + Q_F = Q_H + Q_E + \Delta Q_S \qquad \text{(eq.2)}$$

This balance accounts for all energy exchanges within a city that affect net radiation (Q^*). Q^* is the sum of total radiation arriving at ($\downarrow$) or exiting from ($\uparrow$) a surface. Q^* includes radiative **fluxes** (both incoming shortwave (K) and outgoing longwave (L) radiation), and it also describes turbulent atmospheric sensible (Q_H) and latent (Q_E) fluxes, as well as energy stored or withdrawn from the surface substrate (ΔQ_S). Heat fluxes represent the movement of energy for a given area at a fixed unit of time. An additional term included for cities is the heat added by anthropogenic waste heat (Q_F) (See eq. 2). Examples of Q_F include heat emissions from vehicles, industrial plants, and air conditioners, among other sources. In most cities, however, anthropogenic waste heat is a relatively small component of the urban-energy balance when compared to Q_H or ΔQ_S.

Flux - rate of flow of some quantity.

Table 1 demonstrates how various factors influence the urban surface-energy budget, and therefore, the UHI. The UHI is essentially caused through alterations of the urban surface-energy balance and impacted by a myriad of factors. For example, changes in land uses or land cover, say in terms of the amount and extent of asphalt applied over areas, will affect the amount of storage heat flux and have the tendency to increase heat. Understanding typical city features and how they vary within urban

TABLE 1: Suggested causes of the UHI through alterations of the urban energy balance, together with (1) typical urban features associated with the change, and (2) direct urban climate effects on UHI formation (based on Oke, 1982).

Surface energy balance equation symbol	Surface energy balance variable	Typical associated urban features	Direct urban climate effects
Increased K*	Shortwave radiation	Canyon geometry	Increased surface area and multiple reflection
Decreased L*	Longwave radiation	Air pollution	Greater absorption and re-emission
Increased L↓	Longwave radiation	Canyon geometry	Reduced sky view factor
Addition of Q_F	Anthropogenic waste heat	Buildings and traffic	Direct addition of heat
Increased ΔQ_S	Storage heat flux	Construction materials	Increased thermal admittance
Decreased Q_E	Latent heat flux	Construction materials	Increased water-proofing
Decreased ($Q_H + Q_E$)	Sensible and latent heat fluxes	Canyon geometry	Reduced wind speed

Thermal admittance - a surface thermal property that quantifies the rate at which a material stores or releases heat. It is the square root of the product of thermal conductivity and heat capacity.

Urban canyon - an artificial "canyon" formed by two vertical walls of buildings with a horizontal street or pavement surface.

Sky view factor (SVF) - the fraction of sky "seen" from a point on the ground up. It ranges from 0 (completely obscured) to 1 (completely visible).

Central business district - the commercial and often geographic center of a city.

areas is critical in explaining how the UHI is caused. Increases in the use of certain construction materials (such as concrete, glass, asphalt, and steel) reduce the potential for evapotranspiration and increase **thermal admittance**. Thermal admittance is the ability of a surface to store and release heat. This term explains why materials like concrete and asphalt store and later radiate more heat to the environment over a longer period, especially when compared to vegetated surfaces such as urban parks. Even greater levels of traffic within confined areas and other sources of waste heat contribute to the UHI. Increased urban air pollution through the creation of smog, for instance, can also reduce the rate of surface radiative loss creating more surface heat.

There are also two other urban features that influence UHI—**urban canyons** and the **sky view factor** (Figure 4). Urban canyons are characterized by tall buildings on either side of long, narrow streets typical of most **central business districts**. These artificial canyons increase the total urban surface area for energy storage and reduce urban wind speed. They can also reduce the sky view factor. This term illustrates how much of the sky is seen from a surface, and lower sky view factor reduce surface radiative loss, especially at night.

Additional Factors Influencing UHI Intensity

ΔT_{u-r} is strongly affected by the prevailing regional climate over a city. Higher wind speeds, increased cloud cover, and lower cloud heights have been shown to reduce magnitudes of ΔT_{u-r} (Arnfield, 2003). These meteorological factors disrupt surface cooling in different ways. Higher wind speeds increase near-surface turbulent mixing, which decreases the efficiency of surface radiative cooling. Increased cloud cover limits surface longwave radiation loss, with low-level clouds (e.g., stratus and cumulus) having greater impact compared to high-level clouds (e.g., cirrus and cirrostratus). Maximum UHI intensities are thus generally associated with periods having clear and calm weather.

The size and geographic location of cities also affect the maximum magnitude of ΔT_{u-r}. Generally, the bigger the urban population, the larger the maximum UHI intensity (Oke, 1973). Cities located in temperate climates typically have higher maximum ΔT_{u-r} compared to tropical, subtropical, and highland cities, with population size held constant. Of interest is that tropical cities experiencing more precipitation appear to have lower observed maximum ΔT_{u-r} compared to tropical cities with pronounced dry seasons, which suggests a strong impact of surface moisture on attenuating UHI intensity (Roth, 2007).

Water bodies and topographic features located next to a city can also affect the UHI's shape and intensity. Cities located by the coast are subject to a regular daily cycle of land and sea breezes. Typically, moister and cooler air masses over the ocean are advected into warmer urban areas in the early evening, resulting in a distinct temperature gradient seen in cities such as Vancouver, British Columbia (Runnalls and Oke, 2000). Similarly, cities located in valleys may be subject to daily cold air drainage flow patterns. These flows— also known as katabatic flows—are usually strongest at night and can directly affect urban temperatures in complex topography.

The temperature of the surface of the Earth is controlled by energy transfers from the sun. Energy enters the Earth's atmosphere from the sun in the form of **shortwave radiation** where the energy is either absorbed or reflected back into the atmosphere. The energy that was absorbed is radiated back into the atmosphere as longwave

Shortwave and longwave radiation - energy enters the Earth's atmosphere from the sun in the form of shortwave radiation, which is either absorbed or reflected back into the atmosphere; energy that was absorbed is radiated back into the atmosphere as longwave radiation

FIGURE 4: A dense urban canyon (i.e. two walls + street) of downtown Singapore that is typical of most central business districts (left), and a fish-eye lens picture that represents the low sky view factor (SVF) seen at the surface of the street (right).
Source: Author – WTLC .

(infrared) radiation. Solar energy accounts for approximately 99.97 percent of energy entering the Earth's atmosphere (other energy sources include geothermal, tidal, and anthropogenic waste heat). **Albedo** refers to the percent of incoming solar radiation that is reflected back to space. Albedo values vary depending upon surface materials and are expressed as a percentage ranging from zero (no reflection) to 100 (complete reflection). Light surfaces such as snow and ice are highly reflective and report albedo values in the range of 80–95 percent. In contrast, dark-colored materials such as asphalt have low levels of solar reflectance and report albedo values in the range of 5–10 percent. The interactions in the long wavelengths of radiation to and from the Earth are critical to the planet's sustainability, because, in essence, the atmosphere acts as a greenhouse that keeps the planet warm. Scientists have calculated that without this greenhouse effect, Earth's temperatures would be some 30° Celsius (C) cooler than present.

> **Albedo** - the fraction of Earth's incoming solar radiation that is reflected back to space.

Understanding the influence of albedo is important in **sustainability science** for two reasons. The first reason is that surfaces with low albedo values absorb large quantities of solar energy, while high albedo surfaces reflect sunlight back into the atmosphere. Second, albedo values associated with various building materials and land uses and land covers are critical when introducing or replacing features in urban environments. For instance, converting an asphalt parking lot (a low albedo surface material) to a park or open green space (a moderate albedo surface material) will increase the solar reflectance of that parcel of land and thus reduce local heat-storage capacity.

> **Sustainability science** - a field of research dealing with the interactions between natural and social systems, and with how those interactions affects the challenge of sustainability.

Impacts of the UHI on Cities

While the UHI effect is a near-universal phenomenon in cities, its resulting impacts— and whether such impacts are "good" or "bad" for urban residents' quality of life—depend on factors such as geographic location and season. Increased urban warmth can be beneficial for residents in high-latitude cities (e.g., Moscow) with cold winters, but detrimental to city dwellers in hot subtropical cities (e.g., Las Vegas, Phoenix) with hot summers. This section discusses three UHI-derived impacts on urban residents, which are: 1) thermal discomfort and vulnerability to increased heat stress; 2) changes to urban energy and water use; and, 3) impacts on urban economic output (Kunkel et al., 1999).

The UHI effect, coupled with naturally occurring summer **heat waves**, is linked to negative impacts on human health and well-being, such as morbidity (illness) and mortality (death) (Rosenzweig et al., 2005). The UHI increases thermal discomfort and is particularly hazardous to human health and well-being when summer temperatures are elevated and sustained over multiple consecutive days. Excessive exposure to heat already accounts for more deaths in the United States than any other weather-related phenomenon (CDC, 2006; Kalkstein and Sheridan, 2007). Research shows that mortality rates and hospital admissions for cardiovascular, respiratory, and other preexisting illnesses increase in conditions of very hot weather (Semenza et al., 1999). The dangerous impacts of excessive exposure to extreme heat are evident from two historic heat waves: 1) the Chicago, Illinois heat wave in July 1995 that claimed over 700 lives (Semenza et al., 1996; Klinenberg, 2002), and 2) the 2003 heat wave that gripped Western Europe resulting in between 22,000 and 52,000 deaths, many of them occurring in large cities (Larson, 2006).

A warmer urban climate could also translate into increased demands on energy and natural resources, such as water. These increased demands are very likely to occur in cities subject to seasonal high temperatures in the summer or located in equatorial climates with relatively hot year-round temperatures. For example, increases in the UHI intensity in metropolitan Phoenix, Arizona have coincided with increased total and peak-energy demand for residential and commercial cooling from the period between 1950 and 2000 (Golden, 2004). Energy demands increase because of more residents using air-conditioning units at higher demands and for longer periods to provide thermal comfort during the warm summer season. Although air-conditioning systems provide interior relief from summer temperatures, they also release large quantities of anthropogenic waste heat (and produce greater emissions of air pollutants, thus worsening urban air quality while contributing to urban warming) into the surrounding outdoor environment. Warmer temperatures in metropolitan Phoenix are also likely to increase demands on local water systems. For instance, demand on local water resources is greatest during summer months when residents irrigate outdoor vegetation and fill their pools to provide relief from intense summer temperatures (Guhathakurta and Gober, 2007; Wentz and Gober, 2007). A secondary demand on the water system relates to energy production and consumption. Higher energy demands translate to increased demand on water resources because of the large quantities of water consumed when producing electricity.

Despite the extensive environmental and human benefits associated with the mitigation strategies outlined in Table 2, several challenges are entailed with successfully implementing these tactics. For example, implementing any mitigation or adaptation strategy requires an initial financial investment, which many individual homeowners and city officials may be reluctant to make, particularly in a depressed or flat economy.

A second challenge is the issue of sovereignty. For instance, the choices of individual homeowners are often limited by the covenants, codes, and restrictions (CCRs) governing a community or neighborhood that are enforced by Homeowners Associations. In some instances, homeowners would like to install solar panels on their roof or install a solar hot-water heater, but these actions may violate the CCRs and thus individuals are unable to implement the adaptation or mitigation strategy that would simultaneously reduce fossil-fuel energy demands, and improve local air quality, while providing an economic incentive to the homeowner.

Another challenge is the suitability of a given UHI mitigation/adaptation strategy in a local geographic context. A UHI mitigation strategy that is perfect for residents living in Portland, Oregon may be an inefficient and/or counter-productive strategy when implemented in Phoenix, Arizona. Thus, UHI mitigation and adaptation strategies must be considered by individual cities based on the resources and natural advantages of a given city. Perhaps the biggest challenge to implementing a given UHI mitigation or adaption strategy is conducting a cost-benefit analysis. The many benefits of expanding an urban forest need to be evaluated against the costs: increased pollen (allergies), tree maintenance services, and a greater demand on water resources, which is highly problematic in arid environments (Gober, 2006; Shashua-Bar et al., 2009). The use of alternative energy systems, such as solar thermal energy (STE) systems, is an increasingly popular method for meeting residential and commercial energy needs with reduced greenhouse gas emissions, but the current systems are highly water-intensive, which must be considered when siting STE plants and allocating water resources (Hu et al., 2010).

UHI Mitigation Strategies

Several mitigation strategies are designed to reduce the UHI effect. Table 2 provides a list of various mitigation strategies that cities and individuals have employed to combat the UHI effect. UHI mitigation strategies include the creation of urban forests that offer a number of environmental benefits, such as sequestering or storing carbon, retaining storm water during rain events, and improving air quality. Urban forests also provide a number of benefits to local residents. These benefits are often described as **health co-benefits,** such as providing shade and increasing thermal comfort, while simultaneously creating green spaces for recreation and relaxation. Improved air quality from urban forests, increased green spaces, and reduced fossil fuel consumption will help restore ecosystems and provide a healthier living environment, which has been found to stimulate physical activity among residents. A more active lifestyle translates into lower rates of obesity and reduced cardiovascular disease, as well as improved mental health (Besser and Dannenberg, 2005; West et al., 2006; Nurse et al., 2010). In addition to direct benefits of a particular mitigation or adaptation strategy, there are a number of wide-ranging co-benefits among urban residents. This concept of redesigning cities to reduce or mitigate UHIs through the understanding of sustainability science needs to be broadened. Advancing sustainable solutions for one problem area may be utilized to support other benefits through a wider articulation of goals. For example, reducing the UHI through additional vegetative cover in cities can also support urban wildlife corridors, rainfall runoff management, and urban farming, thus making for healthier cities.

Health co-benefits - multiple benefits of a program whereby one of the domains benefits the public health sector, such as providing shade and increasing thermal comfort.

Conclusions

The field of sustainability science offers valuable tools and insights to help address social and environmental concerns associated with the UHI effect. Although there are numerous definitions for the terms sustainability and sustainable development,

TABLE 2: Illustration of mitigation strategies to reduce the urban heat island effect with health co-benefits.

mitigation strategy	environmental outcome	examples	human health co-benefit
Urban Greening	carbon sequestration, enhanced stormwater management and water quality, air quality improvement, reduced energy use	**Urban Forest:** Chicago, IL has implemented an urban forest to improve air quality while reducing the UHI effect	increased shade and thermal comfort, less heat-related illnesses, improved quality of life
		Community Garden: Boston, MA is using community gardens to capture carbon, increase green space throughout the city, and provide fresh fruit and vegetables locally	improved nutrition, increased community engagement
		Green Roofs: Toronto (Canada) utilizes green roofs to help reduce local outdoor temperatures while providing insulation and cooling capacity inside buildings	less heat-related illnesses
Urban Fabric Modification	reduced energy consumption, reduced air pollution and greenhouse gas emissions by lowering energy use	**Cool Roofs:** the City of Phoenix implemented a Cool Roofs program to coat 70,000 square feet of the city's existing rooftops with reflective materials	less heat-related illnesses, improved human comfort
		Cool Pavement: Sacramento's pervious concrete parking lot at Bannister Park is one of the first in the state of California to use cool pavement	less heat-related illnesses, lower tire noise, better nighttime visibility, improved human comfort
Urban Structure Modification	improved air quality, ventilation and solar access	**Building orientation:** Singapore's Marina Bay Financial Centre aligns its arterial roads along the predominant wind direction to improve wind flow at street level, and staggers building heights to increase wind downwash that removes air pollutants	Less exposure to air pollutants, increased shade, and improved thermal comfort

Intragenerational - fair or just access (or exposure) to a given resource within the same generation.

it is generally agreed upon that there are three components of sustainability: 1) environmental conservation; 2) equity (inter and **intragenerational**); and 3) economic development. An anthropocentric paradigm often exploits one sector for the benefit of another, such as harvesting a resource beyond its natural rate of production for economic gain. Sustainable development initiatives aim to simultaneously maximize all three values.

Why is the UHI concept important from the larger framework of sustainability and the idea of maximizing the three values of sustainability—environment, equity, and economics? How we design cities, the materials used for construction and infrastructure, the extent of vegetative open space, and the nature of public transportation systems will affect the intensity of the UHI. But we also learned that we can construct and/or redesign neighborhoods and individual buildings in addition to establishing mitigation policies aimed at reducing the impacts of the UHI. In the case study section on Phoenix, the natural environment has been significantly altered through the process of urbanization, which has produced a well-defined UHI. Land use and land cover change transformed the native Sonoran Desert into an urban concentration, and the resulting alterations in the local urban climate system present new challenges and vulnerabilities to local residents. The degree of change in the intensity and spatial coverage of the UHI will depend on the ways in which a given city is built (or rebuilt) and the materials that are used to construct various features within the urban environment.

The variability of temperatures within a given city represents issues of both inter- and intragenerational equity. For instance, **intergenerational** equity refers to longitudinal access of a given resource, in this case, climate. The increase of minimum temperatures in the urban environment compromises the ability of future generations to enjoy a comparable climate. Intragenerational involves variability within the same generation. In the case of UHIs, some parts of a city are significantly warmer compared to other neighborhoods or areas of the city. The distribution of temperatures within a given city is often concerning because the burden of temperatures is not evenly distributed among social groups. Research shows that minority and low-income populations are often exposed to the worst environmental conditions, yet they possess the fewest resources to cope with extreme heat.

Intergenerational - fair or just access to a given resource across multiple generations

The economic sector is also intimately related with UHIs. Suburbanization is a significant contributor to UHI formation, and the expansion of urban areas into sprawling megacities is largely driven by economics. Rather than introduce a growth boundary, redevelop an existing lot, or increase density (through vertical development), residential development often occurs on the urban fringe where land is relatively cheap. Although economics has contributed to the development of UHIs, this sector also offers opportunities to increase the efficiency of cities. For instance, city efforts to introduce or enhance public transportation systems would provide local employment opportunities, commuting options for residents and visitors, and reduce dependency on automobiles and fossil fuel consumption, in addition to improving air quality. There are also wide-ranging opportunities for the private sector to provide services and innovative solutions for sustainable development, such as solar technologies.

CASE STUDY: The Phoenix, Arizona UHI

The Phoenix metropolitan area is an ideal city to investigate the physical and **social dimensions** of the UHI effect due to its hot subtropical climate coupled with the rapid increase in population and alterations in land use and land cover (Chow et al., 2012). This case study examines the Phoenix UHI from three distinct perspectives. The first perspective investigates physical changes throughout metropolitan Phoenix by analyzing temperature readings from local and regional

Social dimensions - the impacts of urban heat islands on the quality of life of individuals and their families living in a given city.

Continued

weather stations. The second perspective explores human dimensions of the Phoenix UHI by examining exposure to heat stress and thermal discomfort within the urban area. The third perspective introduces an atmospheric model to demonstrate and inform planning scenario alternatives for neighborhoods throughout metropolitan Phoenix.

Changes in the Physical Landscape

The physical dimension of the Phoenix UHI is visible temporally (e.g., change over time) and spatially (e.g., within the study area). From the temporal perspective, Figure 5 shows minimum and maximum annual temperatures for the Phoenix regional weather station from 1900–2008. Note that temperatures vary from year to year for both minimum and maximum temperatures. Variability occurs naturally; however, the time series shows a strong departure from normal beginning in the mid-1960s when the mean annual minimum temperature rises sharply over the next 50 years. The rise in annual minimum temperature is highly correlated with the population growth and land use land cover change that occurred within Phoenix during this period of time. In addition to examining mean annual minimum and maximum temperature trends, two temperature **thresholds** were investigated for the Phoenix regional weather stations (Parmesan et al., 2000). Results are shown in Figure 6. "Frost days" refer to daily minimum temperature of less than 0 °C (32 °F). "**Misery days**," a local measure of excess heat, is defined as daily maximum temperature greater than or equal to 43.3 °C (110 °F). Results show a major regime shift in the annual number of frost and misery days during the 109-year study period. Note the fluctuation in both frost days and misery days from 1900–1970, but beginning around 1970, there is a strong departure from historical trends. We observe a steady rise in the annual number of misery days and a rapid decline in the annual number of frost days.

Thresholds - levels in underlying controlling variables of a system in which feedbacks to the rest of the system change.

Misery days - a temperature threshold of thermal comfort. A misery day in Phoenix, Arizona is when the daily maximum temperature is greater than or equal to 110 °F (or 43.3 °C).

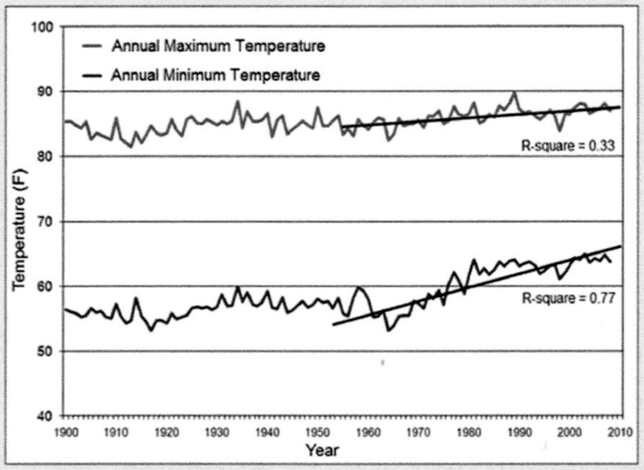

FIGURE 5: Mean Annual Temperature for Phoenix, AZ Regional Weather Station from 1900-2008.

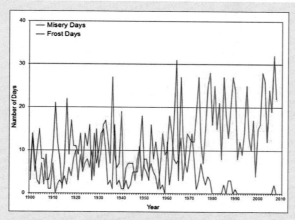

FIGURE 6: Annual Number of Threshold Temperatures for Phoenix, AZ Regional Weather Station from 1900–2008.

Analyses of the spatial structure of the Phoenix UHI also reveal changes in the physical landscape (Figure 7). The graph of monthly mean minimum air temperature patterns from 1990 to 2004 (in five-year increments) illustrates changes in the Phoenix UHI. Results show three distinct findings. The first finding is that the UHI effect is becoming more intense. We find a rise in mean minimum air temperatures from 22 °C (71.6°F) in the 1990–1994 time-step up to 24 °C (75.2°F) in the 2000–2004 time-step. Second, the Phoenix UHI is expanding with the majority of temperature change occurring on the urban fringe where suburbanization replaces desert landscapes. For instance, the area reporting temperatures of 22 °C during the period from 1990–1994 is merely a fraction of the area reporting temperatures of 22 °C (or even 23 °C) in the 2000– 2004 period of analysis. Third, the spatial distribution of the UHI effect exhibits heterogeneity. In other words, there are pockets (or bands) of warmer/cooler temperatures within metropolitan Phoenix, which means people and places within metropolitan Phoenix are exposed to variant levels of heat stress.

Inequity in the Social Landscape

Sustainability scientists have only recently begun to explore social dimensions of UHIs. This section briefly explores exposure to temperatures among different social groups within metropolitan Phoenix and its implications in the area of **spatial equity**, a fundamental concept in sustainability. Census block group data for year 2000 were combined with output from a sophisticated atmospheric model (the Weather Research and Forecast climate model) to investigate correlations between exposure to air temperature and the social characteristics of people living in the warmest/coolest places within metropolitan Phoenix. The model was used to create a Heat Intensity Index to compare exposure to extreme heat among 40 neighborhoods throughout metropolitan Phoenix. The heat index was divided into three classes: low exposure, medium exposure, and high exposure. Four census block group variables were examined—density, income, ethnicity, and age—and all four

Spatial equity - the concept of spatially equitable living conditions within a given urban area.

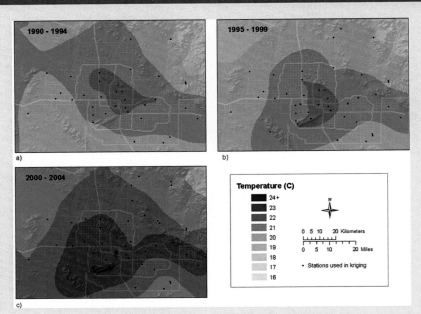

FIGURE 7: Monthly mean minimum air temperature patterns (using ordinary kriging methods) from 1990 to 2004 in 5 yr increments.

From Climate Research Journal, Volume 33: 172-182, February 22, 2007 by Anthony Brazel et al. Copyright © 2007 by Inter-Research. Reprinted by permission.

TABLE 3: Population Characteristics of Neighborhoods by Heat Intensity Class (Modified from Ruddell et al. 2010).

Demographics	Heat Intensity Class		
	Low	**Medium**	**High**
N Neighborhoods	15	10	15
Density			
Population per sq mi	3,569	3,757	7,550
Socioeconomic Status			
Household income	$71,903	$62,669	$38,621
Ethnicity			
% minority	20.7	25.9	44.7
Age			
% ages 65 and over	9.8	20.4	17.5

Source: 2000 US Census.

were highly correlated Heat Intensity Index (Table 3). The population per square mile of the high-heat intensity class is almost double the population density of the low and medium intensity classes. Median household income is considerably higher in the low- and medium-heat intensity classes compared to the high-heat intensity class. The percentage of ethnic minorities is significantly larger in the high-heat intensity class relative to the low and medium classes. Finally, the medium- and high-heat intensity classes reported relatively large percentages of elderly residents, which is a concern, because physiologically, the elderly are one of the most vulnerable groups to extreme temperatures. In short, extreme heat is not evenly distributed among all social groups within the urban environment. Residents exposed to the worst environmental conditions tend to be low-income, minority, and elderly.

Simulating Alternative Planning Scenarios

Scientists utilize climate models to assess proposed UHI mitigation measures at different temporal and spatial scales to analyze outcomes of various "what-if" scenarios. These modeling techniques provide assistance and insight into planning and/or redesigning more efficient living environments. A recent study by ASU scientists investigated the impact of urban form on afternoon temperatures during the summer season among neighborhoods throughout metropolitan Phoenix by using the microclimate model ENVI-met Middel et al., 2014). Air temperature simulations at a fine spatial resolution of 1 meter were conducted for typical residential neighborhoods in Phoenix, classified into five local climate zones (Figure 8). The study found that neighborhoods comprised of mesic landscaping (e.g., grass, trees, and shrubs) were cooler than residential areas with xeric landscaping (e.g., drought-tolerant), but at the micro-scale, urban form had a more discernable impact on temperatures than the amount of vegetation. Dense urban forms were more beneficial in terms of daytime cooling than sprawled or sparsely built urban forms, mainly because of reduced incoming solar radiation and more shading. This study supports the finding that dense urban areas can have an oasis effect and create a local cool island in mid-afternoon.

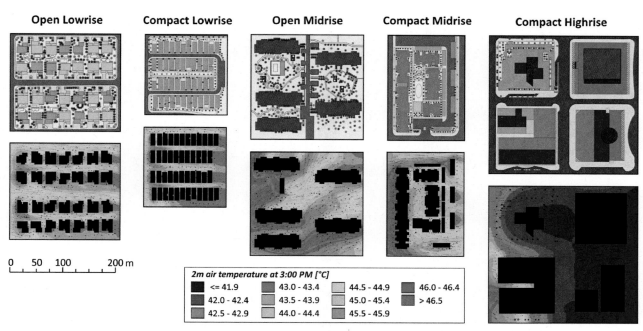

Figure 8: 2-meter air temperature simulation for five residential neighborhoods in Phoenix, Arizona.

Reprinted from Landscape and Urban Planning, Vol 122, Ariane Middel et al, Impact of urban form and design on mid-afternoon microclimate in Phoenix Local Climate Zones, Pages 16-28, Copyright 2014, with permission from Elsevier.

References

Chow, W.T.L., Brennan, D., Brazel, A.J., 2012. Urban Heat Island research in Phoenix, Arizona: Theoretical contributions and policy applications. Bulletin of the American Meteorological Society 93, 517–530.

Parmesan C, Root TL, Willig MR 2000. Impacts of extreme weather and climate on terrestrial biota. Bulletin of American Meteorological Society 81:443–450.

Assessing Urban Sustainability: Using Indicators to Measure Progress

Devon McAslan

Introduction

Indicators have become an important tool for policy makers in the realm of sustainable development. Without the ability to accurately and effectively measure progress towards sustainability, how are we to know whether our efforts and policies are in fact creating more sustainable communities and improving the well-being of people? Indicators allow us to measure and track progress in achieving sustainability goals. This chapter will discuss the history of indicator use in public policy and how indicators became a part of the sustainable development movement. Further, it will explore the many dimensions of what indicators are and why they are important in sustainability planning efforts. The key characteristics of indicators will be examined and how individual indicators are used to develop indicator programs will be explored. The chapter will conclude by providing an overview of multiple ways in which indicators have been used to measure and assess sustainability at different geographic and political scales.

What is an Indicator?

An **indicator** is any form of information that allows a decision maker to quickly and effectively determine the state of a system or what is being measured. An indicator usually consists of a single number and is sometimes presented as a ratio. Some commonly used indicators are the unemployment rate, income, poverty rates, and air pollution levels. Increasingly, many indicators are used together to provide a more complete picture of a system, as is the case with sustainable development. The data triangle (Figure 1) shows how an indicator relates to other types of information. They are more specific than raw data or statistics of which they are comprised. Likewise, a number of indicators can be combined into an index. The purpose of an indicator, or set of indicators, is to help policy makers evaluate whether their actions are having the desired or intended effect. Indicators are measurements that can be compared across time and space and have policy implications and societal importance. As we will see, some indicators are viewed as more effective at accomplishing these requirements than others. As a result, such indicators are relied upon more frequently than others. As indicators have increasingly been used to assess the progress of sustainable development policies, the use of certain types of indicators, such as traditional economic or environmental monitoring indicators, has been questioned because clear links between policies and outcomes are much more difficult to establish when considering social, environmental, and economic goals simultaneously. Increasingly, indicators for sustainability are

> **Indicator** - An Indicator is a piece of information that can help to determine the state of a system quickly and effectively.

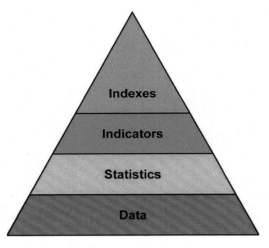

FIGURE 1: The data triangle.
Source: Newton, 2001.

used at the urban level. It is widely accepted that cities are pivotal to achieving a sustainable future. As such, it is within cities where it is most important to measure sustainability.

When we discuss the use of indicators for sustainable development, we are referring to the use of social indicators. A social indicator is any indicator that has social (or societal) significance. A social indicator may be defined as a "direct and valid statistical measure which monitors levels and changes over time in a fundamental social concern" (OECD, 1976). Nearly all indicators used by policy makers today to track sustainable development can be considered **social indicators** since sustainable development is a major social concern.

Social Indicators - Any indicator that measures and reports on something of social importance in a specific context.

Index - An index is a single number that combines multiple indicators in order to provide a general trend of a system.

A distinction should be made between indicators and indexes, as both can be used to measure sustainability. Like indicators, indexes are often presented as single numbers, but there are notable differences between indicators and indexes. An **index** is created when two or more indicators are combined in order to give a summary that shows a general trend of a system. Some examples of common indexes include GDP, the Consumer Price Index (CPI), and the Human Development Index (HDI). The numbers that these indexes provide are useful for achieving a general understanding of what they represent. Unlike indicators, an index is not useful for policy makers when making decisions about which specific policies to implement. This is because indexes are comprised of multiple, often unrelated, indicators. In order to make effective policies, the individual components of an index must be known. For example, the HDI is comprised of measures that assess health, education, and income. Two countries may have very similar scores, but each could require altogether different policies in order to improve their HDI score. Because knowing the HDI score does not mean we know how a country is doing in each of the index's component parts, we cannot accurately or effectively use the HDI to develop new policies. This is why indicators are so important – because their specificity allows for better policies to be developed and implemented.

Indicators: A Brief History

The use of indicators in public policy is not a recent phenomenon. In fact, the first use of what we now recognize as social indicators can be traced back to the early 1800s. It was at this time when indicators were used by social reformers in an attempt to improve public health and social conditions in industrial cities. The first use of statistical indicators can be traced back to 1810 in Philadelphia with the purpose of prison reform. There was, however, little understanding of how the measurements used could affect social policy and the reformers assumed the numbers would speak for themselves. By mid-century there was a better understanding of how to use statistical measurements. These measurements were used to show causal relationships between various social factors – largely in an effort to support different social views. In the later part of the 19th century, wages, unemployment and conditions of the working class became important political issues and as a result labor statistics were among the first officially gathered social statistics. Labor bureaus were established in order to collect these statistics and how these early agencies defined their roles would affect the indicator movement for nearly a century. Initially, the statistical indicators were used to support political viewpoints and make arguments, based on the statistics, in favor of labor reform. However, this practice did not persist when the labor reform movement collapsed. By the end of the 19th century there was a consensus that statistical indicators needed to be neutral to politics and should be used simply to report the data. These two opposing viewpoints continue to be an issue today when trying to define what indicator programs should aim to achieve.

In 1910 the Russell Sage Foundation developed the first set of that we would now call community indicators. They developed survey methods that were initially used to gauge industrial conditions in Philadelphia. After the success of this first survey, they began to consult other organizations around the US in conducting their own surveys. As a result of their efforts, over two thousand local surveys were conducted on education, recreation, public health, crime and general social conditions (Cobb and Rixford 1998). Generally, the authors of these surveys hoped that social reform would result from the information collected and reported to the public, thus mobilizing people around the key issues revealed by the data (Cobb and Rixford 1998). However, this rarely occurred, and for this reason, these types of community indicators were relatively ineffective in promoting policy changes in the first part of the 20th century.

During the 1920s there was a shift away from local community organized indicator collection towards collection at the national level. The federal government continued to collect social indicators, but it also improved its collection of business and economic data. In 1929 the federal government released *Recent Economic Changes in the United States*; and, in 1933 it released a similar report on social issues called *Recent Social Trends*. These social reports served as little more than a compendium of demographic, health and education conditions and they "offered little insight into how to understand or solve the huge problems brought on by the Great Depression" (Cobb and Rixford 1998). Due to the inability of social indicators in and of themselves to provide solutions for social problems, there was a shift away from the use of social indicators towards collection of solely economic statistics, such as unemployment rates and GDP. These indicators were based on economic principles that were well defined and widely accepted and proven to work. Like the indicators that came before them, they remained objective and value neutral and proved useful in attempting to predict economic cycles and affecting policy (Cobb and Rixford 1998). The use of these economic indicators remained popular during the post war period as international organizations began to focus on growth and development in developing countries. Economic growth was viewed by many as a way to improve the overall social conditions, especially in developing countries. The ability of objective economic indicators to affect economic policies was seen as highly beneficial.

In the 1960s a renewed interest in social indicators developed as a result of the success economists experienced in using economic indicators to guide economic policy (Cobb and Rixford 1998). Proponents of social indicators argued that economic indicators alone were not an adequate measure of the full array of social issues. Initially, it was thought that the social indicators should remain objective, since this was how economic indicators had achieved success (Cobb and Rixford 1998). Two government reports were published in the 1960s that focused exclusively on social issues. The first was *Social Indicators* (1966) published by NASA to determine the secondary benefits of the space program and the second was *Towards a Social Report* (1969) published by the US Department of Health and Welfare. Both reports used a descriptive and objective approach in collecting and reporting on social issues. The authors of *Towards a Social Report* believed that indicators "should tell us if we are moving in the right direction, be relevant to policy setting and help evaluate the effectiveness of social programs" (Cobb and Rixford 1998). In 1968, the Russell Sage Foundation and the Social Science Research Council published *Indicators of Social Change* which promoted an inductive approach to indicators. Many proponents of social indicators wanted to establish a Council of Social Advisers, just as a Council of Economic Advisers had been created. However, one of the authors of *Indicators of Social Change* argued that social indicators could not follow in footsteps of economic indicators because "social goals were more ambiguous than economic ones, social problems were less clearly understood and the theoretical foundations of economics were much clearer than those underlying the analysis of social problems" (Cobb and Rixford 1998). The development and use of social indicators flourished in the 1970s but often had little effect on policy resulting generally from a lack of understanding of the underlying causes of social problems (Cobb and Rixford 1998).

During the 1970s, with the increased public awareness of widespread environmental degradation, the development and use of environmental indicators became an important goal of the federal government. The Environmental Protection Agency (EPA) was created in 1970 and led the way in developing environmental indicators and continues this role today. The EPA, and other environmental organizations, began to publish 'state of the environment' reports. Similar to early social reports, these environmental reports were comprehensive, reported on many statistics, and remained largely objective. As their comprehensiveness made their content not readily accessible to policy makers, these reports did not achieve the desired influence on environmental policy after the initial wave of environmentalism.

During the 1980s the federal government shifted away from the use of social indicators. This resulted from a number of factors – a growing concern about national economic conditions, the continued inability of social indicators to be useful in shaping public policy and the lack of a theoretical framework for interpreting social indicators (Cobb and Rixford 1998). However, the use of social indicators did not halt altogether. During the 1980s locally organized community groups once again began to make use of indictors, as happened at the start of the 20th century. They began to focus on quality of life concerns which incorporated not only social issues but also economic and environmental issues (Sawicki and Flynn 1996). This is the start of what many refer to as the modern community indicators movement which has since branched into the sustainability indicator movement.

Community Indicators

Community indicators emerged in the early 1980s after national interest in indicator development began to decrease. The term **community indicator** is a broad term for an indicator that measures any aspect of a community's well-being. Community indicators are "measurements of local trends that include all three dimensions of what it takes to build a healthy community – economic, environmental and social" (Redefining Progress 1997). The scale of use in community indicators varies depending how *local* and *community* are defined. Community indicators are used at many geographic scales, including neighborhoods, cities, counties, regions and even states. Community indicators have been used by nonprofit organizations, private businesses, neighborhood associations, government departments within cities, school districts, city governments, counties, regional planning councils and state governments. Community indicators use a bottom-up approach, contrasting with the top-down social and environmental indicators movements of the 1960s and 1970s. At the urban level, community indicators often looked at the overall quality of life within a city or region. When sustainable development was introduced into development practices, it became the focus of many community indicator programs. These differing perspectives for indicator work have become frameworks around which indicators are developed.

Community Indicator - A specific type of indicator that measures any aspect of a community's well-being.

Sustainable Development and Indicators

In 1987, the World Commission on Environment and Development released *Our Common Future*, in which the concept of sustainable development was introduced as a new way of thinking about growth and development, in both economic and social terms, and integrating it with concerns about environmental wellbeing and natural resource depletion. In addition to defining sustainable development, this report suggested that new ways of measurement needed to be developed in order to monitor progress towards sustainable development. Five years later, in 1992, the UN Conference on Environment and Development released *Agenda 21*. This document stated that:

> "40.4. Commonly used indicators such as the gross national product (GNP) and measurements of individual resource or pollution flows do not provide adequate indications of sustainability. Methods for assessing interactions between different sectoral environmental, demographic, social and developmental parameters are not sufficiently developed or applied. Indicators of sustainable development need to be developed to provide solid bases for decision-making at all levels and to contribute to a self-regulating sustainability of integrated environment and development systems." (UN CED 1992)

Agenda 21 provided the necessary motivation to accelerate the early community indicator movement of the 1980s into an appreciably more widespread movement. It did this since it directly stated that indicators could be used for measuring sustainable development. Up to this point, indicators had largely been used to measure economic conditions, basic social characteristics, and the state of the environment, but did so without recognizing the connections between these areas, which is a fundamental part of sustainability. In section 40.2, *Agenda 21* states that "more and different types of data need to be collected . . . indicating the status and trends of the planet's ecosystem, natural resource, pollution and socio-economic variables" (UN CED 1992). These new types of data combined with previously used indicators would paint a more accurate picture, which could be used in indicator programs and would assist in improving development policies. In addition to new indicator programs being developed to measure progress towards sustainable development, a new type of indicator emerged: *sustainability indicators*. These *sustainability indicators* are based on an integrated concept of sustainability and recognize the linkages between the environment, society and the economy in a single measurement.

Agenda 21 also emphasized the fact that indicators should be used for decision making at different levels of government, which suggests a top-down approach to developing sustainable development policies. *Agenda 21* did not, however, specify how indicators should be used within policy making, whether they should remain objective, as they often had been in the past, or if they should provide detailed analyses and outline policy agendas. This continues to be a point of contention within indicator programs. Many programs continue simply to report the data, while others dig deeper and investigate the root cause of the state of a particular indicator and suggest possible routes to improvement.

Agenda 21 further stated that sustainable development was a goal towards which both national governments *and* local governments needed to work. *Agenda 21* recognized the "general lack of capacity, particularly in developing countries, and in many areas at the international level, for the collection and assessment of data, for their transformation into useful information and for their dissemination" (UN CED 1992). The UN attempted to address this concern by working on both national and local indicators. In 1993 the UN Human Settlements Program (UN Habitat) developed an indicator set specifically for urban areas. This program created a Global Urban Observatory which established and worked with national and local data observatories to collect and analyze data. In 1996 the UN Commission on Sustainable Development developed a comprehensive set of national level sustainable development indicators which could be adopted by national governments to assess their own progress (UN DESA 2007). Both of these programs helped to maintain interest in the development of indicators and continued monitoring.

In the US, an interagency working group was organized in 1994 and subsequently published *Sustainable Development in the United States: An Experimental Set of Indicators* (1998). Shortly after the release of this report, there was decreasing support for national sustainable development strategies and indicators in the US. This was due, in part, to a continued lack of a universal definition of sustainable development and also to the growing recognition that local and regional efforts were most important for achieving sustainable development at the national and global level. Local governments, motivated by *Agenda 21*, began to develop local plans and indicator programs for sustainable development. By this time, the community indicator movement had already begun to address sustainable development and several sustainable development indicator programs had been developed. Although both local governments and community organizations have had success in developing urban sustainability indicator programs, the question remains regarding their overall effectiveness as policy tools and whether they actually help to create sustainable cities.

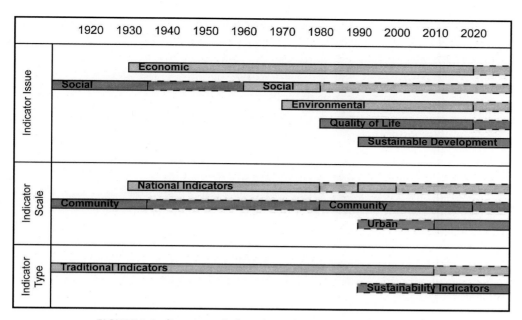

FIGURE 2: Indicator evolution chart showing prevalent issues.

Figure 2 summarizes the evolution of indicators over the last 100 years since the Russell Sage Foundation (which continues its work in the social sciences today) first developed community surveys in 1910. It shows three parallel tracks – the issue being emphasized, the scale of measurement, and the type of indicators that are most prevalent. Social indicators at the local level quickly became less important than national indicators that measured economic issues. By the 1960s and 1970s social and environmental issues became increasingly important issues at the national level. In the 1980s, however, there was a shift back to community indicators which focused on quality of life concerns. Each of these movements used traditional indicators that measured a single aspect of a community. In the 1990s three trends emerged. First, the introduction of sustainable development shifted the development of indicators towards this issue. Second, indicators became much more focused on urban areas than they had been previously. And third, the development of *sustainability indicators* introduced new indicators and measurements that provided a more holistic and integrated perspective of urban systems.

Why do we use Indicators?

Indicators are used to assess sustainable development because of their ability to alert policy makers, and the public, to the state of a system and the trend within that system – whether it is improving or getting worse. Almost any number can be an indicator, but that does not necessarily mean it will be a good indicator. Much effort has gone into determining what makes a good indicator. These efforts have yielded a number of criteria used to gauge whether an indicator is (or will be) useful for policy making. These characteristics are discussed below.

A good indicator is one with a high overall usefulness to a community. In order to achieve this, an indicator must possess several characteristics. Many authors and organizations have discussed what characteristics indicators should possess or what criteria should be used to select indicators for use within a program (see Levett 1998; de Vries 2001; Innes and Booher 2000; Miller 2000; Redefining Progress 1997; Phillips 2003; Leitmann 1999; and Maclaren 1996). The most widely cited characteristics include:

- Being Relevant: Indicators must be relevant to the community and to policy and decision making. An indicator has relevance when it "tells you something about the system you need to know and is meaningful to the community (Redefining Progress 1997)." When the indicator is important to the community then the information it portrays can be used by decision makers to choose policies that will improve the condition reflected by the indicator.

- Valid: A valid indicator means that the indicator is based on sound data and accurately depicts a real situation (Phillips 2003). The data used in measuring the indicator must be collected in a scientific or controlled manner and "methodological rigor is needed to make the data credible for both experts and laypeople (Miller 2000)."

- Simple and Easy to Understand: This means the indicators should be presented in ways allowing the user, without difficulty, to know what is being measured. Even if the issue is complex, a good indicator has the capacity to clearly present the information to users (Miller 2000). The indicator should also be understandable by a diverse group of people (Leitmann 1999; Phillips 2004; Reed et al. 2006). Further, each indicator should be "simplified as much as possible," permitting all stakeholders to communicate effectively about community issues (Zhang et al. 2008).

- Measurable: If the data needed to measure an indicator cannot be collected, then the indicator cannot be reported. The data should be already available (Leitmann 1999) or a practical method for collecting the data must be available are able to be developed (Redefining Progress 1997).

- Cost Effective: Indicators should make use, where possible, of already available data and by doing so, they can lower overall costs. The cost of collecting data should not be overly expensive (Phillips 2003) and the indicator itself should be worth the time and money used to produce it (de Vries 2001).

- Able to Show Trends: Indicators need to have consistent and reliable time series data. By tracking an indicator over a period of time, the user is able to detect trends for the indicator. These trends can provide indirect information about future conditions (Maclaren 1996). Knowing whether a system is improving or worsening allows a user to make a decision to improve the state of that indicator. In order to best show trends, the collection of data must be consistent and reliable (Redefining Progress 1997).

- Sensitive to Change: An indicator should have the capacity to measure changes (de Vries 2001). It must be able to alert users to this change quickly, especially if the condition is worsening, so that policies can be evaluated to determine the cause of the observed change and what action(s) can be taken to improve the system.

- Comprehensive: A single indicator should represent many aspects of an issue and in doing so reduce the number of total indicators needed (Phillips 2003). Although indicators should be comprehensive, they should still remain simple and understandable.

Objective and Subjective Indicators

Indicators can be classified and sorted in many different ways depending on their composition and function. One of the most important distinctions to make when using indicators is between objective and subjective indicators. There are two main differences between these two types of indicators – their purpose and the source of the data that is used.

Objective indicators, also called quantitative indicators, are used to measure concrete aspects of a system and are based on observed statistical data. These are observable and measurable phenomenon, such as air quality or crime levels. Objective indicators comprise a majority of indicators currently used to assess sustainable development.

Subjective indicators, also called qualitative or perceptual indicators, report peoples' opinions and feelings about their lives and about their communities. The data for these indicators are gathered through field surveys in which citizens are asked about their perceptions or feelings about things such as their perception of air quality or perception of crime. Increasingly, the scope of these surveys has been expanded to include other questions, such as overall well-being or happiness.

Although subjective indicators offer insight to the views of urban residents, it has been noted that they also often can create confusion, particularly among policy makers who want to rely upon facts and data. The confusion (or lack of understanding) can arise when "there are disparities between what people say they want and need and what the objective conditions indicate (Dluhy and Swatz 2006)." Instead of causing confusion and a lack of understanding, it is possible that these discrepancies can offer valuable insight for policy makers if those who develop indicators can more clearly identify and explain possible areas where perceptions and measurable data may differ.

Taken together, quantitative and qualitative indicators are useful to policy makers to assist them in decision making that has a greater overall affect. This is especially true of indicator programs that seek to measure quality of life, well-being and happiness in addition to sustainability. To achieve a more viable approach, however, it is better to strive for a balance of the two types and not rely on subjective indicators. This is because subjective indicators are often more expensive and more time consuming to gather data on since they must be collected locally and be specific to local concerns. In other words, the data for these is not readily available for use within indicator programs. As a result, a majority of programs do not use these types of indicators and instead rely on objective quantitative indicators. However, as indicator programs have evolved over the past decade, a greater number of organizations are collecting subjective indicators, largely with the help of the internet. Regardless of the whether a program uses objective or subjective indicators or a mix of the two, they must all adhere to the characteristics that result in good indicators.

Objective Indicator - An indicator that reports on concrete and observable phenomena.

Subjective Indicator - An indicator that measures individuals' opinions and perceptions about their community.

Sustainability Indicators versus Traditional Indicators

Another distinction that we must make when talking about indicators is the difference between **traditional indicators** and **sustainability indicators**. Traditional indicators, which includes the large majority of indicators, are one dimensional. In general, this means that they only pertain to one part of a community, and often at the cost of other parts (Hart 1995). The integrated nature of sustainability (integrating economic, social and environmental decisions) required a new type of indicator that had not previously been used. Sustainability requires indicators that emphasizes linkages between different sectors of a community. With respect to sustainability indicators, they should capture multiple aspects of a community in a single measurement, hence offering a more holistic perspective of the system. Sustainability indicators are more meaningful since they tend to highlight why an indicator is important why we care about what the measurement tells us.

Sustainability indicators, as we have defined them here, are essentially the same as traditional indicators in the way they are presented. The difference resides in their embodiment of multiple aspects of a community in a single measurement.

Indicator Programs

While a single indicator might be useful to look at a single variable, an urban system is complex and comprised of many components. In order to assess sustainability in urban areas, multiple indicators are combined into what is called an **indicator program**. A program, in general, is any activity designed to reach a designated goal. In the case of a sustainability indicator program the goal is to measure progress towards a future that is more sustainable than the present. These programs can contain anywhere from several to a few hundred individual indicators. The scale varies based on the goals and objectives of the program. Most sustainability indicators programs focus on the urban scale – both municipal and metropolitan areas. There are however a number of indicator programs and organizations that measure sustainability at a national scale. Increasingly, these programs are becoming inactive as more programs are developed to measure the sustainability of urban areas.

Sustainability indicator programs are developed by a range of organizations. Governments, such as a municipal government or a regional council of governments, and community based organizations, such as a local non-profit organization, are the two types of groups that primarily develop indicator programs in an urban setting to measure sustainability. Universities and nongovernmental organizations (distinguished from community based organizations by the fact that they do not necessarily have origins within the community in which they are operating) have also been involved in the development of indicator programs. Increasingly in the US, local and regional governments are developing sustainability indicator programs.

A number of specific steps need to be taken when developing an indicator program. Many authors and organizations have suggested different steps and phases to creating indicator programs (see Redefining Progress 1997 and 2002; Maclaren 1996; and Reed, et al 2006). The most important steps to consider when developing an indicator program include:

- Set Goals: Community goals and targets should be identified. Without them we cannot determine whether the community is improving or getting worse on any given indicator. Additionally, the indicator program itself should have goals and objectives, whether to assist policy makers or to simply monitor the community.

- Select Framework: Every indicator program needs some type of framework around which its indicators are organized. There can be considerable variation in the structure of these frameworks, but having an appropriate framework around which to develop the program that reflects community goals is important to the success of the program.

- Community Participation: Community participation and stakeholder engagement is a key element of an indicator program as it ensures that the community has a vested interest in what is being measured. It also increases awareness of the indicator program within the community.

- Select Indicators: The indicators chosen to be the program must be appropriate for the community for which they are meant to measure progress.

- Publish Report: A reporting mechanism that is issued regularly and is easily accessible to the public and to policy makers is perhaps the most important part of an indicator program. Without ongoing monitoring and updating of the indicators, we cannot determine the state of the community and whether it is improving or worsening.

Program and Community Goals

An urban indicator program is intended to measure progress towards a future urban condition. These goals need to be established before an indicator program can be developed if that program is to have a chance at being effective. The goals are usually developed by the organization managing the indicator program. They can be general goal statements, such as decrease air pollution or increase the number of industries in the local economy. Likewise, they can be more specific and include the use of targets, such as reduce traffic congestion by 20 percent or reduce CO_2 levels to 2000 levels. When an indicator uses a target, it is necessary to establish a baseline for that indicator, meaning a starting point against which future measures of that indicator will be measured. If a target is not established, an indicator usually compares future data against the data collected in the first report. This is the more common method since many communities and indicators do not necessarily have preexisting data to gather baselines from. Increasingly, the goals that are established are part of a local or regional sustainability plan or comprehensive plan, which provide long term (usually 20-30 years) plans for the future development of a city or region. Additionally, these plans are generally required by law to be updated regularly meaning that the goals are updated as communities evolve over time. Another important trend in indicator development shows that more indicator programs are now being developed as part of comprehensive plans, as opposed to simply adopting the same goals.

Program Frameworks

An indicator framework is a system which provides "a structure for indicator selection and development (Frederiksen and Kristensen 2008)." The types of frameworks used by indicator programs vary greatly. The selection and use of an appropriate framework is a key component of an indicator program since it is what allows for the logical

Sustainability Indicators for Australia

Social and Human Capital

Skills and Education

Educational attainment*
Primary education (literacy and numeracy)
Early development
Research and development

Health

Self-reported physical health
Life expectancy
Mental health
Smoking
Obesity

Institutions, Governance and Community Engagement

Level of trust in core institutions
Volunteering
Cultural activity attendance
Participation in sport
Community engagement by persons with a disability

Employment

Under-employment
Unemployment
Hours worked
Employment to population ratio

Security

Feelings of safety
Incidence of personal crime
Incidence of household crime

Natural Capital

Climate and Atmosphere

Air quality
Greenhouse gas emissions
Observed climate change
Energy intensity
Carbon stored in the landscape

Land, Ecosystems and Biodiversity

Extent of native vegetation
Ground cover
Ecosystem protection (protected areas)

Water

Water quality
Water consumption
Water availability to meet demand

Waste

Waste disposed to landfill
Recycling rate

Natural Resources

Fish stocks
Timber resources
Mineral and fossil fuel reserves

Economic Capital

Wealth and Income

Household net worth
Income disparity
Financial stress

Housing

Housing supply
Housing affordability

Transport and Infrastructure

Vehicle and passenger kilometres travelled
Travel time to work
Mode of transport to work
Broadband internet connections

Productivity and Innovation

Productivity
Business innovation

* **bold** denotes a headline indicator.

In addition, the following contextual indicators will provide key demographic information to assist with interpretation of the sustainability indicators:

Topic	Population	Cultural Diversity	Regional Migration	Land Use
Indicator	Population size	Proficiency in spoken English	International migration	Land use change
	Population density	Indigenous population	Domestic migration	
	Gender and age profile	Country of birth		

Framework developed by Australia's Measuring Sustainability.

From Fact Sheet: Measuring Sustainability Program (October 2012) by Australian Government, Department of Sustainability, Environment, Water, Population and Communities. Copyright © 2012 by Australian Government. Reprinted by permission.

organization of indicators as well as helping in guiding their selection. Gudmundsson (2003) distinguishes between two types of frameworks: conceptual frameworks and utilization frameworks. Conceptual frameworks provide the inner structure of the indicator program, while utilization frameworks refer to outside relations.

Conceptual frameworks are used to "give focus for what is important to measure (Dluhy and Swartz 2006)" and to establish a logic for the "selection of indicators and contains the supporting technical definitions, metrics and linkages… it prescribes a specific worldview with associated categories, system boundaries and 'blind spots' (Gudmundsson 2003)." Strong conceptual frameworks are needed so that a city can identify how it is doing and what interventions are needed to work towards shared goals (Dluhy and Swartz 2006).

Utilization frameworks are defined "with regard to the presence of mechanisms to ensure that information from indicators is used, or in other words the presences of accountability mechanisms (Gudmundsson 2003)." There are three types of utilization frameworks: information frameworks, monitoring frameworks, and control frameworks. Information frameworks present indicators to a broad audience who may choose to use that information or not, and they typically use descriptive methods and lack accountability measures (Gudmundsson 2003). State of the environment reports and other comprehensive indicator programs tend to use information frameworks. Monitoring frameworks track the progress of policies and programs in order to enable feedback and use both descriptive and performance indicators and may have accountability measures (Gudmundsson 2003). Monitoring frameworks are used by many quality of life indicator programs and other community based programs that aim to track community progress but have no control over policy. Control frameworks are used to closely regulate policy making in terms of where and how to act; measure results through use of performance indicators which are compared to a standard, target, or benchmark; and have regulative mechanisms for accountability purposes (Gudmundsson 2003). Local governments that have developed indicator plans alongside their comprehensive plans often use a control framework since they have the ability to directly change policies and allocate resources to meet their goals.

Maclaren (1996) identifies six types of frameworks, which have been used in various reporting systems and are essentially types of conceptual frameworks. These frameworks include: (1) domain based frameworks, which develop indicators around the key dimensions of sustainability; (2) goal based, which require the identification of specific sustainability goals and then identifies indicators; (3) sectoral, which develop indicators to measure sustainability in different sectors which a municipal government has responsibility over; (4) issue based, which are organized around specific issues within the community; (5) causal, which show a cause and effect relationship among indicators; and (6) combination frameworks, which use two or more of the previous frameworks. These six frameworks are useful in that they help to determine the organizational structure of the indicators in that program, once the overall conceptual framework has been established.

Within urban focused indicator programs, sustainability is but one of the conceptual frameworks frequently used. Other important frameworks include quality of life, healthy cities, and livability. While the focus and intention of these different frameworks may vary slightly, in practice these four frameworks are all quite similar and contain many of the same measurements. Each framework also utilizes both traditional indicators and sustainability indicators (as discussed above). They differ in their organizing principles and outlook on the community. It could be argued that each of these frameworks is simply a different way of measuring sustainability. This is in part because the policy choices that are made and the outcomes in the built environment are often very similar. Each approach, in its own way, helps to make cities more sustainable in the long run.

Quality of Life

Quality of life is "the level of enjoyment and fulfillment derived by humans from the life they live within their local economic, cultural, social and environmental conditions (Redefining Progress 1997)." Quality of life programs tend to have a broad scope and cover all aspects of a community that affect its residents. As a result, these program often contain many indicators, often upwards of 100 indicators or more. Quality of life frameworks are often regarded as ineffectual in policy making because it becomes difficult to discern trends and to prioritize issues. It is common for that different indicators draw the attention of policy makers or the public each year (Dluhy and Swartz 2006). Additionally, quality of life programs can sometimes rely heavily on subjective views of urban citizens and policy makers often find it more challenging to base policy decisions on individuals' perspectives. Despite such shortfalls, many community quality of life indicator programs are well established, with some lasting more than 30 years. Quality of life indicators provide valuable information about urban conditions, and many programs have been modified over the years to become more effective when used as a basis for changing policy.

Sustainability

An indicator program using a sustainability or sustainable development framework typically reflects the three broad areas of concern within sustainability – environment, society and economy. Indicators are typically grouped into these three categories, and sometimes links between the different indicators are made. Much of the focus of sustainable development has been on the environmental aspect of development. As such, some indicator programs tend to be more environmentally focused rather than evenly distribute the indicators among the three sectors.

Healthy Cities

The healthy cities conceptual framework originated from the World Health Organization's Healthy Cities Program (Phillips 2003). Such programs use indicators that examine the overall health of a population, such as life expectancy or leading causes of death. They also use indicators that measure factors that affect the health of the population, such as air or water quality, access to medical care, or nutrition. In this way, these indicator programs touch upon social, environmental and economic areas. Like quality of life indicators, healthy community indicator programs have tended to have a broad scope and include many indicators, and as a result have not been useful in shaping urban policy. In the US, the Center for Disease Control (CDC) and the Department of Health and Human Services have begun to help cities develop indicator programs to assess the health of their populations. These programs also closely mirror many quality of life and sustainability programs.

Livability

The concept of livability is closely related to both sustainability and quality of life. Livability deals with urban characteristics such as walkability, human scale, and safety of urban spaces (Hankins and Powers 2009). Livability pertains to the relationships between people and the environment, both the natural and the built environment, and how the environment can enhance human wellbeing (both as individuals and as a society). "Urban livability suggests that there is an ideal relationship between the urban environment and the social life it sustains" (Hankins and Powers 2009). Public transit, for example, is promoted within sustainable development primarily because it eliminates emissions from automobiles. Within a livability perspective, public transit is developed to enhance the lives of people by reducing congestion, making streets safer for pedestrians, and allowing more time for social interaction, with the ecological benefit being a secondary consideration. Livability could be viewed as integrating different perspectives of quality of life and sustainable development and does so specifically within the context of urban environments. Due to its urban focus, the concept of livability has been a growing area within urban development practices, and the fact that urban indicator programs have used it as a conceptual framework supports this. Chapter 2 discusses the sustainability, livability and resiliency indicator systems.

Community Participation

It is widely agreed that citizen involvement in the development of urban indicator programs is a key to their success. However, there is little consensus on the extent to which, and with which steps, of the indicator development process citizens should be involved. Two main reasons exist as to why citizen involvement has been advocated. First is the belief that "participatory processes are necessary for a city to produce a durable and operational definition of sustainability (Portney 2003)," or in other words, the idea of sustainable development is subjective and is defined locally. Second is the belief that "greater civic engagement is itself an integral part of what it means for a city to be more sustainable" (Portney 2003). Both of these views come into play when developing an urban indicator program and the ways in which citizens are involved in developing urban indicator programs can vary greatly among programs.

Citizens may be involved at different individual or multiple phases of the indicator program development process. The most important step in which citizens can be involved is in defining community goals and developing a vision for the future for which the indicator program is measuring progress (Maclaren 1996; Redefining Progress 1997). This is often done in a comprehensive development plan, which uses broad community participation. An indicator program may be integrated into this development plan, or it may simply adopt the same community goals. An indicator program may also choose to adopt different goals if it has a more specific purpose, such as public awareness.

Citizens are also usually involved in the actual development and selection of indicators. Maclaren (1996) suggests that an initial set of indicators should be selected by stakeholders engaged in the process with technical input from experts, with a final set of indicators be selected by experts using specified evaluation criteria. Redefining Progress (2002) suggests that citizens select possible indicators from an initial set of indicators, and then technical advisors review this narrowed list. The idea behind involving many citizens in the actual selection of indicators is that it offers them a sense of ownership over the process and the final outcome (Gahin, et al. 2003; Dluhy and Swartz 2006). This ownership can further establish a commitment and a willingness among citizens to seek policy changes (Dluhy and Swartz 2006).

The inclusion of citizens in the development and selection of indicators has been criticized. Some experts argue that including citizens in the development and selection of indicators raises concerns based on the relative lack of citizen knowledge on technological, ecological, sociological, economic, and other issues (Alibegovic and de Villa 2008). Some programs are viewed as having chosen "simplicity and participation over complexity and depth of understanding (McAlpine and Binie 2003)."

This concern over citizen knowledge highlights a conflict between two types of approaches to developing indicator programs: bottom-up citizen driven and top-down expert driven. This dichotomy stems from the fact that the social indicator programs of the 1960s were government operated and informed by trained experts or top-down and expert driven. Early community indicator projects emerged from a growing concern over local issues, and so they used a bottom-up citizen driven approach. It has been noted (Eckerberg and Mineur 2003) that expert driven programs focus largely on performance assessment and measuring effectiveness of programs, while citizen oriented programs aim to start a dialogue among citizens. Community indicator programs are "not only about providing information to policy makers but also about empowering and engaging citizens (Gahin and Paterson 2001)." The solution can entail a middle ground approach where citizens and experts work together. As sustainability concepts have been adopted by local governments, empowerment and civic engagement have become key components of development practices. As such, local government 'experts' tend to engage the public and act as facilitators in the development of sustainability indicator programs. Citizen driven indicator programs have also sought expert input in the development of their indicator programs.

Overall, the role of citizens in developing a sustainability indicator program is important. Many citizen driven indicator programs have been quite successful in informing decision makers and shaping urban policy, partly because of their broad community participation. Likewise, government agencies that have developed indicator programs, and have sought to make community participation a key aspect, have also been successful.

Selecting Indicators

In order to be an effective program, the individual indicators must be appropriate for use in that program. This appropriateness has several dimensions. The indicators need to be appropriate, in that they match the political, institutional, and jurisdictional contexts in which the program is used (Phillips 2003). They need to be appropriate and sensitive to the cultural and social contexts of the city or region. They also need to measure something of value to or something that is of concern within the community. Usually these are reflected in the community's goals, and so using indicators that relate to and measure progress towards these goals, will help ensure their appropriateness. A good conceptual framework will also help to ensure that the right indicators are used. The indicators must also accurately measure variables at the correct scale. In order to ensure this, lists of criteria have been developed on which to judge possible indicators for use within a program. The most important criteria or characteristics (discussed above) are that indicators should be relevant, valid, simple and understandable, measurable, cost effective, consistent and reliable in regard to time series data, sensitive to change, and comprehensive. If an indicator has multiple characteristics listed here, is meaningful to the community, and makes sense contextually, then it is an appropriate indicator and will help to ensure the program is effective.

Indicator Program Reports

The final part of an indicator program is the report. While much effort must be taken in developing goals, selecting a framework, choosing indicators, and seeking community involvement, the report is the final product of all the preceding efforts and is the physical product which is used in the community by citizens and policy makers. The guiding principles for developing the report should be clarity, accessibility, interest, and graphic appeal (Redefining Progress 2002). "At the very minimum, the report should contain a description of each indicator, why it is important, historical trends or anticipated changes (Maclaren 1996)" as well as whether the indicator demonstrates improving or worsening conditions. The report should highlight the urgent issues and should explore and discuss the linkages among various indicators (Redefining Progress 2002). Policy recommendations can also be made within the report. The inclusion of recommendations will depend largely on whether the indicator program uses value neutral and informative approach or an approach which promotes a specific agenda. It is also important that the report be made available to a broad audience, as well as being clear and concise so that different audiences can understand it. With the increase in computer and internet use over the last decade, many indicator programs have developed interactive websites, with multiple benefits. It has reduced the cost to publish and update reports. It also allows the indicators to be more accessible to a larger audience. The use of GIS mapping has also been increasing. This allows the authors to connect specific indicators to geographic areas of the city or region. In doing so, policy makers are made aware of general trends as well as where disparities exist within the city or region. For these reasons, the report is a vital component of an indicator program. It must be clear and understandable, highlight the important information, and appeal to a broad audience.

Indicators in Practice

Indicator programs have become quite common in many communities around the world and the prevalence of their use is increasing, especially in the US. This next section will provide some case studies of sustainability indicator programs. It will discuss a range of programs developed at national, regional and local metropolitan scales by a range of organizations.

National Indicator Programs

National Indicator programs, in a manner similar to international programs, can have different scales of analysis – either the nation as a whole, or cities or regions within the nation.

United States: STAR Communities Rating Program

The STAR Communities (Sustainability Tools for Assessing and Rating Communities) program is a framework for nationwide sustainability monitoring designed for urban areas. The program began development in 2008 after a partnership was formed between several organization – ICLEI Local Governments for Sustainability, the US Green Building Council, the National League of Cities and the Center for American Progress. The goal of this partnership was to develop a common framework for sustainability that cities, towns, and counties could utilize (STAR 2012). The STAR Communities program combines a framework for assessing sustainability, a rating system that drives continuous improvement and fosters competition, and an online system to track progress (STAR 2012). The program is a points based rating system, similar to the US Green Building Council LEED programs – points are gained for achievement in each measure. The program relies on cities to self-report on the sustainability. Since the program is voluntary and cities must be paid subscribers in order to gain the full benefit of being a STAR Community. The program is organized around seven goal areas which contain 44 objectives that each have an evaluation measure. Points are earned, and a community is rated, based on a community's performance on these evaluation measures.

The program was partially implemented in 2010 with ten beta communities that provided feedback and guidance on the program's feasibility, framework, and design, as well as its goals and evaluation measures. The beta communities also helped to develop the online system for monitoring. Since the program became fully implemented in 2012, a number of communities around the US have joined the program. There are various levels to which a community can participate in the program. Participating communities certify their intent to use the STAR Community program. A reporting community is one that has registered their intent to report on the sustainability measures and have met the prerequisite of achieving points in at least one objective in each goal area (50-199 points). Certified communities can become 3-, 4- or 5-STAR rated based on the number of points they achieve (200-399 for 3-STAR, 400-599 for 4-STAR and 600 or more for 5-STAR). There are currently 74 cities town and counties participating in the STAR Communities program – 26 participating communities, 36 reporting communities, seven 3-STAR communities, four 4-STAR communities, and one 5-STAR community.

This program is noteworthy as it represents the only active program designed to assess sustainability in cities across the entire US. It offers a common framework and indicators for cities to adopt, which allows them to be compared to each other. It also encourages the development of locally specific indicators, which increases relevance to each community. However, one objective of the program is to "inform and advance a 'race to the top' for the quality of life of residents," meaning that a sense competition is built into the program. Additionally, the program is subscription based, which means only cities willing to use their resources to take part in the program will be assessed. The STAR Communities program is relatively new, but has gained a wide following in only a couple years. It will likely remain a significant program in sustainability indicator development in the US for the foreseeable future.

Regional and Metropolitan Indicators

Regional sustainability indicators focus on metropolitan areas, which can be defined in various ways. In the US, regional indicator programs are often developed by community organizations. Increasingly, however, regional councils of government are developing sustainability plans and developing indicator programs to measure progress at a regional level. Unfortunately, both these types of organizations often lack direct control of local policies that would actually move the region towards a more

Built Environment	Climate & Energy	Economy & Jobs	Education, Arts & Community	Equity & Empowerment	Health & Safety	Natural Systems
Ambient Noise & Light	Climate Adaptation	Business Retention & Development	Arts & Culture	Civic Engagement	Active Living	Green Infrastructure
Community Water Systems	Greenhouse Gas Mitigation	Green Market Development	Community Cohesion	Civil & Human Rights	Community Health & Health System	Invasive Species
Compact & Complete Communities	Greening the Energy Supply	Local Economy	Educational Opportunity & Attainment	Environmental Justice	Emergency Prevention & Response	Natural Resource Protection
Housing Affordability	Industrial Sector Resource Efficiency	Quality Jobs & Living Wages	Historic Preservation	Equitable Services & Access	Food Access & Nutrition	Outdoor Air Quality
Infill & Redevelopment	Resource Efficient Buildings	Targeted Industry Development	Social & Cultural Diversity	Human Services	Indoor Air Quality	Water in the Environment
Public Spaces	Resource Efficient Public Infrastructure	Workforce Readiness		Poverty Prevention & Alleviation	Natural & Human Hazards	Working Lands
Transportation Choices	Waste Minimization				Safe Communities	

STAR Communities Rating System goals (top row) and objectives (columns).

From Star Community Rating System Version 1.1, January 2014 by Star Communities. Copyright © 2014 by Star Communities. Reprinted by permission.

sustainable future. One exception is California, which as of 2008 and the passage of Senate Bill 375, has required regional councils of government to be more active in developing integrated land use and transportation plans as well as consider the location and development of new housing and to address environmental concerns such as their contribution to climate change.

Two regional indicator programs that have been largely successful are *Sustainable Seattle* and the *Central Texas Sustainability Indicators Project*, both of which were developed by community organizations that gained popular support within their communities.

Seattle, Washington: Sustainable Seattle

Sustainable Seattle is a nonprofit organization that was founded in 1991 whose goal is to promote urban sustainability in Seattle, the US, and internationally (sustainableseattle.org). Their mission is "to create healthy communities, economies, and ecosystems by serving as an incubator for emerging people, projects, and ideas, as a convener of diverse citizens and practitioners, and as a catalyst for turning indicators into action (sustainableseattle.org)." In 1993 Sustainable Seattle released their first indicator report containing 20 indicators developed over the course of the previous year by a panel of stakeholders. In 1995 and 1998 they released a second and third report which both contained a total of 40 indicators, the original 20 plus 20 additional ones that had been developed. After the release of the 1998 report Sustainable Seattle decided to reassess its indicator program. There was concern that merely publishing the indicators was no longer an adequate goal (sustainableseattle.org). Instead, a "successful program should include programs which support actions by citizens, businesses and policy makers to affect the trends documented by the indicators (sustainableseattle. org)." At this same time Sustainable Seattle also looked towards creating a set of indicators for use at the neighborhood level.

In 2008 Sustainable Seattle released a fourth version of its indicators called B-Sustainable, an online interactive website. B-Sustainable contains just over 100 indicators (103) divided into four main goal areas – the natural environment, built environment, social environment and personal environment. Each of the individual indicators falls into one of these categories and monitors progress towards the specific goals in each section. Each indicator page defines the indicator, describes the basis of the data, and discusses the present trend for that indicator. Since the 2008 development of the website, the *Sustainable Seattle* program has not been updated or modified. This is in part because their efforts as an organization have evolved. They have greatly increased awareness of sustainability issues among decision makers and citizens in the Seattle region and now focus more of their work towards assisting other communities to developing sustainability measures.

Austin, Texas: Central Texas Sustainability Indicators Project

The Central Texas Sustainability Indicators Project (CTSIP) is a community based organization that began in 1999. The overall mission of the CTSIP is to "promote sustainability using community indicators (CTSIP 2012)." The organization has grown from including only three counties in the region to now tracking progress in six counties. Initially, reports were published every year, but in 2005 they switched to biennial reports so that they could focus on other goals, such as supporting other regional efforts like Envision Central Texas, a nonprofit which addresses the concerns of regional growth. Also, CTSIP took steps to ensure that local decision makers and community leaders have access to the information provided in the indicators reports so that they actually help to create better policies addressing regional sustainability concerns. To this end, CTSIP has partnered with a number of community organizations in the region, as well as some governmental agencies, which provide the technical support needed for CTSIP to compile their indicator reports. CTSIP is also forging a stronger partnership with the Center for Sustainable Development at the School of Architecture at UT Austin (CTSIP 2009), which will introduce further expertise and resources to the program. Each of these partnerships is important because they increase awareness of the indicator reports as well as general sustainability concerns.

The 2012 CTSIP report is the most recent report. The indicator program is organized into eight categories: (1) public safety; (2) education and children; (3) social equity; (4) civic engagement; (5) economy; (6) environment; (7) health; and (8) land use and mobility. There are a total of 40 composite indicators that include multiple measures (close to 150 individual indicators). The most recent reports have highlighted certain themes which become apparent in the review of the indicators themselves. This indicator program has become a valuable resource in the community and has helped policy makers guide policies in more sustainable directions.

City Indicators

Local governments produce city indicators. Local governments of all sizes, from the largest US cities to suburbs of major US cities to small towns, have developed sustainability indicators. Many of these indicator programs have been developed alongside local sustainability plans or comprehensive plans. It is important to note here that while many of these programs may seem beneficial, their overall impact might not be strong. This is because many local government account for only a small percent of a region's total population and land area. As a result, efforts at this scale might be negated unless there are broader regional efforts to become more sustainable. This raises the question of what scale is best for promoting sustainable development. Regardless, many cities have been proactive in promoting sustainability policies and measuring their progress. Three cities are highlighted below.

New York, New York: PlaNYC 2030

In April 2007 the NYC Mayor's Office released the PLANYC 2030. The plan resulted from months of planning and asking people in New York City what goals they though were important for creating a sustainable future. These efforts resulted in ten goals which are outlined in the 2007 sustainability plan. They include: (1) create homes for almost a million new residents, while making housing more affordable and sustainable; (2) ensure that all residents live within a ten minute walk of a park; (3) clean up all contaminated sites; (4) open 90 percent of waterways for recreation by reducing water pollution and preserving other natural areas; (5) develop back-up systems for the aging water network to ensure long term reliability; (6) improve travel times by adding transit capacity for millions more residents; (7) reach a state of good repair on NYC roads, subways and rails for the first time in history; (8) provide cleaner more reliable power by upgrading energy infrastructure; (9) achieve the cleanest air of any big city in America; and (10) reduce global warming emissions by more than 30 percent. The plan also outlines 127 initiatives that work towards reaching these goals. They are coordinated and monitored by the Mayor's Office of Long-Term Planning and Sustainability.

As part of the plan, an initial set of 80 indicators in 7 different categories (land, water, transportation, energy, air, waste and climate change) was developed to monitor progress towards the goals. In 2011 the plan was updated with new initiatives and a smaller set of only 27 indicators. Different departments within the city are responsible for reporting on the indicators, while the Mayor's Office coordinates efforts.

Minneapolis, Minnesota: Minneapolis Sustainability Indicators

The City of Minneapolis adopted a sustainability plan in 2005 which was incorporated into the city's comprehensive plan and has been used to guide city long term investments in infrastructure as well as daily operations. As part of the plan, the City adopted key indicators and corresponding 10 year targets for each. In early 2012 the indicators were revised and new 10 year targets were set.

In 2006 the first annual sustainability report was released which reported on the indicators adopted in 2005. The indicator set was originally comprised of 25 indicators in three major categories – a healthy life, which addresses citizen health; greenprint, which addresses environmental concerns and transportation; and a vital community, which looks at education, housing and other social issues. Currently, the indicator program remains focused on these three categories and contains indicators in 26 topic areas within these categories, with each topic containing between one and three indicators. The current program contains nine health indicators, 26 environmental indicators, and 14 indicators on pressing social issues.

In 2012, the City stopped publishing an annual report on their indicators and instead now uses an internet based approach. This indicator program shows that the number of indicators does not need to be extensive in order to measure sustainability. It also highlights the fact that in order to remain effective and relevant, the indicator program must evolve and adapt to new circumstances and technologies. The City has revised their indicators and targets for each as well as switching from an annual report to an internet based report.

Tucson, Arizona: Livable Tucson Vision Program and Plan Tucson: City of Tucson General and Sustainability Plan

In 1997 the City of Tucson began its Livable Tucson Vision Program (LTVP). The goal of the program involved the development of "a long-term, community-driven vision for Tucson that would help to shape the city's budget and provide a framework for developing programs and services that address the real concerns of the community (City of Tucson 2000)." After a series of community workshops, 17 goals were developed. In 1998 the city began work to create a set of 55 indicators, although many indicators were used for multiple goals, making the actual number of indicators appear larger. The City however, never fully developed the program or published an official report. Instead, the City incorporated the 17 goals from the LTVP into their 2001 General Plan Update. In 2006 the City of Tucson created an Office of Conservation and Sustainable Development, which has been working to advance sustainability goals as well as the goals and policies from the LTVP and the General Plan and has released a number of sustainability reports.

The current general plan for the City of Tucson was adopted in fall 2013 and incorporates sustainability as its main organizing theme with sections on the social environment, the economic environment, the built environment, and the natural environment. As part of the plan implementation process, a series of indicators have been selected which will be used to measure progress towards meeting the goals outlined in the plan. The indicators include locally significant indicators, as well as indicators used by the STAR Communities Rating Program, which has the benefit of showing comparisons to other cities using the program. The General Plan has developed a 'sustainability indicators matrix' that examines the linkages between different indicators and specific policies, which is important for decision makers so they can better understand what impacts their actions might have.

This latest comprehensive plan demonstrates the most current way in which sustainability indicators can be more effective in policy making efforts. The Tucson case also shows how the use of indicators has changed since the 1990s. It also highlights the trend found in many US cities – the increasing use of indicators in conjunction with comprehensive planning.

Summary

Indicators are an important tool in the current age of sustainable development. Measuring sustainability is necessary so that we know whether our actions are having the intended and desired effects and whether society is in fact moving towards being more sustainable. Indicators are valuable tools for policy makers so that they can be more knowledgeable about the state of their community and make better informed decisions.

Sustainability can be measured in different ways. Sustainability indexes and single measures have been developed to measure sustainability at a global and national scale. Indicator programs have been developed to measure national and subnational sustainability. Urban indicator programs have become the most common type of sustainability measurements during the last 20 years. Increasingly in the US, these programs are closely tied to local and regional sustainability and comprehensive plans. This approach ensures a greater degree of policy relevance. It will also likely result in better outcomes that move cities and regions towards sustainability since local governments that develop sustainability goals will allocate more resources in order to meet these goals and create more sustainable communities.

Examining Urban Sustainability through Urban Models

Subhrajit Guhathakurta

Understanding Models and Modeling

Models are the microcosms of real world phenomena that cannot be experienced or examined in their actual spatial and/or temporal contexts. We use different models for different purposes. Yes, some are indeed human models used by the fashion design and media industries to promote overpriced products. When Georgiou Armani or Calvin Klein want to convey how you might look and feel when you buy their newly designed outfits, they will find a human model to demonstrate these outfits. Of course, what is being modeled is far from our reality given that many of us would probably look uncomfortable or unseemly in the same outfit. In this case, the reality that is being modeled may only exist in peoples' imaginations.

Most models are not meant to cater to the imaginary world, but are designed to bring our imaginations to conform to reality. They are usually quite distinct from the objectified humans described above. Scientists, innovators, and researchers often use physical models to test critical properties of a designed or engineered product before the product is actually used. For example, scaled-down airplane models are tested in a wind tunnel to examine how the shape and structure of the model perform under different wind conditions. Similarly, structural engineers use miniaturized models of buildings designed with different materials and technologies on a vibrating platform to test how these structures perform for different intensities and types of earthquakes. In both cases, models allow us to test, under laboratory conditions, the robustness of our critical infrastructure. They also offer researchers the ability to improve on the existing designs.

Models can be concepts, ideas, or plans. These nonphysical models are expressed through words or symbols—or sometimes not expressed at all. When I leave my home in the morning to go to work, I use a mental map, or a model, that I use to choose my mode and route of travel to my destination. This model mostly remains in my unconscious since I have used it hundreds of times (until I am asked to describe the journey). We use such informal "**mental models**" to accomplish most of our tasks. Without a mental model, we are unable to act deliberately.

Our mental models are often inadequate when we face novel or complex situations. In such cases, we tend to formalize them so that they can be examined and perfected. Take, for example, traveling to various destinations in a new country. Most travelers in new situations will study maps and make copious notes of places to halt for

Mental models - an image we hold in our minds about how processes and events are related to each other.

conveniences or sightseeing and alternative routes in the case of road closures. These maps and notes together form a formal model of travel in a relatively strange land.

Complex processes and organizations require **formalized models**. It would be difficult, for example, to have a clear understanding of how a city functions with only mental models. Our mental models may provide bits and pieces of the total picture—we may know that population growth and an auto-oriented culture will lead to high levels of traffic congestion. We could also intuit that high levels of congestion may induce some people to seek homes closer to work—or, in the long run, seek out options in other cities that offer a better quality of life. Each of these processes triggers other changes in individual and social behavior that can either reinforce congestion levels or counteract them. Reinforcing processes are known as **positive feedback** loops, while the counteracting processes offer **negative feedback**. When individuals try to leave the pollution and noise of congested roads by fleeing to the suburbs, they may actually be reinforcing congestion levels by increasing commute distances. On the other hand, when enough commuters decide to give up on driving (because it is no fun to drive at five miles an hour and be abused by other irate drivers) and choose to travel by public transit, congestion levels may ease. This would be a negative feedback of congestion. Our mental models are inadequate to tease out the interactions among all the direct, indirect, and induced feedback loops of individual and social behavior in a city. In such complex situations, we use formal models with specific syntax and notations. These formalized models can both illustrate the interactions among the different parts of the system (such as individual and social decisions) and communicate how the system can change under different scenarios.

One such model of a city was developed by Jay Forrester, who became interested in questions about urban policies and how they affect the quality of life of urban populations in the long run. He wrote a book called **Urban Dynamics** based on his findings from this modeling exercise (1969). This model incorporated specific kinds of syntax, notations, and mathematics; known as **system dynamics** that Forrester himself developed to examine logistical aspects of firm growth and decline. Through his system dynamic model of the city, Forrester demonstrated that policies meant to alleviate urban problems like housing shortages, unemployment, or neighborhood decline in fact exacerbate those problems. These models show that our intuitive "mental models" are often wrong when situated in a complex dynamic context.

As you can guess, there is a reason why I am using models of urban areas as prime examples of formalized models. Formalized models with complex mathematical expressions are used in numerous domains—from power systems to meteorology to economics. But urban areas pose a specific challenge given that the dynamics of urban processes include complex interactions among human, social, and natural systems. **Urban models** can never capture the richness of all interacting processes within an urban region. However, they can be useful in predicting future location and intensity of activities based on prior trends and show how different decisions we make today might play out in the future. Also, importantly, this chapter is about modeling urban sustainability. In the next few pages, I will demonstrate how to examine future sustainability impacts with the help of **urban-environmental models**. Before I delve into the questions of sustainability, a brief background on urban modeling is warranted.

Formalized models - a specific set of procedures or mathematical formulae that show how different processes result in a particular outcome or a set of outcomes.

Positive feedback - a connected causal chain of events in a closed loop where the intensity or scale of the initial driving force increases with each cycle.

Negative feedback - a connected causal chain of events in a closed loop where the intensity or scale of the initial driving force decreases with each cycle.

Urban dynamics - changes in the total connected urban system induced by changes in one component of this system. It is also the title of a book on examining a systems model of an urban region by Jay Forrester.

System dynamics - a methodological approach for characterizing a connected system of processes and events and examining how changes in one component of this system affect all other parts of the system.

Urban models - mathematically derived expressions for connecting aspects of urban processes, most commonly the relationship between land use and transportation.

Urban-environmental models - connecting urban models with environmental processes such as determining air quality from land use and transportation attributes.

The First Generation of Urban Models

While Forrester was developing his system dynamic framework, another form of urban model was already transforming land use and transportation planning in large urban regions across the United States. This type of model was based on the concept of "**spatial interaction**," which assumed that activities that were closer together had a higher intensity of interaction than those further away. This premise was an analogue to the Newtonian law of gravitation, which stated that every mass in the universe attracts every other mass by a force equal to the product of their masses and inversely proportional to the square of the distance between them. In mathematical terms, this translates to:

$$F \propto \frac{m_1 m_2}{d^2}$$

Where: F = Force of attraction between two masses; m_1 and m_2 = masses of the two bodies; and D = distance between m_1 and m_2.

If you are wondering whether the inverse relationship with distance is always to the second power for all situations, your suspicion is not without merit. In fact, a more generalized version of the above equation is:

$$F = K \frac{m_1^{\alpha} m_2^{\beta}}{d^{\lambda}}$$

In this case, α, β, λ, and K are constants to be determined. Note that both the numerator and the denominator have power values that are not fixed but determined through empirical observations for each context of their use. If you now consider that m_1 and m_2 can also represent intensity of activities (e.g., number of people working, living, or shopping, in an area), it is not difficult to see how the interactions among these activities can be modeled as an extension of the general spatial interaction model shown above. Consider, for example, that you want to allocate future population growth to three neighborhoods in a small city (which has only three neighborhoods). Also, you expect that the attractiveness of these neighborhoods to be based on the amount of space available in them for accommodating new housing units (a proxy for price of entry) and how close the neighborhoods are to employment locations relative to the number of jobs in these locations. In other words, the *accessibility* (A_j) of a neighborhood j to employment locations is proportional to the sum of the number of jobs in these employment locations ($E_1, E_2,$ and E_3), each weighted by the inverse of distance to the neighborhood j (d_{ij}). That is:

$$A_j = K \sum_{i=1}^{3} \frac{E_i}{d_{ij}^{\lambda}}$$

Where K and l are constants estimated empirically.

Once the accessibility of each neighborhood is known, the allocation of growth to these neighborhoods can be apportioned according to the ratio of the product of land availability and accessibility of each neighborhood, in relation to the total of similar products of all neighborhoods. Again, in mathematical terms this would be:

$$G_j = G_T \left(\frac{L_j A_j}{\sum_{i=1}^{n} L_j A_j} \right)$$

Where L_j is the indicator of amount of space available; G_j = Growth allocated to j; and G_T = Total growth in the city

The Lowry Model

In 1964, Ira Lowry of the Rand Corporation unveiled a land-use and transportation model that became the precursor to the first generation of such models. These first-generation models allocated activities spatially using some form of the generic spatial interaction model described above.

The Lowry model included jobs and housing, and their location relative to each other as in the example above. There were, however, several key innovations. First, Lowry distinguished between two types of jobs—*basic* and *non-basic*. The basic jobs were jobs employed in the export-oriented sectors. That is, the product of this sector was mostly consumed outside the region, such as the output of manufacturing, mining, agriculture, tourism, and other similar economic activities. All other jobs were considered non-basic, which indicated that they were mostly serving the local population. The number of basic jobs and their locations, current and future, are provided as *exogenous* inputs to the model (i.e., decided outside the model). The model then figures out where the non-basic jobs and households will be located *endogenously* (i.e., estimated by the model).

The Lowry model consists of two sub-models. The first, known as the *economic base sub-model*, jointly determines the additional service-related jobs and the increment in households and population because of new basic employment. The second sub-model is the *spatial allocation sub-model* that allocates the new households, population, and service employment to zones using the familiar spatial interaction format. As you can tell, there is positive feedback between new households and new service-related jobs. As we add households of basic employees, more service-related jobs are needed, which in turn generates more households (families of those service employees), and subsequently, more service jobs in a chain effect. This iterative process is stopped when additional increments are too small to account for. A simple schematic of this process in provided in the Lowry model.

The Lowry model inspired a surge of successors that improved upon its basic framework. Within a period of about six years from Lowry's publication of "A Model of Metropolis,"[1] about a dozen such models were formulated both in the United States and in Europe. These included 1) Time-Oriented Metropolitan Model (TOMM 1964); 2) Bay Area Simulation Study (BASS I 1965); 3) The Cornell Land Use Game (CLUG 1966); 4) A Dynamic Model for Urban Structure (TOMM II 1968); 5) Projective Land-Use Model (PLUM 1968); and 6) a portfolio of eight models developed by various individuals for different regions in the United Kingdom.[1] (see Goldner 1971 for detailed review.) Even today, over 50 years past the initial Lowry formulation, aspects of his approach continue to be applied in urban land-use and transportation models (such as in DRAM, EMPAL, and METROPILUS models by Putnam 1983, and Putnam and Chen 2001).

The subsequent developments in urban land-use change models included several innovations that extended the theoretical and empirical scope of the Lowry model. Most of these models included a more disaggregated set of households and jobs. Many broke away from the rigid square grid and adopted census tracts for zones.

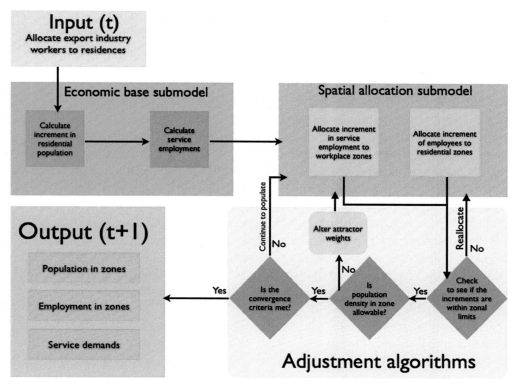

Lowry Model.

Several later models also experimented with different forms of land-use constraints and limitations on household behavior and budgets. In addition, new techniques for calibration and evaluation were also introduced to make the models better "fit" the data available for specific places.

Despite the relatively rapid pace of development of the first generation of urban models, these models were perceived as being too large, too expensive, too reliant on extensive data, and therefore, inadequate in offering critical and reliable information planners needed in formulating long range plans. A seminal article written by Douglas Lee in 1973 called "Requiem for Large Scale Models" was significant in substantially slowing down research and application of urban models. Lee noted "seven sins of large scale models" that together rendered the first generation of models irrelevant to the new directions in which planning was headed.[2,3] Regardless, urban models continued to progress and mature, while computers became more powerful and data management, less onerous with the advent of Geographic Information System (GIS) technologies. A second generation of models began to take shape, albeit more self-consciously and with more humble objectives.

The Second Generation of Urban Models

The second-generation urban models followed two general approaches. The first is rule-based **land classification** that would assign all land parcels a "suitability" score for various forms of development. The second approach follows from the well-known **discrete choice models** developed by Daniel McFadden, which won him the Nobel

Land classification - a system for categorizing land according to the use and the physical attributes of that piece of land. Several such schemes are now used; the most common being the USGS Anderson Land Classification Scheme.

Discrete choice models - models examining choices between two or more alternatives such as choosing between different modes of transport or between different residential locations.

Prize in economics. Both these approaches were enabled by rapid advances in computing and geographic information systems technologies, together with the proliferation of the Internet, which brought high performance computing to individual desktops.

The **suitability score** approach originated from landscape analysis, particularly through Ian McHarg's most celebrated book called "Design with Nature" (1969). McHarg popularized the "overlay method" in which transparent map layers, each containing information about one particular aspect of land (slope, soil type, land use, vegetation, floodplain, drainage, etc.), are overlaid to identify suitable areas that can be developed with minimum disruption to the natural environment. This approach became one of the primary functions of Geographic Information Systems (GIS), especially in the formative years of Arc/Info (ESRI). The overlay approach was also the foundation for the **Land Evaluation/Site Assessment (LESA)** technique adopted by the U.S. Department of Agriculture (USDA) in evaluating the suitability of land parcels for agriculture, conservation or development. This technique essentially assigned scores to a set of land attributes (land evaluation, or LE) and site characteristics (site assessment, or SA), which were individually weighted according to their importance for a particular use. These scores were then aggregated to determine which parcels were most suitable for that use.

The basic tenets of the land-suitability approach (adopted for the urban context) is implemented in an urban model called "What If?" developed by Richard Klosterman of What If?, Inc.[4,5] The approach incorporated development capability of different predetermined spatial units of land reflected in a suitability score. While the technique relies on significant amount of user input, the process is primarily based on assumptions about growth, public policies, and decision rules supplied by the users, mostly as weights for physical and locational characteristics of parcels that are suitable for particular developments or for conservation. Klosterman emphasizes that the "What if" method is not a forecasting tool but a planning support tool that shows *What* would happen *If*: a) particular development policies are enacted; b) growth assumptions prove to be true; and 3) the user supplied suitability scores are appropriate and reasonable.

A variation of the suitability approach was implemented in California Urban Futures (CUF 1) model developed by John Landis and his team at Berkeley.[6,7] Suitability for development in this model was based on "profitability" rather than physical and environmental constraints assumed by the user. In CUF 1, as in What If?, the units of land were synthetically created from land attributes; hence, they have no legal existence. These parcels are constructs generated from spatial intersection and /or union of various land attributes such as zoning, slopes, density, distance from transport infrastructure, and others. Landis called them developable land units or DLUs. These DLUs ranged in size from one to several hundred acres.

In CUF 1, each DLU was assigned a profitability score based on estimated costs of development in that land unit. Only residential developments were considered in this first version. The future residential growth in the region (calculated separately for counties and cities) was then allocated according to profitability rankings of the DLUs. A subsequent process examined the growing DLUs adjacent to the urban areas to determine if they should be incorporated within the city boundaries. The process stopped when all residential growth was allocated to the cities and unincorporated areas in the county. Although CUF1 adopted a market-based approach, it assumed that profitability is independent of demand characteristics and purely a function of costs of residential development. In other words, the initial estimate of growth was not affected by demand parameters, which would presumably impact congestion levels and cost of living and thereby moderate growth.[8] Also, given that no other types of land uses were considered, other types of development (commercial, retail, industrial, etc.) could not compete for land parcels (DLUs). Therefore, CUF 1 was quite limited in its scope and ability to capture land-market dynamics.

The second generation of California Urban Futures model, CUF 2, made several improvements over its predecessor, CUF-1, described above. First, it incorporated and predicted different land-use types, including commercial, single- and multi-family residential, industrial, and so on. This version of the model predicted land use transitions from vacant to each of the above-mentioned land use types and also redevelopment from one use to another. Second, the spatial unit of analysis was now 100m × 100m (1 hectare) grid cells instead of the DLUs of CUF-1. Third, it generated job forecasts for each of the three-digit NAICS industry sectors through separate econometric models to determine employment growth. The employment growth parameters are then used to drive the demand in commercial and industrial land uses.

Finally and importantly, CUF-2 was among the first land-use models to implement a statistical framework based on a theory called the "random utility theory," which allowed estimation of probabilities of discrete events. Discrete events are unique and exclusive activities within a set of possible activities that can occur. For example, a commuter can choose among a set of unique mode choices such as self-driven auto, carpool, or transit. Only one option (a discrete event), say, self-driven auto, is finally chosen, at which point the others, carpool and transit, are rejected (exclusive). Land-use change is also a similar discrete event since each type of land use is unique and exclusive. Once a group of parcels is designated as "residential," we would (at least in theory) eliminate all other uses. CUF-2 implemented a statistical technique known as "multinomial logit" to estimate the probabilities of land use change to any one of the discrete land use types or between them. This form of modeling based on "random utility" theory using "multinomial logit" techniques is now pervasive in the current generation of urban and transportation models.

The New Era of Urban Environmental Models

The evolution of urban and environmental models has accelerated since the new millennium. Advances in computation can now allow complex dynamic simulations at a fine spatial and temporal scale. So, we can now look closely at how neighboring land uses and activities are influencing a specific parcel and how this influence is changing at regular temporal intervals (yearly, quarterly, etc.). Also, as discussed previously, the random utility theory has been instrumental in expanding the range of competing activities we can model. A good example of such a highly disaggregated and spatially as well as temporally dynamic model that is becoming a "gold standard" in metropolitan planning organizations is *UrbanSim*.[9,10] UrbanSim has been in active development since the late-1990s, first at the University of Washington and now at the University of California at Berkeley. In 2005, UrbanSim was completely re-engineered to adopt a more extensible and modular platform called OPUS based on the Python code. As of this writing, OPUS is already in version 4.4 (http://urbansim.org).

UrbanSim

UrbanSim introduced several innovations in the field of urban environmental models. First, it is a highly disaggregated model with each household, business, and developer behaving as a "decision-making agent." The interplay of these individual decisions leads to the final outcome of their location in space. This form of modeling from the bottom-up is also known as "agent-based" modeling. UrbanSim explicitly models each household's decision to locate in or relocate to a neighborhood in the metropolitan area. Similarly, every business is identified and location and relocation decisions estimated.

Second, new developments in the real estate sector are predicted by modeling the change in land prices. Previously, few urban models included real estate prices in their estimation. Third, the changes in travel behavior and its impact on locational and development decisions are explicitly incorporated in the modeling platform by interfacing UrbanSim with a travel demand model. Therefore, UrbanSim is usually run in tandem with a separate travel demand model given that this feature is not included in the current platform.

Finally, UrbanSim and OPUS are under active development with new features being added in relatively quick succession. UrbanSim now includes a graphical user interface (GUI) that shows all the models and datasets in one place, provides drop-down, user selectable commands to run the models, and shows geographic information systems based maps of the output. The most recent version also includes a module to "evolve" the households as they age over the period of the simulation. That is, households are no longer static entities throughout 20- or 30-year horizons, but grow and or split up due to marriage, educational choices, dissolution of marriages, new births, and deaths. Very soon, a 3-D platform will also be included with the UrbanSim portfolio of tools for immersive visualization and scenario development.

Several other models are also being developed and tested at different parts of the world. Some, such as TLUMIP2 (Oregon) and IRPUD (Dortmund, Germany), are similar to UrbanSim in their approach in terms of their level of spatial disaggregation and the explicit modeling of individual agent behavior. Other modeling approaches include **cellular automata** (such as CLUE and SLEUTH) and system dynamics (similar to Forrester's model described earlier). Many previous studies have categorized

Cellular automata - a collection of "cells" on a grid where each cell is affected by the condition of its neighboring cells according to a set of predetermined rules.

Courtesy of Paul Waddell

UrbanSim San Fransisco Buildout.

and evaluated urban land use / transport / environmental models based on attributes such as the level of disaggregation, the ability to incorporate dynamics, methodological approach, and whether they are region specific or generic. Readers are especially directed to the reviews by Haase and Schwarz,[11] and Wegener[12] for more in-depth examination of the different model characteristics.

Modeling with Cellular Automata

Cellular automata consists of an array of similar "cells" that are arranged in a two-dimensional lattice where each cell is affected by changes in the state of its neighbors. Cells in the automata have different discrete states (e.g., dead or alive; residential, commercial, industrial, or vacant). Also, the state of a cell changes based on the aggregate changes in adjacent cell states according to a predetermined rule. Imagine, for example, a neighborhood with a group of identical houses and one of the houses in the middle of this neighborhood is abandoned and falls into disrepair. Very soon, the households in the houses immediately adjacent to it will begin to resent this eyesore and move out of the neighborhood by underpricing their houses (since buyers will demand a discount to have the abandoned property next door). This in turn affects other houses adjacent to the first wave of home sales, and they drop in value as well. This devaluation will continue until the values are low enough for an investor to buy up several of the properties and redevelop them to the latest standards, which triggers a virtuous cycle in home values. Cellular automata models can capture this process of decline and redevelopment of housing.

One of the most celebrated examples of a land-use model based on cellular automata is SLEUTH. The acronym is based on the six attributes that the model uses to drive urban growth—slope, land use, exclusion, urban extent, transportation, and hillshade. These six types of data are provided as input tables for a gridded map, where each grid represents a "cell." Based on several years of information on these parameters, five rules of transition for each cell are determined. These transition rules are based on: a) diffusion (controlling overall scatter of growth); b) breed (likelihood of new settlements being generated); c) spread (growth outward and inward from an existing cluster); slope (a resistance parameter and threshold beyond which development does not happen); and roads (an attraction parameter). The process of figuring out the appropriate parameters for the five transition rules is called calibration. The calibration process actually proceeds in three sequential stages where at each stage, 13 different goodness-of-fit measures are evaluated and the best values for the transition rules extracted. The final calibration parameters are used for simulating future changes in land use.

Advancing Sustainability through Urban Models

How do urban models help us in making decisions about urban sustainability? In the early years of urban modeling, sustainability was not a term that was part of an urban planner's lexicon. Regardless, the objective of urban models was to illustrate, in visual and tabular form, how the future of urban regions will evolve based on past trends and an assumed set of social and individual decisions over the simulation period. This orientation toward a future that is deliberately planned to provide adequate resources for meeting the needs of future populations makes the process of urban modeling also appropriate for discussing issues of sustainability. A substantial component of sustainability falls within the narrow concerns of land use and transportation, which has been the bedrock of all urban models. The distribution of human activities within urban space as reflected in land-use patterns impact a range of core issues of sustainability including energy use, open space preservation, protection of ecological resources, pollution, and social equity, among others. Travel behavior is substantially influenced by land use patterns; hence land use and transportation are modeled together. The transportation sector consumes 28% of carbon-based energy in the United States and responsible for commensurate amount of greenhouse gas emissions. Transportation is therefore among the most important components of urban sustainability.

Most metropolitan planning organizations (MPOs) in the United States have invested in developing urban modeling capacity in-house to coordinate regional planning efforts. One principle impetus for using urban models at this level of metropolitan governance is to meet air quality standards as mandated by the Environmental Protection Agency (USEPA). Failure to meet the air quality standards triggers a series of actions that could result in withholding federal highway dollars for the region. Urban land-use and transportation models are used to demonstrate how a non-complying region will improve air quality through a coordinated set of actions such as increasing carpooling and transit use and reducing self-driven automobiles. MPOs also use urban models for engaging the community in making long-range decisions by showing how the decisions they make result in urban growth scenarios and the implications of such growth for the environment and quality of life.

The new generation of urban models is bringing ecological, urban, and social dynamics closer together. Critical challenges of integrating the different modeling domains remain since each developed under different theoretical and methodological traditions. For example, ecological models examine competition among species to predict abundance, distribution, and other characteristics of organisms co-located in a habitat. These models reflect nonlinear dynamics and critical thresholds through time. In contrast, socio-behavioral models are often based on economic theories of static equilibrium, such as equating demand and supply of goods and services. Recent advances in **agent-based models** have brought the two traditions closer together.

Agent-based models mimic the goal-seeking behavior of autonomous agents who interact with each other to maximize their utility while generating higher-level patterns and rules. Therefore, these models are highly disaggregated and built from the bottom up. The process of building such models involves assigning each agent with a set of rules based on the specific attributes of its environment (which includes other agents). For example, one rule might be "if another agent or an obstacle is sensed directly in front on the path of motion, move to the right." Yet another could be "if more than two agents or a large obstacle is sensed in front on the path of motion, turn around and head back." Highly complex agent-based models will have a large set of such "if—then" rules for each type of agent—and there could be many different types of agents. The larger objective of building such models is to determine if simple rules of behavior of different agents lead to more complex "emergent" properties that we may or may not have expected.

A simple example of an agent-based model can illustrate its basic principles. Consider a metropolitan region comprising two types of agents—city households and

Agent-based model - a class of computational models that simulate the behavior of autonomous agents in relation to each other and observe the patterns that emerge from such interaction.

suburban households. Both these types of households tend to remain in their present location unless they realize that they are better off moving. City households move to the suburbs if they find that the taxes they are paying compared to the investments in city infrastructure is higher in the city than in the suburbs. In other words, city households move to the suburbs if, for example, more and more people end up moving to the suburbs (with far fewer jobs moving in that direction) or the transportation infrastructure gets congested and commutes get longer. At some point, many suburban households will move to the city to get relief from long and stressful commutes. Equilibrium will be reached when the number of households coming from the city matches the number moving back to the city from the suburbs. At this point, the size of the city and suburb will stabilize until taxes and investments are changed again. For simplicity, no increase in population through natural growth or migration from other regions is considered in this model.

This phenomenon of city-suburb dynamics and subsequent equilibrium can be represented by the model shown here. The figure depicts a very specific form of graphic representation of stocks, flows, and influences, pioneered by Jay Forrester mentioned earlier. City households and suburban households are represented by boxes or stocks since they "contain" households that flow in or out of them based on the rules suggested above. All other variables, such as taxes, investments, congestion levels, and other derived variables, influence the rate of suburbanization and centralization. We begin exploring this model by setting up some reasonable parameters such as:

Starting number of city households: 100,000

Suburban households: 10% of the city (so 10,000)

Total infrastructure investments (annual): $10,000,000

Percent of total investments for city: 60% (the rest goes to the suburbs)

Taxes for city dwellers (annual): 1000/household

Taxes for suburban dwellers (annual): 500/household

Using the values above to drive the model in Figure 4, we find that the trend to suburbanize at low levels of congestion is strong, but increasing the congestion levels leads to an equilibrium condition where the flows out of the city to the suburbs equals the flows in the reverse direction. Suburbs gain population at the expense of the city under most circumstances. However, in one scenario, city gains population when it receives 90% of the total investments, but imposes a tax that is only 50% of what suburban households pay.

Once the model is set up and offering logically consistent results, it can be used to address questions through experimental (trial-and-error) methods. For example, one obvious question that arises from the model runs above is: *What level of taxation and investment would make the relative movement of people between the city and suburb negligible?* By making small adjustments to the parameters and checking the results, one can incrementally arrive at the answer to the question. It turns out that if the city residents were paying about 11% lower taxes per household than suburban residents but receiving 90% of the total investments (remember, they are 90% of total metropolitan population), then the city population (and concomitantly, the suburban population) remains more or less unchanged.

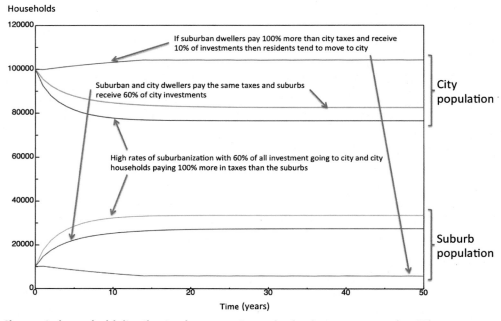

Change in household distribution between city and suburb over 50 years for different tax and investment scenarios.

Understanding where people are choosing to live and why provides a critical input for estimating sustainability parameters of the region. One obvious implication of how the population and employment are distributed in a region is the resulting impact on travel behavior. If housing is dispersed and jobs are concentrated in the center, a significant number of people may be experiencing long commutes. Assuming that these commuters drive to work (which is more than 85% of all trips), the resulting implications for energy demands, fossil fuel use, air pollution, and climate-changing carbon emissions would make the region less sustainable. However, if alternative forms of mobility, such as transit systems, were available, the adverse impact on the environment would be lower.

Besides impacting travel, the location and distribution of jobs and housing also influence several other aspects of sustainability. As a city sprawls and develops low-density suburbs, it encroaches upon agricultural land and compromises biodiversity by destroying some habitats. The low-density form of development with its concomitant long commutes reduces social contacts and increases isolation of social groups. Large private yards also require more water for maintenance and upkeep. On the other hand, high-density developments in central areas can also have adverse effects on sustainability if the high concentration of heat-absorbing materials, such as concrete and asphalt, leads to urban-heat island effects. These materials absorb the radiant energy of the sun during the day and release that in the night thereby keeping the night-time temperatures higher than surrounding areas. The high nighttime temperatures lead to higher levels of air pollution, higher energy demands for cooling, more water, and more heat related illnesses. Therefore, determining the optimum levels of density and dispersal of different land uses to achieve urban sustainability requires the use of sophisticated urban models that can balance the multiple positive and negative influences and offer guidance for planning.

Where Are We Headed?

We are now witnessing the confluence of several technological and social trends that is revolutionizing the way we interact with our physical surroundings and with each other. High-speed communication networks, mostly in the urban locations, have integrated many of the city functions such as transport, service delivery, and emergency management. Devices that sense locations, see objects, and measure the ambient environment (temperature, noise, air quality, and other activities) are everywhere. You are probably holding one such device in your hand, which is also known as a smartphone. It is now possible to track the flow of people and crowds through different parts of the city with the help of cellphone records. This could be complemented with information about the most significant events that are happening by capturing the data from social media like Twitter feeds.

Supplemental Readings

Batty, M. (2005) Cities and Complexity: Understanding Cities Through Cellular Automata, Agent-Based Models, and Fractals. Cambridge, MA: MIT Press.

Miller, E. J. (2009). Integrated urban models: theoretical prospects. *The Expanding Sphere of Travel Behaviour Research: Selected Papers from the 11th International Conference on Travel Behaviour Research.* Edited by Ryuichi Kitamura, Toshio Yoshii and Toshiyuki Yamamoto. Bingley, U.K.: Emerald Group Publishing Limited. Chapter 14, pp. 351–384.

Santé, I., García, A. M., Miranda, D., & Crecente, R. (2010). Cellular automata models for the simulation of real-world urban processes: A review and analysis. *Landscape and Urban Planning*, 96(2), 108–122. doi:10.1016/j.landurbplan.2010.03.001

Schwarz, N., Haase, D., & Seppelt, R. (2010). Omnipresent sprawl? A review of urban simulation models with respect to urban shrinkage. *Environment and Planning B-Planning and Design*, 37(2), 265–283.

Can We Teach an Education for Sustainable Development? Measuring the Fourth *"E"*

Chad P. Frederick and K. David Pijawka

Introduction

This chapter explores why the measurement of learning outcomes in education for sustainable development is necessary and how it can be approached. First, it will help to illustrate the distinction between an education for sustainable development (ESD) and the traditional model of education. While ESD and traditional education are similar in some respects, there are many important differences between them. In both approaches, students accumulate facts about the world. These facts allow students to have the information necessary to be competent citizens in society. Students also develop mental skills, such as mathematics and language. This allows them to be competent workers in the economy.

The differences between the two models may be found in how we situate the student in relation to the facts and for which skills we try to develop competencies. In order to study complex systems, traditional education has a tendency to start the learning process by simplifying and characterizing systems as collections of discrete elements. This method has been successful in the natural and physical sciences, such as chemistry and physics, where reducing systems into elements allows students to observe critical interactions. This method, however, has also been applied to many other academic fields, including the ecological and social sciences with mixed results. In the traditional educational approach, people generally are treated as distinct and separable from the systems in which they live and independent of the goods and services they consume. Although there may be educative goals achieved by this approach, the separation fosters a disconnection between our consumption and the social and ecological environments where these goods and services are produced and consumed—a principal idea when considering sustainability. Further, it allows us to treat as separate whatever impacts the remains of our material consumption may have after we discard them. It even allows us to think of the products as separate from the processes used to produce them (Jensen, 2008, pp. 293–305).

In contrast, education for sustainable development promotes **systems thinking** in our students. In systems thinking, products and services are not only seen as interconnected to their production and consumption, but also to their consequences throughout their lifecycle. This enables students to critically inspect their own relationships to the socio-ecological systems in which they live and those which they affect (Colucci-Gray, Camino, Barbiero, & Gray, 2006). For example, automobiles are seen not only

Systems thinking – the ability to recognize the existence of complex networks, and to think in terms of multiple relationships within networks, as opposed to being limited in thought to isolated actions and reactions.

as products providing utility for their owners, but are also a source of pollution, and even as a force for shaping urban forms which, in turn, has accessibility and equity implications for those without automobiles (Boone, 2014).

Traditional education mostly focuses on acquiring technical skills, while ESD also strives for **affective competencies**. This is because it has become evident that people use their attitudes, ethics, and values when analyzing facts and making decisions (Kollmuss & Agyeman, 2002). Reflecting on our ethics and values allows us to see if they are accurately aligned with our habits and actions and if they are helping us to make informed decisions. Education for sustainable development requires we consider more than knowledge but also attitudes, ethics, values, and behaviors. This distinction is important because it calls into question the very purpose of education and can lead toward the empowerment of 'actively engaged citizens' (Jickling & Wals, 2008).

There is a growing literature on learning outcomes related to sustainability education. In this chapter we address what the dimensions are of sustainability education outcomes and how these can be achieved. Utilizing one undergraduate course in a sustainability program, *Sustainable Cities, we address the question of how to measure these outcomes using pre and post course* surveys as the methodology. We begin the chapter by articulating the meaning of the learning outcomes expected in education for sustainability and ways in which to achieve them and then we demonstrate a case where the outcomes are measured for a particular course. *Sustainable Cities,* is one of the largest courses in the School of Sustainability at Arizona State University with just less than 1000 students annually. The course purposively tries to be interdisciplinary through co- instructors from different disciplines, invited lecturers from various disciplines on campus and outside campus, and collaborative student team exercises/ assignments with students both from different disciplines and levels of educational achievement. Various methods of instruction are introduced including assignments that require individual responses that focus on ethical issues and complex systems understanding, as well as dissuasions of how to change current consumer patterns toward sustainable solutions. One important assignment—Community—based research is also is expected of these students at the undergraduate level through an student Honors section added to the course. *Critical Thinking* is introduced throughout each topic covered in the course through questions on the readings and specially developed assignments. The course is built around these sustainability education outcomes and we offer how we tried to apply them to this course and measure the level of success.

Learning Outcomes

Before exploring goals of the *Sustainable Cities* course, it may be helpful to review what we mean by **learning outcomes**. Learning outcomes can be found in three domains: cognitive, affective, and psychomotor. While often overlapping, there are some distinctions among these domains. Psychomotor skills involve physical movement. Cognitive skills are fundamentally about thinking, while affective skills employ feelings. Many actions involve all three (Kraiger, Ford, & Salas, 1993). For example, consider having to escape from a wild animal. Being surprised by a wild animal might make you frightened, which activates the physical responses necessary to jump and run. Simultaneously, your mind determines ways to evade the animal and calculates whether or not you have the skills to perform the required movements. On the other

Learning outcomes – the set of knowledge and abilities that students aspire to master and that educators aspire to deliver.

hand, some situations (for example, determining how many purchases to make in a store) seem to require only one, such as simple addition. Still, how we perceive our capacity to perform cognitive skills often affects our overall ability to execute them (Dweck, Mangels, & Good, 2004). All three domains can be trained for improvement. Indeed, one old maxim regarding problem-solving is that people do not "rise to the occasion"—rather, they tend to "fall to the level of their training."

Learning Outcomes in Education for Sustainable Development

Most learning outcomes in traditional education involve the performance of cognitive competencies such as recalling the content learned in class or demonstrating abilities such as applying mathematical operations and constructing coherent, convincing paragraphs. In contrast, education for sustainable development calls for students to exercise affective skills, as the complex nature of many sustainability problems require affective competencies to solve them (Wiek, Withycombe, & Redman, 2011). For example, a sustainability problem might call for specialists from three wholly different occupational fields to work together, with each applying their own distinct expertise, to work toward its resolution. Such **interdisciplinary** teamwork means that the specialists will need to respect each other's input, which is largely an affective capacity.

Interdisciplinarity – the practice of distinct fields of knowledge working together to produce new knowledge that cannot be produced by the fields on their own.

Still a young field, it is challenging to describe the exact list of appropriate learning outcomes for ESD (Sterling & Thomas, 2006). Furthermore, sustainability educators also recognize that this list of outcomes is likely to evolve over time. Finally, much like the need to master basic mathematical skills before attempting more advanced operations, it is likely that some affective competencies provide a sound basis for more advanced skills (Shephard, 2008). Unfortunately, there is little research or theory in this area. Nonetheless, scholars in the field of ESD have identified a wide range of beneficial outcomes for which to strive and have developed useful frameworks for pursuing these outcomes.

The *Sustainable Cities* course has adapted elements of these frameworks to satisfy its unique goals, and we encourage scholars to draw on these resources as needed to support their own specific pedagogic goals. Although these lists of ESD competencies have been described as unwieldy, Wiek, Withycombe, & Redman (2011) have reviewed these frameworks and from them have identified five general competency categories: systems thinking, anticipatory, normative, strategic, and interpersonal competencies. Further, de Haan's concept of *Gestaltungskompetenz* (2010) views problem-solving in ESD as a general competency which involves the interaction of twelve cognitive and affective sub-skills. These sub-skills include **self-reflection** and interdisciplinarity, as well as increased empathy and motivation. And, Svanström, Lozano-García, and Rowe (2008) also outlined a set of learning outcomes drawn from various institutions supporting sustainability in higher education. For them, knowledge is supplemented by characteristics for change agency in ESD. Similarly, interdisciplinarity, reflectivity, systems thinking, and ethical reasoning are among their central concerns. Indeed, sustainability scholars Sterling and Thomas (2006) remarked regarding ESD learning outcomes, "[while] authors often use different words, there is often a strong similarity in the meaning." In this course, we adopted the Sterling and Thomas idea that, in addition to affective learning outcomes, it is also critical students develop a personally meaningful *definition of sustainability*.

Self-reflection – the process of critically reflecting on own personal ideals, goals, and actions, and objectively evaluating the impact those actions have on the world around us.

We agree with Wiek, et al. that attempting to establish all five domains of learning outcomes would be overwhelming for both the student and instructors especially in one course, but these outcomes need to be driving factors for a learning program in sustainability(Pijawka et al., 2013) Therefore, it is critical to strive for those learning outcomes that are achievable. After all, each individual outcome is a challenge and is complex.. Boix-Mansilla & Dawes-Duraisingh (2007) dismantles interdisciplinarity into three components: 1) appreciating and understanding the methods of different disciplines, (2) understanding and valuing the contribution of disciplines as they relate to the students' discipline, and (3) understanding the limitations of their own disciplines, as well as others. Untangling the complexities of individual learning outcomes will assist in constructing more effective instruments with which to estimate their delivery to students.

Essential Outcomes and Assessments in *Sustainable Cities*

Achieving greater urban sustainability is considerably more than a technical exercise. It will require people who have the cognitive and affective skills necessary to apply sustainable solutions (Murray & Murray, 2007). Therefore, *Sustainable Cities* strives to enable the affective outcome of *environmental conscientiousness*, which allows for positive environmental behavior. By adapting various frameworks of learning outcomes in ESD, we have identified five central outcomes, achievable over the course of a semester, which also supports the development of positive environmental behavior.

Concept vocabulary. One of the foundations of creating sustainable policies and environments is the ability to effectively discuss sustainability (Orr, 1992). Since sustainability has developed independently in several different academic fields over the past 50 years, attaining a common vocabulary has been difficult. Without a shared understanding of the concepts that support sustainability, people will be unable to work together successfully. Therefore, the course first tries to develop a core vocabulary for students to use in articulating their goals, and importantly, to bring with them into their other academic fields.

Interdisciplinary understanding. Working together on sustainability is essential, as problems are unlikely to be solved by the use of a single academic or occupational specialization. However, few professionals have experience working across disciplines and are only rarely taught how to work collaboratively across fields. In *Sustainable Cities*, we emphasize the need for cooperation by illustrating how a team can produce results amounting to more than the sum of its parts. This process involves illustrating the multi-dimensional nature of sustainability problems by linking it to the diverse perspectives that a team (comprised of multiple disciplines) can bring into focus.

Ethical conceptualization. Working together is not enough to solve sustainability problems. To tackle the complex problems challenging society, we need people with the ability to reason ethically from a sustainability perspective (Tilbury, 2004). Without ethical reasoning, we are otherwise tempted to solve only the immediacy of the problem, or view it as intrinsically an environmental problem, when in fact it may be a social problem as well. Instead of developing a solution to the problem, this tends to move the problem geographically. This means that the crisis merely becomes someone else's problem. Of course, many sustainability problems are difficult to contain, or are global in nature regardless of where they are geographically concentrated. An ethical reasoning can recognize our interconnectedness, and thus permit the consideration of people's welfare everywhere, and even the people of future generations.

Definition of sustainability. While it is understandable that some desire a strict definition of sustainability, we should recognize such strictness would limit our capacity to adapt to new situations and new considerations. Given the varied needs faced by those engaging with sustainability issues, developing a strict definition seems unlikely. That said, resolving sustainability problems would likely always require at least a basic and mutually understood basis bounded by vocabulary, interdisciplinary efforts, and ethical reasoning. When a student reflects on his/her values for ethical reasoning and interdisciplinarity, it helps the individual to develop an enhanced personal concept of sustainability. While having a personal definition of sustainability seems to conflict with achieving broader goals (Djordjevic & Cotton, 2011), it actually allows for sharing and adapting several perspectives, increasing effective communication and diversifying the ability to recognize problems. As McKeown and her colleagues (2002) conclude, many of the great concepts in human society, such as democracy and justice, are difficult to define or are culturally relative. This neither reduces their importance, nor does it prevent their further exploration. In essence, what is most important for sustainability education is that an informed, personally relevant definition will support a meaningful basis for environmental conscientiousness.

Environmental conscientiousness. One central goal of *Sustainable Cities* is to provide students with the opportunity for positive environmental behavior, or to become change agents for improving their world. While establishing an environmental conscientiousness alone is insufficient to create behavior change, it is supportive. Some scholars have cautioned against promoting environmental conscientiousness, suggesting it undemocratically removes choice. However, allowing for the possibility for change and demanding it are separate notions: Not providing students with the skills and information to behave environmentally limits their choice to one: only acting unsustainably; and, it could be argued, this is far less democratic. With an ESD, students actually have more choices: from business-as-usual, to various amounts of environmental conscientiousness, and change agency. We are confident that the ability to reflect on values opens the door for change.

Measuring Cognitive and Affective Learning Outcomes

Another central difference between traditional education and ESD is that, because they deliver primarily cognitive learning outcomes, traditional courses typically measure success in passed examinations, successfully completed homework assignments, and final grades. Unfortunately, there is very little research on how to accurately measure affective learning outcomes. The available research points toward cumbersome instruments of unclear validity. In this regard, ESD is breaking new ground. Drawing on the lessons of diversity, the faculty of *Sustainable Cities* has taken a different approach drawing on the research principle of *triangulation*. Since direct measurements with single instruments are largely unavailable, a diverse set of limited tools can be used to develop a sense of the impact the course has on student learning outcomes (Buissink-Smith, Mann, & Shephard, 2011). This allows faculty to more nimbly adjust their toolbox of instruments gathered while teaching the course.

While there are numerous ways to analyze student learning outcomes, we present a few that can be easily incorporated into course construction and evaluation. If this is not possible, perhaps they will assist in the development of new assessment techniques. While measuring qualitative and affective characteristics can prove difficult, this does not mean it should not be attempted; rather, the results should be interpreted very carefully. Improved measurement techniques are unlikely to occur without attempting to develop them, however limited the initial attempts prove to be (Rode & Michelsen, 2008).

Surveys

One of the goals of Education for Sustainable Development concerns the need for an increase in change agency. The 'before and after' survey design is an ideal way to measure change, especially attitudinal change (Kraiger et al., 1993). However, developing accurate instruments can be complicated and requires some background. If you do not have training in constructing survey instruments, it is advisable to have a colleague review it before giving it to students or have someone assist in its development. In any case, create simple surveys that are fairly straightforward. The students should complete the first survey before the first lecture, to avoid that experience from biasing the later results. You also weigh the length of the survey against interest in completing it, so survey space is at a premium and care should taken in selecting questions.

Asking a series of questions at the beginning of the course can help capture an impression of the students' opinions, skills, and feelings they have at that time. Asking the same questions at the end of the course can tell you how much your course impacted the students. Of course, many other influences can transpire over the course of a semester, but very few can be expected to happen to all students. Certain rare, history-making events, such as the fall of the Berlin Wall, or the landing of astronauts on the Moon can affect the entire classroom.

Journals

Having students turn in periodic electronic journal entries is a good way to amass considerable data that can be easily analyzed. These can also be completed at the end of each class to assess what students found to be the most important lesson of the lecture (Abbott, 2012). When these entries are submitted electronically, instructors can scan them for keywords, and measure how much the use of the words changes or what words are associated with them. There are very advanced software packages available for qualitative research such as Atlas Ti, but oftentimes even simple programs like Microsoft Word can be used effectively if the journal entries are designed appropriately.

Measuring Learning Outcomes in *Sustainable Cities*

Concept Vocabulary

Concept mastery is foundational. Measuring student mastery in examinations is not always accurate, as the pressure of the exam can alter their performance. Furthermore, most exams are not conversational, whereas one of the main purposes of developing

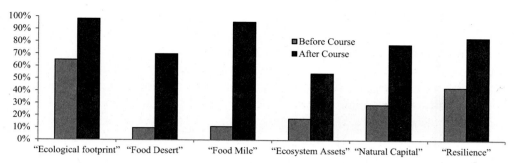

FIGURE 1: Change in Student Comfort in Defining Concepts – Before and After Course.

a mastery of key terms is to be able to communicate with one another and develop solutions. Nevertheless, vocabulary is largely a cognitive skill, and is therefore fairly easy to measure.

One of The simplest methods is to just ask students how confident they are in explaining the concept, as this can be compared to how much lecture time is devoted to the various concepts. This can aid in the review of how much time is needed for teaching each concept, and whether or not there are better learning episodes for presenting the terms. Factors contributing to understanding can also be determined. For classes like Sustainable Cities, which are open enrollment, this can be quite informative.

One semester we wanted a raw score of *Sustainable Cities* student understanding of key concepts and to determine what factors play a role in their mastery. We chose six terms to investigate: ecological footprint, food desert, food-miles, ecosystem assets, natural capital, and resilience (see Figure 1, below). Through the use of regression models, we discovered that academic year played the largest role in differences in student concept acquisition. This is important because the course usually contains a sizable proportion of upperclassmen. Being a senior led to a 19% greater likelihood to master an additional concept over juniors. Sophomores had a 9% chance to master an additional term than freshmen. Academic major also played a role. For example, Art and Architecture students had a nearly 16% greater odds of acquiring an additional term. Other factors such as a student's initial self-reported environmental conscientiousness had an impact. The main takeaway is that knowing student class levels and majors is important for helping to structure the class in ways that help effectively deliver the learning outcome of vocabulary.

Interdisciplinary Understanding

Accurately measuring a level of interdisciplinarity abilities in students is extremely problematic. Research in this area is limited. Several factors make this type of measurement problematic., For example, some pairs of disciplines are considered 'farther apart' than are other pairs. All things being equal, taking art and architecture students might find it much easier to work together than art students and mathematicians. Different disciplines also tend to hold various methodologies in differing levels of esteem.

As a competency, interdisciplinarity is both an affective and cognitive skill. It requires having an ability to work in an interdisciplinary fashion and having the desire to do so. As a cognitive skill, it entails both understanding what interdisciplinarity is and how to approach it. As an affective ability, it requires respecting the contribution and mind-sets of others and being able to envision the multidimensionality of sustainability problems. Measuring student regard for interdisciplinarity is different from, and much easier than, assessing their skill at using it. However, neither is impossible to assess.

For assessments of cognitive skills, inferences can be made as to the degree of cooperation that has been achieved by a) analyzing how much students achieve toward resolving an issue, b) illustrating their own unique contribution, and also c) remarking on their team's disciplinary composition. This exercise can be repeated over the semester to gauge changes in this skill.

For assessments of affect, we can compare student attitudes before and after the course regarding various disciplinary contributions toward understanding sustainability. For example, you might use a survey instrument to simply ask students to rank or rate the contribution of different lectures toward their understanding of the transdisciplinary nature of sustainability. A well-delivered course should show an increase in student regard for the contribution of different disciplines. If students largely dismiss the contribution of what is known to be a key component in the resolution of some sustainability problems, you might consider a different approach toward delivering this fact. One approach could involve selecting an ideal team of three or four specialists for tackling different sustainability problems and describing how each member will contribute to their solutions.

An indirect method (which works in conjunction with other methods) entails asking if the course ever encouraged the students to consider altering their academic plan. The results can be compared to their existing major if that information is available from the survey instruments. This question can then be followed by another open-ended question asking which additional component they would add and why. We found that up to 25% of students considered adding a minor, and an additional 15% would have considered it but were too far along in their studies to alter their plan (see Figure 2, below). While this is not a measure of interdisciplinarity, it does demonstrate whether or not the course creates a new acknowledgement of the utility of other disciplines and on whom it has that effect. When combined with and compared to other data, it can help instructors gauge the impact of the course.

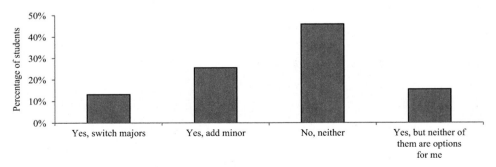

FIGURE 2: Impact of course on academic plan.

Ethical Conceptualization

A student's ethical contribution toward resolving a problem in sustainability is also difficult to ascertain. Although there is more research on this topic than exists for measuring interdisciplinarity, the available research is either difficult to implement in a classroom setting or of mixed value. However, again, this should not deter us from trying to develop an understanding of the impact our efforts have but, rather, that we should be cautious of the results.

Assessments can be useful when built into an assignment. It is helpful to embed the assessment into the assignment in such a way as to not draw attention to the instrument itself as undo attention will corrupt the results. Assignments can be designed to measure the level of ethical reasoning that students apply toward resolving of a set of sustainability problems by positioning ethical dilemmas as merely part of the overall solution. For example, students can be asked to describe in which ways the problems are ethical, environmental, or economic in nature. Furthermore, students can be asked to what degree are each of the "three e's" (i.e., equity, ecology, and economy) are involved in their resolution, and why. The important part is to follow up afterward with students as to why the problems might be ethical in basis when they seem to be more straightforward.

Assessment instruments can be extremely simple and yet still provide a wealth of information. As part of an assignment for using the online Ecological Footprint tool, we asked students whether or not people have a 'right to consume' products and services as they wished. It would not be highly informing to ask outright for a 'yes' or 'no' answer and have the students simply check a box. In this situation, we asked the students to reply with a well-thought out paragraph justifying their answer. This allows students to unpack their ethical positions, giving instructors a more valid response. The teaching assistants (under supervision) formed a rubric, read a random sample of responses together to provide a level of continuity, and then coded the remainder according to the rubric. The results were surprising: we found that students overwhelmingly responded with "no," while only a small percentage unequivocally said "yes." An additional 27% responded that people do have a right to consume as they please, but that such attitudes are either irrational or harmful, and that acting on that right was detrimental to the public well being (see Figure 3, below).

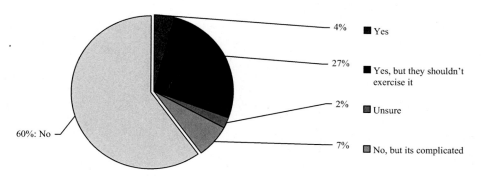

4% ■ Yes

27% ■ Yes, but they shouldn't exercise it

2% ■ Unsure

7% ■ No, but its complicated

60%: No

FIGURE 3: "Do people have a 'right to consume'?"

Definition of Sustainability

Determining the changes in students' definitions of sustainability is much easier, although it can be a bit more work, and almost certainly involves qualitative coding. However, the results are quite definitive. In both the before-course and after-course surveys, students are asked to give a brief definition of sustainability using a sentence or two. (Alternatively, you might give them a word count of perhaps 30 or 40 words. If the course is generating a personal, ethical definition, then you will almost certainly see a shift in the types of words used.) For example, in a recent semester of *'Sustainable Cities'* the use of words reflecting environmental concerns decreased dramatically from before to after the course and were replaced by a wider range of words concerned with equity and economics (see Figure 4).

Student Definitions of Sustainability: Frequency of Change in Key Words[1]

	Before Count	Adj. Count[2]	After Count	Percent Change
future	73	64.97	205	215.53%
*consci-**	8	7.12	19	166.85%
generation	54	48.06	125	160.09%
lifestyle	8	7.12	15	110.67%
change	12	10.68	18	68.54%
*socie-**	16	14.24	23	61.52%
*social**	30	26.7	36	34.83%
action	17	15.13	19	25.58%
preserve	26	23.14	29	25.32%
planet	20	17.8	22	23.60%
world	42	37.38	45	20.39%
plan*	32	28.48	32	12.39%
conserve*	16	14.24	16	12.36%
survive	15	13.35	15	12.36%
impact	20	17.8	19	6.74%
econo-*	23	20.47	21	2.59%
health	17	15.13	14	−7.47%
earth	51	45.39	41	−9.67%
sustain*	311	276.79	239	−13.65%
human	41	36.49	30	−17.79%
enviro-*	123	109.47	84	−23.27%
resource	158	140.62	107	−23.91%
system	21	18.69	14	−25.09%
natur-*	51	45.39	34	−25.09%
maint-*	38	33.82	22	−34.95%
green	20	17.8	11	−38.20%
effici-*	33	29.37	17	−42.12%
produc-*	18	16.02	8	−50.06%
material	15	13.35	5	−62.55%
build	15	13.35	5	−62.55%
waste	15	13.35	4	−70.04%
tech-	16	14.24	4	−71.91%
energy	36	32.04	9	−71.91%
renew*	22	19.58	2	−89.79%

1 words with a count over 15 in either the before- or after course surveys
2 Adjusted count to reflect decrease in total word count
* Root words used to capture student intent. Specific contexts were evaluated.
Italicized words reflect an overall increase in usage.

FIGURE 4: Changes in the types of words used from before to after course in articulating students' personal definitions of sustainability.

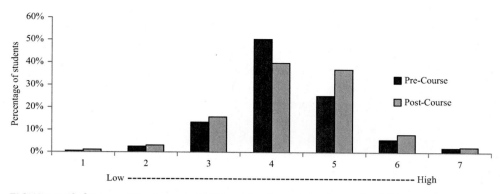

FIGURE 5: Shift toward Environmental Conscientiousness when asked, "How environmentally conscientious do you consider yourself?"

This shows a broadening of the meaning of sustainability to encompass more than core environmental issues. We also found that the word count dropped as well, from over 26 words per response in the before course survey, to less than 23 in the after course response; a drop of 12%. Looking closely at the responses, we determined that students resolved the matter with more precision.

Environmental Conscientiousness

By incorporating research from the cognitive sciences and environmental psychology, we know that behavioral change requires more than a conscientious desire but also requires the development of new habits. However, asking students to develop new habits is beyond the scope of the Sustainable Cities course. Instead, we ask students to report how environmentally conscious they consider themselves to be at the beginning of the course and compare it to their answers at the end of the course (see Figure 5). Survey prompts are categorized in bins that feature short descriptions of each level (e.g., how much consideration they give the environment when making decisions, various levels of consumption, buying new vs. used and engaging socio-ecological organizations). Results should be compared with parallel data to reduce two major concerns. First, many students initially rank themselves as highly conscientious only to learn during the semester that in reality they were not as environmentally conscientious as they initially thought. The second concern is the opposite: some did not know how environmentally conscientious they in fact were before taking the course. While we found a statistically significant shift overall toward greater conscientiousness using this one metric despite these concerns, we can see that additional questions proved to be valuable for uncovering these two concerns. A simple question in the after-course survey asking how accurately they think they answered the before-course question about conscientiousness would help.

Conclusions

In this chapter, we have attempted to provide a modest sampling of the techniques used in *Sustainable Cities* to measure the impact of the course and the achievement of student affective learning outcomes. In the absence of simple and verified direct measures of affective learning outcomes, we suggest developing a toolbox of measurements and using them in concert to develop an understanding of the course's efficacy. This "triangulation of methods" can easily adapt to course content changes, student demographic changes, evolving learning outcomes, and other adjustments. In order to be effective, it is important that ESD course instructors ask themselves, "Does this course teach an education for sustainable development and how well does it do it?"

Instructors of ESD courses have access to a world of easily implementable diagnostic methods. Student surveys provide critical data that will help keep course content suitable to the important societal events students experience. Surveys also inform instructors as to slight changes that emerge in the composition of student demographics. Finally, we recognize that we have just exited the United Nations' *Decade of Education for Sustainable Development* (2005–2014) that impacted student awareness of sustainability issues in K-12 education nationwide. Reflexive surveys will help determine if content should be adjusted as more students enter college with a basic knowledge of sustainability concepts.

In short, sustainability instructors should not dismiss the impact of collecting triangulated data that informs their pedagogy. We hope that this brief excursion into our methods will aid in the development of individual, customizable toolboxs of instruments for the measurement of affective and cognitive learning outcomes.

Supplemental Readings.

Groves, R. M., Fowler Jr., F. J., Couper, M. P., Lepkowski, J. M., Singer, E., & Tourangeau, R. (2013). *Survey methodology*. John Wiley & Sons.

Gibbs, J. C., Basinger, K. S., Fuller, D., & Fuller, R. L. (2013). *Moral maturity: Measuring the development of sociomoral reflection*. Routledge.

China's Pursuit: Smart Sustainable Urban Environments

Douglas Webster, Feifei Zhang, Jianming Cai

Introduction

This chapter outlines the issues facing China's cities as they pursue smart, sustainable futures in an economy moving from manufacturing to services. Then, ongoing sustainable initiatives, of both national and local (primarily municipal) governments are described and assessed. A major Chinese city at the forefront of locally driven sustainability efforts, Hangzhou is profiled to provide more on-the-ground level detail. (This will permit comparisons with other sustainable international cities as profiled in Chapter 2.) Because the national government of China is an important innovator and supporter of sustainable urbanization, probably more so than in western countries such as the United States, where local (city and state) governments tend to be the leaders in the sustainable movement, an important aspect of this chapter is documenting the role of China's national government in propelling sustainability momentum at the local level.

Context

China's spectacular economic growth and rise to become the second largest economy in the world (after the United States), propelled by the market reforms that started around 1980, has been one of the great global success stories of the late twentieth and early twenty-first centuries.[1] According to the World Bank, this growth has lifted over 500 million people out of poverty since 1978 – an unprecedented feat.[2] The economic growth and poverty alleviation is almost entirely the product of urbanization; in fact, China's rural agricultural sector remains very inefficient. China's urban areas, including their peri-urban industrial peripheries became the "factory of the world" after 1980, resulting in massive migration of approximately 234 million people to the nation's cities. Rural to urban migration raised the income of a worker by at least four times immediately. Now, China is becoming a service economy; in 2013 the output of the service sector became larger than manufacturing for the first time since the Communist Party of China took power in 1949.

However, China's urban propelled economic rise did not come without cost. China's rise to become the "factory of the world" was associated with the high dependence on coal for generation of electricity, energy inefficient production, lax emission controls, and rapid motorization (China is the leading producer and consumer of automobiles in the world). The result now is severe water and air pollution, soil contamination, and the exacerbation of water shortages, especially in the north. An emphasis on quantity, e.g., massive production of housing, rather than quality of housing and community design, resulted in less livable communities than could have been the case for the same level of investment.[3]

The costs of China's rapid urban-centered economic growth to Chinese residents have been high. Up to 500,000 Chinese urban residents die prematurely each year from air pollution;[4] In 2007, the World Bank reported that 12 of the 20 most air polluted cities in the world were in China. However, this appears no longer to be the case; 2012 data released by the World Health Organization (WHO) indicates that India's cities are, in general, more polluted. However, this not cause for complacency, only 1 percent of China's urban population live in urban areas that meet the EU's minimum air quality standard.[5]

River pollution from upstream industrial emissions and spills, human waste, and agriculturally associated pollutants such as animal waste, pesticides, and fertilizer, have made the majority of China's great rivers severely polluted, sometimes causing complete shutdowns of urban water supplies, such as in Harbin in 2005 and in Lanzhou in 2014. The Yellow River, birthplace of Chinese civilization is so polluted for most of its length that it is not safe for swimming. Globally, China produces more Green House Gases than any other nation; however, much of this GHG, as well as localized pollution and use of scarce water is associated with exports. Arguably, in terms of equity, this export oriented pollution should be charged to the consuming countries.

There is nothing new about the severe urban environmental problems and shortcomings in terms of urban quality of life that China has experienced while becoming a great industrial power – a similar trajectory has been seen during other industrial and subsequent motorization revolutions. This relationship between economic development and environmental problems and conditions is known as the **Environmental Trajectory** – see Figure 1. In a nutshell, almost invariably urban environmental quality deteriorates rapidly to a very low point during its middle-income stage as a country industrializes, then people and governments react, using financial resources acquired from economic success to dramatically improve the quality of the urban environment. In the 1950s in London, killer fogs were frequent – people could not see their

Environmental Trajectory - The Environmental Trajectory is a useful conceptual framework that indicates that cities and countries experience the worst environmental conditions when they have recently industrialized and are in the lower-middle income stage. Afterwards, urban environmental conditions usually improve as cities transform into service economies, then post-industrial amenity based economies. As cities move up the environmental trajectory more resources become available to address environmental problems, and residents and investors demand higher quality environments.

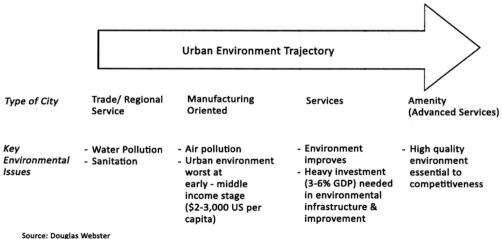

Type of City	Trade/ Regional Service	Manufacturing Oriented	Services	Amenity (Advanced Services)
Key Environmental Issues	- Water Pollution - Sanitation	- Air pollution - Urban environment worst at early - middle income stage ($2-3,000 US per capita)	- Environment improves - Heavy investment (3-6% GDP) needed in environmental infrastructure & improvement	- High quality environment essential to competitiveness

Source: Douglas Webster

FIGURE 1: Urban Environmental Trajectory.

hands in front of them, and thousands of deaths occurred; Los Angeles in the 1970s experienced deadly smog (ozone based) primarily associated with automobile emissions under inversion meteorological conditions. Rivers caught fire in the US, e.g., the Cuyahoga River outside Cleveland in 1969. Japan experienced the mercury poisoning (Minamata Disease) incident in Niigata Bay in 1965. In both the US and Japanese cases, such incidents were catalysts that led to a massive regulatory push to clean up the environment, and creation of agencies with strong mandates, such as the Environmental Protection Agency (EPA), established in the United States in 1970. What is different about the Chinese case is that its industrial revolution was compressed into about 40 years, a process that took approximately 150 years in the Western experience, such as the United Kingdom. Secondly, the numbers are much bigger, both in terms of levels of production and population, so the impacts are proportionately higher – China's population is about four times as large as the United States, and its economic growth rate about three times as large. China's population is about 1.36 billion (2014), of which 54 percent are urban - 730 million people or approximately twice the entire population of the United States.

The current situation is both sweet and sour. As noted, China's cities are not currently healthy, nor sustainable. However, much is being initiated by both government and private sector actors that is very encouraging. China has more installed solar capacity than any country on earth, that grew at an annual rate of 89.5% between 2010 and 2015, as well as installed wind capacity (76 gigawatts at the end of 2012), growing at an expected annualized compound rate of 26.4% since 2010.[6] New Chinese companies such as BYD, researching and manufacturing electric cars, are pioneering new environmental technologies. China is the world's largest producer of solar panels, exporting inexpensive solar equipment to the world. Both national and local governments are taking dramatic actions to improve the situation, e.g., phasing out the use of coal in Beijing;[7] creating financial incentives for purchase of electric cars; undertaking investments to increase the percentage of future electricity generation from nuclear, natural gas, hydro and alternative sources dramatically; applying hi-tech in urban waste treatment; relocating polluted manufacturing firms into industrial zones where they are required to adopt cleaner technologies and become more energy efficient or be shut down. Throughout China, **Smart Cities** and sustainable cities are the new mantra. And a big tail wind supportive of sustainable cities is gaining momentum, namely the shift in the country's economy from a heavy reliance on manufacturing (generally of low cost consumer goods), often energy and resource inefficient, to a higher-value service economy (person consumption of services such as medicine and leisure, tourism, business and professional services, knowledge activities such as higher education and research, etc.). Service economies almost invariably consume much less energy and produce considerably less pollution per unit of economic output, thus making achievement of high and sustainable urban environmental quality much easier to achieve.

Until recently, urban populations accepted high levels of pollution, the benefits of rapid household income growth and poverty alleviation. These outweighed the costs of pollution and less attractive cities than could have been the case. The vast majority of urban Chinese understood pollution was a sacrifice to enable China to develop its economy. However, now that most Chinese cities have achieved middle-income status, and leading coastal cities, such as Shanghai, are essentially first-world cities,

Smart Cities - A Smart City is characterized by the extensive use of information technologies to achieve efficient urban outcomes; smart cities extensively deploy sensors to monitor the status of the city in real time, and adjust sub-systems accordingly; smart city technologies frequently incorporate "internet of things" sub-systems. Smart cities frequently use such technologies to achieve efficient traffic flows, public lighting, irrigation, police surveillance, e-governance, etc.

public attitudes are changing. The nature of this change reflects a cultural preference in China (and East Asia) to associate environmental quality with public health rather than with bio-diversity, wilderness, etc., as in the West. Especially since the extreme air pollution crisis in Beijing in January 2013, the population is demanding much high quality urban environments – especially in terms of air quality and the livability of their immediate residential neighborhoods. This change in public opinion coincides with increased national government emphasis on urban environmental quality, especially since 2011. Three major drivers underlying this change can be identified.

Firstly, China has developed a very large urban middle class over the last three decades (according to the McKinsey Institute, over 460 million people in 2013, forecast to rise to 650 million by 2022) as the country has achieved middle-income status. As has happened, virtually everywhere urban middle-income status has been achieved, and this more affluent, better-educated large cohort exhibits changed values. Although household income, material goods, and opportunity (especially for their children) are still valued highly, there appears to be a shift in values and preferences among China's urban middle class toward less tangible goods and services, e.g., clean air, less time wasted traveling, attractive and interesting neighborhoods, and public spaces, especially parks. However, no substantive research has yet been done on this topic.

The second factor is the exponential growth in use of social media in China, e.g., "We Chat", the equivalent of Twitter, tens of millions of Micro Blogs, etc., especially among the rapidly expanding urban middle classes. When air quality in Chinese cities plummets, tens of millions of people take to the social media complaining and demanding action, primarily from government. The government takes such "direct democracy" seriously.

However, thirdly, for change to occur, especially in the world's most populous country, where the national government plays a key role in guiding development and allocating resources, there is need for political and administrative will, and action. Increasingly, the leadership of the Communist Party of China, which governs China, is placing a priority on cleaning up the environment, especially in urban areas. This change was noted as early as in the 11th Five Year National Development Plan period (2006-2010), but is very pronounced in the current 12th National Development Plan period (2011-2015). The current President of China, Xi Jinping, has forcefully indicated that China needs to restructure its economy, and reorder its values, consistent with the priority the Government places on environmental quality and sustainability.

It will not be easy for the National Government to achieve sustainable urbanization, as there are deep structural constraints to changing environmental behavior that even the President, the Politburo, and the State Council (equivalent to a Western national cabinet) will need to struggle hard to overcome through reform. One of the most serious is that civil servants are promoted (or not) based on economic growth (GDP) in their jurisdictions. Despite some change in this regard, economic growth is still the standard by which local governments are primarily judged. Secondly, although the National Government formulates progressive guidelines and laws to improve the environment, based on international best practices (China is very open in international expertise, e.g., from the World Bank), local governments, which are fiscally powerful, often choose to largely ignore them. In China it is said, "the mountains are high and the emperor is far away". Lastly, but very important, State Owned Enterprises (SOEs) have grown very powerful as China's economy has boomed, further strengthened by the SOE reforms of the 1990s. Often these institutions, e.g., Petro China, are among the most powerful institutions in the country and may ignore environmental dictates of the national government.

What are the Key Environmental / Sustainability Issues Facing China's Cities?

The most critical issue is *air pollution*: 500,000 people are estimated to die prematurely each year in urban China because of severe air pollution in the major metropolitan regions according to scientific Chinese sources.[8] The burning of coal, primarily to generate electricity, is the main source of air pollution (and associated Green House Gases [GHG]), followed by vehicle emissions and industrial emissions, although the relative importance of different sources varies city by city. Air pollution in Beijing rose to a record high on January 12, 2013, sparking criticism of the Government's handling of air pollution. Although there has been a trend toward moving coal-fired electrical generation plans away from large cities, this has no effect on GHG gas emissions, and does not improve urban air quality as much as might be expected because a portion of particulates, etc., are blown back on cities by winds. For example, relocation of coal-fired thermal plants to less settled regions north of Beijing, still results in pollution impacts on Beijing when the wind is blowing from the north.

Water pollution, particularly of rivers, is another major issue. Impacts are especially severe as these rivers flow through cities. Coastal water pollution occurs as these rivers empty into the ocean. The problem is exacerbated by the fact that China overall is short of fresh water, especially so in the north, where the Capital Region, Beijing, is located.[9] More expensive treatment costs of polluted surface water make it more expensive to supply Chinese homes and workplaces with safe potable water. Urban water pollution problems are exacerbated by the fact that river pollutants impacting cities are from point sources upstream, e.g., chemical plants, which are often located in different municipalities or even provinces, making remediation difficult because the upstream polluters are outside the jurisdictional control of the impacted city (Municipality). (Although there are national standards, these national standard vary by jurisdiction; furthermore, Municipalities with large wealthier cities tend to have higher standards than Municipalities (or their rural equivalent Prefectures) that lack sophisticated cities.) In addition upstream sourced human and agricultural waste worsens water pollution problems. Groundwater under and near most cities is being harvested beyond sustainable rates and groundwater supplies are often polluted, especially in metropolitan areas. For example, 44.1% of the groundwater under the North China Plain is polluted to various degrees.[10]

Energy inefficiency is a major threat to urban sustainability in China. The problem is both supply side (as noted, China is the most coal dependent nation on earth), but also demand side. Governments in China recognize the coal problem, and are taking action to reduce coal dependency, e.g., phasing out the burning of coal in Beijing. On the demand (consumption) side, there increasingly exists a significant commitment by national and local governments to improve the efficiency of industrial processes and to improve the energy efficiency of residential and (to a lessor extent) commercial buildings. Industries and firms are being required to meet higher energy efficiency standards, e.g., in the case of new industrial parks, known as Economic and Technological Development Zones. Residential buildings are subject, both through regulation and voluntary compliance to higher standards, to meet the energy efficiency standards of the China Green Building Council or LEEDS. The low energy efficiency of industry and of the residential stock has historical roots. In the case of industry, until recently, China's economy competed on large-scale low-cost production, which often led to overlooking inefficient energy consumption and other **Environmental Externalities**. In the case of the urban housing stock, construction was often of low quality during the 1960s and 1970s. Rapid urbanization, starting in the 1980s led governments and property developers to emphasize the quantity of housing rather than quality, including energy efficiency. In particular, much of China's residential building stock is not well insulated, which is especially wasteful of energy in cities with extreme climates, e.g., Harbin, with its very cold winters.

Although the foregoing environmental issues may sound alarming, and they are serious, from a futures perspective, there is considerable room for optimism. As noted, China is already the largest generator of solar and wind energy in the world, and capacity continues to grow very rapidly. Thirty-one nuclear reactors are under construction to reduce coal dependence; plus it is possible that China could exploit its shale resources to produce more less-polluting natural gas, as North America is doing. (A major constraint to shale gas production in China is that it is very water consumptive, and China is very short of water.)

Soil contamination is a problem nationwide, in both rural and urban areas. The problem has gained a high profile recently with the release of a major report on the problem.[11] In urban areas, soil pollution is a major issue, especially in former industrial areas, where heavy metals may be present. (Rural soil contamination tends to be related to fertilizer, pesticide use, etc.). Because urban land markets did not exist prior to the 1980s, factories often were located in the center of cities; although virtually all such factories have been dispersed to peri-urban areas, the high-value land left behind often has high levels of pollution. For example, the Shanghai 2010 World Expo site along the Huangpu River (the city's historic and contemporary axis) had to be cleaned up before the fantastic array of Expo pavilions were constructed; the site had been a major industrial site for close to a century. The Taopu Smart City to be constructed in north-west Shanghai represents a similar case. The area was known for heavy industry, particularly large petro-chemical complexes, so a major soil rehabilitation effort is underway, before the Smart City can be constructed (see Image 1).

Integrating urban transport and land use in smart efficient ways is key

Courtesy Douglas Webster

Land clearing underway in the Taopu area of north-West Shanghai. The formerly heavy industry area is being redeveloped into a "Smart City".

Environmental Externality - Environmental Externality refers to benefits or costs from an investment or activity that are not reflected in the pricing of a product. For example, a coal-fired thermal plant may damage the health of nearby residents causing them costs, but this externality is not reflected in the price of the electricity sold. Or, a new park in a city may increase the value of residential buildings surrounding it, but the beneficiaries (the home owners) do not have to pay for the benefit.

to urban sustainability. For example, in some global cities, transport generates over half of the Green House Gase emissions, but this can be reduced below 10% with skillful integrated transport / land use planning. In this realm of urban sustainability, sometimes referred to as **Smart Growth**, China is a world leader. The Ministry of Housing and Rural and Urban Construction's recommended **Population Density** for cities is 10,000 persons per square kilometer, much higher than in North American, or even Western European, urban densities. For example, the average density of US cities is 905 persons per square kilometer. The densest city, Los Angeles,[12] has a density of 2,702 persons per square kilometer.[13] Amazingly, even with rampant motorization, densities on the suburban periphery of major Chinese cities are remaining high, e.g., in the range of 7,000 persons per square kilometer in Beijing. Core city densities are even higher in most large Chinese cities, around 8,000-12,000 persons per square kilometer. High densities are extremely conducive to sustainable urbanization, enabling lower unit costs of infrastructure, higher building energy efficiency, reduced trip distances, and positively affect urban transport mode share (toward mass transit and walking). China is near completion of the world's most extensive High Speed Rail (HSR) system, learning from the dramatically positive outcomes in Western Europe, Japan, and South Korea, which will enable enormous energy savings in travel between cities and, new to the world, within **Megapolitan Regions**.[14] (Disappointingly, the United States has been very slow to adopt this transport mode, which is key to megapolitan and inter-urban sustainability, although an important exception is the expected start of construction of a California HSR system in late 2014 which will have 800 miles of track by 2029, connecting all leading urban centers of the State.[15]) China is also currently engaged in a major nation-wide mass transit subway initiative. Subway routes of 2,400 kilometers in 2013 will increase to an astounding 6,100 kilometers by 2020.[16] Already, Shanghai has surpassed cities such as Tokyo, Seoul, New York, and London to have the most extensive subway system in the world, creating a **Saturation Mass Transit** system. Beijing and Guangzhou are are not far behind, and second-tier cities such as Wuhan are building extensive mass rail transit systems. Since rail based transportation is extremely energy efficient (even more efficient than bicycling), China's cities have the opportunity to become the global pace-setters in terms of sustainable transportation.

Of course, all is not perfect in regard to the transport – land use interface in urban China. A major problem is that **Transit-Oriented Development** (TOD) is not as developed as it should be: (i) Population densities should be higher, (ii) Land / building use should be mixed, and (iii) Micro connectivity should be intense (moving sidewalks/ escalators, small vehicle feeders, lack of pedestrian obstacles) around mass transit stations. In terms of motorization, the major story is that despite China being the largest consumer and producer of private vehicles in the world, mass transit mode share remains surprisingly high in the leading cities, e.g., 40.9% in Beijing, 49% in Guangzhou, and 33% in Shanghai (2011 data). The shift to electric vehicles is slow in China, as in most of the world, however, the government has introduced policies to support use of electric cars, and BYD, a Chinese company is a global pioneer researching and producing electric cars.

A significant driver of urban land efficiency in China is the fact that a strict agricultural land protection quota has been put into effect. This policy indicates that China must retain at least 120 million hectares of agricultural land. The importance of this threshold is indicated by the fact that it is referred to as the "red line". However, this "red line" is being threatened by a variety of factors, including urbanization,

Smart Growth - Smart Growth refers to land use pattern characteristics, e.g., contiguity, higher densities, compactness; and land use – transportation integration, e.g., transit-oriented development, which minimize consumption of urban land, and contributes to less energy consumption, pollution and shorter travel times.

Population Density - Population Density refers to the number of people per unit of land. In the United States, this is usually measured as number of residents per square mile; in most of the world, the standard measurement is number of residents per square kilometer.

Megapolitan Regions - A Megapolitan Region consists of at least two metropolitan areas that are strongly inter-connected through transport, communications and economic systems, and has a population of at least 10 million people, such as the Pearl River Delta Region of China which contains three large metropolitan areas (Hong Kong, Guangzhou, Shenzhen), all of which are within one hour's travel time of each other using HSR; the Region has a total population of over 60 million people.

Saturation Mass Transit - When over 80% of residents of the built-up area of a city live within 600 meters of a rapid transit station, e.g., a subway station, this is known as Saturation Mass Transit.

Transit Oriented Development (TOD) - Transit Oriented Development is characterized by mixed land/building use, extreme connectivity (e.g., pedestrian overpasses, escalators, local feeder vehicles, and higher employment (workplace), and higher residential densities than the area norm, surrounding a rapid transit station. Normally, TOD developments are planned, and are frequently found where mass transit lines intersect or where stations serve an existing vital urban sub-center.

through extensive rural-urban land conversion, including on some arable lands. Thus future urbanization in China will need to be land efficient and be steered away from arable land – if the red line is not to be crossed. This policy to protect agricultural land is very important to China because arable land constitutes 12 percent of the country's area at most, considerably lower than the United States, where arable land 18 percent of the surface area, yet China's population is approximately four times that of the United States.[17]

Sectoral Hierarchical Institutions Set the Framework for Environmental Policy

In China, governance and policy implementation is hierarchical with principles and guidelines established at the national level, while implementation occurs, in descending order at the Provincial, Municipal, and District (Urban) and County (Peri-Urban and Rural) levels. At each of these levels, equivalent bureaus to national ministries usually exist, e.g., Development Reform Agencies (the equivalent of the national planning agency, the National Development and Reform Committee [NDRC]), and Environmental Protection Bureaus. From an urban sustainability perspective, the most important levels of government are the *National*, because of its authority and technical capabilities, and the *Municipal*, because Municipalities are large in size, over-bounding most metropolitan regions and smaller urban agglomerations, as well as headquarters of major economic engines/players and massive financial resources – both public and private.

However, this vertical governance hierarchy is not as simple as it may appear because the key ministries and their local counterparts operate independently from each other to a certain extent. In today's governance jargon, they are "silos". The key agencies in terms of urban environmental quality and sustainability, represented at most spatial levels are the Ministry of Environment Protection (MEP), established in 2008,[18] the National Development and Reform Commission (NDRC), and the Ministry of Housing and Urban/Rural Construction (MHUR), formerly the Ministry of Construction. Overall national development policy, including for the environment is set forth in the Five Year Development Plans; China is currently in its 12th national development plan period. The national plans are Strategic, rather than Command and Control (as was formerly the case) in orientation, reflecting China's change in the 1980s from a command and control to nationally guided market economy. In turn, sectoral or thematic agencies, such as the MHUR, set more detailed guidelines, policies, targets, etc., for their areas of responsibility. Within ministerial vertical lines of authority, local targets, plans, etc., are established at Provincial and Municipal Bureaus of the ministries in question.

Most directly involved in establishing urban environmental targets, policies, initiatives, and monitoring the foregoing, is the Ministry of Environmental Protection.

The Ministry of Housing and Urban / Rural Construction is responsible for the built environment, i.e., establishing standards for buildings, highways, and civil infrastructure, such as sewer and mass transit systems. (Through subsidiary companies at different spatial levels it is also indirectly involved in construction of the urban environment.) Although some of its guidelines are ambiguous, the MHUR has an important role to play in establishing energy efficiency standards for buildings and influencing transportation mode choice in cities, which can have a very significant impact on the environment. Under the MHURC, Urban Planning Bureaus are active players at the Municipal level (and other spatial levels, e.g., urban districts), e.g., for Shanghai; the Urban Planning Bureaus play an important role in pursuing land use efficiency (highly important in addressing energy efficiency and pollution concerns) with varying degrees of success across the country.

The National Development Framework for Urban Environment Quality

The National Development Reform Commission (NDRC) establishes overall strategic guidelines for the development of China in its Five Year National Development plans. The current 12th Five Year Plan includes, among its priorities, a framework emphasizing environmental quality improvement, with the urban environment as a key concern. The Plan showcases a more sustainable approach toward development, given the environmental stresses that have resulted from "fast and unguided economic growth" and "social tensions" (including public demonstrations) caused by environmental incidents.

The main thrust of the current national development framework is to recognize that different places in China require different responses, based on their resource endowments, economic development situation, and strategic positioning of each region. In the future, it is hoped that population and economic activity will be distributed in a more rational manner, e.g., agricultural land should be protected, while fragile eco-systems should not be the site of rampant urbanization. In practice, for example, this means different pollution emission caps and environmental standards for different parts of the country. For example, a high amenity city such as Hangzhou (discussed below) should have higher environmental standards, to be set locally above national minimum standards, than a heavy industry area, such as the string of cities along the Yangtze River in Anhui Province (The Wanjiang Region City Belt Industrial Transfer/Relocation Demonstration Zone which covers nine cities), which might have standards closer to national minimums. However, factories relocating to industrial re-

location areas in the Interior, such as the Wanjiang Belt would be subject to higher environmental standards than was the case of their old former factories on the coast (See Image 2.) Given China's enormous manufacturing economy located in peri-urban areas, the plan emphasizes the importance of production efficiency, energy savings, pollution reduction, and environmental protection.

Importantly, and new thinking in China, the Plan recognizes that some areas, e.g., eco-functional areas providing environmental services and/or valued for scenic value will

Recently relocated factories in Xuancheng in the Wanjiang Industrial Relocation Zone. In the moving process, factories upgrade their environmental performance.

not be judged by the GDP criteria that has been the pervasive measure of "progress" in China since the reforms of the 1980s. In such areas, other indicators will prevail, e.g., preservation of scenery; value of environmental services; and integrity of nature and culture, including preservation of historical buildings. This new initiative should be a major step forward. In the past, high amenity / tourist areas such as Hainan Island (China's major sub-tropical resort island) and western tourist cities, such as Dali in Yunnan, were blighted by concurrent industrial development (often heavy and polluting), which was designed to raise local GDP, but in the longer-run, actually did the opposite, undermining the amenity (tourism; Meetings, Incentive Travel, Conferences, Exhibtions [MICE]; amenity migration) economy, which had much more potential economic value than heavy industry.

China's **Urbanization Level**, currently at 54%, has been rising by about one percentage basis point per year. The Plan views continued relatively rapid urbanization as a positive (as do we), but advocates a steady urbanization rate, not a rapid acceleration of the current rate. Urbanization is to be focused on appropriate locales from an environmental point of view, and "comprehensive" infrastructure is to be put in place in anticipation of need, to absorb population growth, which is mainly the result of rural-urban migration to China's cities, rather than natural increase. Better planning and effective early infrastructure investment, e.g., subway systems, waste water systems, will increase the carrying capacity of cities as they grow. A national "New Urbanization Development Plan (2014-2020)", released in March 2014 further refined these concepts.

The current 12th Five Year Plan indicates that the guiding principles underlying sustainable urban development are that cities should be human-oriented, land and energy saving, safe for residents, and promote the unique features of individual places, especially by preserving each place's culture and natural legacy. The Plan advocates improvement in the quality of urban planning. At present most urban planning services are provided by Urban Design Institutes, which need to be more effective, locally oriented, and creative. In our opinion, China would benefit from the growth of a private urban planning sector, which could result in more localized planning, and higher quality designs resulting from more competition within the profession.

The 12th Five Year Plan importantly advocates that urban construction standards should be improved, e.g., in terms of energy efficiency, seismic (earthquake) resilience, etc. In general, new urban construction should be more carefully regulated, monitored, and standards enforced.

Similar to the case in Germany, and in some North American cities (e.g., Vancouver, Canada; and Portland, USA), the Plan advocates that **Growth Boundaries** should be designated and enforced around cities. **Smart Growth** policies are advocated in the Plan to increase land efficiency. Although China's cities are already dense, the plan calls for higher urban densities. (The Chinese normative urban density guideline, from the Ministry of Housing and Rural/Urban Construction] is 10,000 people per square kilometer.) Increased urban population densities would lower unit costs of infrastructure, enable saturation mass transit (primarily subways and LRT), and reduce rural-urban land conversion on the peripheries of Chinese cities.

Given the lack of arable land in China and the fact that the national agricultural land quota red line will soon be threatened, the Plan pays particular attention to the rural-urban fringe, i.e., peri-urban areas. Also, given that peri-urban areas are

Urbanization Level - The Urbanization Level refers to the percentage of people in a nation (or other geographic jurisdiction such as a continent, state or province) who live in urban settlements, i.e., cities and towns. This term is not to be confused with the Urbanization Rate, which is the percentage increase in the urban population of a nation (or other geographic jurisdiction) year-on-year.

Growth Boundaries - Growth Boundaries are designated boundaries around cities, restricting urban growth beyond the boundaries. They are usually enforced through zoning regulations and building codes. Similar, and sometimes utilized in conjunction with Growth Boundaries, but different in terms of implementation mode, are Service Boundaries. Service Boundaries restrict delivery of services, e.g., water and sewer supply, or garbage pickup beyond the Service Boundaries, but are not geared to land use per.

transitioning away from manufacturing dominated economies,[19] the Plan calls for re-development of these areas, reflecting their new functions.

The Plan indicates that planning should not just be two dimensional, but that the third dimension is important to cities. As virtually all of China's largest metropolitan areas achieve extensive, even saturation, rapid transit networks by 2020, the vertical dimension will become more important. For example, Transit Oriented Development involves complex, highly connected mixed use urban development below and above ground near transit stations.

The Plan advocates more urban public space, particularly green space. Urban villages (formerly collective rural villages enveloped by the growth of large cities) should be redeveloped. The urban construction investment and financing system shall be reformed, incorporating innovative financing approaches such as **Public-Private Partnerships** (PPP). Cities should become smart, i.e., digitized, to enable local e-governance, support economic development, and enable resource-saving city management, e.g., sensor based management of irrigation, traffic, and lighting.

Public Private Partnerships (PPP) - A Public Private Partnership is a mechanism whereby government (usually local government) and a private firm(s) co-operate to construct and/or operate a needed piece of catalytic infrastructure, e.g., a toll expressway or LRT line, or large-scale development, e.g., a new urban sub-center in a city. The co-operation may involve land (often from government), finance, technology, etc. For example, the redevelopment of the historic core of Foshan, China was a co-operative project of Shui On Land (a private corporation) and Foshan Municipality.

The Plan recognizes the close relationship between urban economic structures, including production processes, and local environmental quality. Accordingly, high energy-consumption economic sectors should be constrained in their growth. Economic instruments should be deployed to encourage firms to use energy more efficiently and reduce pollution, as well as caps on overall emissions of major polluters. To facilitate the effectiveness of these market mechanisms (economic instruments), energy saving technologies should be developed and their use encouraged. A cyclical economy based on recycling is promoted. In particular, given that China leads the world in industrial solid waste, construction waste and agricultural waste, initiatives to reuse as much of this waste as possible are advocated. Given that most manufacturing in China, and much of the R&D and scientific activity is located in Industrial Parks, known as Economic and Technology Development Zones (ETDZs) and Science Parks, these areas should be carefully planned, built and renovated (in the case of existing industrial zones) to support the cyclical economy, achieve intensive land use, generate energy through co-generation, promote waste water recycling, and centralized treatment of pollutants. The overall re-use rate of industrial solid waste should reach 72%.

The Plan promotes Green consumption and a green living style. Consumers are encouraged to buy energy and water saving products, energy saving and environmentally friendly automobiles (including alternatively powered vehicles, such as electric vehicles made by the Chinese BYD company), and energy and land saving housing. The use of disposable products should be reduced and over-packaging restricted. Treatment capacity for urban wastewater and solid waste should be improved so that the treatment rate will reach 85% and 80% respectively.

The Plan recognizes the importance of regional scale management of water and airsheds – a city itself cannot control these larger atmospheric and hydrological ecosystems. Accordingly, institutional mechanisms are proposed related to the planning and management of key **Watersheds**, **Airsheds**, and trans-boundary water systems. Environmental risks will be reduced by enhancing the monitoring and warning of risks related to natural hazards.

Watershed - According to the United States EPA, a Watershed is the area of land where all the water that is under it or drains off of it goes into the same place.

Airshed - An Airshed is part of the atmosphere that behaves in a coherent way with respect to the dispersion of emissions. As a geographical area within which the air frequently is confined or channeled, all parts of the area are thus subject to similar conditions of air pollution. Airsheds typically form an analytical or management unit.

The Plan advocates that resource pricing mechanisms should be reformed to improve energy and resource use efficiency, and to support a more equitable society. Resources, such as water, should be priced to reflect their real value (scarcity value), which may in itself eliminate certain low-end industries that essentially sell subsidized products because inputs are priced below market value. In support of more equitable outcomes, stepped pricing for basic human needs such as electricity and water should be introduced, meaning that the first units of consumption, needed to meet basic human needs, are priced lower than additional units consumed. Waste treatment fees should be increased, and up-front financial subsidies to build needed urban infrastructure, e.g., waste treatment facilities, should be increased. Environment taxes should be promoted, including those based on higher taxation of products, which are damaging to the environment.

Urban Environmental Policies of the Ministry of Housing & Rural and Urban Construction

As indicated, the MHRUC is responsible for overseeing planning and regulating the built form of Chinese cities. Like the national planning ministry's policies, described above, the MHRUC has become much more focused on urban sustainability issues. Accordingly the MHRUC has launched a series of theme-oriented 12th "Five-Year" Plans , that include: (i) a Green City and Lighting Plan, (ii) an Urban Disaster Prevention and Reduction Plan, and (iii) an Urban Building Energy Conservation Plan.

In addition, MHRUC has established guidelines to provide technical assistance to cities. In particular, guidelines have been prepared for sustainable planning of resource-oriented cities, e.g., coal mining cities, methods for low-carbon eco-city planning, and historical preservation.

Urban Environmental Policies of the Ministry of Environmental Protection

One of the most important functions of the Ministry of Environmental Protection is to establish enforceable environmental standards and targets for environmental protection. Figure 2 describes such targets in the current 12th Five Year Plan of the national of the Ministry of Environmental Protection.

The MEP proposes to implement Environmental Impact Assessment (EIA) processes (similar to those in the United States) in key cities for major projects, and to explore development of Urban-Rural Environmental Master Plans, which would focus on the dynamic peri-urban fringes of cities, and more far flung recreational and agricultural hinterlands of major cities.

Key 12th Plan policies of the MEP related to urban environmental improvement include:

1. An *"Eco-civilization" Development Index* shall be integrated into the evaluation system of local governments and their staff. A major constraint to achieving sustainable cities in China is that cities and their staff are now evaluated primarily on economic growth criteria. Environmental protection should be accorded more power in local governance, including veto power over projects that will do serious environmental damage. Furthermore, officials who fail to meet defined environmental targets will be denied promotion.

No.	Indicator	2010	2015	Total increase from 2010 to 2015
	Key Indicators for Environmental Protection in China's 12th FYP Period.			
1	Total emissions of Chemical Oxygen Demand (COD) (in 10,000 tons)	2551.7	2347.6	−8%
2	Total emissions of ammonia nitrogen (in 10,000 tons)	264.4	238.0	−10%
3	Total emissions of sulfur dioxide (in 10,000 tons)	2267.8	2086.4	−8%
4	Total emissions of nitrogen oxide (in 10,000 tons)	2273.6	2046.2	−10%
5	Proportion of state-controlled sections of surface water with quality below Grade V (%)	17.7	<15	−2.7 percentage points
	Proportion of state-controlled sections of the seven watersheds with quality above Grade III (%)	55	>60	5 percentage points
6	Proportion of county-level cities with air quality above Grade II (%)	72	≥80	8 percentage points

State Council of China [2011] No.42. 12th Five-Year Plan for National Environmental Protection, Box 1

FIGURE 2: Key Indicators for Environmental Protection in the 12th Five Year National Development Plan.

2. Enhance *environmental standards* and improve the effectiveness of the regulatory system, including enforcing regulations through an enhanced *environmental legal system.*

3. Improve the *technical quality of environmental economic policies*, addressing key issue areas, such as subsidies for electricity pricing, construction of waste water facilities. Develop "zero-discharge" policies. Relate environmental performance of firms to the banking system and credit access. A green rating system should be developed for use by banks and other financial institutions. Given that Chinese governments are multi-billion dollar consumers of products, promote government green procurement. Early steps in this direction are already underway, e.g., mandatory purchase of electric vehicles by some urban governments for certain functions, and government financial incentives to purchasers of hybrid and electric vehicles. Still, only five million of the over 260 million vehicles expected to be on China's roads by 2020 will be hybrid, electric, or fuel cell.[20]

4. Develop a major *environmental protection industry*. China already possesses a well-developed environmental protection industry in areas such as water treatment, wind and solar power, meter technology, etc. The objective is to grow this industry plus move into more technologically sophisticated areas such as "smart city" information technologies.

5. Improve *access to environmental information* and encourage *public participation*. Information on urban environmental quality, key pollution sources, drinking water quality, the environmental performance of enterprises, and nuclear power plant security should be freely available and well publicized. (This is a looming issue in that 31 nuclear reactors are now being built in China – 40% of the world's total.[21]) Enterprises discharging toxic and/or

harmful pollutants should be subject to compulsory disclosure. Clear complaint channels need to be established at all levels of government. Environmental prosecutions should be undertaken to resolve the most serious cases of environmental damage.

Locally Driven Sustainability Planning

Not all urban environmental initiatives are driven by top-down planning and administrative processes as described above. Cities, usually at the powerful Municipal level, are increasingly developing their own sustainability strategies that reflect local geography, financial resources, culture, preferences, and levels of motorization, etc. Usually these locally driven sustainability strategies contain targets that are stricter, i.e., more ambitious, than the targets and standards found in the national plans. They are usually branded, e.g., *Beautiful Hangzhou*, and implemented through changing public behavior, policies, plus investment in catalytic environmental projects.

Broad-based urban environmental / sustainability strategies are springing up in many Chinese cities across a wide variety of urbanization contexts. Contexts range from wealthy (first world in terms of economic development), high amenity cities such as Shanghai, Qingdao, Xiamen, Chengdu, and Hangzhou to cities that are known as some of the most polluted in the world, e.g., Taiyuan and Chongqing.

For example, in terms of broad-based environmental / sustainability strategies, Chongqing, a Municipality of 32 million people (urbanization level: 58% in 2014) in western China, known for its heavy industry and air pollution, in 2010 announced that it would

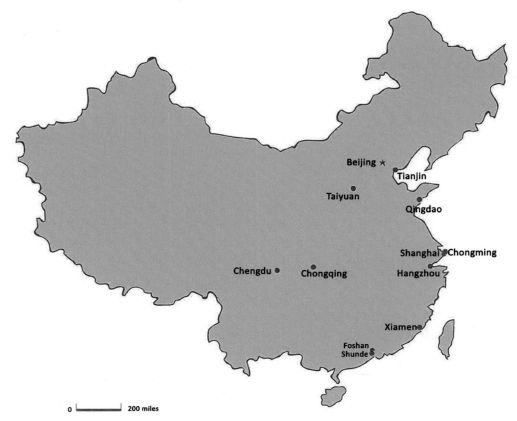

become a "National Environmental Protection Model City". The objectives of this strategy were to improve air quality, achieving over 300 days of blue sky annually; improve the water quality of the Yangtze, Jialing and Wujiang Rivers which flow through the Municipality to meet the Chinese Class II water quality standard;[22] to achieve 100% public access to safe potable water; to reduce urban ambient and road traffic noise to within 55 and 68 decibels respectively; and to engage in large-scale tree planting and ecological restoration.

The Chonqing Xintiandi Retail/Lifestyle Complex Along the Reforested Valley of the Jialing River: Part of Chongqing's Environmental Protection Model City Initiative.

Courtesy Douglas Webster

Tianyuan Municipality is infamous throughout China for its polluted environment. Home to approximately 30% of China's coal reserves, the industrial-based economy, polluted environment and lack of amenities have kept Taiyuan a third-tier city of approximately 4.25 million residents. However, in co-operation with the national government, the Municipality has declared its intentions to become Taiyuan "Eco Garden City". This new Taiyuan is envisioned as offering a high standard of living for residents, with international brands and high-class amenities, as well as branding Taiyuan as a cultural destination, similar to Xi'an (home of the terra cotta warriors), through the renovation, marketing and expansion of historic areas such as Jinci Temple. Upgrading the image of Taiyuan includes rebranding the metropolis as an environmentally robust city, anchored by the creation of a massive ecological preserve around Jinci Temple and protecting the water sources in the north that feed the Fen River.[23]

At the other end of the urban development spectrum, Xiamen, a high amenity city, has introduced a number of sustainability-oriented initiatives, which have focused on it being a "smart" city. Thus PM2.5 monitoring for the whole city proper was introduced in 2012, and a comprehensive air quality index was continuously available beginning in 2013. To improve performance against these, and other indicators, strong measures have been taken of late. For example, vehicles without Environmental Protection (EP) labels were banned from the city starting in 2012, 409 energy efficient public vehicles are being introduced, starting with 40 hybrid powered buses in 2011; and construction of its LRT system was accelerated. These actions follow up on a green strategy earlier in the century, for which Xiamen won the 2003 Nations in Bloom Award in 2003 and the UN Habitat Scroll of Honor Award in 2004.

In the early twenty-first century, China's preferred route to local sustainability was through the creation of model eco-cities, almost environmentally utopian in nature. (To a considerable extent this reflected the Chinese development policy of testing policies in a limited geographic areas, e.g., the establishment of the initial four "open special economic zones" in the early 1980s in South China to test market economy and opening up principles.) Unfortunately, these model eco-cities have a mixed record, at best.

Dongtan Eco City on Chongming Island (see Map 1), an island and urban district of Shanghai was one of these early attempts; its construction has been essentially halted, despite construction of a bridge and tunnel to the island in 2009. The city was to be carbon neutral, and communities were to be composed of attractive, highly livable mid-rises with care and attention being given to the landscape around their footprints, while still achieving relatively high density. The forecast population for 2050 was 500,000. The causes of the failure of the Dongtan Eco City are not completely clear, however, confusion over funding and a corruption scandal are normally cited as the reasons for the failure of this Eco City.

The Sino-Singapore Tianjin Eco City (see Map 1) near Tianjin Metropolis is another such "protected" environmental city. The Sino-Singapore Eco City is still being developed, it is too early to judge its success. Purposely built on a dumping ground for toxic waste along the coast, it is designed to house 350,000 inhabitants by 2020. If successful, the city will be low carbon, using a variety of alternative energy technologies including wind turbines (five installed), solar for lighting and ground source heat pumps for energy, which exploit differences in ground temperatures. Because it is a joint project between the Chinese and Singapore Governments, the Sino-Singapore Tianjin Eco City has a greater chance of success than other model eco cities in China. Nearby, the Yujiapu Financial Center, under construction, is intended to be a low carbon model central business district, as part of APEC's green growth initiative. Its future is also problematic, given strong challenges to its intended financial economic base for Lujiazui, Shanghai's financial center.

During the 11th and 12th Five Year Plans the focus has shifted to local sustainability initiatives focused on *existing* metropolitan areas, e.g., the Hangzhou case described below, or for initiatives, particularly Smart Cities (which perform well environmentally based on sensors, internet of things, etc.) within the *existing urban fabric*, e.g., Minhang District in Shanghai and Shunde District in Foshan. New Smart City initiatives continue to spring up, e.g., the proposal to create a Taopu Smart City in Putou Urban District of Shanghai. In our opinion, this movement away from model protected eco cities toward sustainability interventions in complex existing metropolitan environments is more realistic and likely to yield positive sustainability outcomes faster.

Beautiful Hangzhou

Hangzhou (see Map) home to beautiful West Lake, one of China's prime tourist attractions, is one of China's richest and most beautiful cities, known for its entrepreneurship, further along the urban development trajectory than less-developed cities in the interior and west China. With a population of approximately 8.8 million, it is not one of China's largest cities. Nevertheless, in 2011, it had the eighth highest GDP among Municipalities in China. By Chinese standards, densities are relatively low with the *city proper* area (essentially the built-up city) being 3,068 persons per square kilometer. (Nevertheless, Hangzhou's density is high by Western urban standards.) Hangzhou has a long history, being the largest city in the world during the thirteenth and fourteenth centuries during the Southern Song and Yuan Dynasties, the terminus of China's historical Grand Canal.

In 2013, Hangzhou launched its *Beautiful City* strategy. President Xi Jinping gave a speech about "beautiful China" when he visited Hangzhou earlier in the year, and he encouraged Hangzhou to base its development on a "beautiful city" model. Hangzhou's leadership took up the challenge, and developed a "Beautiful City"

Courtesy Zhang Feifei

River banks in Hangzhou have been restored, including wetland areas.

Courtesy Zhang Feifei

Organic wastewater treatment in Peri-Urban Hangzhou.

sustainability strategy. The importance of Hangzhou's focus on sustainability goes beyond the local; because it is one of China's most developed cities. Other cities in China can learn from Hangzhou's experience. Furthermore, it illustrates the principle that once wealth is achieved, the work of development is not over, the environmental quality, livability, and amenity of a city becomes a value and objective of equal developmental importance to GDP growth.

The Policy Research Department of Hangzhou Municipal Government together with the Hangzhou Environmental Protection Bureau, in consultation with two top national think tanks in sustainable development,[24] crafted the strategy. The team did a thorough study on the most pressing environmental issues affecting Hangzhou, establishing targets to be achieved. The research team reviewed global best practice in metropolitan scale sustainable development. To obtain local opinion, a questionnaire was administered to 1,200 people in Hangzhou, including locals, migrants, and tourists. Respondents were asked about their expectations in regard to the six dimensions (see below) of a, *Beautiful Hangzhou*, to identify the gap between current reality and expectations, then indicate what actions should be taken.

In terms of environment, among water, air, noise, solid waste and greening, 52.6% are not satisfied with the air quality; the most urgent things should be done are cleaning the air and improving drinking water quality.

The environmental standards in the *Beautiful Hangzhou* sustainability strategy are higher than equivalent national ones and higher that those of most other Chinese cities. Interestingly, indicators that are not included in the national plan, are included in the Hangzhou strategy, e.g., "swimmable and fishable water". This was to address a complaint heard in Hangzhou, and elsewhere in urban China, that "the official environmental indicators show improvement, but the environment feels (seems) worse". The premise of the *Beautiful Hangzhou* sustainability strategy is that Hangzhou needs to have a higher quality sustainable environment to outperform cities with whom it competes. Thus the strategy is based both on an intrinsic rationale (a higher amenity, healthier Hangzhou for people) and an economic one. Care was taken to include the needs of migrants in the strategy, to increase the plan's level of social inclusion.

A prime objective was to create a sustainability strategy that truly reflected Hangzhou's context, issues, and its population's preferences. A major problem in China is that urban sustainability strategies tend to be similar, produced in a "cookie cutter" fashion; Hangzhou wanted to avoid this outcome. "Cookie cutter" urban sustainability plans in China are often the result of lack of qualified local personnel to produce a plan for a city that is crafted from the reality on the ground upwards.

The Plan contains progressive targets to achieve the goal of "beautiful Hangzhou". By 2015, the spatial planning, strategic thrusts, and policies should be established, to enable Hangzhou to compete for the title of National Eco-City, awarded by the Ministry of Environmental Protection. Awards are a key motivator for Chinese cities to perform well, including in terms of environmental performance. By 2020, ecosystem restoration should be well underway, while real results in terms of the environmental quality of the metropolis should be evident. By 2030, the city hopes to achieve a natural-economic-social virtuous circle, the equivalent of sustainability.

Plan Content

There are *six dimensions* to the Hangzhou strategy. The key dimensions and indicators/targets associated with each dimension are as follows:

1. *A complete ecosystem*, protecting picturesque scenery of the mountains and rivers. The forestry cover (percentage of Municipal land area) is to be stabilized at 65%, 90% of existing wetlands are to be protected

2. *A healthy environment* with blue sky and clean soil. Objectives for drinking water source compliance rates with national standards (safe potable water) objectives are 100% for urban and 99% for rural areas within the Municipality. The ratio of city waters (lake, inner rivers, and the Grand Canal) achieving Grade IV water quality is to be 90%, and the days when air quality is above Grade II should be over 300 per year.[25]

3. *A green and low carbon industrial system.* Services will constitute 60% of the GDP, and the output of ten major targeted desired economic activities will account for more than 55% of the GDP. Related to this shift in the structure of the urban economy, carbon emission intensity will decrease by more than 50% compared to 2005, while emission intensity of major pollutants such as COD and SO_2 per 10 thousand GDP are to be under 1.5 kg and 1.0 kg respectively

4. *Pleasant habitat.* Buildings over 50 years old should be reviewed for historical protection before being torn down. The mode share of public transportation should be over 50%; the green community rate (number of neighborhoods) should reaches 50%;[26] 550 "beautiful villages" should exist; while 75% of the building stock should meet the green building standard of the MHURD;

5. *The education system will teach respect for nature*, the target is for at least 90% of Hangzhou's residents to be aware of key environmental concepts;

6. *Happy and harmonious quality life.* The average (mean) labor force educational attainment rate is to reach 13 years. The Gini Index of urban income distribution is to be under 0.3;[27] while the average life expectancy is expected to be 82; medical insurance should covers all municipal residents, both urban and rural residents; while the *green travel rate* (mode share of walking, cycling, mass transit) should be over 80%.

Implementation

Achieving the foregoing targets will not be easy. Implementable priority policies include the following:

1. *Low carbon city*. To restructure its economy, Hangzhou has identified economic clusters that will be strongly supported. As noted, environmental quality in any city is as much a product of the economic structure, as the regulatory environment. In the case of Hangzhou, the ten economic clusters that will be supported will include culture and creativity, tourism and recreation, financial services, e-commerce, information and software, advanced equipment manufacturing, the Internet of Things, bio-pharmaceutical, energy saving and environmental protection equipment, new energy. Low carbon buildings will be incentivized, including solar roof-top installations and green roof-tops.

2. *Two banks of Three Rivers Ecological Planning*. The length of river banks in Hangzhou is 436 km. Corridors 200 to 500 meters from the river banks will be protected, a total area of about 602 square kilometers. Underway are river bank ecological rehabilitation projects and beautification projects at some points along the river. A riverside scenic *slow green* pathway system (walking, biking; interpretative stations) will be developed to promote water front tourism and recreational industries.

3. *Public bicycle System*. Hangzhou has the most sophisticated public bicycle system in the country. To solve the "last 1 kilometer" problem of the public bus system, starting in 2008, Hangzhou built its public bicycle system. By the end of 2011, there were 2,200 rental points distributing 65,000 bicycles. Based on research by the Chinese Academy of Social Science, the Hangzhou public bicycle system saves 7,500 tons of gasoline and reduces CO_2 emission by 23,897 tons per year. Hangzhou was "one of the eight best public bicycle cities" in the world according to a BBC report in 2011. Interestingly, Hangzhou is the only city in China to sell carbon credits based on GHG reduction through bicycling. (China has already introduced pilot regional carbon trading markets, but will establish a national market in 2016.)[28]

4. *Trash sorting, Collecting, Clean Transporting and Recycling*. Citizens are encouraged to sort trash; newly designed transfer stations and direct transport of solid waste, virtually eliminate leakage. Kitchen waste is reused, through efficient composting.

5. *Wetland Organic Restoration*. Building densities in the Xixi Wetland have been lowered, to reduce environmental pressure. Now Xixi wetland, with an area of eleven square kilometers, is the first urban wetland park in China, and an attractive destination for high-end tourists.

To smoothly implement the plan, Hangzhou established a "building a beautiful Hangzhou" mechanism, which includes a committee that coordinates the main tasks, meshing the *Beautiful Hangzhou* plan with Hangzhou's economic and social development plan, annual budgeting, and the Master Land Use Plan. This committee also takes responsibility for integrating the plan with a number of industrial policies related to requirements for economic restructuring, public hearings, and consultant's expertise, etc. Based on the *Beautiful Hangzhou* plan, a three-year action plan and an annual implementation plan for each year are developed, and the detailed implementation instructions are assigned to a wide variety of government departments. Implementation results relative to targets are important in evaluating the performance of government departments and officials.

To access financing, the government encourages private enterprises and banks to invest in *Beautiful Hangzhou* development. An eco-compensation system is being established to compensate communities along the Qiantang and Tiaoxi Rivers for limiting their own development to protect downstream water quality and ecological integrity.

But the Beautiful Hangzhou Plan is not without critics. Is the Plan wasteful of land with its emphasis on greening, massive forest cover, and beautiful peri-urban villages? Is it naïve? Can urban governments in China, or anywhere in the world, really impact income distribution and the Gini coefficient? Would transformation to a much more energy-efficient post-industrial economy not occur through market forces, without the existence of a formal sustainability strategy?

The Foreseeable Future: Chinese Sustainability Initiatives

In China, there is a need for bottom up and top down approaches to urban sustainable to coalesce. Much of the sustainability expertise is in the national agencies in Beijing, where talent tends to concentrate, and where access to international expertise is more readily available. Wealthy municipalities such as Hangzhou, Shanghai, and Xiamen are developing customized sustainability strategies aligned with their problems and strategic competitive positioning. However, many of China's less developed cities tend to copy the environmental sustainability plans of other cities, domestic and international, because they lack expertise or ideas. (As talented university graduates in China increasingly settle in second and third tier cities, the talent pool in the urban environmental field is likely to improve in lower tier cities.) Often little research is done to determine the most effective mix of strategic thrusts and policies in local sustainability plans, nor is there enough prioritization, given the magnitude of the environmental issues that Chinese cities face. This needs to be corrected over time with local (Municipal Governments) more aggressive in customizing plans to local conditions, undertaking more research (evidence-based planning), and applying prioritization techniques constrained by human resource, financial, and other realities. Central agencies, such as the Environmental Protection Bureau, will need to continue to play a strong supporting role.

Amenity - Urban Amenity refers to the attractiveness of an urban area. Frequent attributes of cities used to measure amenity include climate, scenery, environmental quality, culture, urban design, leisure facilities, and cuisine. The level of Amenity of a place is of considerable concern to people and policy makers because Amenity affects the level and mix of migration, and the types and level of investment in a city.

Increasingly, Chinese cities will aspire to be smart cities,[29] and will incorporate these concepts into their plans, supported by declining costs associated with the Internet of Things, sensors and monitors, etc. This is a positive trend in that sensor based technologies can do much to save energy, water, and human time. –Xiamen is a leader in this regard.

A major trend starting to influence inter-urban migration and urban sustainability planning in China is the growing importance of **Amenity**, i.e., the availability and pull of attractive, stimulating, vital environments in which to live, work, and play.[30] As populations become wealthier and basic environmental needs such as clean water and air are met, the focus of sustainability strategies tends to move in the direction of meeting amenity objectives. This orientation can be seen in cities such as Singapore, San Francisco, and Stockholm. Hangzhou's emphasis on river corridors, slow bike paths, beautiful peri-urban villages, appealing wetlands, etc., reflects an awareness of amenity preferences among the city's increasingly well-off populace. For example, Kunming in the Himalayan foothills of south-west China is currently orienting its sustainability policies toward amenity, for example improving the water quality of Caohai Lake and making the lake accessible to tourists and local residents, see Image 6.

Image by douglas Webster

North Caohai Lake in Kunming, China's City of "Eternal Spring" is being cleaned up and the Lake Shore is being beautified and made accessible as part of Kunming's Amenity.

Urban environmental governance in China increasingly will change, but it is not clear exactly how. Chinese cities lack well-developed civil society in contrast with strong government and private sectors. Will civil society become populated by NGOs, etc., creating a third voice? Or will China's urban civil society be the discourse of social media – already very developed and dense in Chinese cities, more so than in Western cities. As noted in this chapter, government ministries in China associated with urban environmental planning are formally advocating more public participation in plan making, especially the Ministry of Housing and Rural/Urban Construction. As noted in the Hangzhou case, extensive surveying was undertaken. And the last two cycles of the national five-year developmental planning process have incorporated citizen feedback through the internet – officials were surprised by the high value citizens placed on green space during the eleventh plan preparation process. Currently, air pollution is at the top of citizens' urban environmental agenda, reflected both in official surveying and discourse on social media.

Another area of urban environmental governance that will likely change is finance, China's economy will grow slower over the next two decades (it is harder to grow fast as a country moves up the economic trajectory), probably growing in the range of 5–7% annually as opposed to the approximate 10% annual growth experienced over the last 35 years. This situation, positive in many respects, will require environmental project mix selection to be more evidence-based, there will be an increased need to find the most cost-effective path to meet targets. Secondly, there will be a need to tap innovative finance. This will need to go beyond local bond issuance and dependence on "few questions asked" borrowing from domestic banks, etc., which has created a national scale problem of local debt, present in most Chinese cities. There needs to be more emphasis on Public Private Partnerships, not only to tap the resources of China's capital rich private sector, but to benefit from private sector expertise. PPP approaches to city building, including in areas such as historical preservation, river front development, and knowledge zones is already underway, but needs to be vastly enhanced. PPP approaches to city building in China are advocated in the 12th National Development Plan, but quality PPP urban developments are still relatively small in number. There are vast sums of capital in China associated with insurance funds, pension holdings, etc. There are positive trends in this direction, e.g., the massive Ping'An insurance company is becoming involved in urban adaptive reuse historical preservation in cities such as Qingdao. However, there is still a tendency for Chinese local governments to cling to public sector dominated projects. Governments alone cannot create sustainable cities; they need substantial involvement of the private sector and the citizenry.

At present, Chinese bureaucrats, academics, and experts are debating urban environmental policy priorities for the 13th Five-Year Development Plan period. Based on citizen concerns, the leading issue is air quality – the urban populace is no longer willing to tolerate the smog that envelops many Chinese cities. Another high profile issue is water quality, particularly of rivers, many of which are black and odorous as they wind through metropolitan regions. The urban population has concerns over food and drinking water safety. Another concern of the urban citizenry is garbage dumps (not well-managed land fills) that are increasingly overflowing with uncovered waste; this is particularly a concern in peri-urban areas, where the problem is most rampant. In general, while past generations in China (from 1980 to the early twentieth century) valued economic growth and growth in household income above all, there is a profound shift occurring in the urban Chinese populace. "Growth at all costs" is no longer the dominant mantra.

At the more technocratic bureaucratic level, there is an increased concern with public health, and increasing research on links between public health and the status of urban environments, e.g., the O_3 issue. Efforts to control emissions (air and water) will continue to be a priority in the 13th Plan period, based on more realistic regional spatial scales. Increased monitoring of emissions and disclosure of information to the public is likely to be advocated. We concur with this public health emphasis – it should be the first order of business.

The 12th Plan period advocacy of new environmental governance and financing mechanisms, such as PPP is likely to be refined and continued. Within the urban environmental governance sphere, more emphasis will be placed on outcomes. Economic instruments are likely to be even more strongly advocated as a means to address environmental problems. Economic mechanisms are likely to go beyond conventional instruments such as polluter pays to embrace natural resource ownership and pricing, compensation for use of environmental resources or environmental damages caused, environmental and natural resource auditing, lifetime responsibility for environmental damage, etc.

Another area likely to receive attention is support to environmental protection industries. China's environmental challenges are a potential source of economic growth, so there is much room for growth of companies producing environmental products—both hardware and software - given the scale of China's urbanization and the magnitude of the challenge.

China's urban environmental initiatives will continue to be target oriented, and current targets will be adhered to, or even increased. Current targets are already ambitious. For example, the Air Pollution Prevention and Control Action Plan calls for the PM10 density to decrease by more than 10% by 2017 compared with that of 2012, and for the number of days with blue skies to increase each year across China's 333 Prefecture (Municipal) level cities. PM2.5 density in metropolitan regions such as Beijing-Tianjin-Hebei, the Yangtze River Delta, and the Pearl River Delta should be targeted to decrease by 25%, 20% and 15%, respectively.

Conclusions

China's cities, along with India's, have the most challenging urban environmental conditions on earth. In both cases the impact is multiplied by the very large, and increasing, urban populations involved.

On the positive side, much has been achieved. Soon most Chinese cities will have water supply and wastewater systems that cover their entire built up areas. This contrasts with some highly economically developed cities in East Asia, e.g., Bangkok, that still lack city-wide sewer systems. China's cities now lead the world in total subway tracks, Shanghai has more subway line than any city on earth. China has constructed the most extensive high speed rail system in the world. These intra and inter-urban rail systems make China potentially the most environmentally efficient people moving system in the world, if people can increasingly be induced away from private vehicles in cities and off highways and airplanes between cities. China has more installed solar and wind capacity than anywhere in the world; 28 nuclear reactors are under construction, the latter evoking concern among some elements in the population re safety issues.[31]

In sum, Chinese cities present a contradiction to those working to make them more sustainable. In some areas, such as mass transit and solar they lead the world. On the other hand, air pollution is deadly – literally.

In our opinion, China has correctly shifted its sustainability emphasis from protected experimental eco cities to a policy stance that focuses on existing metropolitan areas. Real cities are more realistic test beds.

Given the complexity and the size of the challenge, environmental governance and financing needs to be improved. As everywhere, there is need for more horizontal integration across government agencies. Especially important will be closer co-operation between the private sector and government – both to tap capital and expertise. More evidence-based cost-effective strategies to meet objectives and targets need to be formulated.

Last, but not least, Chinese urban sustainability stakeholders need to keep their eye on future trends – China's cities can completely remake themselves in ten to twenty years, as shown by China's urban track record in economic and physical development. Urban environmental sustainability will enjoy a significant tailwind thanks to an accelerating economic restructuring toward a high value service economy, with the factory of the world role becoming relatively less important. New challenges will likely involve amenity migration. In the United States, people moved from the industrial mid-west to the sun belt, creating a completely transformed urban geography that included boom cities and rust belts (the percentage of the US population living in the Sunbelt area increased from 32.2% in 1930 to 41.6% in 2010)[32]; China's citizenry will develop new urban sustainability preferences, increasingly centered on quality of life

Rural-Urban Transition - Rural-Urban Transition is the process by which a country moves from being primarily rural (e.g., an urbanization level of 20%) to being completely urbanized (usually an urbanization level between 75 and 85%). South Korea experienced the fastest rural-urban transition in history, moving from an urbanization level of approximately 20% to one of 80% in 40 years

and amenity as the current seemingly overwhelming challenges of air, water, and soil pollution are addressed successfully. This shift in preferences, in the Chinese context, could create overwhelming pressures on tourist and amenity migration locales, while at the same time create a greater gap between highly successful –luxury cities and poorly performing depressed cities, especially given the fact that the overall Chinese population will decrease between 2040 and 2050 according to official Chinese and UN forecasts, and the Chinese **Rural-Urban Transition** will be essentially over by the 2030s, with the population of most Chinese cities peaking by the 2030s, meaning that fixed sum game dynamics will apply to the Chinese urban system, when China will have an urbanization level of at least 70%.

Sustainability in Indian Country: A Case of Nation-Building Through the Development of Adaptive Capacity

Judith Dworkin

Introduction

A sustainable, resilient, and adaptable community is a worthwhile objective for all people. For Indian people and for Indian nations[2] located within the United States, these concepts are bound up in a 225-year history of inconsistent and often abject treatment of Indian people and their communities by the United States government. In the past, the concepts related to a sustainable and resilient community could be translated into the goal of mere survival as an identifiable Indian nation. Over this timespan, some Indian nations did not survive but most did. But, in order to survive, Indian people were forced to adapt: relinquishing significant portions of their ways of life and livelihood, cultures, languages and economies. Hence, during much of the history of the United States, the definition and meaning of a sustainable Indian community constituted the mere survival of people, government and culture.

During the last three decades, Indian nations have been engaged in transformative changes of their economic, governmental, social, and cultural capacities. Revitalizing Indian culture has recently become a critical component of a sustainable future and requires a definition of sustainability that is more expansive than mere survival, maintenance, or economic development. Studies performed on types of 'ethnic reorganization' indicate that cultural restoration and resurgence is helping tribes to re-engage with their culture.[3] Indian nations are more inclined now to practice their language and traditional culture in order to promote a sustainable community culture for the future. This strong sense of belonging and community may even result in positive health and economic effects. As Hill describes it, the "sense of belonging as connectedness occurs through the dynamics of relationships between everything in the creation/universe. It is a deep spiritual connection to family, community, nature, the Creator, land, environment, ancestors and traditional way of life."[4]

Today, Indian nations planning for a sustainable future are able to consider the multiple needs of their members which may include on-reservation employment opportunities, sufficient housing, a reliable transportation system, safe and adequate water supplies, appropriate wastewater systems, access to electricity, Internet access, higher education centers, and cultural expression. Balanced with planning for the economic needs of their communities, Indian nations are committing resources to **cultural activities and institutions** which may include restoration of language, reintroduction of ceremonies, protection of sacred places, cultural storytelling and education.

Cultural Activities and Institutions - Culture is the set of values and beliefs people have about the world works as well as the norms of behavior derived from that set of values. Cultural activities and institutions include language, religion, cuisine, social habits, music and arts. It also includes economic decisions such as investment in education and willingness to contribution to public goods.

Despite a palpable legacy of political and economic adversity, Indian nations and Indian people have outlived the tragedies of colonization and marginal existence. Today, Indian nations are actively engaged in **nation-building** to ensure sustainability.

Indian nations have begun to emerge from a subsistence mentality to rebuild their communities, restore their Indian identity, and build **resilient institutions** that strengthen economic, social and environmental capital to enhance needed governance. Some Indian nations are located in close proximity to large cities and have successful casinos; other Indian nations have abundant supplies of natural resources for development; some Indian nations have developed a significant tourist industry due to a unique resource or historic site; and yet other Indian nations are located in remote locations with limited opportunities. In each of these situations, the government of the Indian nation has the task of developing a sustainable and resilient economy that is reflective of the specific Indian culture at the same time adapting and insulating themselves from outside economic influences in order to build a stronger community.

This chapter uses a detailed case analysis of the Tohono O'odham Nation to demonstrate how one Indian nation has developed institutional capacity and promoted nation-building by responding to a culturally-driven cry to "bring our elders home." In order to set the stage for this case, the chapter provides the reader with (i) an overview of the special relationship between the United States government and Indian nations and the various federal Indian policies to which Indian nations have been subject during the past 225 years and (ii) certain statistics regarding American Indians and Indian nations. With the recent emergence and importance placed on developing resilient communities (See Chapter 6) as part of sustainability, this chapter explores the evolution of adaptive capacity building and its importance in enhancing resilience.

An Overview of Federal Indian Policy

Indian nations have a unique relationship with the United States within this country's system of federalism. Indian nations were sovereign powers at the time the Europeans "discovered" America. Each Indian nation consisted of a unique group of people with a distinct language and a distinct culture and religious structure. It controlled a specific geographical area and possessed governmental powers acknowledged by its people and enforced by governmental authority. These Indian nations negotiated treaties with other Indian nations and with foreign governments and after the break from European colonial powers, with the newly formed United States. While the earliest of treaties were negotiated as between two equal sovereigns, the United States government quickly came to fully embrace the Doctrine of Discovery by which title to newly discovered lands lay with the government whose subjects discovered new territory.[5] Under this doctrine, Indian nations that came in contact with these original colonists were "discovered." Sovereignty and discovery became fundamental features of federal Indian policy and are important, even today, in understanding the underlying factors and decisions of an Indian nation to create its own sustainable future.

These early expressions in treaties of the relationship between the United States and the Indian nations were further documented by Justice John Marshall, writing for the United States Supreme Court and referred to as the "Marshall Trilogy." Justice Marshall established three key principles regarding the sovereignty of Indian nations or tribes: (1) "tribes are "domestic, dependent nations," (2) tribes have the right of

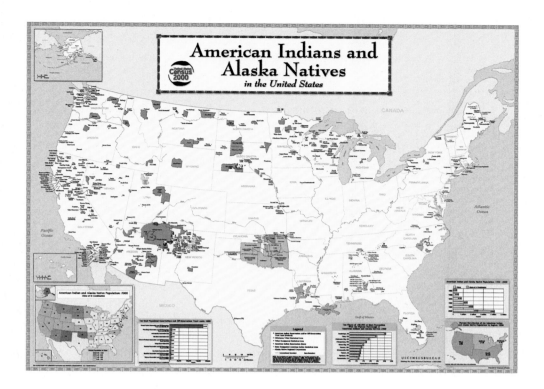

occupancy but not fee ownership in their lands, and (3) the rights of a tribe are always subject to diminishment by Congressional plenary power.[6] Based upon these concepts, the scope of **tribal sovereignty** has waxed and waned with changes in federal Indian policy over time.

Today there are 566 federally recognized Indian nations or tribes within the United States.[7] These Indian nations have survived a series of federal Indian policies that, at times, sought to eliminate their very existence.[8] Among the most notable federal Indian policies include the following:

- The Treaty Period (1789–1871). During the Treaty Period, the United States negotiated treaties with Indian nations in which the overriding goal of the United States entailed obtaining Indian lands and fixing the boundaries of the Indian nation in return for the delivery of goods and services by the United States. Common among these goods and services were livestock and farming tools and health and educational services. A fundamental principle developed during this period called for the United States to have a special trust responsibility to Indians.

- The Removal Period (1815–1846). The Removal Act of 1830 authorized the President to negotiate with selected tribes to induce them to move from their homelands in the southeastern portion of the United States to substitute reserves west of the Mississippi into Oklahoma, Kansas, and Nebraska. With the discovery of gold in California and the need to develop safe routes to western acquired lands, reservations were re-established and tribes were moved to even more remote locations or confined to smaller reservations.

Tribal Sovereignty - Tribal sovereignty refers to a tribe or Indian nation's right to govern itself, define its membership, manage its property, both real and personal, and regulate tribal business and domestic relations.

- The Allotment Period (1887–1934). The General Allotment Act of 1887, known as the Dawes Act, redistributed substantial landholdings to Indians as individuals allowing portions of the existing reservations to be sold off as "surplus" land to settlers. The concept to convert Indian allottees from traditional hunters to farmers was an abject failure. Allotments were small and often fractionated by familial descent. Additionally, Indian allottees had neither the farming experience nor the capital needed to buy the appropriate equipment and supplies; further, their limited allotments often failed to have access to necessary water supplies. Indian allottees frequently found it necessary to sell the land once it had been converted to fee. Over the next 50-year period, some ninety million tribal acres were acquired by non-Indian parties either directly as surplus land or indirectly through the acquisition of land from Indian allottees.

- Indian Reorganization (1928–1942). This period was marked by a shift away from assimilation policies and toward the recognition of Indian sovereignty. In 1934, the Indian Reorganization Act was passed by Congress and stopped any further allotment of lands, establishing restraints on alienation for trust lands, establishing mechanisms for the organization of tribal governments and tribally owned businesses, and recommitting the federal government to the strengthening of tribal sovereignty. Unfortunately, by this time, reservation life had "plunged into a downward spiral of poverty, disease and despondency."[9]

- Termination (1943–1961). A 1943 study entitled *Survey of Conditions Among the Indians of the United States* found that conditions on reservations were deplorable, that the Bureau of Indian Affairs bore responsibility for extreme mismanagement and that assimilation of Indian peoples should be expedited.[10] Termination of tribes became an express federal Indian policy in 1952 when the House of Representatives directed the Committee on Interior and Insular Affairs to conduct a full investigation into Bureau of Indian Affairs activities and to formulate legislative proposals "designed to promote the earliest practicable termination of all federal supervision and control over Indians."[11] The following year, on August 1, 1953, Congress adopted House Concurrent Resolution 108 which spurred legislation terminating 70 tribes and Indian bands. The termination legislation ended the special relationship between the United States and the Indian nations. Federal programs were discontinued so that education, health, welfare and housing assistance, as well as other social programs, were no longer available to Indians. The impact on the lands of the terminated Indian nations was dramatic. Most terminated tribes ultimately relinquished or lost their land. While the governments of the terminated Indian nations were not expressly extinguished, once the land base was lost, most were unable to exercise governmental power over their Indian members. Therefore, termination weakened the sovereignty of the terminated tribes.

- Relocation (1952–1972). After World War II, between 1952 and 1972, approximately 100,000 Indians were relocated to targeted urban cities such as Minneapolis, Denver, Chicago, San Francisco and Seattle. Senator

Arthur V. Watkins of Utah, chairman of the Senate Committee on Indian Affairs expressed the sentiments of Congress: "The sooner we can get the Indians into the cities, the sooner the government can get out of the Indian business."[12] Many of those Indians moved back to the reservations – only to find rampant poverty and unemployment there.

Notwithstanding the assault on tribal sovereignty by the loss of substantial portions of their land holdings, many tribes did manage to survive. After nearly 225 years of land dissipation; ethnocentric regulatory mauling; religious, educational, and the economic force-feeding and destabilization of tribal governments; most reservations and cultures still existed, albeit, with varying degrees of integrity.[13] Much communal land had been lost; chaotic land holding patterns had been created; poverty had become entrenched; and language, customs, and traditions had been lost. Yet, despite such profound losses and dislocations, the embers of these remarkably resilient tribal cultures still smoldered.[14]

In 1970, President Richard Nixon declared a new Indian policy of **Indian self-determination** and tribal sovereignty. Subsequent administrations have supported Nixon's government-to-government policy between the federal government and Indian tribes. President Barack Obama has similarly confirmed his administration's commitment "to strengthening and building on the Nation-to-Nation relationship between the United States and tribal nations."[15] It is within this current government-to-government Indian policy that we consider the ability of Indian nations to promote sustainable community practices and institutions.

Indian Self-determination - Indian self-determination was first used by the National Congress of American Indians in 1966 and refers to three interrelated concepts of tribal self-rule, cultural survival and economic development.

An Overview of Indian Demographics

Indians are some of the most disadvantaged people within the United States as compared to the United States population in general or the "Non-Hispanic White" population. These statistics are collected by the United States Census, as well as other federal agencies. According to the U.S. Census Bureau in 2011 there were approximately 5.1 million American Indians and Alaska Natives ("AI/AN),[16] representing 1.6 percent of the U.S. total population. Of that population, 22 percent lived in American Indian reservations, other trust lands, or Alaska Native Villages. Indian nations have a higher proportion of children than the general population: 30.0 percent of the population on reservations is under 17 years of age, compared to 24.6 percent nationwide. The median age of the AI/AN population is 31.3 years, which is younger than the median age of 37.3 for the U.S. population. Multigenerational homes are more common in Indian country. Over 56 percent of grandparents on reservations who live with their grandchildren are solely responsible for them, as compared to 41 percent nationwide who are solely responsible for their grandchildren. The median income of AI/AN households in 2011 was $35,192 as compared to $50,502 for the United States as a whole.

The Indian Health Service reports that American Indian/Alaska Natives are 2.2 times as likely to have diabetes as compared to non-Hispanic Whites. There was a 110 percent increase in diabetes from 1990-2009 in AI/AN youth aged 15-19 years.[17] The Center for Disease Control and Prevention collects and reports statistics regarding trends in health disparities and inequalities. AI/AN mothers had the second largest infant death rate compared with other mothers, 48 percent greater than the rate among white mothers.[18] In 2007, AI/AN population had the highest death rate due to motor vehicle injuries, a suicide rate among one of the largest, and the second highest death rate due to drugs (including illicit, prescription, and over the counter) compared with other racial/ethnic populations. In 2009, AI/AN adults were among those with the largest prevalence of binge drinking, one of the largest number of binge drinking episodes per individual, and the largest number of drinks consumed during binge drinking compared with other racial ethnic populations. In 2009, only adult (18 years and older) Hispanics in the same age group were less likely to have completed high school than AI/AN adults. In a 1990-91 study of 9,000 children aged 5-18 years living on or near an Indian reservation, found 39.3 percent of AI/AN to be overweight or obese.[19]

Unemployment rates on certain Indian reservations are the highest in the United States. In the aggregate, only 58 percent of individuals ages 15-64 living on reservations are employed, compared to 70 percent nationwide. In 2009, the percentage of AI/AN adults living in poverty was among the largest compared with other racial/ethnic populations (and was similar to African American and Hispanic percentages). Twelve percent more AI/AN adults lived below the federal poverty level, as compared to white adults. The three counties with the highest poverty rates in the United States are all located in South Dakota and all are wholly or predominantly comprised of Indian reservations: Ziebach County (Cheyenne River Indian Reservation and Standing Rock Indian Reservation) poverty rate is 50.1 percent, Todd County (Rosebud Indian Reservation) poverty rate is 49.1 percent, and Shannon County (Pine Ridge Indian Reservation) poverty rate is 47.3 percent.[20] Residents of Indian reservations utilize food stamps at approximately twice the national rate.

The cumulative effect of federal Indian policies has resulted in extreme poverty, isolation, and health problems unique to Indian Country. Despite the efforts to assimilate and destroy Indian culture and communities, Indian people have resisted and have undertaken efforts to reverse these statistics in order to provide long-term sustainability for their people. The development of community resilience is a cornerstone of these efforts and the basis for this case study.

A Sense of Identity

Notwithstanding this history of concerted efforts aimed at acquiring Indian lands and assimilating Indian peoples into the melting pot of America and the failed efforts of the Bureau of Indian Affairs to honor the federal government's trust responsibility, Indian nations have survived. The research literature informs us that survival comes through adaptability and resilience. Resiliency can be defined as the "capacity of a complex structured system such as a tribe to survive, grow, adjust, and thrive in the face of unforeseen change and catastrophic events"[21] It is also the ability of a system to adapt and cope with long, drawn out events such as climate change or economic restructuring that are not abrupt in nature, but require a community to adapt in order to survive and thrive. "Resilient systems expand and contract with variable cycles of growth, accumulation, crisis, and renewal."[22] "A resilient social system resists disorder and the unexpected by accepting and planning for episodic catastrophes, crisis and abundance."[23] Resilience theory teaches that a resilient community, such as an Indian nation, will embrace the reality of continuous, unpredictable future change, and look for ways to adapt in order to survive the irreversible changes that have already been made or that will occur.[24] Resilience is the capacity of a complex system (such as an Indian nation) to survive, grow, adjust, and thrive in the face of unforeseen change and catastrophic events, such as colonial contact, placement onto a reservation, or destruction of a community's land base.[25]

Some communities within the United States simply disappeared when people moved away, and once vibrant communities become ghost towns as communities did during the Dust Bowl era and after the Gold Rush.[26] In contrast, the survival of Indian nations is "inextricably tied to the sense of community"[27] which helps to build place-based social capital, a key aspect of resiliency. For the past century, and in some instances for time immemorial, that sense of place is most closely connected to land and the "reservations" which are Indian peoples' "homelands." For some, the Indian reservation may be all or a portion of their traditional homelands, for others it may be located far from the traditional homeland.

It is within these reservations that Indian sovereignty has been allowed to exist and thrive. "Native people traditionally perceive themselves as embedded in a web of dynamic and mutually-respectful relationships among all of the natural features and phenomena of their homelands."[28] Within the jurisdiction of the reservation, Indian people can govern themselves with their own laws utilizing their sovereign rights. Research indicates that many Indian nations perceive their environment as sacred and fundamentally important to their society.[29] Reservation boundaries can be a reminder that the reservation lands "typically represent a fraction of what previously constituted the custodial lands of pre-colonial indigenous populations."[30] At the same time, within the Reservation, members of an Indian nation understand that this creates a special sense of place and Indian identity as well as conferring intergenerational responsibilities.[31]

Research is affirming that "the knowledge, practices, values and languages of indigenous people are intimately linked to sustainable living."[32] Indigenous people "know a great deal about flora and fauna and they have their own classifications systems and versions of meteorology, physics, chemistry, earth science, astronomy, botany, pharmacology, psychology and the sacred. Sustainability concepts of preserving the environment and saving it for future generations are included and celebrated in their rituals and spirituality."[33] The study of ecosystems in relationship to community health has recently been applied to studies of Indigenous peoples. King and Hood note "Indigenous people have much to teach us about the connection among ecosystems and community health and about integrated ways for managing environments and people."[34] Additionally, researchers are working on indicators to determine the overall health of communities and its role within a Reservation ecosystem.[35] This is an important research direction for Indian nations, particularly as they work to create a broader vision of a sustainable future.

Revival of language is but one of a suite of critical components of any cultural restoration projects by Indian nations. "American Indian people are faced with daily reminders of loss: reservation living, encroachment of Europeans on their reservation lands, loss of language, loss and confusion regarding traditional religious practices, loss of traditional family systems, and loss of traditional healing practices."[36] The status of Indian languages is constantly changing. In general, Indian nations are becoming more aware of the need to restore and preserve their languages.[37] Many schools located on reservations are implementing language immersion programs into their curriculum. In addition, many schools, including head start and pre-school, have started to teach native languages to children at a young age to familiarize them with their traditional language.[38]

Establishing a sustainable future for tribal communities requires recognizing and enhancing traditional and customary principles with contemporary legal, economic, and political strategies. In recent years, many Indian nations have established legal and judicial systems under which community discord and commercial disputes are resolved and they have defined the parameters of their own programs and services.[39] For some Indian nations, Americans' apparent passion for gaming activities, the passage of the Indian Gaming Regulatory Act and the negotiation of gaming compacts between the Indian nations and the states have produced an economic engine not previously seen in Indian country. Gaming revenues have contributed positively toward mitigating the absence of tax revenues – as well as the overall lack of funds for basic infrastructure, including funding for roads, housing, public safety, sanitation, education, and health.[40] The implementation of gaming activities, however, cannot be the sole basis for a sustainable future. Indian nations control millions of acres of land throughout the United States that are rich in natural resources, including reserves of oil, gas, coal, timber, minerals, and renewable resources like wind and solar energy. Yet, resource development must incorporate cultural values and traditions and at the same time produce development and employment that is sustainable. Indian nations have historically been seen as conscientious land stewards, based on their deep respect for, and intimate relationship with, the environment.[41] As the former Chairman and President of the Navajo Nation, Peterson Zah explained: "on the reservation, land means everything. It touches religious beliefs and spiritual reality."[42]

Land use planning is key to developing a sustainable future—for economic development, housing, education, and healthcare. Indian legal principles stemming from the Doctrine of Discovery to allotment and assimilation impact the practical development of land by both an Indian nation and its members. Because most reservation land is held in trust by the federal government for the benefit of the Indian nation and individual Indians, land development is challenging. Tribal trust land generally may not be sold, taxed or encumbered without the approval of the Secretary of the Interior. Because the land is held in trust, tribal members and the Indian nation cannot use the land for collateral in order to obtain loans for development purposes, even to build much needed housing. In many instances, tribal members inherit fractionated land that was distributed during the allotment period resulting in numerous allottees with ownership interests in a parcel of land. Because the federal government disfavors partitioning of land for the benefit of tribal members, many tribal members are left without options to develop a homesite.[43]

The challenge for each Indian nation is determining the vision for its people. As the governing body, the Indian nation is charged with considering how to restore the health of its members, to provide opportunities within the reservation for employment, and to revitalize the customs and traditions of the Indian nation in accordance with community values. Nation-building and creating a sustainable future can take many forms. In some instances, the Indian nation has successfully established a comprehensive community planning effort. The Spokane Tribe of Indians and the Navajo Nation are two recent examples.[44] In other instances, the Indian nation has focused attention on specific economic development activities. The following is a case study of the Tohono O'odham Nation and the institutional capacity building which began with the Nation's response to a need driven by the O'odham people's cultural values to "bring their elders home." However, what this case actually demonstrates is that the expression of a cultural need led to the building of institutional capacity and resiliency through newly developed governance structures.

The Case of the Tohono O'odham Nation: Capacity Building

The Background

The Tohono O'odham Nation is located in the Sonoran Desert of southern Arizona along the United States-Mexican border. It is the second largest reservation in Arizona in both population and geographical size. Comprised of three non-contiguous reservations and additional parcels of land, the Tohono O'odham Nation controls a land base of 2.8 million acres or 4,460 square miles of land. Its boundaries begin south of Casa Grande and continue south for about 90 miles to the United States-Mexico International border. The southern boundary of the Nation runs for 75 miles against the United States – Mexico International border. The closest urban populations are Tucson (population: 520,116), Casa Grande (population: 49,591), and Gila Bend (population: 1,922).

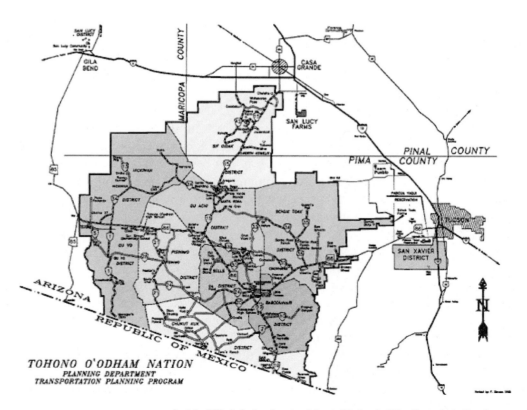

TOHONO O'ODHAM NATION
PLANNING DEPARTMENT
TRANSPORTATION PLANNING PROGRAM

The Tohono O'odham members have inhabited portions of the Sonoran Desert for thousands of years. The Spanish established the San Xavier mission in the seventeenth century to minister to the O'odham Indians and convert them to the Roman Catholic religion. Many indigenous traditions remained, adapted into a unique form of "Sonoran Catholicism."[45] Over time, the O'odham language and culture adapted and survived. The Tohono O'odham Community Action organization ("TOCA") describes the Tribe's culture and language as "Endangered but Intact."[46]

In 1853, the Gadsden Purchase by the United States split the O'odham people between the United States and Mexico. In the twentieth century, federal Indian policies brought greater mobility to O'odham people, some voluntary and others forced, including programs involving boarding schools, migrant labor, and World War II. After World War II, numerous O'odham families were moved to cities like Oakland, California and Chicago, Illinois.[47]

The rural nature of the Tohono O'odham lands is further seen in the number of people per square mile as compared to the county in which the majority of the lands are located (Pima County) and the State of Arizona. The population density of the Tohono O'odham Reservation is only 2 persons per square mile, as compared to the population density of Pima County with 107 persons per square mile, and Arizona with 56 persons per square mile.

The Tohono O'odham Nation is divided into 12 political districts and 83 villages. Nine of these districts are located on the Sells Tohono O'odham Reservation (established in 1917 by Executive Order and expanded in 1931 by Congressional Act). The community of Sells, centrally located within the Sells Reservation, is the seat of the central government. The remaining districts are the San Xavier District (established by Executive Order in 1874), which covers the entirety of the San Xavier Reservation; the San Lucy District, located on the Gila Bend Indian Reservation (established by Executive Order in 1882, modified by Executive Order in 1909); and the Hia-Ced District created in 2012 and located on a parcel of land near Why, Arizona and placed in trust in February 2009. The Sells, San Xavier, Gila Bend Reservations and other parcels of land held by the Nation are referred to as the "Reservation."

According to the 2010 U.S. Census, roughly 22,000 of the 30,000 enrolled tribal members live on the Reservation. More than 3,300 of the enrolled members are 55 years of age or older, 1,800 of whom reside on the Reservation. Multigenerational families are common. Thus, children on the Tohono O'odham reservation are 15 times more likely to live with grandparents as compared to urban Arizona communities.

Health is a major concern on the Reservation. The Tohono O'odham Community Action organization reports that until the 1960's, no tribal member had ever suffered from type-2 (adult onset) diabetes. Today, more than 50 percent of all Tohono O'odham adults have the disease, which is reported to be the highest rate in the world. Beginning in the 1990's childhood-age onset began to rise. The percentage of diabetics is expected to exceed 75 percent for O'odham children born after 2002. It is closely correlated with childhood obesity. According to the Arizona Bureau of Public Health Services, the death rate due to type-2 diabetes among Arizona's native population is three times that of the state average.

Tohono O'odham life expectancy is more than six years less than the U.S. average, according to a 2010 study published in *The New England Journal of Medicine*, which analyzed the longitudinal health data of 4,857 Pima and Tohono O'odham children born between 1945 and 1984. (The Indian Health Service had records of 40 years of children's vital signs.) The average age of the children was 11 years old when they were first examined for glucose levels, BMI, blood pressure, and cholesterol information. Decades later, researchers traced health records of the 4,857 individuals to see how long they actually lived. The researchers documented high rates of premature death, with life expectancies cut to only 55 years of age. The adults who, as children, had been measured at the highest body mass indices (BMI) were 2.3 times more likely to die prematurely. Those with the highest glucose levels were 73 percent more likely.[48]

The self-reported health status among the Tohono O'odham elders shows that 57 percent of O'odham elders rated their health as fair or poor as compared to only 27 percent of non-Native American elders. And, those who rated themselves as "fair" or "poor" tended to have one or more illnesses or conditions considered as predictors for future medical intervention and skilled healthcare. These include diabetes (61.9 percent reported) and obesity (47 percent reported).

The health of O'odham members is further complicated by disadvantaged living conditions. Many of the villages scattered throughout the Nation lack paved roads, making travel difficult. Housing is limited and often not built according to accepted building codes. According to the Indian Health Service Division of Sanitation, hundreds of homes on the Nation still lack indoor plumbing and telephone service, which means that often the poorest elders live in homes without adequate plumbing, heating, and cooling.

Health care services on the Tohono O'odham Reservation are quite limited. There are limited acute care services available at the Sells Area Indian Health Service Hospital, but O'odham members did not have access to reservation-based hospital care, post-hospital care, or long-term care services. This situation has been particularly problematic for O'odham elders. Elders admitted to the Sells Area Indian Health Service Hospital for acute care and subsequently requiring long term skilled nursing care would be discharged to a nursing home facility located in the Tucson, Arizona area (most of which are located more than one and one-half hours away from the majority of O'odham families). In some cases, the ailing elder went directly to a Tucson hospital for his or her initial care and then would be discharged for post-hospital recovery to a Tucson nursing home. The end result, in either case, left O'odham elders isolated in nursing homes located in Tucson, far away from their families. Many elders do not speak English which further complicated their off-Reservation care. The facility caregivers could not speak to these residents in the O'odham language and O'odham residents were not offered traditional foods to eat, could not easily seek the assistance of "medicine people," and were not able to spend their remaining days in the desert environment to which they were accustomed. While statistics are not readily available, it is not hard to conclude that placing an ill and frail O'odham elder in a foreign and often time isolated facility hastens both further debilitation and death.

The O'odham people asked their government to "bring their elders home." In 1978, the Tohono O'odham Nation responded to the demands of its members and funded the development of a master plan to build a "nursing home" within the boundaries of the Nation, which would bring the elders back home. Unfortunately, the cost of constructing and operating a skilled nursing facility was not feasible in 1978. But the voices in support of this goal continued for the next 15 years, with those most passionate about the goal forming an advisory committee, which became recognized by the government as the "Tohono O'odham Nation Nursing Home Advisory Committee."

Institutional Capacity Building and Cultural Sustainability

The 1970's brought a new era of self-determination on the part of Indian nations and a new federal Indian policy that addressed Indian nations on a government-to-government relationship. It was, however, the enactment of the Indian Gaming Regulatory Act in 1988, which enabled the Tohono O'odham Nation to amass substantial revenues supplementing the historic revenues of the Tohono O'odham Nation's government. The first casino, located in the metropolitan Tucson area, opened in 1993, followed by two additional casinos that opened in 1999 and 2003. In 1993, due in part to the financial success of the casinos, the Nation allocated funding to commence the process of building a skilled nursing facility on the Reservation.

An important aspect in regard to the adaptive aspects of resiliency is the notion of economic resiliency which refers to a diversified economic base and the reinvestment of funds back into the community. While many Indian nations heavily rely on a casino-based economy with the Tohono O'odham Nation being no different, Indian nations are also taking the economic gains that come from the casinos and investing them back into their communities. Keeping money and reinvesting that money back in the community is a cornerstone of resiliency. It not only strengthens a community's economic base, it also helps to strengthen the community as a whole by buffering it from outside shocks and strengthens it from within. The Tohono O'odham Nursing Care Authority is an important example of this process in action.

In December 1998, the Tohono O'odham Nation established the Tohono O'odham Nursing Care Authority ("TONCA") as a tribal enterprise of the Nation. The Nation could have operated the skilled nursing facility through its Department of Health and Human Services but the formation of TONCA was an enlightened decision that expanded the institutional capacity of the Nation and promoted nation-building.

TONCA's Charter demonstrates the dual objectives of the Nation in building a skilled nursing facility: operating the facility (i) as a modern twentieth century facility meeting all of the national licensing requirements and (ii) in compliance with the Nation's culture referred to as ***O'odham Himdag*** (the Tohono O'odham way of life). The Guiding Principle of TONCA as established in the Charter is defined as "All people deserve to live and die in dignity. Life, death, and dignity are uniquely defined by one's own culture." The study of *O'odham Himdag*, which refers to "a way of life inclusive of terms such as culture, heritage, history, values, traditions, customs, beliefs and language" is an integral part of the O'odham lifestyle.[49] Each person is expected to live their life in reverence of the *Himdag*. The *Himdag* promotes cultural sustainability in all aspects of life including tribal government departments even in indirect ways, including "fostering strength and wellness in their community by translating increased economic self-sufficiency and resources derived from gaming into social, health, and educational services which maintain their tribal traditions, thereby providing and effective path toward the maintenance of cultural identity, or *O'odham Himdag*."[50] This example is consistent with the general acknowledgement that for Indian nations, sustainability cannot be addressed without a consideration of culture.[51] *O'odham Himdag* has been a tool of resiliency for the Tohono O'odham people.

TONCA was envisioned as a mission-driven institution that, on behalf of the Nation, would have the ability and adaptability required to successfully develop and

O'odham Himdag -
O'odham Himdag is roughly translated as the Desert People's lifeway or way of life. It refers to the traditional cultural skills and knowledge of the O'odham people.

operate the skilled nursing facility <u>and</u> advocate for other needed health care programs on the Reservation. The Preamble to the Charter establishes the breadth of the responsibilities delegated to the TONCA Board.[52] "Health is more than the absence of disease. It is a complete combination of intellectual, physical, psychological, social, and spiritual states which form the condition of wellness."[53] This was the foundation for sustainable well-being with broad-based responsibility for this newly-formed organization—TONCA. In satisfying its dual objectives, TONCA recognized that elder care should be of the highest quality but also be provided in a language the residents understand and in harmony with the cultural values and customs of *O'odham Himdag*. The skilled nursing facility is located in the Sonoran desert and offers residents traditional foods, some purchased from a cooperative farm located on the reservation. Medicine people visit residents and also bless the facility. Young people have the opportunity to learn traditional stories and improve their O'odham language skills from the elder residents. The facility respects residents' desires to die with family around them in accordance with O'odham tradition. TONCA encourages non-O'odham employees to learn rudimentary O'odham language.

The Nation's lawmakers intended for TONCA to operate independent of the Nation's government but not to be independent of the Nation's government. The Charter clearly provides that TONCA control its own budget; have the authority to open bank accounts, hire professionals including legal counsel, invest funds, establish a capital improvement fund, develop an annual budget, form subsidiary organizations and otherwise operate without requiring consent of the government. Importantly, however, TONCA requires and benefits from an annual subsidy from the Nation. This ongoing duality of independence and dependence encourages the maintenance of close, positive relationships among TONCA and the Nation's members, the governing bodies of the 12 districts, the Executive Branch of the Nation's government, and the Legislative Council. These productive relationships have enhanced TONCA's ability to meet its long and short-term objectives. The financial dependence encourages transparency and regular communications. Further, this independent control encourages resiliency through adaptability and institutional connections.

In establishing TONCA, the Nation created a long-term mission aimed to improve the health care services that are available to O'odham members on the Tohono O'odham Nation. For many Indian nations, the years of abject poverty and the change away from traditional foods have led to some of the worst health statistics in the overall United States population. "The extent to which sustainable development benefits a community is closely tied to its level of health, as health is a product of economic social, political and environmental factors, as well as of health services."[54] Improvements in health and health services contribute to sustainable development. Effective health services must be accessible and offer good quality care, which requires good organization, sufficient resources, and a capacity for strategic support and effective mobilization of personal action and technological development to improve health.[55] "Poverty leads to ill-health, but possibly ultimately more debilitating is the negative impact of poor health on development."[56] In contrast, good health enhances development and results in higher productivity among healthier workers and higher rates of savings and investment.[57] In summary, effective health services are those services that are accessible and offer good quality care, requiring the right focus on health needs, and "equitable distribution, good organization and sufficient resources (human, physical and supplies)."[58]

Recognizing that healthcare is more than just skilled nursing, the Nation charged TONCA with assuming "a leadership role in providing a continuum of care and services designed to enhance the physical, spiritual, emotional, social and intellectual qualities of life for aging O'odham and other members of the Nation."[59] As such, TONCA seeks to ensure that services are provided without duplication, fragmentation, or gaps—a seamless system integrating health with nation-building.

There are substantial barriers to improving the health of O'odham members. These barriers include:

- *Lack of Financial Resources.* Half of O'odham elders live below the poverty line.

- *Far Distances to Healthcare.* Primary health care services are centralized requiring patients to spend inordinate amounts of time traveling to receive treatment. Distances lead to postponement of preventive and primary care, resulting in treatable and chronic illnesses being first diagnosed at a later stage as compared to non-Natives, thus increasing the needs and costs of invasive treatments, as well as less satisfactory outcomes.

- *Limited and Undependable Transportation.* The Tohono O'odham Nation does not have a public transportation system and many families do not have a personal vehicle.

- *Lack of Readily Available In-home, Locally Based Services.* Elders need help with basic activities of daily living, which is particularly true for the 16% of elders who live alone.

- *Language Barriers.* Language is still a barrier to healthcare for the many O'odham elders for whom the O'odham language is still the primary language spoken. The prevalent use of the native language requires healthcare workers who can either understand the language or can have an interpreter assist with communication, either of which is often unavailable.

- *Limited Understanding of Traditional Medicine by Healthcare Team.* Many non-Indian healthcare workers, doctors, and administrators often misunderstand the use and benefit of traditional medicine. Seventy percent of O'odham elders desire to include traditional medicine as a component of their compliment of healthcare resources.

- *Treatment Instead of Prevention.* Treatment of healthcare conditions continues to have priority over prevention and early intervention, resulting in health care needs that progress unchecked until the related treatment is acute and costly, and the condition becomes debilitating.

- *Poor communication and Coordination.* Poor communication and coordination of services lead to the fragmentation of healthcare services. In such an environment, the quality of care is compromised.

- *Supportive Housing Options.* The housing stock on the Reservation is insufficient and lacks the quality necessary to support the needs of elders. There is a clear need for a robust program of home repair and home rehabilitation including the modification of homes to meet accessibility standards for changing needs of aging elder residents. The need for long-term care services and supportive housing facilities continues to rise, resulting in a demand that surpasses the supply of such services and facilities on the Reservation. The ultimate result is that O'odham members who require this type of help cannot be guaranteed the access to on-Reservation options. Additional forms of housing include group homes; independent living where meals, housekeeping, and maintenance are provided; and assisted living that can extend the independent living services to include modest health related services.

TONCA seeks to address these barriers as it expands its leadership role in its continuum of care mission.

Growing Institutional Capacity and Adaptability

When the Nation formed TONCA, it had a single specific objective: open and operate a skilled nursing facility. Its long term mission would need to rely on the developing capabilities of the institution. In 1998, it would have been difficult to predict the significant success of the organization 16 years later.

<u>The Skilled Nursing Facility</u>

In November 2002, the Archie Hendricks, Sr. Skilled Nursing Facility opened to its first four residents. Since 2002, it has operated at or near the 60 bed capacity providing short and long-term care to O'odham members. The majority of the admissions to the facility come from hospitals in Tucson, Casa Grande, and Sells. As of Spring 2014, 586 O'odham members had been admitted and discharged from the facility.

TONCA faced many challenges including staffing, physical infrastructure, and training needs. Senior professional staff including a licensed administrator, Director of Nursing, and a Business Office Manager had to be recruited from outside of the Nation, as there were no O'odham members with the appropriate qualifications who were seeking employment. The lack of employee housing inhibited recruiting efforts. The closest housing for employees was either 45 minutes away in Casa Grande or 90 minutes away in Tucson. Additionally, the Skilled Nursing Facility's building had some construction defects. And, finally, some of the O'odham members who were hired in managerial positions were in need of mentorship to be able to meet the challenges of their positions.

TONCA was able to overcome these challenges. First, it began operations with non-O'odham members in key positions with the understanding that over time it would replace those individuals with O'odham members. Employee housing was constructed in order to facilitate the task of hiring and retaining both O'odham and non-O'odham staff. Building defects that resulted from the initial construction were corrected. TONCA started a mentorship program to help facilitate the management training needs of its O'odham employees. This series of initial challenges and practical solutions reflect what would become a defining resiliency characteristic of TONCA: its ability to be vigilant for current or future problems and the adaptability in changing previous plans in order to overcome or prevent such issues.

Staying Relevant, Having the Capacity to be Adaptive, and Being Responsive

In establishing TONCA with the mission "to take a leadership role" its founding board offered broad flexibility to the institution to stay relevant and be adaptive while staying true to its core value to provide services in accordance with O'odham culture and customs. Organizations that focus on the healthcare necessities of a community encounter needs that change as the health dynamics of a community evolve over time. Such organizations must be alert to these trends so that their services can be ready to meet such needs when they arise. This is one of several respects in which TONCA may be viewed as a proactive organization.

In order to ensure that the provision of services continues to meet the needs of the Nation's members and to determine if new services need to be included, the Board methodically revisits the provision of services by TONCA and other service providers on the Reservation. The Board projects the healthcare needs of the Nation's members and evaluates the need for future endeavors. The Board sets relevant goals for its programs, acquires data that relates to the goals and programs, evaluates the data in light of the issue being addressed, and reaches a strategic plan of action. And, after the implementation of a course of action, the Board evaluates whether the results were consistent with the expected outcomes and modifies its course of action when necessary. These intensive levels of attentiveness, feedback and flexibility ensure that its programs remain relevant to the O'odham community; further, it insures that TONCA is an institution that supports a sustainable future for the Tohono O'odham Nation. TONCA's focus is expanding healthcare services and improving O'odham health; the bi-product of its efforts is the growth of institutional capacity and the outcome is nation-building.

Over the course of its 16 year existence, TONCA has seen the population demographics change and the healthcare needs shift on the Reservation and it has established and collaborated with other institutions in a number of programs in response to the changing demographics and shifting needs. Such programs include hospice services, assisted living, and pre-hospice services. TONCA was a founding member of a consortium of healthcare providers that serves the Nation's population. Today, TONCA is reaching out to other Indian nations to establish an organization that can advocate for needed resources in the U.S. Congress. Each of these additional services enhances the knowledge base and experience of TONCA, provides additional health services so necessary to members of the Tohono O'odham Nation, and contributes to the sustainable development of the Nation.

Hospice Services: Shortly after the Skilled Nursing Facility opened its doors, TONCA became aware of the lack of reliable hospice services on the Reservation. In 2007, the Board expanded TONCA's services to provide hospice care, making its first hospice admission on November 16, 2007. The Tohono O'odham Hospice brings together a team of traditional healers, doctors, nurses, social workers, chaplains, and volunteers to meet the physical, emotional, and spiritual needs of those at the end of life and their families. Hospice patients, and by extension family members, receive services either in their own homes or at the Skilled Nursing Facility, which allows the patient to complete his or her life in the presence of family and community and in accordance with O'odham traditions.

Desert Pathways: With a small grant from the Robert Wood Johnson Foundation, TONCA began "Desert Pathways," to help O'odham members and their families address the challenges of facing a serious illness. In the 2013 fiscal year, Desert Pathways staff made 336 visits to 65 members of the Nation and their families. Grant funds have been exhausted and there is no obvious source of funding at the same time as the need for these services continues to increase with the growing number of O'odham members with long-term conditions, such as diabetes and obesity.

Assisted Living Facility: By 2008, TONCA recognized that many of the residents of the Skilled Nursing Facility no longer needed skilled nursing care but were unable to be discharged from the facility because they could not live independently, and there were no options for them on the Reservation. Assisted living costs less than half of the average daily cost of a skilled nursing facility to operate. A new master plan was developed for TONCA's 30-acre site that provided for 4 assisted living buildings of 10-12 residents each. After several years of unsuccessfully seeking to obtain funding to construct the first building, in July 2011, the TONCA Board resolved to commit monies from its Board directed fund to construct a single ten-resident assisted living facility. In February 2013, the Assisted Living Facility opened with 4 residents and, by the end of 2013, 10 O'odham members were living in this residence. Some of these residents transferred from the Skilled Nursing Facility and others came from the O'odham community.

The Elder Care Consortium and a Health Care Network: As an advocate for enhancing the quality of life for O'odham elders, TONCA set out to identify the full spectrum of needed services, identify gaps in service, and advocate for filling the gaps by coordinating with other service providers to create a shared plan for the O'odham Nation. In order to accomplish its mission, it required the collaboration of other service providers. TONCA became a founding member of the Tohono O'odham Elder Care Consortium (the "ECC"), which also included the Tohono O'odham Nation's Department of Health and Human Services ("HHS"), the Tohono O'odham Community College ("TOCC"), a tribal enterprise of the Nation, and the Tucson Area Indian Health Service ("IHS"), a Federal health care agency. In April 2009, the ECC members executed a Collaborative Agreement by which the members agreed to cooperate in grant applications and program development and to prepare and disseminate position statements, reports, and other written materials. The ECC created an opportunity for representatives of these entities and the Community College to meet and discuss issues, breaking down the "silo" behavior of these organizations. The ECC has also improved the skilled healthcare workforce on the Reservation. Before the ECC, the Nation sent students to off-Reservation programs to receive health care training and certifications. With the support of TONCA, TOCC offers an entry-level health care course to certify students as caregivers. Graduates are eligible to work in assisted living facilities, including TONCA's assisted living facility. Several of the initial graduates have found employment with TONCA's Assisted Living Facility.

The Future

The Tohono O'odham Nation has developed an institution, TONCA, that has grown, developed and performed well, while also learning to take on larger, ever evolving health care challenges. The national trends suggest skilled nursing facilities will see (i) a growing requirement for more sophisticated care and treatment and (ii) an increasing number of requests for short-term rather than long-term skilled nursing care. Though the Indian Health Care Improvement Act signed by President Obama on March 23, 2010, as part of the Patient Protection and Affordable Care Act, expands the extent of IHS responsibilities to include long term care, Congress has not provided any appropriations that would ensure the delivery of such services.

TONCA continues to maintain vigilance over the current and projected healthcare-related needs. This allows the Board to make informed decisions regarding future services and administrative and funding needs. The current dynamic healthcare topics with which TONCA must contend include the changing healthcare landscape, the needs associated with physical infrastructure construction and maintenance, recruiting qualified staff, and securing the funding to continue operating.

The Changing Healthcare Landscape: The incidence of chronic health conditions continues to rise, which results in elders needing longer and more-intensive care. Given this trend, the roles of skilled nursing and assisted living are expected to change so that skilled nursing facilities will be handling the "sickest" O'odham members in the near future as an alternative to hospital stays. Assisted living facilities will function more like skilled nursing facilities.

Physical Infrastructure: A continuing challenge will entail finding capital funds to complete the remaining, and needed, assisted living buildings and to expand the wastewater system to service the additional buildings. The current wastewater system is operated at (or near) maximum capacity. TONCA has been seeking to partner with the housing authority of the Nation to collaborate on a regional wastewater facility that would meet TONCA's needs as well as those of a proposed neighboring housing project.

Staffing: The location of TONCA's facilities, about 100 miles from the urban centers of Tucson and Phoenix, continues to be a challenge in hiring and retaining professional staff. TONCA is always looking for ways in which it can improve the quality of staff and increase O'odham employment. The Board remains ready to consider alternative employment arrangements in order to obtain the highest quality of care providers.

Financial Resources: Funding is an ever-present concern for any organization or program. TONCA continually looks for ways to secure the financial resources that keep its programs running. Its primary source of funding comes from the Nation through an annual allocation and it has successfully modified the funding cycle so that it receives funding on a five-year plan whereby the Nation agrees to provide annual support prior to the start of the fiscal year in a single lump sum. Currently, TONCA is in the third year of the latest five-year cycle and it has started the process of seeking support for the next five-year resolution well before the current five-year cycle ends.

Conclusion

The Tohono O'odham Nation established TONCA to "enhance the physical, spiritual, emotional, social and intellectual qualities of life for aging O'odham and other members of the Nation in need of skilled nursing care." In achieving its initial objective, it gained the institutional capabilities necessary to expand its services. Healthcare needs, like many other types of needs, operate in a fluid environment in which resilient and adaptable institutions are better able to support the dynamics of a sustainable foundation for the Tohono O'odham Nation.

The shifting healthcare needs and TONCA's responses are a prime example of the type of institution that can successfully support a sustainable future for an Indian nation. People, society, regulations, and technology evolve thus requiring institutions and their leadership teams and administrators to focus on new trends and prepare for the impact of such trends. TONCA achieves this through: (1) constantly seeking data on new healthcare and regulatory needs within and outside of their community, (2) analyzing the data to make appropriate plans, and, (3) evaluating current programs for effectiveness in meeting current goals. This practice ensures that TONCA is able to stay true to its vision while also staying versed in on-the-ground needs and trends of its community. In the pursuit of a mission, many organizations face challenges that require them to re-evaluate the effectiveness of existing procedures. This often becomes a stumbling block for the organizations that are hesitant to consider new paths and forego outdated plans. The adaptability inherent in TONCA's operating culture means that it is able to quickly respond to an issue in order to meet its ultimate objective. Improvements in health services contribute to sustainable development of the Nation.

The Tohono O'odham Nation's reliance on *O'odham Himdag* demonstrates how traditional cultural norms can be used to develop sustainable communities. Health services that are delivered consistent with the O'odham culture and values further support a sustainable future. The process by which the skilled nursing facility was established and those charged with elder care were permitted to expand beyond the initial objective to "bring the Elders home" shows a clear connection to the tenets of resilient thinking: expanding a healthcare system in a holistic manner that engages the community, government, and tribal members. The case of the Tohono O'odham Nation and the Tohono O'odham Nursing Care Authority is being replicated in other locations throughout Indian country as Indian nations pursue sustainable futures consistent with their own cultures and customs.

REFERENCES

Chapter 1

1. Diamond, J.M. 2006. *Collapse: How Societies Choose to Fail or Succeed.* New York: Penguin group

2. FAO. 2013. The State of Food Insecurity in the World. Summary Report

3. Global Footprint Network. 2012. National Footprint Accounts. Working Paper

4. Meadows et al. 2004. "World Scientists Warning to Humanity." A note in *Limits to growth: The Thirty-year Update.* Chelsea Green Publishing Company, UT

5. United Nations. 2013. World Population Prospects, New York

6. United Nations. 2014. World Urbanization Prospects. New York

7. World Commission on Environment and Development (WCED). 1987. Our Common Future. New York: Oxford University Press

Chapter 2

1. Ahmadi, F., Toghyani, S. 2011. The Role of Urban Planning in Achieving Sustainable Urban Development. OIDA International Journal of Sustainable Development, 2(11): 23–25.

2. Beatley, T. 2010. *Biophilic Cities: Integrating Nature into Urban design and Planning.* Washington DC: Island Press

3. Berggren, C. 2013. Stockholm, Sweden: An Urban Planner's Dream City. http://sustainablecitiescollective.com/planningphotographycom/179351/stockholmsweden-urban-planners-dream-city (accessed 8.12.2014)

4. Bündnis 90/Die Grünen. 2014. http://www.gruene.de/startseite.html (accessed 8.15.2014)

5. C40. 2014. *C40 Cities: Climate Leadership Group.* http://www.c40.org/ (accessed 8.15.2014)

6. Caine, T. 2011. *The Garden City vs the Green City.* Sustainable Cities Collective http://sustainablecitiescollective.com/tcaine/21809/garden-city-vs-green-city (accessed 8.15.2014)

7. City Climate Leadership Awards. 2014. Stockholm: Hammarby Sjöstad. http://cityclimateleadershipawards.com/stockholm-hammarby-sjostad/ (accessed 8.12.2014)

8. City of Freiburg, 2014. http://www.freiburg.de/pb/,Lde/205243.html (accessed 8.15.2014)

9. City of Stockholm. 2011. The Walkable City: Stockholm City Plan. http://international.stockholm.se/Future-Stockholm-Stockholm-City-Plan/ (accessed 1.25.2012)

10. City of Stockholm. 2012. Urban Mobility Strategy. Stockholm, SE: City of Stockholm, the City of Stock-holm Traffic Administration.

11. City of Stockholm. 2014. Welcome to the Capital of Scandinavia. http://international.stockholm.se/ (accessed 8.12.2014)

12. City of Vancouver, 2011, Downtown Separated Bicycle Lanes Status Report, http://bettercities.net/sites/default/files/penv2DowntownSeparatedBikeLanes StatusReportSummer2011.pdf (accessed 8.15.2014)

13. City of Vancouver, 2012, Greenest City 2020 Action Plan, http://vancouver.ca/ files/cov/Greenest-city-action-plan.pdf (accessed 8.15.2014)

14. City of Vancouver, 2014, http://vancouver.ca/ (accessed 8.15.2014)

15. Demographia. 2014. http://www.demographia.com/ (accessed 8.15.2014)

16. Fourteenislands.com.2014. Bicycle Paths http://www.fourteenislands.com/bicycle-paths/ (accessed 8.12.2014)

17. Future Communities, 2014. Hammarby Sjostad, Stockholm, Sweden, 1995 to 2015: Building a 'Green' City Extension. http://www.futurecommunities .net/case-studies/hammarby-sjostad-stockholm-sweden-1995-2015 (accessed 8.12.2014)

18. Green City Freiburg. 2014. Freiburg Green City Brochure.

19. http://www.fwtm.freiburg.de/servlet/PB/menu/1182949_l2/index.html (accessed 8.15.2014)

20. Grossvenor. 2014. Resilinet Cities: A Grosvenor Research Report. www. grosvenor.com (accesd 8.15.2012)

21. Howard, E. 1902. *Garden Cities of To-Morrow*. Harvard University: S. Sonneschein & Company, Limited.

22. Ignatieva, M.E., Berg, P. 2014. . Hammarby Sjöstad—A New Generation of Sustainable Urban Eco-Districts. http://www.thenatureofcities.com/2014/02/12/ hammarby-sjostad-a-new-generation-of-sustainable-urban-eco-districts/ (accessed 8.12.2014)

23. The London School of Economics and Political Science (LSE). 2013. Stockholm: Green Economy Leader Re-port. London, UK: LSE Cities, London School of Economics and Political Science.

24. Nelson, A. 2014. Stockholm, Sweden: City of Water http://depts.washington.edu/ open2100/Resources/1_OpenSpaceSystems/Open_Space_Systems/Stockholm_ Case_Study.pdf (acceassed 8.12.2014_

25. Newman, P., Beatley, T., & Heather, B. 2009. Resilient Cities: Responding to Peak Oil and Climate Change. Washington DC: Islandpress.

26. Organization for Economic Cooperation and Development (OECD). 2013. Green Growth in Stockholm, Sweden, OECD Green Growth Studies, OECD Publishing. http://dx.doi.org/10.1787/9789264195158-en (accessed 8.12.2014)

27. Parsons, K.J., Schuyler, D. 2002. *From Garden City to Green City: The Legacy of Ebenezer Howard*. Baltimore: John Hopkins University Press.

28. Port Metro Vancouver website, 2014, http://www.portmetrovancouver.com/ (accessed 8.15.2014)

29. Statistics Canada, Census 2011, http://www12.statcan.gc.ca/census-recensement/2011/dp-pd/hlt-fst/pd-pl/Table-Tableau.cfm?LANG=Eng&T=303&SR=1&S=51&O=A&RPP=9999&PR=0&CMA=933 (accessed 8.15.2014)

30. Statistikomstockholm. 2013. Stockholm Gacts & Figures 2013. http://www.statistikomstockholm.se/attachments/article/21/facts%20and%20figures%202013_webb.pdf (accessed 8.12.2014)

31. The Economist Intelligence Unit. 2012a. The Green City Index: A summary of the Green City Index research series. Munich: Siemens AG

32. The Economist Intelligence Unit (EIU). 2012b. A Summary of the Livability Ranking and Overview. http://www.tfsa.ca/storage/reports/Liveability_rankings_Promotional_August_2013.pdf (accessed 8.15.2014)

33. TreeKeepers, 2012, http://www.treekeepers.ca/ (accessed 8.15.2012)

34. The EcoTipping Points Project. 2011. Germany – Freiburg – Green City. http://www.ecotippingpoints.org/our-stories/indepth/germany-freiburg-sustainability-transportation-energy-green-economy.html (accessed 8.15.2014)

35. United Nations (UN) Habitat. 2012. State of the World's Cities 2012/2013. http://mirror.unhabitat.org/pmss/listItemDetails.aspx?publicationID=3387 (accessed 8.15.2012)

36. Vauban. 2014. www.vauban.de: Stadtteil Vauban, Freiburg. http://www.vauban.de (accessed 8.15.2014)

37. Vince, G. 2012. *Sustainability in the new urban age*. Smart Planet http://www.bbc.com/future/story/20121214-greening-the-concrete-jungle (accessed 8.15.2014)

38. Winters, M., Babul, S., Becker, H.J., Brubacher, J.R., Chipman, M., Cripton, P., Cusimano, M.D., Friedman, S.M., Harris, M.A., Hunte, G., Monro, M., Reynolds, C.C., Shen, H., Teschke, K., 2012, Safe cycling: how do risk perceptions compare with observed risk? Canadian Journal of Public Health, 103(9 Suppl 3):eS42-7.

39. Zottis, L. 2014. Cidades planejam-se para mudanças climáticas, aponta MIT. http://thecityfixbrasil.com/2014/06/10/cidades-buscam-resiliencia-mit/ (accessed 8.15.2014)

Chapter 3

1. Adams, W. M. 2006. The future of sustainability: Re-thinking environment and development in the twenty-first century. Report of the International Union for Conservation of Nature (IUCN) Renowned thinkers meeting, 29–31 January 2006.

2. Balboa, M. W. 1973. United Nations Conference on the Human Environment. *Women Law. J.*, *59*, 26.

3. Boone, C., & Modarres, A. 2006. *City and environment*. Temple University.

4. Brown, L. R. 2011. *World on the edge: How to prevent environmental and economic collapse.* New York: Earth Policy Institute.

5. Carson, R. 1951. *The sea around us*. New York: Oxford University.

6. Carson, R. 1962. *Silent spring*. New York: First Mariner.

7. Clark, W.C. 1999. Sustainability science: A room of its own. *PNAS, 104*(6), 1737–1738.

8. Commoner, B. 1963. *Science and survival*. New York: Viking.

9. Commoner, B. 1971. *The closing circle: Confronting the environmental crisis*. London: Cape.

10. Cronon, W. 2011, April 13. The riddle of sustainability: a surprisingly short history. Lecture presented at Wrigley Lecture Series. Arizona State University, Tempe, AZ.

11. Diamond, J. 2006. *Collapse: How societies choose to fail or succeed*. New York, NY: Penguin Group.

12. Du Pisani, J. A. 2006. Sustainable development: Historical roots of the concept. *Environmental Science 3*(2), 83–96.

13. Egan, M. 2007. *Barry Commoner and the science of survival: The remaking of American environmentalism*. Cambridge, MA: M.I.T.

14. Ehrlich, P. 1968. *The population bomb*. New York: Ballantine.

15. Grober, U. 2012. *Sustainability: A Cultural History*. UIT Cambridge Limited.

16. Guthrie, W., & Guthrie, W. 1988. *Dust bowl ballads*. Rounder.

17. Hardin, G. 1968. The tragedy of the commons. *Science, 1623859.*, 1243–1248.

18. Hay, P. R. 2000. *Main currents in western environmental thought*. Bloomington: Indiana University.

19. Hempel, L. C. 2012. Evolving concepts of sustainability in environmental policy. *The Oxford Handbook of US Environmental Policy*, 67.

20. Hopwood, B., Mellor, M., O'Brien, G. 2005. Sustainable development: Mapping different approaches. *Sustainable Development 13*(1), 38–52.

21. IUCN, U. (WWF). 1980. World conservation strategy. World Conservation Union, United Nations Environment Programme, Word Wide Fund for Nature, Gland.

22. Kates, R. W., & Clark, W. C. 1999. *Our common journey: A transition toward sustainability*. Washington, DC: National Academy.

23. Kates, R.W., & Parris, T.M. 2003. Long-term trends and a sustainability transition. *Proceedings on the National Academy of Sciences, 100*(14), 8062–8067.

24. Leopold, A. 1949. *A Sand county almanac: And sketches here and there*. Oxford: Oxford University.

25. Malthus, T. R. 1898. *An Essay on the Principle of Population Or a View of Its Past and Present Effects on Human Happiness, an Inquiry Into Our Prospects Respecting the Future Removal Or Mitigation of the Evils which it Occasions by Rev. TR Malthus*. Reeves and Turner.

26. Meadows, D. H., Meadows, D. L., & Randers, J. 1972. *Beyond the limits: Global collapse or a sustainable future*. Earthscan.

27. Meadows, D., Randers, J., & Meadows, D. 2004. *Limits to growth: The 30-year update*. Chelsea Green.

28. Meadows, D. H., Meadows, D. L., Randers, J., & Behrens III, W. W. 1972. The limits to growth: A report for the club of Rome's project on the predicament of mankind. Nova York, New American Library.

29. Miller, C. 2009. The once and future forest service: Land-management policies and politics in contemporary America. *Journal of Policy History* *21*(1): 89–104.

30. Minteer, B. A. 2006. *The landscape of reform: Civic pragmatism and environmental thought in America.* MIT Press.

31. Minteer, B. A. 2011. *Refounding environmental ethics: Pragmatism, principle and practice.* Philadelphia: Temple University.

32. Naess, A. 1973. The shallow and the deep, long-range ecology movement. A summary. *Inquiry*, *16*(1–4), 95–100.

33. Naess, A., & Sessions, G. 1984. Basic principles of deep ecology. *Ecophilosophy*, *6*(3), 7.

34. Odum, E. F. 1971. The fundamentals of ecology (3rd ed). Philadelphia: Suanders.

35. Orr, D. W. 2002. Four challenges of sustainability. *Conservation Biology. 16* (6), 1457–1460.

36. Osborn, F. 1948. *Our plundered planet.* Our plundered planet.

37. Oxford English Dictionary Online (*OED*). 2014. Oxford University Press. Retrieved June 4, 2014, www.oed.com.

38. Radkau, J. 2009. *Nature and power. A global history of the environment.* New York: Cambridge University.

39. Redman, C. L., Grove, J. M., & Kuby, L. H. 2002. Integrating social science into the long-term ecological research (LTER) network: social dimensions of ecological change and ecological dimensions of social change. *Ecosystems*, *7*(2), 161–171.

40. Rees, W. E. 1992. Ecological footprints and appropriated carrying capacity: what urban economics leaves out. *Environment and urbanization*, *4*(2), 121–130.

41. Rees, W. E., & Wackernagel, M. 1996. Urban ecological footprints: Why cities cannot be sustainable- and why they are a key to sustainability. *Environmental Impact Assessment Review*, 16(4), 223–248.

42. Rittel, H. W., & Webber, M. M. 1974. Planning Problems are Wicked. *Polity, 4*, 155–69.

43. Sale, K. 1993. *The green revolution: The environmental movement 1962-1992.* New York: Macmillan.

44. Steinbeck, J. 1939. *The grapes of wrath.* Penguin.

45. Summit, E. 1992. Agenda 21. *The United Nations Programme for Action from Rio.*

46. Thoreau, H. D. 1949. On the duty of civil disobedience [resistance to civil government]. Rockville, MD: Manor.

47. Thoreau, H. D. 2006. *Walden.* Yale University Press. [Originally published in New York: Tinker & Co., 1854.]

48. Von Carlowitz, H. C. 1732. *Sylvicultura Oeconomica Oder Haußwirthliche Nachricht und Naturmäßige Anweisung zur Wilden Baum-Zucht Nebst Gründlicher Darstellung Wie... dem allenthalben und insgemein einreissenden Grossen Holtz-Mangel, Vermittelst Säe-Pflantz-und Versetzung vielerhand Bäume zu rathen . . . Worbey zugleich eine gründliche Nachricht von dem in Churfl. Sächß. Landen Gefundenen Turff . . . befindlich* (Vol. 1). Bey Johann Friedrich Brauns sel. Erben.

49. World Commission on Environment and Development (WCED). 1987. *Our common future: Report of the world commission on environment and development. The Brundtland Commission.* Oxford: Oxford University.

50. Williams, R. 1976. *Keywords: A vocabulary of culture and society.* London: Fontana

51. Wilson, E. O. 1998. *Consilience: The unity of knowledge.* New York: Vintage.

52. Wilson, E. O. 2002. *The future of life.* London: W.W. Norton & Co.

53. Worster, D. 1979. *Dust bowl: the southern plains in the 1930s.* Oxford, UK: Oxford University.

54. Worster, D. 1985. *Rivers of empire: Water, aridity, and the growth of the American West.* Oxford, UK: Oxford University.

55. Worster, D. 1994. *Nature's economy: A history of ecological ideas.* Cambridge University.

Chapter 4

1. Diamond, J. 2005. *Collapse: How societies choose to fail or succeed.* New York, NY: Penguin Group.

Chapter 5

1. Archer, D., Rahmstorf, S. 2010. *The Climate Crisis: An Introductory Guide to Climate Change.* Cambridge, NY : Cambridge University Press

2. Calthorpe, P. 2011. *Urbanism in the age of climate change.* Washington D.C: Island Press.

3. City of Chicago. 2008. Chicago Climate Action Plan: Our City.Our Future. http://www.chicagoclimateaction.org (accessed 5/20/2014)

4. City of Portland. 2001. Local Action Plan Global Warming. Portland: Office of Sustainable Development & Department of Sustainable Community Development.

5. CNN. 2013. Hurricane Sandy Fast Facts. http://www.cnn.com/2013/07/13/world/americas/hurricane-sandy-fast-facts/ (accessed 6/5/2014)

6. CNU. 2014. Charta of the New Urbanism. Congress for the New Urbanism Online. http://www.cnu.org/charter (accessed 5/24/2014)

7. Doha. 2012. COP 18/CMP8. http://www.cop18.qa/ (accessed 6/5/2014)

8. FAO. 2008. Climate Change and Food Security: A Framework Document. Rome, Italy: Food and Agriculture Organization of the United Nations.

9. Global Food Security Index. 2014. Ranking and Trends. New York: The Economist Intelligence Unit Confirmation http://foodsecurityindex.eiu.com/Index (accessed 6/5/2014)

10. Fuerth, L.S. 2009. Foresight and anticipatory governance. *Foresight, 11 (4),* 14–32.

11. Intergovernmental Panel on Climate Change (IPCC). 2007. Climate Change 2007: The Physical Science Basis. Contribution of Working Group 1 to the Fourth Assessment Report of the Intergovernmental Panel on Climate Change. Cambridge, UK and New York, NY, USA: Cambridge University Press

12. Intergovernmental Panel on Climate Change (IPCC). 2013. Climate change 2013: The Physical Science Basis. Contribution of Working Group 1 to the fifth Assessment Report of the Intergovernmental Panel on Climate Change. Cambridge, UK and New York, NY, USA: Cambridge University Press.

13. Intergovernmental Panel on Climate Change (IPCC). 2014a.Climate Change 2014: Impacts, Adaptation, and Vulnerability. Contribution of the Working Group 2 to the fifth Assessment Report of the Intergovernmental Panel on Climate Change. Cambridge, UK and New York, NY, USA: Cambridge University Press.

14. IPCC. (2014b). Climate Change 2014: Mitigation of Climate Change. Contribution of the Working Group 2 to the fifth Assessment Report of the Intergovernmental Panel on Climate Change. Cambridge, UK and New York, NY, USA: Cambridge University Press.

15. Millard-Ball, A. Where the Action Is. Planning, 76(7), 16–21.

16. National Aeronautics and Space Administration (NASA). 2010. NASA Research Finds Last Decade was warmest on Record, 2009 One of Warmest Years. *National Aeronautics and Space Administration.* http://www.nasa.gov/home/hqnews/2010/jan/HQ_10-017_Warmest_temps.html (accessed 9/1/2010)

17. National Oceanic and Atmospheric Administration (NOAA). 2005. Stratospheric Ozone Layer Depletion and Recovery. http://www.esrl.noaa.gov/research/themes/o3/ (accessed 6/4/2013)

18. National Oceanic and Atmospheric Administration (NOAA). 2013. State of the Climate: Global Analysis - Annual 2013. http://www.ncdc.noaa.gov/sotc/global/2013/13 (accessed 6/4/2013)

19. National Research Council (NRC) 2009. Driving and the Built Environment: The Effects of Compact Development on Motorized Travel, Energy Use, and CO2 Emissions, Special Report 298: Committee for the Study in the Relationships among Development Pattern, Vehicle Miles Traveled, and Energy Consumption.

20. National Research Council (NRC). 2010. Advancing the Science of Climate Change. Washington, DC.: The National Academic Press

21. NBC. 2005. Bush: Kyoto treaty would have hurt economy. http://www.nbcnews.com/id/8422343/ns/politics/t/bush-kyoto-treaty-would-have-hurt-economy/#.U5CuPXJdV8E (accessed 6/4/2013)

22. Pittock, B. A. 2009. Climate Change: The Science, Impacts and Solutions. London: Earthscan.

23. Quay, R. 2010. Anticipatory Governance: A Tool for Climate Change Adaptation. *Journal of the American Planning Association, 76 (4), 496–511.*

24. Rosenzweig, C., Solecki, W.D., Hammer, S.A., Mehrotra, S. 2011. Climate Change and Cities: First Assessment Report of the Urban Climate Change Research Networks. Cambridge, NY: Cambridge University Press.

25. Smart Growth Network. 2014. Smart Growth Overview. Smart Growth Online. http://www.smartgrowth.org/about/overview.asp (accessed 5/24/2014)

26. Stern, N. 2006. *The Economics of Climate Change: The Stern Review - Executive Summary.*

    a. Cambridge: Cambridge University Press.

27. United Nations. 1998. Kyoto Protocol to the United Nations Framework Convention on Climate Change. http://unfccc.int/resource/docs/convkp/kpeng.pdf (accessed 5/20/2014)

28. United Nations Framework Convention on Climate Change (UNFCCC). 2008. *Report of the Conference of the Parties on its thirteenth session, held in Bali from 3 to 15 December 2007.* United Nations: UNFCCC Framework Convention on Climate Change http://unfccc.int/resource/docs/2007/cop13/eng/06a01.pdf (accessed 5/20/2014)

29. United Nations Framework Convention on Climate Change (UNFCCC). 2009. *Copenhagen Accord.* United Nations: UNFCCC Framework Convention on Climate Change http://unfccc.int/resource/docs/2009/cop15/eng/l07.pdf (accessed 5/20/2014)

30. United Nations Framework Convention on Climate Change (UNFCCC). 2011. *Report of the Conference of the Parties on its sixteenth session, held in Cancun from 29 November to 10 December 2010.* United Nations: UNFCCC Framework Convention on Climate Change http://unfccc.int/resource/docs/2010/cop16/eng/07a01.pdf#page=4 (accessed 5/20/2014)

31. United Nations Framework Convention on Climate Change (UNFCCC). 2014. United Nations Framework Convention on Climate Change. https://unfccc.int/2860.php (accessed 5/20/2014)

32. The United States Conference of Mayors. 2014. Organization Overview. http://www.usmayors.org/about/overview.asp (accessed 5/20/2014)

33. United States Department of Commerce. 2013. Economic Impact of Hurricane Sandy. Washington D.C: Economics and Statistics Administration http://www.esa.doc.gov/Reports/economic-impact-hurricane-sandy (accessed 5/20/2014)

34. U.S. Green Building Council (USGBC). 2014. Leadership in Energy and Environmental Design. U.S. Green Building Council Online. http://www.usgbc.org/ (accessed 5/24/2014)

35. Warsaw. 2013. COP19/CMP 9 http://www.cop19.gov.pl/ (accessed 6/4/2014)

Chapter 6

1. Adger, W. N., 2000. "Social and ecological resilience: Are they related?", in *Progress in Human Geography* 24(3): 347–364.

2. Beatley, T, 2009. *Planning for Coastal Resilience: Best Practices for Calamitous Times.* Washington, D.C: Island Press

3. Brand, R. and F. Graffikin, 2007. "Collaborative Planning in an Uncollaborative World." in *Planning Theory.* Vol. 6(3): 282–313.

4. Cutter et al. 2003. "Social Vulnerability to Environmental Hazards." in *Social Science Quarterly* 84(1): 242–261.

5. Davoudi, S., K. Shaw, L.J. Haider, A. Quinlan, G. Peterson, C. Wilkinson, H. Funfgeld, D. McEvoy, L. Porter, and L. Porter and S. Davoudi, 2012. "Resilience: A Bridging Concept or a Dead End? 'Reframing' Resilience: Challenges for Planning Theory and Practice Integrating Traps: Resilience Assessment of a Pasture Management Systems in Northern Afghanistan Urban Resilience: What

does it Mean in Planning Practice? Resilience as a Useful concept for Climate Change Adaptation? The Politics of Resilience for Planning: A Cautionary Note." in *Planning Theory and Practice.* Vol. 13(2): 299–333.

6. Enelow, Noah, 2013. *The Resilience of Detroit: An Application of the Adaptive Cycle Metaphor to an American Metropolis.* Economics for Equity and the Environment Network

7. Folke, C., 2006. "Resilience: The emergence of a perspective for social–ecological systems analyses, Resilience, Vulnerability, and Adaptation." *A Cross-Cutting Theme of the International Human Dimensions Programme on Global Environmental Change.* 16(3), 253–267.

8. Gallopín, Gilberto C., 1991. "Linkages between vulnerability, resilience, and adaptive capacity", in *Global Environmental Change,* Vol. 16 (3): 293–303.

9. Grosvenor Group, 2014. *Resilient Cities: A Grosvenor research report. New York:* Grosvenor Group Limited.

10. Holling, C. S., 1973. "Resilience and stability of ecological systems", in A*nnual Review of Ecology and Systematics* 4, 1–23.

    a. 1996. "Engineering Resilience versus Ecological Resilience." In P.C. Schulze (Ed) *Engineering Within Ecological Constraints.* P31-44 Washington DC: National Academy Press.

11. Magis, K., 2010. "Community Resilience: An indicator of social sustainability." In *Society and Natural Resources.* Vol. 23: 401–406.

12. Maguire, B. and Cartwright, S. 2008. *Assessing a community's capacity to manage change: A resilience approach to social assessment.*

13. Margerum, R., 2011. *Beyond Consensus: Improving Collaborative Planning and Management.* Cambridge: MIT Press.

14. Norris, F. and S. Stevens, 2007. "Community Resilience and the Principles of Mass Trauma Intervention." In *Psychiatry.* Vol. 70(4): 320–328

15. Olsson, P., Folke, C. and F. Berkes. 2004. "Adaptive co-management for building resilience in socio-ecological systems." in *Environmental Management.* 34: 75–90.

16. Pelling, M., 2003. *The vulnerability of cities. Natural disasters and social resilience.* London, Sterling, VA: Earthscan Publications.

17. Putnam, R, 2001. *Bowling Alone: The Collapse and Revival of American Community.* New York: Simon and Schuster.

18. Quay, R, 2010. "Anticipatory Governance". In *Journal of the American Planning Association.* Vol. 76 (4): 496–511.

19. Resilience Alliance: 2007. *Assessing Resilience in Social-Ecological Systems: A Workbook for Scientists.*

    a. 2007b. *Urban Resilience: Research Prospectus.* A Resilience Alliance Initiative for Transitioning Urban Systems towards Sustainable Futures.

    b. 2014. *The Adaptive Cycle, resalliance.org/index.php/adaptive_cycle*

    c. 2014b. *Bounding the System: Describing the Present, http://wiki.resalliance.org/ index.php/Bounding_the_System_-_Level_2*

20. The Rockefeller Foundation, 2014. *100 Resilient Cities.* http://100resilientcities. rockefellerfoundation.org/

21. Sachs, Jeffrey D., 2014. *Courcebook, Chapter 14: The SDGs. Coursera: The Age of Sustainable Development.* Available at https://d396qusza40orc.cloudfront.net/ susdev/ISD%20Chapter%2014.pdf

22. Sherrieb, K., F. Norris, and S. Galea, 2010. "Measuring Capacities for Community Resilience." In *Soc. Indic. Res.* Vol. 99: 227–247

23. Smith, S., Morris, W. and Voorhees, R. W. (eds), 1998. *New international webster's comprehensive dictionary of the English language,* Trident Press International.

24. Turner, B. L., R.E. Kasperson, P.A. Matson, J.J. McCarthy, R.W. Corell, L.Christensen, N. Eckley, J.X. Kasperson, A. Luers, M.L. Martello, C. Polsky, A. Pulsipher and A. Schiller 2003. "A framework for vulnerability analysis in sustainability science", in *Proceedings of the National Academy of Sciences,* 100(14): 8074–8079.

25. United Nations Human Settlements, 2008. *Global Report on Human Settlements 2007.* Vol. 3 UN-Habitat

26. Wilson, G., 2012. *Community Resilience and Environment Transitions.* London: Routledge

Chapter 7

1. Alberti, M. 2005. The effects of urban patterns on ecosystem function. International Regional Science Review, 28:2 pp 168–192.

2. Asbirk, S. and S. Jensen. 1984. An Example of Applied Island Theory and Dispersal Biology. In: P. Agger and V. Nielson (Editors). Dispersal Ecology. Naturfredningstradet of Fredningsstrylsen,: Copenhagen, pp. 49–54.

3. Benedict, T. and R. McMahon. 2006. Green Infrastructure. Island Press: Washington

4. Boutequila, L., J. Miller, J. Ahern and K. McGarigal. 2006. Measuring Landscapes. Island Press: Washington. 118 pp.

5. Bowler, D., L. buyung-Ali, T. Knight and A. Pullin. 2010. Urban greening to cool towns and cities: A systematic review of empirical evidence. Landscape and Urban Planning. 97: 147–155.

6. Carr, M., D. Lambert and P. Zwick. 1994. Mapping of Continuous Biological Corridor Potential in Central America: Final Report. Pase Pantera. University of Florida: Florida.

7. Cook, E.A. and H.N. van Lier (Editors), 1994. Landscape Planning and Ecological Networks. Elsevier: Amsterdam. 354 pages

8. Cook, E. A. 2002. Landscape structure indices for assessing urban ecological networks. *Landscape and Urban Planning*, 58:269–280.

9. Cook, E. A. 2007. Green site design: strategies for stormwater management. *Journal of Green Building.* Vol. 2: Number 4. pp. 46–56.

10. Daily, G.C. (Editor) 1997. Nature's Services, societal dependence on natural ecosystems. Island press: Washington DC.

11. Diaz, E. (Editor). 2008. Microbial Biodegradation: Genomics and Molecular Biology. Caister Academic Press.

12. Dramstadt, E.W., Olson, J.D. and Forman, R.T.T., 1996. Landscape Ecology Principles in Landscape Architecture and Land Use Planning. Island Press: Washington DC

13. Ewing, J. 2005. The Mesoamerican Biological Corridor: A Bridge Across the Americas. Ecoworld. December 19, 2005. www.ecoworld.com/home/articles2.cfm?tid=377.

14. Forman, R.T.T., 1995. Land Mosaics. Cambridge University Press: Cambridge

15. Forman, R.T.T. 2008. Urban Regions: Ecology and Planning. Cambridge University Press: Cambridge

16. Forman, R.T.T. and Godron, M., 1984. Landscape Ecology. John Wiley: New York. 619 pages.

17. Hellmund, P. and D. Smith. 2006. Designing Greenways. Island Press: Washington

18. Huling, S. and B. Pivetz. 2006. In-situ chemical oxidation. Engineering Issue of EPA, August 2006

19. Hough, M. 1984. City form and Natural Process. Routledge: New York

20. Jongman, R. and G. Pungetti (Editors), 2004. Ecological Networks and Greenways: Concept, Design, Implementation. Cambridge University Press, Cambridge. 345 pp.

21. Jongman, R., I. Bouwma, A. Griffioen, L. Jones-Walters and A. Doorn. 2011. The Pan European Ecological Network: PEEN. Landscape Ecology, 26:3 pp. 311–326.

22. Lyle, T. 1985. Design for Human Ecosystems: Landscape and Natural Resources. Island Press: Washington DC

23. Lyle, T. 1995. Regenerative Design for Sustainable Landscapes. Wiley: New York

24. McGarigal, K. and B.J. Marks, 1995. FRAGSTATS: Spatial pattern analysis program for quantifying landscape structure. Gen. Tech. Rep. PNW-GTR-351. US Department of Agriculture, Forest Service: Portland, OR, 122 pp.

25. McHarg, I. 1969. Design with Nature. Doubleday: New York

26. McPherson, E. 1992. Accounting for benefits and costs of urban green space. Landscape and Urban Planning 22:1 pp 41–51.

27. Miller, K. E. Chang and N. Johnson. 2001. Defining Common Ground for the Mesoamerican Biological Corridor. World Resources Institute.

28. Noss, R. F. 2004. Can urban areas have ecological integrity? Proceedings 4th International Urban Wildlife Symposium.

29. Odefy, J., S. Detwiler, K. Rousseau, A. Trice, R. Blackwell, K. O'Hara, M. Buckley, T. Souhlas, S. Brown and R. Raviprakash. 2012. Banking on Green. American Rivers, The Water Environment Federation, The American Society of Landscape Architects and ECONorthwest.

30. Pagano, M. and A. Bowman. 2000. Vacant land in cities: an urban resource. The Brooking Institute survey series. Pps. 1–7.

31. Palazzo, D. and F. Steiner. 2012 Urban Ecological Design. Island Press: Washington DC

32. Schultz, F. 2005. Yellowstone to Yukon: freedom to roam. Mountaineers books: Seattle.

33. Steiner, F. 2008. The Living Landscape: An Ecological Approach to Landscape Planning: Island Press: Washington DC

34. Steiner, F. 2002. Human Ecology: Following Nature's Lead, Island Press: Washington DC

35. Steiner, F. 2011. Design for a Vulnerable Planet. University of Texas Press: Austin

36. Suresh, B. and G. Ravishankar. 2004. Phytoremediation – a novel and promising approach for environmental cleanup. Critical Reviews of Biotechnology, 24:2–3, pp 97–124.

37. Van der Ryn, S. and S. Cowan. 1996. Ecological Design. Island Press: Washington DC

38. Werquin, A., B. Duhem, G. Lindholm, B. Oppermann, S. Pauleit and S. Tjallingii (Editors). 2005. Green Structure and Urban Planning: Final Report. European Commission: Brussels

Chapter 8

1. Food Agriculture Organization (FAO). 2006. Food security: Policy brief, Food and Agriculture Organization of the United Nations no. 2. ftp://ftp.fao.org/es/ESA/policybriefs/pb_02.pdf

2. Food Agricultural Conservation and Trade Act of 1990, no. 101–624,104 Stat. 3359. 28 November 1990.

3. Miller, T. G. 2007. *Living in the environment* (15th ed.). Belmont, CA: Thomson Learning.

4. Conway, G. 1998. *The doubly green revolution: Food for all in the 21st century.* Ithaca, NY: Cornell University Press.

5. Grey, M. A. 2000. The industrial food stream and its alternatives in the United States: An introduction. in *Human Organization, 59*(2), 143–150.

6. Conway, G. 1997. *The doubly green revolution: Food for all in the twenty-first century.* Ithaca, NY: Comstock Publishing Associates.

7. Hoppe, R., MacDonald, J., & Korb, P. 2010. Small farms in the United States; persistence under pressure. United States Department of agriculture, Economic Research Service. Retrieved from http://www.ers.usda.gov/publications/eib63/

8. Pimentel, D., & Pimentel, M. 2003. Sustainability of meat-based and plant-based diets and the environment. *American Journal of Clinical Nutrition, 78*, 660–663.

9. Pirog, R., & Benjamin, A. 2003. Checking the food odometer: Comparing food miles for local versus conventional produce sales to Iowa institutions. Leopold Center for Sustainable Agriculture. Retrieved from http://www.leopold.iastate.edu/pubs/staff/files/food_travel072103.pdf.

10. Heller, M. C., & Keolian, G. A. 2003. Assessing the sustainability of the US food system: A life cycle perspective. *Agricultural Systems, 76*, 1007–1041.

11. McMichael, A., Powles, J., Butler, C., & Uauy, R. 2007. Food, livestock production, energy, climate change, and health. *The Lancet, 370*, 1253–1263.

12. Postel, S. 2000. Entering an era of water scarcity: The challenges ahead. *Ecological Applications, 10*(4), 941–948.

13. Canfield, D. E., Glazer, A. N., & Falkowski, P. G. 2010. The evolution and future of earth's nitrogen cycle. *Science, 330*, 192–196.

14. Pretty, J. 2008. Agricultural sustainability: Concepts, principles and evidence. *Philosophical transactions of the Royal Society, 363*, 447–465.

15. Nord, M., Andrews, M., & Carlson, S. 2009. *Household food security in the United States 2008.* United States Department of Agriculture, Economic Research Service, Economic Research Report no. 83.

16. Pretty, J. Agricultural sustainability.

17. Nord, M., Andrews, M., & Carlson, S. 2003. Household food security in the United States, 2003. Food Assistance and Nutrition Research Report No. 42.

18. Barrett, C. B. 2010. Measuring food insecurity. *Science, 327*(5967), 825–828.

19. Ploeg, M. V., Breneman, V., Farrigan, T., Hamrick, K., Hopkins, D., Kaufman, P., . . . E. Tuckermanty. 2009. Access to affordable and nutritious food: Measuring and understanding food deserts and their consequences. *Economic Research Service.* Retrieved from http://www.ers.usda.gov/Publications/AP/AP036/AP036.pdf

20. Powell, L. M., Slater, S., Mirtcheva, D., Bao, Y., & Chaloupka, F. 2007. Food store availability and neighborhood characteristics in the United States. *Preventive Medicine, 44*, 189–195.

21. Glanz, K., Sallis, J. F., Salens, B. E., & Frank, L. D. 2007. Nutrition environment measures survey in stores (NEMS-S): Development and evaluation. *American Journal of Preventative Medicine, 32*(4), 282–289.

22. Larson, N. I., Story, M. T., & Nelson, M. C. 2009. Neighborhood environments: Disparities in access to healthy foods in the U.S. *American Journal of Preventative Medicine, 36*(1), 74–81.

23. 23. Peters, C. J., Bills, N. L., Wilkins, J. L., & Fick, G. 2008. Foodshed analysis and its relevance to sustainability. *Renewable Agriculture and Food Systems*, 1–7.

24. 24. Dubbeling 2009.

25. 25. Heckman, J. 2006. A history of organic farming: Transitions from Sir Albert Howard's to war in the soil to USDA national organic program. *Renewable Agriculture and Food Systems, 21*(3), 143–150.

26. National Organic Program (NOP). *National organic program: Background information.* United States Department of Agriculture, NOP, 2008. Retrieved from http://www.ams.usda.gov/AMSv1.0/getfile?dDocName=STELDEV3004443

27. 27. Economic Research Service (ERS). 2008. U.S. certified organic farmland acreage, livestock numbers, and farm operations. *Economic Research Service.*

28. Trevwas, A. 2001. Urban myths of organic farming: Organic agriculture began as an ideology, but can it meet today's needs? *Nature, 410*, 409–410.

29. Hole, D. G., Perkins, A. J., Wilson, J. D., Alexander, I. H., Price, G. V., & Evans, A. D. 2005. Does organic farming benefit biodiversity? *Biological Conservation, 122*, 113–130.

30. Pimentel, D., Hepperly, P., Hanson, J., Douds, D., & Seidel, R. 2005. Environmental, energetic, and economic comparisons of organic and conventional farming systems. *BioScience, 55*(7), 573–582.

31. Heller, M. C., & Keolian, G. A. 2003. Assessing the sustainability of the US food system: a life cycle perspective. *Agricultural Systems, 76*, 1007–1041.

32. Pimentel, D., & Pimentel, M. 2003. Sustainability of meat-based and plantbased diets and the environment. *American Journal of Clinical Nutrition, 78*, 660–663.

33. Topp, C. F. E., Stockdale, E. A., Watson, C. A., & Rees, R. M. 2007. Estimating resource use efficiencies in organic agriculture: A review of budgeting approaches used. *Journal of the Science of Food and Agriculture, 87*, 2782–2790.

34. Williams, C. M. 2002. Nutritional quality of organic food: Shades of grey or shades of green? *Proceedings of the Nutrition Society, 61*, 19–24.

35. Hoefkens, C. 2009. A literature-based comparison of nutrient content and contaminant contents between organic and conventional vegetables and potatoes. *British Food Journal, 111* (10), 1078–1097.

36. Miller, T. G. 2007. *Living in the environment* (15th ed.). Belmont, CA: Thomson Learning.

37. Pimentel, D., et al. 2005. Environmental comparisons. *BioScience, 55*(7).

38. Kirchmann, H., Bergstrom, L., Katterer, T., Andren, O., & Andersson, R. (Springer, 2008). Can organic crop production feed the world? In H. Kirchmann, & L. Bergstrom (Eds.), *Organic crop production – Ambitions and limitations*.

39. Pimentel, D., et al. 2005. Environmental comparisons. *BioScience, 55*(7).

40. Oberholzter, L., Dimitri, C., & Greene, C. 2005. Price premiums hold on as U.S. organic produce market expands. United States Department of Agriculture. Retrieved from http://www.ers.usda.gov/publications/vgs/may05/vgs30801/vgs30801.pdf

41. Lin, B. H., Smith, T. A., & Huang, C. L. 2008. Organic premiums of US fresh produce. *Renewable Agriculture and Food Systems, 23*(3), 208–216.

42. Kirchmann, H., & Others. Price premiums.

43. Connor, D. J. 2008. Organic agriculture cannot feed the world. *Field Crops Research, 106*, 187–190.

44. Dimitri, C., & Oberholtzer, L. 2009. Marketing U.S. organic foods: Recent trends from farms to consumers. *Economic Research Service*. Retrieved from http://www.ers.usda.gov/publications/eib58/eib58.pdf

45. Ibid.

46. Heimlich, R. E., & Anderson, W. D. 2001. *Development at the urban fringe and beyond: Impacts on agriculture and rural land.* United States Department of

Agriculture: Economic Research Service, Agricultural Economic Report no. 803. Retrieved from http://www.ers.usda.gov/publications/aer803/aer803.pdf

47. Hoppe, R., MacDonald, J., & Korb, P. Small farms. *Economic Information Bulletin, 63*.

48. Martinez, S., Hand, M., De Pra, M., Pollack, S., Ralston, K., Smith, T., . . . Newman, C. 2010. *Local food systems: Concepts, impacts and issues*. United States Department of Agriculture, Economic Research Service Report 97. Retrieved from http://www.ers.usda.gov/publications/err-economic-researchreport/err97.aspx

49. Taylor, C., & Aggarwal, R. 2010. Motivations and barriers to stakeholder participation in local food value chains in Phoenix, Arizona. *Urban Agriculture Magazine, 24*, 46–48.

50. Martinez, S. et al. (2010, May). Local food. Economic Research Report Number 97.

51. Hand, M. S., & Martinez, S. 2010. Just what does local mean? *Choices: The Magazine of Food, Farm and Resource Issues, 25*(1).

52. Feagan, R., & Morris, D. 2009. Consumer quest for embeddedness: A case study of Brantford Farmer' Market. *International Journal of Consumer Studies, 33*(3).

53. Goland, C. 2002. Community supported agriculture, food consumption patterns, and member commitment. *Culture & Agriculture, 24*(1), 14–25.

54. Hunt, A. R. 2007. Consumer interactions and influences on farmers' market vendors. *Renewable Agriculture and Food Systems, 22*(1), 54–66.

55. Wolf, M. M., Spittler, A., & Ahern, J. 2005. A profile of farmers' market consumers and the perceived advantages of produce sold at farmers' markets. *Journal of Food Distribution Research, 36*(1), 192–201.

56. United States Department of Agriculture (USDA). 2009. 2007 Census of agriculture: United States summary and state data. *The Geographic Area Series*, vols. 1 part 51. Retrieved from http://www.agcensus.usda.gov/Publications/2007/Full_Report/usv1.pdf

57. Griffin, M. R., & Frongillo, E. A. 2003. Experiences of farmers from Upstate New York farmers' markets. *Agriculture and Human Values, 20*, 189–203.

58. Jarosz, L. 2008. The city in the country: Growing alternative food networks in Metropolitan areas. *The Journal of Rural Studies, 24*, 231–244.

59. Barney and Worth 2008. page 12.

60. Henneberry, S. R., & Agustini, H. N. (2004, 18 February). *An analysis of Oklahoma direct marketing outlets: Case study of produce farmers' markets*. Selected Paper prepared for presentation at the Southern Agricultural Economics Association Annual, Tulsa, Oklahoma.

61. Bryld, E. 2003. Potentials, problems, and policy implications for urban agriculture in developing countries. *Agriculture and Human Values, 20*, 79–86.

62. Cofie, O., van Veenhuizen, R., & Drechsel, P. 2003, March 17. Contribution of urban and peri-urban agriculture to food security in sub-saharan Africa. Presented at the Africa session of 3rd World Wildlife (WWF), Kyoto.

63. Born, B., & Purcell, M. 2006. Avoiding the local trap: Scale and food systems in planning research. *Journal of Planning Education and Research, 26*, 195–207.

64. Kneafsey, M. 2010. The region in food – important or irrelevant? *Cambridge Journal of Regions, Economy and Society, 3*(2), 1–14.

65. Winter, M. 2003. Embeddedness, the new food economy and defensive localism. *Journal of Rural Studies, 19*, 23–32.

66. Hill, H. 2008. Food miles: Background and marketing. ATTRA – National Sustainable Agriculture Information Service. Retrieved from https://attra.ncat.org/attra-pub/PDF/foodmiles.pdf

67. Heller, M. C., & Keolian, G. A. 2003. Assessing the sustainability of the US food system: A life cycle perspective. *Agricultural Systems, 76*, 1007–1041.

68. Mariola, M. 2008. The local industrial complex? Questioning the link between local foods and energy use. *Agriculture and Human Values, 25*, 193–196.

69. Edwards-Jones, G., Mila I Canals, L., Hounsome, N., Truninger, M., Koerber, G., Hounsome, B., … Jones, D. L. 2008. Testing the assertion that 'local food is best': The challenges of an evidence-based approach. *Trends in Food Science and Technology, 19*, 265–274.

70. Lyso, T., & Guptill, A. 2004. Commodity agriculture, civic agriculture and the future of U.S. farming. *Rural Sociology, 69*(3), 370–385.

71. Milestad, R., Westberg, L., Geber, U., & Björklund, J. 2010. Enhancing adaptive capacity in food systems: Learning at farmers' markets in Sweden. *Ecology and Society, 15*(3).

72. Hinrichs, C. C., Gillespie, G. W., & Feenstra, G. W. 2004. Social learning and innovation at retail farmers' markets. *Rural Sociology, 69*(1), 31–58.

73. Allen, P., Guthman, J., & Morris, A. 2006. Research brief #9: Meeting farm and food security needs through community supported agriculture and farmers' markets in California. *Center for Agroecology and Sustainable Food Systems.*

74. Guthman, J. 2008. Bringing good food to others: Investigating the subjects of alternative food practice. *Cultural Geographies, 15*, 431–447.

75. FAO. Food security.

76. Barrett, C. B. 2010. Measuring food insecurity. *Science, 327*(5967), 825–828.

77. Arnould, E. J., & Thompson, C. J. 2005. Consumer culture theory (CCT): Twenty years of research. *Journal of Consumer Research, 31*(4), 868–882.

78. Conner, D. S., Colesanti, K. J. A., & Smalley, S. B. 2010. Understanding barriers to farmers' market patronage in Michigan: Perspectives from marginalized populations. *Journal of Hunger and Environmental Nutrition, 5*, 316–338.

79. Grace, C., Grace, T., Becker, N., & Lyden, J. 2007. Barriers to using urban farmers' markets: An investigation of food stamp clients' perceptions. In *Journal of Hunger & Environmental Nutrition, 2*(1), 55–75.

80. Dale, V. H., & Polansky, S. 2007. Measures of the effects of agricultural practices on ecosystem services. *Ecological Economics, 64*, 286–296.

81. Swinton, S. M., Lupi, F., Robertson, G. P., & Hamilton, S. 2007. Ecosystem services and agriculture: Cultivating agricultural ecosystems for diverse benefits. In *Ecological Economics, 64*, 245–252.

82. Deelstra, T., & Girardet, H. 2000. Urban agriculture and sustainable cities. *Growing Cities, Growing Food*, Retrieved from http://www.trabajopopular.org.ar/material/Theme2.pdf

83. Ibid.

84. Cordell, D., Drangert, J.-O., & White, S. 2009. The story of phosphorus: Global food security and food for thought. *Global Environmental Change, 19*, 292–305.

85. United Nations Environment Progamme (UNEP). 2011. Phosphorus and food production. *UNEP Yearbook 2011*, 35–45. http://www.unep.org/yearbook/2011/pdfs/phosphorus_and_food_productioin.pdf

86. Eaton, R. L., Hammond, G. P., & Laurie, J. 2007. Footprints on the landscape: An environmental appraisal of rural and urban living in the developed world. *Landscape and Urban Planning, 83*, 13–28.

87. Bryld, E. 2003. *Agriculture in developing countries. Agriculture and Human Values, 20*(1), 79-86(8).

88. Cordell, D., Drangert, J.-O., & White, S. 2009, May. The story of phosphorus. *Global Environmental Change, 19*(2), 292–305. Traditional Peoples and Climate Change.

89. Deelstra, T., & Girardet, H. Urban Agriculture.

90. Colding, J. 2007. Ecological land-use complementation for building resilience in urban ecosystems. *Landscape and Urban Planning, 81*, 46–55.

91. Ricketts, T., & Imhoff, M. 2003. Biodiversity, urban areas and agriculture: Locating priority ecoregions for conservation. *Conservation Ecology, 8*(2).

92. Colding, J. Ecological land-use.

93. Bryld, E. Agriculture in developing countries.

94. Ministry of Agriculture Botswana (website). 2006. Retrieved from http://www.moa.gov.bw/?nav=. Bengston et al. 2004. *Landscape and Urban Planning, 69*, 271–286.

95. American Farmland Trust. 1997. Bengston et al. 2004. *Landscape and Urban Planning, 69*, 271–286.

Chapter 9

1. Schoenauer, N. 2003. *6,000 Years of Housing, revised and expanded ed.* W. W. Norton & Company.

2. Conservation measures. Las Vegas Valley Water District. Retrieved from htpp://www.lvved.com/conservation/drought.html

Chapter 10

1. Joint Monitoring Programme for Water Supply and Sanitation. 2012. *Progress on drinking water and sanitation: 2012 update.* New York, NY: World Health Organization and UNICEF.

2. Vorosmarty, C. J., McIntyre, P. B., Gessner, M. O., Dudgeon, D., Prusevich, A., Green, P., ... Davies, P. M. 2010. Global threats to human water security and river biodiversity. *Nature, 467*, 555–561.

3. World Bank. 2007. *Cost of pollution in China: Economic estimates of physical damages.* Washington, DC: World Bank.

4. Falkenmark, M., & Molden, D. 2008. Wake up to realities of river basin closure. *Water Resources Development, 24*(2), 201–215.

5. The Worldwatch Institute. 2004. *State of the World 2004.* New York, NY: W. W. Norton.

6. Shiklomanov, I. A. 1993. World fresh water resources. In P. H. Gleick (Ed.), *Water in crisis: A guide to the world's fresh water resources* (Vol. 33, pp. 13–24). New York, NY: Oxford University Press.

7. Diamond, J. M. 2005. *Collapse: How societies choose to fail or succeed.* New York, NY: Penguin Books.

8. Kenny, J. F., Barber, N. L., Hutson, S. S., Linsey, K. S., Lovelace, J. K., & Maupin, M. A. 2009. *Estimated use of water in the United States in 2005* (p. 1344.). U.S. Geological Survey Circular.

9. Swift, B. L. 1984. Status of riparian ecosystems in the United States. *Journal of the American Water Resources Association, 20*, 223–228.

10. Milly, P. C., Betancourt, J., Falkenmark, M., Hirsh, R. M., Kundzewicz, Z. W., Lettenair, D. P., Stouffer, R. J. 2009. Climate change: Stationarity is dead: Whither water management? *Science, 319*(5863), 573–574.

11. Quay, R. 2010. Anticipatory governance—A tool for climate change adaptation. *Journal of the American Planning Association, 76*(4), 496–511.

Chapter 11

1. Pisarski, A. E. 2006. *Commuting in America III, Transportation Research Board* (3rd ed.). Washington, DC: Transportation Research Board.

2. Pucher, J., & Dijkstra, L. 2000. Making walking and cycling safer: Lessons from Europe. *Transportation Quarterly, 54*(3), 25–50.

3. Delucchi, J., & McCubbin, D. 2010. External cost of transport in U.S. In A. de Palma, R. Lindsey, E. Quinet, & R. Vickerman (Ed.), *Handbook transport economics*, UK: Edward Elgar Publishing Ltd.

4. Ibid.

5. Ibid.

6. Oak Ridge National Laboratory. 2010.

7. United States Environmental Protection Agency (EPA). 2010. *Our Nation's Air-Status and Trends through 2008.* Research Triangle Park, NC: EPA.

8. United States Environmental Protection Agency (EPA). 2012. *Inventory of U.S. Greenhouse Gas Emissions and Sinks: 1990–2010.* EPA.

9. Freund, P. E. S., & Martin, G. T. 1993. *The Ecology of the Automobile* (p. 18). Montreal, QC: Black Rose Books.

10. Etkin, D. S. 2001. *Analysis of oil spill trends in the United States and worldwide*. Presentation at the International Oil Spill Conference, Tampa, Florida.

11. Ewing, R., Bartholomew, K., Winkelman, S., Walters, J., & Chen, D. 2010. *Growing cooler—the Evidence on Urban Development and Climate Change* (p. 7). Urban Land Institute.

12. Ibid.

13. Ibid, 12.

14. Ardila-Gomez, A. 2004. *Transit planning in curitiba and bogota: Roles in interaction, risk and change* (PhD Thesis). Massachusetts Institute of Technology.

15. 15. Lublow, A. 2007. The road to curitiba. *The New York Times Magazine*. New York, NY: The New York Times.

16. 16. Ewing, R., & Others. 2010. *Growing cooler—the evidence on development*. Urban Land Institute.

17. 17. Mohl, R. A. 2004. Stop the road: Freeway revolts in American cities. *Journal of Urban History, 30*(5), 674–706.

18. Shaheen, S., Cohen, A., & Chung, M. 2009. North American carsharing: A tenyear retrospective. *Journal of the Transportation Research Board, 2110*, 35–44.

19. Ibid.

20. Cervero, R., Golub, A., & Nee, B. 2007. City carshare: Longer-term travel demand and car ownership impacts. *Journal of the Transportation Research Board*, 1992, 70–80. Transportation Research Record.

21. Golub, A., & Henderson, J. 2011. The greening of mobility in San Francisco. In M. Slavin (Ed.), *Sustainability in America's cities: Creating the green metropolis*. Washington, D.C.: Island Press.

22. San Francisco Municipal Transportation Agency (SFMTA). 2009. 2008 San Francisco State of Cycling Report, San Francisco, CA: San Francisco Bicycle Program, Department of Parking and Traffic, Municipal Transportation Agency.

23. United States Department of Transportation (USDOT). 2010. *The National Bicycling and Walking Study: 15-Year Status Report* (22). Washington, DC: USDOT.

24. Harry Wray, J. 2008. *Pedal power: The quiet rise of the bicycle in american public life*. Boulder, CO: Paradigm Publishers.

25. SFMTA, *San Francisco Cycling Report, 2009*, 22 and SFMTA, 2010 *San Francisco State of Cycling Report*, San Francisco: San Francisco Bicycle Program, Department of Parking and Traffic, Municipal Transportation Agency, 2010), 22.SFMTA. 2009. 22.

26. The name was inspired by Return of the Scorcher, an independent documentary film that included a narrative observing hundreds of cyclists bunching at an intersection in China and pushing their way into traffic. Bicyclists would wait until they had "critical mass" to push into the stream of cross-traffic, and the phrase was borrowed by local activists organizing the monthly ride.

27. Switzky, J. 2002. Riding to See. In C. Carlsson (Ed.), *Critical mass: Bicycling's defiant celebration* (pp. 186–192). Oakland, CA: AK Press.

28. Ardila-Gomez, A. Transit planning in Curitiba and Bogota. (PhD Thesis).

Chapter 12

1. The Energy Sector Management Assistance Program (ESMAP) 1983 is a global, multidonor technical assistance trust fund administered by the World Bank and cosponsored by 13 official bilateral donors. http://www.esmap.org/Energy_Efficient_Cities

2. http://en.wikipedia.org/wiki/China_National_Highway_110_traffic_jam

3. http://www.forbes.com/sites/hengshao/2013/08/05/could-bringing-back-bicycles-fixbeijings-traffic-woes/

4. There were so many bicycles—9 million—that it was put to song "Nine Million Bicycles". http://en.wikipedia.org/wiki/Nine_Million_Bicycles http://www.azlyrics.com/lyrics/katiemelua/ninemillionbicycles.html

5. China: A Kingdom Of Bicycles No Longer by Robert Dreyfuss, Nov 25, 2009.1 http://www.npr.org/templates/story/story.php?storyId=120811453

6. http://en.wikipedia.org/wiki/Transport_in_Beijing

7. In 2013, the Bay Area Rapid Transit (BART) system in the San Francisco Bay Area, with 104 miles (167 km) of track and 44 stations totaled about 20 million rides. http://en.wikipedia.org/wiki/Bay_Area_Rapid_Transit.

8. No Chinese cities ranked in the top 20 most polluted cities, despite thick, gray smog filling its cities and millions of residents commuting behind surgical masks. Beijing reported 56 micrograms of PM2.5. Source: Top 20 most polluted cities in the world. By Madison Park, CNN updated 6:03 AM EDT, Thu May 8, 2014. http://www.cnn.com/2014/05/08/world/asia/india-pollution-who/. And the world's most polluted city is . . . By Simon Busch, CNN updated 4:00 AM EST, Fri January 31, 2014 http://www.cnn.com/2014/05/08/world/asia/india-pollution-who/. American Lung Association. State of the Air. http://www.stateoftheair.org/2013/city-rankings/most-polluted-cities.html

9. http://aceee.org/local-policy/city-scorecard

10. As identified on the website of the EIER: http://www.eifer.uni-karlsruhe.de/spip.php?article6.

11. Amory Lovins 1977. *Soft Energy Paths,*

12. U. S. Energy Information Administration. 2011. Rankings: total energy consumed per capita, 2011. http://www.eia.gov/state/rankings/?sid=US

13. California Energy Commission. Energy efficiency programs. http://www.energy.ca.gov/efficiency/.

14. http://www.usgbc.org/leed

15. http://www.usgbc.org/articles/infographic-leed-world

16. Craig Morris. Denmark surpasses 100 percent wind power. 08 Nov 2013 http://energytransition.de/2013/11/denmark-surpasses-100-percent-wind-power/

17. Curious about these numbers? Take a look at this web page: http://www.americanforests.org/assumptions-and-sources/

18. http://en.wikipedia.org/wiki/Arcosanti.

Chapter 13

1. Arnfield AJ 2003. Two decades of urban climate research: a review of turbulence, exchanges of energy and water, and the urban heat island. International Journal of Climatology 23:1–26.

2. Besser LM, & Dannenberg AL 2005. Walking to public transit: steps to help meet physical activity recommendations. *American Journal of Preventive Medicine*, 29:273–280.

3. Brazel AJ, Selover N, Vose R, Heisler G 2000. The tale of two climates-Baltimore and Phoenix urban LTER sites. Climate Research 15:123–135.

4. United States Census Bureau 2014. Available at: www.census.gov.

5. Centers for Disease Control and Prevention (CDC) 2006. Extreme heat: a prevention guide to promote your health and safety. http://www.bt.cdc.gov/disasters/extremeheat/heat_guide.asp; accessed 4/29/09

6. Davis M 2006. Planet of Slums. London Verso.

7. Gober PA 2006. Metropolitan Phoenix place making and community building in the Desert. University of Pennsylvania Press, Philadelphia, PA.

8. Golden JS 2004. The built environment induced urban heat island effect in rapidly urbanizing arid regions – a sustainable urban engineering complexity. *Environm Sci. – J. Integr. Environm. Sci.*, 1(4), 321–349.

9. Guhathakurta S, Gober PA 2007. The impact of the Phoenix urban heat island on residential water use. Journal of the American Planning Association 73:317–329.

10. Howard L 1833. *The Climate of London, Volume 1*. Joseph Rickaby.

11. Hu E, Yang YP, Nishimura A, Yilmaz F, & Kouzani A 2010. Solar thermal aided power generation. *Applied Energy*, 87:2881–2885.

12. Kalkstein, A. & Sheridan, S. 2007. The social impacts of the heat–health watch/warning system in Phoenix, Arizona: assessing the perceived risk and response of the public. *International Journal of Biometeorology*, 52, 43–55.

13. Klinenberg E. 2002. Heat wave: a social autopsy of disaster in Chicago. Chicago: University of Chicago Press.

14. Kunkel KE, Pielke Jr. RA, Changnon SA 1999. Temporal fluctuations in weather and climate extremes that cause economic and human health impacts: A review. American Meteorological Society 80:1077–1098.

15. Landsberg HE 1981. *The Urban Climate*. New York: Academic Press.

16. Larson J 2006. Setting the record straight: more than 52,000 Europeans died from heat in summer 2003. Earth Policy Institute. Available at http://www.earth-policy.org/Updates/2006/Update56.htm. Accessed October 19, 2009.

17. Masson, V. 2006. Urban surface modeling and the meso-scale impact of cities. Theoretical and Applied Climatology, 84(1–3), 35–45, DOI: 10.1007/s00704-005-0142-3

18. Middel, A., Häb, K., Brazel, A.J., Martin, C., Guhathakurta, S., 2014. Impact of urban form and design on microclimate in Phoenix, AZ. Landscape and Urban Planning 122, 16–28.

19. Nurse J, Basher D, Bone A, & Bird W 2010. An ecological approach to promoting population mental health and well-being – a response to the challenge of climate change. *Prospectives in Public Health*, 130: 27–33.

20. Oke, T.R., 1995. The heat island of the urban boundary layer: Characteristics, Causes and Effects, in Cermak, J.E., et. al. (eds.) *Wind Climate in Cities*, Kluwer, 772 pp.

21. Oke, T.R., 1987. *Boundary Layer Climates*, 2nd ed. Routledge, 435 pp.

22. Oke TR 1982. The energetic basis of the urban heat island. Quarterly Journal of the Royal Meteorological Society 108:1–24.

23. Oke TR 1973. City size and the urban heat island. Atmospheric Environment 7: 769–779.

24. Rosenzweig, C.,W.D. Solecki, L. Parshall, M. Chopping, G. Pope, and R. Goldberg. 2005. Characterizing the urban heat island in current and future climates in New Jersey, Global Environmental Change Part B: Environmental Hazards, 6(1):51–62. DOI: 10.1016/j.hazards.2004.12.001.

25. Roth, M 2007.: Review of urban climate research in (sub)tropical regions. *Int. J. Climatol.*, **27**, 1859–1873.

26. Ruddell DM, Harlan SL, Grossman-Clarke S, Buyanteyev A 2010. Risk and exposure to extreme heat in microclimates of Phoenix, AZ. In P. Showalter & Y. Lu (Eds.), Geospatial techniques in urban hazard and disaster analysis. Springer, pp. 179–202.

27. Runnalls KE & Oke TR 2000. Dynamics and controls of the near-surface heat island of Vancouver, British Columbia, Physical Geography 21(4): 283–304

28. Semenza JC, McCullough JE, Flanders WD, McGeehin MA, Lumpkin JR 1999. Excess hospital admissions during the July 1995 heat wave in Chicago. American Journal of Preventive Medicine 16:269–277.

29. Semenza JC, Rubin CH, Falter KH, Selanikio JD, Flanders WD, How HL, Wilhelm JL 1996. Heat-related deaths during the July 1995 heat wave in Chicago. American Journal of Preventive Medicine 16:269–277.

30. Shashua-Bar L, Pearlmutter D, Erell E 2009. The cooling efficiency of urban landscape strategies in a hot dry climate. *Landscape and Urban Planning*, 92:179–186.

31. Stewart, I.D., Oke, T.R., 2012. Local Climate Zones for Urban Temperature Studies. Bulletin of the American Meteorological Society 93, 1879–1900.

32. Wentz EA, Gober PA 2007. Determinants of Small-Area Water Consumption for the City of Phoenix, Arizona. Water Resources Management 21:1849–1863.

33. West JJ, Fiore AM, Horowitz LW, & Mauzerall DL 2006. Global health benefits of mitigating ozone pollution with methane emission controls. *Preceedings of the National Academy of Sciences*, 103:3988–3993.

Chapter 14

1. Alibegovic, Dubravka Jurlina and Zeljka Kordej de Villa. 2008. The Role of Urban Indicators in City Management: A Proposal for Croatian Cities. *Transition Studies Review*. 15 (1): 63–80.

2. Australian Government Department of Sustainability, Environment, Water, Population and Communities. 2012. "Fact Sheet: Measuring Sustainability Program." Accessed June 26, 2014. http://www.environment.gov.au/system/files/pages/35b3f5fc-fe28-4f44-ab5f-073f3963a2ff/files/fs-measuring-sustainability.pdf.

3. Central Texas Sustainability Indicators Project (CTSIP). 2012. *2012 Data Report*. Austin, TX: Central Texas Sustainability Indicators Project.

4. City of Minneapolis. 2014. "Sustainability Indicators." Accessed June 27, 2014. http://www.minneapolismn.gov/sustainability/indicators/index.htm.

5. City of New York. 2007. *PlaNYC: A Greener, Greater New York*. New York: The City of New York.

6. City of New York. 2011. *PlaNYC: A Greener, Greater New York*, Update April 2011. New York: The City of New York.

7. City of Tucson. 2000. "Livable Tucson Vision Program." Accessed April 4, 2010. http://cms3.tucsonaz.gov/livable.

8. City of Tucson. 2013. *Plan Tucson: City of Tucson General and Sustainability Plan 2013*. Effective November 13, 2013. Tucson, AZ: City of Tucson. Available online http://pdsd.tucsonaz.gov/integrated-planning/plan-tucson.

9. Cobb, Clifford W and Craig Rixford. 1998. *Lessons Learned from the History of Social Indicators*. San Francisco: Redefining Progress.

10. De Vries, Willem F.M. 2001. Meaningful Measures: Indicators on Progress, Progress on Indicators. *International Statistical Review* 69 (2): 313–331.

11. Dluhy, Milan and Nicholas Swartz. 2006. Connecting Knowledge and Policy: The Promise of Community Indicators in the United States. *Social Indicators Research* 79 (1): 1–23.

12. Eckerberg, Katerina and Mineur Eva. 2003. The Use of Local Sustainability Indicators: Case Studies in Two Swedish Municipalities. *Local Environment* 8 (6): 591–614.

13. Frederiksen, Pia and Peter Kristensen. 2008. "An Indicator Framework for Analysing Sustainability Impacts of Land-Use Change," in *Sustainability Impact Assessment of Land Use Changes*, eds. Helming, et al., 293–305. New York: Springer.

14. Gahin, Randa and Chriss Paterson. 2001. Community Indicators: Past, Present and Future. *National Civic Review* 90 (4): 347–361.

15. Gahin, Randa, Vesela Veleva and Maureen Hart. 2003. Do Indicators Help Create Sustainable Communities? *Local Environment* 8 (6): 661–666.

16. Gudmundsson, Henrik. 2003. The Policy Use of Environmental Indicators – Learning from Evaluation Research. *The Journal of Transdisciplinary Environmental Studies* 2 (2): 1–12.

17. Hankins, Katherine and Emily Powers. 2009. The Disappearance of the State from 'Livable' Urban Spaces. *Antipode* 41 (5): 845–866.

18. Hart, Maureen. 1995. *Guide to Sustainable Community Indicators*. North Andover, MA: QLF/Atlantic Center for the Environment.

19. Innes, Judith E. and David E. Booher. 2000. Indicators for Sustainable Communities: A Strategy Building on Complexity Theory and Distributed Intelligence. *Planning Theory and Practice*. 1 (2): 173–186.

20. Leitmann, Josef. 1999. Can City QOL Indicators Be Objective and Relevant? Towards a Participatory Tool for Sustaining Urban Development. *Local Environment* 4 (2): 169–180.

21. Levett, Roger. 1998. Sustainability Indicators—integrating quality of life and environmental protection. *Journal of the Royal Statistical Society, Series A.* 161 (3): 291–302.

22. Maclaren, Virginia W. 1996. Urban Sustainability Reporting. *Journal of the American Planning Association.* 62 (2): 184–202.

23. McAlpine, Patrick and Birnie Andrew. 2003. Is there a Correct Way of Establishing Sustainability Indicators?; The Case of Sustainability Indicator Development on the Island of Guernsey. *Local Environment* 10 (3) 243–257.

24. Miller, Clark A. 2000. *Creating Indicators of Sustainability: A Social Approach.* Winnipeg, Manitoba, Canada: International Institute for Sustainable Development.

25. Newton, Peter. 2001. "Urban Indicators and the Management of Cities," in *Urban Indicators for Managing Cities*, Matthew Westfall and Victoria de Villa (eds). Manila, Philippines: Asian Development Bank.

26. Organization of Economic Cooperation Development (OECD). 1976. *Measuring Social Well-Being: A Progress Report on the Development of Social Indicators.* Paris, France: OECD.

27. Phillips, Rhonda. 2003. *Community Indicators.* Chicago, IL: American Planning Association.

28. Portney, Kent. 2003. Civic Engagement and Sustainable Cities in the United States. *Public Administration Review* 65 (5): 577–589.

29. Redefining Progress. 2014. Accessed June 26, 2014. http://rprogress.org/index.htm.

30. Redefining Progress. 1997. *The Community Indicators Handbook: Measuring Progress Toward Healthy and Sustainable Communities.* Oakland, CA: Redefining Progress.

31. Redefining Progress. 2002. *Sustainability Starts in Your Community: A Community Indicators Guide.* Oakland, CA: Redefining Progress.

32. Reed, Mark S, Evan DG Fraser and Andrew J Dougill. 2006. An Adaptive Learning Process for Developing and Applying Sustainability Indicators with Local Communities. *Ecological Economics* 59 (4): 406–418.

33. Sawicki, David S and Patrice Flynn. 1996. Neighborhood Indicators. *Journal of the American Planning Association.* 62 (2): 165–183.

34. STAR Communities. 2012. *STAR Communities Rating System.* Washington, DC: STAR Communities. Available online at http://www.starcommunities.org/rating-system.

35. STAR Communities. 2014. Accessed July 2, 2014. http://starcommunities.org/.

36. Sustainable Measures. 2010. Accessed June 26, 2014. http://www.sustainable measures.com/.

37. Sustainable Seattle. 1998. *Indicators of Sustainable Community 1998*. Seattle, WA: Sustainable Seattle.

38. Sustainable Seattle. 2014. "Historical Indicator Work." Accessed June 27, 2014. http://sustainableseattle.org/.

39. United Nations Conference on Environment and Development (UN CED). 1992. *Agenda 21*. New York: United Nations.

40. World Commission on Environment and Development. 1987. *Our Common Future*. Oxford: Oxford University Press.

41. Zhang, Kunmin, Zongguo Wen, Bin Du, and Guojun Song. 2008. "A Multiple Indicators Approach to Monitoring Urban Sustainable Development," in *Ecology, Planning and Management of Urban Forests: International Perspectives*, eds. M.M. Carreiro et al., 35–52. New York: Springer.

Chapter 15

1. Lowry, I. S. 1964. *A model of metropolis*. Santa Monica, CA: Rand Corporation.

2. Goldner, W. 1971. The lowry model heritage. *Journal of the American Institute of Planners, 37*(2), 100–110.

3. Guhathakurta, S. 1999. Urban modeling and contemporary planning theory: Is there a common ground? *Journal of Planning Education and Research, 18*(4), 281.

4. Wegener, M. 1994. Operational urban models state of the art. *Journal of the American Planning Association, 60*(1), 17–29.

5. Asgary, A., Klosterman, R., & Razani, A. 2007. Sustainable urban growth management using What-if? *The International Journal of Environmental Research, 1*(3), 218–230.

6. Klosterman, R. E. 2008. A new tool for a new planning: The What if?™ planning support system. In R. K. Brail (Ed.), *Planning support systems for cities and regions* (pp. 85–99). Cambridge, MA: Lincoln Institute of Land Policy.

7. Landis, J. D. 1994. The California urban futures model: A new generation of metropolitan simulation models. *Environment and Planning B, 21*, 399–399.

8. Landis, J. D. 1995. Imagining land use futures: Applying the California urban futures model. *Journal of the American Planning Association, 61*(4), 438–457.

9. Landis, J. D., & Zhang, M. 1998. The second generation of the California urban futures model. Part 2: Specification and calibration results of the land-use change submodel. *The Environment and Planning B, 25*, 795–824.

10. Waddell, P. 2002. UrbanSim: Modeling urban development for land use, transportation, and environmental planning. *Journal of the American Planning Association, 68*(3). http://lab.geog.ntu.edu.tw/lab/errml/%E5%A4%A7%E5%B0%88%E9%A1%8C/03021%E5%8E%9F%E6%96%87.pdf

11. Waddell, P. 2000. A behavioral simulation model for metropolitan policy analysis and planning: Residential location and housing market components of UrbanSim. *Environment and Planning B, 27*(2), 247–264.

12. Haase, D., & Schwarz, N. 2009. Simulation models on human—Nature interactions in urban landscapes: A review including spatial economics, system dynamics, cellular automata and agent-based approaches. *Living Reviews in Landscape Research, 3*(2), 1–45.

13. Wegener, M. 2004. Overview of land use transport models. *Handbook of transport geography and spatial systems, 5*, 127–146.

Chapter 16

1. Abbott, Laurie. 2012. Tired of Teaching to the Test? Alternative Approaches to Assessing Student Learning. *Society for Range Management Rangelands, 34*(3), 34–38.

2. Boix Mansilla, Veronica, & Dawes Duraisingh, Elizabeth 2007. Targeted Assessment of Students' Interdisciplinary Work: An Empirically Grounded Framework Proposed. *jhe The Journal of Higher Education, 78*(2), 215–237.

3. Boone, Christopher G. 2014. Justice and Equity in the City. In C. E. Colten & G. L. Buckley (Eds.), *North American Odyssey: Historical Geographies for the Twenty-first Century* (pp. 413): Rowman and Littlefield.

4. Buissink-Smith, N., Mann, S., & Shephard, K. 2011. How Do We Measure Affective Learning in Higher Education? *Journal of Education for Sustainable Development, 5*(1), 101–114.

5. Colucci-Gray, Laura, Camino, Elena, Barbiero, Giuseppe, & Gray, Donald. 2006. From Scientific Literacy to Sustainability Literacy: An Ecological Framework for Education. *Science Education, 90*(2), 227–252.

6. de Haan, G. 2010. The Development of ESD-Related Competencies in Supportive Institutional Frameworks. *International Review of Education, 56*(2–3), 315–328.

7. Djordjevic, A., & Cotton, D. R. E. 2011. Communicating the sustainability message in higher education institutions. *International Journal of Sustainability in Higher Education, 12*(4), 381–394.

8. Dweck, Carol S., Mangels, Jennifer A., & Good, Catherine. 2004. Motivational effects on attention, cognition, and performance. *Motivation, emotion, and cognition.*

9. Jensen, Jon. 2008. Educating for ignorance. In B. Vitek & W. Jackson (Eds.), *The Virtues of Ignorance–Complexity, Sustainability, and the Limits of Knowledge* (pp. 307–322). Lexington: University Press of Kentucky.

10. Jickling, Bob, & Wals, Arjen E. J. 2008. Globalization and Environmental Education: Looking beyond Sustainable Development. *Journal of Curriculum Studies, 40*(1), 1–21.

11. Kollmuss, Anja, & Agyeman, Julian. 2002. Mind the gap: why do people act environmentally and what are the barriers to pro-environmental behavior? *Environmental education research, 8*(3), 239–260.

12. Kraiger, Kurt, Ford, J Kevin, & Salas, Eduardo. 1993. Application of cognitive, skill-based, and affective theories of learning outcomes to new methods of training evaluation. *Journal of applied psychology, 78*(2), 311.

13. McKeown, R., Hopkins, C. A., Rizi, R., & Chrystalbridge, M. 2002. *Education for sustainable development toolkit*. Knoxville, TN: Energy, Environment and Resources Center, University of Tennessee.

14. Murray, Paul E., & Murray, Sheran A. 2007. Promoting sustainability values within career-oriented degree programmes: A case study analysis. *International Journal of Sustainability in Higher Education, 8*(3), 285–300.

15. Orr, David W. 1992. *Ecological literacy: Education and the transition to a postmodern world*: SUNY Press.

16. Pijawka, D., Yabes, R., Frederick, C., and White, P. 2013. Integration of Sustainability in Planning and Design Programs in higher education: Evaluating learning outcomes, Journal of Urbanism p. 1–13.

17. Rode, Horst, & Michelsen, Gerd. 2008. Levels of indicator development for education for sustainable development. *Environmental Education Research, 14*(1), 19–33.

18. Shephard, K. 2008. Higher education for sustainability: seeking affective learning outcomes. *International Journal of Sustainability in Higher Education, 9*(1), 87–98.

19. Sterling, S, & Thomas, I. 2006. Education for sustainability: the role of capabilities in guiding university curricula. *IJISD International Journal of Innovation and Sustainable Development, 1*(4).

20. Rowe, D., Svanström, M., & Lozano-García, F. J., 2008. Learning outcomes for sustainable development in higher education. *International Journal of Sustainability in Higher Education, 9*(3), 339–351.

21. Tilbury, Daniella. 2004. Environmental education for sustainability: a force for change in higher education. In P. B. Corcoran & A. E. Wals (Eds.), *Higher education and the challenge of sustainability*. Dordrecht: Kluwer Academic Publishers.

22. Wiek, A., Withycombe, L., & Redman, C. L. 2011. Key competencies in sustainability: a reference framework for academic program development. *Sustainability Science, 6*(2), 203–218.

Chapter 17

1. China's national compound annualized economic growth rate from 1980 to 2012 was 10%.

2. Source: *China Overview*, Washington: The World Bank, 2014 (Information Sheet)

3. Douglas Webster, Cai, J., Xie, L., "Pivoting from Quantity to Quality: A new Suburban Community Development Paradigm in China, *Asia Pacific Housing Journal*, Volume 7, #23, April-June 2013, pp 17–28

4. Zhu Chen, Jin-Nan Wang, et al. China tackles the health effects of air pollution. *Lancet*: 2013: 382: pp 1959–1960

5. For details (and sources) re the air pollution discussion in this paragraph, see: Asian Development Bank, *Green Urbanization in Asia*, Manila: 2013, pp 10–12

6. Source: State Council of China, *12th Five Year Plan on Energy Development*, Beijing: State Council of China, 2013

7. The coal ban (and for other types of high pollution fuel) for Beijing is being introduced by urban districts: Dongcheng (before 2015), Xicheng (before 2015), Shijingshan (before 2017), Chaoyang, Haidian, and Fengtai before 2020), Beijing Economic & Technology Development Zone (before 2014); plus 10 new towns in the outer suburbs districts will be banning the listed fuel in steps. By 2020, 80% of the areas in Beijing will be coal-free. This ban is part of the air pollution prevention and control action plan, which was launched in early 2014. It places pressure on enterprises that use high polluting fuel.

8. Zhu Chen, Jin-Nan Wang, et al. China tackles the health effects of air pollution. *Lancet*: 2013: 382: pp 1959–1960.

9. China's Renewable internal freshwater resources were 2,093 cubic meters per capita in 2011, which is ¼ the global per capita supply; equivalent to, 3% of Canada's per capita freshwater resources and 23% of America's. By this measure, China ranks around 130 in the world.

10. Data Source: Chinese Academy of Geological Sciences

11. *National Soil Contamination Situation Bulletin*, Beijing: Ministry of Environmental Protection, Ministry of Land Resources, Government of China 2014.

12. Ironically, most Americans and foreigners perceive Los Angeles to be the epitome of urban sprawl, when it is the densest city in the US, ahead of San Francisco and New York SMSAs.

13. Data Source: 2010 US Census, US Census Bureau. Data is for Standard Metropolitan Statistical Areas (SMSAs)

14. Because land was not available in the heart of many Chinese cities for HSR stations, they tend to be in suburban areas, creating secondary urban centers, such as the Hongqiao Hub on the western periphery of Shanghai. Given the fact that the largest metropolitan areas in China are almost invariably embedded in megapolitan regions, HSR is collapsing distance among cities, and dramatically reducing energy and travel time costs. *National Soil Contamination Situation Bulletin*, Beijing: Ministry of Environmental Protection, Ministry of Land Resources, Government of China 2014.

15. Jon Davis, "Chugging Into the 21St Century: A Report on High-Speed Rail in California and Beyond", *Planning* (American Planning Association), May 2014, pp 220–25

16. Source: National Development Reform Commission, *2012-2013 Urban Subway Development Report*, Beijing: Transportation Institute of the NDRC, 2013

17. Source: *World Development Indicators*, World Bank, 2014 Data Set: Arable Land

18. The State Environmental Protection Administration (SEPA) was established in 1998 and upgraded to ministerial status (MEP) in 2008

19. Douglas Webster, Cai J., Muller L., "The New Face of Peri-urbanization in East Asia: Modern Production Zones, Middle-class Lifestyles and Rising Expectations", *Journal of Urban Affairs*, Volume 36, 2014, Number S1, pp 1–19

20. Hiscock, Geoff, *China's Auto Affair Drives Oil Demand*, CNN Internet News, Accessed December 27, 2013

21. Larson, C., "China Wants Reactors, and Lots of Them", *Bloomberg Businessweek*, February 25—March 13 2013, pp 10–11 (This article indicates that 29 nuclear reactors are under construction in China; however, the actual number is 31, based on information from China's Ministry of Environmental Protection.)

22. To measure water quality and set targets, the Ministry of Environmental Protection utilizes a five grade scale based on 24 biological indicators. Class 1 is best (source water), Class 2 is suitable for drinking water source, Class 3 is suitable for swimming and as secondary drinking water source, Class 4 is for industrial use, boating, etc., while Class 5 is for irrigation.

23. Material in the foregoing paragraph is derived from, Dolins, Sarah-Laura, *Metropolitan Fusion or Folly: The Creation of A Multiple-Nodal Metropolis in Taiyuan, Shanxi, China,* Masters Thesis, School of Geographical Sciences and Urban Planning, Arizona State University, 2014

24. The China Ecological Civilization Research and Promotion Institute, and the Chinese Academy for Environmental Planning

25. To measure air quality and set targets, the Ministry of Environmental Protection utilizes a three grade scale based on 10 atmospheric indicators (of which 6 are basic indicators). Grade 1 air quality is considerably better than Grade 2, while Grade 2 air is considered unsatisfactory. Thus cities set standards in terms of number of Grade 1 and Grade 2 days to be achieved.

26. The MEP has a Green community guideline, based on the ISO14000 environmental management standards. It basically refers to a community that meets certain environmental standards, and exhibits an effective environmental management system, including participation mechanisms. Standards relate to green buildings, green space, solid waste sorting, waste water treatment, water and energy efficiency.

27. The Gini Index measures the extent to which the distribution of income within an economy deviates from a perfectly equal distribution. Thus a Gini index of 0 represents perfect equality, while an index of 100 implies perfect inequality.

28. Reuters News Service, "China Plans a Market for Carbon Permits", *New York Times*, September 1 20–14, pg B2

29. There is some confusion between the term, Smart Cities, and Knowledge Cities, the latter are cities with economies based on creativity, and creation of knowledge.

30. Douglas Webster, Cai J., Muller, L., Wen, T., "Early Stage Amenity Dynamics in China: The Yunnan Amenity Corridor, in Moss, L. (Editor), *Amenity Migration: A Global Perspective*, New Ecology Press, 2014

31. China's nuclear construction process was temporarily suspended immediately after the Japanese Fukushima nuclear incident.

32. Data Source: US Censuses, Bureau of the Census, US Government

Chapter 18

1. Portions of this chapter were prepared for Harvard University Honoring Nations Program as a case profile, authored jointly by Judith Dworkin and Frances Stout and edited by Niina Haas.

2. There are a number of terms that Indian people have used to describe their political entities. Some, like the Navajo and the Tohono O'odham use the term "nation." Others, particularly where more than one Indian ethnic group occupy the same land area, describe themselves as "community," such as the Gila River Indian Community or the Salt River Indian Community. Many use the term "tribe," such as the Hopi Tribe or the San Carlos Apache Tribe. The term "tribe" has legal as well as ethnic significance. In this chapter the term "Indian nation" is used throughout unless reference is made to a specific tribal entity.

3. Nagel, Joane & Snipp, Matthew C. 1993. Ethnic reorganization: American Indian social, economic, political and cultural strategies for survival. *Ethnic and Racial Studies*, 16(2), 203–235.

4. "In 1823, Chief Justice Marshall of the United States Supreme Court justified the taking lands from Indian nations using the "Doctrine of Discovery." *Johnson v. McIntosh,* 21 U.S. 543 1823. Under the "doctrine of discovery," *Oneida II,_* 470 U. S. 226, 234 1985., "fee title to the lands occupied by Indians when the colonists arrived became vested in the sovereign—first the discovering European nation and later the original States and the United States," *Oneida I,* 414 U. S. 661, 667 1974. In the original 13 States, "fee title to Indian lands," or "the pre-emptive right to purchase from the Indians, was in the State." *Id.,* at 670; see *Oneida Indian Nation of N. Y. v. New York,* 860 F. 2d 1145, 1159–1167 (CA2 1988). Both before and after the adoption of the Constitution, New York State acquired vast tracts of land from Indian tribes through treaties it independently negotiated, without National Government participation. See Gunther, Governmental Power and New York Indian Lands—A Reassessment of a Persistent Problem of Federal-State Relations, 8 Buffalo L. Rev. 1, 4–6 (1958–1959) (hereinafter Gunther)." *City of Sherrill v. Oneida Indian Nation of New York*, 544 U.S. 197, 203-04 at n.1 2005.

5. *Johnson v. McIntosh,* 21 U.S. 543 1823.; *Cherokee Nation v. Georgia ,*30 U.S. 1 1831.; and *Worcester v. Georgia,* 31 U.S. 515 1832.

6. Federal recognition of an Indian tribe authorizes that tribe to be eligible to receive services from the U.S. Department of the Interior, Bureau of Indian Affairs. *See* Federally Recognized Tribes List Act, Pub. L. No. 103–454 1994.; Indian Entities Recognized and Eligible To Receive Services From the United States Bureau of Indian Affairs, 79 Fed. Reg. 4748 (Jan. 29,2 014). Some Indian nations have received state recognition but not federal recognition while many Indian nations are unrecognized by either the federal government or a state.

7. For a summary of the history of Federal Indian policies, *see History & Background of Federal Indian Policy*, Cohen's Handbook of Federal Indian Law, chapt. 1 2012.

8. P.H. Kunesh, "Constant Governments: Tribal Resilience and Regeneration in Changing Times," 19 Fall Kan. J. L. & Pub. Pol'y 8, 18 1991.

9. S. Rep. No. 78–310 1943.

10. H.R. Rep. No. 82–2503 1952.

11. *Id.* At 25.

12. Ragsdale, Jr. Indian Reservations and the Preservation of Tribal Culture: Beyond Wardship to Stewardship," 59 UMKC Law Review 503, 510 1991.

13. *Id.*

14. *Id. at 31–32.*

15. The U.S. Census collects data for Americans Indians and Alaska Natives in a single category.

16. American Diabetes Association; http://www.diabetes.org/living-with-diabetes/ treatment-and-care/high-risk-populations.

17. CDC Report, CHDIR: (2006 data).

18. Jackson MY, "Height, Weight, and BodyMass Index of American Indian Schoolchildren, 1990-1991." *Journal of the American Dietetic Association*, 93(10): 1136–40, 1993. The reference information for this study was the Centers for Disease Control and Prevention's 1970 definitions for children who were at or above the 85th percentile of body mass index (BMI) on sex- and age-specific growth charts. www.leadershipforhealthycommunities.org

19. U.S. Census Bureau 2010 small Area Income and Poverty Estimates.

20. Spokane Tribe of Indians, Sustainable Community Master Plan: the ST01 2012 Comprehensive Plan @ pp. 2–3 (Draft: September 26, 2012)(citing to Hollings, Crawford S., "Engineering Resilience versus Ecological Resilience," In Engineering with Ecological Restraints. National Academy of Sciences, pp. 31–43. Retrieved from www.nap.edu/openbook).

21. *Id.*

22. *Id.*

23. *Id.*

24. (Holling 1996) [Spokane Tribe of Indians, Sustainable Community Master Plan, p.2]

25. Chapter 3, *infra.*

26. Jonathan Placito, "Native American tribal Rights: How Arizona's Looming Water-Shortage Threatens Tribal Sovereignty." Rebecca Tsosie, *Land, Culture, and Community: Envisioning Native American Sovereignty and National Identity in the 21st Century.* 2 International Social Science Review. 180 2001.

27. Cajete, G. 2000. Native Science, Natural laws of Interdependence. Santa Fe, NM: Clear Light Publishers. p. 178.

28. Martinez, Dennis. 1998. First People—Firsthand Knowledge. *Winds of Change*, 13(3), 1–4.

29. Hibbard, Lane & Rasmussen, 2008, p. 141.

30. Semken, Steven. 2005. Sense of Place and Place-Based Introductory Geoscience Teaching for American Indian and Alaska Native Undergraduates. *Journal of Geoscience Education*, 53(2), 149–157.

31. Roland, Margaret & Semali, Ladi. 2010. Intersections of Indigenous Knowledge, Language and Sustainable Development. CIES Perspectives Newsletter: Florida International University, p.1.

32. *Id.* at 2.

33. King, Leslie A. & Hood, Virginia L. 1999. Ecosystem Health and Sustainable Communities: North and South. *Ecosystems Health* (1), 49–57, 56.

34. Trosper, Ronald L. 2002. Northwest coast indigenous institutions that supported resilience and sustainability. *Ecological Economics*, 41, 329–344.

35. Whitbeck, L.B., Adams, G.W., Hoyt, D.R. and Chen, X. 2004. Connceptualizing and Measuring Historical Trauma Among Indian People. *American Journal of Community Psychology*, (33 Nos. 3/4), 119–130, at 121.

36. Reyhner, J., Cantoni, G., St. Clair, R.N. & Yazzie, E.P. (Eds.). 1999. Proceedings from *5th Annual Stabilizing Indigenous Languages Symposium*. KY: Northern Arizona University; McCarty, T.L., Romero-Little, M.E. & Zepeda, O. 2006. Native American Youth Discourses on Language Shift and Retention: Ideological Cross-currents and Their Implications for Language Planning. *The International Journal of Bilingual Education and Bilingualism*, 9(5), 659–677.

37. Reyhner, Cantoni, Clair & Yazzie 1999.

38. Kunesh, at 39.

39. Mariella, P. & DeWeaver, N. 2007. Tribes in Arizona: Growth and Land Use. In: *Land use: Challenges and choices for the 21st century.* (pp 63–71). Phoenix: Arizona Town Hall. Retrieved October 4, 2011, from http://www.aztownhall.org/pdf/Complete_91st_Report_FINAL.pdf.

40. Hibbard, M., Lane, M. & Rasmussen, K. 2008. The split personality of planning: Indigenous peoples and planning for land resource management. *Journal of Planning Literature*, 23(2), 136–151.

41. Community pursues development at its own pace. (2007, June 23). *The East Valley Tribune*. Retrieved August 29, 2011, from http://www.eastvalleytribune.com/article_0ef8a52b-aa65-5101-bc16-b4f5b32fa343.html.

42. Smith, L. 2008. Indigenous geography, GIS, and land use planning on the Bois Forte Reservation. *American Indian Culture and Research Journal,* 32(3), 139–151.

43. Spokane Tribe of Indians, Sustainable Community Master Plan: the ST01 2012 Comprehensive Plan @ pp. 2–3 (Draft: September 26, 2012); Gardner, J., D. Pijawka, and E. Trevan. 2014. Recommendations for Updating the Community-Based Chapter Land Use Plans for the Navajo Nation. Final Report. Office of the President. Navajo Nation.

44. Id.

45. Id.

46. *Id.*

47. TOCA Tohono O'odham Communicty Action; http://www.tocaonline.org/our-community.html.

48. *Id.* at 242.

49. Woods, Teri K., Blaine, Karen & Francisco, Lauri. 2002. O'odham Himdag as a Source of Strength and Wellness among the Tohono O'odham of Sothern Arizona and Northern Sonora, Mexico. *Journal of Sociology and Social Welfare*, 29(1), 35–53, at 36.

50. Seivertson, Bruce Lynn. 1999. History/Cultural Ecology of the Tohono O'odham Nation. (Unpublished doctoral dissertation). University of Arizona: Tucson.

51. A seven member Board of Directors, whose directors are appointed by the Chairperson of the Nation and confirmed by the Legislative Council, governs TONCA. The Board of Directors is viewed as the policy-making entity and delegates the day-to-day operation of the programs under TONCA to the programs' professional staff.

52. TONCA Preamble to Charter, codified at Tohono O'odham Code, Title 17, Ch. 2.

53. Background Paper: "Health and Sustainable Development, Meeting of Senior Officials and Minsters of Health, Johannesburg, South Africa, 19-22, January 2002, Summary Report at 35.

54. *Id.* at 29–40.

55. *Id.* at 33.

56. *Id.*

57. *Id.* at 37–38.

58. TONCA Charter, Title 17, ch. 2, Preamble.

CONTRIBUTOR BIOGRAPHIES

Rimjhim Aggarwal

Dr. Rimjhim Aggarwal's research explores global dimensions of sustainability such as the links between globalization, local ecosystems, and poverty in less-developed countries. She has conducted extensive field work on groundwater-irrigation institutions in India; her recent research examines the emerging tradeoffs between water availability and the growing demands of agriculture in dry-land regions of the world.

Anthony Brazel

Dr. Brazel is Professor Emeritus at Arizona State University's School of Geographical Sciences and Urban Planning and is a Senior Sustainability Scientist in the Global Institute of Sustainability. His areas of expertise include physical geography and urban climatology, and he is coauthor of Environmental Sciences: A Student's Companion. He was Director of the Southwest Center for Environmental Research & Policy (which was supported by the U. S. EPA). He has authored numerous articles on mitigating the urban heat island effect, urban climatology, and vulnerability to climate change, and received the Helmut A. Landsberg Award from the American Meteorological Society for distinguished work on urban climate of desert environments.

Stephen Buckman

Stephen Buckman holds a PhD in Urban Geography and an MPA in Public Administration and presently is Post-Doctoral Research Fellow at the Taubman College of Architecture and Urban Planning at the University of Michigan. His doctoral work centered on issues of small neighborhood based developments on canal banks to increase density and create walkability within polycentric landlocked urban environments. His present research pertains to community resiliency and climate change as it relates to Great Lake communities and their master planning process.

Jianming Cai

Jianming Cai is Professor in the Institute of Geographical Sciences and Natural Resources Research at the Chinese Academy of Sciences. He holds a PhD in Urban Geography & City Planning from the University of Hong Kong, and has published more than 140 papers & chapters since 2000 both in Chinese and English. He frequently serves as a senior advisor or consultant on urbanization, sustainable regional and urban development, urban agriculture and food security to both international agencies such as World Bank, ADB, EU, Ford, Lincoln Land Institute and Chinese national and local governments.

Winston T.L. Chow

Winston T.L. Chow is an Assistant Professor in the Department of Geography, National University of Singapore. Previously, he completed his Ph.D. in Geography and postdoctoral training in Engineering at Arizona State University. His areas of published research expertise include investigating the urban heat island and in applying sustainable concepts in urban climatology, which include assessing methods and techniques in minimizing detrimental impacts of the heat island towards residents in cities. Apart from being the news editor of Urban Climate News, the quarterly magazine of the International Association for Urban Climate, Dr. Chow has also taught lower- and upper-level undergraduate courses on geography and meteorology, which include courses examining sustainability at the human-environment interface.

Edward A. Cook

Dr. Edward A. Cook is a Landscape Architecture faculty member in The Design School at Arizona State University where he teaches courses on urban ecological design, landscapes and sustainability, and landscape ecological planning. He has published books and articles focused on his research in urban ecology, green/ecological networks and sustainable urbanism. He has worked on projects on landscape ecological planning throughout the world and was one of the pioneers in developing planning and design strategies for ecological networks in urban landscapes. He has a PhD from Wageningen University in the Netherlands, a Master of Landscape Architecture degree from Utah State University and a Bachelor of Science in Landscape Architecture from Washington State University.

Judith Dworkin

Judith Dworkin is the managing partner of the Scottsdale law firm of Sacks Tierney P.A. Her practice is devoted primarily to Indian law and water resources law issues. Dr. Dworkin has been selected for inclusion in Best Lawyers of America in the fields of water law and Native American law and selected among Arizona's "50 Most Influential Women in Business" by AzBusiness magazine. She received her M.A. and Ph.D. degrees in geography from Clark University and her J.D. degree, cum laude, from Arizona State University. She clerked for the Honorable William C. Canby, Jr. of the Ninth Circuit Court of Appeals. She is admitted to the Arizona and Navajo Nation bars and is admitted to practice in the courts of the Tohono O'odham Nation, Gila River Indian Community, Hopi Tribe and Hualapai Tribe. Dr. Dworkin lectures regularly and publishes on topics relating to water resource management and economic development on Indian Reservations. She is an adjunct professor in the Sandra Day O'Connor College of Law and the School of Geographical Sciences and Urban Planning at Arizona State University where she teaches graduate courses in water and natural resources law and planning.

Chad Frederick

Chad Frederick, MUEP, is a doctoral candidate in urban and public affairs, and a university fellow at the University of Louisville. His masters thesis explored measuring learning outcomes in a large, introductory urban sustainability course. His dissertation identifies the potential contribution of public affairs and urban planning for a new paradigm in K12 civic education focused on metropolitan governance. Dovetailing with these research agendas is a line of study that explores planning pedagogy, curriculum development, and course construction in education for sustainable development.

Aaron Golub

Aaron Golub is an Associate Professor in the School of Geographical Sciences and Urban Planning and the School of Sustainability at Arizona State University. He teaches courses on urban transportation planning and policy, research methods, international development, and environmental justice. His research focuses on the social contexts of urban transportation systems, explored in three ways: 1. the effects on social equity of current transportation planning practices – how do people participate in planning, and who wins and who loses from transportation plans; 2. planning, research and activism in support of alternatives to the automobile (car-sharing, public transportation and bicycles); and, 3. the historical roots of automobile dependence in the United States. He worked as a researcher, consultant and advocate in California for a decade on projects related to public transit, car-sharing, and social justice issues in transportation finance. He has worked in Brazil, Mexico and Colombia as a consultant on various transportation advocacy and planning projects. He sits on two national research committees related to environmental justice in transportation and transportation planning in developing countries. Dr. Golub received his Ph.D. in Civil Engineering from UC Berkeley in 2003. His masters and bachelor's degree were earned in mechanical engineering at the Massachusetts Institute of Technology and Virginia Polytechnic Institute, respectively.

Subhrajit Guhathakurta

Dr. Subhrajit Guhathakurta is the Director of the Center for Geographic Information Systems (CGIS) and Professor of City and Regional Planning at the Georgia Institute of Technology. Dr. Guhathakurta has spent twenty years undertaking research on various dimensions of urban sustainability that included housing, energy, transportation, urban climate, and water use. He was among the founding members of the School of Sustainability at Arizona State University where he also served as Associate Director of the School of Geographical Sciences and Urban Planning. Dr. Guhathakurta is Co-Editor of the Journal of Planning Education and Research, which is the flagship journal for the Association of Collegiate Schools of Planning (ACSP). His publications include over 70 journal papers and several edited books including Integrated Land Use and Environmental Models (2003) and Visualizing Sustainable Planning (2009), both published by Springer.

Bjoern Hagen

Bjoern Hagen's research focuses on climate change mitigation and adaptation, including public risk perceptions and risk communication. Hagen's research aims to increase the capacity of urban areas to adapt to climate change and offers decision makers the capacity tools to do it. Hagen's work focuses on understanding human-natural systems, combining social science theory with applications. He is currently carrying out a survey on an international scale, examining public perceptions of climate change and public willingness to support climate change policies in nine different countries. This study will provide decision-makers with information crucial to crafting environmental policies and strategies. Hagen is also currently working on a study about how hydro-meteorological disasters impact Americans' climate change perceptions. Before coming to ASU, Hagen worked on sustainable development in Germany, including the redesign of the UNESCO World Heritage site Völklingen Ironworks as well as various projects with the Development Agency of Rhineland Palatinate (Entwicklungsagentur Rheinland-Pfalz e.V).At Arizona State University, Hagen regularly teaches Sustainable Cities, Planning and Climate Change, and Sustainability on Film. He holds a M.Sc. in Spatial and Environmental Planning from the University of Kaiserslautern, Germany, and a Ph.D. in Environmental Design and Planning from Arizona State University. He currently is a Lecturer in the school of Geographical Sciences and Urban Planning at Arizona State University.

Devon McAslan

Devon McAslan is a doctoral student at the University of Michigan studying urban and regional planning in the Taubman College of Architecture and Urban Planning. He has a master's degree in urban and environmental planning from Arizona State University. His research focuses on a range of urban sustainability issues. His master's thesis evaluated the effectiveness of quality of life and sustainability indicator programs and he has published several articles on quality of life indicators. He is continuing his research on sustainability metrics and advocates for their further development and refinement for better and more accurate policy making.

John Meunier

John Meunier came to Arizona State University in 1987 to be Dean of the College of Architecture and Environmental Design, a position he held until 2002 when he returned to the faculty as Professor of Architecture. Previously he was Director of the School of Architecture and Interior Design at the University of Cincinnati, having been Head of the Department of Architecture there from 1976 to 1979. He started teaching architecture at Cambridge University in England where he was on the faculty from 1962 to 1976, and was Acting Head from 1973–4. While in Britain Professor Meunier was a widely published practicing architect. His work was exhibited at the Paris Biennale in 1967, and he and his partners, Barry Gasson and Brit Andresen won the competition and commission for the Burrell Museum in Glasgow in 1972. The building was completed in 1983.

Professor Meunier studied at Liverpool University from which he graduated with a first-class honors degree, B.Arch, in 1959. He then received a Frank Knox Fellowship to the Graduate School of Design at Harvard from which he graduated with a Masters of Architecture in 1960.

During his career Professor Meunier has been a Visiting Critic and Lecturer at many schools of architecture but has spent extended periods as a visitor at McGill, Harvard, Yale, San Luis Obispo, and Charlotte, North Carolina. He is a registered architect in West Germany and Britain and has received reciprocal certification in the U.S.A. from the National Council of Architectural Registration Boards. He is a registered architect in the State of Arizona and a member of the A.I.A. He is a Fellow of the Royal Society of Arts and was a Fellow of Darwin College, Cambridge. He is a Past-President of the Association of Collegiate Schools of Architecture, and was also a member of the National Architectural Accrediting Board. In 2005-6 he was Interim Director of the School of Architecture at Clemson University while on leave from ASU.

Ariane Middel

Ariane Middel received her Ph.D. in Computer Science from a German National Science Foundation (DFG) funded international graduate school at the University of Kaiserslautern, Germany and holds a M.Sc. in Geodetic Engineering from the University of Bonn, Germany. Dr. Middel is currently a Research Professional in the Julie Ann Wrigley Global Institute of Sustainability at Arizona State University. Her primary research interests are directed toward developing climate adaptation strategies in urban environments, specifically addressing the challenges of sustainable urban form, design, and landscape in the face of climatic uncertainty in rapidly urbanizing regions. For the past four years, she has been working on sustainability issues related to urban heat islands, thermal comfort, water use, wastewater reuse, and human-climate interactions in cities.

Martin J. Pasqualetti

Dr. Martin J. Pasqualetti's work blends 40 years of experience in the academic, administrative, and business sides of the energy industry. He has advised several US government agencies, including the National Research Council, the Department of Energy, and the Nuclear Regulatory Commission. He has conducted energy research in China, the United Kingdom, Mexico, Canada, the Czech Republic, among others. He helped establish two energy firms: EcoGroup and Strategic Solar Energy. Professor Pasqualetti has authored books, chapters, and articles on energy, and is in demand as a public speaker. At Arizona State University, Dr. Pasqualetti regularly offers four energy courses, including The Thread of Energy, Energy and Environment, Solar Energy Policy, and Energy in the Global Arena. A constant theme in all his courses is the form and function of cities as an energy organism.

Ray Quay

Ray Quay is a Research Professional with the Decision Center for a Desert City a unit of the Julie Ann Wrigley Global Institute of Sustainability at Arizona State University. Professor Quay is involved in research on urban planning, water resources, climate change, urban heat island, regional growth policy issues and scenario analysis. Previously he was the Assistant Director of Water Services and Assistant Director of Planning for Phoenix Arizona, and Assistant Director of Planning for Arlington and Galveston Texas. He is a Fellow of the American Institute of Certified Planners and has authored numerous books and articles related to urban planning and water resources including "Anticipatory Governance: A Tool for Climate Change Adaptation", "Managing water resources: The central issue for sustaining life", and coauthored Master Change with Bruce McClendon. He holds a BS from Baylor University, a MS from University of Texas at Austin, and a PhD from Arizona State University.

Nelya Rakhimova

Nelya Rakhimova is a PhD candidate at the Dresden Leibniz Graduate School in Germany that has a focus on urban and regional resilience. Her first degree at Tyumen State University in Russia was in environmental management. In 2011 she received a master's degree in Urban and Environmental Planning at Arizona State University as a Fulbright scholar. During her studies she participated in various scientific activities around the world that gave her opportunities to learn about different prospectives and approaches to current global economic, social and environmental issues. Currently, she is investigating how American cities are coping with demographic and economic changes and how communities are prepared to meet the needs of the most vulnerable populations. In particular, her work evaluates community resilience of the elderly poor.

Charles Redman

Charles Redman has been committed to interdisciplinary research since as an archaeology graduate student he worked closely in the field with botanists, zoologists, geologists, art historians, and ethnographers. Redman received his BA from Harvard University, and his MA and PhD in Anthropology from the University of Chicago. He taught at New York University and at SUNY-Binghamton before coming to Arizona State University in 1983. Since then, he served nine years as Chair of the Department of Anthropology, seven years as Director of the Center for Environmental Studies and, in 2004, was chosen to be the Julie Ann Wrigley Director of the newly formed Global Institute of Sustainability. From 2007-2010, Redman was the founding director of ASU's School of Sustainability. Redman's interests include human impacts on the environment, sustainable landscapes, rapidly urbanizing regions, urban ecology, environmental education, and public outreach. He is the author or co-author of 14 books including Explanation in Archaeology, The Rise of Civilization, People of the Tonto Rim, Human Impact on Ancient Environments and, most recently, co-edited four books: The Archaeology of Global Change, Applied Remote Sensing for Urban Planning, Governance and Sustainability, Agrarian Landscapes in Transition, and Polities and Power: Archaeological Perspectives on the Landscapes of Early States. Redman is currently working on building upon the extensive research portfolio of the Global Institute of Sustainability and teaching in the School of Sustainability which is educating a new generation of leaders through collaborative learning, transdisciplinary approaches, and problem-oriented training to address the environmental, economic, and social challenges of the 21st Century.

Darren Ruddell

Darren Ruddell is an Assistant Professor and Director of Undergraduate Studies at the Spatial Sciences Institute at the University of Southern California. Ruddell teaches and develops curricula in GeoDesign and advanced online programs in Geographic Information Science and Technology. GeoDesign is a forward-thinking, interdisciplinary framework that pairs planning, design, and environmental systems with geospatial technologies to explore ways to build a better world. Ruddell earned his Ph.D. from the School of Geographical Sciences and Urban Planning at Arizona State University, and his research efforts utilize geospatial technologies to investigate issues of urban sustainability and resiliency.

Craig Thomas

Craig Thomas studied engineering at West Point for two years, graduated cum laude in English literature from Ohio State University (BA), and holds graduate degrees in creative writing from the Naropa Institute (MFA), and in sustainability and environmental management from Harvard University (MLA). He has written articles and given presentations on water resource management, climate adaptation, and the history of sustainability at national conferences; and published climate-change and regional-policy related articles in the Sierra Sun and Tahoe Daily Tribune. He was an editor of the literary journal, Bombay Gin, and has published short stories in Jumbo Shrimp and The Murray Meaning, as well as being a finalist for the Scribner's Best of the Fiction Workshops. From 2000-2007, Craig toured Southeast Asia and taught advanced English and American literature and writing courses at Toko University. While at Harvard he was the secretary then president of the Harvard Extension Environmental Club, and also worked for Alexandria Cousteau as the Director of Angkor Wat Research for the non-profit group, Blue Legacy: Telling the Story of Our Water Planet featured on the National Geographic Channel. He is currently a teaching fellow and PhD Candidate at the School of Sustainability at Arizona State University.

Douglas Webster

Douglas Webster is Professor in the School of Geographical Sciences and Urban Planning at Arizona State University. He holds a PhD in City Planning from the University of California, Berkeley. As Senior Advisor to the National Planning Agency, Thailand from 1993–2003, he managed the Asian Development Bank's trend-setting large-scale initiative, Planning for Sustainable Urbanization in Thailand. Since 2000 Professor Webster's work on urban sustainability has focused on China - in partnership with the Institute of Geographical Sciences and Natural Resources Research at the Chinese Academy of Science. Professor Webster is a frequent advisor on smart city building in East Asia to major international development organizations, corporations, and NGOs. He is author of many publications, both academic and practice-oriented, on the urban environment, resilience, and sustainability in East Asia.

Feifei Zhang

Feifei Zhang is a PhD student in Urban Planning at Arizona State University. She holds a dual Masters degree in International Co-operation and Urban Development from the Technical University of Darmstadt, Germany and Rome University, Tor Vergata, Italy. Before joining ASU, she worked as a Senior Researcher in the Chinese Academy for Environmental Planning (CAEP), Chinese Ministry of Environmental Protection. Her work experience includes research on China's National and Regional Medium-to-Long Term Environmental Protection Strategic Planning, and Environmental Master Planning for Cities and their hinterlands, from a sustainable point of view. Ms. Zhang has extensive experience working as a consultant on large-scale urban projects in major cities oriented to improving the amenity of Chinese cities.